COGNITIVE INTERFERENCE

Theories, Methods, and Findings

The LEA Series in
Personality and Clinical Psychology
Irving B. Weiner, Editor

Exner • Issues and Methods in Rorschach Research

Gacono/Meloy • The Rorschach Assessment of Aggressive and Psychopathic Personalities

Ganellen • Integrating the Rorschach and the MMPI-2 in Personality Assessment

Hy/Loevinger • Measuring Ego Development, Second Edition

Sarason/Pierce/Sarason • Cognitive Interference: Theories, Methods, and Findings

Zillmer/Harrower/Ritzler/Archer • The Quest for the Nazi Personality: A Psychological Investigation of Nazi War Criminals

COGNITIVE INTERFERENCE
Theories, Methods, and Findings

Edited by

Irwin G. Sarason
University of Washington

Gregory R. Pierce
Hamilton College

Barbara R. Sarason
University of Washington

Routledge
Taylor & Francis Group
LONDON AND NEW YORK

First published 1996
by Routledge
2 Park Square, Milton Park, Abingdon, Oxon OX14 4RN

Simultaneously published in the USA and Canada
by Routledge
711 Third Avenue, New York, NY 10017

Routledge is an imprint of the Taylor & Francis Group, an informa business

First issued in paperback 2016

Reprinted 2009 by Routledge

Library of Congress Cataloging-in-Publication Data

Cognitive interference : theories, methods, and findings / edited by
Irwin G. Sarason, Gregory R. Pierce, Barbara R. Sarason.
p. cm.
Includes bibliographical references and indexes.
ISBN 0-8058-1624-0 (alk. paper)
1. Interference (Perception) 2. Cognition. 3. Cognitive
psychology. I. Sarason, Irwin G. II. Pierce, Gregory R.
III. Sarason, Barbara R.
BF323.I52C64 1996
153–dc20 95-40959
CIP

Books published by Lawrence Erlbaum Associates are printed on acid-free paper, and their bindings are chosen for strength and durability.

ISBN: 978-0-805-81624-2 (hbk)
ISBN: 978-1-138-99145-3 (pbk)

CONTENTS

PREFACE

We all know that what people think about influences their behavior. Recognizing this, cognitive researchers have emphasized the need to demonstrate empirically the relationship between specific types of cognitive events and processes, on the one hand, and actions, on the other. For example, we now know that whether individuals focus their attention primarily in an inward self-oriented direction or on the task confronting them has a significant impact on their behavior. We also know that stress often produces an increase in the amount of off-task thinking and that some individuals seem to be generally prone to have thoughts that interfere with what they want to do. This volume is about the role unwanted thoughts play in people's lives, particularly with regard to effective performance and happiness. Our contributing authors are among the leaders in the study of various types of unwanted thoughts. They have done pioneering work in identifying both personality and situational variables that increase or decrease intrusive cognitions.

People differ in the kinds of cognitive interference they experience—images, thoughts, doubts, impulses. This book tells why certain cognitive events occur and what influences them. Although we all know that it is good to be task-oriented, attentive to what is going on in the situations with which we deal, and analytical in our approach to solving problems, we also know that this does not always happen. A person may be so anxious, depressed, or angry that rationality and planfulness are not possible. These personal affective responses can be due to the kind of people we are, the situation we find ourselves in, or both. An example of the role played by individual differences is the situation created by the instructions on an appliance we are considering buying. The instructions might say "Some assembly needed," and evoke a wide range of cognitive responses ranging from "This should be fun" to "I can't do this" to "What fool made up these instructions?"

The contributors to this book have thought constructively and creatively about cognitive intrusions and have confronted a number of important questions. These include:

1. What keeps people from controlling, regulating, and minimizing the cognitive interference they experience?
2. How is cognitive interference related to motivation and emotion?
3. Can cognitive interference be influenced in either positive or negative directions by particular situational factors?
4. How does cognitive interference relate to performance?
5. How can clinicians most effectively identify unwanted cognitions that misdirect and perhaps ruin people's lives, find out what activates these cognitions, and, ultimately, modify them?

It is clear that cognitive interference doesn't just materialize. It is not just an annoyance. It is part of the natural world of human thought and behavior. Understanding the process of cognitive interference might help move us along a path toward a psychology of productive thinking.

This book not only recognizes the legitimacy and importance of questions about intrusive thinking, but also reflects current theoretical and empirical efforts to answer them. Pertinent efforts are occurring in many areas of psychology that superficially might seem unrelated to each other. Yet, as the chapters show, there are common threads in such varied domains as the clinic, the classroom, the workplace, and the laboratory. If this volume has a message it is the call for a coherent approach to unwanted—often disturbing—thoughts in different domains of life. We hope we have taken a step toward needed integration of the exciting findings emerging in various domains.

We have organized the volume into three sections: (1) theoretical analyses of cognitive interference, (2) the role cognitive interference plays in influencing performance and social behavior, and (3) the pervasive and debilitating manifestations of cognitive interference that clinicians treat. Building on empirical evidence, contributors to the first section review and discuss the role of intrusive thinking in the natural flow of cognitive activity and how that unwanted activity might be assessed. Worry, self-doubt, self-focus, and distractibility are issues the contributors analyze. They ask many tantalizing questions including: "How can concepts of self-regulation incorporate the processes pertinent to cognitive interference?" "Can people learn to be more task-focused?" The second section deals with the relationship between cognitive interference and performance and the roles played by situational factors and individual differences. Intellective task performance, sports and other motor skills, social behavior (for example, shyness and loneliness), reactions to failure, and the acquisition of coping skills are among the topics contributors to this section deal with. The concluding section concerns seriously maladaptive behavior in which cognitive intrusions play an important role—depression, dissociation, anxiety, and post-traumatic stress reactions.

Flow charts like:

Task → Attention to task → Problem solving →
Action → End of sequence

are idealizations (occasionally, oversimplifications) because they fail to take account of or recognize the roles played by false starts, blind alleys, and mistaken judgments that occur in varying degrees every step of the way in cognitive-behavioral sequences. One of our major goals is to present important conceptualizations of cognitive-behavioral sequences that involve thoughts that usually hurt rather than help us.

If cognitive interference is not just an annoyance, accident, or glitch, then what is it? We think there is growing evidence that it is a superordinate concept that encompasses intrusive thinking in diverse situations and in people with particular characteristics. Self-oriented thoughts seem especially important in causing cognitive interference. They reduce the storage and processing capacity of the working memory system in laboratory, school, social, and work settings. The theoretical and research challenges posed by cognitive interference include the definition of classes of cognitions that lower personal effectiveness, identification of situations that bring them above threshold, and specification of pertinent risk factors. Increasing numbers of researchers are taking up these challenges.

This is the first volume to review comprehensively the topic of intrusive thought and its effects on people's lives. We hope it answers some questions and raises others. Although the phenomenon of cognitive interference is not new, its scientific study is. The chapters should be of interest to researchers and practitioners of various types—for example, clinicians and educators—whose efforts are directed to fathoming cognitions that interfere with people reaching their goals and helping them strengthen their cognitive repertories.

ACKNOWLEDGMENTS

We are indebted to many people who helped us directly or indirectly in editing this book. Most of all, we are indebted to the book's contributors who responded so enthusiastically to the invitation to participate in the project. We asked the contributors to review relevant research and to present their own conceptualizations about the contents of interfering thoughts and the processes by which these thoughts influence behavior. While we believed that these reviews and conceptualizations would contribute to the integration of wide-ranging evidence about intrusive thinking, it was not until we received the authors' contributions that we realized their depth and breadth and value for researchers and practitioners.

The book is the product, not only of our own thinking about the topic of cognitive interference, but also of the suggestions of colleagues. We have learned a lot from many people.

As usual, Betty Johnson has done a magnificent job of supporting our efforts. She has been there every step of the way.

Irwin G. Sarason
Gregory R. Pierce
Barbara R. Sarason

COGNITIVE INTERFERENCE
Theories, Methods, and Findings

PART I

Cognitive Interference and Information Processing

CHAPTER

1

THE CONTENTS OF THOUGHTS: INTERFERENCE AS THE DOWNSIDE OF ADAPTIVE NORMAL MECHANISMS IN THOUGHT FLOW

Eric Klinger
University of Minnesota

Cognitive interference takes many forms: attentional bias and distraction, memory lapses of various kinds, and several different kinds of intrusive or otherwise objectionable thoughts or thought patterns. This chapter discusses the last of these, the anomalies of thought content that are variously labeled mindwandering, daydreaming, worry, rumination, and obsessive thought.

These all have much in common. Much of the time they make adaptive—indeed, indispensable—contributions to living. At other times, they intrude on consciousness in ways that interfere with task performance and social relationships (Sarason, Sarason, Keefe, Hayes, & Shearin, 1986). The author regards them as consequences of the normal mechanisms that govern the flow of thought, albeit sometimes with self-destructive impact. This need not surprise us. Many pathways toward disease are laid down as protective processes that may sometimes go awry, as with fevers that protect but may get out of hand, or immune responses that protect but may begin to devastate the host. To begin with, then, the chapter reviews the normal mechanisms that govern thought flow and then examines the ways in which the thought patterns they engender come to take on troublesome forms.

NORMAL MECHANISMS OF SHIFTS IN THOUGHT CONTENT

Human thought normally shifts focus at a high rate, at least in the case of Minnesota students. Judging from thought-sampling studies with subjects trained to estimate the duration of their thoughts, the median length of time during which thought content remains on the same specific topic is about 5 seconds, with a mean of about 14 seconds (Klinger, 1978). This indicates that on average people shift thought content about 4,000 times per 16-hour day; or, putting it another way, engage in about 4,000 distinct thoughts a day.

Therefore, rapidly shifting thought content is the human norm. It becomes troublesome and can be considered to be interference when the content to which it shifts gets in the way of the individual's immediate goals. For example, if the person is trying to accomplish some task from which thought content keeps drifting away, and if that interferes with completing the task in a timely and effective manner, then the individual is likely to declare him or herself to be in a state of one or more of the following: mindwandering, preoccupation, worry, or inability to concentrate. If thought keeps shifting to images that the individual finds disturbing, such as particular violent or unacceptable sexual images, s/he may ponder the possibility of becoming mentally ill or may simply become self-condemnatory; and if he or she consults a psychodiagnostician, a case of obsessive-compulsive disorder may be diagnosed. Yet, in most such instances, the problem will turn out to be not a defect in the thought-shifting mechanism itself but a conflict between the conditions that govern the normal functioning of that mechanism and the individual's self-stated goals and possibly self-concept.

A Model of the Thought-Shifting Mechanism

In a nutshell, the model used here asserts that thought content shifts when an individual encounters a cue that arouses emotion because of its association with one of the individual's current concerns. The thought so triggered is likely to pertain to the respective concern. There are a number of qualifications to this generalization, but let us first explicate the core of the model.

A root assumption of this model is that animal life—including human life—consists of a series of goal pursuits. The term *current concern* (Klinger, 1971, 1975, 1977, 1987a) denotes a construct that refers to the *latent state* of an organism between the two time points of commitment to striving for a particular goal and either goal attainment or disengagement from that goal. The construct by itself does not refer to conscious content; although concerns are presumed to exert extensive influence on attention, recall, thought content, and action, the construct is different from—is presumed to underlie—these effects. This view posits a separate concern corresponding to each of a person's current goal pursuits. The goal in question may be as short- or long-term, as narrow or broad, and as trivial or lofty as the person may conceive of it, whether buying a new shirt, making new friends, winning an election, or attaining salvation.

A major property of a current concern is sensitization to cues associated with the goal or with the means for attaining it. This sensitization takes the form of emotional reactivity to those cues, accompanied by cognitive and often motor responses directed at advancing toward the goal. If the situation permits the person to take action toward the goal without unacceptable costs, the response will include such action. For example, if the goal is to attend a sold-out concert and the cue is an acquaintance who wishes to sell a ticket at a reasonable price, one is likely to buy the ticket on the spot. If the situation permits cognitive work aimed at later action toward the goal, this becomes part of the response. For example, if the cue is an acquaintance who intends to use the ticket, one may briefly ponder how to induce him to sell it. If the situation permits neither kind of operant response, the response remains respondent—simply spontaneous thought in reaction to the cue, without intended purpose. Such spontaneous responses are often dubbed "daydreaming." For example, the conversation comes around to the concert, no one there has a ticket, and one imagines trying to find a ticket just before the performance, or enviously imagines the crowd having a good time at the concert. In other words, emotionally arousing cues instigate goal-related responses, which may be restricted to spontaneous, apparently idle cognitive responses in the absence of acceptable opportunities to accomplish more.

The existence of emotional reactivity to cues associated with goal pursuits does not mean a full-blown emotional reaction to each cue that might be so associated. Rather, there are several levels at which cues are screened. At the lowest level, the individual processes gross features of a cue and, if an association with a goal pursuit exists, responds with a purely central, nonconscious *protoemotional response*. This response ushers in further cognitive processing which may confirm or disconfirm the relevance of the cue. In the case of disconfirmation, processing ends, whereas in the case of confirmation, processing proceeds further or is channeled into action, depending on the extent of cognitive closure about the cue and on the situation. At various points in this process, the cue may still be dismissed, terminating processing; or, as the meaning of the cue becomes clearer, the protoemotional process may gradually recruit other components of emotional response—glandular (e.g., adrenal, dermal), effector (e.g., facial, postural), and conscious components, including associated thought content.

The cues may be either external, such as speech, writing, or nonverbal events, or they may be internal, such as features of the ongoing stream of thought. "Thought" throughout this chapter includes mental imagery, whether verbal or not.

Qualifications to the Model

There are at least two kinds of qualifications to these generalizations. First, because individuals often encounter cues while engaged in some other activity, processing the cue sets up a conflict with the processing required by the already existing activity. Ongoing activity is accompanied by, for competing responses, reduced access to consciousness, to effectors, and probably to other resources. That is, competing activity, including conscious attention to something other than the ongoing activity, is to some extent inhibited. The inhibition is far from total, but it does raise the threshold for whatever criteria a competing response process must surmount to gain access. Therefore, concern-related, emotionally arousing cues may be processed without entering consciousness unless they pass certain elevated criteria for interrupting the ongoing stream.

A second qualification arises from the observation that emotionally arousing cues may produce conscious mental content even when they are not associated with a *current* concern. The cues may elicit hard-wired emotional responses, or they may elicit conditioned emotional responses that have not yet been extinguished. In most instances, however, emotional responses reflect current concerns—joy that goal pursuits are going well, fear when they are threatened, anger when they are first blocked, and disappointment, sadness, depression, or grief after they are clearly lost.

Implications for Shifts in Mental Content. This delineated model suggests both a mechanism for normal shifts in thought content and the variables that might occasion shifts that are experienced as interference. When a person is trying to work, for instance, the model would predict difficulty in keeping one's mind on the job in situations rich in cues for one's other current concerns, or when one is in the grip of an important current concern that produces powerful emotional responses to a wide range of cues, including those in one's own thought stream, but with a different goal from the goal of the task at hand. With this model, it is easy to see why concentrating on work is difficult while in love, in grief, or anticipating an imminent vacation. Later sections of this chapter explore these implications further.

Evidence for the Model

Evidence That Concern-Related Cues Elicit Conscious Content. Initial investigations of this model employed dichotic listening to two simultaneous 15-minute narratives, one to each ear, both of them taken from the same literary work. At intervals, the narratives were modified by inserting words that would presumably be associated with one of the subject's current concerns in one channel and synchronously the opposite narrative was modified to allude to another individual's concern, designated here as a nonconcern. These conditions were, of course, balanced with respect to side. Subjects used a toggle switch to signal the channel to which they were currently listening. A few seconds after each of these modified passages (embedding sites), the tape stopped with a signal tone, at which point subjects reported and rated last thoughts and also reported the last segments of the tape they could recall hearing. This provided information regarding attentional direction, recall, and thought content. Methods for assessing concerns included interviews at first and subsequently questionnaires (Klinger, 1987b), including currently the Motivational Structure Questionnaire (Cox & Klinger, 1988; Klinger & Kroll-Mensing, 1995).

The effects of conditions were quite powerful (Klinger, 1978). Subjects spent significantly more time listening to passages associated with their concerns, recalled those passages much more often, and had thought content that (by ratings of blind judges) was much more often related to them than to the nonconcern passages opposite them. Judges found hardly any resemblance of thoughts to passages that subjects had not yet heard, indicating that the cuing effect of concern-related stimuli accounted for the differences. Furthermore, when subjects were exposed to tapes created for other subjects, the embedded passages had no detectable effect, indicating that embedded text as such could not account for the effects.

To investigate whether this responsivity to concern-related cues required a conscious cognitive process or was reasonably automatic, we conducted a sleep experiment (Hoelscher, Klinger, & Barta, 1981). Sleeping subjects received spoken words or brief phrases that related to concerns or nonconcerns, as assessed on a previous day. A few seconds later, they were awakened for a dream report. Subjects much more often reported dreams related to concern-related than to nonconcern-related cues. Again, a control rating of how much dreams resembled cues not yet heard found little resemblance, indicating that the concern-related cues were responsible for the effect. These results confirmed that the effects of concern-related cues on cognitive processing are substantially automatic. That is, they occurred in reaction to concern-related cues without the intercession of waking consciousness or of deliberate decision-making.

Other data link current concerns to electrodermal responses of the kind often identified as orienting responses; they suggest that responses to internally generated cues follow the pattern shown for external cues (Nikula, Klinger, & Larson-Gutman, 1993). When subjects were induced to listen to strings of three-word clusters, those that alluded to one of the subject's current concerns evoked significantly more skin conductance responses than did those chosen to allude to a nonconcern. Furthermore, subjects thought-sampled just after a spontaneous skin conductance response—that is, a skin conductance response during a period without external cuing—were significantly more likely to report just having thought about a current concern than when they were thought-sampled during electrodermally inactive periods.

Evidence That Concern-Related and Emotionally Arousing Cues Compel Processing Even in the Absence of Intent or Consciousness. There are a number of investigations whose results show that encountering concern-related or emotionally arousing cues places an extra processing burden on cognitive activity, enough to slow down processing for the subject's main task. In one case, the cues were probably not even consciously perceived. Young's (1987) subjects were to decide as quickly as possible whether each occurrence of a letter string on a computer screen was an English word. Button-press answers provided reaction time. The left side of the screen was taken up by a patch containing computer-related verbal garbage that subjects were instructed to ignore (which they seem to have done) but which sometimes contained a word planted to relate to one of a subject's current concerns. When the target string was indeed a word, reaction time of reporting this was significantly slower if the distractor patch contained a concern-related word. Thus, concern-related stimuli seem to impose an extra cognitive-processing load even when they are peripheral and subjects are consciously ignoring them. This finding adds a further facet to the automaticity of the effect: it is not readily suppressed by disattention, but is instead to some degree irresistible.

This effect was shown in yet another cognitive process, using reaction time with either a modified Stroop or a quasi-Stroop procedure. In one of these investigations (Riemann & McNally, in press), student subjects were asked to name the colors of words that varied according to whether they were emotionally neutral or were highly or only slightly related to subjects' positive or negative current concerns. Responses were quickest for neutral words and slowest for words highly related to concerns, regardless of whether the concerns were positive or negative. In another such investigation (Johnsen, Laberg, Cox, Vaksdal, & Hugdahl, 1994), alcoholics and nonalcoholics named the colors of computer-displayed neutral words (e.g., "window"), alcohol-related words (e.g., "whiskey"), and, in the standard Stroop manner, mismatched color words (e.g., "red" written in green letters). Reaction times were slower in naming the colors of alcohol-related words (which for alcoholics were presumably also concern-related) than of neutral words for the alcoholics but not for the nonalcoholics. For the alcoholics, the effect was as powerful as was the standard Stroop manipulation. In the quasi-Stroop investigation (Cox, Blount, & Cools, unpublished data), alcoholic inpatients were presented with pairs of words, one of them a color word (e.g., yellow), and pressed one of two buttons to indicate the identity of the color word. The noncolor word was in either of five conditions: neutral, "color friction" (e.g., lemon—a marker condition), alcohol-related (e.g., drunk), other concern-related (e.g., daughter), or presumptively emotionally arousing (e.g., death). The three presumably concern-related conditions, taken as a group, produced significantly slower reactions than neutral words.

The interference of incidental concern-related stimuli with cognitive processing appears to be a general phenomenon, at least when the cognitive task is less than fully automatized. It has been shown to occur, in addition to the instances described above, with stimuli constructed to remind anxious subjects of their anxieties, subjects with self-concept problems of the discrepancy between the way they view themselves as being and the way they think they ought to be, and eating- or body-image-disordered subjects of their bodies (Newman et al., 1993).

Other investigations have shown that the effects of encountering emotionally arousing stimuli are similar to those of encountering concern-related stimuli. Thus, subjects pressed buttons to distinguish *X*s from *Y*s when they appeared one at a time on the lower half of a computer screen (Schneider, 1987). Distractor stimuli often appeared above them at the fixation point, many of them words, which subjects were instructed to ignore. After this procedure, subjects rated how much each distractor word aroused them emotionally. More emotionally arousing distractor words were associated with significantly slower reaction times. That this effect really was attributable to something emotional is supported by another feature of the investigation: Subjects who scored high on the Affective Intensity Measure (Larsen & Diener, 1987) were slowed by emotionally arousing distractors significantly more than other subjects were.

Evidence parallel to the above findings has come from investigations using social-psychological conceptions of attitudes, which presumably have a strong emotional component. Thus, to demonstrate that strongly held attitudes are activated automatically upon exposure to the objects of those attitudes, investigators (Fazio, Sanbonmatsu, Powell, & Kardes, 1986) presented subjects with "attitude objects" (e.g., "cake") which subjects had previously rated as "good" or "bad," followed 300 ms after stimulus onset by a positive or negative evaluative adjective (e.g., "awful"), which they were similarly to rate as "good" or "bad." They were also asked to keep rehearsing the word for each attitude object while evaluating the ensuing adjective. When the attitude object was regarded as strongly positive or negative (inferred from response speed in the first rating task), it slowed down response to an ensuing adjective of the opposite valence. The short time interval between them indicated that the effect had to be automatic—that the evaluation evoked by the attitude object could not have been decided deliberately.

Modifications in this procedure resulted in similar findings for objects of both strongly and weakly held positive and negative attitudes. This suggests that the effect is quite general. However, in one experiment (Bargh, Chaiken, Govender, & Pratto, 1992, Experiment 3), in which objects of both strongly (quickly evaluated) and weakly (slowly evaluated) held attitudes exerted effects on reaction time, the effects were stronger for the stronger than for the weaker attitudes, as would be predicted from an emotional-arousal standpoint.

Evidence That the Effects of Concerns Are Mediated by Emotional Responses. There is no direct evidence on emotional mediation of thought content, but there is such evidence with regard to effects on recall. Subjects were asked to perform any of several tasks with word stimuli, such as to judge their length, pronounceability, abstractness, or emotional arousal value. After a buffer task, subjects were given a free recall test for the words, after which they all rated them for their emotional arousal impact and their relatedness to subjects' individual current concerns. Words rated as either relatively emotionally arousing or concern-related were recalled significantly more often than other words (Bock

& Klinger, 1986; Klinger, Bock, & Bowi, 1990). Concern-relatedness and emotional arousal value of words were strongly intercorrelated. However, looking at words that were above average for a subject on one variable but below average on the other, it was possible to examine which combination of highs and lows produced the best recall. For words that had been processed with attention to their meanings, when their emotional arousal value was high, recall was superior regardless of the rating on concern-relatedness. Concern-relatedness, cleaned of emotional arousal variance, had no significant effect on recall. These results suggest that the effect of current concerns on recall is mediated by the emotional responses that the concerns largely potentiated. It seems likely that effects on thought content are similarly mediated by emotion.

COGNITIVE INTERFERENCE IN ANXIETY AND DEPRESSION

Among the most powerful sources of cognitive interference are states of anxiety and depression. Both, though in somewhat different ways, interfere with ability to concentrate, and both are experienced to a substantial degree in terms of the kinds of thoughts identified with them.

In view of the model described above, the cognitive interference experienced in anxiety and depression is readily understandable. Anxiety is a response to indications that goal pursuits are threatened (Gray, 1982). Under those circumstances, people are sensitized to cues regarding the threatened goal pursuit and to respond to them with mental content that works over their options and apprehensions. Anxious mentation therefore tends to be forward-looking (Kroll-Mensing, 1992). Depression is a result of realizing that an important goal pursuit is blocked, probably irretrievably (Klinger, 1975, 1977). It accompanies the process of disengaging from the lost goal, which is most likely a process of gradually inhibiting emotional responses to cues associated with the failed goal pursuit. Until disengagement is complete, the individual continues to respond emotionally to those cues, but with mental content that reviews the failed efforts to attain the goal, draws implications for one's ability to attain other such goals, reassesses one's self-concept, and seeks relief from emotional distress. Depressed mentation therefore tends to be backward-looking (Kroll-Mensing, 1992). Given a task that is unrelated to such mentation, and in view of the above theory of shifts in mental content, the anxious or depressed individual can be expected to find frequent anxiety- and depression-related intrusions on the process of carrying out the task.

Evidence on Cognitive Interference During Anxiety and Depression

Mounting behavioral evidence supports the connection between affect and cognitive processing, including attention, recall, and thought content. Given the model of content shifts proposed above, whatever factors influence attention are also likely to influence thought content, and recall may provide a post hoc indication of previous attentional focus. Thus, evidence on the way anxiety and depression influence attention and recall is also relevant to influences on thought content.

Retrieval has repeatedly been shown to be biased in the direction of mood-congruent content (Bower, 1992). This bias is not just a matter of valence—positive versus negative—but is specific to the type of negative affect: depressed individuals tend to recall depressive content, and anxious individuals tend to recall anxious content (Ingram, Kendall, Smith, Donnell, & Ronan, 1987). (A somewhat similar specificity can be seen in Stroop interference patterns: Carter, Maddock, & Magliozzi, 1992.)

The mood variable used in these studies has generally been assessed rather than induced, so that this evidence is purely correlational; but selective recall of anxious material by panic-disorder patients is enhanced by experimentally induced physical arousal (McNally, Foa, & Donnell, 1989), which suggests a causal influence. Furthermore, not only is there a consistent finding that people in depressed moods recall more negatively toned autobiographical memories, this effect is likelier a state than a trait effect (Lewinsohn & Rosenbaum, 1987), because it does not show up after the depression has remitted. It is therefore probably attributable to mood states rather than to any more enduring cognitive traits of the individual, such as accessibility of particular constructs.

In the case of attention, depressed individuals are more attentive to depressive cues than are nondepressed individuals (Gottlib, McLachlan, & Katz, 1988); and anxious individuals respond more quickly to threat-related than to nonthreat-related stimuli (using a probe method) in ways that indicate greater attentiveness to threat cues (Broadbent & Broadbent, 1988; Fox, 1993). It is presumably this differential attentiveness that accounts for panic-disorder patients' selectively slower color-naming of threat words in a Stroop-like task (Ehlers, Margraf, Davies, & Roth, 1988).

The cognitive impairments associated with anxiety and especially with depression have sometimes been interpreted as attributable to a narrowing of attentional focus (e.g., Hartlage, Alloy, Vázquez, & Dykman, 1993). The precise nature of this attentional narrowing has not been pinned down empirically with much precision, but the pattern of evidence (Hartlage et al., 1993) seems consistent with the view (also labeled a "resource allocation" model: Ellis, 1990; Ellis & Ashbrook, 1991) that depressed (and probably anxious) individuals display certain kinds of performance decrements as a result of preferring to process material related to their lost or threatened goals rather than the material associated with a different task. This view is especially strengthened by the pattern of evidence indicating that depressed individuals display their decrements when working with tasks requiring mental effort but not with tasks eliciting overlearned, "automatically" accessible responses. Particularly, even on mentally effortful tasks there are generally no decrements and there may even be enhancements of performance when the content of the task is to learn negatively valenced material (Hartlage et al., 1993)—that is, material more relevant to the depressed subjects' concerns.

An alternative view holds that depression produces cognitive interference because depressed individuals are unable to let go of unmet goals (Kuhl & Helle, 1986, 1994). They therefore continue to be preoccupied with their previous intentions, and these interfere with new activities. In this study, subjects were enlisted in a task of cleaning up a messy table, but were then diverted from being able to do so. Strongly as compared with slightly depressed subjects subsequently showed a significantly reduced memory span and reported thinking much more about the messy table. This explanation is consistent with the current concerns approach, but it also adds an individual-differences component: depressed individuals have trouble letting go of blocked goal pursuits other than the one(s) that may have depressed them in the first place.

Naturally Occurring Thought Content in Anxiety and Depression

The evidence described above was collected largely in experimentally controlled situations, which leave the implications for everyday experience untested. However, there are now also experience-sampling data on the thought-content correlates of anxiety and depression (Kroll-Mensing, 1992). These data were collected by having subjects take beeper wristwatches into their everyday lives for three days and to record the thoughts and feelings they experienced just before each signal.

Looking at individual differences, people who were more depressed than others reported a lower proportion of deliberate, directed, thoughts. Their thoughts were more focused on the past and more often on some kind of loss. Those who were more anxious than others experienced their thoughts as less controllable. Their thoughts were more often focused on the future and more often on failure. Both, in various ways, experienced their thoughts as more dysphoric and reported more imagined interactions with others than did nondepressed, nonanxious individuals, and their imagined interactions generated on average less positive feeling than did those of the nondepressed and nonanxious.

Looking at variation within individuals, when these subjects were feeling more depressed than usual, they rated their thoughts as vaguer and as containing less visual imagery, including less color, and slightly less auditory imagery. Their thoughts were somewhat more preoccupied with past or present losses.

When these subjects were feeling more anxious than usual, they rated their thoughts as feeling less controllable and modifiable and as more inappropriate. Their thoughts were more focused on future anticipated losses and problems and on present or past failure. The interactions they imagined having with others left them less satisfied with their imaginary partners.

Both kinds of moods were associated with more dysphoric thoughts, decreased comfort, and more focus on self. They both were associated with less positive feelings during imagined interactions with others.

Many of these findings are consistent with the view that the effects of anxiety and depression reflect what is happening to people's goal pursuits. As these are threatened, thereby generating anxiety, thoughts focus on the future problems this presents and become more intrusive. As goal pursuits are stymied, thereby generating depression, thoughts become less directed and flaccid—perhaps a kind of surrender to the inevitable—and more focused on the loss, thus facilitating the process of disengagement from the goal.

WORRY AND RUMINATION

People are often preoccupied with important events in their lives. Whether this is healthy or maladaptive for them depends very much on the circumstances of the preoccupation. There is a continuum of preoccupation that is at least three-dimensional.

One dimension, of course, is simply the proportion of time a person spends on a certain topic. By itself, this dimension tells one nothing about health or adaptiveness. Even extensive preoccupation with something can be healthy and adaptive if it maintains positive affect and helps to solve life's problems.

The second dimension is the valence of the affect associated with the preoccupation. Someone preoccupied with a lover may experience predominantly positive affect; someone preoccupied with a pregnancy may experience predominantly positive or predominantly negative affect or a mix of affect; someone preoccupied with a failed relationship or a failed career will experience predominantly negative affect—emotions such as anger, anxiety, shame, guilt, disappointment, or depression. This dimension certainly bears on health, in that negative affect is unpleasant and tends to lower resistance to disease; but its bearing on adaptiveness is complex, because some negatively valenced processing may be necessary for successful disengagement from failed goals (Beckmann, 1993, 1994; Klinger, 1975, 1977, 1990). Negatively valenced preoccupation is generally labeled "worry" (e.g., Borkovec, 1985).

The third dimension is the amount of utility or redundancy of the mental content. When worry becomes unduly repetitive and stereotyped, it ceases to contribute to problem solving while maintaining a high level of negative affect, and it crowds out more adaptive, pleasant mental content. Thus, this is the dimension that contains most of the evaluation regarding the adaptiveness of preoccupation. Overly repetitive worry is generally labeled "rumination" (e.g., Lyubomirsky & Nolen Hoeksema, 1993; Martin & Tesser, 1989).

Although healthy preoccupation, worry, and rumination have become separate categories in the psychological literature, there is no reason to suppose that they follow different sets of principles. All can be regarded as special cases of the general model of content shifts described above. They are differentiable chiefly in terms of the goal pursuits they represent. All reflect important goal pursuits whose cues are capable of eliciting strong emotion, although they vary in the type of emotion they typically elicit. Hypothetically, healthy preoccupation is the result of the general model when the goal pursuit is going reasonably well and the dominant emotional responses are interest and joy. Worry is the result of perceiving threats to one's goal pursuits (Vasey & Borkovec, 1992). As a major component of anxiety, its dominant emotional responses are the negative ones of fear, anger, etc. (e.g., Davey, 1994; Eysenck & Van Berkum, 1992). Rumination is associated with goal pursuits that are mired down or in the process of disengagement, and its dominant emotional responses are anger, sadness, and fear. Rumination is a characteristic symptom of depression and other states related to major stressful life events (Tait & Silver, 1989).

Within the present model, individuals with especially pressing goals are disposed by their concerns to respond readily with strong emotion to cues associated with those concerns, and many of these cues occur within the individual's own thought stream. Normally, such cues trigger responses that pertain to a variety of the individual's concerns. In preoccupation, however, the potentiation of strong emotional responses to the one class of cues is so strong that the thoughts about the topic of the preoccupation keep cueing further emotional responses and further accompanying mental content within the same topic area.

It is as yet unclear just how a goal pursuit comes to command the degree of emotional responsivity that leads to preoccupation. However, Martin and Tesser (1989) argue that goals high in a goal hierarchy, whose attainment or loss would affect a correspondingly larger portion of an individual's life, are more important in this respect than goals low in their respective hierarchies.

Clearly, individual differences in personality will influence the disposition toward each of the styles of preoccupation. Hypothetically, extraversion (or its component positive emotionality) should dispose toward healthy preoccupation; neuroticism (negative emotionality) should dispose toward worry and rumination. This is consistent with factor analyses of daydream styles, which have consistently found individual-difference factors commonly labeled "positive-constructive daydreaming" and "guilty-dysphoric daydreaming" (Segal, Huba, & Singer, 1980; Singer & Antrobus, 1972).

In possible contradistinction to this model of content shifting, Lyubomirsky and Nolen-Hoeksema (1993) argue that, once caught up in rumination, depressed individuals are motivated to continue ruminating, at least to the extent of being less likely to switch to a nonruminative activity that they would normally enjoy. However, there are reasons to question this conclusion, especially inasmuch as depressed individuals find their daydreams unpleasant and boring (Giambra & Traynor, 1978). Lyubomirsky and Nolen-Hoeksema's (1993) evidence came from an experimental manipulation in which subjects were induced to ruminate or not to ruminate, after which they indicated the likelihood that they would engage in any of a list of activities. Those subjects induced to ruminate averaged lower likelihoods of engaging in the nonruminative tasks. However, depressive rumination itself depresses mood further (Nolen-Hoeksema & Morrow, 1993), and depression is associated with a disinclination to engage in pleasurable activities (Klinger, 1993a). Therefore, the lowered likelihood of experimentally induced ruminators might just reflect their differentially depressed moods rather than any motivation to ruminate as such.

SUPPRESSION, SELF-MONITORING, AND OBSESSIVE MENTATION

"Obsessional thought" refers to the classic clinical phenomenon of unwanted, anxiety-provoking thoughts that keep intruding on consciousness. For example: "I used to walk down the street thinking of choking women I saw or grabbing at men's dicks. I don't know how often I'd have these thoughts, probably hundreds of times a day. These thoughts sometimes terrified me. I was afraid I'd do it. Yet I knew I didn't want to. I had no control over the thoughts, had no idea of where they came from or why I couldn't get rid of them" (Morphy, 1980).

Despite the alarm with which people often greet such obsessional ideas, and apart from their interference with other cognitive activity, they tend to be innocuous. Individuals who are obsessional in this sense rarely act out their obsessional images. What distinguishes these experiences from snatches of ordinary daydreams is the reaction to them—the individual's anxiety and sense of having lost control. People are less likely than with worry to experience them as triggered by ordinary events (Turner, Beidel, & Stanley, 1992). Given that nearly half of thoughts are predominantly spontaneous, that is, undirected (Klinger, 1990; Klinger & Cox, 1987–1988), it is not at all unusual for mental content to "pop into" one's consciousness. Most likely, the property that makes obsessional thoughts feel especially out of control is their ego-dystonic character and the anxiety that this evokes. The fact that they are ego-dystonic also indicates that these thoughts, which are usually heavily imaginal, represent feelings and motivation that the individual fails to acknowledge.

Careful clinical analysis tends to show that obsessional thoughts arise under specific circumstances, following specific cues that are associated with particular concerns (e.g., Tallis & de Silva, 1992). In other words, obsessional thoughts can be accommodated by the general model of content shifts described previously. Supportive of this view is evidence that "at best, there is a continuum between obsessions and worry, and . . . at worst, obsessions and worry overlap to such a degree that the distinction is meaningful only in pure cases" (Freeston et al., 1994, p. 29).

This view is also supported by the nature of the behavioral methods that are effective in treating obsessional patients. These include satiation (paying close attention to each occurrence), paradoxical intention (deliberately creating the obsessional images), and connecting the images with the feelings and goals they reflect. All of these methods have in common the kind of exposure—focusing on the obsessional thought, which in this instance is the source of anxiety, without permitting escape—that is the common denominator of effective behavioral treatments for other anxiety disorders (Klinger, 1993b). This both extinguishes the anxiety such thoughts evoke and, by eliminating attempts to suppress them, reduces their frequency. Connecting them to their underlying motivational and emotional nexus furthermore obviates the need for them and eliminates them.

The idea that trying to suppress thoughts increases their tendency to occur has found substantial experimental support in recent years (Wegner, 1989). However, the reason for this may have to do with the paradox inherent in suppression: if one is to suppress a thought, one must continuously monitor one's consciousness to police its occurrence. Monitoring, of course, maintains sensitization to the thought. It may be the act of monitoring for the to-be-suppressed thought that accounts for its increased tendency to occur (Salkovskis & Campbell, 1994; Wegner, 1989).

There are undoubtedly other factors than those discussed here that contribute to clinically significant obsessional thoughts, including those that are emerging in neuropsychology (Otto, 1992). Presumably, obsessional individuals are more prone to negative emotions and may evince other individual differences in behavior that have so far not been identified. Nevertheless, these other factors may well have their impact chiefly by modifying the response parameters in the general model of content shifting described in this chapter.

OTHER STATE AND INDIVIDUAL DIFFERENCES IN SUSCEPTIBILITY TO COGNITIVE INTERFERENCE: ACTION VERSUS STATE ORIENTATION

The previous sections have indicated conditions and states that conduce to interference with the content of thought. Additionally, some individuals appear to be consistently more susceptible to this kind of interference than others. Accumulating evidence provides steadily increasing support for a dimension of *action versus state orientation* (Kuhl & Beckmann, 1994). This dimension theoretically denotes both states and more enduring individual differences. Operationally, however, it is most commonly investigated as a trait.

Action orientation refers to "the ability to facilitate the enactment of context-adequate intentions . . . whenever it is appropriate" (Kuhl, 1994a, p. 10). State orientation refers to a focus on one's current state in ways that interfere with continuing volitional activity, including "debilitating effects on individuals' volitional abilities to plan, initiate, and complete intended activities: Intrusive and perseverating thoughts focusing on an experienced state can impair those volitional functions, at least temporarily" (Kuhl, 1994a, p. 9).

Although neither orientation is considered inherently adaptive or maladaptive—for example, state-orientedness would facilitate deliberating about a complex decision—state orientation is strongly correlated with anxiety (Bossong, 1994; Hautzinger, 1994; Kammer, 1994; Klinger & Murphy, 1994) and depression (Hautzinger, 1994; Kammer, 1994). The dimension is "moderately related to fundamental personality dimensions such as conscientiousness, negative emotionality (sometimes called "neuroticism"), anxiety, especially its worry component, intro- versus extraversion, etc." (Kuhl & Beckmannn, 1994, p. 3). Nevertheless, Kuhl and Beckman view the construct as having sufficient variance independent of such other personality dimensions, and sufficient independent relatedness to yet other variables, including neurophysiological ones (Kuhl, 1994a), as to warrant a separate theoretical identity.

The dimension of action versus state orientation is assessed as a trait by the Action Control Scale (ACS; Kuhl, 1994b), factor analyses of which have yielded three factors: preoccupation (with past events), hesitation (regarding the future), and volatility (tendency to alternate activities or do more than one thing at a time) (Kanfer, Dugdale, & McDonald, 1994; Kuhl, 1994b). The first two factors are strongly intercorrelated, but they are uncorrelated with the third. Volatility sounds conceptually the inverse of absorption (Tellegen & Atkinson, 1974), but it is essentially uncorrelated (Klinger & Murphy, 1994) with the Absorption scale of the Multidimensional Personality Questionnaire (MPQ; Tellegen, 1985).

State-oriented individuals are characterized by a number of attributes relevant to cognitive interference. The Preoccupation and Hesitation scales of the ACS are strongly correlated (Klinger & Murphy, 1994) with the Poor Attentional Control scale of the Short Imaginal Processes Inventory (Huba, Singer, & Aneshensel 1982) and with the MMPI Schizophrenia scale, and moderately correlated in one of two studies with a thought-sampling measure of vagueness of thoughts and mistrust for their memory of their thoughts (Klinger & Murphy, 1994). They require more time to process the attainment of a goal or the failure to attain it before being ready to go on to the next one (Beckmann, 1994). Under induced failure, state-oriented individuals employ fewer efficient strategic plans and more inefficient task strategies than action-oriented individuals, they experience less self-confidence, give themselves fewer instructions, and are more preoccupied with loss of control (Brunstein, 1994).

Despite their apparently greater immersion in their own thoughts, state-oriented individuals are not less defensive or more favorably inclined toward daydreaming than the action-oriented; on the contrary, they espouse less favorable attitudes toward daydreaming, feel less free to disclose either their daydreams or their past actual experiences, and feel less comfortable when they imagine doing so (Klinger & Murphy, 1994).

In addition to displaying these cognitive attributes, state orientation is also associated with a number of volitional peculiarities. Despite the fact that state-oriented individuals ruminate more about their intentions, they are actually more likely to forget them and less likely to carry them out; and they are more likely to be confused as to whether their activities were assigned by others or are what they themselves intended (Kuhl & Goschke, 1994). They have more difficulty in making choices and take longer to decide among alternative activities (Stiensmeier-Pelster, 1994).

Some of the cognitive deficits associated with state orientation can be related to the content-shifting model with which this chapter began. The common denominator of these deficits appears to be attentional focus on thoughts other than those best suited to facilitating action. That is, state-oriented individuals are more subject than others to intrusions of thought content extraneous to what it would be most adaptive to focus on. Their content shifting mechanism seems relatively underinhibited by a task focus or by the operant demands of a present situation.

One possible explanation for this apparent underinhibition is that state-oriented individuals may respond with stronger emotion to cues of their various other goal pursuits. State orientation has, in fact, been found correlated with Affective Intensity Measure (AIM; Larsen & Diener, 1987) scores. In two studies, correlations of AIM with ACS preoccupation and hesitation scores (with state orientation at the low end of the scale and action orientation at the high end) have ranged from –.13 to –.39 (Kanfer, Dugdale, & McDonald, 1994; Klinger & Murphy, 1994). To the extent that an individual responds with stronger emotion to concern-related cues other than those relevant to a task at hand, task-irrelevant thoughts will keep outmatching the inhibitory constraints and keep intruding on consciousness. This may be one manifestation of what Kuhl (1994a, p. 39) calls the "role of the septo-hippocampal system . . . in mediating maintenance ("perseveration") of cognitive" and other processes.

(2) State-oriented individuals may possess a weaker capacity for inhibition. Both preoccupation and hesitation scores of the ACS (with state orientation at the low end of the scale and action orientation at the high end) are, in fact, correlated in two studies with MPQ Control, with coefficients ranging from .33 to .47 (Klinger & Murphy, 1994). Whether these relationships entail a different capacity for inhibition is, however, impossible to determine from these relationships. It is furthermore an oversimplification to speak in terms of across-the-board differences in inhibitory strength. However, if state orientation were associated with a deficiency in nonconscious ("automatic") inhibition of task-irrelevant thoughts, that would not only lead to more intrusions, but would also force a more massive, partly conscious effort to suppress them, which might further interfere with task performance or with the volitional resources required to get on to a new activity (Kuhl, 1994a). There is evidence that processing failure is compressed, presumably automatically, by the prospect of having.to begin a new task soon (Beckmann, 1993). That kind of clearing of the mental decks appears to come harder to the state-oriented.

Action- and state-oriented individuals do differ neurophysiologically in their reactions to failure (Haschke, Tennigkeit, & Kuhl, 1994), with the state-oriented displaying a positive slow-potential shift in their EEGs over a 5 s period following failure feedback as compared with success feedback. Whether this represents a failure to inhibit responses to the feedback is, however, uncertain.

CONCLUSIONS

Thought content typically jumps from one topic to another at a rapid pace. One model that appears to accommodate much of what is known about content-shifting asserts that thought content shifts when an individual encounters a cue that arouses emotion because of its association with one of the individual's current concerns. The cue may be external or an internal part of the individual's ongoing conscious stream. The thought so triggered is likely to pertain to the respective concern. Substantial evidence has accumulated both for the directing and sensitizing role of current concerns and for the mediating role of emotional responses. The content-shifting mechanism is to some extent constrained by the demands of ongoing task activity.

The cognitive interference associated with anxiety and depression can be viewed as special cases of this general model, in which anxiety states potentiate strong responses to threat-related cues, with the accompanying thoughts being relatively more often future oriented, whereas depression potentiates strong responses to loss-related cues, with the accompanying thoughts relating more often to past events. In the latter case, depression is seen as evidence that the individual has not yet completed disengagement from major lost goals.

Preoccupation, with its intrusions on thought content, can be described along three dimensions: proportion of time spent on a topic, quality of the affect accompanying those thoughts, and their utility (versus redundancy). Rumination, which falls high on the first two dimensions but low on the third, is consistent with the content-shifting model under conditions of strong negative emotional responsivity to cues of a threatened or lost goal. Obsessive thoughts also probably fit within the content-shifting model, differing from other thought content primarily in their ego-dystonic quality and the consequent horror with which the individual having them reacts.

Individuals vary in their susceptibility to cognitive interference, a difference addressed by the concept of action versus state orientation. State-oriented individuals experience more thoughts irrelevant to ongoing tasks and situational demands intruding on their thought streams, along with a number of other cognitive and volitional attributes. The cognitive attributes can be understood within the current-concerns-based content-shifting model as associated with affectively more intense responses to concern-related cues and relatively weakened automatic inhibition of task- and situation-relevant thought content.

REFERENCES

Bargh, J. A., Chaiken, S., Govender, R., & Pratto, F. (1992). *Journal of Personality and Social Psychology, 62*, 893–912.

Beckmann, J. (1993). *Ruminative thought and the disengagement from an intention.* Unpublished manuscript.

Beckmann, J. (1994). Volitional correlates of action versus state orientation. In J. Kuhl & J. Beckmann (Eds.), *Volition and personality: Action versus state orientation* (pp. 155–166). Seattle: Hogrefe & Huber.

Bock, M., & Klinger, E. (1986). Interaction of emotion and cognition in word recall. *Psychological Research, 48*, 99–106.

Borkovec, T. D. (1985, December). What's the use of worrying? *Psychology Today, 19*, 58–60, 62–64.

Bossong, B. (1994). Scholastic stressors and achievement-related anxiety. In J. Kuhl & J. Beckmann (Eds.), *Volition and personality: Action versus state orientation* (pp. 397–406). Seattle: Hogrefe & Huber.

Bower, G. H. (1992). How might emotions affect learning? In S.-A. Christianson (Ed.), *The handbook of emotion and memory: Research and theory* (pp. 3–32). Hillsdale, NJ: Lawrence Erlbaum Associates.

Broadbent, D., & Broadbent, M. (1988). Anxiety and attentional bias: State and trait. *Cognition and Emotion, 2*, 165–184.

Brunstein, J. (1994). Dispositional action control as a predictor of how people cope with academic failure. In J. Kuhl & J. Beckmann (Eds.), *Volition and personality: Action versus state orientation* (pp. 341–350). Seattle: Hogrefe & Huber.

Carter, C. S., Maddock, R. J., & Magliozzi, J. (1992). Patterns of abnormal processing of emotional information in panic disorder and major depression. *Psychopathology, 25*, 65–70.

Cox, W. M., & Klinger, E. (1988). A motivational model of alcohol use. *Journal of Abnormal Psychology, 97*, 168–180.

Davey, G. C. L. (1994). Worrying, social problem-solving abilities, and social problem-solving confidence. *Behaviour Research and Therapy, 32*, 327–330.

Ehlers, A. M., Margraf, J., Davies, S., & Roth, W. T. (1988). Selective processing of threat cues in subjects with panic attacks. *Cognition and Emotion, 2*, 201–220.

Ellis, H. C. (1990). Depressive deficits in memory: Processing initiative and resource allocation. *Journal of Experimental Psychology: General, 119*, 60–63.

Ellis, H. C., & Ashbrook, P. W. (1991). The "state" of mood and memory research: A selective review. In D. Kuiken (Ed.), *Mood and memory: Theory, research and applications* (pp. 1–21). Newbury Park, CA: Sage.

Eysenck, M. W., & Van Berkum, J. (1992). Trait anxiety, defensiveness, and the structure of worry. *Personality and Individual Differences, 13*, 1285–1290.

Fazio, R. H., Sanbonmatsu, D. M., Powell, M. C., & Kardes, F. R. (1986). On the automatic activation of attitudes. *Journal of Personality and Social Psychology, 50*, 229–238.

Fox, E. (1993). Allocation of visual attention and anxiety. *Cognition and Emotion, 7*, 207–216.

Freeston, M. H., Ladouceur, R., Rheaume, J., Letarte, H., et al. (1994). Self-report of obsessions and worry. *Behaviour Research and Therapy, 32*, 29–36.

Giambra, L. M., & Traynor, T. D. (1978). Depression and daydreaming: An analysis based on self-ratings. *Journal of Clinical Psychology, 34*, 14–25.

Gottlib, I. H., McLachlan, A. L., & Katz, A. N. (1988). Biases in visual attention in depressed and nondepressed individuals. *Cognition and Emotion, 2*, 185–200.

Gray, J. A. (1982). *The neuropsychology of anxiety: An enquiry into the functions of the septo-hippocampal system.* New York: Oxford University Press.

Hartlage, S., Alloy, L. B., Vázquez, C., & Dykman, B. (1993). Automatic and effortful processing in depression. *Psychological Bulletin, 113*, 247–278.

Haschke, R., Tennigkeit, M., & Kuhl, J. (1994). Personality and task related slow potential shifts: The role of test anxiety and action vs. state orientation in top-ranking soccer players' coping with failure. In J. Kuhl & J. Beckmann (Eds.), *Volition and personality: Action versus state orientation* (pp. 475–483). Seattle: Hogrefe & Huber.

Hautzinger, M. (1994). Action control in the co/ntext of psychopathological disorders. In J. Kuhl & J. Beckmann (Eds.), *Volition and personality: Action versus state orientation* (pp. 209–215). Seattle: Hogrefe & Huber.

Hoelscher, T. J., Klinger, E., & Barta, S. G. (1981). Incorporation of concern- and nonconcern-related verbal stimuli into dream content. *Journal of Abnormal Psychology, 49*, 88–91.

Huba, G. J., Singer, J. L., & Aneshensel, C. S. (1982). *Short Imaginal Processes Inventory Manual.* Port Huron, MI: Research Psychologists Press.

Ingram, R. E., Kendall, P. C., Smith, T. W., Donnell, C., & Ronan, K. (1987). Cognitive specificity in emotional distress. *Journal of Personality and Social Psychology, 53*, 734–742.

Johnsen, B. H, Laberg, J. C., Cox, W. M., Vaksdal, A., & Hugdahl, K. (1994). Alcoholics' attentional bias in the processing of alcohol-related words. *Psychology of Addictive Behaviors, 8*, 111–115.

Kammer, D. (1994). On depression and state orientation: A few empirical and theoretical remarks. In J. Kuhl & J. Beckmann (Eds.), *Volition and personality: Action versus state orientation* (pp. 351–362). Seattle: Hogrefe & Huber.

Kanfer, R., Dugdale, B., & McDonald, B. (1994). Empirical findings on the action control scale in the context of complex skill acquisition. In J. Kuhl & J. Beckmann (Eds.), *Volition and personality: Action versus state orientation* (pp. 61–77). Seattle: Hogrefe & Huber.

Klinger, E. (1971). *Structure and functions of fantasy.* New York: Wiley.

Klinger, E. (1975). Consequences of commitment to and disengagement from incentives. *Psychological Review, 82*, 1–25.

Klinger, E. (1977). *Meaning and void: Inner experience and the incentives in people's lives.* Minneapolis: University of Minnesota Press.

Klinger, E. (1978). Modes of normal conscious flow. In K. S. Pope & J. L. Singer (Eds.), *The stream of consciousness: Scientific investigations into the flow of human experience* (pp. 225–258). New York: Plenum.

Klinger, E. (1987a). Current concerns and disengagement from incentives. In F. Halisch & J. Kuhl (Eds.), *Motivation, intention and volition* (pp. 337–347). Berlin: Springer.

Klinger, E. (1987b). The Interview Questionnaire technique: Reliability and validity of a mixed idiographic-nomothetic measure of motivation. In J. N. Butcher & C. D. Spielberger (Eds.), *Advances in personality assessment* (Vol. 6, pp. 31–48). Hillsdale, NJ: Lawrence Erlbaum Associates.

Klinger, E. (1990). *Daydreaming.* Los Angeles: Tarcher.

Klinger, E. (1993a). Loss of interest. In C. G. Costello (Ed.), *Symptoms of depression* (pp. 43–62). New York: Wiley.

Klinger, E. (1993b). Clinical approaches to mood control. In D. M. Wegner & J. W. Pennebaker (Eds.), *Handbook of mental control* (pp. 344–369). Englewood Cliffs, NJ: Prentice-Hall.

Klinger, E., Bock M., & Bowi, U. (1990). *Emotional mediation of motivational factors in word recall.* Unpublished manuscript.

Klinger, E., & Cox, W. M. (1987–1988). Dimensions of thought flow in everyday life. *Imagination, Cognition and Personality, 7*, 105–128.

Klinger, E., & Murphy, M. D. (1994). Action orientation and personality: Some evidence on the construct validity of the Action Control Scale. In J. Kuhl & J. Beckmann (Eds.), *Volition and personality: Action versus state orientation* (pp. 79–92). Seattle: Hogrefe & Huber.

Klinger, E., & Kroll-Mensing, D. (1995). Idiothetic assessment: Experience samping and motivational analysis. In J. N. Butcher (Ed.), *Clinical personality assessment: Practical approaches* (pp. 267–277). New York: Oxford University Press.

Kroll-Mensing, D. (1992). *Differentiating anxiety and depression: An experience sampling analysis.* Unpublished doctoral dissertation, University of Minnesota, Minneapolis.

Kuhl, J. (1994a). A theory of action and state orientations. In J. Kuhl & J. Beckmann (Eds.), *Volition and personality: Action versus state orientation* (pp. 9–46). Seattle: Hogrefe & Huber.

Kuhl, J. (1994b). Action versus state orientation: Psychometric properties of the Action Control Scale (ACS-90). In J. Kuhl & J. Beckmann (Eds.), *Volition and personality: Action versus state orientation* (pp. 47–59). Seattle: Hogrefe & Huber.

Kuhl, J., & Beckmann, J. (Eds.). (1994). *Volition and personality: Action versus state orientation.* Seattle: Hogrefe & Huber.

Kuhl, J., & Goschke, T. (1994). State orientation and the activation and retrieval of intentions in memory. In J. Kuhl & J. Beckmann (Eds.), *Volition and personality: Action versus state orientation* (pp. 127–153). Seattle: Hogrefe & Huber.

Kuhl, J., & Helle, P. (1986). Motivational and volitional determinants of depression: The degenerated-intention hypothesis. *Journal of Abnormal Psychology, 95,* 247–251.

Kuhl, J., & Helle, P. (1994). Motivational and volitional determinants of depression: The degenerated-intention hypothesis.

Larsen, R., & Diener, E. (1987). Affect intensity as an individual difference characteristic. *Journal of Research in Personality, 21,* 1–39.

Lewinsohn, P. M., & Rosenbaum, M. (1987). Recall of parental behavior by acute depressives, remitted depressives, and nondepressives. *Journal of Personality and Social Psychology, 52,* 611–619.

Lyubomirsky, S., & Nolen-Hoeksema, S. (1993). Self-perpetuating properties of dysphoric rumination. *Journal of Personality and Social Psychology, 65,* 339–349.

Martin, L. L., & Tesser, A. (1989). Toward a motivational and structural theory of ruminative thought. In J. S. Uleman & J. A. Bargh (Eds.), *Unintended thought* (pp. 306–326). New York: Guilford.

McNally, R. J., Foa, E. B., & Donnell, C. D. (1989). Memory bias for anxiety information in patients with panic disorder. *Cognition and Emotion, 3,* 27–44.

Morphy, R. (1980). An inner view of obsessional neurosis. *The Gestalt Journal, 3,* 120–136.

Newman, J. P., Wallace, J. F., Strauman, T. J., Skolaski, R. L., Oreland, K. M., Mattek, P. W., Elder, K. A., & McNeely, J. (1993). Effects of motivationally significant stimuli on the regulation of dominant responses. *Journal of Personality and Social Psychology, 65,* 165–175.

Nikula, R., Klinger, E., & Larson-Gutman, M. K. (1993). Current concerns and electrodermal reactivity: Responses to words and thoughts. *Journal of Personality, 61,* 63–84.

Nolen-Hoeksema, S., & Morrow, J. (1993). Effects of rumination and distraction on naturally occurring depressed mood. *Cognition and Emotion, 7,* 561–570.

Otto, M. W. (1992). Normal and abnormal information processing: A neuropsychological perspective on obsessive compulsive disorder. *Psychiatric Clinics of North America, 15,* 825–848.

Riemann, B. C., & McNally, R. J. (in press). Cognitive processing of personally-relevant information. *Cognition and Emotion.*

Salkovskis, P. M., & Campbell, P. (1994). Thought suppression induces intrusion in naturally occurring negative intrusive thoughts. *Behaviour Research and Therapy, 32,* 1–8.

Sarason, I. G., Sarason, B. R., Keefe, D. E., Hayes, B. E., & Shearin, E. N. (1986). Cognitive interference: Situational determinants and traitlike characteristics. *Journal of Personality and Social Psychology, 51,* 215–226.

Schneider, W. (1987). *Ablenkung und Handlungskontrolle: Eine 'kognitiv-motivationale Perspektive'* [Distraction and action control: A "cognitive-motivational perspective"]. Unpublished diploma thesis, University of Bielefeld, Germany.

Segal, B., Huba, G. J., & Singer, J. L. (1980). *Drugs, daydreaming, and personality: A study of college youth.* Hillsdale, NJ: Lawrence Erlbaum Associates.

Singer, J. L., & Antrobus, J. S. (1972). Daydreaming, imaginal processes, and personality: A normative study. In P. W. Sheehan (Ed.), *The function and nature of imagery* (pp. 175–202). New York: Academic Press.

Stiensmeier-Pelster, J. (1994). Choice of decision-making strategies and action versus state orientation. In J. Kuhl & J. Beckmann (Eds.), *Volition and personality: Action versus state orientation* (pp. 167–176). Seattle: Hogrefe & Huber.

Tait, R., & Silver, R. C. (1989). Coming to terms with major negative life events. In J. S. Uleman & J. A. Bargh (Eds.), *Unintended thought* (pp. 351–382). New York: Guilford.

Tallis, F., & De Silva, P. (1992). Worry and obsessional symptoms: A correlational analysis. *Behaviour Research and Therapy, 30,* 103–105.

Tellegen, A. (1985). Structures of mood and personality and their relevance to assessing anxiety: With an emphasis on self-report. In A. H. Tuma & J. Maser (Eds.), *Anxiety and the anxiety disorders* (pp. 681–706). Hillsdale, NJ : Lawrence Erlbaum Associates.

Tellegen, A., & Atkinson, G. (1974). Openness to absorbing and self-altering experience ("absorption"), a trait related to hypnotic susceptibility. *Journal of Abnormal Psychology, 83,* 268–277.

Turner, S. M., Beidel, D. C., & Stanley, M. A. (1992). Are obsessional thoughts and worry different cognitive phenomena? *Clinical Psychology Review, 12,* 257–270.

Vasey, M. W., & Borkovec, T. D. (1992). A catastrophizing assessment of worrisome thoughts. *Cognitive Therapy and Research, 16,* 505–520.

Wegner, D. M. (1989). *White bears and other unwanted thoughts: Supression, obsession, and the psychology of mental control.* New York: Viking.

Young, J. (1987). *The role of selective attention in the attitude-behavior relationship.* Doctoral dissertation, University of Minnesota.

CHAPTER

2

Cognitive Interference and the Structure of Behavior

Charles S. Carver
University of Miami

The question of how cognitive interference comes to have a disruptive influence on task performance is an important one, and it is a question that's likely to have several answers rather than just one. My goal in this chapter is to present a conceptual structure within which I believe certain kinds of interference effects are readily interpreted. Although this structure is unlikely to provide a basis for understanding all sources of cognitive interference in performance, I think it will provide a useful vantage point for understanding at least some sources.

STRUCTURE OF BEHAVIOR

My view of cognitive interference derives from a more general viewpoint on the nature of behavioral self-regulation (Carver & Scheier, 1981, 1990a, 1990b, 1995). Indeed, I believe that the interference effects addressed in this chapter are specific manifestations of those more general principles. Accordingly, my first step in presenting a framework for discussing the experience of cognitive interference is to sketch out that broader view on the structure of self-regulation.

Goal Directedness

One conceptual starting point for this view is goals. I see human behavior as intrinsically goal directed, even though there are times when (both as observers and actors) we don't know exactly what the goal behind an action is. Goals of various sorts provide the structure that defines people's lives, both in the short term and in the long term. Moreover, many goals are dynamic in nature—not simply end points to be attained, but whole paths to be negotiated. For example, the goal of "having a holiday" is not to emerge relaxed at the other end of a blank 4-day period, but to experience whatever comprises the leisure activities of the holiday. This general view of goals and behavior is certainly not uniquely mine. Many others have expressed similar views (e.g., Cantor & Kihlstrom, 1987; Elliott & Dweck, 1988; Emmons, 1986; Higgins, 1987; Klinger, 1975, 1977; Markus & Nurius, 1986; Palys & Little, 1983; Vallacher & Wegner, 1985; for reviews see Pervin, 1989, or Gollwitzer & Bargh, in press).

Goals can exist at several levels of abstraction. They can be extremely concrete (creating specific levels of muscle tension) or they can be far more abstract (e.g., to manifest the quality of grace or dignity in one's handling of a social situation). Goals can be restricted in scope and quickly attained (e.g., to pick up a pencil) or they can be elaborate and attained slowly (e.g., to acquire a solid reputation in one's work, to develop a sound relationship with a partner). Since most goals imply a need for physical movement, there presumably is a translation process by which abstract aspects of schemas are translated into concrete act qualities. Though the most concrete aspects of behavioral schemas are of great interest to contributors to the literature of motor control (e.g., Adams, 1976; Kelso, 1982; Rosenbaum, 1987, 1991; Schmidt, 1987, 1988), emphasis here is on goals at higher levels of abstraction.

From Goals to Behavior

Goals are important, but they aren't enough by themselves. We've argued in a number of places (e.g., Carver & Scheier, 1981, 1990a, 1995) that goals have their influence on behavior through a process of feedback control (see also MacKay, 1963, 1966; Miller, Galanter, & Pribram, 1960; Powers, 1973). In a discrepancy reducing (or negative) feedback loop, an existing condition is compared against a reference value. If a discrepancy between the two is detected, an output function is engaged. The output creates an adjustment in the existing state of affairs, aimed at diminishing the discrepancy. If the adjustment is effective, subsequent perceptions will align more closely with the reference value. The overall function of the loop is to reduce (or keep reduced) sensed deviations from the comparison value.

I believe these functions are implicit in much of human behavior. Behavior-specifying information is taken as a guide, goal, reference point, or a standard of comparison (terms I'll use interchangeably here). People periodically check on their activities, states, or qualities (input function) and compare the perceptions against the reference values. If the perception or construal of behavior is discrepant with what the person intended to be doing, the result is typically a change in behavior, aimed at diminishing or removing the discrepancy (cf. Norman, 1981).

In the logic of the feedback loop, behavior is inherently purposive (even if the purposes underlying many acts are relatively trivial), undertaken in the service of creating perceptions of conformity to some reference value. Human life is viewed from this perspective as a continuous process of establishing goals and intentions, and adjusting current patterns of behavior so as to more closely match these values, using informational feedback as a guide to progress.

My own interest in this line of reasoning began with an interest in the self-regulatory consequences of self-focused attention (Carver, 1979). Self-focus increases the tendency to compare one's current behavior with salient reference points (Scheier & Carver, 1983). Self-focus has also been found (in a large number of studies) to cause people to adjust their behavior so that it conforms more closely to salient behavioral standards (for reviews see Carver & Scheier, 1981, 1995). Findings of this sort have led us to argue that in many behavioral contexts the effect of self-directed attention is to engage the comparator of the feedback loop that is currently controlling the person's conscious behavior.

Hierarchies in Self-Regulation

Though going farther than goals by themselves, the single feedback loop is also inadequate to account for the elaboration and flexibility of human behavior. Complexity is added, however, by the idea that feedback systems can be interconnected, for example, ordered in a hierarchy. Powers (1973) argued that this sort of organization underlies the self-regulation of behavior in living organisms, and arguments of a similar form have also been made by other theorists focusing on very different aspects of behavior (e.g., Broadbent, 1977; Dawkins, 1976; Gallistel, 1980; Vallacher & Wegner, 1985, 1987). We find aspects of this argument interesting and have adopted it as a conceptual heuristic.

In a hierarchical organization of feedback systems, there are relatively superordinate feedback loops and relatively subordinate loops. The output function of the superordinate system consists of the resetting of reference values at the next lower level of abstraction. To put it differently, higher order systems "behave" by providing reference values to the systems just below them in the hierarchy. The reference values that are being specified become more concrete and restricted as one moves from higher to lower levels of a hierarchy. Control at each lower level reflects regulation of some quality that contributes to the quality controlled at the next higher level. Each level monitors input at a level of abstraction that is appropriate to its own functioning, and each level adjusts output so as to minimize discrepancies at that level. Powers (1973) argued that such a hierarchy underlies the physical execution of action.

Our own interest is in the implications of the hierarchy at relatively high levels of abstraction. At the highest level proposed by Powers are such values as the global sense of idealized self. Self isn't the only reference value that occurs at this level, though it may be the most intuitive example of the type of standard that occurs here and may also be the most often used reference value at this level. Other possibilities include the idealized sense of a relationship (cf. Read & Miller, 1989), or of a society.

Values at this level are very abstract. A reasonable question is what behavioral outputs might be relevant to the attempt to self-regulate toward such a value. How does a person act so as to minimize discrepancies between these abstract values and behavior? Powers (1973) suggested that the behavioral output of this highest order system consists of providing reference values to the next lower level, which he termed the level of principle control. People act to be who they think they want to be by using any of several guiding principles implied by the idealized self to which they aspire. The makeup of the idealized self to which the person aspires obviously will differ from person to person. Thus, the principles that will be specified as output will also vary.

Principles begin to provide form for behavior. They are aspects of behavior for which we have names (essentially, trait labels) in everyday language—for example, honesty, responsibility, thrift, and expedience. They are still fairly abstract, however. Principles are not specifications of acts, but rather of qualities that can be manifest in acts of many types (just as traits can be manifest in a wide range of different acts—cf. Carlston & Skowronski, 1994; Read, Jones, & Miller, 1990; Shoda, Mischel, & Wright, 1989). People do not just go out and "do" honesty, or responsibility, or thrift, or expedience. Rather, people can manifest any one (or more) of these qualities in their behavior by doing any number of specific activities.

These specific activities, in which behavior finally becomes more recognizable as behavior, are termed programs. A program specifies a course of action, but with many of the details left blank. The details are left unspecified because what is done at a particular point in the script depends on what circumstances are encountered at that point. Clearly, much of what people do in their day-to-day lives appears program-like in character. Going to the grocery store, cooking dinner, writing a report, taking a walk, taking an exam—all these are programs.

Programs are the sort of activities that most people take for granted as "behavior." Although they often are undertaken in order to attain relatively abstract goals, the programs themselves are sufficiently concrete and overt that they are easily recognizable as actions. Enacting a program, however, is more complex than it might seem. In the model proposed by Powers (1973), programs act by specifying yet more restricted qualities as reference values to lower level control structures, which ultimately result in changes in patterns of muscle tensions. One might think of this model as representing a set of "be" goals, which are attained by specifying and attaining a set of "do" goals, which in turn are attained by specifying and attaining a set of motor-control goals (Fig. 2.1). When a given goal is engaged in behavior, so are all the constituent goals below it that contribute to its realization.

This is the essence of the notion of hierarchicality in this model. This line of thought has been given support by a body of work conducted by Vallacher and

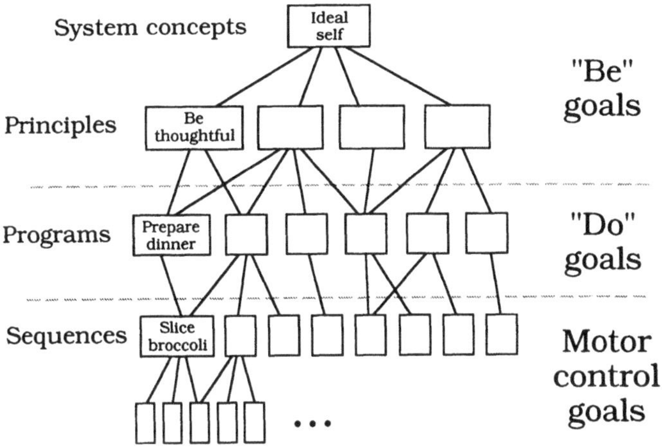

FIG. 2.1. Four-level hierarchy depicting the organization of goals and control processes of a person attempting to behave in accord with an idealized sense of self, by behaving in line with a principle of thoughtfulness, which is presently being realized by the act of preparing dinner for a friend, which involves a series of action sequences including the cutting up of broccoli for steaming (adapted from the logic of Powers, 1973). Lines indicate the contribution of lower level goals to specific higher level goals. The lines can also be read in the opposite direction, indicating that a given higher order goal specifies more-concrete goals at the next lower level. The hierarchy involves goals of "being" particular ways, which are attained by "doing" particular actions (from Carver & Scheier, 1995).

Wegner (1985, 1987) and their colleagues. Their work appears to argue strongly for the viability of the notion of hierarchical organization, at least as applied to relatively high levels of control. Vallacher and Wegner noted that people can identify any given act in a variety of ways, some of which are concrete and some more abstract. Furthermore, the level of abstraction at which people identify their actions can have predictable influences on behavior. Research stemming from Vallacher and Wegner's theory is interesting in its own right, but the point I wish to make about their work here is that it seems to bear out the usefulness of a hierarchical view of behavior. Furthermore, most of the behavioral qualities by which variations in act identification have been illustrated are easily assimilated to levels of control in the hierarchy proposed by Powers (1973).

Nor is this line of research the only one that fits with the notion that behavior is hierarchically organized. A great many theories are based on the idea that people are motivated by a desire to have high levels of self-esteem, and the further assumption that various aspects of behavior are responsive to how best to maintain such a positive self-evaluation (see, e.g., Snyder, Higgins, & Stucky, 1983; Steele, 1988; Taylor & Brown, 1988; Tesser, 1980, 1986, 1988). Such theories would appear to represent hierarchical models in which one attains a fit between one's perceived self and desired self by making particular behavioral choices at a more concrete level.

Hierarchicality: A Further Issue Regarding High Level Control

The notion of hierarchicality is a potentially useful one, but there is a danger of assuming more than is warranted. In particular, it is important to recognize that higher levels of the hierarchy are not necessarily engaged at all times. There are many circumstances in which action isn't guided by the superordinate sense of self, or even a principle, but rather by reference values at the level of program control. Moderately low levels of control thus are *functionally* superordinate when the person's current concern resides at that lower level (cf. Klinger, 1975; Shallice, 1978; Vallacher & Wegner, 1985, 1987). This would appear to be the case, for example, when people engage in the "maintenance" activities of life—for example, shopping for groceries, washing dishes, or driving to work. During such actions people may lose sight of higher order goals as they focus on the concrete realities of the situations confronting them (cf. Norman, 1981).

Thus, in considering many kinds of action, the actor can be controlling a behavior at any of several levels of abstraction. Sometimes trying a new task is simply trying a new task (a program of action). But sometimes the person who's trying the new task isn't focused on the trying of a new task. What he's really trying to do is live up to his idealized self-image. This is an altogether different thing to be doing, even if the physical motions that take place are exactly the same. The hierarchical view assumes that whichever level of abstraction the person is focused on while doing the behavior is the level that's functionally superordinate, with action qualities at lower levels of abstraction being subsumed and engaged automatically by that one (for broader discussion see Carver & Scheier, 1995; Carver, Lawrence, & Scheier, in press). I suspect that which level of abstraction the person is focusing on may turn out to have implications for the experience of cognitive interference.

EXPECTANCIES AND DISENGAGEMENT

A model in which goal-directedness is so important needs to deal with at least one further issue. Specifically, sometimes people have difficulty in moving forward toward their goals. Sometimes they get stuck in corners. For a goal-based view of behavior to provide an adequate account of the human experience, it must include some provision for how people extricate themselves from such situations.

Interruption and Assessment

We've suggested that when people experience adversity in their attempts to move forward toward their goals, they periodically interrupt their task-directed efforts to assess the likelihood of a successful outcome (e.g., Carver & Scheier,

1981, 1990a, 1990b, 1995). In effect, they suspend the behavioral stream they're in the midst of, step outside it, and evaluate the likely outcome of continued efforts, in a more deliberated way than takes place while acting. This may happen once, or it may happen often. It may constitute only a momentary check, or it may represent a more extended thinking through of the situation. The outcome of this process is a sense of favorable versus unfavorable expectancy concerning the desired outcome.

There are several questions that might be asked about this postulated interruption and assessment. One question is what circumstances induce it? Clearly such interruption is not inherent in all activity. For example, the experience of "flow" (Csikszentmihalyi, 1990) seems to be one in which behavior occurs smoothly, with no thought at all being given to the question of whether the outcome of the behavior will be as desired. Interruptions probably occur when obstacles are encountered, particularly unexpected obstacles. Indeed, it may often be the sudden halt to progress that such obstacles can create that causes people to stop and wonder—if only for a moment—whether they will be able to get around the roadblock they are facing.

Though interruptions often occur in the midst of behavior, they can also come before the action commences. People often engage in deliberative assessment of outcome likelihood before undertaking behaviors (cf. Gollwitzer, 1990), particularly if it's known ahead of time that the task is going to be difficult. Indeed, in such cases the perceived likelihood of success may be one determinant of the decision whether to undertake the behavior or not.

Individual differences surely exist in the tendency to engage in expectancy assessment. Some people are prone to step outside the behavioral stream and lapse into assessment repeatedly (cf. Kuhl's 1981, 1985 concept of state orientation)—the virtual opposite of a flow experience. Others only rarely take this step. These differences in the process of questioning seem to be tied to the individual's level of confidence. A fundamental effect of confidence seems to be to preempt the question of whether an action (or a program of action) will be successful. The issue is simply less likely to arise for a confident person than for a person with greater doubts. Here is one simple place in the structure of action where relative confidence may relate to differences in cognitive interference.

A second question about expectancy assessment concerns the source of the expectancies that emerge from it. In this process of more consciously assessing the probability of the desired outcome, people presumably depend to a large extent on memories of prior outcomes in similar situations. They may also consider a number of other issues. For example, an important question is what additional resources they might bring to bear on the problem they're confronting (cf. Lazarus, 1966). Another possibility is whether there is an alternative approach to the problem they might take. People also make use of social comparison information in assessing what the eventual outcome might be (e.g., Wills, 1981; Wood, 1989; Wood, Taylor, & Lichtman, 1985).

Some of the influences on the expectancies that emerge stem from variations in the situation. Others are a product of personality. Dispositional biases can have a large influence on people's expectations, even when the situation being confronted is the same for everyone. For example, the personality disposition of optimism versus pessimism represents a dimension of generalized expectancies for the occurrence of good versus bad outcomes in one's future (Scheier & Carver, 1985, 1992; Scheier, Carver, & Bridges, 1994). Stable biases in expectancies also play a role in cognitive theories of vulnerability to depression (e.g., Beck, 1972).

Consequences of Assessment: Basic Theory

Although the processes of creating expectancies and of locating expectancy-related information in memory are of interest in their own right, the question that may be of greatest interest is what follows from the assessment of expectancies. We've argued for some time that the outcome of people's expectancy assessments are reflected in the behaviors that occur subsequently (Fig. 2.2). In particular, if expectations of a successful outcome are sufficiently positive, the result is a return to efforts at moving toward the goal. If expectations are sufficiently negative, the result is an impetus to disengage from further effort, and potentially to disengage from the goal itself (Carver & Scheier, 1981, 1990a, 1990b, 1995; see also Klinger, 1975; Wortman & Brehm, 1975).

One more element of theory in this context concerns the role of self-directed attention in situations of this sort. As noted earlier, in many circumstances self-focus induces *task* focus: more intense or more careful efforts to match one's behavior to the reference value that's salient in the situation. This principle remains in effect when people confront adversity with confidence of overcoming

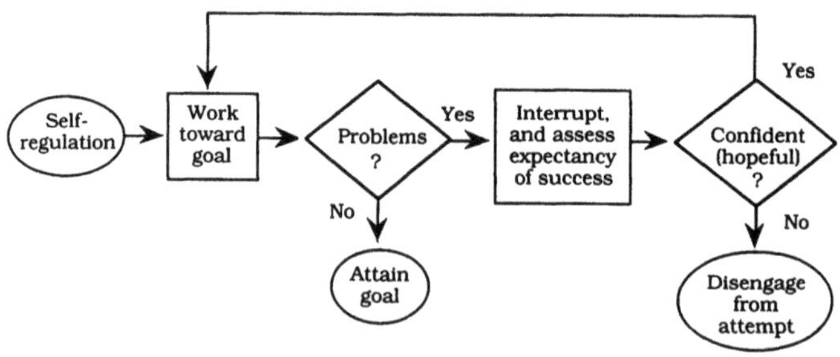

FIG. 2.2. Flow-chart depiction of self-regulatory possibilities, indicating that action sometimes continues unimpeded toward goal attainment, that obstacles to goal attainment sometimes induce a sequence of evaluation and decision making, and that if expectancies for eventual success are sufficiently unfavorable the person may disengage from further effort (adapted from Carver & Scheier, 1981).

it. In such cases, self-focus can be expected to result in more intense task engagement. When people are doubtful about overcoming the adversity, however, self-focused attention has a different effect: When expectancies are sufficiently unfavorable, self-focus enhances the tendency to *disengage* from the goal.

This interactive principle is reflected in several distinguishable ways, through several distinct kinds of outcome variables. All of them, however, seem ultimately to be reflections of a single basic self-regulatory dimension of psychological response: continued engagement with the goal versus disengagement from it. In the sections that follow, I briefly describe several laboratory projects that examined the effects of these variables in a variety of contexts. The projects were chosen in part to illustrate the interactive effects of self-focus and expectancies.

Disengagement From Comparisons

I argued earlier that self-focus enhances the functioning of the comparator in the feedback process. The case for that idea is based in part on a series of studies showing that people are more likely to engage in active comparisons between their present behavior and some comparison value when self-focus is higher than when it's lower (Scheier & Carver, 1983). One such comparison involved seeking out information about test norms. By choosing to work on test items for which norms were available, subjects higher in self-focus made themselves better able to compare their upcoming performances to relevant standards of comparison.

Somewhat later we conducted another study, which examined the role of expectancies in this phenomenon (Carver, Antoni, & Scheier, 1985). Subjects were given a similar opportunity to choose test items, from among sets for which norms were available and sets for which no norms were yet compiled. In this case, however, subjects' expectancies about how well they thought they would do on this task were manipulated by a previous success or failure on what was portrayed as a closely related task. Self-focus interacted with this manipulation of expectancy, in the following way: Among subjects who thought they would do well, self-focus enhanced the tendency to seek out the norms-available items, just as in the earlier research. Among subjects who thought they would do poorly, self-focus led them to avoid the items for which norms were available. In this way, these subjects showed evidence of disengaging themselves from the goal of performing well. This is one of several instances in which unfavorable expectancies have been shown to give rise to a turning away from information relevant to comparisons between the subjects' behavior and their goal (see also Butler, 1993; Scheier et al., 1989).

Responses to Fear

Turning away from goal relevant information isn't the only consequence of doubt. There are also effects on overt actions. The idea that self-focus interacts with confidence level to influence overt behavior has been tested in several ways. One of these studies also helps to establish the additional point that the temporary, ephemeral doubts associated with negative emotion can be overridden by a more firmly established sense of confidence about the ultimate outcome. This study employed people who reported themselves to be moderately fearful of snakes (Carver, Blaney, & Scheier, 1979a), a level of preexisting fearfulness that was identical for all subjects. Subjects differed, however, in how they said they thought they would react if asked to pick up and hold a nonpoisonous snake. Some of them (confident) chose the response "I'd do it, but I'd feel a little queasy about it," whereas the other subjects (doubtful) chose "I'm not at all sure that I'd do it."

That, of course, is exactly what they were asked to do in individual sessions later on. The snake was in an aquarium at the end of a hall. Self-focus was increased among half the subjects by the presence of a mirror. Nine levels of approach were predefined, and an observer (outside the subject's view) determined how far in the approach sequence the subject got before stopping. Subjects then made self-reports concerning their "contents of consciousness" during the task.

Two aspects of the findings of this study are important. First, though the manipulation of self-focus made all subjects more aware of their situational fear, that was the only difference in fear level among groups. In particular, confident subjects reported just as much fear as doubtful subjects. In contrast to this main effect, self-focus and confidence had an interactive effect on approach behavior. Self-focus caused doubtful subjects to stop sooner in the approach sequence, but it tended to *enhance* the performances of confident subjects. Analysis of postexperimental reports revealed that self-focus caused confident subjects to attend more to comparisons between their behavior and their goal (picking up and holding the snake), whereas it caused doubtful subjects to focus less on that comparison. Instead, the doubtful subjects under high self-focus attended more to signs of fearfulness inside themselves.

These findings indicate that residual confidence provided one group of subjects the wherewithal to overcome the very real fear they were experiencing in order to stay focused on the behavior they intended to execute. Thus, one of the points made by this study is that the increased fear levels among the confident subjects failed to impair their task concentration. The other group, lacking this confidence, turned their attention away from the task. Their response—avoidance of the behavior–goal comparison—is very similar to the pattern found in research on information seeking described in the previous section. However, the attentional target for the doubtful subjects in this study wasn't as benign as it was in the study described previously. In this study, the doubtful subjects focused on their fearfulness and inadequacy. This is a point to which I return a bit later.

Persistence

Other research has examined persistence at task-related efforts as a function of self-focus and expectancies (Carver, Blaney, & Scheier, 1979b). Subjects in this research were told that they were participating in a project that was evaluating several tests of abstract reasoning. Each subject was to work on portions of two of the tests. The first task subjects received was a set of anagrams, which were presented along with bogus norms from previous testing. The norms indicated that the anagram set was relatively easy. In reality, however, the anagrams were extremely difficult and in some instances impossible. As a result, all subjects performed poorly. The experimenter noted the poor performance, ensuring that it was salient for all subjects.

By now, there was a substantial discrepancy between subjects' desired performance and their actual performance. At this point, the experimenter manipulated expectancies for future success by indicating that the subject's second task tended to produce scores that either were very similar to, or were not very similar to, scores on the anagrams task. The subject then was taken to a second room, where a second experimenter took over. The second task was a line tracing problem originally developed to measure persistence (Feather, 1961). The first problem was impossible to solve according to the instructions. The measure was how long the subject tried to complete it before going to the second problem. This was determined unobtrusively by the experimenter from a point outside the subject's view. Subjects attempted the task at a table where a mirror either was or was not directly in front of them.

As was true of the work described previously, this study yielded an interaction between the manipulations of expectancy and self-focus. Self-focus enhanced persistence among subjects who believed they would be able to make up for their earlier failure (conceptually replicating the many cases in which self-focus has caused enhanced conformity to standards). In contrast, self-focus reduced persistence among subjects who had been induced to have doubts about being able to do well on the second task.

Mental Disengagement, Task Performance, and Negative Rumination

Although there are circumstances in which people are able to withdraw behaviorally from tasks they've taken up, sometimes this isn't easy to do. For one thing, social constraints may be in place that prevent this from happening. In such cases, the disengagement impulse is sometimes expressed in terms of mental disengagement—off-task thinking, daydreaming, and so on (cf. Diener & Dweck, 1978). Although this mental disengagement may sometimes be useful (for example, self-distraction from a feared stimulus may permit anxiety to abate), it can also create problems. If the situation is one with time pressure, the result of mental disengagement can be impairment of performance, as time is spent on task-irrelevant thoughts instead of the task. In accord with this line of thought, an interaction between self-focus and expectancies similar to that shown for persistence has been shown for measures of performance (Carver, Peterson, Follansbee, & Scheier, 1983; Carver & Scheier, 1982).

A further point about this mental disengagement is that even when it occurs it cannot always be sustained (Fig. 2.3). Mental disengagement may remove the person psychologically from the situation temporarily, but life is often structured in ways that cause this psychological removal to be overridden. For example, a person in a performance setting must continue to reconfront the unfinished task. Daydreaming won't make the task go away. As the person reconfronts the task, there may be a briefly renewed effort, which quickly gives way to expectancy reassessment, and thus renewed awareness of the doubts that prompted the disengagement impulse in the first place.

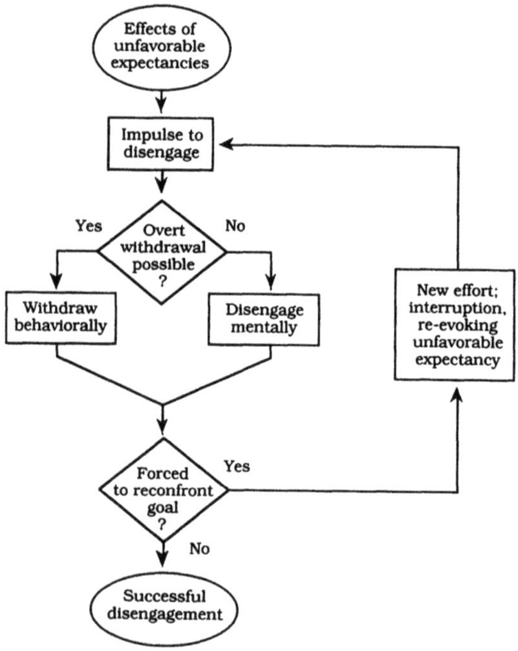

FIG. 2.3. Sometimes a behavioral withdrawal or a mental disengagement is successful in separating people from the goals they are doubtful about moving toward. Sometimes, however, the structure of the situations that people are in the midst of forces them to reconfront the goal; this may induce new effort, but if the effort continues to meet with difficulty, the result is likely to be fresh interruption, a renewed awareness of the doubts, and a renewal of the attempt to disengage.

This reconfrontation with doubt and the disengagement impulse is likely to be experienced as a phenomenology of continuing or repetitive negative—and often self-deprecatory—rumination (cf. Wine, 1971, 1980). It is this experience that I believe constitutes one of the most important classes of events that fall under the heading of cognitive interference. I believe that to understand this experience, however, means understanding the dynamic that lies behind it.

Hierarchicality Can Impede Disengagement

Although disengagement is sometimes precluded by situational constraints (Fig. 2.3), it isn't only situational constraints that prevent disengagement. Another aspect of this problem stems from the idea that behavior is hierarchically organized and that goals are increasingly important as they bear on higher levels of the hierarchy. Presumably disengagement from values low in the hierarchy of control is often easy. Indeed, the nature of programs of action is such that disengagement from efforts at subgoals is quite common, even while the person continues to pursue the program's overall goal. For example, if attacking a problem from one angle doesn't work, people often back up and consider another angle of attack.

Lower order goals vary, however, in how closely they're linked to values at a higher level, and thus how important they are (Fig. 2.4). To disengage from low-level goals that are closely linked to higher-level goals causes enlargement of discrepancies at the higher level. One cannot disengage from these higher order qualities, or disregard them, or tolerate large discrepancies between those values and currently sensed reality, without either experiencing considerable distress or substantially reorganizing one's value system (Carver & Scheier, 1986; Kelly, 1955; Millar, Tesser, & Millar, 1988). In such a case, disengagement from even very concrete behavioral goals can be quite difficult.

Section Summary

To sum up the ideas reviewed in the preceding sections, there is evidence that having sufficient doubt about being able to move forward toward goals is associated with a variety of outcomes. People with unfavorable expectancies avoid

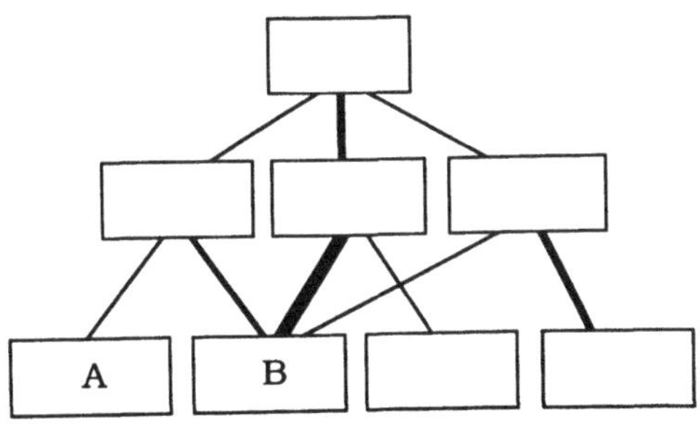

FIG. 2.4. Importance accrues to a given concrete action goal in either of two ways. The action can contribute in a major way to the attainment of a higher order goal (indicated here by a thicker line), or the action can contribute to several higher order goals at once (indicated here by a larger number of upward projections). On both of these criteria, concrete action goal A is relatively unimportant, whereas B is more important (from Carver & Scheier, 1995).

information that would permit them to compare their performances to meaningful reference points related to the goal. They disengage their effort from performance attempts, and may withdraw from the setting, if doing so is easy. They display performance deficits in circumstances in which mental disengagement absorbs time that could have been used for task efforts. And they display off-task thinking and negative rumination when they're unable to withdraw behaviorally or mentally from the situation. These findings are all consistent with a picture in which these people are trying to free themselves from involvement in a feedback loop that would otherwise be aimed at matching a behavioral standard. Sometimes the effort to extricate oneself from the loop is successful, sometimes it isn't. The specific effect that results depends on the pattern of influences channeling the behavior.

COGNITIVE INTERFERENCE

The conceptual model that was developed in the preceding sections leads to at least three kinds of suggestions about places in the structure of behavior where cognitive interference can occur during people's efforts at task performance.

Expectancy Assessment

One place where problems can intrude concerns the very process of stepping outside the behavioral stream and assessing the likelihood of the occurrence of the desired outcome. This event itself is a kind of cognitive intrusion. If it happens once, twice, or a few times during the course of a task performance, it's unlikely to be problematic. The more it happens, though, the more intrusive the self-questioning becomes and the more the process of questioning per se is likely to interfere with performance. This is so for at least two reasons. First, the intrusion of the assessment process can use time and mental resources that are more usefully expended in task efforts. Second, the more frequently the person asks whether the effort will be successful, the more likely it is that the person will begin to answer "no."

That is, as noted in an earlier section, it seems very likely that the frequency of expectancy assessment in a given activity is associated with the intensity of doubt about being able to perform adequately in that activity. People who are more confident are far less likely to engage in this process at all. A case can be made that even a fairly doubtful person would be well advised to stay engaged in the concrete aspects of behavior and try never to question whether he or she will be successful at reaching the desired goal. Simply keep the behavior on track, and find out later whether it worked or not.

Although the tendency to engage in repeated assessments of outcome likelihood is a potential problem, I don't think this problem is as great as the next one, the one that comes into play when the answer from expectancy assessment is "no, you're not going to succeed."

Stifled Disengagement

In discussing the cognitive interference that occurs in this situation, I return to the theoretical arguments made earlier in the chapter. I argued there that a sufficiently unfavorable expectancy leads to an impetus to disengage from further effort—or even further consideration—of the goal toward which one has been attempting to move. I view this impetus as a natural consequence of the fact that as living organisms we need to be able to stop doing things when we find they don't work. In this impetus, however, lies the seed of a particular pattern of cognitive interference. In a sense, the problem is that this natural, functional tendency to cut ourselves loose from goals becomes entangled in the web of the social contexts we create for ourselves.

To return to the theoretical argument, I think that when the person encounters adversity and enough doubt emerges, the disengagement tendency begins to be expressed. Given social settings in which actual physical withdrawal is either precluded or strongly discouraged (which I think is true of most of the performance settings that we have in mind in thinking about this topic), the disengagement tendency is not typically expressed overtly, but covertly. People in this situation have trouble concentrating, because they'd rather be elsewhere. Indeed, their thoughts may focus on actually being elsewhere. They daydream, fantasize, and find themselves distracted by other stray thoughts, sights, or sounds.

This mental disengagement cannot be sustained, however. People in performance settings trying to disengage are continually confronted with reminders that the task remains unfinished before them. Thus, they enter into a recurrent cycle of sporadic effort, interruption, assessment (yielding only evidence of further deepening doubt), and disengagement. The experience of people in this cycle will be manifestly one of cognitive interference, because there is so much going on in their minds that is only indirectly task related. The content of their consciousness will tend to be negatively toned, particularly as the person spends more time in this cycle of failed disengagement and less time in daydreaming. Because the content of consciousness pertains to doubts about one's abilities, it will likely be self-deprecatory. I regard this sort of experience—and even the mere outlines of this experience—as a particularly disruptive kind of cognitive interference.

This characterization of interference and disruption has found support in the literature of test anxiety. For example, Galassi, Frierson, and Sharer (1981) asked subjects with varying levels of test anxiety to report their thoughts while taking an exam. They found that the most frequently reported thought among subjects high in test anxiety concerned the desire to escape from the test situation. Test anxious students don't typically escape, of course. They simply sit in their seats and *wish* to escape (see also Nottelman & Hill, 1977). This finding is very much in line with the theoretical analysis presented here.

We've also conducted studies of our own (Carver et al., 1983) which support the idea that people high in test anxiety are vulnerable both to a lack of persistence and to performance deficits under self-focus. These findings once again hint at the possibility that the phenomenology of test anxiety has at its core the unsuccessful attempt to disengage from the task. Rich and Woolever (1988) have reported data indicating more clearly that the problems in performance among highly test anxious people result from their unfavorable expectancies. They showed that if expectancies are manipulated to be favorable among highly test anxious subjects, self-focus causes enhancement of performance rather than impairment (which occurs when expectancies are unfavorable).

Control From Too High a Level

I believe that another aspect of cognitive interference arises from the attempt to control behavior from too high a level of abstraction. A person who is working on a task as a task must sometimes deal with setbacks in the effort to perform well. A person who is working on a task as a way of trying to maintain self-esteem, however, has a bigger job when performance falters. When self-esteem is on the line, a poor performance (or a poor period of performance within a larger task) is more threatening than it is when the task is nothing more than a task. The greater the implications for the overall self-image, the bigger is the potential threat (Fig. 2.4). The person who is trying to control behavior from too high a level will experience a poor performance not as a task failure but as a failure of the self.

Now consider what happens when the impulse to disengage arises regarding the task that isn't going well. If the task doesn't matter much, the disengagement is relatively easy; the person quits this activity and moves on to something else. The more the task matters, however, the harder it is to disengage and to sustain the disengagement. When the task is maintaining the entire sense of self, it's impossible to disengage without in effect renouncing the desired self. The more a task matters to the sense of self, the more the person is immersed in the phenomenology of being stuck in a behavioral loop that's not moving forward but can't be let go of.

I suspect that people who tend to generalize from a single bad occurrence to the broader sense of self-worth (Carver & Ganellen, 1983; Carver, La Voie, Kuhl, & Ganellen, 1988) are trying to control their behavior from the top level on downward. When a bad thing happens to this person, it doesn't mean merely a bad event. It means a failure of the self. Such generalization from single occurrences to the overall sense of self produces a slightly different kind of cognitive interference than I've been discussing to this point, though it derives from the same set of issues as were discussed in the previous section. Generalization in response to bad outcomes is reflected in cognitions about broad personal inadequacy, rather than inadequacy pertaining to some particular domain of performance. These cognitions by their very nature interfere with further efforts to perform—not just in this context, but more widely. As such, they can be extremely debilitating. It should be no surprise that this pattern of thought is associated with depression (Carver & Ganellen, 1983; Carver et al., 1988).

CLOSING COMMENT: SELF-FOCUS, TASK-FOCUS, AND RUMINATION

I close this chapter with a few brief comments about how the types of interference discussed here have been characterized in the literature. As described in earlier sections, persons confronting adversity sometimes experience a phenomenology of continuing or repetitive negative rumination, which often focuses on perceptions of self-doubt and inadequacy. These are important classes of cognitive interference. I think it's important to be clear, however, about their sources. A number of writers—both from an earlier tradition of cognitive-attentional theories of anxiety (e.g., Sarason, 1975; Wine, 1971, 1980) and some more recent (Ingram, 1990)—have equated this phenomenology of negative rumination with the term "self-focus." I think this is a mistake, because I think it leads to a misconstrual of what's going on in these situations (see also Pyszczynski, Greenberg, Hamilton, & Nix, 1991).

Why does it lead to misconstrual? Because self-focus doesn't always produce interference. As described earlier, there are many cases in which self-focus is associated with *task* focus, as the experience of attention inward engages the feedback process underlying behavioral efforts. Indeed, among confident subjects in the studies that were reviewed earlier, this is precisely what occurred even under conditions of adversity. Self-focus led to higher levels of task efforts, as manifested both in overt behavior and in contents of consciousness. It was only doubtful subjects in whom self-focus led to performance impairment or to negatively toned rumination.

I believe that there is a good reason for that divergence among the effects of self-focused attention. In the conceptualization that was outlined in this chapter, impairment in functioning and negatively toned rumination are not direct consequences of self-directed attention. Rather, they are consequences of a more complex set of influences. These outcomes arise when self-focus occurs in combination with doubt, leading to an impulse to disengage, which is not given full expression. Impairment clearly doesn't occur in all instances of self-focus, only in certain specifiable cases. In sum, it's possible to become distracted by the surface appearance of a phenomenon, and fail to consider the structure of the processes that underlie it. In this case, consideration of the underlying structure provides a way to understand both the facilitating and interfering effects of self-focus on performance. Without understanding both, we understand neither.

ACKNOWLEDGMENTS

Preparation of this chapter was supported in part by grant BNS 90-11653 from the National Science Foundation and grants PBR-56 and PBR-82 from the American Cancer Society. The chapter was written while the author was a Visiting Scholar at the University of California, Los Angeles.

REFERENCES

Adams, J. A. (1976). Issues for a closed-loop theory of motor learning. In G. E. Stelmach (Ed.), *Motor control: Issues and trends* (pp. 87–107). New York: Academic Press.

Beck, A. T. (1972). *Depression: Causes and treatments*. Philadelphia: University of Pennsylvania Press.

Broadbent, D. E. (1977). Levels, hierarchies, and the locus of control. *Quarterly Journal of Experimental Psychology, 29*, 181–201.

Butler, R. (1993). Effects of task- and ego-achievement goals in information seeking during task engagement. *Journal of Personality and Social Psychology, 65*, 18–31.

Cantor, N., & Kihlstrom, J. F. (1987). *Personality and social intelligence*. Englewood Cliffs, NJ: Prentice-Hall.

Carlston, D. E., & Skowronski, J. J. (1994). Savings in the relearning of trait information as evidence of spontaneous trait inference generation. *Journal of Personality and Social Psychology, 66*, 840–856.

Carver, C. S. (1979). A cybernetic model of self-attention processes. *Journal of Personality and Social Psychology, 37*, 1251–1281.

Carver, C. S., Antoni, M., & Scheier, M. F. (1985). Self-consciousness and self-assessment. *Journal of Personality and Social Psychology, 48*, 117–124.

Carver, C. S., Blaney, P. H., & Scheier, M. F. (1979a). Focus of attention, chronic expectancy, and responses to a feared stimulus. *Journal of Personality and Social Psychology, 37*, 1186–1195.

Carver, C. S., Blaney, P. H., & Scheier, M. F. (1979b). Reassertion and giving up: The interactive role of self-directed attention and outcome expectancy. *Journal of Personality and Social Psychology, 37*, 1859–1870.

Carver, C. S., & Ganellen, R. J. (1983). Depression and components of self-punitiveness: High standards, self-criticism, and overgeneralization. *Journal of Abnormal Psychology, 92*, 330–337.

Carver, C. S., La Voie, L., Kuhl, J., & Ganellen, R. J. (1988). Cognitive concomitants of depression: A further examination of the roles of generalization, high standards, and self-criticism. *Journal of Social and Clinical Psychology, 7*, 350–365.

Carver, C. S., Lawrence, J. W., & Scheier, M. F. (in press). A control-process perspective on the origins of affect. In L. L. Martin & A. Tesser (Eds.), *Striving and feeling: Interactions among goals, affect, and self-regulation*. Hillsdale, NJ: Lawrence Erlbaum Associates.

Carver, C. S., Peterson, L. M., Follansbee, D. J., & Scheier, M. F. (1983). Effects of self-directed attention on performance and persistence among person high and low in test anxiety. *Cognitive Therapy and Research, 7*, 333–354.

Carver, C. S., & Scheier, M. F. (1981). *Attention and self-regulation: A control-theory approach to human behavior.* New York: Springer-Verlag.

Carver, C. S., & Scheier, M. F. (1982). Outcome expectancy, locus of attributions for expectancy, and self-directed attention as determinants of evaluations and performance. *Journal of Experimental Social Psychology, 18*, 184–200.

Carver, C. S., & Scheier, M. F. (1986). Functional and dysfunctional responses to anxiety: The interaction between expectancies and self-focused attention. In R. Schwarzer (Ed.), *Self-related cognitions in anxiety and motivation* (pp. 111–141). Hillsdale, NJ: Lawrence Erlbaum Associates.

Carver, C. S., & Scheier, M. F. (1990a). Principles of self-regulation: Action and emotion. In R. Sorrentino & E. T. Higgins (Eds.), *Handbook of motivation and cognition: Foundations of social behavior* (Vol. 2, pp. 3–52). New York: Guilford.

Carver, C. S., & Scheier, M. F. (1990b). Origins and functions of positive and negative affect: A control-process view. *Psychological Review, 97*, 19–35.

Carver, C. S., & Scheier, M. F. (1995). *On the self-regulation of behavior.* New York: Cambridge University Press, in preparation.

Csikszentmihalyi, M. (1990). *Flow: The psychology of optimal experience.* New York: Harper & Row.

Dawkins, R. (1976). Hierarchical organisation: A candidate principle for ethology. In P. P. G. Bateson & R. A. Hinde (Eds.), *Growing points in ethology* (pp. 7–54). Cambridge, England: Cambridge University Press.

Diener, C. I., & Dweck, C. S. (1978). An analysis of learned helplessness: Continuous changes in performance, strategy, and achievement cognitions following failure. *Journal of Personality and Social Psychology, 36*, 451–462.

Elliott, E. S., & Dweck, C. S. (1988). Goals: An approach to motivation and achievement. *Journal of Personality and Social Psychology, 54*, 5–12.

Emmons, R. A. (1986). Personal strivings: An approach to personality and subjective well being. *Journal of Personality and Social Psychology, 51*, 1058–1068.

Feather, N. T. (1961). The relationship of persistence at a task to expectations of success and achievement-related motives. *Journal of Abnormal and Social Psychology, 63*, 552–561.

Galassi, J. P., Frierson, H. T., Jr., & Sharer, R. (1981). Behavior of high, moderate, and low test anxious students during an actual test situation. *Journal of Consulting and Clinical Psychology, 49*, 51–62.

Gallistel, C. R. (1980). *The organization of action: A new synthesis.* Hillsdale, NJ: Lawrence Erlbaum Associates.

Gollwitzer, P. M. (1990). Action phases and mind-sets. In R. Sorrentino & E. T. Higgins (Eds.), *Handbook of motivation and cognition: Foundations of social behavior* (Vol. 2, pp. 53–92). New York: Guilford.

Gollwitzer, P. M., & Bargh, J. A. (Eds.). (in press). *The psychology of action: Linking cognition and motivation to behavior.* New York: Guilford.

Higgins, E. T. (1987). Self-discrepancy: A theory relating self and affect. *Psychological Review, 94*, 319–340.

Ingram, R. E. (1990). Self-focused attention in clinical disorder: Review and a conceptual model. *Psychological Bulletin, 107*, 156–176.

Kelly, G. A. (1955). *The psychology of personal constructs.* New York: Norton.

Kelso, J. A. S. (Ed.). (1982). *Human motor behavior: An introduction.* Hillsdale, NJ: Lawrence Erlbaum Associates.

Klinger, E. (1975). Consequences of commitment to and disengagement from incentives. *Psychological Review, 82*, 1–25.

Klinger, E. (1977). *Meaning and void: Inner experience and the incentives in people's lives*. Minneapolis: University of Minnesota Press.

Kuhl, J. (1981). Motivational and functional helplessness: The moderating effect of state versus action orientation. *Journal of Personality and Social Psychology, 40*, 155–170.

Kuhl, J. (1985). Volitional mediators of cognition-behavior consistency: Self-regulatory processes and action versus state orientation. In J. Kuhl & J. Beckmann (Eds.), *Action control: From cognition to behavior* (pp. 101–128). New York: Springer-Verlag.

Lazarus, R. S. (1966). *Psychological stress and the coping process*. New York: McGraw-Hill.

MacKay, D. M. (1963). Mindlike behavior in artefacts. In K. M. Sayre & F. J. Crosson (Eds.), *The modeling of mind: Computers and intelligence* (pp. 225–241). South Bend, IN: University of Notre Dame Press.

MacKay, D. M. (1966). Cerebral organization and the conscious control of action. In J. C. Eccles (Ed.), *Brain and conscious experience* (pp. 422–445). Berlin: Springer-Verlag.

Markus, H., & Nurius, P. (1986). Possible selves. *American Psychologist, 41*, 954–969.

Millar, K. U., Tesser, A., & Millar, M. G. (1988). The effects of a threatening life event on behavior sequences and intrusive thought: A self-disruption explanation. *Cognitive Therapy and Research, 12*, 441–458.

Miller, G. A., Galanter, E., & Pribram, K. H. (1960). *Plans and the structure of behavior*. New York: Holt, Rinehart, & Winston.

Norman, D. A. (1981). Categorization of action slips. *Psychological Review, 88*, 1–15.

Nottelman, E. D., & Hill, K. T. (1977). Test anxiety and off-task behavior in evaluative situations. *Child Development, 48*, 225–231.

Palys, T. S., & Little, B. R. (1983). Perceived life satisfaction and the organization of personal project systems. *Journal of Personality and Social Psychology, 44*, 1221–1230.

Pervin, L. (Ed.). (1989). *The goals concept in personality and social psychology*. Hillsdale, NJ: Lawrence Erlbaum Associates.

Powers, W. T. (1973). *Behavior: The control of perception*. Chicago: Aldine-Atherton.

Pyszczynski, T., Greenberg, J., Hamilton, J., & Nix, G. (1991). On the relationship between self-focused attention and psychological disorder: A critical reappraisal. *Psychological Bulletin, 110*, 538–543.

Read, S. J., & Miller, L. C. (1989). Inter-personalism: Toward a goal-based theory of persons in relationships. In L. Pervin (Ed.), *Goal concepts in personality and social psychology* (pp. 413–472). Hillsdale, NJ: Lawrence Erlbaum Associates.

Read, S. J., Jones, D. K., & Miller, L. C. (1990). Traits as goal-based categories: The importance of goals in the coherence of dispositional categories. *Journal of Personality and Social Psychology, 58*, 1048–1061.

Rich, A. R., & Woolever, D. K. (1988). Expectancy and self-focused attention: Experimental support for the self-regulation model of test anxiety. *Journal of Social and Clinical Psychology, 7*, 246–259.

Rosenbaum, D. A. (1987). Hierarchical organization of motor programs. In S. P. Wise (Ed.), *Higher brain functions: Recent explorations of the brain's emergent properties* (pp. 45–66). New York: Wiley.

Rosenbaum, D. A. (1991). *Human motor control*. San Diego: Academic Press.

Sarason, I. G. (1975). Anxiety and self-preoccupation. In I. G. Sarason & C. D. Spielberger (Eds.), *Stress and anxiety* (Vol. 2, pp. 27–44). Washington, DC: Hemisphere.

Scheier, M. F., & Carver, C. S. (1983). Self-directed attention and the comparison of self with standards. *Journal of Experimental Social Psychology, 19*, 205–222.

Scheier, M. F., & Carver, C. S. (1985). Optimism, coping, and health: Assessment and implications of generalized outcome expectancies. *Health Psychology, 4*, 219–247.

Scheier, M. F., & Carver, C. S. (1992). Effects of optimism on psychological and physical well-being: Theoretical overview and empirical update. *Cognitive Therapy and Research, 16*, 201–228.

Scheier, M. F., Carver, C. S., & Bridges, M. W. (1994). Distinguishing optimism from neuroticism (and trait anxiety, self-mastery, and self-esteem): A re-evaluation of the Life Orientation Test. *Journal of Personality and Social Psychology, 67*, 1063–1078.

Scheier, M. F., Matthews, K. A., Owens, J. F., Magovern, G. J., Sr., Lefebvre, R. C., Abbott, R. A., & Carver, C. S. (1989). Dispositional optimism and recovery from coronary artery bypass surgery: The beneficial effects on physical and psychological well being. *Journal of Personality and Social Psychology, 57*, 1024–1040.

Schmidt, R. A. (1987). The acquisition of skill: Some modifications to the perception-action relationship through practice. In H. Heuer & A. F. Sanders (Eds.), *Perspectives on perception and action* (pp. 77–103). Hillsdale, NJ: Lawrence Erlbaum Associates.

Schmidt, R. A. (1988). *Motor control and learning: A behavioral emphasis* (2nd ed.). Champaign, IL: Human Kinetics.

Shallice, T. (1978). The dominant action system: An information-processing approach to consciousness. In K. S. Pope & J. L. Singer (Eds.), *The stream of consciousness: Scientific investigations into the flow of human experience* (pp. 117–157). New York: Wiley.

Shoda, Y., Mischel, W., & Wright, J. C. (1989). Intuitive interactionism in person perception: Effects of situation–behavior relations on dispositional judgments. *Journal of Personality and Social Psychology, 56*, 41–53.

Snyder, C. R., Higgins, R. L., & Stucky, R. J. (1983). *Excuses: Masquerades in search of grace*. New York: Wiley.

Steele, C. M. (1988). The psychology of self-affirmation: Sustaining the integrity of the self. In L. Berkowitz (Ed.), *Advances in experimental social psychology* (Vol. 21, pp. 261–302). New York: Academic Press.

Taylor, S. E., & Brown, J. D. (1988). Illusion and well-being: A social psychological perspective on mental health. *Psychological Bulletin, 103*, 193–210.

Tesser, A. (1980). Self-esteem maintenance in family dynamics. *Journal of Personality and Social Psychology, 39*, 77–91.

Tesser, A. (1986). Some effects of self-evaluation maintenance on cognition and action. In R. M. Sorrentino & E. T. Higgins (Eds.), *Handbook of motivation and cognition: Foundations of social behavior* (pp. 435–464). New York: Guilford.

Tesser, A. (1988). Toward a self-evaluation maintenance model of social behavior. In L. Berkowitz (Ed.), *Advances in experimental social psychology* (Vol. 21, pp. 181–227). New York: Academic Press.

Vallacher, R. R., & Wegner, D. M. (1985). *A theory of action identification*. Hillsdale, NJ: Lawrence Erlbaum Associates.

Vallacher, R. R., & Wegner, D. M. (1987). What do people think they're doing? Action identification and human behavior. *Psychological Review, 94*, 3–15.

Wills, T. A. (1981). Downward comparison principles in social psychology. *Psychological Bulletin, 90*, 245–271.

Wine, J. D. (1971). Test anxiety and direction of attention. *Psychological Bulletin, 76*, 92–104.

Wine, J. D. (1980). Cognitive-attentional theory of test anxiety. In I. G. Sarason (Ed.), *Test anxiety: Theory, research, and application* (pp. 349–378). Hillsdale, NJ: Lawrence Erlbaum Associates.

Wood, J. V. (1989). Theory and research concerning social comparisons of personal attributes. *Psychological Bulletin, 106*, 231–248.

Wood, J. V., Taylor, S. E., & Lichtman, R. R. (1985). Social comparison in adjustment to breast cancer. *Journal of Personality and Social Psychology, 49*, 1169–1183.

Wortman, C. B., & Brehm, J. W. (1975). Responses to uncontrollable outcomes: An integration of reactance theory and the learned helplessness model. In L. Berkowitz (Ed.), *Advances in experimental social psychology* (Vol. 8, pp. 277–336). New York: Academic Press.

CHAPTER

3

ANXIETY AND COGNITIVE PROCESSES

Colin MacLeod
The University of Western Australia

INTRODUCTION

It now is well established that individuals who report high levels of anxiety often display performance deficits across a wide range of cognitive tasks. Such anxiety-linked deficits have been observed on experimental procedures designed to assess reasoning ability (e.g., Leon & Revelle, 1985), verbal skills (e.g., Zarantonello, Slaymaker, Johnson, & Petzel, 1984), arithmetic competence (e.g., Calvin, Koons, Bingam, & Fink, 1953), memorial functioning (e.g., Darke, 1988; Knox & Grippaldi, 1970; Mueller, 1976; Zatz & Chassin, 1985), and a variety of other cognitive operations (cf. Eysenck, 1982, 1992). The likelihood of finding such performance deficits in anxious individuals increases with task difficulty. Indeed, in reviewing this literature, Eysenck (1982) has reported over twenty studies in which anxious subjects showed substantially impaired functioning on a difficult version of a cognitive task without being greatly impaired on a simple version of that task. While a variety of different theories have been proposed to account for this pattern of anxiety-linked performance deficits, a common feature of many such accounts is the suggestion that anxious individuals may be characterised by a reduction in the amount of information that can be processed (e.g., Easterbrook, 1959; Eysenck, 1982; Eysenck & Calvo, 1992; Humphreys & Revelle, 1984; Sarason, 1988).

Early models attributed reductions in cognitive performance to the arousal component of anxiety, and proposed that restrictions in the amount of information that could be processed by anxious individuals were due to the narrowing of attentional focus characteristic of high arousal states (Easterbrook, 1959). That is, it was considered that the processing restriction associated with anxiety operated peripherally, and reduced the amount of information that could gain access to the central cognitive system. According to this type of account, anxiety impairs performance most on difficult tasks because such tasks require the intake of more information, and hence the narrowing of attentional focus is more likely to result in a failure to encode task-relevant cues.

There is some evidence to suggest that anxious individuals do indeed appear less likely than control subjects to process all the available information when performing cognitive tasks. For example, anxious subjects sometimes show less beneficial effects of additional task-relevant cues, and less adverse effects of additional task-irrelevant cues, than do such control subjects (e.g., Bruning, Capage, Kozuh, Young, & Young, 1968; Zaffy & Bruning, 1966). However, the common observation that, on many tasks, anxious subjects display increased levels of distractability (e.g., Dornic, 1977; Dornic & Fernaeus, 1981; Eysenck, 1988; Pallack, Pittman, Heller, & Munson, 1975) seems inconsistent with the argument that attention is overly focused in anxious individuals. Furthermore, evidence has accumulated to suggest that it is the worry component of elevated anxiety, rather than the arousal component, which is most strongly predictive of impaired cognitive performance (e.g., Deffenbacher, 1980; Morris, Davis, & Hutchings, 1981).

More recent models of anxiety-linked performance deficits have placed increasing emphasis upon the possibility that the critical restriction in information processing capacity occurs centrally within the cognitive system, rather than resulting from a peripheral narrowing of attention. Such accounts typically attribute this reduction in central cognitive capacity to the effects of task-irrelevant processing (e.g., Eysenck, 1982, 1992; Sarason, 1984, 1986, 1988; Wine, 1971, 1982). For example, Eysenck (1992) has reviewed considerable evidence which supports his proposal that the locus of the processing restriction in anxiety lies within working memory, a limited capacity central system responsible for both active processing, and the transient storage of intermediary products, during the performance of many (but not all) cognitive tasks (Baddeley, 1986). Eysenck's review indicates that anxiety-linked performance deficits are most likely to be observed on those tasks which plausibly rely to the greatest extent upon working memory capacity, while such deficits typically are not found on tasks that make no demands upon working memory. In accounting for this observation, Eysenck suggests that elevated anxiety does not actually reduce working memory capacity per se, but rather is associated with a tendency to employ working memory to sustain certain types of task-irrelevant processing operations, thus leaving less capacity available to support the execution of the main experimental tasks. Thus, according to this account, performance deficits associated with anxiety represent the result of *cognitive interference*, produced by task-irrelevant processing. Sarason, Sarason, and Pierce (1994) defined cognitive interference as "thoughts that intrude on task-related activity and serve to reduce the quality and level of performance" (p. 2). Simply put, therefore, the cognitive interference hypothesis proposes that certain types of intrusive thoughts are characteristic of anxiety, and that these thoughts can disrupt experimental task performance in anxious individuals.

While the cognitive interference hypothesis provides an attractive account of anxiety-linked performance deficits, it also raises interesting research issues. Obviously, it is necessary to empirically evaluate the claim that certain types of intrusive thoughts are characteristic of anxious individuals, and to assess the evidence for the proposal that such thoughts can account for the patterns of performance deficits shown by such subjects. If it is confirmed that certain patterns of thinking do differentiate high from low anxious individuals, and may account for the differing levels of functioning displayed by these subjects, then it becomes important to determine the underlying differences in cognitive processing that might sustain these discrepant patterns of thinking. The next section provides a brief review of the fairly compelling evidence that certain types of intrusive thinking are indeed characteristic of anxious individuals, while the remainder of this chapter considers the patterns of selective information processing that plausibly might give rise to this cognitive content in anxious subjects.

THE COGNITIVE CONTENT OF ANXIETY

A considerable amount of research has investigated the types of thoughts commonly experienced by clinically anxious patients, and has supported the contention that such individuals do indeed experience a range of intrusive negative thoughts. For example, assessment of thought content through clinical interview has led researchers to conclude that generalized anxiety disorder patients tend to experience, with exceptional frequency, thoughts concerning imminent danger (e.g., Beck, Laude, & Bohnert, 1974; Hibbert, 1984). Such conclusions also have been drawn by researchers who have assessed thought content in these patients using more reliable structured questionnaire assessment measures (e.g., Sutton-Simon & Goldfried, 1979). Similar thought content has been recorded within other classes of clinically anxious patients such as agoraphobics (e.g., Chambless, Caputo, Bright, & Gallagher, 1984), simple phobics (e.g., Mizes, Landolf-Fritsche, & Grossman-McKee, 1987), and individuals suffering from panic disorder (e.g., Ganellan, Matuzas, Uhlenhuth, Glass, & Easton, 1986).

This tendency to experience an elevated frequency of threatening thoughts is not restricted to clinically anxious individuals, but also is characteristic of normal subjects who report high levels of anxiety. Parkinson and Rachman (1981) employed a thought recording technique to assess the cognitive content of women who were anxious because their children were about to undergo surgery. These women reported a striking elevation in the frequency of catastrophic thoughts concerning the possibility of harm befalling their children, and described these threatening thought as having a highly intrusive quality. An inflated frequency of intrusive thoughts concerning the likelihood of social or physical trauma also has been reported by anxious students (e.g., Davidson, Feldman, & Osborn, 1984; Sewitch & Kirsch, 1984), and schoolchildren (e.g., Francis, 1988; Kendall, 1993).

Probably the largest body of research concerning the association between intrusive thinking and anxiety in normal subjects has resulted from the study of test anxiety. For example, using both a standardized questionnaire (Cognitive Interference Questionnaire, CIQ; Sarason & Stoops, 1978), and a custom designed thought recording procedure, Blankenstein, Toner, and Flett (1989) reported that high test-anxious students experienced more worry-laden thoughts, which they rated as highly interfering, than did low test-anxious students, when performing a demanding cognitive task. Similar findings have been reported by Zatz and Chassin (1985) who contrasted thought content reported by high and low test-anxious schoolchildren in an evaluative situation.

There is reasonable evidence, therefore, that anxious individuals do show an increased frequency of certain types of thoughts, which typically are described as being both emotionally threatening and intrusive in nature. Furthermore, there is also evidence that the presence of such idiosyncratic thoughts is associated with the occurrence of performance deficits on intellectually demanding tasks. For example, it often has been observed that the frequency with which test-related worries are experienced under test-like conditions correlates negatively with performance on such intellective tasks (e.g., Bruch, Kaflowitz, & Kuethe, 1986; Hunsley, 1987; Nichols-Hoppe & Beach, 1990; Sarason & Stoops, 1978). Of course, the demonstration of such an association provides no direct support for the proposal that cognitive interference resulting from these threat-related thoughts actually *causes* the observed performance deficits. Indeed, it could be argued that the causal nature of the association might even be in the reverse direction, with those individuals who are experiencing difficulty performing the task tending to worry more as a *consequence* of this poor task performance. Against this alternative causal account of the association between intrusive threatening thoughts and impaired task performance, however, stands the finding that direct manipulation of the former can serve to modify the latter. For example, when the attention of test-anxious subjects has been directed away from their worrying thoughts through modeling (e.g., Sarason, 1973), or desensitization (e.g., Naveh-Benjamin, 1991), then these subjects have been found to show disproportionate improvement on intellective task performance relative to the improvement shown by low test-anxious subjects undergoing the same attentional manipulations.

It seems reasonable to conclude, therefore, that the patterns of performance deficits often shown by anxious subjects may indeed be caused by the increased frequency with which such individuals experience intrusive thoughts concerning threat or danger. That is, it appears plausible that anxious individuals may be poor at performing difficult experimental tasks because their cognitive systems instead preferentially process task-irrelevant information relating to threat. Recent research that has directly investigated individual differences in the selective processing of emotional information has produced very strong support for the hypothesis that vulnerability to anxiety is associated with a selective processing bias operating at an automatic level within the cognitive system in a manner that favors threat-related information (cf. Mathews & MacLeod, 1994). This processing bias not only may explain the preponderance of intrusive thoughts concerning threat that are experienced by anxious individuals, but may even represent the cognitive substrate of anxiety vulnerability, serving to mediate emotional responses to stressful events.

SELECTIVE INFORMATION PROCESSING AND ANXIETY

The cognitive interference account of anxiety-linked performance deficits implies that elevated anxiety should be associated with distorted *selective* processing, rather than with an overall reduction in processing ability. It is not surprising, therefore, that many researchers recently have turned their interest to the study of selective information processing in anxious subjects. The most common experimental approach has been to present high and low anxious subjects with emotionally toned stimulus materials, and to compare the patterns of selective encoding, selective interpretation, or selective retrieval, shown by these subject groups. This chapter provides a review of the main findings that have emerged from this research over the past decade or so.

Selective Encoding and Anxiety

Probably the simplest technique adopted to assess selective encoding in anxious subjects has involved presenting threatening and nonthreatening words under conditions that make their perception difficult, and requiring that anxious and nonanxious subjects attempt to identify (or detect) certain emotional target words. Typically, clinically anxious patients have been found to show an enhanced ability, relative to normal control subjects, to identify or detect the more threatening target words, suggesting that these anxious individuals display an increased ability to encode emotionally threatening information. For example, Burgess et al. (1981) gave agoraphobic and social phobic patients a dichotic listening task, within which separate lists of words were presented simultaneously to each ear through headphones. These subjects were required to detect emotionally threatening and emotionally neutral target words which could appear in either channel. In contrast to normal control subjects, who displayed no differential ability to detect these two classes of target words, the clinically anxious patients showed an increased ability to detect the threatening targets relative to the neutral targets. Burgess et al. concluded that these anxiety patients were characterized by a selective encoding advantage for threatening information. The same conclusion was drawn by Foa and McNally (1986) who employed a similar dichotic listening paradigm to compare the performance of obsessive-compulsive patients against that of control subjects. The clinically anxious patients again showed a disproportionate ability to detect threatening target words relative to neutral words, once more suggesting that elevated anxiety is associated with an enhanced capacity to encode threatening information.

While these findings are consistent with the existence of an anxiety-linked encoding advantage for threatening information, it seems possible that performance on such detection tasks may be influenced by guessing biases. The anxiety patients might simply have been more inclined than the control subjects to guess, under conditions of uncertainty, that a threat related target had been presented. Such a response bias would result in an increased hit rate for the threat targets, but would not represent an encoding advantage for threatening stimuli. Converging evidence for the existence of an anxiety-linked encoding advantage favoring threatening information has been provided, however, by research that has assessed selective encoding through the study of interference effects. In this approach, anxious and nonanxious subjects have been given a central task to perform in the presence of distracting information which they are instructed to ignore. Sometimes the distracting information consists of threat-related stimuli, while sometimes the distracter information is neutral in emotional tone. The degree to which subjects are able to successfully ignore each type of distracter information can be inferred by assessing the degree to which these different classes of distracters interfere with performance on the central task. For example, Mathews and MacLeod (1986) presented generalized anxiety patients and normal control subjects with a central simple reaction time, which had to be performed while subjects attempted to ignore lists of words played through headphones. On half of the reaction time trials, the distracter words were emotionally threatening (e.g., "cancer," "danger") while on the other half of the trials these distracters were emotionally neutral in content (e.g., "dancer," "ranger"). The reaction times displayed by the anxiety patients on the central task were slowed disproportionately in the presence of the threatening distracter words, suggesting that these anxiety patients found it particularly difficult to avoid the encoding the threatening distracter information.

The interference task that has been used most commonly to assess selective encoding in anxiety has been an adapted version of the Stroop task (Stroop, 1938), within which subjects are presented with colored emotional words, and are instructed to name the color of each word while attempting to ignore its semantic content. It is assumed that any difficulty avoiding the processing of word content will be revealed by delayed color-naming responses. A great many studies have confirmed that clinically anxious patients, compared to nonanxious control subjects, do show a disproportionate slowing to color naming emotionally threatening words relative to emotionally neutral words, suggesting that these anxious individuals find it difficult to avoid encoding the threat word content. This effect now has been demonstrated for generalized anxiety disorder patients (e.g., Mathews & MacLeod, 1985; Mogg, Mathews, & Weinman, 1989), panic disorder patients (e.g., McNally et al., 1994), posttraumatic stress disorder patients (e.g., Cassiday, McNally, & Zeitlin, 1992; Thrasher, Dalgleish, & Yule, 1994), obsessive-compulsive patients (e.g., Lavy, van Oppen, & van den Hout, 1994), spider phobics (e.g., Lavy, van den Hout, & Arntz, 1993; Watts, McKenna, Sharrock, & Trezise, 1986), and social phobics (e.g., Hope, Rapee, Heimberg, & Dombeck, 1990; Mattia, Heimberg, & Hope, 1993).

Clearly, this is a very reliable finding and, because the task does not require that subjects attempt to identify the emotional stimuli, the effect cannot readily be attributed to an anxiety-linked guessing bias. Nevertheless, the observation that anxiety patients display exaggerated interference effects in the presence of threatening distracters does not necessitate the conclusion that these anxious individuals are selectively encoding this threatening distracter information. Indeed, as has been pointed out by several researchers (e.g., MacLeod, 1990; de Ruiter & Brosschot, 1994), it could even be proposed that prolonged color-naming latencies might result from an attempt to avoid processing the threatening stimuli, if this avoidance response were so pronounced that it impaired the encoding of all stimulus information including color. A couple of recent observations have added some credibility to this alternative explanation. First, it has been found that individuals who score high on questionnaire measures of "repression," a personality trait that traditionally has been assumed to reflect a tendency to avoid processing aversive information, also take disproportionately long to color name threat words relative to neutral words (e.g., Dawkins & Furnham, 1989). Second, when Lavy and van den Hout (1994) directly instructed normal subjects to selectively avoid processing a certain class of semantic information (i.e., number words, such as "two," or "seven"), they found that this instructional manipulation served to selectively increase the color naming latencies shown on this class of stimulus materials. Therefore, it is difficult to be fully confident that the inflated color naming interference typically shown on threatening words by anxiety patients necessarily reflects a tendency for these individuals to selectively encode the threatening content of such stimulus materials.

However, more direct measures of selective attention have added still further support for the hypothesis that anxious individuals do show a selective encoding bias that favors threatening information. For example, MacLeod, Mathews, and Tata (1986) exposed subjects to word pairs on a VDU screen. Each pair contained one threatening and one neutral word, and these words each were presented in a different screen location. On some trials, following the termination of the word display a small dot probe appeared on the screen in the same location as either of the two previously presented words. Subjects were required simply to indicate detection of these probes by making a button pressing response, and their detection latencies were recorded. Adopting the assumption that subjects would be fastest to detect probes that appeared within attended screen areas, MacLeod et al. were able to infer attentional responses to emotional stimuli by assessing patterns of probe detection latencies. Generalized anxiety patients displayed a pronounced speeding to detect the probes that appeared in the same location as the emotionally negative, rather than the emotionally neutral words, suggesting that these anxious subjects did indeed move attention selectively towards these threatening verbal stimuli. In contrast, nonanxious control subjects showed the opposite pattern, displaying slowed detection latencies for probes in the vicinity of the threat words compared to probes in the vicinity of neutral words, which suggests that these individuals may have selectively withdrawn attention from the threatening stimuli. The tendency for anxiety patients to show speeded detection latencies for probes appearing within the vicinity of threat stimuli appears to be a reliable effect, which recently has been replicated by Mogg, Mathews, and Eysenck (1992).

In conclusion, therefore, despite the interpretative problems associated with some previous approaches to the study of selective encoding, strong and consistent converging evidence has accrued to indicate that clinically anxious patients do indeed show an exaggerated tendency to selectively encode threatening information. It seems possible that this selective encoding bias may contribute to the development and maintenance of the intrusive threatening thoughts commonly reported by such anxious individuals. That is, the threatening character of these thoughts plausibly may reflect the overrepresentation of threat cues within the information that anxious subjects encode from their environment. Furthermore, the intrusive quality of these threatening thoughts might result from this same attentional bias. If one considers a thought to be an internal stimulus, then it would be expected that anxious subjects' attentional bias towards threatening stimuli should make it particularly difficult for these individuals to ignore their threatening thoughts. This may be one of the reasons why the threatening thoughts experienced by anxious individuals tend to interfere with, and disrupt, task performance.

Selective Interpretation and Anxiety

Of course, the construction of thoughts requires more than the simple encoding of external information. Often, the information that we encode is ambiguous and our thought content will reflect the interpretations that we impose upon this ambiguity. Therefore, the preponderance of threatening thoughts reported by highly anxious individuals possibly may result not only from the selective encoding of threat cues, but also from a tendency to selectively impose threatening interpretations on ambiguous information. The hypothesis that anxious subjects may display an interpretative bias of this sort has been the focus of considerable experimental scrutiny, and has received a fair degree of empirical support.

An early approach to the study of interpretative processing in emotionally disordered patients involved presenting such subjects with brief descriptions of ambiguous scenarios, and requiring them to select their preferred interpretations from a set of predetermined options (e.g., Butler & Mathews, 1983; Krantz & Hammen, 1979). Butler and Mathews presented clinically anxious patients and control subjects with passages describing hypothetical events which could be interpreted in more or less threatening ways, together with a set of alternative possible resolutions for the ambiguity. For example, one passage described the central actor awakening in the night to hear a noise coming from another room, and the alternative resolutions included the threatening interpretation that a burglar was in the house, and the nonthreatening interpretation that a window was knocking in the wind. When asked to select the interpretation that they would be most likely to draw in such situations, the anxiety disordered patients showed a greater tendency than nonanxious control subjects to select the more threatening options.

Although such findings are consistent with the possibility that anxious subjects may selectively impose threatening interpretations on ambiguity, it is difficult to place great faith in findings from such self-report tasks for at least two reasons. First, these tasks assume that subjects can introspect accurately about the interpretations that they would actually make within hypothetical situation, and this assumption may be entirely unwarranted. Though the limits of introspection remain the subject of some debate, Nisbett and Wilson's (1977) influential review of this issue has clearly demonstrated that subjects often are extremely inaccurate when attempting to introspectively report on their own cognitive processes, indicating the need for caution when assessing the significance of Butler and Mathews' results. Second, the transparency of these self-report measures of interpretation introduces the very real possibility that demand effects may contaminate the results. Clinically anxious patients (who in Butler and Mathews' study were attending for treatment), may feel some obligation to demonstrate the severity of their disorder by endorsing the more negative interpretations, thus giving rise to the pattern of effects observed in this type of self-report task.

In view of these problems, more recent studies have moved away from self-report methodologies, and have attempted to assess the interpretation of ambiguity in more direct ways. For example, in what was conveyed to subjects as a test of verbal ability, Eysenck, MacLeod, and Mathews (1987) presented anxiety patients and normal control subjects with homophones, embedded within a long list of other words recorded on audio tape, and required these subjects simply to write down each word as it was spoken. The critical homophones each had two possible spellings, one pertaining to a relatively threatening meaning and one to a more neutral meaning (e.g., Die/Dye, Groan/Grown,

Guilt/Gilt, Pain/Pane). Subjects' spelling lists were examined to determine the meanings that they had imposed upon these ambiguous stimuli. Eysenck et al. found that the proportion of threatening spellings produced by subjects correlated more that 0.7 with a questionnaire measure of trait anxiety, indicating that heightened vulnerability to anxiety was associated with a heightened tendency to write down the threatening meaning of these ambiguous words. More recent research by Mathews, Richards, and Eysenck (1989), employing this same homophone task, has confirmed that generalized anxiety disorder patients show a greater tendency to spell the homophones in their more threatening form than is shown by nonanxious control subjects.

Clearly, the findings obtained using this homophone task are consistent with the hypothesis that anxious individuals tend to interpret ambiguity in a disproportionately negative manner. However, it is not impossible that the different patterns of spellings observed on this task may reflect an anxiety-linked response bias, rather than a genuine interpretative bias. If all subjects occasionally become aware of both meanings of a homophone, and hence must select one option to utilize as their response in the spelling task, then any tendency for the more anxious subjects to select the more threatening response option would result in the observed effects. However, such a bias would not reflect any differences in the actual interpretation of the ambiguous stimuli. Richards and French (1992) recently used a lexical priming paradigm to assess the meanings that were semantically activated when high and low trait-anxious subjects processed ambiguous words. Subjects were exposed to prime-target pairs, and were required to perform a lexical decision on the target stimulus. It is well established that the latency to correctly decide that a target stimulus is an English word is reduced when that target is preceded by a prime word which is semantically associated with the target (e.g., Neely, 1977). In Richards and French's study the critical prime words were homographs, each of which had one threatening and one neutral meaning, such as "Sentence" (jail term vs. grammatical structure), or "Club" (weapon vs. social group). These researchers contrasted the magnitude of the semantic priming effects observed when such words were followed by targets related to either of their possible meanings, thus making it possible to infer the meanings of the primes that had been semantically activated as a result of their exposure. At the shortest prime-target stimulus onset asynchrony (500 msec) both high and low trait-anxious subjects showed equivalent priming effects for targets related to either meaning of these ambiguous primes. However, at the longer stimulus onset asynchrony of 750 msec the most pronounced priming effects were shown by the high trait-anxious subjects, and only for those targets related to the threatening meanings of the primes. These results suggest that while both possible representations of the ambiguous prime stimuli appear to have been accessed initially by all subjects, high trait-anxious subjects maintained the semantic activation of the more threatening representation to a disproportionate degree. Thus it would appear that there is, indeed, an increased tendency for anxious individuals to impose threatening interpretations on ambiguous words.

Evidence supporting the presence of an anxiety-linked interpretative bias also has been provided by studies that have employed rather more complex verbal materials. For example, Eysenck, Mogg, May, Richards, and Mathews (1991) presented generalized anxiety patients and nonanxious control subjects with an audiotaped set of sentences in an initial encoding task, then subsequently tested their capacity to correctly recognize written versions of these sentences. The critical sentences exposed in the encoding task were ambiguous, and were amenable to both threatening and nonthreatening interpretations (e.g., "At the refugee camp the week/weak would soon be finished"). The recognition test presented only disambiguated versions of such sentences (e.g., "At the camp the sick would soon be dead" or "At the camp the weekend had nearly arrived"). Eysenck et al. observed that the anxiety patients showed an exaggerated tendency to falsely "recognize" the threatening disambiguations of the ambiguous sentences, suggesting that these anxious patients had originally interpreted these ambiguous sentences in their more threatening manner. Also using ambiguous sentences, MacLeod and Cohen (1993) studied interpretative processing in high and low anxious subjects using an online text comprehension task. Subjects read short passages at a self-paced rate on a VDU screen, pressing a button to receive each sentence. By timing the intervals between presses, it was possible to record the comprehension latencies shown on every sentence. One sentence in each passage was ambiguous, and permitted either a threatening or a nonthreatening interpretation (e.g., "The doctor examined little Emily's growth"). The subsequent sentence appeared in either of two forms, one providing a meaningful continuation only for the threatening interpretation of the ambiguous sentence, and one providing a meaningful continuation only for the neutral interpretation of that ambiguous sentence (e.g. "Her tumor/height had changed little since last visit"). It was assumed that subjects would show elevated comprehension latencies on those continuation sentences that violated their initial interpretation of the ambiguous sentence. In keeping with the experimental prediction, high trait-anxious subjects alone demonstrated relatively fast comprehension latencies for those continuation sentences that were consistent with the threatening, rather than with the nonthreatening interpretation of the ambiguous sentence. The reverse pattern was shown by low trait-anxious subjects. MacLeod and Cohen concluded from this study, therefore, that high trait-anxious individuals do impose threatening interpretations upon ambiguous information during the comprehension process.

On the basis of this brief review, it can be concluded that there is considerable evidence to suggest that anxious individuals selectively impose threatening interpretations upon ambiguous information. It seems likely that this interpretative bias may contribute to the patterns of thought content which appear to interfere with anxious subjects' performance of intellective tasks. Many aspects of test taking situations require subjects to deal with information that is inherently ambiguous. Whether or not individuals evaluate their performance favorably and experience positive thoughts and heightened subjective confidence, or evaluate their performance negatively and experience the types of self-critical thoughts that interfere with task execution, will depend on how those individuals interpret such ambiguity. Anxious individuals' tendency to interpret ambiguous information in a threatening manner, therefore, could account for the preponderance of worry-related thoughts reported by these individuals, and hence could give rise to to the high levels of cognitive interference experienced by these subjects when performing such tasks.

Selective Memory and Anxiety

The possibility that anxious individuals may display facilitated retrieval of past threatening events from memory offers yet another potential explanation for the threatening thought content reported by such subjects. Not surprisingly, therefore, a good deal of research has addressed the hypothesis that anxious subjects may demonstrate a recall advantage for emotionally threatening information. Despite this effort, however, very little convincing support for this hypothesis has been obtained.

Many of the studies described earlier, which have assessed patterns of color naming latencies shown on emotional words, also subsequently assessed memory for the contents of these words (e.g., Mathews & MacLeod, 1986; Mogg et al., 1989; Watts et al., 1986). In none of these studies, however, were the anxious subjects found to show any relative recall advantage for the emotionally threatening words. Several carefully constructed studies designed specifically to compare selective memory in anxious and nonanxious subjects also have failed to find any evidence for such a memory bias. For example, Rapee, McCallum, Melville, Ravenscroft, and Rodney (1994) contrasted social phobic and normal control subjects in a series of four experiments which assessed recall and recognition of emotional stimulus words, recall of criticism and praise given in response to earlier task performance, and retrieval of emotional events from autobiographical memory. Across all experiments, no differential patterns of selective memory were observed between the anxious and the control subjects.

Indeed, occasional findings have been reported which suggest that anxious individuals may show disproportionately poor memory for emotionally threatening stimuli. For example, Watts and Dalgleish (1991) found that spider phobics display a selective memory impairment for spider-related information. Such spider phobics show both a selectively impaired ability to recall words related to spiders (Watts, 1986), and an impaired capacity to recognize actual spiders that have been exposed previously (Watts et al., 1986). A similar memory deficit for threat-related stimulus information also has been reported within generalized anxiety disorder patients. For example, Mogg, Mathews, and Weinman (1987) used a simple self-referent encoding task to present such patients, and control subjects, with trait adjectives which differed in emotional tone. Following this encoding procedure, an unexpected incidental recall test was given to test the hypothesis that the anxiety patients would show enhanced memory for the anxiety-relevant trait adjectives. In fact, however, the anxiety patients, relative to the control subjects, showed disproportionately poor memory for the more negative trait adjectives, and this memory impairment was most pronounced for those adjectives that were most closely related to anxiety. Foa, McNally, and Murdock (1989) reported similar effects when they used an equivalent self-referent encoding task and incidental recall test to assess selective memory in speech phobic subjects experiencing elevated state anxiety because they were about to deliver a talk. Not only did these anxious subjects show no increased ability to recall the anxiety-related words in the incidental recall task but, indeed, those individuals who showed the greatest elevations in state anxiety (as assessed by heart rate elevation) displayed the poorest relative ability to recall the anxiety-related trait words, compared to the neutral trait words.

Only very infrequently has it been found that anxious patients display enhanced memory for threatening stimulus information, and this usually occurs when these words are threatening only for the patients, and not for the control subjects (e.g., Nunn, Stevenson, & Whalen, 1984; Zeitlin & McNally, 1991). For example, Nunn et al. observed that a group of agoraphobics showed a relative recall advantage for words such as "travel" or "supermarket," when compared against normal control subjects. However, the fact that such words would have held no emotional connotations whatsoever for the control subjects means that this effect cannot be assumed to reflect group differences in memory for emotionally negative stimuli. In any case, such effects often prove difficult to replicate. Pickles and van den Broek (1988), for example, have failed to replicate Nunn et al.'s original findings. For some time, it did look possible that panic disorder patients may show a more reliable memory advantage for threatening information (e.g., McNally, Foa, & Donnell, 1989; Cloitre & Leibowitz, 1991). However, recent failures to replicate this effect also have been reported (e.g., Beck, Stanley, Averill, Baldwin, & Deagle, 1992), casting considerable doubt on the validity of this proposal.

The most appropriate conclusion, therefore, would seem to be that anxious subjects show no reliable memory advantage for emotionally threatening information. Consequently, there is no reason to believe that the intrusive thoughts concerning threat and danger, which appear to interfere with anxious subjects' performance on intellective tasks, result from the selective retrieval of threatening memories. Nevertheless, it seems reasonable to suppose that these interfering thoughts may result from anxious subjects' heightened tendencies to selectively encode threat cues from their environment, and to selectively impose threatening interpretations upon ambiguous information.

SPECIFICITY OF ANXIETY-LINKED SELECTIVE PROCESSING BIASES

Many researchers have argued that the patterns of negative thinking reported by anxious individuals are quite specific to anxiety, and do not represent a ubiquitous characteristic of dysphoric emotion in general. In particular, it has been suggested that future-oriented thoughts concerning personal danger are peculiar to anxiety (e.g., Beck & Clark, 1988; Clark, Beck, & Brown, 1989). Consistent with this proposal, there is convincing evidence that thoughts of this type do predict the presence of anxiety symptoms rather than the presence of depressive symptoms, which are better predicted by past-oriented negative thoughts concerning loss and failure (e.g., Jolly & Dykman, 1994; Sewitch & Kirsch, 1984; Wickless & Kirsch, 1988). Given the apparent specificity of anxiety-linked negative thought content, then if selective processing biases do contribute to the development of this thought content it might reasonably be expected that anxiety-linked selective processing biases also ought to be highly specific in nature.

It is indeed the case that the profile of processing biases associated with elevated anxiety appears to be quite different from that associated with elevated depression. The characteristic encoding advantage for negative information shown by anxiety patients typically is not evidenced by depressed patients (e.g., MacLeod et al., 1986; MacLeod, Tata, & Mathews, 1987; Gotlib, MacLachan, & Katz, 1988; McCabe & Gotlib, in press). Furthermore, depressed subjects display a robust recall advantage for emotionally negative information (e.g., Blaney, 1986; Denny & Hunt, 1992) which is not shown reliably by anxious individuals. It seems plausible that the future-oriented nature of anxiety-linked negative thought content might reflect the fact that such thoughts result primarily from the selective encoding bias characteristic of anxiety, which increases the perception of potential threats within the immediate environment. In contrast, the selective memory bias shown by depressed subjects, which operates to favor the recall of previously encountered negative events, may be more likely to produce the types of past-oriented negative thinking which characterizes this rather different emotional condition.

It also appears to be the case that the particular semantic domains from which negative information is selectively encoded by different classes of anxious subjects may correspond very closely to the specific types of negative thought content experienced by these individuals. For example, Mogg, Mathews, and Eysenck (1992) classified a sample of generalized anxiety disorder patients according to the degree to which they tended to worry about social concerns (such as coping with the demands and expectations of others) or about physical concerns (such as the possibility of illness or injury). Using the dot probe technique, Mogg et al. then assessed the subjects' attentional responses to emotional stimuli which included both negative words related to social threat (e.g., "rejected" and "criticized") and negative words related to physical threat (e.g., "disease" and "mutilated"). These researchers found that, although the anxiety patients showed speeded detection latencies for probes occurring in the vicinity of threat words in general, the degree of speeding to detect probes in the vicinity of social threat words in particular was significantly correlated with subjects' reported tendencies to worry greatly about social concerns. Similar conclusions have been supported by findings from the color-naming interference task (e.g., Mathews & MacLeod, 1985; Mogg et al., 1989). For example, Mogg et al. divided their generalized anxiety disorder patients into those who reported worrying most about social concerns, and those who worried most about physical concerns, and found that the former anxious subgroup showed inflated color-naming latencies only on words related to social threat, while the latter subgroup showed inflated color-naming latencies only on words related to physical threat. Thus, those generalized anxiety disorder patients whose negative thought content revolved around the theme of social threat were particularly likely to be characterized by a selectively encoding advantage for information pertaining to social threat, while those patients whose thought content revolved around the theme of physical threat were better characterized by a selective encoding advantage information for information related to physical threat.

Further evidence suggesting a strong correspondence between the semantic domains from which anxiety patients selectively encode threatening information, and the types of concerns that characterize these patients, is revealed when one contrasts findings across different classes of clinical anxiety disorders. Using the color-naming interference task to assess selective encoding, Watts et al. (1986) found that spider phobics showed elevated color-naming latencies only on threat words related to spiders, and not on general threat words unrelated to this topic. Similarly, Hope et al. (1990) found that their social phobic patients only displayed elevated color-naming latencies on threat words specifically related to social threat. Likewise, it appears that panic disorder patients show color-naming interference only on threat words concerning aversive bodily sensations, subjective symptoms of panic, and physical catastrophes, and do not show any tendency to display color-naming interference on more general categories of threat words (Ehlers, Margraf, Davies, & Roth, 1988; McNally, Riemann, & Kim, 1990; McNally, Riemann, Louro, Lukach, & Kim, 1992). Finally, it has been observed that posttraumatic stress disorder patients show a specific elevation of color-naming interference only on trauma-related threat words, which correspond closely to the content of these patients' intrusive thoughts (e.g., Foa, Feske, Murdock, Kozak, & McCarthy, 1991; McNally, Kaspi, Riemann, & Zeitlin, 1990; Thrasher, Dalgleish, & Yule, 1994). For example, in their study of rape victims suffering from posttraumatic stress disorder, Foa et al. found that these subjects (but not rape victims without PTSD) showed elevated color-naming interference on threat words related to rape, but did not display such interference on equally threatening words unrelated to this topic. Similarly, McNally et al. reported that their combat veteran PTSD patients were disproportionately slow to color name only threat words related to combat, while Thrasher et al. observed slowed color-naming responses within their PTSD patients, who were all survivors of a ferry disaster, only on disaster-related threat words.

Across all of these studies, therefore, the particular domain of concern that has characterized each type of anxious subject has closely matched the semantic domain from which that class of anxious subject has tended to selectively encode threatening information. While appreciating that a causal interpretation cannot be inferred from a simple association, it nevertheless is tempting to speculate that discrepancies in the precise negative thought content associated with each of these various types of anxiety disorders may result from the specificity of the selective encoding biases shown by these different categories of patients. If the threatening thought content associated with elevated anxiety does result from an anxiety-linked tendency to selectively process threatening information, then it seems likely that individual differences in the semantic domains within which these selective processing biases are most pronounced may contribute to the precise character of such threatening thoughts. The precise nature of these threatening thoughts, in turn, might be expected to influence the precise symptomatology displayed by these anxious individuals (MacLeod, 1991).

AUTOMATICITY OF ANXIETY-LINKED SELECTIVE PROCESSING BIASES

Within the burgeoning clinical literature that has attempted to assign a causal role to negative thought content in the genesis of emotional pathology, the claim often has been made that the threatening thoughts experienced by anxious individuals occur quite automatically, in the sense that their presence is not mediated by conscious intention (e.g., Beck, Emery, & Greenberg, 1986). Certainly, this proposal is consistent with the cognitive interference literature, given that cognitive interference typically is considered to involve unwanted thoughts. If we accept the premise that the thoughts that contribute to cognitive interference in anxious subjects occur automatically, and we continue to entertain the notion that such thoughts may represent the products of anxiety-linked biases in selective encoding and interpretation, then it is easy to develop the hypothesis that these anxiety-linked selective processing biases must themselves occur automatically. What evidence is there to support this hypothesis?

The automaticity of the interpretative bias shown by anxious individuals has not been well established, in part because there is no simple way to restrict subjects' opportunity to employ consciously mediated interpretative strategies when performing the tasks that have been employed to assess interpretation.

The study of selective interpretation which probably bears most directly upon this issue is the lexical priming experiment reported by Richards and French (1992). The results of this study do not offer strong support for the hypothesis that patterns of anxiety-linked selective interpretation represent the consequence of an automatic processing bias. Neely (1977) has established that automatically mediated priming effects can be detected at prime-target onset asynchronies of 250 msec or below, while longer asynchronies lead to an increasing contribution from intentionally mediated strategic processes. In Richards and French's study, however, the group differences in the relative magnitude of the priming effects, which suggested the presence of an anxiety-linked interpretative bias, were not evidenced at stimulus-target onset asynchronies of 500 msec, and only appeared when these asynchronies were extended to 750 msec. Thus, there is little evidence as yet to indicate that the biased interpretation shown by anxious individuals occurs automatically.

There is, however, considerable evidence that the encoding advantage for threatening information shown by anxious subjects does occur quite automatically, without requiring mediation by conscious awareness. For example, in Mathews and MacLeod's (1986) dichotic listening version of the interference paradigm, despite the fact that the anxious subjects were disproportionately slow to perform the central reaction time task when threat-related distracters were presented through the headphones, these subjects nevertheless were entirely unable to recall, or to accurately recognize, the identity of these distracter stimuli. Indeed, all subjects professed to have been completely unaware of the distracter words' semantic content. Even more impressive evidence that this anxiety-linked selective encoding bias occurs without conscious mediation has been provided by studies that have employed backward masking techniques to prevent awareness of the emotional stimulus words (cf. Turvey, 1973). Backward masking involves presenting stimulus words very briefly (20 msec or less), before replacing them with a random pattern "mask" consisting of rotated and inverted letter fragments. Under such conditions, subjects typically report no conscious awareness of words having been presented, though there is considerable evidence that the semantic content of masked stimuli nevertheless is encoded (e.g., Marcel, 1983). Despite their lack of conscious awareness for the semantic content of masked stimuli, anxious subjects continue to show evidence of an encoding bias favoring the emotionally threatening stimulus words.

MacLeod and Rutherford (1992) employed a masked version of the color-naming interference task, in which colored emotional words were exposed for only 20 msec before being replaced by masks presented in the same color. Subjects were entirely unable to accurately determine whether or not a word had been presented under this masked presentation condition, but had no difficulty naming the ink color used in each trial. Despite their lack of awareness for the identity of the emotional words, highly anxious individuals nevertheless displayed disproportionately slow color naming latencies on those trials within which threat words were presented. Using this same methodology, MacLeod and Hagan (1992) confirmed that the masking procedure was effective in eliminating subjects' ability to consciously detect the presence of the emotional words. However, these researchers found that the degree to which color naming latencies were slowed on threat word trials, relative to neutral word trials, correlated positively and significantly with questionnaire measures of anxiety. Using a slightly different version of this masked color naming task, in which the emotional words were exposed for only 1 msec, Mogg, Bradley, Williams, and Mathews (1993) found that generalized anxiety disorder patients, relative to normal control subjects, still displayed a relative slowing of color naming latencies on trials within which threat words were presented. Indeed, Mogg et al. found that the magnitude of this anxiety-linked threat interference effect was just as great under the masked exposure condition as it was under an unmasked exposure condition which permitted full awareness of the word content.

The above findings lend considerable support to the hypothesis that anxious subjects' tendency to selectively encode threatening stimuli is not mediated by conscious awareness. Given the interpretative problems associated with the color-naming task, however, it would be reassuring to see these findings conceptually replicated using more direct measures of selective attention, such as that provided by the dot probe methodology (MacLeod et al., 1986). As yet, no published studies have reported results from masked versions of this dot probe task, though preliminary findings within the author's laboratory strongly suggest that masking the stimulus words does not modify the pattern of detection latencies displayed by anxious subjects. For example, Churcher (1992) employed a version of the probe task that was virtually identical to that used by MacLeod et al., except that on half of the trials the two stimulus words were presented for only 20 msec, and were followed by a pattern mask. Although this exposure condition prevented conscious awareness of these words' presence, it did not decrease the tendency demonstrated by highly anxious subjects to display a reduced detection latencies for probes appearing in the location of the threat words, relative to probes appearing in the location of neutral words.

Thus it would appear that the attentional bias towards threatening stimuli that characterizes anxious individuals does indeed proceed automatically, in the sense that it operates outside conscious awareness. Of course, it seems likely that while the bias itself may operate outside of awareness, it will have a profound influence upon what ultimately becomes represented within conscious awareness. That is, the preconscious orientation of attention towards threat-related information shown by anxious subjects would be expected to result in those subjects becoming disproportionately aware of the more threatening elements of their environment. This, in turn, may give rise to the conscious thoughts concerning the imminence of danger which appear to be characteristic of anxiety. Therefore, although this anxiety-linked encoding advantage for threatening information appears to function nonconsciously, it nevertheless may contribute causally to the development of the distinctive pattern of thinking that characterizes the content of consciousness in anxious individuals.

DO ANXIETY-LINKED SELECTIVE PROCESSING BIASES REFLECT TRAIT OR STATE VARIABLES?

The preceding review of selective information processing in anxiety has focused primarily upon research that has contrasted clinically anxious patients against normal control subjects. Typically, clinically anxious patients show higher current levels of anxious mood state than do normal control subjects, and also are characterized by a greater than normal trait disposition to experience such anxious moods. That is, clinically anxious patients tend to show higher levels of both state anxiety and trait anxiety (cf. Spielberger, Gorsuch, & Lushene, 1970) than do normal control subjects. Consequently, it is difficult to determine whether anxiety patients' elevated tendency to selectively encode threatening information, and to interpret ambiguity in a threatening manner, is a characteristic of their elevated state anxiety, their elevated trait anxiety, or both.

Studies that have investigated the cognitive changes that accompany the elimination of anxious mood state in clinical patients, achieved through effective therapeutic intervention, can shed some light on this issue. The results of such studies strongly suggest that the selective information processing biases shown by clinically anxious patients are, to some extent, associated with their elevated levels of state anxiety. Some researchers have taken a cross-sectional approach, and have contrasted groups of recovered anxiety patients against both currently anxious patients and normal control subjects. For example, in Mathews et al.'s (1989) homophone study, designed to assess selective interpretation of ambiguous words, it was found that, while clinically anxious patients produced a greater proportion of threatening spellings than did normal control subjects, the proportion of threat spellings produced by a group of recovered anxiety patients fell midway between the proportions shown by the other two groups, and differed significantly from neither. In the false recognition paradigm used by Eysenck et al. (1991) to assess the selective interpretation of ambiguous sentences, a group of recovered anxiety patients showed an equivalent pattern of recognition judgments to that shown by normal control subjects. The fact that current anxiety patients showed a pattern of recognition judgments that indicated a greater tendency to have imposed threatening interpretations on the ambiguous sentences than was shown by the recovered anxiety patients suggests that elevated state anxiety may be implicated in the mediation of this interpretative bias.

There also is evidence from recovery studies that elevated state anxiety may be critical in determining the presence of a selective encoding advantage for threatening information. Again, cross-sectional designs sometimes have been employed to address this issue. For example, Mogg et al.'s (1992) dot probe study included a group of recovered clinical anxiety patients in addition to currently anxious patients and control subjects. While the currently anxious patients showed a greater speeding to detect probes in the location of threat words than did normal controls, the recovered patients showed a pattern of latencies which fell between these extremes, and which did not differ significantly from the pattern shown by either of these other two groups. Even more convincing evidence that state anxiety plays a role in the mediation of attentional biases comes from longitudinal studies, which have followed a cohort of clinical patients through treatment. Most of these studies have employed the color-naming interference task, and have found that clinically anxious patients' tendency to display slowed color-naming latencies on threat words, relative to neutral words, is substantially attenuated when state anxiety levels are reduced therapeutically. Watts et al. (1986) found that reducing state anxiety through exposure treatment eliminated the selective slowing to color name spider words shown by spider phobic subjects. Indeed, Lavy et al. (1993) have demonstrated that the elevated color-naming interference shown on spider words by such patients can be significantly reduced by even a single session of exposure therapy. The elimination of selective color-naming interference through the successful treatment of the anxiety state has been observed not only in spider phobics, but also in obsessive compulsive patients (Foa & McNally, 1986), and in panic disorder patients (Beck et al., 1992). Furthermore, the elimination of this selective interference effect has been observed across a wide range of intervention approaches. For example, Mattia et al. (1993) found that their social phobics showed reduced color-naming interference on social threat words, relative to control words, as their state anxiety levels declined, regardless of whether this mood change occurred in response to cognitive-behavior therapy, group therapy, phenelzine, or placebo.

The evidence reviewed above strongly suggests that elevated state anxiety is implicated in the mediation of the selective processing biases shown by clinically anxious patients. However, this demonstration that state anxiety plays a role in the mediation of these effects in no way excludes the possibility that trait anxiety also may make an important contribution. The finding that clinically anxious patients do not show selective processing advantages for threatening information unless they are experiencing elevated levels of state anxiety, does not permit the conclusion that elevated state anxiety will be associated with the presence of such selective processing biases in all subjects, regardless of their level of trait vulnerability. In fact, studies which have directly examined the patterns of selective processing elicited by elevated state anxiety in normal subjects have demonstrated clearly that the cognitive correlates of elevated state anxiety differ markedly as a function of subjects' trait anxiety levels.

MacLeod and Mathews (1988) employed the dot probe task to assess selective attention in two groups of students who differed in their levels of trait anxiety. These subjects were tested twice, once when state anxiety was low (near the beginning of semester), and once when state anxiety was high (in the week preceding end of semester examinations). The patterns of probe detection latencies shown in the low state anxiety test session did not discriminate the two trait groups, and revealed no tendency for either group to attend towards or away from the emotionally threatening stimulus words. The elevation of state anxiety observed in the high state anxiety session elicited, in the high trait anxious subjects only, speeded detection latencies for probes presented in the vicinity of exam threat words, suggesting that these high trait-anxious subjects responded to this state anxiety elevation by developing an attentional bias towards stress relevant threat stimuli. In contrast, this elevation of state anxiety elicited the opposite pattern of effects in the low trait-anxious subjects who, in the high state anxiety session, showed disproportionately slow detection latencies for probes appearing in the vicinity of the exam threat words. This suggests that low trait-anxious subjects may respond to elevations in state anxiety by developing an attentional avoidance response to stress relevant threatening information. Using this same dot probe paradigm, Broadbent and Broadbent (1988) also concluded that the likelihood of elevated state anxiety being associated with increased attentional orientation towards threat stimuli, rather than away from such threat stimuli, is a positive function of trait anxiety level.

A similar interactive function of state and trait anxiety has been observed on the color-naming interference task also. Richards, French, Johnson, Naparstek, and Williams (1992) employed an experimental mood manipulation to induce either positive affect, or elevated state anxiety, in high and low trait-anxious subjects, who then were required to color name threatening and nonthreatening words. For the high trait subjects, the state anxiety induction increased their color-naming latencies on threat words relative to control words, suggesting that these individuals found it more difficult to ignore the threat word content as they became state anxious. For the low trait-anxious subjects, however, the pattern of observed effects was in the opposite direction, with the state anxiety elevation tending to reduce color-naming interference on threat words relative to control words. MacLeod and Rutherford (1992) obtained very similar results using a masked version of the color-naming task. High trait-anxious students were found to respond to state anxiety elevations, elicited by exam proximity, by showing slower color-naming latencies on trials exposing masked threat words, relative to trials exposing masked neutral words. Low trait-anxious subjects, in contrast, responded to the same state anxiety elevations by showing speeded color-naming latencies on the masked trials that exposed threat words rather than neutral words. Thus, while elevated state anxiety may elicit an automatic attentional bias towards threat in high trait-anxious subjects, it appears not to elicit this effect in low trait anxious. Indeed, the evidence suggests that, in low trait-anxious subjects, elevated state anxiety is more likely to elicit automatic attentional avoidance of threatening information.

These trait-linked differences in the patterns of selective processing elicited by elevated state anxiety may go some way towards explaining individual differences in tendency to experience cognitive interference during the performance of stressful intellective tasks. It is well documented that some subjects experience more intrusive negative thoughts than others during intellective test performance, and those subjects who experience most negative thoughts also tend to experience the greatest anxiety elevations (cf. Sarason, Sarason, & Pierce, 1994). Although it is likely that this variability may, in part, reflect individual differences in the degree to which subjects experience any initial slight elevation of state anxiety within test settings, it also is possible that individual differences in the patterns of selective processing elicited by such slight initial elevation in state anxiety could contribute to the variance. Suppose, for example, that all subjects tend to become slightly state anxious when entering a test situation, but that only some respond to this anxious mood state by showing an increased tendency to selective encode threatening information and to selective impose threatening interpretations upon ambiguity. For those subjects who do display this response, it is likely that the types of threatening thoughts resulting from such processing biases will further elevate state anxiety, thus intensifying the processing bias, and further increasing the presence of intrusive negative thoughts. Therefore those subjects, even if they did not show initially intense anxiety reactions to the test situation, will be characterized by spiraling levels of state anxiety, and by increasingly severe cognitive interference. In contrast, those subjects who respond to heightened state anxiety by developing a tendency to avoid processing threatening information may experience the same initial elevation of state anxiety in a test setting without this resulting either in cognitive interference or in any escalation of this anxious mood state. Essentially, what is being suggested here is that stable individual differences in the patterns of selective processing that are elicited by elevated state anxiety might provide a causal explanation for individual differences in anxiety vulnerability. The final section of this chapter considers this intriguing possibility in a little more detail.

CAUSAL NATURE OF ASSOCIATION BETWEEN SELECTIVE PROCESSING AND ANXIETY VULNERABILITY

Across the past two decades, the study of emotion and cognition has been characterized by a marked shift of emphasis. Until the late 1970s, researchers within this field primarily were interested in studying the cognitive effects of emotional states such as anxiety, and hoped that an understanding of these effects might illuminate the nature of the cognitive system in general, and may permit the development of optimal task designs within stressful work environments. However, since the advent of the "cognitive revolution" within clinical areas of our discipline (cf. MacLeod, 1993), many researchers have become more interested in exploring the cognitive basis of emotion, and seek an understanding of the cognitive processes that may contribute causally to different forms of emotional vulnerability in the hope that this may inform the development of clinical therapies designed to modify such vulnerability.

Many of the phenomena reported within this chapter appear to represent cognitive effects of state anxiety, given that they are elicited by those manipulations that directly induce this mood state. Nevertheless, the observation that the cognitive effects of state anxiety vary across subjects, and the fact that such variations are closely associated with individual differences in trait anxiety level, suggest the possibility that individual differences in the patterns of selective processing elicited by stress may constitute the cognitive basis of variations in anxiety vulnerability. Consider, for example, the individual who responds to elevated state anxiety by showing an increasing tendency to selectively process threatening information. If one assumes that the increased processing of threatening information will further elevate state anxiety, then it is inevitable that for this individual brief episodes of mild state anxiety will tend to escalate rapidly, with the resulting intense anxiety becoming relatively stable. It is precisely this self-reported tendency to commonly experience intense and stable state anxiety elevations which results in this individual being classified as highly trait anxious. In contrast, the individual who responds to elevations in state anxiety by increasingly avoiding the processing of threatening information will enjoy the benefits of a homeostatic mechanism that should prevent escalations of state anxiety, and which should ensure that any episodes of elevated state anxiety are short lasting. It is precisely this self-reported tendency to experience few, slight, and transient episodes of elevated state anxiety which results in this individual being classified as low trait anxious. Thus, individual differences in the tendency to selectively process threatening information when state anxious plausibly can provide a functional explanation for individual differences in anxiety vulnerability.

Given that it highlights a possible cognitive target for therapeutic manipulation, this cognitive explanation of anxiety vulnerability is rather exciting, though it must await experimental confirmation. Meanwhile, however, MacLeod and Hagan (1992) have reported findings that are consistent with a minimal prediction resulting from this account. Specifically, they tested the hypothesis that initial measures of subjects' tendencies to selectively encode threatening information when stressed should powerfully predict later individual differences in the distress produced by a subsequent negative life event. MacLeod and Hagan used a masked version of the color-naming interference task to assess patterns of selective encoding in a group of state anxious women about to undergo colposcopy investigation. At this initial test session, conventional questionnaire measures of emotional vulnerability also were taken. Those 15 women who some time later received a diagnosis of cervical pathology were followed up, and the degree to which their diagnosis elicited emotional distress was assessed using a questionnaire instrument. As predicted by the hypothesis that individual differences in the patterns of selective encoding elicited by state anxiety may functionally mediate emotional reactions to stressful events, it was found that the strongest predictor of the degree of distress elicited by the subsequent diagnosis was the degree to which subjects were initially slow to color name masked threat words relative to masked neutral words. Indeed, this interference measure alone accounted for more than 25% of the variance in emotional reactions to the subsequent diagnosis.

More recently, MacLeod and Ng (1995) have used a similar approach when trying to predict individual differences in emotional reactions to the acculturation stress experienced by overseas students on their arrival to commence tertiary studies in Australia. In an initial assessment session, given in their home country (Singapore) several weeks prior to their departure, subjects performed the color-naming interference task under both high and low stress conditions. At this same time, they were also given conventional questionnaire measures of emotional vulnerability and mood state. The day after their arrival in Australia, these subjects again had their mood state assessed, enabling calculation of the extent to which state anxiety levels had been elevated by the transition. The measure of selective encoding provided by the color-naming interference task on the initial assessment session, which quantified the degree to which subjects had responded to stress by showing increased color-naming latencies on threat words, relative to neutral words, was the only independent predictor of individual differences in the magnitude of these later state anxiety responses to this subsequent stressful transition event.

Such findings are entirely consistent with the hypothesis that individual differences in the patterns of selective information elicited by stress may functionally mediate emotional reactions to real life stressful events. However, demonstrating an association between two measures cannot impute causation, even when these two measures are taken at different times. Despite these encouraging findings, therefore, it remains uncertain whether individual differences in the processing biases elicited by stress represent the cognitive substrate of anxiety vulnerability, or are merely cognitive correlates of such vulnerability. Clearly, this is an important issue that needs to be addressed by future research.

SUMMARY AND CONCLUSIONS

Evidence has been presented to suggest that the patterns of impaired performance shown by anxious subjects on many demanding cognitive tasks are caused, at least in part, by cognitive interference resulting from intrusive threat-related thoughts. This chapter has developed the proposal that the elevated frequency of intrusive threatening thoughts reported by anxious individuals may itself be a consequence of certain low level selective processing biases that are associated with anxiety. Both clinically anxious patients and high trait-anxious normals experiencing elevated state anxiety display a striking tendency to selectively encode threatening information from the environment, and also show an inflated likelihood of selectively imposing threatening interpretations upon ambiguous information. Although the anxiety-linked selective encoding bias appears to operate outside awareness, it seems likely that this bias will powerfully influence the contents of consciousness. Consistent with the possibility that this selective encoding bias may make a functional contribution to thought content, it has been found that those anxious subjects who show a restriction of the selective encoding bias to particular semantic domains also tend to experience threatening thoughts associated with those same semantic domains. While rather less research has investigated the automaticity and specificity of the interpretative bias demonstrated by anxious individuals, it is plausible that this systematic tendency to resolve ambiguity in a threatening manner also might contribute to the intrusive negative thought content characteristic of anxious subjects.

In clinically anxious patients, the selective processing advantage for threatening information is eliminated by reductions in state anxiety. However, state anxiety elevations only serve to elicit such a selective processing bias in those normal subjects who report a high level of trait vulnerability to anxiety. Indeed, low trait-anxious individuals often respond to elevated state anxiety by showing selective avoidance of threatening information. In the light of such observations, it seems possible that variations in subjects' tendencies to experience cognitive interference from intrusive negative thoughts under stressful test situations may be accounted for by individual differences in the patterns of selective information processing elicited by elevated state anxiety. Furthermore, it is feasible that such individual differences in selective processing may play a functional role in mediating emotional experience, and thus may represent the cognitive substrate of trait anxiety.

The degree to which individuals show an increased tendency to selectively process threatening information when state anxious does, in fact, powerfully predict the degree to which these individuals later experience dysphoric emotionally responses to subsequent stressful life events. Such findings are consistent with the hypothesis that individual differences in patterns of selective processing serve to functionally mediate emotional vulnerability. However, the critical test of this hypothesis only can be provided by studies designed to directly manipulate patterns of selective encoding, and to assess the impact of such manipulations upon later emotional responses to stressful events. Consequently, the development of training techniques capable of modifying selective information is an important goal for researchers working within this field. If such techniques do indeed prove capable of manipulating anxiety vulnerability, then this not only will greatly advance our theoretical understanding of anxiety proneness, but also will offer clinicians a range of new procedures that may prove valuable in the treatment of anxiety disorders.

REFERENCES

Baddeley, A. D. (1986). *Working memory.* New York: Oxford University Press.

Beck, A. T., Emery, G., & Greenberg, R. C. (1986). *Anxiety disorders and phobias: A cognitive perspective.* New York: Basic Books.

Beck, J. G., Stanley, M. A., Averill, P. M., Baldwin, L. E., & Deagle, E. A. (1992). Attention and memory for threat in panic disorder. *Behaviour Research & Therapy, 30,* 619–629.

Beck, A. T., & Clark, D. M. (1988). Anxiety and depression: An information processing perspective. *Anxiety Research, 1,* 23–36.

Beck, A. T., Laude, R., & Bohnert, M. (1974). Ideational components of anxiety neurosis. *Archives of General Psychiatry, 31,* 319–325.

Blaney, P. H. (1986). Affect and memory: A review. *Psychological Bulletin, 99,* 229–246.

Blankenstein, K. R., Toner, B. B., & Flett, G. L. (1989). Test anxiety and the contents of consciousness: Thought listing and endorsement measures. *Journal of Research in Personality, 23,* 269–286.

Broadbent, D. E., & Broadbent, M. H. P. (1988). Anxiety and attentional bias: State and trait. *Cognition and Emotion, 2,* 165–184.

Bruch, K. R., Kaflowitz, N. G., & Kuethe, M. (1986). Beliefs and the subjective meaning of thoughts: Analysis of the role of self-statements in academic test performance. *Cognitive Therapy and Research, 10,* 51–69.

Bruning, J. L., Capage, J. E., Kozuh, G. F., Young, P. F., & Young, W. E. (1968). Socially induced drive and range of cue utilization. *Journal of Personality and Social Psychology, 9,* 242–244.

Burgess, I. S., Jones, L. N., Robertson, S. A., Radcliffe, W. N., Emerson, E., Lawler, P., & Crow, T. J. (1981). The degree of control exerted by phobic and nonphobic verbal stimuli over the recognition behaviour of phobic and nonphobic subjects. *Behaviour Research and Therapy, 19,* 223–234.

Butler, G., & Mathews, A. (1983). Cognitive processes in anxiety. *Advances in Behaviour Research and Therapy, 5,* 51–62.

Calvin, A. D., Koons, P. B., Bingam, J. L., & Fink, H. H. (1953). A further investigation of the relationship between manifest anxiety and intelligence. *Journal of Consulting Psychology, 19,* 280–282.

Cassiday, K. L., McNally, R. J., & Zeitlin, S. B. (1992). Cognitive processing of trauma cues in rape victims with post-traumatic stress disorder. *Cognitive Therapy & Research, 16,* 283–295.

Chambless, D. L., Caputo, G. C., Bright, P., & Gallagher, R. (1984). Assessment of fear in agoraphobics: The Body Sensations Questionnaire and the Agoraphobic Cognitions Questionnaire. *Journal of Consulting and Clinical Psychology, 52,* 1090–1097.

Churcher, M. (1992). *Manipulating automatic and strategic attentional biases in anxious subjects.* Unpublished master's thesis, Department of Psychology, The University of Western Australia.

Clark, D. A., Beck, A. T., & Brown, G. (1989). Cognitive mediation in general psychiatric outpatients: A test of the content specificity hypothesis. *Journal of Personality and Social Psychology, 56,* 958–964.

Cloitre, M., & Leibowitz, M. R. (1991). Memory bias in panic disorder: An investigation of the cognitive avoidance hypothesis. *Cognitive Therapy & Research, 15,* 371–386.

Darke, S. (1988). Anxiety and working memory capacity. *Cognition and Emotion, 2,* 145–154.

Davidson, G. C., Feldman, P. M., & Osborn, C. E. (1984). Articulated thoughts, irrational beliefs, and fear of negative evaluation. *Cognitive Therapy and Research, 8,* 349–362.

Dawkins, K., & Furnham, A. (1989). The colour naming of emotional words. *British Journal of Psychology, 80,* 383–389.

de Ruiter, C., & Brosschot, J. F. (1994). The emotional Stroop interference effect in anxiety: Attentional bias or cognitive avoidance? *Behaviour Research and Therapy, 32,* 315–319.

Deffenbacher, J. L. (1980). Worry and emotionality in test anxiety. In I. G. Sarason (Ed.), *Test anxiety: Theory, research and applications* (pp. 131–159). Hillsdale, NJ: Lawrence Erlbaum Associates.

Denny, E. B., & Hunt, R. R. (1992). Affective valence and memory in depression: Dissociation of recall and fragment completion. *Journal of Abnormal Psychology, 101*, 575–580.

Dornic, S. (1977). *Mental load, effort, and individual differences.* Reports from the Department of Psychology, The University of Stockholm, Number 509.

Dornic, S., & Fernaeus, S. E. (1981). *Individual differences in high load tasks: The effect of verbal distraction.* Reports from the Department of Psychology, The University of Stockholm, Number 569.

Easterbrook, J. A. (1959). The effect of emotion on cue utilization and the organization of behavior. *Psychological Review, 66*, 183–201.

Ehlers, A., Margraf, J., Davies, S., & Roth, W. T. (1988). Selective processing of threat cues in subjects with panic attacks. *Cognition and Emotion, 2*, 201–220.

Eysenck, M. W. (1982). *Attention and arousal: Cognition and performance.* Berlin: Springer.

Eysenck, M. W. (1988). Anxiety and attention. *Anxiety Research, 1*, 9–15.

Eysenck, M. W. (1992). *Anxiety: The cognitive perspective.* Hove, UK: Lawrence Erlbaum Associates.

Eysenck, M. W., & Calvo, M. G. (1992). Anxiety and performance: The processing efficiency theory. *Cognition and Emotion, 6*, 409–434.

Eysenck, M. W., MacLeod, C., & Mathews, A. (1987). Cognitive functioning in anxiety. *Psychological Research, 49*, 189–195.

Eysenck, M. W., Mogg, K., May, J., Richards, A., & Mathews, A. M. (1991). Bias in interpretation of ambiguous sentences related to threat in anxiety. *Journal of Abnormal Psychology, 100*, 144–150.

Foa, E. G., & McNally, R. J. (1986). Sensitivity to feared stimuli in obsessive-compulsives: A dichotic listening analysis. *Cognitive Therapy and Research, 10*, 477–486.

Foa, E. B., McNally, R., & Murdock, T. B. (1989). Anxious mood and memory. *Behaviour Research and Therapy, 27*, 141–147.

Francis, G. (1988). Assessing cognition in anxious children. *Behaviour Modification, 12*, 267–280.

Ganellan, R. J., Matuzas, W., Uhlenhuth, E. H., Glass, R., & Easton, C. R. (1986). Panic disorder, agoraphobia, and anxiety-relevant cognitive style. *Journal of Affective Disorders, 11*, 219–225.

Gotlib, I. H., McLachan, A. L., & Katz, A. N. (1988). Biases in visual attention in depressed and nondepressed individuals. *Cognition and Emotion, 2*, 185–200.

Hibbert, G. A. (1984). Ideational components of anxiety: Their origin and content. *British Journal of Psychiatry, 144*, 618–624.

Hope, D. A., Rapee, R. M., Heimberg, R. G., & Dombeck, M. J. (1990). Representations of the self in social phobia: Vulnerability to social threat. *Cognitive Therapy & Research, 14*, 177–189.

Humphreys, M. S., & Revelle, W. (1984). Personality, motivation and performance: A theory of the relationship between individual differences and information processing. *Psychological Review, 91*, 153–184.

Hunsley, J. (1987). Cognitive processes in mathematics anxiety and test anxiety: The role of appraisals, internal dialogue, and attributions. *Journal of Educational Psychology, 79*, 388–392.

Jolly, J. B., & Dykman, R. A. (1994). Using self report data to differentiate anxious and depressed symptoms in adolescents: Cognitive content specificity and global distress? *Cognitive Therapy & Research, 18*, 25–37.

Kendall, P. C. (1993). Cognitive-behavioural therapies with youth: Guiding theory, current status, and emerging developments. *Journal of Consulting and Clinical Psychology, 61*, 235–247.

Knox, W. J., & Grippaldi, R. (1970). High levels of state or trait anxiety and performance on selected verbal WAIS subtests. *Psychological Reports, 27*, 375–379.

Krantz, S., & Hammen, C. (1979). Assessment of cognitive bias in depression. *Journal of Abnormal Psychology, 88*, 611–619.

Lavy, E., van den Hout, M., & Arntz, A. (1993). Attentional bias and spider phobia: Conceptual and clinical issues. *Behaviour Research and Therapy, 31*, 17–24.

Lavy, E. H., van Oppen, P., & van den Hout, M. (1994). Selective processing of emotional information in obsessive compulsive disorder. *Behaviour Research and Therapy, 32*, 243–246.

Lavy, E. H., & van den Hout, M. A. (1994). Cognitive avoidance and attentional bias: Causal relationships. *Cognitive Therapy & Research, 18*, 179–191.

Leon, M. R., & Revelle, W. (1985). Effects of anxiety on analogical reasoning: A test of three theoretical models. *Journal of Personality and Social Psychology, 49*, 1302–1315.

MacLeod, C. (1990). Mood disorders and cognition. In M. W. Eysenck (Ed.), *Cognitive psychology: An international review* (pp. 9–56). Chichester, England: Wiley.

MacLeod, C. (1991). Clinical anxiety and the selective encoding of threatening information. *International Review of Psychiatry, 3*, 279–292.

MacLeod, C. (1993). Cognition in clinical psychology: Measures, methods, or models? *Behaviour Change, 10*, 169–195.

MacLeod, C., & Cohen, I. (1993). Anxiety and the interpretation of ambiguity: A text comprehension study. *Journal of Abnormal Psychology, 102*, 238–247.

MacLeod, C., & Hagan, R. (1992). Individual differences in selective processing of threatening information, and emotional responses to a stressful life event. *Behaviour Research & Therapy, 30*, 151–161.

MacLeod, C., & Mathews, A. (1988). Anxiety and the allocation of attention to threat. *Quarterly Journal of Experimental Psychology: Human Experimental Psychology, 38*, 659–670.

MacLeod, C., Mathews, A., & Tata, P. (1986). Attentional bias in emotional disorders. *Journal of Abnormal Psychology, 95*, 15–20.

MacLeod, C., & Ng, V. (1995). *Initial attentional bias to threat predicts later emotional response to acculturation stress.* Manuscript in preparation.

MacLeod, C., & Rutherford, E. M. (1992). Anxiety and the selective processing of emotional information: Mediating roles of awareness, trait and state variables, and personal relevance of stimulus materials. *Behaviour Research and Therapy, 30*, 479–491.

MacLeod, C., Tata, P., & Mathews, A. (1987). Perception of emotionally valenced information in depression. *British Journal of Psychology, 26*, 67–68.

Marcel, A. J. (1983). Conscious and unconscious perception: Experiments on visual masking and word recognition. *Cognitive Psychology, 15*, 197–237.

Mathews, A., & MacLeod, C. (1985). Selective processing of threat cues in anxiety states. *Behaviour Research and Therapy, 23*, 563–569.

Mathews, A., & MacLeod, C. (1986). Discrimination of threat cues without awareness in anxiety states. *Journal of Abnormal Psychology, 95*, 131–138.

Mathews, A., & MacLeod, C. (1994). Cognitive approaches to emotion. *Annual Review of Psychology, 45*, 25–50.

Mathews, A., Richards, A., & Eysenck, M. (1989). Interpretation of homophones related to threat in anxiety states. *Journal of Abnormal Psychology, 98*, 31–34.

Mattia, J. I., Heimberg, R. G., & Hope, D. A. (1993). The revised Stroop color-naming task in social phobics. *Behaviour Research and Therapy, 31*, 305–313.

McCabe, S., & Gotlib, I. H. (in press). Selective attention and clinical depression: Performance on a deployment-of-attention task. *Journal of Abnormal Psychology.*

McNally, R. J., Amir, N., Louro, C. E., Lukach, B. M., Riemann, B. C., & Calamari, J. E. (1994). Cognitive processing of idiographic emotional information in panic disorder. *Behaviour Research & Therapy, 32*, 119–122.

McNally, R. J., Foa, E. B., & Donnell, C. D. (1989). Memory bias for anxiety information in patients with panic disorder. *Cognition and Emotion*, 3, 27–44.

McNally, R. J., Kaspi, S. P., Riemann, B. C., & Zeitlin, S. B. (1990). Selective processing of threat cues in panic disorder. *Behaviour Research & Therapy, 28*, 407–412.

McNally, R. J., Riemann, B. C., & Kim, E. (1990). Selective processing of threat cues in panic disorder. *Behaviour Research and Therapy, 28*, 407–412.

McNally, R. J., Riemann, B. C., Louro, C. E., Lukach, B. M., & Kim, E. (1992). Cognitive processing of emotional information in panic disorder. *Behaviour Research & Therapy, 30*, 143–149.

Mizes, J. S., Landolf-Fritsche, B., & Grossman-McKee, D. (1987). Patterns of distorted cognitions in phobic disorders. *Cognitive Therapy and Research, 11*, 583–592.

Mogg, K., Bradley, B. P., Williams R., & Mathews, A. (1993). Subliminal processing of emotional information in anxiety and depression. *Journal of Abnormal Psychology, 102*, 304–311.

Mogg, K., Mathews, A., & Eysenck, M. W. (1992). Attentional bias to threat in clinical anxiety states. *Cognition & Emotion, 6*, 149–159.

Mogg, K., Mathews, A., & Weinman, J. (1987). Memory bias in clinical anxiety. *Journal of Abnormal Psychology, 96*, 94–98.

Mogg, K., Mathews, A., & Weinman, J. (1989). Selective processing of threat cues in anxiety states: a replication. *Behaviour Research and Therapy, 27*, 317–323.

Morris, L. W., Davis, M. A., & Hutchings, C. H. (1981). Cognitive and emotional components of anxiety: Literature review and a revised worry-emotionality scale. *Journal of Educational Psychology, 73*, 541–555.

Mueller, J. H. (1976). Anxiety and cue utilization in human learning and memory. In M. Zuckerman & C. D. Spielberger (Eds.), *Emotions and anxiety: New concepts, methods and applications* (pp. 262–291). Hillsdale, NJ: Lawrence Erlbaum Associates.

Naveh-Benjamin, M. (1991). A comparison of training programs intended for different types of test-anxious students: Further support for an information processing model. *Journal of Educational Psychology, 83*, 134–139.

Neely, J. H. (1977). Semantic priming and retrieval from lexical memory: Roles on inhibitionless spreading activation and limited capacity attention. *Journal of Experimental Psychology: General, 106*, 226–254.

Nichols-Hoppe, K. T., & Beach, L. R. (1990). The effects of test anxiety and task variables on predecisional information search. *Journal of Research in Personality, 24*, 163–172.

Nisbett, R. E., & Wilson, T. D. (1977). Telling more than we can know: verbal reports on mental processes. *Psychological Review, 84*, 231–259.

Nunn, J. D., Stevenson, R., & Whalan, G. (1984). Selective memory effects in agoraphobic patients. *British Journal of Clinical Psychology, 23*, 195–201.

Pallack, M. S., Pittman, T. S., Heller, J. F., & Munson, P. (1975). The effect of arousal on Stroop color-word task performance. *Bulletin of the Psychonomic Society, 6*, 248–250.

Parkinson, L., & Rachman, S. (1981). Speed of recovery from an uncontrived stress. *Advances in Behaviour Research and Therapy, 3*, 119–123.

Pickles, A. J., & van den Broek, M. D. (1988). Failure to replicate evidence for phobic schemata in agoraphobic patients. *British Journal of Clinical Psychology, 27*, 271–272.

Rapee, R. M., McCallum, S. L., Melville, L. F., Ravenscroft H., & Rodney, J. M. (1994). Memory bias in social phobia. *Behaviour Research & Therapy, 32*, 89–99.

Richards, A., & French, C. C. (1992). An anxiety related bias in semantic activation when processing threat/neutral homographs. *Quarterly Journal of Experimental Psychology, 45A*, 503–525.

Richards, A., French, C. C., Johnson, W., Naparstek, J., & Williams, J. (1992). Effects of mood manipulation and anxiety on performance of an emotional Stroop task. *British Journal of Psychology, 83*, 479–491.

Sarason, I. G. (1973). Test anxiety and cognitive modelling. *Journal of Personality and Social Psychology, 28*, 58–61.

Sarason, I. G. (1984). Stress, anxiety and cognitive interference: Reactions to tests. *Journal of Personality and Social Psychology, 46*, 929–938.

Sarason, I. G. (1986). Test anxiety, worry, and cognitive interference. In R. Schwarzer (Ed.), *Self-related cognitions in anxiety and motivation* (pp. 19–33). Hillsdale NJ: Lawrence Erlbaum Associates.

Sarason, I. G. (1988). Anxiety, self-preoccupation and attention. *Anxiety Research, 1*, 3–7.
Sarason, I. G., Sarason, B. R., & Pierce, G. R. (1994). Cognitive interference: At the intelligence-personality crossroads. In D. Saklofske & M. Zeidner (Eds.), *International handbook of personality and intelligence* (pp. 2–34). New York: Plenum.
Sarason, I. G., & Stoops, R. (1978). Test anxiety and the passage of time. *Journal of Consulting and Clinical Psychology, 46*, 102–109.
Sewitch, T. S., & Kirsch, I. (1984). The cognitive content of anxiety: Naturalistic evidence for the predominance of threat related thoughts. *Cognitive Therapy and Research, 8*, 49–58.
Spielberger, C. D., Gorsuch, R. L., & Lushene, R. E. (1970). *Manual for the State-Trait Anxiety Inventory*. Palo Alto, CA: Consulting Psychologists Press.
Stroop, J. R. (1938). Factors affecting speed in serial verbal reactions. *Psychological Monographs, 50*, 38–48.
Sutton-Simon, K., & Goldfried, M. R. (1979). Faulty thinking patterns in two types of anxiety. *Cognitive Therapy and Research, 3*, 193–203.
Thrasher, S. M., Dalgleish, T., & Yule, W. (1994). Information processing in post-traumatic stress disorder. *Behaviour Research & Therapy, 32*, 247–254.
Turvey, M. (1973). On peripheral and central processes in vision: Inferences from an information-processing analysis of masking with patterned stimuli. *Psychological Review, 80*, 1–52.
Watts, F. N., & Dalgleish, T. (1991). Memory for phobia related words in spider phobics. *Cognition & Emotion, 5*, 313–329.
Watts, F. N., McKenna, F. P., Sharrock, R., & Trezise, L. (1986). Colour naming of phobia related words. *British Journal of Psychology, 77*, 97–108.
Watts, F. N. (1986). Cognitive processing in phobias. *Behavioural Psychotherapy, 14*, 295–301.
Wickless, C., & Kirsch, I. (1988). Cognitive correlates of anger, anxiety and sadness. *Cognitive Therapy and Research, 12*, 367–377.
Wine, J. (1971). Test anxiety and direction of attention. *Psychology Bulletin, 76*, 92–104.
Wine, J. D. (1982). Evaluation anxiety: A cognitive-attentional construct. In W. Krohne & L. Laux (Eds.), *Achievement, stress and anxiety* (pp. 78–102). Washington, DC: Hemisphere.
Zaffy, D. J., & Bruning, J. L. (1966). Drive and the range of cue utilization. *Journal of Experimental Psychology, 71*, 382–384.
Zarantonello, M., Slaymaker, F., Johnson, J., & Petzel, T. (1984). Effects of anxiety and depression on anagram performance, ratings of cognitive interference, and the negative subjective evaluation of performance. *Journal of Clinical Psychology, 40*, 20–25.
Zatz, S., & Chassin, L. (1985). Cognitions of test-anxious children under naturalistic test taking conditions. *Journal Consulting and Clinical Psychology, 53*, 393–401.
Zeitlin, S., & McNally, R. J. (1991). Implicit and explicit memory bias for threat in post-traumatic stress disorder. *Behaviour Research & Therapy, 29*, 451–458.

CHAPTER

4

INTEGRATING COGNITIVE, PERSONALITY, AND SOCIAL APPROACHES TO COGNITIVE INTERFERENCE AND DISTRACTIBILITY

Penny L. Yee
Jonathan Vaughan
Hamilton College

Psychologists have long been interested in the nature, determinants, and consequences of mental activity. Examples include William James' (1890) focus on phenomenological aspects of mental life and Sigmund Freud's work (1900/1953, 1901/1960, 1940) on the unconscious determinants of everyday behavior and clinical phenomena. Current research and theory on cognitive interference and distractibility can be traced to these and other early contributions in the history of psychology. One important feature of contemporary investigations of interference and distractibility is the presence of multiple paradigms from which to examine these issues. The mainstreams of cognitive and social/personality psychology in particular have each evolved rich and robust sets of programmatic and cumulative research. Not surprisingly, however, theoretical and methodological developments generated in these paradigms have not influenced trends in the other as much as they might have. The purpose of this chapter is, therefore, to encourage an integration of approaches to the topics of cognitive interference and distractibility and their influence on behavior. In order to achieve this integration, the chapter is divided into three sections. In the first section, theoretical and methodological contributions that have been inspired by research traditions in personality and social psychology, on the one hand, and cognitive psychology, on the other, are described. Because social and personality perspectives are developed elsewhere in this volume this chapter devotes proportionately less discussion to them and more to cognitive perspectives. The second section describes and evaluates two influential models of cognitive interference and performance and the third identifies needs for future research in these domains of inquiry.

COGNITIVE INTERFERENCE AND DISTRACTIBILITY: THEORETICAL AND METHODOLOGICAL DISTINCTIONS

It is no accident that the title of this chapter includes the terms "cognitive interference" and "distractibility." They represent related but different topics that have been investigated in parallel fashion by personality/social psychologists, and cognitive psychologists, respectively. Broadly speaking, in the lexicon of social/personality psychology cognitive interference refers to conscious thoughts that impede task performance; these thoughts may or may not be directly relevant to the task at hand. Distractibility, a term more frequently used by cognitive psychologists, refers more generally to decrements in performance that result from inattention to the task at hand; this inattention may be a result of either conscious or unconscious processes. Research on cognitive interference and distractibility are described separately in the following section; later in the chapter their potential integration into a more general theory of cognitive processing and task performance is discussed.

Cognitive Interference

As a psychological construct, research on cognitive interference is closely linked with research on the topic of anxiety. Personality and social psychologists have identified two components of anxiety: an emotional component and a cognitive component (Liebert & Morris, 1967). Researchers have called the cognitive component of anxiety *cognitive interference* to reflect both its source and its debilitating impact on behavior.

Definitions

Broadly defined, cognitive interference refers to thoughts that detract from on-task activity. Under this definition a wide range of psychological phenomena may be considered cognitive interference. For many social and personality psychologists 'cognition' refers to the phenomenological experience of conscious thought—the internal voice one "hears" during ruminative thought. Thus, cognitive interference is the conscious thought entertained while performing some task. The content of the thoughts determines their effects. For instance, are the thoughts that one experiences related or unrelated to the task at hand? Do the thoughts reflect worry or anxiety about the level of one's performance of a task?

Within the social/personality perspective the distraction experienced by an individual is internally generated. The worrisome thoughts arise from within the person rather than from the external environment. Individuals who are experiencing high levels of cognitive interference believe that they are performing poorly or worry about what the experimenter or teacher may think of them when evaluating their performance. The thoughts or worries are not explicitly introduced by an outside observer, though they may be indirectly manipulated by an experimenter, for example, by contriving a failure situation.

Individuals may possess a general tendency for experiencing cognitive interference, or they may experience cognitive interference only occasionally or in particular situations, as for example, while taking a test. These two situations reflect trait and state characteristics of cognitive interference, respectively.

Thus, key elements in the definition of cognitive interference for personality and social psychologists are (1) the salience of the thoughts, that is, the thoughts occur at a conscious level, (2) the content of the thoughts, that is, those thoughts typically concerned with worry, and (3) the origins of the thoughts, that is, they are internally generated from within and the person is presumably aware of them. This perspective also acknowledges the state and trait aspects of cognitive interference.

Assessment of Cognitive Interference

Several kinds of measures of cognitive interference are used. As in many other areas of personality and social psychology, investigators often rely on self-report measures of intrusive thinking to assess the prevalence of interfering thoughts. With these methods the thoughts experienced before, during, or after the performance of some task are typically assessed. Verbal protocols, retrospective accounts and posttask questionnaires are commonly used for determining the extent to which one experiences intrusive cognitions (Sarason, Sarason, & Pierce, 1990). The Cognitive Interference Questionnaire (CIQ; Sarason & Stoops, 1978; I. Sarason, B. Sarason, Keefe, Hayes, & Shearin, 1986), the Thought Occurrence Questionnaire (TOQ; Sarason et al., 1986), the Cognitive Failures Questionnaire (CFQ; Broadbent, Cooper, Fitzgerald, & Parkes, 1982), and the Reactions to Tests questionnaire (RTT; Sarason, 1984) are commonly used measures for assessing the degree to which individuals experience intrusive thoughts during a task.

The CIQ is designed to assess the degree to which one experiences intrusive thoughts within a well-defined window of time. The TOQ and the CFQ are designed to measure general tendencies to experience intrusive thoughts and to lose one's train of thought. And the RTT focuses on a person's reactions in testing situations in general. Thus, the TOQ, CFQ, and RTT represent trait measures of cognitive interference, while the CIQ reflects a state measure. These questionnaires, and others like them, ask subjects to indicate the degree to which they engaged in certain types of off-task thinking in the performance of a task. Because they are administered at the end of a session these responses are strictly retrospective in nature.

Research on Cognitive Interference

Although a person may report experiencing high levels of interfering thoughts on these questionnaires, not all irrelevant thoughts have been shown to produce cognitive interference during performance. Intrusive thoughts concerning how well one is doing in the task and how others will evaluate the individual tend to interfere with performance (Deffenbacher, 1980; Morris, Davis, & Hutchings, 1981), while thoughts that are unrelated to personal evaluation or performance do not. Thus, only those thoughts which pose a threat to an individual's self-esteem detract from on-task performance. This particular type of thinking is classified as 'worry' by most experts in the field (Humphreys & Revelle, 1984; Liebert & Morris, 1967; Sarason, 1984; Wine, 1971, 1982). Findings like these have led researchers in the field to narrow the definition of cognitive interference to include only thoughts about worry.

Individual Differences in Cognitive Interference. As mentioned earlier, cognitive interference is closely linked with the concept of anxiety. Individuals who are high in trait anxiety are more prone to experience high levels of cognitive interference (e.g., Zarantonello, Slaymaker, Johnson, & Petzel, 1984). Because the worrisome thoughts revolve around concerns of evaluation and personal performance, the experience of cognitive interference has been linked with measures of personality adjustment such as depression (Beck, 1967; Ingram, 1984), and attributional style (Seligman, 1974). Individuals' quality of adjustment or coping is related to the extent to which they dwell on negative cognitions about themselves. These findings strongly suggest that the frequency and salience of intrusive thoughts depends on self-schemas; consequently the experience of cognitive interference will vary from person to person.

Situational Factors. Although individual differences in the experience of cognitive interference are well documented, the particular situation can frequently moderate the level of cognitive interference. Several studies have shown that the perceived availability of a supportive individual can ameliorate the occurrence and the negative effects of cognitive interference on performance (Goldsmith & Albrecht, 1993; Sarason, 1981; Sarason & Sarason, 1986).

Strengths and Limitations of the Personality/Social Approach

An attractive feature of this approach to cognitive interference is its face validity. People are readily able to identify the irrelevant thoughts that they believe may have impaired their performance in a task in which they have been engaged. Self-report measures are useful because they provide a means of assessing what an individual's experiences, conscious thoughts, and intentions are. There are, however, dangers in this method. People are not always privy to the workings of their own minds. Many mental operations proceed outside of our awareness. Consequently, the almost exclusive reliance on self-report may not be an optimal means of uncovering the mechanisms that may cause impairments in performance. The use of retrospective reports also introduces problems of memory distortions (e.g., Bem & McConnell, 1970; Glucksberg & King, 1967; Greenwald, 1980; Henry, Moffitt, Caspi, Langley, & Silva, 1994; Loftus & Palmer, 1974). How accurate are the retrospective self-reports? How much self-handicapping may be present in subjects' responses? Thus, while the approach adopted by social and personality psychologists has uncovered interesting psychological relationships, it is unlikely that this approach alone will produce a thorough understanding of the mechanics or the processes by which cognitive interference exerts its effects on performance.

Distractibility

Among researchers there is convergence towards the idea that performance deficits related to cognitive interference reflect impairments in the functioning of attention (Easterbrook, 1959; Eysenck, 1982, 1988; Wine, 1971). Consequently, the discussion in this section is focused on traditional cognitive measures and current conceptions of attentional processes. Most human experimental psychologists have been concerned with understanding how people interact with the environment and with the limitations of human performance. As a consequence, cognitive psychologists' research on distractibility contrasts with the self-report measures of cognitions used by social/personality psychologists. Cognitive psychologists are more typically concerned with how people deal with the external events that the world (or an experimenter) thrusts upon them. Consequently, they rely on measures of performance in attention tasks to assess the degree to which individuals have been distracted. In these tasks the investigator exerts control over the nature of the extraneous stimuli, and therefore can evaluate the relationship between distraction and the nature of the distractor. This perspective is not surprising considering the origins of the information processing approach.

Definitions

Within this perspective, thinking (i.e., cognition) is not always considered a conscious process (Lachman, Lachman, & Butterfield, 1979). Early research in the field of attention demonstrated that a considerable amount of information from the environment is processed outside of conscious awareness, and these unconscious processes can influence what becomes conscious (Corteen & Wood, 1972; Lewis, 1970; MacKay, 1973; Stroop, 1935; Treisman, 1960). These findings challenged earlier assumptions and caused many researchers to redefine thinking as the "processing of information" (Lachman, Lachman, & Butterfield, 1979). This represents a more inclusive definition of "cognition" than simply "conscious thought." This shift acknowledged the vast amount of mental activity that seemed to occur unbeknownst to the person. There are many examples from research in memory and problem solving that reflect the belief that a considerable degree of thinking proceeds at an unconscious level. This aspect of cognition has been documented repeatedly in research on the tip-of-the-tongue phenomenon (Brown & McNeill, 1966) and on incubation (Silveira, 1971) which presumes that the mind is actively searching, retrieving and integrating information in the absence of direction from conscious thought. Similarly, it has often been shown that subjects' intuitions about how their mental processes affect their performance are incorrect. For example, in memory search most subjects believe they are engaged in a search that terminates when the target is found, whereas chronometric evidence shows that this belief is not true (Sternberg, 1966, 1969). Search for a target occurs in a serial, exhaustive fashion, where each item is evaluated even after a match has been found. In the area of attention there have been numerous demonstrations to illustrate the amount of processing carried out automatically, at unconscious levels. Thus, within the contemporary cognitive perspective, thinking refers to all mental processes both conscious or unconscious, and intentional or unintentional. Distraction from on-task performance can stem from any one of these forms of processing. Thus, in contrast to the personality/social psychology approach to cognitive interference, (1) distraction can arise from conscious or unconscious thoughts (both may interfere); (2) the nature of the distracting thoughts are often features of the task itself, for example, an irrelevant word or message presented concurrently with the relevant event, rather than a worrisome thought; and (3) the origins of distracting thoughts are typically external to the person.

Measures of Distractibility

To assess the degree to which an individual has thoughts about irrelevant, distracting events, cognitive psychologists rely on performance measures in various selective attention tasks. Given the orientation of the field, these tasks are typically perceptual in nature. One is assumed to have been distracted during a task, if one's response time (RT) or accuracy in completing the task is impaired. The more distraction experienced, the greater the impairment in completing the test trial (i.e., longer response times, or more errors, or both). Typically, the experimenter varies the nature of the task (e.g., more difficult or easy) and the distractor (e.g., more or less similar to the task relevant information) across trials. Frequently the goal is to determine the degree to which the irrelevant information has detracted from performance in the primary task. Based on these methods, one could argue that the distraction measured trial by trial represents a transient state of distraction, while comparisons across individuals of the size of distraction, across all trials would reflect a more traitlike characteristic. However, the experimental design in many studies (within-subjects) is intended to minimize and ignore the subject-specific distractibility that is frequently of primary interest to the social or personality psychologist.

The distinction among different types of mental processes (conscious, unconscious, intentional, and unintentional) is important in this context because it is clear that one's performance in a task can be disrupted by unintentional processes operating at an unconscious level. This has been demonstrated in a number of attentional phenomena. Several classic research paradigms have been useful in revealing the extent to which distracting information is processed.

The Stroop Task. The Stroop color-naming paradigm (Stroop, 1935) stands out as one of the most frequently cited examples of automatic processes affecting a person's behavior. In this task, performance is influenced by the internal activation of irrelevant concepts (i.e., the written color word). Even though individuals direct their efforts toward one aspect of the task (the ink color of the word), it is apparent that they cannot avoid thinking about the word printed in front of them. In the Stroop task participants are asked to report the ink color in which a word is written. Interference in naming the color (reflected in naming times) is observed when the word names a different color, for example, the word "BLUE" written in red ink. Regardless of subjects' intentions, they find it very difficult to ignore the written word when naming the color. Several researchers concluded that subjects unintentionally read the word. Activation of the word meaning occurs, despite the conscious desire to ignore it. This unconscious activation interferes with subjects' ability to report accurately and efficiently the color they see. Because this activation occurs in direct opposition to subjects' own intentions, investigators have argued that the activation of the word occurs automatically; it is outside of a person's direct control (see MacLeod, 1991). Variations of this paradigm have demonstrated that the unconscious activation of meanings is not restricted to the color word alone. Semantic and color associates of the written word are also activated and become a source of interference in color naming (Klein, 1964; also see MacLeod, 1991, for an extensive historical review of the literature on the Stroop phenomenon).

Dichotic Listening Tasks. In the Stroop task the word and color names originate from the same stimulus. Do we still process irrelevant information when it originates from separate and distinct sources? Early attention research suggests that we do.

In dichotic listening tasks subjects receive two distinct auditory messages over a set of headphones. Their task is to report the message received in one ear and ignore the other. Initially, Cherry (1953) reported that subjects were unaware of the content of the ignored message. Subjects reported being aware of only the gross physical features of the ignored message, for example, the sex of the speaker. But subsequent investigators demonstrated that more complex processing of the message was being performed. Unknowingly, the subjects had activated the meanings of the words and sentences of the irrelevant message (e.g., Corteen & Wood, 1972; Lewis, 1970; MacKay, 1973; Treisman, 1960). This unconscious thought activation was shown to influence performance in concurrent tasks. For instance, Treisman (1960) had subjects shadow the message presented in one ear. Shadowing requires that subjects monitor and recite a message heard through one ear while ignoring the message to the other ear. During the session the messages presented to the two ears were switched such that the left ear received the message that had begun in the right ear. Subjects frequently erred and began shadowing the message in the unattended ear. Such errors show that the subjects must have been processing the content of the message received in the ignored ear; how else could they have formed the connection and continued with the wrong ear?

Studies like this suggest that unconscious thoughts can be triggered by ignored external events and that these thoughts can influence performance in an ongoing task. The effects that these "unattended" events have on concurrent performance provide strong evidence that the people were indeed thinking about the ignored information. These early studies led the way in altering cognitive psychologists' conceptions about thinking and the use of performance as a measure of thought processes.

Negative Priming Tasks. In the above studies the presence of unintended thoughts was demonstrated by the amount of interference observed in a concurrent task. More recently, however, Driver and Tipper (1989) have demonstrated that processing of irrelevant information does not always produce interference, but the effects of the irrelevant information can be demonstrated nonetheless. Their study was based on a selective attention study of a phenomenon called "negative priming." Negative priming provides indirect evidence of the operation of selective attention. When an individual selectively attends to one of several possible sources of information, attention must operate to filter out unwanted distraction. We have already seen in the Stroop and dichotic listening studies that the filtering process does not block the distracting information from activating high level conceptual representations. What happens to the irrelevant information once these conceptual representations have been activated? Some mechanism must suppress this activation to allow the relevant information to drive a person's behavior. Neill (1977) and Tipper (1985; Tipper & Cranston, 1985) have proposed an attentional mechanism that functions to inhibit the activation of information that is not selected for conscious processing. Indirect evidence of this inhibitory process has been observed in the form of negative priming effects.

In a typical negative priming trial a subject is presented with a target and a distracter item. The target on each trial is identified by a feature such as its color or position in space. If the distracter on a previous trial becomes the target on the present trial, a negative priming effect is observed; the time to name the current target is slowed significantly relative to a control situation in which the target had not been seen before. Table 4.1 illustrates the relevant conditions used in Neill's (1977) early demonstration of this phenomenon. Neill (1977) reported negative priming effects with a Stroop color naming task. As in the classic Stroop procedure, subjects were to name the ink color of a written word.

TABLE 4.1
Sample Conditions From Neill's (1977) Stroop Study Demonstrating Negative Priming Effects

	Trial n		*Trial n + 1*	
Condition	*Stimulus*	*Correct Response*	*Stimulus*	*Correct Response*
Negative Priming	BLUE (in green ink)	"Green"	RED (blue)	"Blue"
Control	YELLOW (in green ink)	"Green"	RED (blue)	"Blue"

If the stimulus on trial *n* was the word "BLUE" written in green ink, the correct response would be "green." If on trial *n* + 1 the target was the word "RED" written in blue ink the correct response would be "blue." Saying "blue" on trial *n* + 1 after having ignored the word "BLUE" on trial *n* constitutes a negative priming trial. Naming times for "blue" following the word "BLUE" are slower relative to a control situation in which the word "BLUE" had not previously appeared. The negative priming effect is measured by the difference between reaction times in control trials and in negative priming trials. The observation of elevated reaction times to negative priming trials shows that the ignored information must have gained access to higher levels of memory representations and that it must have been suppressed. The fact that the responses to previously ignored distracters were slower suggests that an important mechanism in selective attention processes is the inhibition of irrelevant, distracting events.

Negative priming effects have been observed in a variety of tasks; for example, letter matching (Neill, Lissner, & Beck, 1990), word and picture naming (e.g., Dalrymple-Alford & Budayr, 1966; Neill, 1977; Tipper, 1985), and lexical decision (Yee, 1991). Negative priming effects have also been demonstrated with a wide range of stimuli; for example, letters and pictures (Allport, Tipper, & Chmiel, 1985; Neumann & DeSchepper, 1991; Tipper & Cranston, 1985; Tipper & Driver, 1988), random shapes (DeSchepper & Treisman, 1991), and spatial location (Connelly & Hasher, 1993; Tipper, Brehaut, & Driver, 1990; Tipper, Lortie, & Baylis, 1992; Tipper, Weaver, Cameron, Brehaut, & Bastedo, 1991). (Also see Neill, Valdes, & Terry, 1995, for a review of the negative priming literature.) Thus, the phenomenon appears to be linked to a wide range of fundamental cognitive abilities. Given the primary role of selective attention processes in behavior and the presumed role of negative priming in the selective attention process, the negative priming paradigm provides an alternative means by which one can gauge the extent to which ignored, irrelevant events have been processed and ultimately suppressed.

Using a negative priming paradigm, Driver and Tipper (1989) reported a situation in which the presentation of a distracter did not interfere with performance in a trial, but still produced negative priming in the following trial.

The observation of negative priming indicated that the distracter item had indeed activated higher level semantic representations in long-term memory and had been successfully ignored, even though the irrelevant elements of the display did not interfere with immediate responses to the target item.

In contrast to the interference effects described in the Stroop and dichotic listening studies, negative priming effects reflect an indirect measure of the distraction experienced during a task. Large negative priming effects indicate that irrelevant items were inhibited or suppressed from expression in a person's behavioral response. Small or weak negative priming effects suggest that irrelevant events were filtered less effectively and were therefore more distracting to the person.

Negative priming paradigms appear to be reliable measures of selective attention performance. The observed effects strongly suggest that a fundamental mechanism in our ability to attend to certain events or thoughts is inhibitory in nature. The inhibition measures in negative priming tasks may reflect a process that is crucial for effective filtering (i.e., ignoring) of irrelevant, distracting mental activity. The irrelevant information appears to be directly inhibited and suppressed from representation in working memory. This inhibition process leaves traces which are detected later in time in the form of negative priming. Thus, cognitive psychologists have at least two performance measures for assessing the presence of irrelevant, distracting information; interference effects in concurrent processing (as in Stroop or shadowing studies), and negative priming effects.

Research on Distractibility

To summarize, the distraction investigated by cognitive psychologists originates in the external, physical environment and not from within the person as emphasized by social and personality approaches to cognitive interference. This does not mean that the phenomena addressed by the two lines of research are distinct. The two approaches may reflect different aspects of a more general trait of "distractibility."

A Distractibility Trait. Distractibility may be defined as the inability to ignore irrelevant information. This information can take on the form of internal thoughts (e.g., "I'm really doing terribly at this task") or environmental events (e.g., the drippy faucet or the neighbor's barking dog). The notion of distractibility as an important individual differences factor has been proposed by many researchers in the area of anxiety (Alting & Markham, 1993; Dornic, 1977; Dornic & Fernaeus, 1981; Easterbrook, 1959; Eysenck, 1982, 1988; Pallak, Pittman, Heller, & Munson, 1975). For example, Alting and Markham (1993) found that people who were either high or low in trait anxiety differed in their level of distraction to external events. Generally, more anxious and more aroused individuals tend to be more distracted. If there is a general distractibility trait, one would expect some measurable relationship to exist between the cognitive measures of unconscious processing of ignored information and the self-report measures of a person's tendency to be distracted in more complex human social behaviors. In the section that follows evidence is presented that relates measures of distractibility to performance in broader behavioral contexts.

Correlates of Distractibility. There exists a growing body of research suggesting that selective attentional processes are related to self-report measures of the broader social behaviors of people. Tipper and Baylis (1987) demonstrated a relationship between the size of an individual's negative priming effects in a semantic categorization task and the person's score on Broadbent's Cognitive Failures Questionnaire (CFQ; Broadbent, Cooper, Fitzgerald, & Parkes, 1982). The CFQ is a self-report instrument designed to measure the degree to which individuals engage in absent-minded behaviors such as losing their keys or entering a room and forgetting what they were looking for. If the selective attentional mechanism measured by negative priming tasks is related to the efficiency with which individuals focus attention and ignore distraction then performance in the attention task should correlate with CFQ scores. Thus, if one is a good filterer of distracting information, negative priming effects should be larger and fewer cognitive failures should be experienced. In line with this prediction Tipper and Baylis (1987) observed significant correlations, such that the higher an individual's score on the CFQ (indicating a higher frequency of cognitive failures) the smaller the person's negative priming effect. In other words, high CFQ scorers, because of their distractibility, tend not to suppress distracting elements in negative priming tasks. A person who experiences many cognitive failures, one who is forgetful and loses track of one's thoughts easily, exhibits smaller negative priming effects, suggesting a difficulty in suppressing irrelevant events.

Neill and Westberry (1987) also reported a relationship between the negative priming observed in a Stroop color-naming task and individuals' scores on the Tellegen-Atkinson Absorption Scale. The Absorption Scale is a measure of how well a person concentrates or focuses on a current task, that is, the extent to which a person can become completely absorbed in what he or she is doing, and has been used as an indicator of how susceptible a person is to hypnosis. Neill and Westberry observed that the higher a person's score on the absorption scale the larger the individual's negative priming effect. Thus, one who has high focusing skills shows a greater likelihood of suppressing irrelevant elements in a selective attention task.

Systematic effects have also been reported between the performance of schizophrenics and normal subjects on negative priming tasks. A characteristic symptom of schizophrenia is difficulty in maintaining and controlling one's attention. In short, schizophrenic patients are easily distracted (Freedman, 1974). In line with the predictions outlined for cognitive failures, schizophrenic patients should perform similarly to individuals who experience high levels of cognitive interference in a negative priming task; that is, they should show smaller negative priming effects. Indeed, investigations with schizophrenics (Beech & Claridge, 1987; Beech, Powell, McWilliams, & Claridge, 1989) indicate that they exhibit significantly smaller negative priming effects than do normal subjects. This pattern is consistent with the presumed role that inhibitory mechanisms play in attentional processes. If one's ability to suppress the processing or activation of irrelevant events is impaired, then these events will be more likely to intrude into a person's working memory or conscious awareness. These findings suggest that behaviors performed in larger social contexts can be traced back to performance in selective attention tasks.

Developmental Changes in Distractibility. If distraction represents a more general trait, one might expect to observe developmental changes as our attentional systems mature. As young children we lack the ability to control our impulses and urges. This behavioral pattern is evident in a number of empirical studies using tasks such as Stroop color naming (Comalli, Wapner, & Werner, 1962), and dichotic listening (Doyle, 1973). Children exhibit more interference from the distracting items; they make more errors by naming events that should be ignored. Given these observations, it seems clear that inhibitory mechanisms may be less developed or perhaps underutilized in children. People appear to become less susceptible to distraction as they develop, but what is the underlying mechanism that makes this possible? In a study with grade school children, Tipper, Bourque, Anderson, and Brehaut (1989) compared the performance of second-graders (7 and 8 years of age) with adults in a Stroop color-naming task. While the children showed sizable interference effects (proportionately more than the adults), the negative-priming effect was negligible in comparison to that observed with the adult subjects. This finding is consistent with the notion that children have more difficulty than adults in dealing with distractions. It may be the case that children at this age lack the biological or strategic development to utilize the necessary inhibitory mechanisms.

A different pattern emerges in the literature on the elderly, however. Age-related decrements in memory and cognitive performance have been noted by psychologists for some time now (see Burke & Light, 1981; and Craik, 1977, for reviews). Hasher and her colleagues (Hartman & Hasher, 1991; Hasher, Stoltzfus, Zacks, & Rypma, 1991; Hasher & Zacks, 1988) have argued that a fundamental mechanism responsible for the decline lies in the ability to suppress "no-longer-relevant thoughts." In a series of reports they argue that the efficiency of working memory processes is highly dependent on a person's ability to control the access and temporary maintenance of task-irrelevant information. Consequently, any failure to inhibit irrelevant information will degrade the contents of working memory (conscious awareness) and the retention of the information. As noted above, negative-priming measures of inhibitory processes are observable in normal young adults. However, a number of investigations of older adults have failed to observe similar inhibitory effects (Hasher et al., 1991; Hasher & Zacks, 1988; McDowd & Oseas-Kreger, 1991; Tipper, 1991). Thus, one consequence of aging may be a breakdown of the inhibitory mechanisms involved in selective attention.

The relationship between the developmental changes in behavior and the empirically measured negative-priming effects strongly suggests that an important element in the distraction construct measured by cognitive psychologists may be biological in nature. The inhibitory mechanisms that prevent intrusive thoughts from entering working memory and impairing task performance may lie in the physiology of the larger attentional system. The observed links with self-report measures and investigations with special populations are encouraging in that they establish connections between the broader behavioral patterns exhibited by people and the inhibitory mechanisms of attention. The mechanisms responsible for suppressing irrelevant information from the outside world, as measured by cognitive psychologists, may be more tightly linked with processes involved in suppressing internal worries than previously suspected. The research suggests that the ability to ignore distractions is an important component in the overall normal functioning of human behavior.

The presence of this relationship should not be surprising since both life stress and performance in laboratory attention tasks have been shown to correlate with real-life job performance (Gopher, 1982; Gopher & Kahneman, 1971; Green, 1985; Kahneman, Ben-Ishai, & Lotan, 1973). Worrisome thoughts arising from stressful life events are likely to detract attentional resources from important tasks at hand. Green (1985) reported that life stress (e.g., worries concerning marital problems or career decisions) may be a major contributor to aircraft pilot errors. Similarly, Yee, Edmondson, Begg, Santoro, and Hunter (1995) have observed systematic relationships among reports of life-stress, cognitive interference, and performance in a sentence comprehension task. Individuals who reported high levels of life-stress also reported experiencing more intrusive thoughts while performing a simple sentence verification task. Life-stress and cognitive-interference measures correlated with response times and accuracy in the verbal task. Furthermore, an attentional task requiring the rapid switching and refocusing of attention in a dichotic listening task was shown to be highly predictive of performance in the real life operation of complex machinery. Gopher and Kahneman demonstrated that performance in a dichotic listening task correlated with proficiency in operating high-speed aircrafts (Gopher, 1982; Gopher & Kahneman, 1971). Good performers on the dichotic listening task were more likely to complete a highly competitive two year training program. Scores also correlated with other tests of pilot selection. Kahneman, Ben-Ishai, and Lotan (1973) also demonstrated that performance in this same task correlated with reports of bus driver accidents.

These studies clearly suggest that there is a meaningful relationship between the performance measures used by cognitive psychologists in assessing an individual's effectiveness in controlling attention in simple tasks and more global behaviors.

Strengths and Limitations of the Cognitive Approach

The merits of the cognitive approach to distractibility lie in the development of paradigms designed to investigate the underlying processes that are disrupted by distracting thoughts. The reliance on behavioral measures of performance, rather than self-report, allows investigators to examine mental operations that are not necessarily accessible for introspective reports. The combination of these two features allows cognitive psychologists to explore the role of specific cognitive mechanisms in dealing with interference in the performance of various tasks. This approach, however, is limited in its focus on distracting elements that are present in the experimental paradigm. Performance in all tasks is undoubtedly influenced by personality variables such as anxiety and motivation, as well as situational factors such as the presence of others and the occurrence of recent life events. This is understandable given the focus adopted by cognitive psychologists on nomothetic rather than ideographic theories of behavior. A complete understanding of the role of distraction in performance and human behavior, however, will need to consider the nature and content of interfering thoughts and not simply their presence or absence.

COGNITIVE INTERFERENCE AND DISTRACTIBILITY: THE SEARCH FOR AN INTEGRATIVE APPROACH

The literature presented thus far suggests that the different approaches to cognitive interference adopted by social/personality and cognitive psychologists are not as disparate as they might seem initially. There is growing evidence that performance measures of attention on simple tasks relate to more complex human behavior. Worrisome cognitions experienced during a task, as measured by self-report instruments, can impair performance. Given the evidence for these relationships, the next step is to determine the mechanism or process responsible for that relationship. Is there a single mechanism or are there many? Are there particular mental processes more susceptible to impairment by the presence of distracting thoughts? Answers to these questions will be helpful in understanding the link between the behaviors studied by social and personality psychologists and those studied by cognitive psychologists. We now take a close look at two dominant theories that have addressed the relationship between cognitive interference and performance.

Two Existing Models

Because 'worry' is presumed to impair performance by interfering with cognitive function and because it is considered a significant component of anxiety, models of the relationship between anxiety/arousal and performance are relevant to the discussion of cognitive interference. At present there are two comprehensive models addressing the relationship between anxiety and performance that make explicit predictions regarding the processes and cognitive components affected by anxiety or arousal. These are the processing efficiency theory proposed by Eysenck (1982) and Eysenck and Calvo (1992), and another initially proposed by Humphreys and Revelle (1984), and later modified by Revelle (1987), and Revelle and Loftus (1990). In the development of both of these models, the investigators carefully examine performance in tasks that place different demands on the cognitive system. There are many processes involved in the performance of any task. For instance, some are conscious, such as the intention to read a story and comprehend the sentences on the page, and some are unconscious, for example, the retrieval of the meaning of a particular word.

In general, models of interference emphasize the limited capacity of certain components of the information processing system. For example Baddeley's Working Memory model (1986) comprises three components; a central executive that controls active processing (often equated with attention), an articulatory loop for rote rehearsal of verbal information, and a visual-spatial scratch-pad for processing visual-spatial information. Each of these components has limited resources available for performing its functions. Processing that relies on the central executive is often referred to as controlled processing, while processing that can proceed without direct control or intention of the person has been called automatic processing. The working memory system serves two major functions: It is a temporary storage buffer for information, and it is directly concerned with the active, conscious (direct) processing of information. The following two models rely on a system such as this to explain the interactions between anxiety and performance.

Eysenck's Processing Efficiency Model. In Eysenck's Processing Efficiency Model (Eysenck, 1979, 1982; Eysenck & Calvo, 1992) of anxiety/arousal and performance, self-preoccupation plays an important role because it represents the cognitive component of state anxiety. The cognitive system targeted in this theory is the Working Memory system (Baddeley, 1986). A primary assumption of the Processing Efficiency Theory is that worry has two major effects. One effect is on the capacity of the working memory system. A second effect is on motivational level. In terms of the working memory system, worry draws resources away primarily from the central executive but also from the storage systems. Thus, tasks with high control processing demands will be more adversely affected than other tasks with lesser demands. Worry may, paradoxically, improve performance by increasing the processing resources that are allocated to a task by elevating motivational levels. Thus, a highly anxious individual can at least partially offset the debilitating effects if highly motivated. According to the processing efficiency theory, motivation operates as a self-regulatory control system that continually monitors the current level of performance and compares it to the expectations or goals of the subject. If a large discrepancy is observed, steps are taken to increase the resources available to working memory. This can be achieved in one of two ways. A person can deal directly with the worry or concern (e.g., ask experimenter how one is performing) or a person can increase the effort exerted in the task. Thus, in the processing efficiency model, the impact of intrusive thoughts lies in its draw on mental resources for both storage and processing.

Humphreys and Revelle's Model. The Humphreys and Revelle model (1984) of anxiety/arousal and performance emphasizes the nature of the tasks being performed. According to this model, tasks can be classified as primarily Sustained Information Transfer tasks (SIT) or Short-Term Memory tasks (STM) depending on the demands placed on subjects during performance. In SIT tasks "the subject is required to process a stimulus, associate an arbitrary response to the stimulus, and execute the response. Furthermore, there is no appreciable retention required" (Humphreys & Revelle, 1984, p. 161). An example of a SIT task is detecting the presence or absence of a specified target letter and pressing a button once detection (or nondetection) occurs. STM tasks, on the other hand, "require subjects to either maintain information in an available state through rehearsal or other processes or retrieve information that has not been attended for a short time" (p. 164). Thus, according to this model, the effects of worry will be most detrimental in STM tasks because of the drain in on-task effort and storage capacity. Therefore, this model, indirectly, also implicates the limited resources available to the central executive in accounting for deficits due to anxiety or arousal. SIT tasks are believed to exhibit smaller effects of anxiety because the drop in available resources can be offset by the facilitative effects that arousal is presumed to have on SIT performance. In contrast, both anxiety (worry) and arousal are assumed to have a negative effect on STM tasks.

A Critical Evaluation

These models have led to the identification of fundamental mental processes affected by intrusive thoughts. They have been instructive in organizing the literature and in identifying significant mechanisms to guide research. The convergence of Eysenck's and Humphreys and Revelle's models of working memory attests to the significance of these components in understanding behavior. But there are limitations in these models. Their explanations still focus on a relatively broad level of processing. It would be useful to identify specific processes that may be affected by the presence of distracting or irrelevant thoughts and that are also crucial for the effective functioning of working memory. The distractibility trait discussed earlier may be relevant here. Investigations of inhibitory processes that filter or suppress unwanted thoughts may provide new insights into the role of cognitive interference in performance.

A second limitation is that these models avoid explanations of why some individuals may experience more cognitive interference than others when placed in stressful situations. Distractibility research suggests that a maturational (biological) factor may account for some of the individual variation observed. The cognitive systems of different age groups appear to operate at different levels of efficiency. This pattern, however, does not explain the variation observed within age groups. Within the populations of younger children and younger and older adults are individuals who predictably experience more intrusive thoughts than others. The question not addressed by the above models is why this is so.

DIRECTIONS FOR FUTURE RESEARCH

Individuals may differ in the extent to which they are capable of ignoring irrelevant information. One explanation may be that some individuals may be particularly vulnerable to cognitive interference in general because they are more prone to distraction at all levels of processing. The impact of stress or anxiety may not necessarily be an increase in the number of irrelevant thoughts experienced, but an impairment in the functioning of a person's inhibitory processes of selective attention. A consequence of this impairment is that a person will experience more intrusive thoughts at a conscious level. This explanation does not imply that those with a tendency to experience more cognitive interference have more worrisome thoughts than other people. At an unconscious level the internal concern over performance and evaluation may be the same. The difference may lie in the extent to which these thoughts break into working memory or consciousness and further detract from task performance. This view is consistent with a strictly cognitive approach to the effects of cognitive interference on performance. However, it is more likely that individuals do differ in the degree to which internally generated thoughts arise. For this reason it is important to consider the role of personality in understanding the interaction between intrusive thoughts and performance. In addition to the maturational development of a person's attentional system, there are no doubt other learned behaviors or experiences that lead individuals to have concerns about their level of performance or public image. In line with this approach a fuller understanding would be gleaned by consideration of how individuals respond in different situations, that is, in the presence or absence of a supportive ally. Based on these observations it is likely that several different mechanisms interact to determine the effectiveness of a person's behavior.

Models of cognitive interference in performance must consider the various cognitive, personality, and social factors that contribute to an individual's behavior. Investigations would benefit from the use of both self-report and behavioral measures of interference to gain insight into the relationship between conscious thoughts or concerns and underlying cognitive operations. An important step may be to investigate more closely the relationship between cognitive interference and negative-priming effects, as this has been shown to be an important mechanism in the suppression of irrelevant information. It is also important not to overlook the content of the intrusive thoughts. Social and personality psychologists have recognized that the nature of the thought (i.e., worry) is an important factor in predicting behavior, while cognitive psychologists have often focused on distractions arising from within the task itself. And lastly, the relationship among cognitive interference, distractibility, and real world situations (e.g., job performance, interpersonal relationships) needs to be more firmly established. Once established, intervention methods can be developed to assist individuals to better cope with distraction from unwanted thoughts.

REFERENCES

Allport, D. A., Tipper, S. P., & Chmiel, N. J. C. (1985). Perceptual integration and post-categorical filtering. In M. I. Posner & O. S. M. Marin (Eds.), *Attention and performance XI* (pp. 107–132). Hillsdale, NJ: Lawrence Erlbaum Associates.

Alting, T., & Markham, R. (1993). Test anxiety and distractibility. *Journal of Research in Personality, 27*, 134–147.

Baddeley, A. D. (1986). *Working memory.* New York: Oxford University Press.

Beck, A. T. (1967). *Depression: Clinical, experimental, and theoretical aspects.* New York: Hoeber.

Beech, A., & Claridge, G. (1987). Individual differences in negative priming: Relations with schizotypal personality traits. *British Journal of Psychology, 78*, 349–356.

Beech, A., Powell, T., McWilliams, J., & Claridge, G. (1989). Evidence for reduced "cognitive inhibition" in schizophrenia. *British Journal of Clinical Psychology, 28*, 109–116.

Bem, D. J., & McConnell, H. K. (1970). Testing the self-perception explanation of dissonance phenomena: On the salience of premanipulation attitudes. *Journal of Personality and Social Psychology, 14*, 23–31.

Broadbent, D. E., Cooper, P. F., Fitzgerald, P., & Parkes, K. R. (1982). The Cognitive Failures Questionnaire (CFQ) and its correlates. *British Journal of Clinical Psychology, 21*, 1–16.

Brown, R., & MacNeill, D. (1966). The "tip-of-the-tongue" phenomenon. *Journal of Verbal Learning and Verbal Behavior, 5*, 325–337.

Burke, D. M., & Light, L. L. (1981). Memory and aging: The role of retrieval processes. *Psychological Bulletin, 90*, 513–546.

Cherry, E. C. (1953). Some experiments on the recognition of speech, with one and with two ears. *Journal of the Acoustical Society of America, 25*, 975–979.

Comalli, P. E., Wapner, S., & Werner, H. (1962). Interference effects of Stroop color-word test in children, adulthood and aging. *Journal of Genetic Psychology, 100*, 47–53.

Connelly, S. L., & Hasher, L. (1993). Aging and the inhibition of spatial location. *Journal of Experimental Psychology: Human Perception and Performance, 19*, 1238–1250.

Corteen, R. S., & Wood, B. (1972). Autonomic responses to shock associated words in an unattended channel. *Journal of Experimental Psychology, 97*, 308–313.

Craik, F. (1977). Age difference in human memory. In J. E. Birren & K. W. Schaie (Eds.), *Handbook of the psychology of aging* (pp. 384–420). New York: Van Nostrand Reinhold.

Dalrymple-Alford, E. C., & Budayr, B. (1966). Examination of some aspects of the Stroop color-word test. *Perceptual and Motor Skills, 23*, 1211–1214.

Deffenbacher, J. L. (1980). Worry and emotionality in test anxiety. In I. G. Sarason (Ed.), *Test anxiety: Theory, research, and applications* (pp. 111–128). Hillsdale, NJ: Lawrence Erlbaum Associates.

DeSchepper, B., & Treisman, A. M. (1991, November). *Novel visual shapes in negative priming.* Paper presented at the meeting of the Psychonomic Society, San Francisco.

Dornic, S. (1977). *Mental load, effort, and individual differences.* Reports from the Department of Psychology, University of Stockholm, No. 509.

Dornic, S., & Fernaues, S. E. (1981). *Individual differences in high-load tasks: The effect of verbal distraction.* Reports from the Department of Psychology, University of Stockholm, No. 569.

Doyle, A. B. (1973). Listening to distraction: A developmental study of selective attention. *Journal of Experimental Child Psychology, 15*, 100–115.

Driver, J., & Tipper, S. P. (1989). On the nonselectivity of "selective" seeing: Contrasts between interference and priming in selective attention. *Journal of Experimental Psychology: Human Perception and Performance, 15*, 304–314.

Easterbrook, J. A. (1959). The effect of emotion on cue utilization and the organization of behavior. *Psychological Review, 66*, 183–201.

Eysenck, M. W. (1979). Anxiety, learning, and memory; a reconceptualization. *Journal of Research in Personality, 13*, 363–385.

Eysenck, M. W. (1982). *Attention and arousal: Cognition and performance.* Berlin: Springer.

Eysenck, M. W. (1988). Anxiety and attention. *Anxiety Research, 1*, 9–15.

Eysenck, M. W., & Calvo, M. G. (1992). Anxiety and performance: The processing efficiency theory. *Cognition and Emotion, 6*, 409–434.

Freedman, B. J. (1974). The subjective experience of perceptual and cognitive disturbances in schizophrenia: A review of autobiographical accounts. *Archives of General Psychiatry, 30*, 333–340.

Freud, S. (1900/1953). *The interpretation of dreams* (Reprint ed., Vols. 4, 5). London, England: Hogarth.

Freud, S. (1901/1960). *Psychopathology of everyday life* (Stanford ed., Vol. 6). London, England: Hogarth.

Freud, S. (1940). An outline of psychoanalysis. *International Journal of Psychoanalysis, 21*, 27–84.

Glucksberg, S., & King, L. J. (1967). Motivated forgetting mediated by implicit verbal chaining: A laboratory analog of repression. *Science, 159*, 517–519.

Goldsmith, D., & Albrecht, T. (1993). The impact of supportive communication networks on test anxiety and performance. *Communication Education, 42*, 142–158.

Gopher, D. (1982). A selective attention test as a predictor of success in flight training. *Human Factors, 24*, 173–183.

Gopher, D., & Kahneman, D. (1971). Individual differences in attention and the prediction of flight criteria. *Perceptual and Motor Skills, 33*, 1335–1342.

Green, R. G. (1985). Stress and accidents. *Aviation, Space, and Environmental Medicine, 56*, 638–641.

Greenwald, A. G. (1980). The totalitarian ego: Fabrication and revision of personal history. *American Psychologist, 35*, 603–618.

Hartman, M., & Hasher, L. (1991). Aging and suppression: Memory for previously relevant information. *Psychology and Aging, 6*, 587–594.

Hasher, L., Stoltzfus, E. R., Zacks, R. T., & Rypma, B. (1991). Age and inhibition. *Journal of Experimental Psychology: Learning, Memory, and Cognition, 17*, 163–169.

Hasher, L., & Zacks, R. T. (1988). Working memory, comprehension, and aging: A review and a new view. In G. H. Bower (Ed.), *The psychology of learning and motivation* (Vol. 22, pp. 193–225). San Diego, CA: Academic Press.

Henry, B., Moffitt, T. E., Caspi, A., Langley, J., & Silva, P. A. (1994). On the "remembrance of things past": A longitudinal evaluation of the retrospective method. *Psychological Assessment, 6*, 92–101.

Humphreys, M. S., & Revelle, W. (1984). Personality, motivation, and performance: A theory of the relationship between individual differences and information processing. *Psychological Review, 91*, 153–184.

Ingram, R. E. (1984). Toward an information-processing analysis of depression. *Cognitive Therapy and Research, 8*, 443–478.

James, W. (1890). *Principles of psychology*. New York: Dover.

Kahneman, D., Ben-Ishai, R., & Lotan, M. (1973). Relation of a test of attention to road accidents. *Journal of Applied Psychology, 58*, 113–115.

Klein, G. S. (1964). Semantic power measured through the interference of words with color-naming. *American Journal of Psychology, 77*, 576–588.

Lachman, R., Lachman, J. L., & Butterfield, E. C. (1979). *Cognitive psychology and information processing: An introduction*. Hillsdale, NJ: Lawrence Erlbaum Associates.

Lewis, J. L. (1970). Semantic processing of unattended messages using dichotic listening. *Journal of Experimental Psychology, 85*, 225–228.

Liebert, R. M., & Morris, L. W. (1967). Cognitive and emotional components of test anxiety: A distinction and some initial data. *Psychological Reports, 20*, 975–978.

Loftus, E. F., & Palmer, J. C. (1974). Reconstruction of automobile destruction: An example of the interaction between language and memory. *Journal of Verbal Learning and Verbal Behavior, 13*, 585–589.

MacKay, D. G. (1973). Aspects of the theory of comprehension, memory and attention. *Quarterly Journal of Experimental Psychology, 25*, 22–40.

MacLeod, C. M. (1991). Half a century of research on the Stroop effect: An integrative review. *Psychological Bulletin, 109*, 163–203.

McDowd, J. M., & Oseas-Kreger, D. M. (1991). Aging, inhibitory processes and negative priming. *Journal of Gerontology: Psychological Sciences, 46*, p340–p345.

Morris, L. W., Davis, M. A., & Hutchings, C. H. (1981). Cognitive and emotional components of anxiety: Literature review and a revised Worry-Emotionality Scale. *Journal of Educational Psychology, 73*, 541–555.

Neill, W. T. (1977). Inhibitory and facilitatory processes in selective attention. *Journal of Experimental Psychology, 3*, 444–450.

Neill, W. T., Lissner, S., & Beck, J. L. (1990). Negative priming in *same-different* matching: Further evidence for a central locus of inhibition. *Perception and Psychophysics, 48*, 398–400.

Neill, W. T., Valdes, L. A., & Terry, K. M. (1995). Selective attention and the inhibitory control of cognition. In F. N. Dempster & C. J. Brainerd (Eds.), *Interference and inhibition in cognition* (pp. 207–261). San Diego, CA: Academic Press.

Neill, W. T., & Westberry, R. L. (1987). Selective attention and the suppression of cognitive noise. *Journal of Experimental Psychology: Learning, Memory, & Cognition, 13*, 327–334.

Neumann, E., & DeSchepper, B. G. (1991). Costs and benefits of target activation and distractor inhibition in selective attention. *Journal of Experimental Psychology: Learning, Memory, and Cognition, 17*, 1136–1145.

Pallak, M. S., Pittman, T. S., Heller, J. F., & Munson, P. (1975). The effects of arousal on Stroop colour-word task performance. *Bulletin of the Psychonomic Society, 6*, 248–250.

Revelle, W. (1987). Personality and motivation: Sources of inefficiency in cognitive performance. *Journal of Research in Personality, 21*, 436–452.

Revelle, W., & Loftus, D. A. (1990). Individual differences and arousal: Implications for the study of mood and memory. *Cognition and Emotion, 4*, 209–237.

Sarason, I. G. (1981). Test anxiety, stress, and social support. *Journal of Personality, 49*, 101–114.

Sarason, I. G. (1984). Stress, anxiety, and cognitive interference: Reactions to tests. *Journal of Personality and Social Psychology, 46*, 929–938.

Sarason, I. G., & Sarason, B. R. (1986). Experimentally provided social support. *Journal of Personality and Social Psychology, 50*, 1222–1225.

Sarason, I. G., Sarason, B. R., Keefe, D. E., Hayes, B. E., & Shearin, E. N. (1986). Cognitive interference: Situational determinants and traitlike characteristics. *Journal of Personality and Social Psychology, 51*, 215–226.

Sarason, I. G., Sarason, B. R., & Pierce, G. R. (1990). Anxiety, cognitive interference, and performance. *Journal of Social Behavior and Personality, 5*, 1–18.

Sarason, I. G., & Stoops, R. (1978). Test anxiety and the passage of time. *Journal of Consulting and Clinical Psychology, 46*, 102–109.

Seligman, M. E. P. (1974). Depression and learned helplessness. In R. M. Friedman & M. M. Katz (Eds.), *The psychology of depression: Contemporary theory and research* (pp.). New York: Wiley.

Silveira, J. (1971). *Incubation: The effect of interruption timing and length on problem solution and quality of problem processing.* Unpublished doctoral dissertation, University of Oregon.

Sternberg, S. (1966). High-speed scanning in human memory. *Science, 153*, 652–654.

Sternberg, S. (1969). Memory scanning: Mental processes revealed by reaction-time experiments. *American Scientist, 57*, 421–457.

Stroop, J. R. (1935). Studies of interference in serial verbal reactions. *Journal of Experimental Psychology, 18*, 643–662.

Tipper, S. P. (1985). The negative priming effect: Inhibitory priming by ignored objects. *Quarterly Journal of Experimental Psychology, 37A*, 571–590.

Tipper, S. P. (1991). Less attentional selectivity as a result of declining inhibition in older adults. *Bulletin of the Psychonomic Society, 29*, 45–47.

Tipper, S. P., & Baylis, G. C. (1987). Individual differences in selective attention: The relation of priming and interference to cognitive failure. *Personality and Individual Differences, 8*, 667–675.

Tipper, S. P., Brehaut, J. C., & Driver, J. (1990). Selection of moving and static objects for control of spatially directed action. *Journal of Experimental Psychology: Human Perception and Performance, 16*, 492–504.

Tipper, S. P., Bourque, T. A., Anderson, S. H., & Brehaut, J. C. (1989). Mechanisms of attention: A development study. *Journal of Experimental Child Psychology, 48*, 353–378.

Tipper, S. P., & Cranston, M. (1985). Selective attention and priming: Inhibitory and facilitatory effects of ignored primes. *Quarterly Journal of Experimental Psychology, 37A*, 591–611.

Tipper, S. P., & Driver, J. (1988). Negative priming between pictures and words in a selective attention task: Evidence for semantic processing of ignored stimuli. *Memory and Cognition, 16*, 64–70.

Tipper, S. P., Lortie, C., & Baylis, G. C. (1992). Selective reaching: Evidence for action-centered attention. *Journal of Experimental Psychology: Human Perception and Performance, 18*, 891–905.

Tipper, S. P., Weaver, B., Cameron, S., Brehaut, J. C., & Bastedo, J. C. (1991). Inhibitory mechanisms of attention in identification and localization tasks: Time course and disruption. *Journal of Experimental Psychology: Learning, Memory, and Cognition, 17*, 681–692.

Treisman, A. M. (1960). Contextual cues in selective listening. *Quarterly Journal of Experimental Psychology, 12*, 242–248.

Wine, J. (1971). Test anxiety and direction of attention. *Psychological Bulletin, 76*, 92–104.

Wine, J. (1982). Evaluation anxiety: A cognitive-attentional construct. In W. Krohne & L. Laux (Eds.), *Achievement, stress and anxiety* (pp. 207–219). Washington, DC: Hemisphere.

Yee, P. L. (1991). Semantic inhibition of ignored words during a figure classification task. *Quarterly Journal of Experimental Psychology, 43A*, 127–153.

Yee, P. L., Edmondson, B., Santoro, K. E., Begg, A., & Hunter, C. (1995). *Cognitive effects of life stress and attributional style.* Submitted.

Zarantello, M., Slaymaker, F., Johnson, J., & Petzel, T. (1984). Effects of anxiety and depression on anagram performance, ratings of cognitive interference and the negative subjective evaluation of performance. *Journal of Clinical Psychology, 40*, 20–25.

CHAPTER

5

THOUGHT CONTROL OF ACTION: INTERFERING SELF-DOUBTS

Ralf Schwarzer
Freie Universität Berlin, Germany

If a student is supposed to write an essay he or she might feel uncomfortable, unable to start or finish it, and might postpone or avoid the task, depending on how much he or she doubts his or her competence to attain the goal that is at stake. Self-doubts are worries about specific coping capabilities in a self-regulatory process. They have a detrimental motivational effect that adds to the reduced information processing efficiency characteristic for anxious individuals.

The present chapter attempts to unite various lines of research on these topics. First, the cognitive anxiety component, "worry," that has been studied in both clinical and educational settings without much communication between the two, is examined. Second, the construct of self-doubts is introduced to overcome the unresolved issue of how anxiety (or worry) is theoretically related to perceived self-efficacy. Third, a motivational and volitional perspective is chosen to illustrate the way individuals adopt, initiate, and maintain difficult actions. Behavioral change, including coping with stress, is seen as a multistage process that is guided by different cognitions at different stages, but that is also impaired by worries or self-doubts at different stages. These doubts interfere with thought control of action.

The first section briefly introduces the underlying action control model, the second elaborates on intrusive thoughts, and the third deals with an integration of such worries into the self-regulatory goal attainment approach.

THE ADOPTION, INITIATION, AND MAINTENANCE OF BEHAVIORS: MOVING THROUGH STAGES

Behavioral change is required when old behavioral routines become inefficient to serve their purposes or when they become incompatible with new goals. Imagine a student who decides to write a paper on a difficult topic. The decision making includes a number of cognitive processes that can be described in terms of different psychological theories. From a transactional stress and emotion theory view (Lazarus, 1991), the student appraises a demanding academic situation that may tax or exceed his or her coping resources. Depending on the characteristics of the situation, failing on that task might be threatening because others would believe that he or she might be incompetent. On the other hand, the task is challenging because success might earn great pride or an attractive scholarship. This "demand appraisal" (What is at stake?) occurs at about the same moment as the corresponding "resource appraisal," that is, the student scrutinizes his or her coping resources (What are my options?), such as academic ability, specific knowledge, time and equipment available, and social support. The degree to which he or she comes up with an overall appraisal of either "challenge" or "threat" is, however, largely determined by the existence and operation of self-doubts. The decision to invest effort, time, and other resources in this academic enterprise relies heavily on confidence in the ability to perform the critical action successfully. Ruminative self-doubts undermine this belief and may postpone the decision to write the paper or may dismiss the project entirely.

The decision making is merely the beginning of a more comprehensive process that includes the planning and preparation of the task, early attempts at writing the paper, actual performance, and difficulties in maintaining it while setbacks occur and other goals distract from the task.

In the stress theory of Lazarus, this regulation process is equivalent to coping in conjunction with multiple reappraisals while the unfolding person-environment encounter is monitored and evaluated. Reappraisals are potential sources of renewed self-doubts that impair the action and might lead to abandoning the goal in favor of other commitments. As in a cybernetic system, feedback occurs continuously at multiple points in time, each appraisal giving rise to either self-doubts or reassurance that, in turn, may stimulate either disengagement or investment of further efforts.

This stress theoretical perspective endorses the crucial role of cognitions before and during a coping process, but due to its diffuse and complex nature it is less suitable to identify persons at transition points that mark the end of one stage and the beginning of another. In particular, when it comes to studying the adoption, initiation, or maintenance of a novel behavior, an action theoretical perspective appears to be more suitable to address debilitating cognitions that prevent the transition from one stage to another. In particular, health behaviors

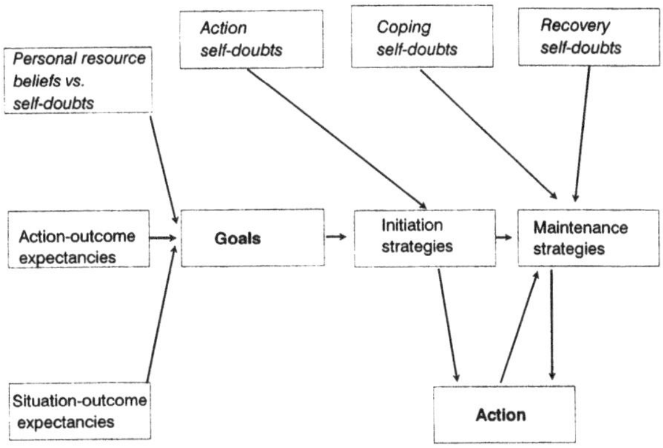

FIG. 5.1. A stage model linking cognitions to the adoption, initiation, and maintenance of actions.

such as dieting, exercising, or quitting smoking can serve as examples for different coping behaviors that go beyond those already practiced actions that require only small amounts of effort instead of an elaborated adoption process.

An action-oriented model is proposed that consists of two stages. According to German action theorists (Gollwitzer, 1993; Heckhausen, 1991; Kuhl & Beckmann, 1994), a motivational process can be distinguished from a volitional process. To put it simply, the former includes the contemplation of alternatives and ends with an intention to act. The latter includes a planning and initiation stage in which individuals elaborate on the means to conduct the behavior and an action stage in which the intended behavior is performed and monitored. These stages could be further subdivided if studied in more detail (see Fig. 5.1).

Such a stage model addresses unresolved issues that plagued former theories, such as the Theory of Reasoned Action (Fishbein & Ajzen, 1975), the Theory of Planned Behavior (Ajzen, 1988), or Protection Motivation Theory (Rogers, 1983); (see Schwarzer, 1992, for a critical review). In the next section, intrusive thoughts are discussed, and later, this model is described in more detail, particularly the crucial role of self-doubts.

THOUGHT INTRUSION, RUMINATION, WORRY, AND SELF-DOUBTS

We all experience self-doubts occasionally and worry about our accomplishments, ruminate about self-worth, and have intrusive thoughts while facing a demanding task. Self-doubts are not only unpleasant in themselves, but also interfere with actions and sometimes persist quite a while. Different authors use the vocabulary differently, and therefore these terms need to be defined for the present chapter. Rumination is defined as the occurrence of repetitive, intrusive, conscious, and aversive thoughts which are unwanted and interfere with normal functioning (Martin, Tesser, & McIntosh, 1993). The content of these intrusive thoughts can be anything that is negative, such as the loss of a loved one, an upcoming surgery, failure at an exam, or peer rejection. Worry has the same nature as rumination, but it is usually less severe or less pathological. It includes concerns about decisions, one's ability, or one's impression upon others. Usually worry impairs optimal functioning. For example, one worries about one's social relationships and cannot fall asleep, or one worries about an exam and cannot study. There is no clear border between worrying and rumination–it is rather a semantic notion of matters of degree. In fact, it is questionable as to whether one should make a distinction here at all.

Worry in Clinical Research

Worry and cognitive interference have been mentioned early in anxiety research (Mandler & Sarason, 1952; Sarason, 1960), but studies on this issue have been conducted more systematically in the last two decades. There are two major lines of research on worry in psychology, one in the field of test anxiety and the other in the field of clinical research. There was almost no communication between these research groups until the recent integrative work by Eysenck (1992). Clinical research on worry became prominent in the early 1980s. Borkovec, Robinson, Pruzinsky, and DePree (1983) defined worry as "a chain of thoughts and images, negatively affect-laden and relatively uncontrollable. The worry process represents an attempt to engage in mental problem solving on an issue whose outcome is uncertain but contains the possibility of one or more negative outcomes. Consequently, worry relates closely to fear process" (p. 9). The authors found a correlation of .67 between the time spent on worrying and the trait of anxiety (see also Borkovec, 1985; Eysenck, 1984; Tallis, Eysenck, & Mathews, 1991). Worry was found to be prevalent in different kinds of patients, in particular those with general anxiety disorder and insomniacs plagued by ruminations that prevent them from falling asleep (Martin, Tesser, & McIntosh, 1993; Roemer & Borkovec, 1993). Meanwhile, it is acknowledged that worry is the cardinal feature of generalized anxiety disorder (GAD). The latter is defined as the presence of excessive and unrealistic worry in at least two domains of life for at least six months (DSM III-R, 1987). Patients with other anxiety disorders, such as phobias, also worry, but they do so less than GAD patients. Partly by definition and partly by empirical evidence it can be concluded that worry represents the key characteristic in GAD as well as in trait anxiety. An example of a psychometric instrument to assess individual differences in worry is the Penn State Worry Questionnaire (Meyer, Miller, Metzger, & Borkovec, 1990), that contains rather general items such as "I have been a worrier all my life" or "My worries overwhelm me." GAD patients scored much higher than a control group on this scale. The measure was highly correlated with trait anxiety (.64), but less so with depression (.36). An attempt to identify diverse content areas of worry was made by Tallis, Eysenck, and Matthews (1992), who designed a 30-item

Worry Domains Questionnaire (WDQ) that refers to ten life domains. In a principal components analysis, two more general dimensions emerged, a strong factor pertaining to worries about one's social-evaluative self-concept, and a weaker one pertaining to worries about physical threat to oneself and others.

Worry in Test Anxiety Research

In test anxiety research, an explicit distinction between worry and emotionality was made about 30 years ago by Liebert and Morris (1967). It became apparent that anxiety could be seen as being composed of these two factors and that worry was more closely related to performance than emotionality. Liebert and Morris (1967) developed the Worry-Emotionality Questionnaire (WEQ), a brief measure designed for making this distinction at the state anxiety level. Spielberger later published the Test Anxiety Inventory (TAI), a measure for these two components at the trait level (Spielberger, 1980). This 20-item measure was translated into many languages and has sparked the idea of separate anxiety components within the test anxiety scientific community (cf. the volumes by Hagtvet & Backer Johnsen, 1992; Sarason, 1980; Schwarzer, van der Ploeg, & Spielberger, 1982, 1987, 1989; van der Ploeg, Schwarzer, & Spielberger, 1983, 1984, 1985). A more refined approach was introduced by Sarason (1984, 1986, 1991) who developed a 40-item inventory called Reactions-to-Tests (RTT) that was composed of four anxiety components, namely worry ("I wonder how other people are doing"), irrelevant thinking ("My mind wanders during tests"), tension ("I feel distressed and uneasy before tests"), and bodily reactions ("I get a headache before a test"). These were two cognitive and two emotional components, and even more detailed distinctions have been made following this model. Schwarzer and Quast (1985), for example, have identified seven facets of test anxiety. However, this could easily become a continuous process until every test item is regarded to represent one specific test anxiety component. Conceptually, two anxiety components may be sufficient to help understand the operating mechanisms of cognitive-emotional processes when individuals face threatening events. The introduction of the component "irrelevant thinking" by Sarason (1984) was innovative in that it aimed at the interfering effect of cognitions while trying to concentrate on a task. Sarason and Sarason (1987) have found very close associations between this component and their Cognitive Interference Questionnaire (CEQ). There is overwhelming evidence that the worry component is responsible for the inhibition of performance in anxious individuals. Three meta-analyses have found negative correlations of academic or physical performance with worry, more so than with emotionality (Hembree, 1988; Kleine, 1990; Seipp, 1990). However, the coefficients are only of moderate size and lie typically near $r = -.21$, depending on the population studied, the measures employed, and other circumstances involved. These correlations do not reflect the full picture of the achievement-debilitating effect because they do not include the actual cognitive processes and the compensating mechanisms that preclude a closer inspection of the impairing procedure. According to Eysenck (1992), worry mainly affects "internal processing efficiency," and less so "external performance effectiveness." The former pertains to what is going on in the mind when intrusive thoughts occur and distract from the task. The latter simply reflects the measurable outcome of a "black-box achievement process" which is additionally influenced by the input of one's resources such as time and effort to attain the desired goals. Worriers may invest more effort to compensate for their lack of concentration: They may study harder because they anticipate failure, and they may persist longer because they cannot afford to lose face by disengaging from an important task, which could result in peer rejection. The gap between "internal processing efficiency" and "external performance effectiveness" narrows if there is no opportunity to invest personal resources. For example, if all individuals, worriers and nonworriers, are suddenly confronted with a challenging or threatening task to be completed immediately, the differences in effort are expected to be smaller than in a situation where there is plenty of time to prepare for the demands. In the preparation or coping period, worriers choose to try harder and make up for their poor concentration by spending more time on the task. Thus, they may come up with the same or even better results than the nonworriers. Depending on the characteristics of such a coping period and on other circumstances, the correlations between anxiety and performance can become negative or positive, low or high. Nevertheless, in terms of information processing, the worriers are at a disadvantage when it comes to accomplishing difficult tasks. On the other hand, they might gain momentum to achieve results while others take an unconcerned stance towards the challenge.

Characteristics of Worry

Why do people worry? According to Borkovec and Lyonfields (1993) the focus on the verbal act of worrying helps to reduce undesired physiological arousal and threatening imagery. Worry can be understood as an attempt to control other unwanted experiences. It "represents a strategic conceptual avoidance response which suppresses the processing of emotional information and thereby guarantees the maintenance of anxiety disorder" (Borkovec & Lyonfields, 1993, p. 102). With conceptual avoidance response it is meant that worry cognitions are rather thoughts than images. Moreover, this response is being used strategically. Fearful imagery as well as unpleasant physiological arousal are suppressed by worrisome activities. It has been found, for example, that subjects who are confronted with phobic scenes suppress their heart rate response when focusing on worry thoughts (Borkovec & Lyonfields, 1993). Unfortunately, the preclusion of an elaborate emotional processing impedes a successful reduction of the threat value. Worry is even reinforced and becomes chronic because most of the ambiguous events that are in mind never actually occur. Thus, worries are superstitiously negatively reinforced by the nonoccurrence of these seemingly dangerous events (Roemer & Borkovec, 1993). This self-reinforcing nature reveals why worry is maladaptive in the long run. The expression of worry precludes successful emotional processing, but choosing to suppress worry instead does not help because suppressed thoughts tend to remain in memory and can even be increased. Suppression may set the stage for obsession. Distraction is also inappropriate since worriers have a tendency to distract themselves with thoughts of other worrisome topics. Instead of expression, suppression, and distraction, it is suggested that relaxation techniques, guided imagery, decatastrophizing, and alternative chains of thoughts are employed (Roemer & Borkovec, 1993).

According to Eysenck (1992), there are at least three functions of worry: (a) an alarm function that initially lets dangerous information become consciously aware, (b) a prompt function that represents thoughts and images about threats in awareness, and (c) a preparation function that allows the individual to be ready for upcoming harm and to have the appropriate coping strategies available. People worry when an event is seen as aversive, likely, imminent, and resource demanding. The threat value of an event is characterized by these aspects, and with increasing threat value worry increases. Eysenck (1992) underscores that not only subjective aversiveness, imminence, and likelihood of a possible event are responsible for its threatening nature, but also the perceived unavailability of "postevent coping strategies," which is about the same as lack of self-efficacy. One need not refer to postevent here, since the prevention of anticipated harm is also at stake. If a student faces an exam, its threat value can be minimized by investing more effort to prepare for it, or the exam can be avoided altogether in favor of alternative commitments. Believing in one's capability to avoid an ambiguous event or to prevent its negative impact may be sufficient to reduce the threat value and, in turn, the amount of time spent on worrying. The onset of worry leads to intensified scanning of the environment for dangers and resources, which can be a self-absorbing and arousing process. Arousal may be triggered by such cognitive activity, which is then in contrast to the theory put forward by Borkovec and Lyonfields (1993), who state that worrying helps to reduce undesired physiological arousal. The performance-impairing effect, however, is mainly due to the cognitive activity that prevents the individual from concentrating on the task.

Worry is closely related to hypervigilance, which is seen as a cognitive vulnerability factor in trait anxiety (Eysenck, 1992; Krohne, 1993; Mathews, 1993). Anxious individuals are inclined to scan their environment constantly for ambiguous or aversive stimuli. This is a bias at the level of attention or preattention, as opposed to the memory recall bias typically found in depressives. Depressives show a bias towards negative processing of information about the self, the world, and the future, for example when retrieving information. They recall more information that is related to loss events or other harmful events that occurred in the past, and they tend to attribute negative events more in a stable, internal, and pervasive fashion. The latter has been coined a depressive explanatory style or "learned pessimism" (Seligman, 1991). In contrast to this explicit memory distortion (elaboration of information), there is an implicit memory distortion (priming of information) for anxious individuals, who attend vigilantly to anticipated aversive stimuli. Their focus is on threat instead of loss. They scan their surroundings in a broad fashion while no danger is identified, but turn to a narrow focus after they have detected a threatening stimulus (Eysenck, 1992). Anxious persons are also highly distractible because they have to divert their attention to a variety of potential sources of harm. The selective attentional bias is seen as one reason for performance deficits of anxious individuals. However, performance is determined by multiple causes, and attention and memory functioning are just some of the influential factors in the learning and achievement process. Interfering thoughts can be detrimental in a structural or quantitative sense by taking away part of the intellectual resources needed for problem solving. Interfering thoughts can also be detrimental in a qualitative manner if their content allows people to make unfavorable decisions. Intrusive thoughts that are related to lack of coping ability, for example, demotivate people, keeping them from investing more effort and persistence into an enterprise and, thus, leading to premature disengagement. The remainder of this chapter, therefore, is devoted to the motivational effect of intrusive thoughts as opposed to the information processing effect.

Specific Content of Worry: Self-Doubts

The fact that worry is very often related to one's social-evaluative concerns and to lack of confidence in the capabilities required for goal attainment suggests that this specific aspect should be elaborated upon further (Tallis et al., 1992). Research on the effect of cognitive processes in anxiety can be supplemented by research on the motivation effects of worry. Sarason (1988, p. 5) has characterized test anxiety in terms of self-focus: "Proneness to self-preoccupation and, most specifically, to worry over evaluation is a powerful component of what is referred to as test anxiety" (see also Carver & Scheier, 1988; Schwarzer, 1986; Schwarzer & Wicklund, 1991). A subset of worry cognitions pertains to negative thoughts about oneself, one's competence, or one's ability to cope with challenging or threatening demands. These are labeled here self-doubts. Self-doubts are unfavorable thoughts that refer to personal deficits in the self-regulation process and, therefore, represent one example of cognitive interference. Self-doubts are specific pessimistic beliefs while facing a stressful encounter, and thus reflect perceived self-inefficacy at the state level of functioning. Examples are "I doubt whether I can solve this problem," "It is difficult for me to make friends," "I am not confident that I can stick to this diet," or "I feel unable to adopt a strenuous exercise regimen." All of these thoughts are self-related and pertain to one's competence or to similar personal coping resources. In contrast, a homemaker who waits nervously for her husband to return home from work may worry about his safety, health, or life, but those are not self-doubts. Self-doubts represent a specific class of worries that are maladaptive in attaining goals because they interfere with an intended self-regulation process. In contrast to rumination or worry, self-doubts are always tied to personal goals. This is why it appears to be suitable for psychologists to study their functioning within an action-theoretical framework.

GOAL SETTING: DEVELOPING THE MOTIVATION TO ACT

Imagine an overweight person who wishes to slim down but does not do anything about it. Nothing will happen unless he or she transforms the wish into a behavioral intention (or goal). The process that leads to setting an explicit goal is labeled "motivation stage." Wishful thinking can be a good starting point ("I wish I were slim"), but motivation relies rather on specific cognitions that arise while contemplating the pros and cons of a remedial action. Intentions (or goals) represent the endpoint of a motivational process (e.g., "I intend to reduce my calorie intake by 30% by next week"). In determining goals, three kinds of expectancies come into play: (a) situation-outcome expectancies, (b) action-outcome expectancies, and (c) personal resource beliefs.

Situation-outcome expectancies pertain to the belief that the situation will change without the individual's intervention. For example, optimistic statements would be: "In the near future, being overweight will become the attractive ideal," and "Slim people will be regarded as less attractive." A pessimistic statement would be "With increasing age I will become more overweight, as most people do." This cognition is similar to a subjective risk assessment in addressing the question, "What is the likelihood that something either beneficial or harmful will happen?" Most people are more optimistic than realistic in this respect. They distort the available information in favor of more positive outcomes, a phenomenon that has been labeled "optimistic bias" or "defensive optimism" (Schwarzer, 1994; Taylor, 1989; Weinstein, 1982). Anxious individuals, however, worry about ambiguous or unfavorable future events, which is more realistic or pessimistic than optimistic: "I am concerned that something terrible might happen."

Action-outcome expectancies are the perception of contingencies between goal-directed behaviors and their consequences. An optimistic statement is "If I reduce my calorie intake then I would lose weight." A pessimistic statement is "Even if I go on a diet and exercise vigorously, I would not lose weight." The last item represents a worry cognition and may become part of constant ruminations, characterizing, however, a depressive mood rather than fearful anticipation.

Only the third kind of cognitions qualifies as self-doubts: Personal resource beliefs (or perceived self-efficacy) refer to one's capability to actually perform a behavior that leads to a desired outcome. This has been theoretically founded by Bandura (1977), and a great deal of research has confirmed the operative power of this construct in various domains of human functioning (Bandura, 1992, 1995). An optimistic example would be, "I am confident that I can run five miles per day even if I am tired." The first part of the sentence refers to the "can-do" notion, while the latter part refers to a barrier that makes the action more difficult (e.g., "... even if it rains, ... if my friends are visiting, ... if nobody would join me," etc.). The physical performance is not the main focus here, but rather the self-regulatory attempt. A pessimistic statement is, "I feel ambiguous about being able to stick to this diet." Obviously, this is the same as self-doubt. Self-inefficacious thoughts (or self-doubts), however, should not be equated with perceived lack of ability ("I know for sure that I cannot swim across the Channel"). It rather refers to the lack of confidence in performing an action that is within the scope of one's abilities. Truly knowing one's limits as opposed to lacking confidence in what is manageable have different motivational implications. The former lead to setting realistic goals and the latter to setting goals too low, undermining the motivation to strive for excellence and giving rise to rumination. Individuals who are plagued by self-doubts procrastinate difficult decisions, fail to develop challenging intentions, and get stuck in a fruitless contemplation process. They may harbor the necessary action-outcome expectancies, that is, they may know the contingent "pathways," but they lack a profound sense of "agency" (Skinner, Chapman, & Baltes, 1988; Smith & Wallston, 1992; Snyder et al., 1991).

There is a triangular relationship among self-efficacy, goal setting, and performance. In a meta-analysis of 14 studies, Locke and Latham (1990) found that, on average, self-efficacy is related to performance at $r = .39$ and to goal setting also at $r = .39$. The latter was also closely associated with performance ($r = .42$). It was assumed that goal setting may serve as a mediator between self-efficacy and performance. Thus, there is not only the well-known direct effect of self-efficacy on performance, but also an indirect one through goal setting. Individuals with self-doubts set lower goals, which leads to fewer accomplishments.

It is, however, not sufficient to examine whether goals are quantitatively high or low. Rather, competent self-regulation requires setting appropriate goals for oneself that are challenging but also within reach (Bagozzi, 1992; Bandura, 1995; Karoly, 1993). Distal goals are less motivating than proximal goals.

Some authors have distinguished between goals and intentions (Locke & Latham, 1990). Intentions are usually seen as being behavioral as for example, a weight loss goal of two pounds within one week pertains to a measurable consequence of a behavior, not the behavior itself, whereas the intention to restrict daily calorie intake to a defined level is clearly behavioral (Ajzen & Fishbein, 1980). It has also been found that there are individual differences in the level of abstraction that people prefer in their strivings. Emmons (1992) has distinguished "low-level strivers" who are concerned with minor daily tasks or challenges (such as household chores) from "high-level strivers" who define their goals as more abstract, diffuse, or philosophical (see also Emmons, King, & Sheldon, 1993).

Another distinction has been made by Gollwitzer (1993): "goal intentions" as opposed to "implementation intentions." A goal intention is, for example, "I intend to compose a chapter"; an implementation intention is, for example, "When I have finished grading the essays tonight I will start writing the chapter by making an outline." Instead of simply describing a desired behavior or behavioral outcome, the latter kind of intention specifies the conditions under which the behavior will be performed. Thus, it is more proximal and precise by referring to the where and when of an action. It has been found that intentions are more likely to be followed by appropriate actions if they are worded in a manner describing the implementation. Moreover, an "implemental mind-set" seems to be typical for the postdecisional phase, whereas a "deliberative mind-set" appears to be more characteristic for the preceding motivation phase (Gollwitzer & Kinney, 1989). When individuals are more deliberative they ponder the alternative options realistically or skeptically before making a decision. When they are in a more implemental mind-set they feel overly optimistic about success and are unaffected by self-doubts.

INITIATING AND MAINTAINING ACTIONS: WHAT WE THINK AFTER WE ARE DECIDED TO ACT

An author who has decided to compose a chapter will not immediately rush to his desk and start writing. Similarly, a smoker who has decided to quit will not immediately discard the remaining cigarettes. Rather, postintentional cognitions will dominate one's mind when an intention has been formed. In this preactional stage, the individual searches for opportunities to act, designs appropriate strategies to start or to try the intended behavior, and compares alternative courses of action that seem to promise success. The question is to what degree such cognitions guide the attempt to change the behavior or lead to procrastination or even disengagement before any action is taken. After the individual has passed through this stage and is acting, the question remains how cognitions can protect the ongoing action from distracting events and under which conditions they fail to maintain the desired behavior and allow relapse into undesired states. The next sections deal with the particular role of self-doubts in debilitating such processes.

Procrastination: Failing to Plan and to Try

In the postintentional preactional stage, mental activities prevail that mainly resemble planning. Therefore, we use the shorter label "planning stage" synonymously. It includes implementation intentions. In planning, one can have explicit trains of thought or implicit images of how the events might unfold. Designing possible courses of action requires attention, mental effort, and creativity. Individuals who harbor self-doubts direct their attention to negative outcomes and to their perceived lack of coping skills when barriers arise. Instead of inventing useful strategies to overcome difficulties they dwell on various kinds of remote possibilities of what could go awry. They imagine failure scenarios in which they see themselves failing at their self-imposed challenges, sometimes with catastrophic consequences. The author who intends to write a chapter doubts his capability to write something valuable at this specific moment and postpones the task until a better opportunity comes up. The smoker does not believe he or she is ready for quitting while stress is imminent and postpones the actual quitting until the "right moment." Directing one's attention to the self and to limitations of one's coping resources inhibits the individual in moving forward and in gaining momentum. This procrastination is a typical consequence of debilitating cognitions after a decision to act has been made. On the other hand, it is not always appropriate to act impulsively because this could jeopardize one's intention by running into unforeseen danger or difficulties. Rather, it is important to plan optimistically and realistically and to examine carefully the options that facilitate success.

As we all know, a good intention is no guarantee for successful action. In particular, rumination about one's capability to actually perform the critical behavior distracts from constructive attempts to find the best possible coping strategy. A lack of effortful attention on pathways for change leads to procrastination or even disengagement from the intention. What is needed, therefore, is self-efficacy to cope with barriers that make the intended action so difficult. Self-efficacious individuals imagine success scenarios where they make fruitful attempts and pass through different courses of action that lead to positive outcomes. They are more creative because, while trusting their capabilities, they see more options and invent more strategies. Optimistic self-beliefs at this stage have been labeled "action self-efficacy" (Marlatt, Baer, & Quigley, 1995). Accordingly, we can refer to the opposite of it as "action self-doubts."

This initiation stage has been widely neglected in previous research which commonly focused on actual performance, not on the immediate cognitive processes that precede the action. A compromise lies in the focus on trying. Finding out how and how often someone tries a difficult or new behavior gives an impression of how strong the goal commitment might be or to what degree self-doubts have been overcome. A Theory of Trying (Bagozzi & Warshaw, 1990) specifically aims at predicting the intention to try and actual trying. It has been designed as an elaboration of the former Theory of Reasoned Action (Fishbein & Ajzen, 1975).

Procrastination means that people fail to plan realistically the details of the intended action and do not even try, whereas someone who tries documents not only that goal commitment is sufficiently high, but also that initial self-doubts have been overcome. Failing to maintain or complete successfully an intended course of action, on the other hand, represents a relapse.

Relapse

When the author eventually sits at his desk and composes the first pages of his self-imposed ordeal, he might feel it difficult to keep writing. The phrases do not come fluently and he feels distracted by a number of stimuli such as hunger, phone calls, heat, and intrusive thoughts. The latter might refer to other business or to this specific task, such as "Can I meet the deadline?", "Am I really competent to write this chapter?", "Would someone else do a better job?", "Why am I so slow?", or "Are my writing skills declining with age?" These are "coping self-doubts" that reflect one's ambiguity about one's competence to carry through a difficult assignment. It refers to one's lack of confidence to cope with critical phases within the process of action when difficulties arise and setbacks occur.

When the smoker is surviving the first smoke-free day(s), he faces withdrawal symptoms and experiences high-risk situations with the frequent urge to smoke. Taking initial action is not enough, one has to maintain abstinence forever as part of a new life-style. Again, coping self-doubts arise that include thoughts such as, "Can I make it?", "Do I have the willpower necessary to stay abstinent?", "Am I able to withstand risky situations?", "Can I resist if someone offers me a cigarette while I'm drinking alcohol?"

This stage is a "volitional" phase where the former intention has to be maintained by a number of supportive means, such as optimistic cognitions, avoidance of high-risk situations, or coping with barriers. Self-doubts are the worst enemy and need to be replaced by self-efficacious thoughts in line with positive accomplishments. Mastery experience is the best way to gain confidence in one's capabilities to perform the difficult action. Therefore, it is essential to set proximal goals that are within one's reach to avoid failure. The course of action could be subdivided into a number of goals with increasing difficulty to ensure goal attainment and positive feedback, which in turn would stabilize one's self-efficacy.

However, setbacks cannot always be avoided. The author realizes that the last pages written in a painful process of self-regulation are below his standards and need to be discarded. This experience "knocks him down," he ruminates for hours, cannot get back to his desk, and finally decides to give up and disengage from this project. He does not believe he would be able to recover from this setback and start again from scratch. His ruminations are filled with "recovery self-doubts."

Similarly, the smoker might have given in to the urge to smoke while enjoying a coffee break during a stressful day. He only wanted to take one or two puffs, but could not stop and went into a full-blown relapse, smoking 20 cigarettes a day as before. This scenario of relapse has been labeled "abstinence violation effect" (Marlatt, Baer, & Quigley, 1995). A minor lapse turns into a major relapse because the individual has not learned to cope with a setback that occurs typically in a high-risk situation. "Recovery self-doubts" let him believe that he has no willpower, cannot stop the downward trend, and is unable to get back on track with some effort.

The distinction among action self-doubts, coping self-doubts, and recovery self-doubts may be a useful attempt to add a time perspective to the experience of worry. Different stages and events within a self-regulatory cycle give rise to intrusive thoughts that deal with ambiguity about one's lack of competence to master a difficult task.

CONCLUSION

It has been found that worry represents the key feature in trait anxiety and in generalized anxiety disorder, and that individual differences in worry can be assessed in various domains of life. Beyond these descriptive facts, it is important to study the causal role of worry when it comes to behaviors and emotions. Past research on anxiety and performance has pointed to worry as the critical component in this relationship: Worry is more closely associated with performance than is emotionality which leads to the conclusion that intrusive thoughts are the causal agent in the achievement impairment process. More recent research has aimed at this explanatory value of the worry construct by examining the actual cognitive processes that take place under more or less stressful conditions.

The present chapter goes further in a different direction by identifying a subclass of worry, labeled self-doubts. When intrusive thoughts occur within a goal attainment process, these thoughts are mostly self-evaluative and refer to the possibility that one's coping resources might not be sufficient to secure mastery of the challenging or threatening demands. The construct of self-doubts has a particular operative power in different areas of human functioning. Worrying about personal resource deficits interferes with goal setting, planning, action initiation, and action maintenance. The focus here is on the motivational pathway to performance impairment, as opposed to the cognitive capacity pathway, which suggests that the processing of threat information does not allow the deployment of sufficient attention to the task. Rather, it is argued that overattending to the self and underestimating one's capability has a motivational and volitional effect that interrupts or changes self-regulatory attempts in goal attainment.

To create a heuristic template for further research, a distinction has been made between action self-doubts, coping self-doubts, and recovery self-doubts. Although the worry content is about the same in all cases, these labels may help to guide stage-specific research. Linking intrusive thoughts to a self-regulatory goal attainment process is a useful means to suggest experimental intervention studies and to discourage cross-sectional correlations studies that cannot shed further light into this field.

ACKNOWLEDGMENTS

This chapter was written while the author was on sabbatical leave at the Chinese University of Hong Kong. The resources provided by the Department of Psychology are gratefully acknowledged.

REFERENCES

Ajzen, I. (1988). *Attitudes, personality, and behavior.* Milton Keynes, CA: Open University Press.

Ajzen, I., & Fishbein, M. (1980). *Understanding attitudes and predicting social behavior.* Englewood Cliffs, NJ: Prentice-Hall.

Bagozzi, R. P. (1992). The self-regulation of attitudes, intentions, and behavior. *Social Psychology Quarterly, 55,* 178–204.

Bagozzi, R. P., & Warshaw, P. R. (1990). Trying to consume. *Journal of Consumer Research, 17,* 127–140.

Bandura, A. (1977). Self-efficacy: Toward a unifying theory of behavioral change. *Psychological Review, 84,* 191–215.

Bandura, A. (1992). Exercise of personal agency through the self-efficacy mechanism. In R. Schwarzer (Ed.), *Self-efficacy: Thought control of action* (pp. 3–38). Washington, DC: Hemisphere.

Bandura, A. (1995). *Self-efficacy: The exercise of control.* San Francisco: Freeman.

Borkovec, T. D. (1985). Worry: A potentially valuable concept. *Behaviour Research and Therapy, 23,* 481–482.

Borkovec, T. D., & Lyonfields, J. D. (1993). Worry: Thought suppression of emotional processing. In H. W. Krohne (Ed.), *Attention and avoidance: Strategies in coping with aversiveness* (pp. 101–118). Seattle, WA: Hogrefe & Huber.

Borkovec, T. D., Robinson, E., Pruzinsky, T., & DePree, J. A. (1983). Preliminary exploration of worry: Some characteristics and processes. *Behaviour Research and Therapy, 21,* 9–16.

Carver, C. S., & Scheier, M. F. (1988). A control-process perspective on anxiety. *Anxiety Research. An International Journal, 1,* 17–22.

DSM III-R. (1987). *Diagnostic and statistical manual of mental disorder.* Washington, DC: American Psychiatric Association.

Emmons, R. A. (1992). Abstract versus concrete goals: Personal striving level, physical illness, and psychological well-being. *Journal of Personality and Social Psychology, 62,* 292–300.

Emmons, R. A., King, L. A., & Sheldon, K. (1993). Goal conflict and the self-regulation of action. In D. M. Wegner & J. W. Pennebaker (Eds.), *Handbook of mental control* (pp. 528–551). Englewood Cliffs, NJ: Prentice-Hall.

Eysenck, M. W. (1984). Anxiety and the worry process. *Bulletin of the Psychonomic Society, 22,* 545–548.

Eysenck, M. W. (1992). *Anxiety: The cognitive perspective.* Hove, UK: Lawrence Erlbaum Associates.

Fishbein, M., & Ajzen, I. (1975). *Belief, attitude, intention, and behavior: An introduction to theory and research.* Reading, MA: Addison-Wesley.

Gollwitzer, P. M. (1993). Goal achievement: The role of intentions. In W. Stroebe & M. Hewstone (Eds.), *European review of social psychology* (Vol. 4, pp. 141–185). Chichester, UK: Wiley.

Gollwitzer, P. M., & Kinney, R. F. (1989). Effects of deliberative and implemental mind-sets on the illusion of control. *Journal of Personality & Social Psychology, 54*, 531–542.

Hagtvet, K., & Backer Johnsen, T. (Eds.). (1992). *Advances in test anxiety research* (Vol. 7). Amsterdam, The Netherlands: Swets & Zeitlinger.

Heckhausen, H. (1991). *Motivation and action*. Berlin, Germany: Springer.

Hembree, R. (1988). Correlates, causes, effects, and treatment of test anxiety. *Review of Educational Research, 58*, 47–77.

Karoly, P. (1993). Mechanisms of self-regulation: A systems view. *Annual Review of Psychology, 44*, 23–52.

Kleine, D. (1990). Anxiety and sport performance: A meta-analysis. *Anxiety Research. An International Journal, 2*, 113–131.

Krohne, H. W. (1993). Vigilance and cognitive avoidance as concepts in coping research. In H. W. Krohne (Ed.), *Attention and avoidance: Strategies in coping with aversiveness* (pp. 19–50). Seattle, WA: Hogrefe & Huber.

Kuhl, J., & Beckmann, J. (Eds.). (1994). *Volition and personality: Action versus state orientation*. Göttingen, Germany: Hogrefe.

Lazarus, R. S. (1991). *Emotion and adaptation*. London: Oxford University Press.

Liebert, R. M., & Morris, L. W. (1967). Cognitive and emotional components of test anxiety: A distinction and some initial data. *Psychological Reports, 20*, 975–978.

Locke, E. A., & Latham, G. P. (1990). *A theory of goal setting and task performance*. Englewood Cliffs, NJ: Prentice-Hall.

Mandler, G., & Sarason, S. B. (1952). A study of anxiety and learning. *Journal of Abnormal and Social Psychology, 47*, 166–173.

Marlatt, G. A., Baer, J. S., & Quigley, L. A. (1995). Self-efficacy and addictive behavior. In A. Bandura (Ed.), *Self-efficacy in changing societies*. New York: Cambridge University Press.

Martin, L. L., Tesser, A., & McIntosh, W. D. (1993). Wanting but not having: The effects of unattained goals on thoughts and feelings. In D. M. Wegner & J. W. Pennebaker (Eds.), *Handbook of mental control* (pp. 552–572). Englewood Cliffs, NJ: Prentice-Hall.

Mathews, A. (1993). Attention and memory for threat in anxiety. In H. W. Krohne (Ed.), *Attention and avoidance: Strategies in coping with aversiveness* (pp. 119–138). Seattle: Hogrefe & Huber.

Meyer, T. J., Miller, M. L., Metzger, R. L., & Borkovec, T. D. (1990). Development and validation of the Penn State Worry Questionnaire. *Behavior Research and Therapy, 28*, 487–495.

Ploeg, H. M. van der, Schwarzer, R., & Spielberger, C. D. (Eds.). (1983). *Advances in test anxiety research* (Vol. 2). Lisse, The Netherlands/Hillsdale, NJ: Swets & Zeitlinger/Lawrence Erlbaum Associates.

Ploeg, H. M. van der, Schwarzer, R., & Spielberger, C. D. (Eds.). (1984). *Advances in test anxiety research* (Vol. 3). Lisse, The Netherlands/Hillsdale, NJ: Swets & Zeitlinger/Lawrence Erlbaum Associates.

Ploeg, H. M. van der, Schwarzer, R., & Spielberger, C. D. (Eds.). (1985). *Advances in test anxiety research* (Vol. 4). Lisse, The Netherlands: Swets & Zeitlinger.

Roemer, L., & Borkovec, T. D. (1993). Worry: Unwanted cognitive activity that controls unwanted somatic experience. In D. M. Wegner & J. W. Pennebaker (Eds.), *Handbook of mental control* (pp. 220–238). Englewood Cliffs, NJ: Prentice-Hall.

Rogers, R. W. (1983). Cognitive and physiological processes in fear appeals and attitude change: A revised theory of protection motivation. In J. R. Cacioppo & R. E. Petty (Eds.), *Social Psychology: A sourcebook* (pp. 153–176). New York: Guilford.

Sarason, I. G. (1960). Empirical findings and theoretical problems in the use of anxiety scales. *Psychological Bulletin, 57*, 403–415.

Sarason, I. G. (1980). *Test anxiety: Theory, research, and applications*. Hillsdale, NJ: Lawrence Erlbaum Associates.

Sarason, I. G. (1984). Stress, anxiety, and cognitive interference: Reactions to tests. *Journal of Personality and Social Psychology, 46*, 929–938.

Sarason, I. G. (1986). Test anxiety, worry, and cognitive interference. In R. Schwarzer (Ed.), *Self-related cognitions in anxiety and motivation* (pp. 19–33). Hillsdale, NJ: Lawrence Erlbaum Associates.

Sarason, I. G. (1988). Anxiety, self-preoccupation and attention. *Anxiety Research. An International Journal, 1*, 3–8.

Sarason, I. G. (1991). Anxiety, self-preoccupation and attention. In R. Schwarzer & R. A. Wicklund (Eds.), *Anxiety and self-focused attention* (pp. 9–13). Chur, Switzerland: Harwood.

Sarason, I. G., & Sarason, B. R. (1987). Cognitive interference as a component of anxiety: Measurement of its state and trait aspects. In R. Schwarzer, H. M. van der Ploeg, & C. D. Spielberger (Eds.), *Advances in test anxiety research* (Vol. 5, pp. 3–14). Lisse, The Netherlands: Swets & Zeitlinger.

Schwarzer, R. (Ed.). (1986). *Self-related cognitions in anxiety and motivation*. Hillsdale, NJ: Lawrence Erlbaum Associates.

Schwarzer, R. (Ed.). (1992). *Self-efficacy: Thought control of action*. Washington, DC: Hemisphere.

Schwarzer, R. (1994). Optimism, vulnerability, and self-beliefs as health-related cognitions: A systematic overview. *Psychology and Health, 9*, 161–180.

Schwarzer, R., Ploeg, H. M. van der, & Spielberger, C. D. (Eds.). (1982). *Advances in test anxiety research* (Vol. 1). Lisse, The Netherlands/Hillsdale, NJ: Swets & Zeitlinger/Lawrence Erlbaum Associates.

Schwarzer, R., Ploeg, H. M. van der, & Spielberger, C. D. (Eds.). (1987). *Advances in test anxiety research* (Vol. 5). Lisse, The Netherlands: Swets & Zeitlinger.

Schwarzer, R., Ploeg, H. M. van der, & Spielberger, C. D. (Eds.). (1989). *Advances in test anxiety research* (Vol. 6). Lisse, The Netherlands: Swets & Zeitlinger.

Schwarzer, R., & Quast, H.-H. (1985). Multidimensionality of the anxiety experience: Evidence for additional components. In H. M. van der Ploeg, R. Schwarzer, & C. D. Spielberger (Eds.), *Advances in test anxiety research* (Vol. 4, pp. 4–14). Lisse, The Netherlands: Swets & Zeitlinger.

Schwarzer, R., & Wicklund, R. A. (Eds.). (1991). *Anxiety and self-focused attention*. Chur, Switzerland: Harwood.

Seipp, B. (1990). *Angst und Leistung in Schule und Hochschule: Eine Meta-Analyse* [Anxiety and performance in school and university: A meta-analysis]. Frankfurt, Germany: Lang.

Seligman, M. E. P. (1991). *Learned optimism*. New York: Knopf.

Skinner, E. A., Chapman, M., & Baltes, P. (1988). Control, means-ends, and agency beliefs: A new conceptualization and its measurement during childhood. *Journal of Personality and Social Psychology, 54*, 117–133.

Smith, C. A., & Wallston, K. A. (1992). Adaptation in patients with chronic rheumatoid arthritis: Application of a general model. *Health Psychology, 11*, 151–162.

Snyder, C. R., Harris, C., Anderson, J. R., Holleran, S. A., Irving, L. M., Sigmon, S. T., Yoshinobu, L., Gibb, J., Langelle, C., & Harney, P. (1991). The will and the ways: Development and validation of an individual-differences measure of hope. *Journal of Personality and Social Psychology, 60*, 570–585.

Spielberger, C. D. (1980). *Test Anxiety Inventory. Preliminary professional manual*. Palo Alto, CA: Consulting Psychologists Press.

Tallis, F., Eysenck, M. W., & Mathews, A. (1991). Worry: A critical analysis of some theoretical approaches. *Anxiety Research. An International Journal, 4*, 97–108.

Tallis, F., Eysenck, M. W., & Mathews, A. (1992). A questionnaire for the measurement of non-pathological worry. *Personality and Individual Differences, 13*, 161–168.

Taylor, S. E. (1989). *Positive illusions: Creative self-deception and the healthy mind*. New York: Basic Books.

Weinstein, N. D. (1982). Unrealistic optimism about susceptibility to health problems. *Journal of Behavioral Medicine, 5*, 441–460.

CHAPTER

6

INFORMATION-PROCESSING PATHWAYS TO COGNITIVE INTERFERENCE IN CHILDHOOD

Michael W. Vasey
Eric L. Daleiden
The Ohio State University

Like their adult counterparts, high-anxious children perform significantly less well than their low-anxious peers on a wide range of tasks. Although numerous, studies of this phenomenon have focused almost exclusively on decrements in the academic performance of test-anxious children (see Dusek, 1980; Wigfield & Eccles, 1990 for reviews). Thus, the need noted by Sarason, Sarason, and Pierce (1995) to expand research and theory to include other domains of performance is particularly pronounced in the study of cognitive interference in childhood. To foster such expansion, this chapter offers a broad information- processing framework for understanding cognitive interference in childhood anxiety.

Expansion of research and theory regarding cognitive interference is best fostered by adopting a broad conceptualization of the phenomenon. Therefore, we propose that cognitive interference refers not only to intrusive thoughts which disrupt task performance, but to all cognitive processes and products that interfere with task-relevant activity. This definition draws attention to the likelihood that a broad range of factors contribute to cognitive interference, including cognitive, emotional, perceptual, and physiological processes. Furthermore, this definition does not assume that the cognitions producing interference are necessarily unintentional, uncontrollable or even unwanted. Although cognitive interference may be produced by such intrusive cognitions, it may also be produced by controlled and strategically enacted operations (Bargh, 1989).

This chapter attempts to broaden the scope of the current literature and refine its research methods by considering a model of the information-processing mechanisms which may underlie cognitive interference. Stated broadly, cognitive interference occurs when information-processing resources (e.g., attention) are diverted from the task at hand, thereby impairing or even preventing effective task performance (Eysenck & Calvo, 1992; Sarason, 1988; Sarason et al., in press). As a context for discussing the factors which may disrupt processing, we review a model of the information-processing sequence. Although each stage of this sequence may contribute to cognitive interference, we emphasize two particular pathways. The first concerns interference related to attentional processes that operate early in the information-processing sequence. Mechanisms of attention may evoke, maintain, or intensify anxiety, and may produce cognitive interference in several ways. The second concerns interference related to anxious children's efforts to cope with anxiety-provoking situations or regulate their own anxiety responses (e.g., worrisome thoughts). Because they consume processing resources, coping and emotional self-regulatory efforts have significant potential to interfere with task performance.

INFORMATION-PROCESSING FRAMEWORK

The model of information-processing adopted for the present discussion is that of Dodge (1991; Crick & Dodge, 1994). Although this model assumes that all stages of processing operate simultaneously (i.e., in parallel), the processing of any single element of information occurs sequentially through a series of six stages. During the *encoding* stage, attentional resources are selectively allocated to encode specific external and internal cues. Encoded cues are passed to the *interpretation* stage during which they are compared to information stored in memory and judgments are made regarding their meaning. After interpretation, a process of *goal clarification* is triggered in which children choose to either revise their current goal in keeping with the new information or to continue pursuit of their preexisting goal. Next, during the *response access or construction stage*, children retrieve possible responses from memory and/or construct new responses to fit the demands of the situation. During the *response selection* stage, responses are evaluated with regard to self-efficacy expectations, outcome expectations, and response appropriateness, and the most positively evaluated response is selected for enactment. Finally, *enactment* is the production of the verbal or motor behavior required to perform the selected response.

Though largely neglected by cognitive psychologists until recently, emotions are now recognized as important determinants of the efficiency and accuracy of information-processing (Bugental, 1992; Crick & Dodge, 1994; Derryberry & Tucker, 1994; Eysenck, 1988). According to Crick and Dodge's model, emotions serve not only to motivate information-processing but also to direct its focus. By doing so, emotions have substantial potential to enhance or interfere with processing. Simply put, if the narrowed focus of processing includes task-relevant stimuli and operations, then efficiency should improve. However, if processing resources are focused on task-irrelevant stimuli, then performance decrements should be observed. Thus, emotions may serve to bias or distort information-processing in ways that produce and/or maintain cognitive interference (Crick & Dodge, 1994).

Because of the potential for emotions to disrupt information-processing, the processes associated with emotional regulation and dysregulation are likely to be important contributors to cognitive interference. Garber, Braafladt, and Zeman (1991) have proposed an information-processing model of emotion regulation and dysregulation based on Dodge's model. In general, these authors argue that emotion regulation requires skills in all stages of information processing. To be effectively regulated, the occurrence of an emotion must first be noticed and its cause accurately interpreted. If the emotion is judged to be excessive or likely to interfere with task-relevant activities, goals will be modified to place priority on regulating the emotion. Regulatory responses will then be generated, evaluated and the response judged most likely to be effective will be enacted. Dysregulated emotion is assumed to result from problems in one or more of these stages. Thus, deficits in the skills of anxiety regulation may contribute to cognitive interference. Moreover, cognitive interference may reciprocally impair the information-processing operations associated with anxiety regulation, thus producing a downward spiral of increasing dysregulation and further interference.

In sum, biases, deficits and distortions at any or all stages of the information-processing sequence have significant potential to contribute to cognitive interference. These effects are likely to occur via a variety of pathways, both direct (e.g., reduction in available processing resources) and indirect (e.g., contributing to increased anxiety). Examples of direct and indirect pathways in each stage of processing are shown in Table 6.1. Unfortunately, an exhaustive discussion of all possible pathways is beyond the scope of this chapter. Instead, we have chosen to focus on two domains of processing which we believe are especially important. The first concerns the role of attentional processes while the second concerns the role of coping responses or emotional self-regulatory processes in mediating cognitive interference.

ATTENTION AND COGNITIVE INTERFERENCE

According to the prevailing cognitive-attentional viewpoint (Sarason, 1988; Wine, 1982), the performance decrements associated with anxiety are due to a reduction in the attentional resources devoted to task performance. In evaluative situations, high-anxious children presumably divert some attentional resources to process internal and external task-irrelevant stimuli, particularly those relevant to the adequacy of their task performance. In contrast, low-anxious children

TABLE 6.1
Examples of Possible Information-Processing Pathways to Cognitive Interference

Stage of Information Processing	*Direct Pathway*	*Indirect Pathway*
Encoding	A selective attentional bias in favor of emotionally threatening information may reduce attentional resources available for encoding task-relevant information. Such an attentional bias may also reduce processing resources available for later stages of processing. In both cases interference will be greatest when demands for effortful processing approach or exceed system limits (Eysenck & Calvo, 1992).	Such a bias may contribute to the maintenance and/or intensification of anxiety, thereby increasing the likelihood of interference in this and other stages of processing.
Interpretation	A bias toward interpreting ambiguous information in a threatening manner and/or overestimating the likelihood of negative out-comes may interfere with problem-solving performance (Davey, 1994). For example, Vasey and Borkovec (1992) showed that chronic worriers generate many more catastrophic outcomes for a given worry topic and rate them as more likely than do nonworriers. Such a tendency might easily make problem-solving more difficult.	Such biases may contribute to increased anxiety. For example, in addition to producing more catastrophic outcomes of their worries, chronic worriers also reported substantially greater anxiety while doing so (Vasey & Borkovec, 1992).
Goal Clarification	Activating a goal of minimizing threatening outcomes may conflict with a goal of maximizing task performance (Hill,1972).	A goal of minimizing threatening outcomes may produce interference by leading to shifts in processing resources to task-irrelevant activities such as increasing processing resources devoted to selective attention toward signals of threat.
Response Access or Construction	Knowledge of strategies for solving problems may be limited such that responses involving avoidance and distraction are overrepresented. Similarly, such strategies may become more accessible in memory than others as children become anxious.	To the extent that the focus of problem-solving efforts is the regulation of anxiety responses (e.g., worrisome thoughts), interference with problem solving may contribute to the maintenance and/or intensification of anxiety.
Response Selection	A bias toward selecting responses involving avoidance and distraction may directly interfere with task performance because such responses are incompatible with demands of the task. Such responses may be chosen due to limited knowledge of alternative responses (see above) or because of low self-efficacy beliefs regarding alternative responses.	Selection of avoidance and distraction strategies may help to temporarily reduce anxiety symptoms such as worrisome thoughts, but such responses are likely to contribute to the maintenance and intensification of anxiety in the long term.
Response Enactment	Even if effective problem-solving responses are generated and selected, they may be enacted ineffectively, perhaps because insufficient processing resources are available for effective performance.	Effective enactment should become particularly difficult as anxiety increases and available processing resources decrease.

narrowly focus their attention on the task at hand and minimize attention to task-irrelevant stimuli (Sarason, 1988; Wine, 1982).

Historically, the cognitive-attentional perspective has approached attention as a generic, undifferentiated processing resource. However, attention is more productively viewed as a multidimensional construct (Eysenck, 1988). Information-processing theorists have identified several dimensions of attention that may provide productive guides for future research. For example, Dodge's model distinguishes between two dimensions of attention: (1) *intensity* refers to the amount of processing resources devoted to encoding cues as opposed to other stages of processing, and (2) *selectivity* denotes the degree to which attentional resources are allocated more toward some cues than others. However, Eysenck's (1988) delineation of four dimensions allows for even greater clarity and differentiation. The first concerns the *content* of the information toward which attention is directed. The second, *capacity*, refers to the total amount of attentional resources available. *Distractibility*, the third dimension, signifies one's ability to maintain attentional focus on a chosen stimulus. Finally, *selectivity* refers to the degree to which attentional resources are focused narrowly on a subset of cues or broadly on many cues.

Each of these dimensions may contribute to or protect against cognitive interference in different ways. For example, assuming a limited pool of processing resources, increased attentional intensity should reduce the resources available for later stages of processing. Similarly, if a large proportion of available resources is devoted to scanning the environment for a specific type of informational content, fewer resources will be available for encoding, interpreting and responding to other types of stimuli (e.g., task-relevant cues).

There is considerable evidence that high-anxious children are more distractible than their low-anxious counterparts and this distractibility appears to impair performance. For example, Dusek, Kermis, and Mergler (1975) found evidence that high-anxious children are more susceptible to the effects of distracting stimuli than their low-anxious peers, suggesting they do indeed devote more attention to task-irrelevant stimuli. Specifically, compared to low-anxious children, high-anxious children's performance on an incidental learning task was significantly more disrupted by the presence of distracting stimuli. Nottelmann and Hill's (1977) finding that off-task glances were more frequent and of longer duration in high- than low- or moderately-anxious children provides more direct evidence of such distractibility. Moreover, high-anxious children performed worse than either low- or moderately-anxious children and the minute-by-minute patterns of performance and off-task glances were closely negatively related. Thus, these authors argued that high-anxious children's performance decrements stem from a reduction in resources available for task performance because attention is directed off-task. Of course, while this may reflect general distractibility, it might also reflect differences in attentional intensity or selectivity. By adopting a differentiated view of attention, future studies can clarify such issues.

In addition to being susceptible to external distracters, anxious children also appear to be distracted by stimuli that originate internally (e.g., worrisome thoughts). For example, several studies have shown that high-anxious children report significantly more off-task thoughts and negative self-evaluations than low-anxious children (Prins, Groot, & Hanewald, 1994; Zatz & Chassin, 1983; 1985). Both types of thoughts were negatively correlated with performance on several tests, suggesting that they serve to distract high-anxious children and contribute to impaired performance. Negative cognitions also appear to be related to performance decrements in social interactions. Johnson and Glass (1989) reported that socially-anxious adolescent boys performed significantly less well than nonanxious peers in a social interaction. These boys were rated by confederates as more anxious and more self-conscious during a conversation than nonanxious boys. Both confederates and objective observers rated high-anxious boys as less socially skilled during the conversation, specifically, exhibiting more pauses and less conversation. Consistent with the cognitive-attentional account, performance was negatively correlated with the frequency of subjects' reports of negative self-evaluative thoughts

Rather than simply reflecting a general tendency to be easily distracted, the findings described above may reflect the operation of a content-specific attentional bias in favor of threat-related stimuli (Eysenck, 1988). For example, high-anxious subjects may be more distractible in part because their attentional focus is disrupted by internal and external signals of threat. Similarly, this bias might result in more worrisome thoughts or promote the diversion of attentional resources to such thoughts (Mathews, 1990). Consistent with the cognitive-attentional theory of test anxiety, this bias could contribute to reduced capacity or increased intensity and may account for much of the cognitive interference experienced by high-anxious individuals (Eysenck, 1988).

Current cognitive theories make clear predictions that high-anxious individuals should show attentional biases *toward* emotionally threatening stimuli, particularly when exposed to stressful situations (Barlow, 1988; Beck & Emery, 1985; Kendall & Ronan, 1990; Mathews & MacLeod, 1994; Williams, Watts, MacLeod, & Mathews, 1988). Consistent with the cognitive-attentional perspective, several theorists also predict that low-anxious individuals should show an attentional bias *away* from threatening stimuli in stressful situations. For example, MacLeod and Mathews (1991) suggested that the attentional bias shown by high-anxious individuals reflects an unusually low threshold for the activation of threat-relevant information in memory. In contrast, the opposite bias of low-anxious children may reflect a high threshold such that activation of threat representations is actually inhibited compared to other information in memory. Presumably, an optimal threshold would serve to filter out minor signals of potential threat, thereby protecting against unnecessary anxiety and disruption of ongoing behavior, but still allow efficient processing of serious signals of threat.

In addition to directly disrupting or supporting an on-task focus, attentional biases may play an important role in anxiety regulation and dysregulation. An attentional bias toward threat is likely to contribute to the maintenance and/or intensification of anxiety. A bias toward threat may promote greater activation of threat-relevant cognitive structures (i.e., threat schemata) which may, in turn, maintain attentional biasing and produce distortions in later stages of processing (Bugental, 1992). By contributing to anxiety dysregulation, this bias might ultimately support the development and maintenance of anxiety disorders. In contrast, an attentional bias away from threat may serve an important function in regulating anxiety. By inhibiting the activation of threat schemata it may serve to protect against unnecessary anxiety and perhaps serve to limit the duration of periods of elevated state anxiety.

Considerable evidence from research with adults indicates that high-anxious individuals do indeed show an attentional bias favoring threatening over neutral stimuli, whereas low-anxious individuals show a bias favoring neutral over threatening stimuli (for reviews see Logan & Goetsch, 1993; MacLeod, this volume; Mathews & MacLeod, 1994). Furthermore, at least one study suggests that the respective biases of both groups increase under conditions of high state anxiety (MacLeod & Mathews, 1988). However, only recently have such attentional biases been studied among children.

Martin, Horder, and Jones (1992) compared 6- to 13-year-old children with and without a fear of spiders. Subjects completed a Stroop color-naming task that included spider-relevant (e.g., web, crawl, etc.) and spider-irrelevant words (e.g., fly, wings, etc.). Researchers have used similar Stroop tasks to demonstrate that anxious adults, color-naming speed is slowed by the presence of threat-relevant words whereas nonanxious adults show no interference (e.g., Mathews & MacLeod, 1985; Watts, McKenna, Sharrock, & Trezise, 1986). As predicted, Martin et al. (1992) found that compared to spider-irrelevant words, spider-relevant words disrupted the performance of children reporting a fear of spiders, but found no interference for children with no fear of spiders.

One explanation for this Stroop effect is that anxious subjects' attention is drawn to the content of threat-relevant words more than neutral words, therefore leaving less attention available for the color-naming task. However, factors other than an attentional bias towards threat may be responsible for interference on Stroop tasks (e.g., MacLeod, Mathews, & Tata, 1986). For example, both high- and low-anxious children may attend equally to threatening words but high-anxious children may experience a more intense emotional reaction to such words, thereby producing greater color-naming interference (MacLeod et al., 1986).

MacLeod et al. (1986) developed an attentional task that resolves this ambiguity. Subjects are presented with two words appearing one above the other in the center of a computer monitor. Word pairs are selected to represent various experimental conditions, such as threat-neutral, neutral-neutral, and neutral-threat. Subjects are instructed to read the upper word in each pair aloud, and attentional allocation is measured by a secondary task requiring detection of a small dot that may subsequently appear in either the upper or lower word position. The time required to detect the dot is an index of the extent to which visual attention was directed to the word location where the dot appeared. If subjects show an attentional bias toward threat, then they should respond faster to probes appearing in the same position as threatening words than to probes appearing in the position of neutral words. However, if subjects show an attentional bias away from threat, then they should respond faster to probes following neutral rather than threatening words.

In our laboratory we have modified the probe detection task of MacLeod et al. (1986) for use with children. We have complete two studies to date using this task. The first (Vasey, Daleiden, Williams, & Brown, 1995) compared a group of 12 clinically-anxious 9- to 14-year-old children to a group of normal controls matched for age, gender, verbal intelligence, reading ability, and socioeconomic status. Our findings indicated that clinically-anxious children were significantly faster at detecting probes in the lower position when they followed threatening words compared to neutral words. In contrast, normal controls responded to probes with equal speed regardless of the content of the preceding words. These findings provide preliminary evidence for an attentional bias toward threat in clinically anxious children but do not support an attentional bias away from threat in normal children. In our second study (Vasey, El-Hag, & Daleiden, in press) we attempted to replicate and extend these findings by comparing samples of high- and low-test-anxious sixth- and eighth-graders. Consistent with the findings of Vasey et al. (1995), high-test-anxious children showed a significant attentional bias toward threatening words. Moreover, in contrast to the findings of Vasey et al. (1995), the study yielded some evidence of an attentional bias away from threat cues among low-test-anxious children.

In sum, the same type of threat-specific attentional biases seen among adults are operative among high- and low-anxious children. From the perspective of Dodge's model, such attentional biases may reflect the activation of specific goals. Dodge views goals as "focused arousal states that function as orientations toward producing particular outcomes" (Crick & Dodge, 1994, p. 76). Historical approaches to children's test anxiety have emphasized the importance of such goals. For example, Hill (1972) argued that high and low levels of test anxiety reflect different patterns of success-failure motives. According to Hill, when high-anxious children perceive information signaling potential failure (e.g., negative feedback), they are likely to experience activation and/or strengthening of a goal directed at minimizing the possibility of failure. In contrast, when low-anxious children perceive information signaling potential failure, they are likely to experience activation and/or strengthening of a goal directed at maximizing the likelihood of success.

Although such goals are consistent with the observed attentional biases, other types of goals may also influence children's use of selective attention. In our laboratory we have begun to explore the influence of children's coping preferences or styles on attentional processing. A number of researchers have argued that such preferences play an important role in anxiety (e.g., Krohne, 1980; Krohne & Rogner, 1982). Miller (1990) divides coping preferences into the categories of monitoring and blunting. High levels of monitoring are characterized by a preference for seeking information concerning imminent threats. In contrast, high levels of blunting are characterized by a preference for avoiding information concerning imminent threats. One pathway by which such goals might contribute to cognitive interference is through their impact on the content upon which attention is selectively focused. When under stress, those high in monitoring should show an attentional bias toward threat cues. In contrast, high blunters should show an attentional bias away from threat cues. Furthermore, because these dimensions are largely unrelated to trait anxiety (Miller, 1990), they may account for variance in attentional bias scores not accounted for by children's level of anxiety.

Preliminary data from our laboratory provide support for this prediction. Using the sample described by Vasey et al. (1995), we examined the relationship between attentional biases and monitoring and blunting. As part of a larger battery, children completed the trait form of the State-Trait Anxiety Inventory for Children (Spielberger, 1973), the Children's Anxiety Sensitivity Inventory (Silverman, Fleisig, Rabian, & Peterson, 1991), the Monitoring and Blunting Scale for Children (Lepore & Kliewer, 1989), and our child version of the probe detection task. Analyses revealed several interesting effects. Although most were only marginally significant, presumably due in part to the small size of the sample, they clearly warrant further study. The dependent variable was a threat bias score which, if positive, represented a bias toward threat and, if negative, represented a bias away from threat (see Vasey et al., 1995). In general, a positive correlation should be found between monitoring and threat bias. Results supported this prediction, $r = .31$, $p < .08$ (one-tailed). In contrast, a negative correlation should be found between blunting and threat bias. However, this prediction was not supported, $r = .15$, *ns*.

To ensure that the correlation between monitoring and attentional bias was not simply due to a correlation between monitoring and anxiety, we conducted two hierarchical regression analyses. In the first, trait anxiety scores, monitoring scores and the trait anxiety X monitoring interaction were entered successively. The interaction was marginally significant (change in adjusted $R^2 = .09$, partial $r = .38$, $p < .10$). However, because the correlation between trait anxiety and bias proved to be nonsignificant ($r = .19$, $p < .20$, one-tailed), a second analysis was conducted which substituted anxiety sensitivity for trait anxiety because it was significantly related to bias ($r = .36$, $p < .04$, one-tailed) and therefore provided a more rigorous test of the independent contribution of monitoring scores. The anxiety sensitivity X monitoring interaction was marginally significant (change in adjusted $R^2 = .11$, partial $r = .40$, $p < .07$). Thus, these results suggest that the effects of monitoring and anxiety on attentional bias are interdependent. Examination of the regression equation revealed that monitoring scores had little effect on attentional bias at low levels of anxiety sensitivity but, at higher levels, high monitoring scores were associated with a bias *toward* threat while low monitoring scores were associated with a bias *away* from threat.

Because low levels of monitoring imply a preference for blunting, we repeated the hierarchical analysis substituting blunting for monitoring scores. However, because this analysis yielded no noteworthy effects, we evaluated the effects of blunting in one other way. Rather than treating the scores independently, Miller (1990) has suggested using a difference score (i.e., monitoring-blunting) which serves as an index of the preference for one or the other style. The interaction between this index and anxiety sensitivity proved to be marginally significant (change in adjusted $R^2 = .08$, partial $r = .36$, $p < .08$). Examination of the regression equation revealed a pattern similar to that described for monitoring alone, but which made the contribution of blunting scores clearer. As before, at low levels of anxiety sensitivity, coping preferences had little impact on attentional bias. However, at higher levels of anxiety sensitivity, a preference for monitoring was associated with a bias *toward* threat while a preference for blunting was associated with a bias *away* from threat cues.

These preliminary results suggest that not all high-anxious children will show an attentional bias toward threat cues. Although such a bias is characteristic of high-anxious children who have a predominantly monitoring coping style, high-anxious children with a predominantly blunting coping style instead appear likely to show a bias away from threat cues. Whether such coping preference effects on attention reflect automatic or strategic allocation of processing resources remains unclear. Recent evidence suggests that the bias toward threat seen among anxious subjects can be suppressed if subjects are allowed sufficient time to consciously process threat cues (MacLeod & Rutherford, 1992). In other words, the effects of monitoring and blunting may be due to strategic efforts to direct attention. This hypothesis could be tested by comparing threat cues presented within and out of awareness. If coping preferences operate at a conscious level they should not be associated with attentional bias when stimuli are presented out of awareness. However, it is equally possible that the effects of coping preference occur automatically. Even if originally reflecting strategic allocations of attention, over time such patterns should become increasingly automatic (Crick & Dodge, 1994).

In sum, an attentional bias towards threat clearly has significant potential to produce cognitive interference via direct pathways such as limiting attentional resources available for task performance and indirect pathways such as interfering with anxiety regulation. By the same token, a bias away from minor threat cues may enhance performance and foster anxiety regulation. However, much remains to be learned about such biases and the roles they may play in producing and preventing cognitive interference. For example, many questions must be asked about the situational determinants of such biases. While adult-based research suggests that stressful conditions (i.e., elevated state anxiety) heighten both biases, this question has not been adequately addressed among children. Furthermore, we currently know little about the relationship between such biases and the level of task performance or the occurrence of other types of attentional problems during task performance.

By no means does the above discussion exhaust the possible links between attention and cognitive interference. For example, although the attentional bias toward threat seen among anxious individuals is generally thought to reflect a tendency for attention to be easily drawn to threatening stimuli, Derryberry and Tucker (1994) have suggested an intriguing alternative. They suggest that instead, the effect may be due to difficulty in disengaging attention from such stimuli once it is directed toward them. These authors argue that the former case should lead to superficial processing of multiple threats that may promote the maintenance of mild, but constant negative affect. However, the latter case should promote in-depth processing of threats once they are perceived, thus leading to a stronger experience of negative emotion, and difficulty redirecting attention to the task at hand. Of course there is no reason that both cannot be characteristic of anxiety. Indeed, it would not be surprising if anxious children were both easily distracted by threat and had difficulty releasing their attention from such stimuli. However, only if these subtle distinctions are considered in future research can such questions be answered.

COPING AND COGNITIVE INTERFERENCE

While children's coping preferences may contribute to cognitive interference through their effects on the focus of attention, coping may also lead to interference via other pathways. For example, several studies suggest the possibility that anxious children's coping efforts contribute to performance decrements by diverting resources away from task-relevant processing. Zatz and Chassin (1985), tested the hypothesis that coping cognitions should be more prevalent among high- than low-anxious children. Coping cognitions were defined as "self-statements reflecting attempts to cope with anxiety and mind-wandering" (p. 395). Because low-anxious children experience few off-task thoughts, they should have little need to make coping self-statements. In contrast, because high-anxious children experience many off-task thoughts they should also report many coping cognitions. As predicted, high-anxious children reported significantly more coping cognitions than low-anxious children. Moreover, coping cognitions were significantly negatively correlated with performance on a math test. Based on their findings, Zatz and Chassin suggested that, at the very least, coping cognitions do not enhance performance and instead may produce cognitive interference by distracting resources from task-relevant processing.

Prins et al. (1994) recently replicated the findings of Zatz and Chassin (1985), showing that high-anxious children reported significantly more coping self-statements as well as more off-task thoughts and negative self-evaluations. As in Zatz and Chassin, coping self-statements were negatively related to math test performance. However, Prins et al. suggested several explanations for this relationship other than that coping cognitions consume processing resources. First, because such thoughts typically contain references to negative aspects of the situations, coping cognitions may serve to focus children's attention further on those negative aspects. Alternatively, high anxiety may independently produce both debilitated performance and coping cognitions without any causal relationship between the two.

In an earlier study, Prins (1986) examined 8–11-year-old children's self-talk during a stressful situation involving jumping from a high-diving board during a swimming lesson. Children were also asked to rate the effectiveness of their attempts at self-regulation and how much they believed fearful emotions could be controlled. Subjects were divided into those who refused to jump off the diving board, those who hesitated, and those who jumped with ease. These groups corresponded with high-, moderate-, and low-anxious classifications, respectively, based on children's self-reports and teacher ratings of anxiety. Self-regulatory thoughts and behaviors were significantly more common in the moderate- than either the high- or low-anxious groups. Furthermore, the majority of high-anxious children reported that fear could not be controlled. Interestingly, those who engaged in self-regulation performed less well than those who did not. However, only low- and moderate-anxious children were included in this comparison because high-anxious children's refusal to perform precluded evaluation of their performance. In summary, among those children who remained in the situation, self-regulatory speech was associated with reduced performance quality.

The results of Zatz and Chassin (1985) and Prins (1986; Prins et al., 1994) seem to suggest that when anxious children use coping thoughts, performance is generally not enhanced and may even be impaired. Unfortunately, these studies actually provide little information about this relationship because the statistical tests necessary to separate the influence of coping cognitions from the effects of negative thoughts were not reported. Examining this relationship is vital because coping cognitions are presumably a self-regulatory response to negative thoughts and appear to be positively correlated with such thoughts (Zatz & Chassin, 1983). To determine whether coping cognitions make any unique contribution to performance decrements, future research should partial out the influence of off-task and negative self-evaluative thoughts. It may be that coping cognitions are indeed independently negatively correlated with performance but the correlation might instead be zero or even positive. A positive partial correlation could occur if coping cognitions actually serve to suppress what would otherwise be an even stronger negative correlation between performance and distracting negative thoughts.

It seems likely that coping cognitions may serve to moderate anxiety-related cognitive interference or even enhance performance under some conditions. A variety of studies have found cognitive interventions to be effective in reducing children's anxiety and improving their task performance (Cradock, Cotler, & Jason, 1978; Kanfer, Karoly, & Newman, 1975; Leal, Baxter, Martin, & Marx, 1981; Stevens & Phil, 1983). By and large, these interventions have taught children new and more effective coping responses. For example, Stevens and Phil compared two cognitive treatments with no-treatment in 42 test-anxious seventh graders. The first cognitive treatment trained children in the skills of problem-solving and cognitive restructuring via verbal self-instructions. The second encouraged students to discuss and develop their own coping strategies. Both treated groups improved significantly compared to the nontreated controls on measures such as the Mazes subtest of the Wechsler Intelligence Scale for Children–Revised (Wechsler, 1974), number of coping strategies generated, and teacher-rated coping ability. Similarly, Kanfer et al. (1975) reported that training in the use of coping self-statements enhanced darkness tolerance in children who feared the dark. Thus, coping skills training appears to be effective for reducing anxiety and may even enhance performance in some situations.

However, the effects of cognitive treatments have not been uniformly positive. Several studies suggest that training children to use coping self-statements may be detrimental (e.g., Denney, 1975; Fox & Houston, 1981). For example, Fox and Houston reported that high-anxious children who received such training were significantly more anxious than untrained high-anxious children prior to and during a public speaking task. These authors suggested that the added burden of having to think about self-instructions may have interfered with cognitive preparation for the task and fostered greater anxiety. One explanation for such interference is that subjects in this study were given very little training and practice (i.e., only one session) in the use of coping self-statements and results might be different if children were given more experience using such strategies (Kendall & Chansky, 1991). When self-statements are first learned, their use is likely to make heavy demands on the limited pool of processing resources and thus interfere with task performance. However, with repeated practice such responses should become increasingly automatic, ultimately requiring little effort and therefore having little potential to interfere with task performance (Kanfer & Hagerman, 1985). In keeping with this view, studies supporting the effectiveness of cognitive interventions have generally provided considerably more opportunity for practice than Fox and Houston (1981). For example, Cradock et al. (1978) provided six and Stevens and Phil (1983) provided ten 1-hour sessions.

Even if we assume that coping cognitions produce cognitive interference, there is much about this relationship that remains unknown. In addition to their frequency, the extent to which coping cognitions disrupt processing may depend on other factors such as the goals and strategies they reflect and beliefs about the controllability of anxious cognitions (Kendall & Chansky, 1991). Furthermore, the types of coping cognitions studied to date reflect only a small subset of the strategies children use to cope with anxiety. Most available studies have been constrained by their decision to study coping cognitions to the exclusion of non-cognitive coping responses and by the type of situation on which they focused (e.g., a math test). The benefits of a less constrained task can be seen in Prins' (1986) study. Although the author focused on coping self-statements, his results reveal another category of coping responses. Prins' diving test allowed children the option of refusing to jump from the high diving board, and high-anxious children consistently chose that option. In other words, they regulated their anxiety by entirely avoiding the demands of the situation. This expanded perspective suggests an alternative interpretation of Prins' findings. Rather than interfering with the quality of their performance, the self-regulatory efforts of the moderate-anxious group may have enabled them to perform despite their anxiety.

Past studies have also been limited by a narrow focus on coping that occurs during task performance and excludes coping that occurs in anticipation of the task. This further limits the type of coping responses seen because much of the interference that occurs during task performance may have its basis in coping failures that occur in anticipation of the task. For example, cognitive interference may disrupt the performance of tasks associated with preparing for an anticipated threatening event (e.g., studying for an exam). These points illustrate the fact that children's coping efforts may contribute to or protect against cognitive interference through a variety of pathways that must be considered in future research.

The types of strategies children use to cope with anxiety-provoking situations and their own anxiety responses may lead to cognitive interference via direct and indirect pathways. First, high-anxious children's performance may suffer directly because the types of coping strategies they choose are incompatible with performance on the task at hand. For example, Houston (1977) suggested that coping strategies such as resignation may reduce anxiety but also reduce motivation while others such as avoidant thinking may interfere with task-focused attention. Second, high-anxious children's performance may suffer indirectly because their anxiety-regulation efforts are ineffective, thereby fostering the maintenance and intensification of anxiety.

A growing body of adult-based research suggests that high-anxious individuals do indeed cope in ways that are likely to be ineffective and conflict with task performance. For example, Houston (1977) collected college students' reports of coping strategies used during stressful situations (i.e., a laboratory stressor and a classroom examination). Judges reviewed subjects' reports and identified each subject's primary coping strategy. Subjects in each coping category were compared with those in each of the other categories on self-reported anxiety and changes in heart rate during the stressful task. The distribution of each type of coping strategy across high- and low-anxious groups was also examined. Strategies involving positive cognitive restructuring were generally associated with the smallest increases in heart rate and self-reported anxiety. In contrast, strategies such as worrying or avoidant thinking were associated with the largest increases. Not surprisingly, worry was significantly more prevalent while intellectualizing (i.e., cognitive restructuring) was significantly less prevalent among high- than low-anxious subjects.

Davey, Burgess, and Rashes (1992) reported that scores on the Fear Survey Schedule (Wolpe & Lang, 1964) were positively correlated with the frequency of avoidance coping and negatively correlated with the problem-focused, cognitive restructuring strategy of threat devaluation. They found similar effects for both panic disordered and simple phobic patients compared to normal controls. Similarly, Genest, Bowen, Dudley, and Keegan (1990) reported significant positive correlations between anxiety levels and subjects' reliance on escape-avoidance strategies and distracting cognitions for coping with anxiety. In contrast, they reported significant negative correlations between anxiety and problem-focused strategies. Since avoidant strategies are likely to preempt or debilitate task performance and problem-focused strategies facilitate performance, anxious adults appear to cope in a fashion that is likely to produce considerable interference.

There are currently few studies of the types of coping strategies used by anxious children but the available findings are consistent with studies of anxious adults. For example, Olah, Torestad and Magnusson (1989) reported a significant positive correlation between trait anxiety and escape-avoidance coping responses. In contrast, they found a significant negative correlation between trait anxiety and constructive coping (e.g. direct problem-solving efforts). Similarly, as noted above, Prins' (1986) results suggest that high-anxious children cope more through avoidance than through self-regulatory self-talk. Thus, it appears that the coping strategies of high-anxious children may be ineffective, likely to interfere with task performance, or both. If possible, high-anxious children will completely avoid task performance, but when they cannot escape task demands, they will likely rely on cognitively avoidant strategies. However, there is clearly need for further research in this area.

Application of the information-processing perspective suggests several pathways that may be relevant to understanding high-anxious children's ways of coping with anxiety. As Garber et al. (1991) noted with regard to depression, the regulation of anxiety requires skills at each stage of processing. For our present purposes we will assume that anxious children are capable of accurately encoding the fact that they are anxious. Indeed it seems likely that many anxious children, especially those who report high levels of anxiety sensitivity, are prone to notice anxiety symptoms earlier than most children.

Anxiety symptoms must be interpreted in order to identify their cause, determine whether that cause represents a significant threat and whether one's anxiety responses require regulation. Another judgment of particular relevance to coping concerns the controllability of the feared outcome and, even more importantly, the controllability of one's own anxiety symptoms or responses

(Kendall & Chansky, 1991). For example, if children believe that worrisome thoughts are uncontrollable and that they can do little about the feared outcome, they should be less likely to use problem-focused strategies and more likely to use emotion-focused strategies such as avoidance and distraction (Compas, Malcarne, & Fondacaro, 1988). Given that existing data suggest that high-anxious children believe that fear is difficult to regulate (Prins, 1986), it seems likely that they will hold very different goals than low-anxious children when they proceed to the response access and construction stage. For example, interpreting feared outcomes and anxiety responses as uncontrollable may trigger a goal state directed at escaping from anxiety in the short term rather than at changing the situation in a constructive manner so that anxiety will be reduced in the long term.

Whether or not high- and low-anxious children enter the response access and construction stage with similar goals, this stage may also contribute to coping difficulties. High-anxious children may be unable to access or generate as many problem-focused strategies as low-anxious children because their knowledge of potential coping options is deficient. This seems to be the view of Hill (1972) who argued that test-anxious children do not learn to cope effectively with the demands of performance situations because their parents are excessively demanding, critical and do not provide proper supports. Similarly, Barrett, Rapee, Dadds, and Ryan (in press) recently found that parents of clinically-anxious children appear to selectively reinforce their children for generating and choosing avoidant coping strategies. Thus, high-anxious children may not acquire developmentally-appropriate knowledge of problem-focused coping strategies (Vasey, 1993).

In addition to or instead of being deficient in knowledge, high-anxious children may be poor at accessing or constructing effective coping strategies because of the cognitive interference associated with anxiety. For example, in a study of fifth graders, Covington (1983) found that trait anxiety was negatively correlated with quality of solutions generated, quality of the single best solution, and total number of solutions generated during problem solving. These correlations remained significant even when IQ was partialled out. Similarly, Nottelman and Hill (1977) and Phillips (1980) suggested that high-anxious children's often perseverative, rigid and stereotyped approach to problems indicates that anxiety interferes with the flexible consideration of different problem-solving strategies. Thus, this stage of coping may be viewed simply as one more cognitive task that is disrupted by anxiety. For example, it may leave too little attention free for effective processing of subtle contextual cues signaling which strategies may be most appropriate. However, this does not preclude the reciprocal influence of ineffective coping from further contributing to cognitive interference. This leads to the prediction that children should become less and less able to cope effectively as anxiety increases and produces greater interference with problem-solving ability.

Even if high-anxious children generate the same type of coping strategies as low-anxious children, they may select different types of strategies as the best available solution. This might reflect the operation of differing goals as discussed earlier. However, it might also reflect deficient understanding of which strategies are most likely to be effective. For example, high-anxious children may not adequately understand the potentially subtle contextual cues that signal which strategies are best in a given situation. If so, high-anxious children may have difficulty choosing strategies to match the demands of the situation. Instead, they may choose strategies that are determined primarily by their emotional state rather than by the demands of the specific situation.

High-anxious children may also choose different strategies because their self-efficacy is low for effectively enacting other strategies. Such low self-efficacy can itself reflect distorted thinking or it may reflect genuine deficits in their ability to enact such strategies. Enacting a given coping strategy is also likely to become much more difficult as anxiety responses become stronger. Effective enactment will require more processing resources even if the strategies enacted are the same and are enacted with similar skill. Prins et al. (1994) expressed a similar opinion, noting that other research suggests that coping cognitions may facilitate performance under moderate levels of anxiety but that higher levels of anxiety may disrupt both task performance and performance of coping responses (Prins, 1986).

As a preliminary attempt to localize coping difficulties, we recently conducted a study focused on the response access and construction stage and the response selection stage. This study compared a sample of 12 clinically anxious children to a matched sample of 12 normal children with regard to their knowledge and use of strategies for coping with worrisome thoughts (Vasey, Daleiden, & Williams, 1992; Vasey, Hilliker, Daleiden, & Williams, 1993). Specifically, we evaluated whether or not anxious children are deficient in their ability to access or generate alternative coping responses and whether or not they select different types of strategies than normal children. With regard to both stages of processing we predicted that strategies directed at immediately reducing worry through avoidance and distraction would be over-represented among the strategies of anxious children compared to normal controls. In contrast, strategies requiring prolonged focus on the worrisome outcome, such as problem-solving or cognitive restructuring, were expected to be underrepresented. In addition, we predicted that, compared to controls, anxious children would view worry as more difficult to control in general and have lower self-efficacy regarding their ability to control their own worries.

Subjects heard a series of vignettes describing situations in which fictional children were experiencing unwanted worrisome thoughts regarding a future threat (e.g. potential failure on a test in school the next day). Children's ability to generate coping strategies was assessed by asking them to describe as many ways as possible that the children in the vignettes could help themselves stop worrying. Subsequently, as a means of studying the types of strategies the children selected for their own use, they were asked how they would help themselves stop worrying if they were worried like the children in the stories.

The numbers of distraction, avoidance, and problem-focused strategies produced were converted to proportions of the total number of strategies produced. Contrary to our expectations, anxious and normal children did not differ in the types of strategies they generated for fictional children. In other words, anxious children appear to be as aware of various types of strategies as normal children, and to generate them in similar proportions. However, with regard to the strategies children said they would use themselves, anxious and normal children differed in the predicted manner. Compared to controls, a significantly larger proportion of anxious children's strategies fell in the distraction and avoidance category and a significantly smaller proportion fell in the problem-focused category (Vasey, Daleiden, & Williams, 1992). Children's parents were also asked how their children would cope with worrisome thoughts and these data replicated the pattern of their children's self-reports. In addition, parents described enough strategies to support analysis in a category labeled "failure to cope" which included responses like resignation or giving up. Consistent with Houston's (1977) findings, such strategies were significantly more prevalent among anxious than normal children.

Contrary to expectations, anxious and normal children did not differ with regard to their ratings of the controllability of worrisome thoughts or their self-efficacy for controlling such thoughts. Both groups rated worries as only "a little bit hard" to control in general and stated that they themselves would have little difficulty controlling such thoughts. However, compared to parents of controls, parents of anxious children rated their children as significantly less able to control such thoughts. The reasons for the discrepancy between parent and child reports are unclear. However, Kendall and Chansky (1991) also reported that anxious children overestimated their ability to cope in comparison to parent ratings. These authors suggested that anxious children's ratings for themselves may reflect an attempt to "fake good" to gain the examiner's approval. Of course, it may also be that anxious children hold inaccurate beliefs regarding their ability to cope with worrisome thoughts. Future research should examine children's beliefs about the controllability of worrisome thoughts as well as other kinds of anxiety responses in greater detail (e.g., distinguishing between controllability and self-efficacy dimensions).

In sum, our preliminary results suggest that anxious children's characteristic coping pattern is related to the strategy choices they make rather than a lack of knowledge or inability to generate effective strategies. They tend to choose strategies that offer immediate relief from anxiety but that also directly interfere with task-focused attention and problem-focused coping efforts that might otherwise enhance performance and reduce anxiety in the long term. Such a pattern is consistent with a two-factor theory account of worry in which worrisome thoughts are associated with increased negative arousal and responses such as distraction, which provide immediate relief, are negatively reinforced. Of course, although anxious children appear to possess adequate knowledge of coping strategies, this does not mean that they can access or construct such strategies adequately when they are actually anxious. Our study assessed their knowledge under optimal conditions and future studies should take care to test children's ability to generate strategies when they are anxious.

SUMMARY AND CONCLUSIONS

Future research may benefit from adopting a broad perspective on the phenomenon of cognitive interference. This approach promotes consideration of disruption in multiple domains of performance (Sarason et al., 1995), as well as multiple pathways to the production of interference. The potential for controlled, strategically enacted cognitions in addition to unintentional, uncontrollable, intrusive thoughts to contribute to cognitive interference merits further investigation. Exploration of the reciprocal relationship between anxious emotion and cognitive interference, and the role of emotional self-regulation in mediating cognitive interference, are vital to a fuller understanding of this phenomenon. The information-processing model elaborated in this chapter may serve as a framework that fosters greater clarity and integration of multiple processes within this broad conceptualization.

In addition to this broad outlook, future research may benefit most from a more differentiated perspective concerning theoretically-relevant constructs. The information-processing approach points to new directions for specifying component processes within the general constructs of attention and coping. Further investigation of the relationship between attention and cognitive interference needs to examine the conditions that exacerbate and minimize high anxious children's attentional bias toward threat and low anxious children's bias away from threat, as well as the role that selective attentional processes may play in emotional self-regulation. Future studies of coping should consider whether anxious children are deficient in their ability to access or construct appropriate coping strategies, tend to select maladaptive strategies, and/or lack the necessary skills to implement effective strategies. Finally, future theoretical and empirical work is needed to elaborate and examine the role of other processes, such as memory, interpretation, and goal clarification, in producing cognitive interference and emotional dysregulation.

REFERENCES

Bargh, J. A. (1989). Conditional automaticity: Varieties of automatic influence in social perception and cognition. In J. S. Uleman & J. A. Bargh (Eds.), *Unintended thought* (pp. 3–51). New York: Guilford.

Barlow, D. A. (1988). *Anxiety and its disorders: The nature and treatment of anxiety and panic.* New York: Guilford.

Barrett, P. M., Rapee, R. M., Dadds, M. M., & Ryan, S. M. (in press). Family of cognitive style in anxious and aggressive children: Threat bias and the FEAR effect. *Journal of Abnormal Child Psychology.*

Beck, A. T., & Emery, G. (1985). *Anxiety disorders and phobias: A cognitive perspective.* New York: Basic Books.

Bugental, D. B. (1992). Affective and cognitive processes within threat-oriented family systems. In I. E. Sigel, J. Goodnow, & A. McGillicudy-deLisi (Eds.), *Parental belief systems: The psychological consequences for children* (pp. 219–248). Hillsdale, NJ: Lawrence Erlbaum Associates.

Compas, B. E., Malcarne, V. L., & Fondacaro, K. M. (1988). Coping with stressful events in older children and young adolescents. *Journal of Consulting and Clinical Psychology, 56,* 405–411.

Covington, M. V. (1986). Anatomy of failure-induced anxiety: The role of cognitive mediators. In R. Schwarzer (Ed.), *Self-related cognitions in anxiety and motivation* (pp. 247–263). Hillsdale, NJ: Lawrence Erlbaum Associates.

Cradock, C., Cotler, S., & Jason, L. A. (1978). Primary prevention: Immunization of children for speech anxiety. *Cognitive Therapy and Research, 2,* 389–396.

Crick, N. R., & Dodge, K. A. (1994). A review and reformulation of social information-processing mechanisms in children's social adjustment. *Psychological Bulletin, 115,* 74–101.

Davey, G. C. L. (1994). Pathological worrying as exacerbated problem-solving. In G. Davey & F. Tallis (Eds.), *Worrying: Perspectives on theory, assessment and treatment* (pp. 35–59). Chichester, England: Wiley.

Davey, G. C. L., Burgess, I., & Rashes, R. (1992). *Coping strategies and phobias: The relationship between fears, phobias, and methods of coping with stressors.* Submitted for publication.

Denney, D. R. (1975). The effects of exemplary and cognitive models on children's interrogative strategies. *Journal of Experimental Child Psychology, 19,* 476–488.

Derryberry, D., & Tucker, D. M. (1994). Motivating the focus of attention. In P. M. Niedenthal & K. Shinobu (Eds.), *The heart's eye: Emotional influences in perception and attention* (pp. 167–196). San Diego: Academic Press

Dodge, K. A. (1991). Emotion and social information-processing. In J. Garber & K. A. Dodge (Eds.), *The development of emotion regulation and dysregulation* (pp. 159–181). Cambridge, England: Cambridge University Press.

Dusek, J. B. (1980). The development of test anxiety in children. In I. G. Sarason (Ed.), *Test anxiety: Theory, research and application* (pp. 87–110). Hillsdale, NJ: Lawrence Erlbaum Associates.

Dusek, J. B., Kermis, M. D., & Mergler, N. L. (1975). Information-processing in low- and high-test-anxious children as a function of grade level and verbal labeling. *Developmental Psychology, 11,* 651–652.

Eysenck, M. W. (1988). Anxiety and attention. *Anxiety Research, 1,* 9–15.

Eysenck, M. W., & Calvo, M. G. (1992). Anxiety and performance: The processing efficiency theory. *Cognition and Emotion, 6,* 409–434.

Fox, J. E., & Houston, B. K. (1981). Efficacy of self-instructional training for reducing children's anxiety in an evaluative situation. *Behaviour Research and Therapy, 19,* 509–515.

Garber, J., Braafladt, N., & Zeman, N. (1991). The regulation of sad affect: An information-processing perspective. In J. Garber & K. A. Dodge (Eds.), *The development of emotion regulation and dysregulation* (pp. 208–240). Cambridge, England: Cambridge University Press.

Genest, M., Bowen, R. C, Dudley, J., & Keegan, D. (1990). Assessment of strategies for coping with anxiety: Preliminary investigations. *Journal of Anxiety Disorders, 4,* 1–14.

Hill, K. T. (1972). Anxiety in the evaluative context. In W. W. Hartup (Ed.), *The young child* (Vol. 2, pp. 225–263). Washington, DC: National Association for the Education of Young Children.

Houston, B. K. (1977). Dispositional anxiety and the effectiveness of cognitive coping strategies in stressful laboratory and classroom situations. In C. D. Spielberger & I. G. Sarason (Eds.), *Stress and anxiety* (Vol. 4, pp. 205–226). New York: Wiley.

Johnson, R. L., and Glass, C. R. (1989). Heterosocial anxiety and direction of attention in high school boys. *Cognitive Therapy and Research, 13,* 509–526.

Kanfer, F. H., & Hagerman, S. M. (1985). Behavior therapy and the information-processing paradigm. In S. Reiss & R. R. Bootzin (Eds.), *Theoretical issues in behavior therapy* (pp. 3–33). New York: Academic Press.

Kanfer, F. H., Karoly, P., & Newman, A. (1975). Reduction of children's fear of the dark by competence-related and situational threat-related verbal cues. *Journal of Consulting and Clinical Psychology, 43,* 251–258.

Kendall, P. C., & Chansky, T. E. (1991). Considering cognition in anxiety-disordered children. *Journal of Anxiety Disorders, 5,* 167–185.

Kendall, P. C., & Ronan, K. D. (1990). Assessment of children's anxieties, fears, and phobias: Cognitive-behavioral models and methods. In C. R. Reynolds & R. W. Kamphaus (Eds.), *Handbook of psychological and educational assessment of children: Vol. 2. Personality, behavior, and context* (pp. 223–244). New York: Guilford.

Krohne, H. W. (1980). Parental child-rearing behavior and the development of anxiety and coping strategies. In I. G. Sarason & C. D. Spielberger (Eds.), *Stress and anxiety* (Vol. 7, pp. 233–245). Washington: Hemisphere.

Krohne, H. W., & Rogner, J. (1982). Repression-sensitization as a central construct in coping research. In H. W. Krohne & L. Laux (Eds.), *Achievement, stress, and anxiety* (pp. 167–194). Washington, DC: Hemisphere.

Leal, L. L., Baxter, E. G., Martin, J., & Marx, R. W. (1981). Cognitive modification and systematic desensitization with test anxious high school students. *Journal of Counseling Psychology, 28,* 525–528.

Lepore, S. J., & Kliewer, W. (1989, August). *Monitoring and blunting: Validation of a coping measure for children.* Poster presented at the 97th Annual Convention of the American Psychological Association, New Orleans, LA.

Logan, A. C., & Goetsch, V. L. (1993). Attention to external threat cues in anxiety states. *Clinical Psychology Review, 13,* 541–559.

MacLeod, C., & Mathews, A. M. (1988). Anxiety and the allocation of attention to threat. *Quarterly Journal of Experimental Psychology, 40,* 653–670.

MacLeod, C., & Mathews, A. M. (1991). Cognitive-experimental approaches to the emotional disorders. In P. R. Martin (Ed.), *Handbook of behavior therapy and psychological science: An integrative approach* (pp. 116–150). New York: Pergamon.

MacLeod, C., Mathews, A., & Tata, P. (1986). Attentional bias in emotional disorders. *Journal of Abnormal Psychology, 95,* 15–20.

MacLeod, C., & Rutherford, E. M. (1992). Anxiety and the selective processing of emotional information: Mediating roles of awareness, trait and state variables, and personal relevance of stimulus materials. *Behaviour Research and Therapy, 30,* 479–491.

Martin, M., Horder, P., & Jones, G. V. (1992). Integral bias in naming of phobia-related words. *Cognition and Emotion, 6,* 479–486.

Mathews, A. (1990). Why worry? The cognitive function of anxiety. *Behaviour Research and Therapy, 28,* 455–468.

Mathews, A., & MacLeod, C. (1985). Selective processing of threat cues in anxiety states. *Behaviour Research and Therapy, 23,* 563–569.

Mathews, A., & MacLeod, C. (1994). Cognitive approaches to emotion and emotional disorders. *Annual Review of Psychology, 45,* 25–50.

Miller, S. M. (1990). To see or not to see: Cognitive informational styles in the coping process. In M. Rosenbaum (Ed.), *Learned resourcefulness: On coping skills, self-regulation, and adaptive behavior* (pp. 95–126). New York: Springer.

Nottelmann, E. D., & Hill, K. T. (1977). Test anxiety and off-task behavior in evaluative situations. *Child Development, 48,* 225–231.

Olah, A., Torestad, B., & Magnusson, D. (1989). Coping behaviors in relation to frequency and intensity of anxiety-provoking situations. *Perceptual and Motor Skills, 69*, 935–943.
Phillips, B. N. (1980). *School stress and anxiety: Theory, research and intervention*. New York: Human Sciences Press.
Prins, P. J. (1986). Children's self speech and self-regulation during a fear-provoking behavioral test. *Behaviour, Research and Therapy, 24*, 181–191.
Prins, P. J., Groot, M. J., & Hanewald, G. J. (1995). Cognitions in test-anxious children: The role of on-task and coping cognitions reconsidered. *Journal of Consulting and Clinical Psychology, 62*, 404–409.
Sarason, I. G. (1988). Anxiety, self-preoccupation and attention. *Anxiety Research: An International Journal, 1*, 3–8.
Sarason, I. G., Sarason, B. R., & Pierce, G. R. (1995). Cognitive interference: At the intelligence-personality crossroads. In S. Saklofske & M. Zeidner (Eds.), *International handbook of personality and intelligence* (pp. 285–296). New York: Plenum.
Silverman, W. K., Fleisig, W., Rabian, B., & Peterson, R. A. (1991). Childhood anxiety sensitivity index. *Journal of Clinical Child Psychology, 20*, 162–168.
Spielberger, C. D. (1973). *Manual for the State-Trait Anxiety Inventory for Children*. Palo Alto, CA: Consulting Psychologists Press.
Stevens, R., & Phil, R. O. (1983). Learning to cope with school: A study of the effects of a coping skill training program with test-vulnerable 7th-grade students. *Cognitive Therapy and Research, 7*, 155–158.
Vasey, M. W. (1993). Development and cognition in childhood anxiety: The example of worry. In T. H. Ollendick & R. J. Prinz (Eds.), *Advances in clinical child psychology* (Vol. 15, pp. 1–39). New York: Plenum Press.
Vasey, M. W., & Borkovec, T. D. (1992). A catastrophizing assessment of chronic worry. *Cognitive Therapy and Research, 16*, 505–520.
Vasey, M. W., Daleiden, E. L., & Williams, L. L. (1992, November). *Coping with worrisome thoughts: Strategies of anxiety-disordered and normal children*. Poster presented at the twenty-sixth annual convention of the Association for the Advancement of Behavior Therapy, Boston.
Vasey, M. W., Daleiden, E. L., Williams, L. L., & Brown, L. (1995). Biased attention in childhood anxiety disorders: A preliminary study. *Journal of Abnormal Child Psychology, 23*, 267–279.
Vasey, M. W., El-Hag, N., & Daleiden, E. L. (in press). Information-processing biases in childhood anxiety: Distinctive patterns of selective attention in high- and low-anxious children. *Child Development*.
Vasey, M. W., Hilliker, D., Williams, L. L., & Daleiden, E. L. (1993, March). *The regulation of worrisome thoughts in anxiety-disordered and normal children: Parental perspectives*. Poster presented at the biennial meeting of the Society for Research in Child Development, New Orleans.
Watts, F. N., McKenna, F. P., Sharrock, R., & Trezise, L. (1986). Colour naming of phobia-related words. *British Journal of Psychology, 77*, 97–108.
Wechsler, D. (1974). *Manual for the Wechsler Intelligence Scale for Children - Revised*. New York: The Psychological Corporation.
Wigfield, A., & Eccles, J. S. (1990). Test anxiety in the school setting. In M. Lewis & S. M. Miller (Eds.), *Handbook of developmental psychopathology* (pp. 237–250). New York: Plenum.
Williams, J. M. G., Watts, F. N., MacLeod, C., & Mathews, A. (1988) *Cognitive psychology and the emotional disorders*. New York: Wiley.
Wine, J. D. (1982). Evaluation anxiety: A cognitive-attentional construct. In H. W. Krohne & L. Laux (Eds.), *Achievement, stress, and anxiety* (pp. 207–219). Washington: McGraw-Hill.
Wolpe, J., & Lang, P. J. (1964). A fear survey schedule for use in behaviour therapy. *Behaviour Research and Therapy, 2*, 27.
Zatz, S., & Chassin, L. (1983). Cognitions in test-anxious children. *Journal of Consulting and Clinical Psychology, 51*, 526–534.
Zatz, S., & Chassin, L. (1985). Cognitions in test-anxious children under naturalistic test-taking conditions. *Journal of Consulting and Clinical Psychology, 53*, 393–401.

CHAPTER

7

DOMAINS OF COGNITIVE INTERFERENCE

Irwin G. Sarason
University of Washington

Gregory R. Pierce
Hamilton College

Barbara R. Sarason
University of Washington

Cognitive interference refers to intrusive thoughts—thoughts that are unwanted, undesirable, and perhaps disturbing. People who experience cognitive interference often describe themselves as troubled and unhappy about their inability to become absorbed in significant aspects of their lives and their performance level may be detrimentally affected by the intrusions. Someone ridden with obsessive thoughts may show impaired performance and may be puzzled and concerned about why the unwanted thoughts occur. People who are unduly worried about what other people think about them may have difficulty feeling comfortable in social situations. Although intrusive thoughts can occur in almost any kind of situation, the undesirable effects of these thoughts have perhaps been studied most intensively in relation to the performance of tasks. Cognitive interference gets in the way of effective performance because it is the opposite of cognitive accessibility. It diminishes attention to the task the individual is performing (Sarason, Sarason, Keefe, Hayes, & Shearin, 1986). Researchers who study cognitive interference face the challenge of discriminating between on- and off-task thoughts—thoughts which reflects task involvement and are directed towards task completion and thoughts which are not (Alting & Markham, 1993).

Thoughts about off-task matters and the general wandering of attention from the task, as well as worries and preoccupations about the task, contribute to performance deficits. For instance, Broadbent and his coworkers focused attention on the negative effects of general absentmindedness, forgetfulness, and the wandering of thoughts while performing a task (Broadbent, Cooper, FitzGerald,

& Parkes, 1982). These researchers found that although absentmindedness appears to be a stable personality characteristic, its effects on performance are seen primarily under stressful conditions. Thus, cognitive intrusions appear to be products of both situational conditions and personality characteristics (Prins, Groot, & Hanewald, 1994). A number of questions, heretofore barely touched upon in the literature, require inquiry and study. These questions include: What are the best ways to get information about interfering thoughts? What are the experiential histories of people who differ in cognitive interference? What role does cognitive interference play in the human information-processing system? What circumstances elicit intrusive thinking?

In the past, cognitive interference was usually approached in one of two ways: (1) as a product of various types of situational and environmental factors (for example, a mother worried about her child's high temperature), or (2) as something that occurs in response to internal processes (for example, obsessive ruminations). An interactional approach to cognitive interference tended to be neglected. From this perspective, cognitive interference is a joint product of exposure to a challenging or stressful situation and vulnerability to self-oriented cognitions (for example, worries, preoccupations, and concerns). Three important issues emerge from an interactional perspective: (1) defining classes of cognitions that heighten vulnerability to interference, (2) identifying situations that bring these cognitions above threshold, and (3) specifying relevant vulnerability factors. Until recently very little was known about the causes of cognitive interference and the mechanisms by which it exerts its influence. The research agenda now needs to deal with these questions: What are the thoughts that cause cognitive interference? What is doing the interfering? What is the process by which cognitive interference takes place?

An interactional approach suggests that when it occurs interference lowers ability to function effectively and heightens personal preoccupation. Ability is usually inferred from how well people perform on certain kinds of tasks. However, poor performance does not necessarily mean low ability. Poor performance could be due to the fact that the individual is upset, thinking about something else, or unmotivated. All of these circumstances can contribute to cognitive interference. Performance can be thought of as being a partial product of personality because it may stimulate personal preoccupations that interfere with attention to the task at hand. Personality can facilitate performance (for example, through high motivation and the ability to become absorbed in tasks) but it can also debilitate it (for example, through worrying about the consequences of failure and being uncooperative with the tester) (I. Sarason, Sarason, & Pierce, 1995).

One might look at the problem of cognitive interference as the loss of control over one's thoughts. This loss of control might be caused by highly valenced thoughts (worries, ambitions) that take precedence over well-focused task involvement. Each person has a hierarchy of needs and values that plays a directive role over behavior—even if that role turns out to be self-defeating. A challenge for the future is the achievement of a better understanding of the loss of control process and finding ways to help people focus their attention on tasks that are important to them.

Another way of approaching cognitive interference is in terms of peremptory thoughts. Peremptory thoughts tend to dominate an individual's thinking and direct her or his behavior. People whose thoughts are dominated by ideas such as "I'm no good," and "People don't like me," have peremptory thoughts related to low self-esteem. Other cognitive themes can also have a peremptory quality. Peremptory thoughts may take on a life of their own and have maladaptive consequences (for example, daydreams that are not task relevant can lead to poor performance). While we do not know whether cognitive interference is directly or indirectly associated with peremptory thinking, it is known that peremptory thought can play a controlling role in a person's life (Katakis, 1990). The role of peremptory thinking is perhaps most evident in instances of clearly abnormal behavior (for example, the fears of the homebound agoraphobic individual and the commanding voices heard by someone who is psychotic). Kazdin (1990) found uncontrollable automatic thoughts to play an important role in childhood depression and Clark (1992) has reported similar results for depressed adults.

Sometimes peremptory thinking can be beneficial to performance as well as adjustment. A scientist who cannot let go of an intriguing question and a composer in pursuit of just the right melody are preoccupied, but their preoccupations are (a) related to events and phenomena outside themselves, and (b) have the potential of contributing to personal happiness and the social good. However, self-preoccupations (for example, worry over performance and social evaluation) may keep an individual from becoming involved in positive ways in important aspects of the worlds of work and social relationships.

Personal schemas and peremptory thoughts play important roles in information processing and behavioral outcomes. The school performance of students and parents' child-rearing practices are products of their schemas of themselves and what it is to be a student or parent. If students overly value success in school their performance might actually suffer and if parents overly value the need for their children to succeed the children's schemas and behavior might be influenced in a negative manner. We need a fuller, more well-rounded picture of how self-preoccupations relate to personal schemas and the situations that activate the schemas.

One way in which peremptory and self-preoccupying thoughts exert their influence is through individuals' goal-setting and motivations. Dweck (1986, 1989) has distinguished between learning-goal and performance-goal orientations. A learning-goal orientation emphasizes the individual's desire to learn and master skills while a performance-goal orientation directs the person's attention to success and worry about failure to achieve goals. Dweck found that differences in goal orientation play roles in both functional and dysfunctional performance. Hoffmann (1992) found that students with performance-goal orientations have more cognitive interference and poorer performance than students with learning-goal orientations.

A first step in studying cognitive interference is its assessment and the specification of conditions that evoke it. Research on stress, particularly the stress of being evaluated, provides a productive context for the study of intrusive cognitions and we turn now to this topic.

STRESS, ANXIETY, AND COGNITIVE INTERFERENCE

Stress has been thought of as a call for action, a person's recognition of the need to do something about a given state of affairs (Sarason, 1984). Calls for action occur in response to situational challenges and threats that lead to either task-relevant or task-irrelevant cognitions. Task-relevant cognitions are likely where a situation or task has been self-selected as a challenge (for example, this would be the case with the mountain climber who seeks adventure). When the call for action is imposed on the individual by either situational demands and constraints or preoccupying goals or demands (for example, students feeling that getting less than an A represents failure) task-irrelevant cognitions are more likely to come to the fore.

The widely studied topic of test anxiety can be approached in terms of individual differences in response to calls for action. Wine (1982) proposed an attentional interpretation of test anxiety according to which people at high and low levels of test anxiety differ in the types of thoughts their attention is directed to in the face of an evaluative stressor. Consistent with this analysis, Ganzer (1968) found that, while performing on an intellective task, subjects with high test anxiety made many more irrelevant comments than did subjects with low test anxiety. A high percentage of these comments were self-deprecatory. Other researchers have found that persons with high test anxiety are more likely than those with low test anxiety to feel less confident in making perceptual judgments (Meunier & Rule, 1967) and set lower levels of aspiration for themselves (Trapp & Kausler, 1958).

There is considerable evidence that the test-anxious person experiences self-preoccupying worry, insecurity, and self-doubt in evaluative situations. It has been argued that these internal distractors lessen attention to the task at hand and contribute to relatively poor performance (Sarason, 1980). From this perspective, anxiety is to a significant extent a problem of intrusive, interfering thoughts that diminish attention to an efficient, rewarding execution of the task at hand. Under neutral conditions, high and low test-anxious subjects often perform comparably, but when an evaluative component is introduced a flag indicating danger goes up for those who are prone to test anxiety. For them, the situation becomes personally threatening.

There usually is more to test anxiety than a history of failure experiences. Test-anxious people process their objective successes and failures in distinctive ways, and their anxiety is related closely to how they, and significant others in their lives, evaluate their test-taking experience. Every teacher can think of bright, successful students who, contrary to what one would expect, spend inordinate amounts of time worrying about whether they can meet the next academic challenge they must face. Proneness to self-preoccupation and, most specifically, to worry over evaluation is a powerful component of what is referred to as test anxiety.

A major development in research on the cognitive view of anxiety has been its application to therapeutic situations. Beck has developed one of the most influential cognitive therapies (Beck & Emery, 1986). He believes that the core psychological problem in anxiety disorders is a vulnerability growing out of the individual's tendency to devalue his or her problem-solving ability as well as to exaggerate the degree of threat in a problematic situation. The anxious individual perceives many threats to social relationships, freedom and self-identity. From this perspective, self-preoccupying thoughts about these perceptions mediate the relationship between eliciting events, on the one hand, and behavioral and physiological response patterns, on the other.

Beck's theory of cognitive therapy argues that each of us has an inner voice. When that voice interferes with our ability to function adequately, the unproductive thoughts must be replaced by productive ones. By correcting thinking errors and having patients work on pertinent homework assignments, they can develop not only improved ways of thinking but also more effective, less anxiety-producing behaviors.

ASSESSING COGNITIVE INTERFERENCE

Although results of research on test anxiety are consistent with cognitive interference as an explanatory mechanism, it would be useful to assess as directly as possible the cognitive interference people experience on particular tasks. Various assessment strategies have been used to obtain information about thoughts that precede, accompany, or follow performance. Cognitive assessment can be carried out in a variety of ways, but most methods have in common a reliance on self-report of thoughts. Pertinent methods include think-aloud procedures, retrospective reports of thoughts in particular situations and posttask questionnaires (I. Sarason, Sarason, & Pierce, 1990). Each of these methods has advantages and disadvantages and requires the subjects' cooperation in giving self-reports regarding cognitive activity.

We have developed two instruments to assess cognitive interference. One provides an index of intrusive thinking in a specific situation. This might be regarded as a state measure of cognitive interference. The other is an assessment of the general tendency to experience preoccupying thoughts. This might be regarded as a trait measure. The Cognitive Interference Questionnaire (CIQ) (Sarason & Stoops, 1978; I. Sarason, Sarason, Keefe, Hayes, & Shearin, 1986) was designed to measure, following performance on a task, the degree to which people experienced various types of thoughts while working on it, and the degree to which these thoughts are viewed as interfering with concentration. The CIQ consists of 22 items, the first 21 of which are rated for frequency of occurrence of particular types of thoughts. Each type of thought is rated on a 5-point scale from 1 (Never) to 5 (Very often). The first 10 items provide postperformance reports of the frequency of occurrence of task-related thoughts that intruded while working on the task (for example, worrying over the adequacy of one's performance). Eleven additional items refer to thoughts whose contents do not refer to the task (for example, thinking about other activities). The final item provides a global rating on a 7-point scale of the degree of mind-wandering experiences while working on the task. Table 7.1 presents the CIQ items together with mean values for 712 undergraduates.

Sarason and Stoops (1978) used the CIQ in a study in which college students who differed in test anxiety performed on a series of tasks presented to them as measures of intelligence. The dependent variables were their performance, estimates they made of how long they had worked on the tasks, and postperformance reports on the CIQ of task-relevant and task-irrelevant thoughts that passed through their minds during performance. Sarason and Stoops found that highly test-anxious subjects under achievement-orienting conditions reported high levels of interfering thoughts, judged the time they spent on the tasks to be longer than the other subjects, and performed at relatively low levels.

I. Sarason et al. (1986) verified by factor analysis that the CIQ measures two types of thoughts, task-oriented worries and off-task thoughts. They found that individuals who describe their customary reactions to testing situations in terms of worry and arousal report high levels of interfering cognitive activity while working on demanding tasks. They also found that the CIQ (particularly task-relevant interfering thoughts) correlated significantly with performance on intellective tasks administered under test-like conditions. Blankenstein, Toner, and Flett (1989) reported that high test-anxious students had more interfering thoughts and mind-wandering while performing on a task than did low test-anxious students. High test-anxious students had especially high scores on CIQ items dealing with self-deprecatory and worry-laden thoughts. These researchers believe that attention to self and self-involvement are key features of anxiety states. The available evidence is consistent with theories that describe the active ingredients of test-anxiety as self-preoccupying thoughts and calls for attention to self and self-involvement as key features of anxiety states (Sarason, 1978, 1980; Wine, 1982).

The Thought Occurrence Questionnaire (TOQ) (Sarason et al., 1986) was designed as an indicator of the habitual tendency to have extraneous thoughts

TABLE 7.1
Cognitive Interference Questionnaire Items and Mean Values for Undergraduates

INSTRUCTIONS: This questionnaire concerns the kinds of thoughts that go through people's heads at particular times, for example, while they are working on a task. The following is a list of thoughts, some which you might have had *while doing the task on which you have just worked.* Please indicate approximately how often each thought occurred to you while working on it by placing the appropriate number in the blank provided to the left of each question.

1 = Never
2 = Once
3 = A few times
4 = Often
5 = Very often

			Mean
__	1.	I thought about how poorly I was doing.	1.44
__	2.	I thought about what the experimenter would think of me.	2.33
__	3.	I thought about how I should work more carefully.	2.03
__	4.	I thought about how much time I had left.	1.74
__	5.	I thought about how others have done on this task.	1.59
__	6.	I thought about the difficulty of the problems.	1.82
__	7.	I thought about my level of ability.	1.92
__	8.	I thought about the purpose of the experiment.	3.08
__	9.	I thought about how I would feel if I were told how I performed.	1.61
__	10.	I thought about how often I got confused.	1.67
__	11.	I thought about other activities (for example, assignments, work).	2.07
__	12.	I thought about members of my family.	2.08
__	13.	I thought about friends.	1.93
__	14.	I thought about something that made me feel guilty.	1.34
__	15.	I thought about personal worries.	1.85
__	16.	I thought about something that made me feel tense.	1.67
__	17.	I thought about something that made me feel angry.	1.28
__	18.	I thought about something that happened earlier today.	1.60
__	19.	I thought about something that happened in the recent past (last few days, but not today).	1.64
__	20.	I thought about something that happened in the distant past.	1.51
__	21.	I thought about something that might happen in the future.	1.99

Please circle the number on the following scale which best represents the degree to which you felt your mind wandered *during the task you have just completed.*

Not at all 1 2 3 4 5 6 7 Very much	2.86

From Sarason, Sarason, Keefe, Hayes, and Shearin (1986, p. 226).

in various types of situations. Construction of the TOQ was based on the idea that people who are generally able to maintain a task focus should be better able than those who are less well focused to meet the demands of a particular assigned task. The 28 items of the TOQ, rated on the same 5-point scale used for the CIQ, provide an index of individuals' general or habitual tendency to misappropriate attention off-task. Table 7.2 presents the TOQ items together with mean values for a large group of college students. Factor analytic studies

TABLE 7.2
Thought Occurrence Questionnaire Items and Mean Values for Undergraduates

INSTRUCTIONS: This questionnaire concerns the kind of thoughts that go through people's heads when they have to concentrate on something, such as working, reading directions, or reading a book. The following is a list of thoughts, which, in your past experience, you may have had while working on various types of tasks. *Please estimate how often each thought has occurred to you by placing the appropriate letter to the left of each item.*

1 = Never
2 = Once
3 = A few times
4 = Often
5 = Very often

			Mean
__	1.	I think about how poorly I am doing.	2.53
__	2.	I think about what someone will think of me.	2.74
__	3.	I think about how I should be more careful.	2.73
__	4.	I think about how well others can do on what I am tying to do.	2.63
__	5.	I think about how difficult what I am doing is.	2.74
__	6.	I think about my level of ability	3.00
__	7.	I think about the purpose of what I am doing.	3.15
__	8.	I think about how I would feel if I were told how I performed.	2.39
__	9.	I think about how often I get confused.	2.08
__	10.	I think about other activities (for example, assignments, work)	3.05
__	11.	I think about members of my family.	2.48
__	12.	I think about friends.	2.85
__	13.	I think about something that makes me feel guilty.	1.92
__	14.	I think about personal worries.	2.81
__	15.	I think about something that makes me feel tense.	2.19
__	16.	I think about something that makes me feel angry.	1.98
__	17.	I think about something that happened earlier in the day.	2.81
__	18.	I think about something that happened in the recent past (for example, in the last few days).	2.69
__	19.	I think about something that happened in the distant past.	2.14
__	20.	I think about something that might happen in the future.	2.82
__	21.	I think about stopping.	2.42
__	22.	I think about how unhappy I am.	1.84
__	23.	I think about how hard it is.	2.54
__	24.	I think about how I can't stand it anymore.	2.02
__	25.	I think about quitting.	2.01
__	26.	I think about running away.	1.44
__	27.	I think about taking something (e.g., pills, a drink) to make it easier.	1.54
__	28.	I think about going to bed/or to sleep.	2.84

From Sarason, Sarason, Keefe, Hayes, and Shearin (1986, p. 226).

have revealed three factors on the TOQ, items relating to worries, social relationships, and escapist thoughts. Research employing this instrument has demonstrated a clear link between the general disposition to experience high levels of interfering thoughts and subpar performance on specific tasks. Those individuals who on the TOQ describe themselves as customarily being worriers and as having a high level of task-irrelevant thoughts, show these tendencies in their CIQ reports of cognitive activities after performance on complex intellective tasks. However, all types of thoughts do not have the same effects. Task-related worries as measured by the CIQ ("I thought about how poorly I was doing") are more predictive of performance than are task-irrelevant thoughts ("I thought about a friend"). This is consistent with other evidence demonstrating that generalized tendencies to have self-deprecatory thoughts and task-related worries are negatively related to task performance under test-like conditions and to cognitive interference (Bruch, Kaflowitz, & Kuethe, 1986; Sarason, 1984). Hunsley (1987), using the CIQ, found this relationship to be particularly strong for performance on mathematics' tasks.

The available evidence provides support for the idea that cognitive interference has negative consequences for task performance; in addition, these intrusive cognitions appear, in part, to stem from traitlike characteristics and to interact with conditions associated with performance. Instruments such as the TOQ might prove to be practically useful in identifying individuals who will later be at high risk for experiencing debilitating preoccupations when confronting the challenges posed by particular situations. However, the occurrence of intrusive thoughts might be influenced by situational parameters? There is evidence suggesting that cognitive interference can be increased by emphasizing the evaluative aspects of the performance situation (Hammermaster, 1989; Sarason, Sarason, & Shearin, 1986).

While there is much evidence that self-deprecation, worry, and self-preoccupation with being evaluated play significant roles in anxiety and performance, other classes of cognition might also play important roles. Galassi, Frierson, and Sharer (1981) found that in an academic performance situation the most frequently reported thoughts of anxious students concerned escaping from the situation. These researchers found little evidence of the devaluing cognitions and worry about evaluation usually attributed to highly test-anxious persons. They speculated that anxiety-lowering interventions may be effective, not so much by directly increasing performance, but by making the test-taking experience less aversive. Geen (1987) found that highly test-anxious subjects were less likely to persist at an anagrams task than were other subjects. These findings raise the possibility that thoughts related to escaping or avoiding an evaluational situation may interfere with attention to the task confronting the individual. Although Mandler and Sarason (1952) suggested this possibility years ago, Geen noted that it has rarely been studied.

We recently performed an experiment in which scores on the TOQ were related to persistence on an assigned task. A series of multiple regressions revealed that escapist thoughts were highly significant predictors of task persistence. This was true even after account was taken of the contribution of scores on the Worry scale of the TOQ. Escapist thoughts as predictors of performance held, not only for task persistence, but for cognitive interference (CIQ) posttask self-reports as well. Why did escapist thoughts make an independent contribution to the prediction of task persistence and cognitive interference? Are escapist thoughts merely products or correlates of fear and worry? Or might they operate through another channel? Escapist thoughts might indicate low frustration tolerance or a tendency to rebel against the requirement to perform. Might escapist thoughts precede anxiety? We do not have the answers to these important questions. However, from this study, it would seem that escapist thoughts are as self-defeating as fears and worries. We now have to find out why people want to escape a situation. Are escapist thoughts expressions of wish fulfillment? If escapist cognitions are a factor in cognitive interference, they need to be assessed and represented in theories that deal with the determinants of performance. The findings reviewed here suggest the need to broaden the concept of cognitive interference to include thoughts of escape and avoidance as well as fear and worry.

Another issue requiring attention concerns the active ingredients of cognitive interference. Because the concept of cognitive interference was originally rooted in research on test anxiety, it is not surprising that many researchers have been primarily interested in intrusive thoughts associated with anxiety. In other words, investigators have devoted the most attention to thoughts that appear to lead to anxiety, such as "I'm going to fail" and "I'm no good at this task." This focus on anxiety-laden thoughts makes intuitive sense and has served to define an important class of cognitions that contribute to poor performance. Yet, we still know little about the mechanisms by which cognitive interference leads to performance deficits. In fact, we do not know whether the cognitions per se or the anxiety associated with them account for problems in task performance. It may be that each aspect of cognitive interference—cognitive and affective—has important behavioral implications. Further research is needed to disentangle the contributions of intrusive thoughts and their associated affective components.

COGNITIVE INTERFERENCE IN SOCIAL SITUATIONS

Just as rarely discussed escapist thoughts may play an important role in cognitive interference and performance, so also might cognitive interference play an important role in situations other than the widely-studied intellective performance tasks. In addition to extending the domain of the content of cognitive interference, the relationship of intrusive thoughts to other aspects of life besides intellective tasks needs to be better understood. For example, what role do intrusive thoughts play in social interactions? While less well specified than concepts like intelligence and performance, social adjustment seems equally central to the lives of people. Cognitive interference can cause attentional dysfunction in a variety of situations, not just intellective ones. For example, many individuals report feeling that they are often unable to enjoy their contacts with others (friends, potential friends) because they spend too much time thinking about how they are affecting the other person and how the other person might be evaluating them.

The authors recently carried out a study of the role of family factors in college students' cognitive interference and found that the quality of parents' relationships with each other was predictive of how much anxiety the student experienced while working on a performance task. Students whose parents had conflictive relationships with each other experienced more cognitive interference than did students whose parents had harmonious relationships. Of particular interest, the students' perception of their parents' relationship was more predictive of their performance anxiety than their perceptions of parent-child relationships. The student's task was to prepare a speech on an assigned topic and give it in front of a television camera. The student's parents were in the laboratory while the speech was being prepared. However, they were not in the same room as the student. It may be that many of the students whose parents did not have a harmonious relationship might have been preoccupied with concerns that their parents might have an unpleasant, perhaps embarrassing, disagreement while in the laboratory.

THE GENERAL PROBLEM OF COGNITIVE INTERFERENCE

A considerable number of experimental studies have been conducted to investigate the role of cognitive interference in task performance. These studies have served to highlight the important role played by features of situations (e.g., their evaluative nature). However, these studies, as a consequence of the use of random assignment to conditions, overlook the possible role individuals play in selecting themselves into, or avoiding, particular types of situations. For example, some individuals, because of a history of anxiety experienced in testing situations, may elect not to pursue further educational opportunities (e.g., college). This outcome would be particularly unfortunate because these individuals would be denying themselves the opportunity for self-corrective experiences. The important point here is that methodologies are needed that allow us to investigate the role of cognitive interference not only in the way in which people respond to situations once they encounter them, but also in the manner in which people either experience or do not experience particular types of situations.

We also need to know more about how cognitive interference relates to the coping strategies an individual employs to confront challenging or threatening situations. For example, are individuals who experience high levels of cognitive interference especially likely to focus their coping efforts on reducing cognitive interference through strategies such as distraction or avoidance? Are they less likely to employ more instrumentally oriented strategies such as redirecting their attention to the task at hand? These questions imply that cognitive interference is linked with a person's response to stressful situations. An adequate understanding of cognitive interference will require specification of its role in conjunction with other features of a person's response to life's challenges.

Subjectively experienced stress is probably a key factor in the dynamics of cognitive interference (for example, the stress of preoccupation with uncontrollable parental conflict). Stress has to do with perceived constraints and demands and intellective and social worries about the unexpected. These perceived constraints, demands, and worries are evoked by particular types of situational challenges. The most adaptive response to stress usually is task-oriented thinking and the ability to set aside personal preoccupations. We need to know more about the personal perceptions of various types of challenges and the self-preoccupations that influence these perceptions and also find out the effects and causes of neglected categories of cognitive interference like escapist thinking. There have been hundreds of studies of worry and anxiety, but only a handful of studies having anything to do with escapist thoughts. Yet, the wish to escape might be a strong, deleterious negative influence. We need to (a) direct our attention to the thoughts in which self-preoccupied persons are absorbed, (b) expand the domains of performance-related cognitions beyond fears and worries, and (c) widen the scope of situations in which cognitive interference is studied. Exploration of these domains might contribute to more realistic and comprehensive theories of cognition-behavior relationships.

Most of the work described in this chapter has to do with important common situations, ones in which people perform in an evaluative context. Individuals who are anxious and worry about being evaluated tend to perform relatively poorly and to report more cognitive interference in evaluative situations. In this type of situation, cognitive interference is usually maladaptive and appears to be a product of self-absorption that keeps the individual from doing what he or she wants or should do. Perhaps people perform best and think most clearly when they are free to become absorbed in people, events, and activities outside themselves. While much work has been carried out on worries and the worrying process, cognitive interference may be a superordinant category of cognitions of which worry is an important but not the sole part. Worry and intrusive thought are not the same thing (Gross & Eifert, 1990). Does cognitive interference always have a detrimental influence over performance? There is some evidence that this may not be the case. For example, Calvo and Carreiras (1993) found that while cognitive interference reduced the working memory capacity available for reading, the amount of information that was acquired was not seriously diminished.

Cognitive interference has been described in terms of peremptory thinking that contributes to loss of control over task involvement. What causes this loss of control? The authors believe it is a joint product of vulnerability and situational factors. The vulnerabilities include personal schemas about self and others that lead individuals to become preoccupied, for example, with pleasing parents, and others, with the achievement of success, and the need to avoid punishment for poor performance. Cognitive vulnerabilities due to schemas of self and others can lead to attentional failures, distractibility, and failure to use coping skills that actually may be in a person's repertory. Situational factors play an important role because the same world can be more dangerous for some people than for others. How people experience and process what goes on in situations depends on their attributions and expectations regarding themselves, others, and the situations. Regardless of how one defines the domain covered by cognitive interference, cognitive interference leads to a failure to become fully absorbed in ongoing activity and to disruptions in information processing (Baum, Cohen, & Hall, 1993; Roche & McConkey, 1990).

This chapter has primarily been about the assessment of cognitive interference and its relationship to performance. But clues concerning the variety of intrusive thoughts and the types of situations (e.g., social ones) in which unwanted thoughts might play a detrimental role have also been considered. The research reviewed in this chapter needs to be extended and elaborated. Equally important, theories of cognitive interference need to be articulated and compared with regard to their predictive power. Intrusive thinking does not just happen. It is a product of internal processes (schemas, working models) that have a peremptory quality. Personal theories of self and the world may provide a path to the causes of cognitive interference.

REFERENCES

Alting, T., & Markham, R. (1993). Text anxiety and distractibility. *Journal of Research in Personality, 27*, 134–137.

Baum, A., Cohen, L., & Hall, M. (1993). Control and intrusive memories as possible determinants of chronic stress. *Psychosomatic Medicine, 55*, 274–286.

Beck, A. T., & Emery, G. (1985). *Anxiety disorders and phobias: A cognitive perspective*. New York: Basic Books.

Blankenstein, K. R., Toner, B. B., & Flett, G. L. (1989). Test anxiety and the contents of consciousness: Thought-listing and endorsement measures. *Journal of Research in Personality, 23*, 269–286.

Broadbent, D. E., Cooper, P. E., FitzGerald, P., & Parkes, K. R. (1982). The Cognitive Failures Questionnaire (CFQ) and its correlates. *British Journal of Clinical Psychology, 21*, 1–16.

Bruch, M. A., Kaflowitz, N. G., & Kuethe, M. (1986). Beliefs and the subjective meaning of thoughts: Analysis of the role of self-statements in Academic test performance. *Cognitive Therapy and Research, 10*, 51–69.

Calvo, M. G., & Carreiras, M. (1993). Selective influence of test anxiety on reading processes. *British Journal of Psychology, 84*, 375–388.

Clark, D. A. (1992). Depressive, anxious and intrusive thoughts in psychiatric inpatients and outpatients. *Behavior and Research Therapy, 30*, 93–102.

Dweck, C. S. (1986). Motivational processes affecting learning. *American Psychologist, 41*, 1040–1048.

Dweck, C. S. (1989). Motivation. In A. Lesgold and R. Glaser (Eds.), *Foundations for a psychology of education* (pp. 87–136). Hillsdale, NJ: Lawrence Erlbaum Associates.

Galassi, J. P., Frierson, H. T., Jr., & Sharer, R. (1981). Behavior of high, moderate, and low test anxious students during an actual test situation. *Journal of Consulting and Clinical Psychology, 49*, 51–62.

Ganzer, V. J. (1968). The effects of audience pressure and test anxiety on learning and retention in a serial learning situation. *Journal of Personality and Social Psychology, 8*, 194–199.

Geen, R. G. (1987). Test anxiety and behavioral avoidance. *Journal of Research in Personality, 21*, 481–488.

Gross, P. R., & Eifert, G. H. (1990). Components of generalized anxiety: The role of intrusive thoughts vs worry. *Behavior and Research Theory, 28*, 421–428.

Hammermaster, C. S. (1989). Levels of performance and cognitive interference in test-anxious subjects. *The Alberta Journal of Educational Research, 35*, 164–170.

Hofmann, D. A. (1992). *The influence of goal orientation on task performance: A substantively meaningful suppressor variable.* Unpublished manuscript, Purdue University.

Hunsley, J. (1987). Cognitive processes in mathematics anxiety and test anxiety: The role of appraisals, internal dialogue, and attributions. *Journal of Educational Psychology, 79*, 388–392.

Katakis, C. (1990). The self-referential conceptual system: Towards an operational definition of subjectivity. *Systems Research, 7*, 91–102.

Kazdin, A. E. (1990). Evaluation of the Automatic Thoughts Questionnaire: Negative cognitive processes and depression among children. *Psychological Assessment: A Journal of Consulting and Clinical Psychology, 2*, 73–79.

Mandler, G., & Sarason, S. B. (1952). A study of anxiety and learning. *Journal of Abnormal and Social Psychology, 47*, 166–173.

Meunier, C., & Rule, B. G. (1967). Anxiety, confidence, and uniformity. *Journal of Personality, 35*, 498–504.

Prins, J. M. P., Groot, M. J. M., & Hanewald, G. J. F. P. (1994). Cognition in test-anxious children: The role of on-task and coping cognition reconsidered. *Journal of Consulting and Clinical Psychology, 62*, 404–409.

Roche, S. M., & McConkey, K. M. (1990). Absorption: Nature, assessment, and correlates. *Journal of Personality and Social Psychology, 59*, 1–11.

Sarason, I. G. (1978). The Test Anxiety Scale: Concept and research. In C. D. Spielberger & I. G. Sarason (Eds.), *Stress and anxiety* (Vol. 5, pp. 193–216). Washington, DC: Hemisphere.

Sarason, I. G. (Ed.). (1980). *Test anxiety: Theory, research, and applications.* Hillsdale, NJ: Lawrence Erlbaum Associates.

Sarason, I. G. (1984). Stress, anxiety, and cognitive interference: Reactions to Tests. *Journal of Personality and Social Psychology, 46*, 929–938.

Sarason, I. G., Sarason, B. R., Keefe, D. E., Hayes, B. E., & Shearin, E. N. (1986). Cognitive interference: Situational determinants and traitlike characteristics. *Journal of Personality and Social Psychology, 51*, 215–226.

Sarason, I. G., Sarason, B. R., & Pierce, G. R. (1990). Anxiety, cognitive interference, and performance. *Journal of Social Behavior and Personality, 5*, 1–18.

Sarason, I. G., Sarason, B. R., & Pierce, G. R. (1995). Cognitive interference: At the intelligence-personality crossroads. In D. Saklofske & M. Zeidner (Eds.), *International handbook of personality and intelligence* (pp. 285–296). New York: Plenum.

Sarason, I. G., Sarason, B. R., & Shearin, E. N. (1986). Social support as an individual difference variable: Its stability, origins, and relational aspects. *Journal of Personality and Social Psychology, 51*, 215–226.

Sarason, I. G., & Stoops, R. (1978). Test anxiety and the passage of time. *Journal of Consulting and Clinical Psychology, 46*, 102–109.

Trapp, E. P., & Kausler, P. H. (1958). Test anxiety level and goal-setting behavior. *Journal of Consulting Psychology, 22*, 31–34.

Wine, J. D. (1982). Evaluation anxiety: A cognitive-attentional construct. In H. W. Krohne and L. Laux (Eds.), *Achievement, stress, and anxiety.* Washington, DC: Hemisphere.

CHAPTER

8

A SELF-REGULATORY SKILLS PERSPECTIVE TO REDUCING COGNITIVE INTERFERENCE

Ruth Kanfer
Phillip L. Ackerman
University of Minnesota

Most people take for granted the notion that an individual's thoughts and emotions can influence task learning and performance; as for example, that worrying about one's performance while taking an examination can divert attention away from the test, and thereby lower performance. Indeed, research in cognitive interference has focused largely on this negative consequence of self-regulation; that is, the detrimental influence of particular types of self-referent cognitions (e.g., worry) on test performance. However, thoughts and emotions may also exert a positive influence on learning and performance. Locke (see Locke & Latham, 1990 for a review) and Bandura (see Bandura, 1991 for a review) suggested that individuals who maintain a strong sense of confidence or self-efficacy during performance show task persistence and higher levels of performance. A comprehensive account of the role of thoughts and emotions must consider the conditions under which self-referent activities help or hinder task learning and performance.

In this chapter a motivational skills framework is used to examine the influence of self-regulatory activities on skill learning and performance. From this individual differences perspective, motivational skills refer to activities that affect the overall efficiency of self-regulation and, in turn, affect task performance. This framework builds on Kuhl's (1985) taxonomy of self-regulatory processes and proposes that individuals differ in the extent to which they develop, modify, and use two fundamental self-regulatory skills during skill acquisition, namely emotion control and motivation control. Consistent with theory and research on cognitive interference, emotion-control skills involve the use of self-regulatory processes to keep performance anxiety and other negative emotional influences (e.g., worry) at bay during task engagement. In contrast, motivation control skills involve self-regulatory processes that keep attention and effort on the task—despite boredom or general satisfaction with current performance.

The first section of this chapter describes a resource-allocation perspective that enables us to make theoretical linkages among the disparate domains of cognitive abilities, motivation, self-regulation, and task demands (skill acquisition). The resource-allocation perspective starts with Kahneman's (1973) model of attention and cognitive resources. The authors adapted this model to represent an individual's performance as a joint function of the individual's relative attentional capacity (i.e., cognitive ability), task demands (i.e., phase of skill acquisition), and the proportion of the learner's total capacity devoted to the task (i.e., motivation) (Kanfer & Ackerman, 1989). Having established the integrated theoretical context for investigation of motivational skills, the next section describes implications of the resource-allocation perspective for the role of motivational skills in learning. In the third section, two studies are described that examined the viability of the motivational-skills perspective and the effectiveness of motivational-skills training for learning and performance. In the final section, problems and prospects of the motivational skills perspective for theory and practice are discussed.

TOWARD AN INTEGRATED RESOURCE-ALLOCATION PERSPECTIVE

The starting point for a consideration of the role of self-regulatory processes in learning and performance is not with motivation or emotion, but rather with the construct of cognitive or attentional resources. Theories of human attention (e.g., Kahneman, 1973) have defined attentional effort as cognitive resources of limited availability. Following from Kahneman (1973), individuals are posited to possess a pool of attentional capacity from which attentional resources are allocated to various activities at two different points; namely, distally, in terms of the proportion of total resources allocated, and proximally, in terms of suballocations of the initial allocation. In the Kahneman model, task performance is related to the extent to which attentional resources are devoted to the task.

The resource-allocation model proposed by Kanfer and Ackerman (1989; see Fig. 8.1) extends Kahneman's model by incorporating cognitive abilities, motivation, and skill acquisition. For example, theory and research by Ackerman (1987, 1988) on the relationship between attentional resources and individual differences in abilities has shown that individual differences in total attentional capacity can be related to individual differences in general cognitive ability. Building upon this work, the integrated resource allocation model states that measures of individual differences in general cognitive ability provide a rough assessment of the upper limit on the availability of attentional resources for

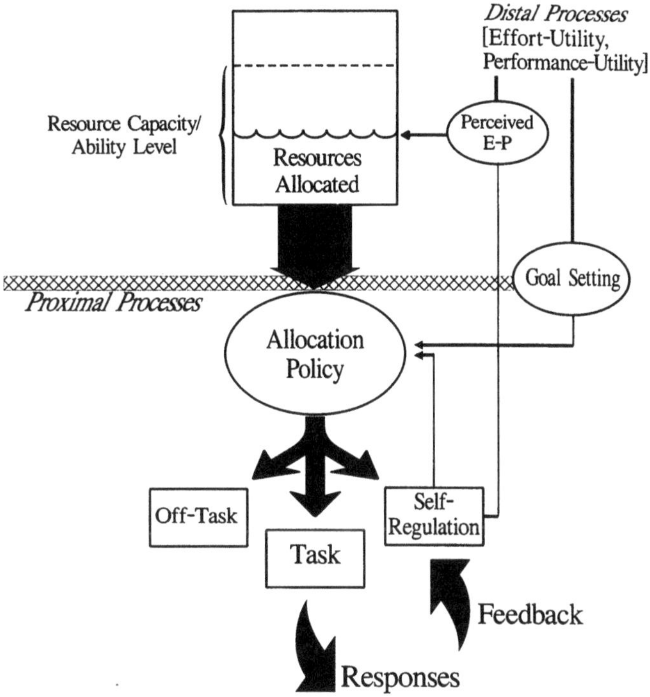

FIG. 8.1. An integrated resource allocation model of ability-motivation interactions for attentional effort. From Kanfer and Ackerman (1989). Copyright American Psychological Association. Reprinted by permission.

task performance. That is, individual differences in general cognitive ability index the amount of attention an individual has to devote to a task (see also Zeaman, 1978).

Motivational processes may also be mapped to the integrated resource-allocation model in terms of their role in allocating attentional resources to tasks. A cognitive resource-allocation approach to motivation permits a distinction between motivational processes affecting an individual's decisions to exert effort (distal), and the volitional processes by which intentions are translated into performance (proximal). In the integrated resource model, distal motivational processes affect the determination of the proportion of an individual's total attentional capacity to be directed toward goal attainment. These distal motivational influences correspond to choice motivation, and set the context for subsequent learning and performance. When performance involves tasks that are well learned or in which the goal can be executed quickly and without difficulty (e.g., getting dressed), no further motivational influences come into play.

In the context of skill acquisition, however, additional motivational influences often operate during task engagement (see, e.g., Kanfer, 1987; Kanfer & Kanfer,

1990). As shown in Fig. 8.1, these influences are represented in the model by the second allocation process, where resources are suballocated to various activities during task engagement. These proximal processes occur during task engagement and represent information-processing strategies that may facilitate or impede goal-directed behavior. Attentional resources at this stage are posited to be allocated among three broad classes of activities: on-task, off-task, and self-regulatory. Allocation of attentional resources to the task is hypothesized to exert a direct, positive influence on performance; resources allocated to off-task activities, such as daydreaming or worry, exert a direct, negative influence on task performance. Allocation of resources to self-regulatory processes, however, may exert a positive or negative effect on task performance depending upon the attentional costs relative to the attentional demands of the task.

In the integrated model, self-regulation plays an essential role in determining on-task attentional allocations in contexts that require sustained effort for learning or performance. In these situations, self-regulation enables changes in both distal and proximal allocation policies as the attentional demands of the task change during skill acquisition. Under ideal conditions, self-regulatory activities permit individuals to effectively adjust attentional resource allocations as task demands change. For example, when the task proves more difficult to accomplish than initially expected, self-regulatory strategies may be used to increase goal commitment (i.e., increase the proportion of total resources devoted to the task) or decrease daydreaming (i.e., decrease resources allocated to off-task activities).

A final aspect of the integrated resource model pertains to the dynamic nature of task demands during skill acquisition. Although learning is typically thought of as a continuous process, learning theorists have often settled on a description of learning that is broken down into phases or stages of skill acquisition (e.g., see Fitts & Posner, 1967). During the first phase of skill acquisition, termed the "cognitive" phase, the individual begins to understand the basic task requirements and the rules for task engagement. In this phase, attentional resource demands imposed by the task are quite high and performance is characterized as slow, attentionally effortful, and error prone (e.g., see Fisk, Ackerman, & Schneider, 1987).

The second phase of skill acquisition, termed the "associative" phase, involves the strengthening of associations formed in the first phase of learning. Performance in this phase is typically marked by a reduction in the attentional demands imposed by the task, substantial increases in the speed of task accomplishment and fewer performance errors. The third phase of skill acquisition, referred to as the "autonomous" phase, is characterized as requiring minimal attentional effort (Fitts & Posner, 1967). At this point, knowledge required to perform the task has become "automatized" and performance is generally fast, accurate, and minimally effortful.

Using the basic outline of skill acquisition described above, Ackerman (1988) has shown that classes of cognitive-intellectual abilities may be mapped to phases of skill acquisition. From this mapping, it then becomes possible to predict the association between individual differences in abilities and individual differences in task performance during skill acquisition. During the first phase of skill acquisition (i.e., the cognitive phase), individual differences in general cognitive abilities play a substantial role in the prediction of performance. However, as trainees develop appropriate strategies for successful task accomplishment (i.e., the associative phase of skill learning), and can eventually meet the task demands with little or no attentional effort (i.e., the autonomous phase), the influence of individual differences in general cognitive ability on task performance declines.

In summary, the resource allocation framework states that attentional and ability demands associated with various phases of skill acquisition interact with individual differences in cognitive (intellectual) abilities and motivational processes to affect learning and performance.

IMPLICATIONS AND EVIDENCE FOR THE MODEL

One basic implication of the integrated model is that self-regulatory processes may help or hinder task performance depending upon task demands and on individual differences in general intellectual ability. Specifically, the model suggests that popular motivational interventions (such as goal setting) that emphasize performance accomplishments can be expected to have few positive or even negative effects on performance during the early phase of complex skill training. During this phase of training, attentional demands of the task are high and trainees must devote as much effort as possible to understanding and mastering basic elements of the task, especially for lower-ability trainees. The imposition of performance goal assignments that trigger self-referent cognitions about one's performance capabilities is hypothesized to divert attentional resources away from the task (i.e., result in cognitive interference). As such, the model predicts that performance goal assignments early in skill training may have the opposite of their intended effect, as the goal instruction focuses attentional resources toward self-evaluation at the time when attentional resource demands of the task are at their highest. Because individuals with lower levels of general cognitive ability have fewer total resources to devote to the task, the debilitating effect of this motivational intervention is expected to be more pronounced among lower ability trainees compared to higher ability trainees.

In contrast, at later phases of skill acquisition, when the attentional demands of the task have declined, goal-setting interventions are predicted to have a positive effect on task performance. During these phases, persons have spare attentional resources that may be redirected back to the task. As a result, at this point in training, goal assignments that promote self-evaluative activities are unlikely to divert critical resources away from the task. At the same time, self-evaluative processing during later phases of skill learning is less likely to generate negative-affective reactions, and can be expected to facilitate performance through self-regulatory activities that emphasize redirection of spare attentional resources back to the task (i.e., motivation control). Again, the predicted positive impact of goal setting at later phases of skill acquisition is expected to be greater for lower ability persons compared to higher ability persons.

Kanfer, Ackerman, and their colleagues (Kanfer & Ackerman, 1989; Kanfer, Ackerman, Murtha, Dugdale, & Nelson, 1994) have provided evidence that supports these predictions in several studies involving training on an air traffic controller (ATC) simulation task (i.e., Kanfer-Ackerman ATC task). The ATC task is a rule-based, real-time computerized task that simulates some of the activities performed by air traffic controllers. The overall objective of the task is for trainees to land planes safely and efficiently. The task requires trainees to accept incoming planes into their airspace, to move planes within a three-level hold pattern, and to land planes on a set of runways as quickly and accurately as possible. An example of the ATC task display is shown in Fig. 8.2. Rules governing task performance address permissible movements of planes in the hold pattern, when planes must be landed, and which plane types may land on which runways under which weather conditions. Trainees are awarded points for each plane successfully landed, and lose points for rule-based errors.

Successful performance on the ATC task requires knowledge of the rules governing plane movements as well as knowledge about how to make plane movements using the computer keyboard. As such, trainee performance on the

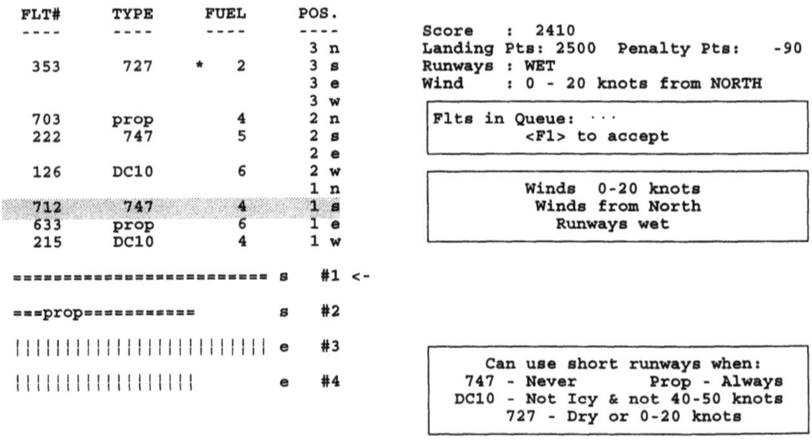

FIG. 8.2. The Kanfer-Ackerman Air Traffic Controller Task. The figure is a literal static representation of the real time display. Copyright (1987) by Ruth Kanfer, Phillip L. Ackerman, and Kim A. Pearson, University of Minnesota. Reprinted by permission.

task over the course of practice is generally characterized by a power function (i.e., large increases early, and diminishing returns with additional practice). The gradual improvement in ATC performance associated with the steady accretion of component skills permits examination of both ability and nonability determinants of skill acquisition. These characteristics of ATC learning and performance provide a distinct advantage over multiple-cue, probability-learning tasks, as well as simple perception, memory, and psychomotor tasks (e.g., simple reaction-time tasks).

Results obtained in the Kanfer and Ackerman studies showed that self-regulatory activities do affect on-task utilization of attentional resources and task performance. Kanfer and Ackerman (1989), for example, compared the pattern of ability-performance correlations for trainees who did and did not receive specific performance goal assignments during the early phase of skill. They found that when the goal manipulation was implemented, the correlation between general ability and performance dropped to a significantly greater degree than occurred in the control condition. That is, self-regulatory processes associated with assignment of specific and difficult performance goals appeared to reduce the role of cognitive-intellectual abilities in determining individual differences in performance.

Kanfer and Ackerman (1989) also found that activation of self-regulatory processing via the assignment of performance goals had differential effects on performance depending on the task demands and individual differences in general cognitive ability. Specifically, the administration of specific and difficult goal assignments during the early, resource-intensive phase of learning impaired performance, whereas administration of assignments during later, or less-resource-demanding phases of skill acquisition facilitated performance, particularly among lower ability trainees.

Further evidence for the influence of self-regulatory processes on task performance was provided by Kanfer et al. (1994) in a study investigating the influence of performance goal assignments in massed and spaced ATC practice conditions. In that study, performance goal assignments interacted with type of practice, such that performance goal assignments exerted a deleterious effect on performance in the massed practice condition, but a positive effect on performance in the spaced practice condition. Self-report results indicated that goal assignments increased cognitive interference (e.g., frequency of negative affective self-reactions) in both the massed and spaced practice conditions. However, trainees in the goal assignment condition reported significantly more on-task information processing during the break periods (spaced practice) than did trainees in the massed practice condition. Taken together, these findings suggest that under certain conditions motivational interventions have context-dependent effects on performance by concomitantly increasing cognitive interference and attentional allocations to the task.

MOTIVATIONAL SKILLS: A CLOSER LOOK AT SELF-REGULATION IN ACTION

Although initial results provided support for the integrated resource allocation model, our early studies did not address questions pertaining to the specific aspects of self-regulatory processing that facilitate or impair task performance. To address this set of issues, the conceptualization of self-regulatory processes was extended within the integrated resource model.

With few exceptions, extant formulations of self-regulation have adopted a structural perspective in which the influence of self-regulatory activities on performance stems primarily from affective and cognitive self-reactions. In Bandura's (1991) model, for example, self-efficacy judgments and performance satisfaction or dissatisfaction represent self-reactions that influence subsequent task learning and performance. Similarly, cybernetic control formulations emphasize the extent to which products of self-regulatory processing (e.g., self-reactions) influence subsequent performance.

In contrast, Kuhl (1985) has proposed a perspective that highlights the focus of self-regulatory activities. Specifically, Kuhl suggested an overlapping set of six self-regulatory strategies that individuals might invoke to facilitate purposive behavior: namely, active attentional selectivity, encoding control, emotion control, motivation control, environment control, and parsimony of information processing. Of the six strategies described, all but environment control involve cognitive processes that modify the direction or allocation of attentional resources. Among these strategies, emotion and motivation control appear to represent broad, meta-motivational strategies that may encompass active attentional selectivity and parsimony of information processing. According to Kuhl (1985), emotion control strategies facilitate performance by inhibiting emotional states that may undermine action. In contrast, motivation control strategies serve to strengthen task attention. In subsequent theorizing, Kuhl (1987) proposed that individual differences in self-regulatory strategies are related to individual differences in action/state orientation.

Following Kuhl's (1985) individual differences perspective, the authors conceptualized self-regulatory processes in terms of integrated skills, rather than specific self-regulatory components or specific self-referent cognitions. In contrast to extant motivational theories that emphasize the direction and intensity of specific emotions or thoughts (e.g., worry, self-efficacy), the skills perspective focuses on the information-processing strategies that underlie resource allocations. As such, individual differences in performance associated with cognitive interference are posited to arise in part from differences in the development and use of self-regulatory skills. In the context of purposive action, the direction and intensity of thoughts and emotions associated with cognitive interference are conceptualized as reflections on the efficiency of self-regulatory skills. Consistent with the integrated resource model, motivational skills are expected to have differential influence on task performance depending on individual capabilities and task demands.

Working from Kuhl's (1985) taxonomy, we selected two fundamental groups of self-regulatory skills, namely, Emotion control and Motivation control. Looking back at earlier research using the ATC simulation task, we noted that poorer-performing trainees also reported higher levels of off-task, emotion-laden cognitions than did higher-performing trainees (Kanfer & Ackerman, 1989). Many of the thoughts reported had a basis in negative emotions and represented distracting intrusions to task concentration. Examples included trainee reports of thinking about doing more poorly than others on the task, dissatisfaction and anger with oneself for making mistakes, and feelings of unhappiness. In contrast, higher performing trainees reported having significantly fewer of these thoughts during task engagement. As such, we identified emotion control as a fundamental set of self-regulatory skills aimed at minimizing negative emotional thoughts and emotions during task engagement.

Our review of previous ATC trainee self-reports also indicated that task interest and commitment often declined during later stages of practice, particularly among higher performing trainees. For many tasks, the early phase of skill acquisition is often both the most demanding and rewarding. Devoting attention and effort to the task at this point in training typically yields readily visible improvements in performance. But as task proficiency develops, initial big gains in performance diminish. Performance improvements continue, but at a less impressive rate, in accord with the "Power Law of Practice" (Newell & Rosenbloom, 1981). Concomitant with performance improvements over practice, task demands on attention for sustaining current performance levels attenuate. That is, with practice, trainees can perform the task at current performance levels with less effort—and often do. From a motivational perspective, these characteristics of later phases of skill training are unfortunate. The task no longer demands effort, and intrinsic rewards associated with readily observed performance improvements are gone. Examples of strategies to overcome such effects include self-set goals, creating imaginary and contrived consequences for performance outcomes, and other practices aimed at the maintenance of high levels of attention and effort toward task performance. Consistent with Kuhl's (1985) theorizing, we considered these to be examples of "motivation control" skills; that is, self-regulatory activities aimed at keeping or strengthening the allocation of attentional resources toward the task, despite boredom or general satisfaction with current performance.

IMPLICATIONS OF A MOTIVATIONAL SKILLS PERSPECTIVE FOR COMPLEX SKILL TRAINING

In general, the motivational skills perspective proposes that individuals may differ in terms of the development and use of two basic, self-regulatory sets of skills; Emotion control and Motivation control. While individual differences in abilities are relatively fixed (at least for adults), motivational skills may be malleable.

In the context of skill acquisition, emotion-control skills are likely to be most important early in training, when task demands for attentional resources are highest. Early in training people often experience failures and displeasure with their behavior and performance. Emotion control skills help to keep such off-task concerns and emotions from diverting attention away from the task. For lower ability trainees, emotion-control skills are particularly important, since these are the individuals who are most likely to experience difficulty early in training.

Late in training, the frequency of failures declines as performance improves. But at this point, a different set of potential motivational impediments to performance arise. Trainees may become bored with the task and fail to exert the effort needed to further improve their performance (just as some students quit practicing their typing skills once they reach an "acceptable" level of performance). Motivation control skills enable individuals to sustain on-task attention and effort. In the standard training environment, motivation-control skills are likely to be most important for higher ability trainees: that is, those who most quickly reach a less effortful (but suboptimal) level of task proficiency.

To assess the viability of the motivational skills perspective for skill acquisition, we conducted two training studies that examined the influence of explicit instruction and pretraining in emotion-control skills and motivation-control skills on performance (see Kanfer & Ackerman, 1990). The procedures and results of these studies are briefly described in the next section. Working from the integrated resource allocation perspective, we expected that emotion-control skills would be more important for lower-ability trainees compared with higher-ability trainees, and that deficits in emotion control would most likely disrupt learning and performance among the lower-ability trainees during the early phase of skill acquisition. In contrast, higher-ability trainees typically reach a satisfactory performance level earlier in practice than lower-ability trainees. Although task skill can still be improved, trainees at this point often become complacent about task performance. With attenuated task demands, the extra attention and effort needed to improve task performance may not be devoted to the task. At this stage of learning, motivation-control skills can be employed to sustain task attention. Thus, we expected that improvements in motivation-control skills would have a pronounced effect on performance among higher-ability trainees, particularly at the later phase of skill acquisition.

ENHANCING PERFORMANCE VIA TASK-EMBEDDED MOTIVATIONAL SKILLS INSTRUCTION

In this study, we looked at the influence of emotion-control and motivation-control skills instructions embedded directly in task training. Two hundred thirty-seven U.S. Air Force basic trainees performed nine, 10-minute trials of the computerized

Kanfer-Ackerman ATC task under one of two randomly assigned instruction conditions; emotion control training and motivation control training. Prior to initial task performance, and during the intertrial intervals, half of the trainees received instructions to control the occurrence of negative emotions during ATC task performance. In particular, trainees were instructed to increase the frequency of positive thoughts and to reduce the frequency of negative emotions, such as worry or upset following errors. The remaining trainees received motivation-control instructions. These trainees were instructed to control and further increase the amount of effort they devoted to the task at all times during the trial. To stimulate self-regulatory processing, trainees in both conditions were assigned specific and difficult performance goals immediately prior to each of the first six ATC task trials. Emotion-control and motivation-control skills instructions were provided following the performance goal assignments. For the final three ATC task trials, trainees were instructed to "do their best," and received no further motivational skills instruction.

Estimates of general cognitive-intellectual ability were derived from the ten test, Armed Services Vocational Aptitude Battery (ASVAB). The ASVAB was completed by trainees several months prior to the experiment and test scores were obtained from personnel records. The global estimate of cognitive ability was obtained using a unit-weighted z-score composite based on all 10 subscales of the ASVAB, and trainees were then divided into higher-ability and lower-ability groups using a median split on the ability composite. This split was used as a two-level blocking factor in subsequent analyses summarized below.

In addition, measures of individual differences on a variety of personality dimensions were obtained from self-report measures administered at the onset of the session (prior to ATC task instruction). These measures included the short form of the Action Control Questionnaire (Kuhl, 1985) and the Control and Stress subscales of the Multidimensional Personality Questionnaire (Tellegen, 1982).

Trainees also completed several brief self-report questionnaires during skill training. Composite scale score measures of goal commitment and self-confidence for goal attainment were obtained immediately after the first goal assignment and prior to task Trial 1, and again prior to Trial 3. Measures of goal attentiveness, performance monitoring, and performance satisfaction were also obtained following completion of the third and sixth task trials. Trainees in all conditions also completed a final self-report questionnaire following the last task trial (Trial 9). This questionnaire included items designed to assess the frequency of various types of thoughts during the final three trials of ATC training. A modification of Sarason's Cognitive Interference Questionnaire (CIQ; Sarason & Stoops, 1978; Sarason, Sarason, Keefe, Hayes, & Shearin, 1986) was used to assess the frequency of on- and off-task thoughts during the past three trials. A subset of adapted CIQ items and new items (e.g., assessing specific self-motivation thoughts and positive self-reactions) were administered using an 8-point

Likert-type rating scale (1 = *never*; 8 = *constantly*). Seven items related to attention to task components (e.g., "I focused my total attention on learning a specific rule"), two items related to negative emotional reactions (e.g., "I got upset when I made a mistake"), four items related to positive emotional reactions (e.g., "I thought about how well I was doing"), four items related to broad, negative affect (e.g., "I thought about how dissatisfied I was with my performance"), two items related to off-task thoughts (e.g., "I let my mind wander while doing the task"), three items related to motivational efforts (e.g., "I pushed myself to do better on each trial"), and four items related to performance evaluation thoughts (e.g., "I thought about how I was doing compared with others"). Internal consistency reliabilities for these composite scales ranged from $r_{xx} = .64$ to .86. As with previous studies using the ATC paradigm, multiple measures of task performance were obtained at each trial, including number of planes landed (Landings), number of rule violations (Errors), number of keystrokes made (Keystrokes), and cumulative performance score (see Ackerman, 1988, 1990; Kanfer & Ackerman, 1989; Kanfer, Ackerman, Murtha, Dugdale, & Nelson, 1994, for further descriptions of the performance measures). Three measures—landings, errors, and keystrokes were used in all analyses of performance.

Results

As expected, trainees in both groups improved in performance with practice. That is, over the course of practice, trainees landed more planes, made fewer errors, and responded more rapidly (making more keystrokes). In addition, lower-ability trainees performed significantly less well than higher-ability trainees on all major performance indicators, particularly during the early phase of skill acquisition.

Of central importance, however, are results related to the effects of motivational skills instruction. The results, shown in Fig. 8.3, indicate that provision of motivation control and emotion control skills instruction during training had significantly different effects on performance among lower-ability trainees, but not higher-ability trainees. As predicted, among lower-ability trainees, those who were given emotion-control skills instruction made fewer errors (and more keystrokes) per trial compared with trainees provided motivation-control skills instruction. As shown in Fig. 8.3, this effect for errors occurred early in training and was sustained throughout practice. Among higher-ability trainees, however, type of training had no significant effect on performance.

Consistent with these results, lower-ability trainees instructed to implement emotion-control skills during task performance reported significantly fewer negative affective self-reactions and fewer attempts to monitor their performance score compared to trainees in the motivation-control-instruction condition.

Examination of the relationship between personality measures and performance showed a stable pattern of relatively small correlations between these

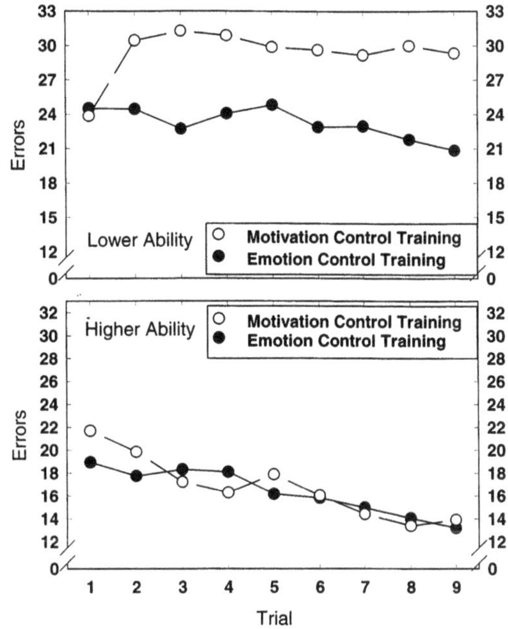

FIG. 8.3. Frequency of errors across ATC task trials by instructional condition and ability group. Motivation control training condition is in open circles. Emotion control training condition is in closed circles. From Kanfer and Ackerman (1990).

measures and performance across practice. Results of tests investigating potential interactive effects of personality measures and training conditions on task performance revealed no significant findings.

The results obtained support a dynamic, skills-based approach to cognitive interference. During the early phase of skill acquisition, when individuals first confront the task and task demands are high, emotion-control instructions had a positive impact on performance, specifically among lower-ability individuals. Interestingly, the beneficial effects of emotion-control skills instruction was demonstrated in the strategic aspects of performance, namely errors and keystrokes. This pattern of results suggests that negative emotional processing may hinder performance through its effects on both speed and accuracy of performance.

Contrary to expectations, however, motivation-control skills instruction did not exert a significant or emergent positive effect on performance among higher-ability trainees during the later period of skill training. Consistent with this finding, no significant differences were observed between emotion-control and motivation-control conditions in self-reports of on-task attention among higher-ability trainees. As shown in Fig. 8.3, we noted that even higher-ability trainees were still improving on their performance at the end of the 1½ hour training session. As such, it might be that motivation-control instructions did not show a beneficial effect for higher-ability trainees because task demands were still high; that is, motivation skills were not yet necessary for sustaining attention and effort on the task.

MOTIVATIONAL SKILLS TRAINING AND NEAR-TRANSFER TASK PERFORMANCE

The objectives of the next study were to extend the examination of skill acquisition to a later phase of training by providing part-task training that enabled greater comprehension of the task prior to ATC task engagement. This part-task training was also used as a context for motivational-skills training in order to go one step further and examine the effects of such skills in a training-transfer paradigm.

Three hundred twenty trainees completed a part-task training module prior to performing the full ATC task. During the part-task training, trainees received approximately 40 minutes of practice in a series of short, structured task trials in one of three randomly assigned conditions: control (baseline), emotion-control training, or motivation-control training. In all conditions, trainees were shown a series of dynamic task scenarios and were instructed to perform operations ranging from simple procedures to more complex procedures. In the two motivational skills training conditions (emotion control and motivation control), the purpose of the part-task training was made explicit; to develop appropriate self-regulatory skills for use in subsequent full ATC task training. After introducing instructions for performing the part-task, trainees in the emotion-control skills training condition received descriptive information on use of an emotion-control strategy and were instructed to practice the strategy when performing each part-task trial. Emotion-control strategy prompts were also provided repeatedly in conjunction with trial feedback and prior to each set of three trials.

Trainees in the motivation-control skills training condition received the same part-task trial instructions as trainees in the emotion-control condition except that instructions in this condition focused on developing and using motivation-control skills. In the control condition, trainees were simply told that the purpose of training was to better prepare them for the ATC training session (and received no motivational skills instructions). After the final part-task trial, trainees in all conditions completed a brief self-report measure assessing frequency of various thoughts during the part-task training.

After completion of the part-task training, all trainees received brief instruction on the full ATC transfer task, and then completed eight, 10-minute full ATC task trials. To investigate the extent to which motivational skills training might be used in a near transfer environment, and in contrast to the previous study, trainees received no motivational-skills instructions during the full ATC task transfer session. As with the previous study, individual differences in general cognitive ability were computed from archival records, and self-report measures were used to assess individual differences in personality dispositions and frequency of various types of thoughts during full ATC task training.

Results

As expected, part-task training did facilitate initial performance on the full ATC transfer task. On the first full ATC task trial, both higher- and lower-ability trainees in the control part-task training conditions made fewer errors, on average, than were made by trainees on Trial 1 in the previous study (shown in Fig. 8.4). These results suggest that the part-task training had been successful in moving trainees along in phase of ATC skill acquisition.

Overall, findings obtained in this study indicated that the part-task emotion-control and motivation-control skills training did transfer to full ATC task performance. Consistent with results obtained in the previous study, the effects of the part-task motivational skills training were most pronounced for error frequency, rather than number of landings. Specifically, results of the repeated measures analyses on error scores indicated that provision of part-task emotion-control and motivation-control skills instruction had significantly different effects on performance among lower- and higher-ability trainees. Among lower-ability trainees, emotion-control skills training was associated with a subsequent beneficial effect on reduction of errors, particularly early in full ATC training. In addition, however, among higher-ability trainees, prior training in motivation control skills training was associated with a subsequent beneficial effect on reduction of errors later in full ATC training. Taken together, these findings support the notion that emotion-control and motivation-control skills represent distinct determinants of learning and performance in skill-acquisition contexts.

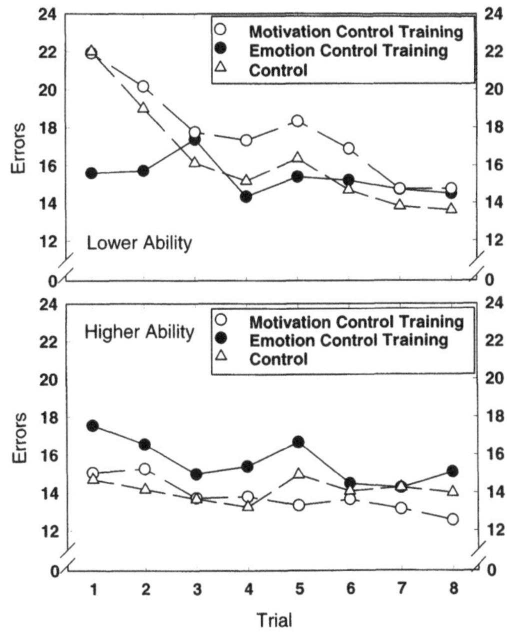

FIG. 8.4. Frequency of errors across ATC transfer-task trials by instructional condition and ability group. Motivation control training condition is in open circles. Emotion control training condition is in closed circles. Control (baseline) condition is in open triangles. From Kanfer and Ackerman (1990).

CONCLUSIONS, PROBLEMS, AND PROSPECTS

In the integrated, resource-allocation perspective, thoughts and emotions influence performance through their impact on the amount (or proportion) of attentional resources devoted to the task. Self-regulatory processes provide the mechanism for allocation of attentional resources across on-task, off-task, and self-referent activities. In this framework, cognitive interference refers to self-regulatory inefficiencies or deficits in the dynamic context of information-processing demands imposed by the task, and individual differences in cognitive abilities and dispositions. Two types of cognitive interference and self-regulatory activity are identified. First, cognitive interference may occur when self-regulatory processing permits diversion of critically needed attentional resources away from the task to negative emotional processing. Cognitive interference of this type occurs early in skill acquisition, when the attentional demands of the task are highest. Cognitive interference in this context typically impairs learning and task performance. A second type of cognitive interference occurs during later phases of skill acquisition, when the attentional demands of the task have declined. In these situations, cognitive interference is associated with self-regulatory processing that fails to redirect attentional resources (no longer demanded in task engagement) back toward the task. In contrast to the first form of cognitive interference, the detrimental influences on performance are expressed in the form of suboptimal learning or lack of performance progress. Self-regulatory efficiency in these later phases of skill acquisition is typically described in motivational terms.

Motivational skills pertain to the purposive patterns of self-regulatory activity. Emotion-control skills refer to self-regulatory patterns aimed at reducing the diversion of attentional resources to emotional concerns, and are most useful when attentional demands of the task are high. In contrast, motivation-control skills refer to self-regulatory patterns directed toward bolstering allocation of attentional resources toward task accomplishment. These skills are most useful when attentional demands of the task have declined during the later phases of skill training. Individual differences in the development and use of these skills are proposed to develop as a joint function of person and situational factors.

Basic tenets of the resource-allocation model underscore the importance of broadening the study of cognitive interference to include learning and skill acquisition contexts. To date, most research on cognitive interference has focused on factors that disrupt performance in testing situations. These contexts are characterized by tasks that impose strong demands on attention, limited opportunity for task engagement, and instigation of strong evaluative concerns. In these situations, emotion-control skills are essential, particularly among lower-ability persons. In the context of learning, however, other factors may disrupt task performance, particularly at later phases of skill acquisition. In learning environments, deficits in motivation-control skills may prevent development of optimal asymptotic levels of performance through failure to sustain attentional effort allocations to the task. Recent evidence by Ericsson, Krampe, and Tesch-Römer (1993), for example, suggested that cognitive interference (associated with deficits in self-regulatory skills that promote sustained allocation of resources to the task) has substantial implications for the development of expertise in a wide variety of life skill domains, such as music, chess, and sports.

The empirical work described in this chapter provides evidence for the role of emotion and motivation skills in learning. Emotion-control skills training had a beneficial effect on performance among trainees most likely to experience difficulties and frustrations when confronting a complex or novel task. In contrast, motivation-control skills training had a beneficial effect on performance among trainees most likely to experience complacency during skill acquisition. Self-report measures provide further evidence that emotion-control and motivation-control skills training had the desired effects on thoughts and emotions during learning.

The results obtained in these studies also indicate the malleability of these skills and the potential of training for subsequent related task learning. Using a near-transfer task paradigm, we found that prior emotion-control and motivation-control skills training continued to have the expected effects in the transfer task. Obviously, these results must be interpreted with caution due to the constraints of the training situation. An important question for future research that has both theoretical and practical implications pertains to the limits of motivational-skills training transfer to diverse learning contexts. For example, it may well be that motivation-control skills training transfers more readily across task contexts than does emotion-control skills training.

The findings also indicate that lower-ability and higher-ability trainees differ in terms of the motivational-skills training most useful in optimizing learning and task performance. Among lower-ability trainees, emotion-control skills appear essential when first confronting a task. Although motivation-control skill training did not appear to exert a deleterious effect on performance among trainees in this group, training methods that attempt to direct attention back to the task using goal assignments or other evaluative incentives, may indeed exert a deleterious effect (see, e.g., Kanfer & Ackerman, 1989). In both of the studies described in this chapter, the benefits of emotion-control skills training for the lower-ability trainees were most pronounced during their initial confrontation with the task. The sharp beneficial effects of emotion-control skills training during early performance in the near-transfer task are particularly interesting, and suggest that difficulties in emotion-control among lower-ability trainees are closely associated with attentional task demands.

The beneficial effect of motivational-skills training, among higher-ability trainees later in skill acquisition, provides support for the notion that thoughts and emotions exert a positive, as well as negative influence on performance. The resource-allocation framework suggests that the beneficial effects of motivation-control skills on performance occur when the task no longer requires substantial attentional resources, but optimal levels of task proficiency have yet to be attained. In the ATC task paradigm, higher-ability trainees were expected to reach this point more quickly than lower-ability trainees. With sufficient practice on the task, however, motivation-control skills would also be expected to enhance performance among lower-ability trainees. That is, the results do not imply that benefits of motivation control skills training are limited to higher-ability trainees, but rather that such skills may not be effective determinants of performance among lower-ability trainees until later in training. Further research in which lower-ability trainees are provided with extended practice (that enables progress to later phases of skill acquisition) is needed to empirically validate this aspect of the model.

The motivational-skills formulation suggests that persons differ in their development and use of basic self-regulatory skills that operate during task learning and performance. As such, individual differences in these skills would be expected to contribute to the prediction of individual differences in performance. Research by Sarason and his colleagues on the CIQ (e.g., Sarason & Stoops, 1978; Sarason, Keefe, Hayes, & Shearin, 1986; see also Sarason, Sarason, & Pierce, 1995) provided convergent evidence for this notion. Ackerman and Kanfer (1993) also provided initial support for this notion in both laboratory and field studies investigating the determinants of air traffic controller training performance and success. In these studies, individual differences in motivational skills (combining motivation- and emotion-control skills) were assessed using a self-report questionnaire. Results of both the laboratory and field studies showed that individual differences in motivational skills added significantly to the prediction of variance in task performance and training success, beyond variance accounted for by individual differences in cognitive abilities. Future research to delineate the relative contribution of individual differences in emotion-control and motivation-control skills represents an important next step in the conceptualization of these skills from a differential perspective.

ACKNOWLEDGMENTS

Research reported here was supported by grants to Ruth Kanfer and Phillip L. Ackerman from the U.S. Air Force Office of Scientific Research (AFOSR 87-0234, AFOSR 89-0242, and AFOSR F49620-93-1-0206). This research program is also supported in part by a grant from the National Science Foundation (NSF/SBR-9223357), Ruth Kanfer, principal investigator.

REFERENCES

Ackerman, P. L. (1987). Individual differences in skill learning: An integration of psychometric and information processing perspectives. *Psychological Bulletin, 102*, 3–27.

Ackerman, P. L. (1988). Determinants of individual differences during skill acquisition: Cognitive abilities and information processing. *Journal of Experimental Psychology: General, 117*, 288–318.

Ackerman, P. L. (1990). A correlational analysis of skill specificity: Learning, abilities, and individual differences. *Journal of Experimental Psychology: Learning, Memory, and Cognition, 16,* 883–901.

Ackerman, P. L., & Kanfer, R. (1993). Integrating laboratory and field study for improving selection: Development of a battery for predicting Air Traffic Controller success. *Journal of Applied Psychology, 78,* 413–432.

Bandura, A. (1991). Self-regulation of motivation through anticipatory and self-reactive mechanisms. In R. A. Dienstbier (Ed.), *Perspectives on motivation: Nebraska symposium on motivation* (Vol. 38, pp. 69–164). Lincoln: University of Nebraska Press.

Ericsson, K. A., Krampe, R. Th., & Tesch-Römer, C. (1993). The role of deliberate practice in the acquisition of expert performance. *Psychological Review, 100,* 363–406.

Fisk, A. D., Ackerman, P. L., & Schneider, W. (1987). Automatic and controlled processing theory and its application to human factors problems. In P. A. Hancock (Ed.), *Human factors psychology* (pp. 159–177). New York: North-Holland.

Fitts, P., & Posner, M. I. (1967). *Human performance.* Monterey, CA: Brooks/Cole.

Kahneman, D. (1973). *Attention and effort.* Englewood Cliffs, NJ: Prentice-Hall.

Kanfer, R. (1987). Task-specific motivation: An integrative approach to issues of measurement, mechanisms, processes, and determinants. *Journal of Social and Clinical Psychology, 5,* 237–264.

Kanfer, R., & Ackerman, P. L. (1989). Motivation and cognitive abilities: An integrative/aptitude-treatment interaction approach to skill acquisition. *Journal of Applied Psychology—Monograph, 74,* 657–690.

Kanfer, R., & Ackerman, P. L. (1990). *Ability and metacognitive determinants of skill acquisition and transfer.* Air Force Office of Scientific Research Final Report, Minneapolis, MN.

Kanfer, R., Ackerman, P. L., Murtha, T., Dugdale, B., & Nelson, L. (1994). Goal setting, conditions of practice, and task performance: A resource allocation perspective. *Journal of Applied Psychology, 79,* 826–835.

Kanfer, R., & Kanfer, F. H. (1991). Goals and self-regulation: Applications of theory to work settings. In M. L. Maehr & P. R. Pintrich (Eds.), *Advances in motivation and achievement* (Vol. 7, pp. 287–326). Greenwich, CT: JAI.

Kuhl, J. (1985). Volitional mediators of cognition-behavior consistency: Self-regulatory processes and action versus state orientation. In J. Kuhl & J. Beckmann (Eds.), *Action Control. From cognition to behavior* (pp. 101–128). New York: Springer-Verlag.

Kuhl, J. (1987). Action control: The maintenance of motivational states. In F. Hallish & J. Kuhl (Eds.), *Motivation, intention, and volition* (pp. 279–291). New York: Springer-Verlag.

Locke, E. A., & Latham, G. P. (1990). *A theory of goal setting and task performance.* Englewood Cliffs, NJ: Prentice-Hall.

Newell, A., & Rosenbloom, P. S. (1981). Mechanisms of skill acquisition and the law of practice. In J. R. Anderson (Ed.), *Cognitive skills and their acquisition.* Hillsdale, NJ: Lawrence Erlbaum Associates.

Sarason, I. G., Sarason, B. R., Keefe, D. E., Hayes, B. E., & Shearin, E. N. (1986). Cognitive interference: Situational determinants and traitlike characteristics. *Journal of Personality and Social Psychology, 51,* 215–226.

Sarason, I. G., Sarason, B. R., & Pierce, G. R. (1995). Cognitive interference: At the intelligence-personality crossroads. In D. Saklofske & M. Zeidner (Eds.), *International handbook of personality and intelligence.* New York: Plenum.

Sarason, I. G., & Stoops, R. (1978). Test anxiety and the passage of time. *Journal of Consulting and Clinical Psychology, 46,* 102–109.

Tellegen, A. (1982). *Brief manual for the Multidimensional Personality Questionnaire.* Unpublished manual. University of Minnesota, Minneapolis, MN.

Zeaman, D. (1978). Some relations of general intelligence and selective attention. *Intelligence, 2,* 55–73.

PART

II

Cognitive Interference, Stress, and Performance

CHAPTER

9

MONITORING AND BLUNTING OF THREATENING INFORMATION: COGNITIVE INTERFERENCE AND FACILITATION IN THE COPING PROCESS

Suzanne M. Miller
Fox Chase Cancer Center

Every day individuals face an enormous array of information about potential risks, threats and dangers to their well being, from hijackers on airplanes and muggers on street corners and layoffs at work to the news the physician gives after reading the test results, or the melanoma signs they might find the next time they look at themselves. When people hear about the symptoms and risks of breast cancer and the frequent fate of the aging prostate gland, do they react in stable ways, some wanting to know more, others quickly running from the news and trying to forget it? If they do, it becomes important to identify the patterns that might characterize individuals' differences in these reactions and to try to understand their psychological implications and consequences (Miller, 1990, 1992a, 1992b, 1995; Miller, Combs, & Kruus, 1993; Miller, Shoda, & Hurley, in press).

In this chapter, selected evidence is reviewed that is obtained from research on individual differences in the tendency to "monitor" or to "blunt" potentially threatening information, especially in medical-health contexts (Miller, Combs, & Stoddard, 1989). Overall individual differences are described that characterize exemplars of these two behavior types, focusing on the cognitive and emotional consequences of their typical ways of dealing with information, and exploring both the costs and the benefits–the interferences and the facilitation–that these patterns seem to produce.

MEASURING MONITORING-BLUNTING: THE MBSS

To identify these two coping types, the Monitor-Blunter Style Scale (MBSS; Miller, 1987) is used (also called the Miller Behavioral Style Scale), which is a written objective self-report measure that describes four hypothetical, relatively uncontrollable scenes that are threat-evoking, such as "imagine you are afraid of flying and have to go somewhere by plane." After each scene, there are eight descriptions of ways of coping with that situation, half of which involve monitoring (e.g., listening for unusual engine noises and looking for unusual behavior by the crew on the plane) and half of which provide blunting options (e.g., watching the inflight entertainment). The complete methodology and scoring—as well as the evidence for the scale's reliability and its convergent, discriminative and construct validity—have been extensively documented and reported elsewhere (e.g., Gard, Edwards, Harris, & McCormack, 1988; Ludwick-Rosenthal & Neufeld, 1993; Miller, 1987, 1990, 1992a; Miller & Mangan, 1983; Miller, Brody, & Summerton, 1988; Miller, Roussi, Altman, Helm, & Steinberg, 1994; Muris & Schouten, 1994; Muris, Zuuren, & Vries, 1994).

Briefly, it has become clear that there are stable individual differences with regard to monitoring-blunting processes, and that individuals who differ in this regard tend to show distinctive patterns of information search, and characteristic ways of responding cognitively and emotionally to potentially threatening information. Moreover, these differences are not simply redundant with, or explicable from, such measures as generally negative affect, depression, or anxiety, although, as expected theoretically, they sometimes are correlated with them (e.g., Davey, 1993; Davey, Hampton, Farrell, & Davidson, 1992; Efran, Chorney, Ascher, & Lukens, 1989; Ludwick-Rosenthal & Neufeld, 1993; Miller, 1987; Miller et al., 1988; Russell & Davey, 1993; Solomon, Mikulincer, & Arad, 1991; Steptoe & O'Sullivan, 1986; Steptoe & Vogele, 1992).

INFORMATION SEARCH: ATTENTION TO SELF-RELEVANT HEALTH INFORMATION

Perhaps the most consistent difference between monitors and blunters is that monitors want to know more and blunters want to know less, especially with regard to potentially bad news about their health and well-being. For example, individuals scoring as monitors typically seek out information relevant to physical and psychological threats. In contrast, individuals identified as blunters typically prefer to avoid and distract from threat-relevant information (Miller, 1987). Consistent findings have been obtained with medical populations, such as gynecologic patients at risk for cervical cancer who were about to undergo colposcopy, an aversive diagnostic procedure, for the first time (Miller & Mangan, 1983). Monitors generally wanted more sensory and procedural information than they had been given. They also desire more information about risks relevant to aversive medical procedures than do blunters (Watkins, Weaver, & Odegaard, 1986).

Similarly, in a sample of women about to undergo gynecologic surgery, monitors wanted more details than did blunters (Steptoe & O'Sullivan, 1986). In the same study, monitors were also found to have significantly more factual knowledge about the procedure. The researchers also compared patient factual knowledge (what they actually knew) with their reported understanding (what they claimed they knew). Whereas monitors who claimed to have better levels of understanding actually gave more correct answers, in blunters factual knowledge was generally low and unrelated to their reported understanding. Among patients visiting a primary care setting for acute medical problems, both monitors and blunters wanted information about the diagnosis and seriousness of their medical problem. However, monitors were significantly more likely to desire additional information pertaining to the cause of their medical problem (Miller et al., 1988). They also wanted to know how healthy they were in general, what they could do to prevent future health problems, and possible medication side effects.

In summary, monitors appear to desire more voluminous and detailed levels of information and preparation than do blunters. Whereas monitors want more information about their health, blunters neither want nor seek such information. The question then becomes: What do monitors do with this information? And what does it do to them? That is, what does it activate in them psychologically, and how do they react to it cognitively, emotionally, physiologically, and behaviorally?

ACTIVATION OF INTERNAL RESPONSES: AFFECT AND GOAL-DIRECTED MOTIVATION

Monitors not only look for more threats externally, but also tend to attend more to their own bodily cues and to amplify them. This is seen in a study (Miller et al., 1988) of patients visiting a primary care setting for acute medical problems (e.g., gastrointestinal problems, influenza), who had experienced new or increased levels of discomfort and dysfunction during the week preceding their medical visit. The results suggest that monitors and blunters differed in the level of seriousness of their actual medical problem. Evaluations by the physicians showed that monitors actually had less severe medical problems than blunters did. Only 9% of the blunters had problems rated "not at all" serious, whereas twice as many monitors had such trivial difficulties.

Although both groups had an equal number of serious problems, one third of the blunters had moderately serious or quite serious problems, while 10% of the monitors had such problems. About three times as many blunters were rated as falling into these upper categories as monitors. Further, the physicians noted that monitors (compared to blunters) had experienced less dysfunction and discomfort prior to the visit, and indicated that their medical problem had contributed less to how they had been feeling. Yet, the monitors sought help.

In part, individuals may have a tendency to monitor as a way of accounting for their greater sensitivity to bodily symptoms (see also Miller, Leinbach, & Brody, 1989). Regardless of the causes, monitors not only scan for external threat-relevant cues more than do blunters, they seem to have lower thresholds for detecting their bodily cues. Consequently, they tend to detect or over interpret new or changing physical symptoms. They also find it difficult to distract themselves from their symptoms, and thus experience more arousal and aversive internal states. In fact, although monitors had less severe medical problems, their self-rated levels of discomfort, dysfunction, and perceived problem seriousness were just like those of the blunters who were more ill. Further, it was the monitors who showed slower and less complete recovery than did the blunters. For example, at a 1-week follow-up after the visit, blunters showed significantly more improvement than monitors in specific medical symptoms, and they rated themselves as manifesting twice as much improvement in their stress-related problems compared to the monitors.

Monitors thus prefer more information, but they do not use it to exert controlling actions themselves (Miller, 1979, 1980; Miller, Combs, & Stoddard, 1989). Instead, these information seekers seem to yield their control to another, more competent individual, that is, the expert, on whom they so easily call. For example, while monitors in a primary care setting typically preferred to have detailed information and reassurance about their medical condition, they did not seem to seek this information for its instrumental value (Miller et al., 1988). Rather, they were more likely to desire to play a passive role in decision-making about their medical care compared to blunters. Perhaps their greater knowledge makes these individuals more acutely aware of the limits of their personal control. Perhaps they seek more information because they sense their own limited self-efficacy and ability to control their fate.

Likewise, in a rare study in which both coping styles and strategies were measured, Carver, Scheier, and Weintraub (1989) found that monitors coped with stress by focusing on and ventilating their emotions. They also did not give up their goals and continued to solve the problem, but they did so not by engaging in more active coping or planning, but by seeking social support for instrumental reasons. That is, they tried to get advice and to find other people who could do something concrete about the problem, or they turned more to religion, seeking the help of God and putting their trust in Him. Thus, while information seekers prefer information, they tend to use it to try to put themselves in the presence of safety signals. For example, they solicit help from medical specialists so that the experts will minimize the aversiveness of the situation for them and provide help, rescuing them from the dangers they so readily perceive.

IMPACT OF CHRONIC ACTIVATING OF NEGATIVE AFFECT: LONG-TERM MORBIDITY

If monitors not only seek bad news, see it pervasively (externally and internally), and amplify its threatening significance, it follows that they will tend to activate high levels of distress and negative affect in themselves (Lerman, Daly, Masny, & Balshem, 1994; Muris & Jong, 1993; Muris & Zuuren, 1992; Zuuren & Wolfs,

1991). Their ruminations about, and rehearsals of, the "bad news" then will create a long-term state of intrusive negative feelings and cognitions (Muris, Jongh, Zuuren, & Horst, 1994; Zuuren & Muris, 1993). This takes many forms and can have substantial psychological and somatic consequences and costs, depending on such factors as the duration and intensity of the life threats experienced, and the interactions between monitoring-blunting strategies and other cognitive social person variables, such as their expectancies, control beliefs, and available coping competencies (e.g., Miller et al., in press).

Some of these negative effects are seen in results from studies of cancer patients' response to various aversive treatment procedures, such as chemotherapy. Significantly more of the monitors undergoing chemotherapy experienced nausea than did blunters and their episodes of nausea lasted more than three times as long (Gard et al., 1988). These differences are especially notable, given that significantly more monitors than blunters received antiemetic medication designed to reduce the severity of these effects (see also Lerman et al., 1990; Ward, Leventhal, & Love, 1988). Moreover, teaching relaxation techniques to patients who are about to undergo chemotherapy proved to be more effective in reducing anticipatory anxiety for blunters than for monitors (Lerman et al., 1990). Monitors seem to need more targeted—or more prolonged—stress management interventions, especially when they face health-related threats and other stressors (Avants, Margolin, & Salovey, 1990; Miller, 1989). Monitors with metastatic cancer also were more dissatisfied with information provided about their tests, symptoms, and conditions (Steptoe, Sutcliffe, Allen, & Coombes, 1991; see also Lerman et al., 1993).

Studies using other, more global, measures of general adaptation and health have yielded data that are less clear. While some show that denial tends to facilitate psychological well-being (Meyerowitz, Heinrich, & Schag, 1983), the instruments used to assess this construct generally have not been well-validated. Theoretically, it is not clear how constructs such as denial link to monitoring-blunting. There is sound evidence that suggests that avoidance strategies, such as denial, may not be beneficial to health status (Carver et al., 1993). Further, people who have trouble expressing negative feelings (especially anger and hostility), and who instead appear more repressed and better adjusted to their disease, may be more likely to develop cancer in the first place or to die of it at a faster rate, according to some studies (e.g., Derogatis, Abeloff, & Melisaratos, 1979; Greer, Morris, & Pettingale, 1979; Jensen, 1987). But, this effect is not consistently found (e.g., Cassileth, Lusk, Miller, Brown, & Miller, 1985; Levy, Lee, Bagley, & Lippman, 1988).

It is difficult to reconcile these findings, in part because it is not clear just which aspects of negative emotion are really toxic: Is the problem rooted in unconscious repression, conscious suppression, strategic nonexpression, or passive nonexpression? Research is still needed to explore in depth and detail exactly what is being attended to or avoided, the mechanisms that underlie these strategies, and their short- and long-term consequences (Miller & O'Leary, 1993; O'Leary & Miller, 1991).

ACTIVATION OF EFFECTIVE PROBLEM-SOLVING COPING STRATEGIES: SOMETIMES, IN SOME PEOPLE

Women at risk for cervical cancer who are monitors tend to use attention-oriented strategies when dealing with an aversive diagnostic procedure (Miller, Rodoletz, Buzaglo, Bales, Mangan, & Sedlacek, 1995). For example, they may focus on bodily sensations, talk with the staff about their physical feelings, ideate about what the physicians are doing, and think how essential the procedure is. They seem to use less self-distraction and generally do not try to relax or think about distractions from the procedure and their gynecologic condition. Compared to blunters, the monitors believe that their coping strategies are less helpful to them and do not necessarily make them feel less anxious, yet they feel compelled to use these strategies (see also Efran et al., 1989).

In the days before their medical visit, monitors report experiencing more intrusive ideation about their gynecologic situation compared to blunters. That is, they are more likely to recurrently relive the stress through intrusive thoughts, images, memories, etc., and to experience intense distress at exposures to reminders of their situation. The monitors also engage in more avoidant strategies in an attempt to curb their thoughts: that is, they are more likely to avoid thinking or talking about it, to push thoughts of it out of their minds, and to try to avoid reminders of it. Monitors who are facing more lethal health threats, such as those who are HIV-positive (Miller, Rodoletz, Buzaglo, Bales, Mangan, & Sedlacek, 1995) or at high genetic risk for breast cancer (Schwartz, Lerman, Miller, Daly, & Masny, 1995), also report greater intrusive and avoidant ideation than do blunters, as well as greater concomitant distress.

These results make sense, because efforts to suppress disturbing thoughts may sometimes have the paradoxical effect of increasing intrusive ideation. Consider, for example, normal subjects instructed to avoid thinking about a white bear and to ring a bell every time they did think about it (Wegner, Schneider, Carter, & White, 1987). These subjects had great difficulty suppressing the thought and, during a subsequent task in which they were explicitly instructed to think about a white bear, they experienced more thoughts about it than a group who had been asked to think the thought from the outset. Monitors may well be especially vulnerable to these paradoxical effects, because they have difficulty spontaneously suppressing unpleasant cognitions and, when they attempt to do so, it may prove to be futile. They therefore may need interventions that provide them with a structure or strategy for tuning out disturbing thoughts. Wegner and colleagues (1987) found, for example, that if subjects were given a specific thought to use as a distractor (the image of a red

Volkswagen) during the initial suppression period, it later eliminated preoccupation with the thought.

In sum, blunters tend to feel more satisfied with their coping efficacy, are less anxious in the face of intrusive ideation, and less concerned with trying to suppress or contain these thoughts, and thus are less victimized by them. In contrast, monitors are more sensitive to their own ruminative ideation, perhaps because they anticipate that they will not be able to modulate this intrusive thinking and will become trapped in an ever-increasing spiral of monitoring which they cannot stop. Consequently, they attend to even minor potential negative consequences and exaggerate them, turning everything into a catastrophe. Unsurprisingly, monitors are more likely to engage in worrying than blunters are (Davey, 1993; Davey et al., 1992; Russell & Davey, 1993), and thus are persistently aware of, and attentive to, possible danger. Interestingly, the relationship between monitoring and worry is found, independent of levels of trait anxiety, suggesting that the adaptiveness of attentionally-oriented processes may depend on different aspects of the threat situation. Hence, in situations in which information seeking is maladaptive, monitors may benefit from intervention techniques that help them learn how to monitor in a way that decreases the salience of threat and that instead focuses them on the positive and reassuring aspects of the situation, and in some cases on the things that they can *do* to effectively cope and solve problems.

DIAGNOSTIC CONDITIONS FOR OBSERVING PROTOTYPIC DIFFERENCES IN COGNITIVE PROCESSING

The subjective and physiological correlates of monitoring and blunting become evident under high threat conditions but not when threat is low or absent. For example, a group of at-risk pregnant women, about to undergo amniocentesis, were assessed with measures of distress obtained after genetic counseling, after amniocentesis, and after obtaining the results which, in all cases, were good (Phipps & Zinn, 1986). After genetic counseling, monitors manifested more anxiety than blunters, and these differences were heightened immediately after amniocentesis. Similar patterns were found on measures of depression and anger. Monitors were more distressed than blunters, both after genetic counseling and immediately after amniocentesis. The monitors' greater arousal dissipated after they heard the good news about their test results. At that point, no differences were found between the different coping style groups. Note also that no differences in affect were found between monitors and blunters at equivalent points in time in a control group of pregnant women who were not at risk, and who did not experience amniocentesis (see also Wardle et al., 1993; Zuuren, 1993).

Studies of physiological arousal yield parallel findings (Sparks & Spirek, 1988). In their research, undergraduate subjects completed the MBSS and 5 weeks later, they watched the frightening film *Nightmare on Elm Street*. Their average skin conductance levels were calculated at baseline, in a beginning low stress segment, in a moderate stress boobytrap segment, at a mild stress segment on descending the stairs, and in a high stress chase segment. Monitors displayed a significantly greater increase in skin conductance from baseline across the entire film segment compared to blunters and, most importantly, the interaction between coping style and time periods was significant. Thus, monitors showed a moderate increase in skin conductance during the moderate stress segment but a large increase in skin conductance during the high stress segment, and their skin conductance did not increase during the low stress and mild stress segments and did not differ from comparable measures in blunters during these segments. Generally, blunters maintained a low level of electrodermal arousal throughout the film.

Within a given stressful situation, monitors and blunters also display distinctive patterns of habituation. They do not differ from each other on initial measures of state or trait distress or on initial measures of psychophysiological arousal, in both laboratory and field settings (Miller, 1979, 1987; Miller & Mangan, 1983; Phipps & Zinn, 1986; Watkins et al., 1986). But the two different coping modes do sometimes display distinctive patterns of emotional responsivity over time. In the laboratory, when faced with the threat of electric shock (to the fingers), monitors and blunters do not differ in their self-reports of tension and anxiety after the first trial (Miller, 1987), but those who attend to information manifest sustained higher arousal and less habituation across trials compared to blunters, who ultimately decrease in arousal.

This differential habituation is also seen when other self-report measures and physiological indices are employed (Miller, 1979, 1987). Miller and Mangan (1983) studied gynecologic patients at risk for cervical cancer who had to undergo an aversive diagnostic procedure (colposcopy). During the 5 days following the procedure, monitors expressed more pain and discomfort than did blunters. Blunters showed a steady decrease in amount of discomfort expressed, but monitors showed a more gradual decline in pain and discomfort.

FLEXIBILITY OF COPING STRATEGIES

Competent self-regulatory coping requires individuals to discriminate the key ingredients of situations that demand different coping strategies and adapt their own behavior in light of the specific requirements of the context (e.g., Mischel & Shoda, 1995). Effective self-regulation thus involves the ability to discriminate variation in situational factors and to adjust one's coping strategies accordingly (Chiu, Hong, Mischel, & Shoda, 1994).

Consider the relationship between the individual's ability to alter an outcome and the corresponding cognitive strategy of choice. Suppose an individual is dealing with a threatening, yet uncontrollable event, such as when the mother gives the family car to a son who does not plan to return home until early next morning. After the child has driven away, this woman cannot change the outcome in any way. If she dwells on the dangers and complications that could befall her son, she will become anxious but to no avail. Instead of ruminating about the awful things that could happen, she would do better to distract herself and focus on how to spend a pleasant evening.

Individuals who persistently monitor for threatening cues place themselves enduringly into the presence of arousing danger signals. Thus, even when these dangers are objectively absent and the individual is externally in a nonaversive situation, he or she may still experience such threatening signals while remaining ignorant of safety signals. Victims of anxiety disorders typically focus on cues about potential dangers (Mathews & MacLeod, 1985) benefit from stress inoculation techniques that teach them how to monitor less and distract more, for example, through deep muscle relaxation, thought stopping, and constructive reinterpretation. These methods also can help extreme monitors to stop focusing on threat and thereby reduce their anxiety (e.g., Goldfried, Decenteceo, & Weinberg, 1974; Meichenbaum, 1992; Meichenbaum & Cameron, 1983; Ross, 1981). It is important, however, to identify strategies that are best for different types of patients and to learn how patients can best be helped to effectively use distraction and related anxiety-reducing techniques, while still effectively processing threats that are real and challenging (Muris, Jong, Merckelbach, & Zuuren, 1993a, 1993b; Steketee, Bransfield, Miller, & Foa, 1989).

Self-distraction is also important when individuals face a frustrating situation. For example, if one orders the house specialty at a French restaurant, one may have to wait quite a while for its arrival. This can produce considerable frustration if one monitors the clock or fails to distract, and the more one thinks about the delayed repast, the more one may be tempted to fill up on bread. Systematic studies of the ability to tolerate frustration in the pursuit of preferred but delayed outcomes show that cognitive transformations of the aversive cues in the situation and strategic self-distraction are essential ingredients of effective goal-directed persistence (e.g., Mischel, Shoda, & Rodriguez, 1989). In contrast, excessive monitoring of reward-relevant cues can generate chronic frustration and plays a role in self-control disorders. Impulsive children tend to respond too quickly and without deliberation to cognitive and other tasks that require patience and forethought, focusing on the "hot," arousing, frustrating textures of the situation, rather than "cooling" and selectively tuning out on them and focusing on what needs to be done in the context (e.g., Rodriguez, Mischel, Shoda, & Wright, 1989). Fortunately, it is also possible to teach impulsive children to divert their attention away from arousing or frustrating stimuli and their self-distraction, in turn, serves to enhance their delay tolerance (e.g., Gallagher, Miller, & Mischel, 1988).

In spite of the large psychic costs of their strategy, monitoring may have a constructive function, helping one to regulate goal-directed efforts under conditions in which the threat is controllable. For example, monitors may change their risk for cancer by giving up cigarettes or reduce potential cancer morbidity and mortality by undergoing routine screening (Christensen, Smith, Turner, & Cundick, 1994; Muris, Zuuren, & Kindt, 1994; Steptoe & O'Sullivan, 1986). In contrast, those who simply ignore or avoid information and distract from the health hazards of continuing to smoke or failing to adhere to screening regimens will not be motivated to change their behavior and thus will endanger themselves. Likewise, people who fail to process extremely traumatic and earth-shattering experiences may also suffer ill effects and show greater and more prolonged disturbance (Solomon et al., 1991), including posttraumatic stress reaction (Foa & Kozak, 1986). Thus, within the present framework, then, the ability to cope effectively with threat and frustration depends not only on monitoring-blunting processes, but also hinges on the individual's ability first to discriminate the relevant situational factors, to identify the necessary problem-solving strategy, and then to execute it in light of the particular situational contingencies. This requires a flexibility in cognitive strategies, rather than rigid oblivion to the demands of the context (Mischel, 1984; Mischel & Shoda, 1995; Shoda, Mischel, & Wright, 1995).

CONCLUSIONS AND NEW DIRECTIONS

The findings reviewed above are not intended as a comprehensive survey and merely illustrate some of the main results obtained in more than 15 years of research with this dimension. Cumulatively, they provide considerable evidence for substantial stable individual differences in the tendency to monitor or to blunt when dealing with potentially threatening information. People who differ in this regard, as identified by their scores on the MBSS, clearly show predictable patterns of information seeking or avoidance, particularly as assessed in health-relevant contexts, such as when they face surgery or information about potential risks to their health and well-being. Although, on the whole, extreme monitoring is often associated with higher psychological and physical costs, both the monitoring and the blunting tendency have distinctive benefits as well as negative consequences, at least under some conditions.

The tendency to monitor, to scan for, and to amplify threatening information easily leads the monitor to experience chronic high levels of anxiety and stress, with aversive intrusive ideation that may become obsessive and habitually ruminative, thereby interfering with effective problem solving and adaptive coping. But although the monitoring tendency does not facilitate a happy-go-lucky life style, and often painfully victimizes those who cannot control themselves, it does have its functional value. For example, monitors are more likely to seek medical help and services, albeit sometimes unnecessarily and in ways that make them medical pests who cry wolf so often that the health care professional may ignore them even when their need is real and urgent.

Conversely, the tendency to blunt is generally associated with less interference from anticipatory anxiety and intrusive, distressing ideation and rumination, thus leaving blunters typically more sanguine and free to deal with diverse everyday issues and problem solving in their life tasks, rather than perpetually scanning for—and finding—danger. On the other hand, blunters also risk whistling in the dark and avoiding screening and other health-protective behaviors that could objectively reduce their health risks.

These findings can easily lead health care professionals to conclude that blunters need to be made to face the facts, and be exposed more to the diverse threats and dangers that are real in health care contexts, whereas monitors need the opposite prescription, so that their anxieties can be reduced by telling them less of the potentially bad news and even glossing over some of the frightening details. Life, however, appears to be more complex. Thus, monitors in fact fare better when given more information, whereas blunters do better given less information when facing a variety of medical procedures. This has been demonstrated in gynecologic patients who were about to undergo colposcopy, a diagnostic procedure to check for the presence of abnormal (cancerous) cells in the cervix and uterus (Miller & Mangan, 1983). Patients were divided into monitors and blunters and half the women in each group were then given extensive information about the forthcoming procedure and its effects, and half were given (the usual) minimal information.

Psychophysiological reactions (like pulse rate), subjective reports, and observer ratings of arousal and discomfort were attained before, during, and after the medical procedure. As predicted, monitors showed much more arousal overall than did blunters. Especially interesting, physiological arousal was reduced when the level of preparatory information was consistent with the patient's coping style. Thus, blunters who received minimal information and monitors who received extensive information experienced the greatest reductions in arousal (see also Christensen et al., 1994; Davis, Maguire, Haraphongse, & Schaumberger, 1994; Efran et al., 1989; Gattuso, Litt, & Fitzgerald, 1992; Jacob, Penn, Kulik, & Spieth, 1992; Litt, Nye, & Schaffer, 1992; Watkins et al., 1986).

To go beyond the broad overall differences that tend to characterize individuals who are relatively extreme with regard to their general tendency to monitor or blunt potentially threatening information requires recognition of the fact that no person is just a monitor or just a blunter: these individuals also differ with regard to diverse other characteristics that importantly interact with their monitoring-blunting strategies in ways that determine their interfering or facilitating impact on the coping process, in response to particular situations and life projects. From the present theoretical perspective, these qualities are conceptualized in terms of such cognitive-affective person variables as their self-concepts and other core personal constructs and encoding patterns, their typical (chronic) affective states (e.g., the ease with which they become depressed), their relevant outcome and efficacy expectations, their major goals and personal values, and their self-regulatory and problem-solving competencies and strategies (e.g., Miller et al., in press; Mischel, 1973; Mischel & Shoda, 1995). For example, discriminative monitoring in potentially controllable, rather than in uncontrollable conditions or regardless of potential control, seems to characterize individuals who are more competent and effective in problem solving (Chiu et al., 1995).

Thus, whether monitoring will or will not facilitate effective coping and problem solving should depend on such considerations as whether the particular situation is encoded as controllable, the activated expectancies (e.g., optimistic-pessimistic; helpless or mastery-oriented) and emotions (e.g., depression, anxiety), and the problem-solving competencies and strategies that are available and accessed (Miller, Hurley, Schwartz, & Schreiber, 1994; Miller, Roussi, Caputo, & Kruus, 1995). The clear implication is that precise predictions of the interference or facilitation produced by monitor-blunting will depend on the interactions among all these person variables in the cognitive-emotional processing of threat-relevant information. To understand these interactions will require conceptual models and measurement strategies that encompass more than one person variable at a time and that focus on the processes through which they are interconnected and activate each other in the mediating system (Miller et al., in press; Mischel & Shoda, in press).

ACKNOWLEDGMENTS

This research was supported, in part, by National Cancer Institute Grants CA46591, CA58999, and CA61280 and American Cancer Society Grant PBR-72 to the author.

REFERENCES

Avants, S. K., Margolin, A., & Salovey, P. (1990). Stress management techniques: Anxiety reduction, appeal, and individual differences. *Imagination, Cognition, and Personality, 10*, 3–23.

Carver, C. S., Pozo, C., Harris, S. D., Noriega, V., Scheier, M., Robinson, D., Ketcham, A., & Moffat, F. (1993). How coping mediates the effects of optimism on distress: A study of women with early stage breast cancer. *Journal of Personality and Social Psychology, 65*, 375–390.

Carver, C. S., Scheier, M. F., & Weintraub, J. K. (1989). Assessing coping strategies: A theoretically based approach. *Journal of Personality and Social Psychology, 56*, 267–283.

Cassileth, B. R., Lusk, E. J., Miller, D. S., Brown, L. L., & Miller, C. (1985). Psychosocial correlates of survival in malignant disease. *New England Journal of Medicine, 312*, 1551–1555.

Chiu, C., Hong, Y., Mischel, W., & Shoda, Y. (1995). Discriminative facility in competent social behavior. *Social Cognition, 13*, 49–70.

Christensen, A. J., Smith, T. W., Turner, C. W., & Cundick, K. E. (1994). Patient adherence and adjustment in renal dialysis: A person by treatment interactive approach. *Journal of Behavioral Medicine, 17*, 549–566.

Davey, G. C. L. (1993). A comparison of three worry questionnaires. *Behaviour Research and Therapy, 31*, 51–56.

Davey, G. C. L., Hampton, J., Farrell, F., & Davidson, S. (1992). Some characteristics of worrying: Evidence for worrying and anxiety as separate constructs. *Personality and Individual Differences, 13*, 133–147.

Davis, T., Maguire, T., Haraphongse, M., & Schaumberger, M. (1994). Preparing adult patients for cardiac catheterization: Informational treatment and coping style interactions. *Heart and Lung, 23*, 140–150.

Derogatis, L. R., Abeloff, M. D., & Melisaratos, N. (1979). Psychological coping mechanisms and survival time in metastic breast cancer. *Journal of the American Medical Association, 242*, 1504–1508.

Efran, J., Chorney, R. L., Ascher, L. M., & Lukens, M. D. (1989). Coping style, paradox and the cold pressor task. *Journal of Behavioral Medicine, 12*, 91–103.

Foa, E. B., & Kozak, M. (1986). Emotional processing of fear: Exposure to corrective information. *Psychological Bulletin, 99*, 20–35.

Gallagher, R., Miller, S. M., & Mischel, W. (1988). *Self-regulatory strategies with delayed rewards: Implications for behavioral adjustment.* Unpublished manuscript, Temple University.

Gard, D., Edwards, P. W., Harris, J., & McCormack, G. (1988). Sensitizing effects of pretreatment measures on cancer chemotherapy nausea and vomiting. *Journal of Consulting and Clinical Psychology, 56*, 80–84.

Gattuso, S. M., Litt, M. D., & Fitzgerald, T. E. (1992). Coping with gastrointestinal endoscopy: Self-efficacy enhancement and coping style. *Journal of Consulting and Clinical Psychology, 60*, 133–139.

Greer, S., Morris, T., & Pettingale, K. W. (1979). Psychological response to breast cancer: Effect and outcome. *Lancet, 2*, 785–787.

Goldfried, M., Decenteceo, E., & Weinberg, L. (1974). Systematic rational restructuring as a self-control technique. *Behavior Therapy, 5*, 247–257.

Jacob, T. C., Penn, N. E., Kulik, T. A., & Spieth, L. E. (1992). Effects of cognitive style and maintenance strategies on breast self-examination (BSE) practice by African American women. *Journal of Behavioral Medicine, 15*, 589–609.

Jensen, M. J. (1987). Psychobiological factors predicting the course of breast cancer. *Journal of Personality, 55*, 317–342.

Lerman, C., Rimer, R., Blumber, B., Cristinzso, M. S., Engstrom, P. F., McElwee, N., O'Connor, K., & Seay, J. (1990). Effects of coping style and relaxation on cancer chemotherapy side effects and emotional responses. *Cancer Nursing, 13*, 308–315.

Lerman, C., Daly, M., Masny, A., & Blashem, A. (1994). Attitudes about genetic testing for breast-ovarian cancer susceptibility. *Journal of Clinical Oncology, 12*, 843–850.

Lerman, C., Daly, M., Walsh, W., Resch, N., Seay, J., Barsevick, A., Birenbaum, L., Heggan, T., & Martin, G. (1993). Communication between patients with breast cancer and health care providers: Determinants and implications. *Cancer, 72*, 2612–2620.

Levy, S. M., Lee, J., Bagley, C., & Lippman, M. (1988). Survival hazards analysis in first recurrent breast cancer patients: Seven-year follow-up. *Psychosomatic Medicine, 50*, 520–528.

Litt, M., Nye, C., & Shaffer, D. (1992). *Distraction from information in coping with oral surgery.* Paper presented at the International Association for Dental Research, Glasgow, Scotland.

Ludwick-Rosenthal, R., & Neufeld, R. J. (1993). Preparation for undergoing an invasive medical procedure: Interacting effects of information and coping style. *Journal of Consulting and Clinical Psychology, 61*, 156–164.

Mathews, A., & Macleod, C. (1985). Selective processing of threat cues in anxiety states. *Behaviour Research and Therapy, 23*, 563–569.

Meichenbaum, D. (1992). Stress inoculation training: A twenty year update. In R. L. Woolfolk & P. H. Lehrer (Eds.), *Principles and practice of stress management* (pp. 373–406). New York: Guilford Press.

Meichenbaum, D., & Cameron, R. (1983). Stress inoculation training: Toward a general paradigm for training coping skills. In D. Meichenbaum & M. E. Jaremko (Eds.), *Stress reduction and prevention* (pp. 115–154). New York: Plenum.

Meyerowitz, B. E., Heinrich, R. L., & Schag, C. C. (1983). A competency-based approach to coping with cancer. In T. G. Burish & L. A. Bradley (Eds.), *Coping with chronic disease* (pp. 137–158). New York: Academic Press.

Miller, S. M. (1979). Controllability and human stress: Method, evidence and theory. *Behaviour Research and Therapy, 17*, 287–304.

Miller, S. M. (1980). Why having control reduces stress: If I can stop the roller coaster I don't want to get off. In J. Garber & M. E. P. Seligman (Eds.), *Human helplessness: Theory and applications* (pp. 71–95). New York: Academic Press.

Miller, S. M. (1987). Monitoring and blunting: Validation of a questionnaire to assess styles of information seeking under threat. *Journal of Personality and Social Psychology, 52*, 345–353.

Miller, S. M. (1989). Cognitive informational styles in the process of coping with threat and frustration. *Advances in Behaviour Research and Therapy, 11*, 223–234.

Miller, S. M. (1990). To see or not to see: Cognitive informational styles in the coping process. In M. Rosenbaum (Ed.), *Learned resourcefulness: On coping skills, self-regulation and adaptive behavior* (pp. 95–126). New York: Springer.

Miller, S. M. (1992a). Individual differences in the coping process: What to know and when to know it. In B. Carpenter (Ed.), *Personal coping: Theory, research, and application* (pp. 77–91). New York: Praeger.

Miller, S. M. (1992b). Monitoring and blunting in the face of threat: Implications for adaptation and health. In L. Montada, S. H. Filipp, & M. J. Lerner (Eds.), *Life crises and experiences of loss in adulthood* (pp. 255–273). Hillsdale, NJ: Lawrence Erlbaum Associates.

Miller, S. M. (1995). Monitoring versus blunting styles of coping influence the information patients want and need about cancer. *Cancer, 76*, 167–177.

Miller, S. M., Brody, D. S., & Summerton, J. (1988). Styles of coping with threat: Implications for health. *Journal of Personality and Social Psychology, 54*, 142–148.

Miller, S. M., Combs, C., & Kruus, L. (1993). Turning in and turning out: Confronting the effects of confrontation. In H. W. Krohne (Ed.), *Attention and avoidance: Strategies in coping with aversiveness* (pp. 51–69). Seattle: Hogrefe & Huber.

Miller, S. M., Combs, C., & Stoddard, E. (1989). Information, coping, and control in patients undergoing surgery and stressful medical procedures. In A. Steptoe & A. Appels (Eds.), *Stress, personal control and health* (pp. 107–130). New York: Wiley.

Miller, S. M., Hurley, K., Schwartz, J., & Schreiber, P. (1994). *Optimism and monitoring in infertile women.* Paper presented at the Society of Behavioral Medicine Fifteenth Annual Scientific Sessions, Boston, MA.

Miller, S. M., Leinbach, A., & Brody, D. (1989). Coping style in hypertensive patients: Nature and consequences. *Journal of Consulting and Clinical Psychology, 57*, 333–337.

Miller, S. M., & Mangan, C. E. (1983). The interacting effects of information and coping style in adapting to gynecologic stress: Should the doctor tell all. *Journal of Personality and Social Psychology, 45*, 223–236.

Miller, S. M., & O'Leary, A. (1993). Cognition, stress, and health. In K. Dobson & P. C. Kendall (Eds.), *Cognition and psychopathology* (pp. 159–189). New York: Academic Press.

Miller, S. M., Rodoletz, M., Buzaglo, J., Bales, T., Mangan, C. E., & Sedlacek, T. V. (1995). *A dispositional model of adjustment to chronic medical conditions.* Paper presented at the Society of Behavioral Medicine Sixteenth Annual Scientific Sessions, San Diego, CA.

Miller, S. M., Roussi, P., Caputo, C., & Kruus, L. (1995). Patterns of children's coping with an aversive dental treatment. *Health Psychology, 14*, 236–246.

Miller, S. M., Roussi, P., Altman, D., Helm, W., & Steinberg, A. (1994). Effects of coping on psychological reactions of low-income minority women of colposcopy. *The Journal of Reproductive Medicine, 39*, 711–718.
Miller, S. M., Shoda, Y., & Hurley, K. (in press). Applying cognitive social theory to breast self-examination in cancer screening. *Psychological Bulletin.*
Mischel, W. (1973). Toward a cognitive social learning of reconceptualization of personality. *Psychology Review, 80*, 252–283.
Mischel, W. (1984). Convergences and challenges in the search for consistency. *American Psychologist, 39*, 351–364.
Mischel, W., & Shoda, Y. (1994). Personality psychology has two goals: Must it be two fields? *Psychological Inquiry, 5*, 156–158.
Mischel, W., & Shoda, Y. (1995). A cognitive-affective system theory of personality: Reconceptualizing the invariances in personality and role of situations. *Psychological Review, 102*, 246–268.
Mischel, W., Shoda, Y., & Rodriguez, M. L. (1989). Delay of gratification in children. *Science, 244*, 933–938.
Muris, P., & Jong, P. de (1993). Monitoring and perception of threat. *Personality and Individual Differences, 15*, 467–470.
Muris, P., Jong, P. de, Merckelbach, H., & Zuuren, F. J. van (1993a). Is exposure therapy affected by a monitoring coping style? *Advances in Behavior Research and Therapy, 15*, 291–300.
Muris, P., Jong, P. de, Merckelbach, H., & Zuuren, F. J. van (1993b). Monitoring coping style and exposure outcome in spider phobics. *Behavioural and Cognitive Psychotherapy, 21*, 329–333.
Muris, P., Jongh, A. de, Zuuren, F. J. van, ter Horst, G. (1994). Coping style, anxiety, cognitions, and cognitive control in dental phobia. *Personality and Individual Differences, 17*, 143–145.
Muris, P., & Schouten, E. (1994). Monitoring and blunting: A factor analysis of the Miller Behavioral Style Scale. *Personality and Individual Differences, 17*, 285–287.
Muris, P., & Zuuren, F. J. van (1992). Monitoring, medical fears, and physical symptoms. *British Journal of Clinical Psychology, 31*, 360–362.
Muris, P., Zuuren, F. J. van, & Kindt, M. (1994). Monitoring coping style, fear of AIDS, and attitudes toward AIDS prevention. *Social Behavior and Personality, 22*, 137–144.
Muris, P., Zuuren, F. J. van, & Vries, S. de (1994). Monitoring, blunting, and situational anxiety: A laboratory study on coping with a quasi-medical stressor. *Personality and Individual Differences, 16*, 365–372.
O'Leary, A., & Miller, S. M. (1991). Stress, immune function, and health: Early settlement of a new frontier. *Clinical Immunology Newsletter, 11*, 177–180.
Phipps, S., & Zinn, A. B. (1986). Psychological response to amniocentesis: II. Effects of coping style. *American Journal of Medical Genetics, 25*, 143–148.
Rodriguez, M. L., Mischel, W., Shoda, Y., & Wright, J. C. (1989). Cognitive person variables in the delay of gratification of older children at risk. *Journal of Personality and Social Psychology, 57*, 358–367.
Ross, A. O. (1981). *Child behavior therapy: Principles, procedures and empirical basis.* New York: Wiley.
Russell, M., & Davey, G. C. L. (1994). The relationship between life event measures and anxiety and its cognitive correlates. *Personality and Individual Differences, 14*, 317–322.
Schwartz, M., Lerman, C., Miller, S. M., Daly, M., & Masny, A. (1995). Coping disposition, perceived risk, and psychological distress among woman at increased risk for ovarian cancer. *Health Psychology, 14*, 232–235.
Shoda, Y., Mischel, W., & Wright, J. C. (1994). Intra-individual stability in the organization and patterning of behavior: Incorporating psychological situations into the idiographic analysis of personality. *Journal of Personality and Social Psychology, 67*, 674–687.
Solomon, Z., Mikulincer, M., & Arad, R. (1991). Monitoring and blunting: Implications for combat related post-traumatic stress disorder. *Journal of Traumatic Stress, 4*, 209–221.

Sparks, G. G., & Spirek, M. M. (1988). Individual differences in coping with stressful mass media: An activation-arousal view. *Human Communication Research, 15*, 191–216.

Steketee, G., Bransfield, S., Miller, S. M., & Foa, E. B. (1989). The effect of information and coping style on the reduction of phobic anxiety during exposure. *Journal of Anxiety Disorders, 3*, 69–85.

Steptoe, A., & O'Sullivan, J. (1986). Monitoring and blunting coping styles in women prior to surgery. *British Journal of Clinical Psychology, 25*, 143–144.

Steptoe, A., & Vogele, C. (1992). Individual differences in the perception of bodily sensations: The role of trait anxiety and coping style. *Behavior Research and Therapy, 30*, 597–607.

Steptoe, A., Sutcliffe, L., Allen, B., & Coombes, C. (1991). Satisfaction with communication, medical knowledge, and coping style in patients with metastatic cancer. *Social Science Medicine, 32*, 627–632.

Ward, S. E., Leventhal, H., & Love, R. (1988). Repression revisited: Tactics used in coping with a severe health threat. *Personality and Social Psychology Bulletin, 14*, 735–746.

Wardle, F. J., Collins, W., Pernet, A. L., Whitehead, M. I., Bourne, T. H., & Campbell, S. (1993). Psychological impact of screening for familial ovarian cancer. *Journal of the National Cancer Institute, 85*, 653–657.

Watkins, L. O., Weaver, L., & Odegaard, V. (1986). Preparation for cardiac catheterization: Tailoring the content of instruction to coping style. *Heart and Lung, 15*, 382–389.

Wegner, D. M., Schneider, D. J., Carter, S. R., III, & White, T. L. (1987). Paradoxical effects of thought suppression. *Journal of Personality and Social Psychology, 53*, 5–13.

Zuuren, F. J., van (1993). Coping style and anxiety during prenatal diagnosis. *Journal of Reproductive and Infant Psychology, 11*, 57–59.

Zuuren, F. J. van, & Muris, P. (1993). Coping under experimental threat: Observable and cognitive correlates of dispositional monitoring and blunting. *European Journal of Personality, 7*, 245–253.

Zuuren, F. J. van, & Wolfs, H. M. (1991). Styles of information-seeking under threat: Personal and situational aspects of monitoring and blunting. *Personality and Individual Differences, 12*, 141–149.

CHAPTER

10

MENTAL RUMINATION AND LEARNED HELPLESSNESS: COGNITIVE SHIFTS DURING HELPLESSNESS TRAINING AND THEIR BEHAVIORAL CONSEQUENCES

Mario Mikulincer
Bar-Ilan University

The phenomenon of human learned helplessness (LH) deals with the performance effects of the exposure to unsolvable problems ("helplessness training"). Theories of LH (Seligman, 1975) have argued that the expectancy of no control is the main antecedent of these deficits. People exposed to unsolvable problems may become convinced that they would fail to control outcomes in the task, which, in turn, reduce effort expenditure in the task and produce performance deficits. However, there is accumulative evidence that these deficits may be also affected by the cognitive process of mental rumination, which involves the conscious processing and elaboration of information related to the failure situation (Kuhl, 1984; Martin & Tesser, 1989). This chapter focuses on the nature of mental rumination during exposure to unsolvable problems and its behavioral consequences.

BASIC DEFINITIONS AND WORKING HYPOTHESES

Before dealing with the role of mental rumination in human LH, the basic constructs of helplessness training and mental rumination are defined and the working hypotheses that guide the organization of this chapter presented. Basically, helplessness training refers to the experience of repeated failures in unsolvable problems. In the author's terms, helplessness training is a typical instance of person-environment mismatches, which sometimes lead to performance deficits and psychopathology and other times to growth and adaptation.

Helplessness training is a goal-oriented setting in which people attempt to solve a problem and implement pertinent instrumental actions that culminate in failure and in a mismatch between what the environment allows them to do and what they want to do. This mismatch implies the loss of control over outcomes and a threat to beliefs about the controllability of the environment and to the sense of self-worth. In this situation, people would mobilize coping actions aimed at restoring the equilibrium with the environment or minimizing the damages of the mismatch, which, in turn, may have immediate positive or negative consequences in their task performance. One of these coping actions is the engagement in mental rumination.

The discussion of the phenomenon of mental rumination is limited to these ruminative thoughts that occur during helplessness training and may affect task performance. In this context, rumination is defined as controlled, purposive thinking on a particular issue over a relatively long period of time (Martin & Tesser, 1989), that reflects a "mindful" state of mind. People actively search for information, encode relevant cues, and retrieve memories that could help in coping with the mismatch created by helplessness training. This is not to say that this rumination would always have positive effects on task performance, only that it can provide help to the coping process that sometimes may improve performance and other times may impair it. In addition, it is important to note that Martin and Tesser have noted that mental rumination is accompanied by some intrusive thoughts that occur without control and accomplish no coping function.

In this chapter, the focus is on two general types of ruminative thoughts: action and off-task thoughts. Action rumination consists of task-relevant thoughts about problem solving. These thoughts are strategic in nature (Kuhl, 1984, 1985). People ruminate on ways to succeed in a task and solve the current problem. They effortfully search and process information dealing with alternative problem solving plans and strategies. They selectively encode task-relevant stimuli, retrieve stored problem solving procedures, and inhibit any off-task cognition.

Off-task thoughts include both state ruminations and task-irrelevant ruminations. The common denominator of these two types of thoughts is that they do not deal with task features or problem solving plans. These off-task thoughts differ, however, in their relationship to the task situation. State thoughts consist of preoccupations with and worries about the implications of failure for the present and future state of the person. They include thoughts about the state of the self, the threats and losses caused by the failure, and failure-related feelings (Kuhl, 1984, 1985). They also include thoughts about the cost and benefit of the current and alternative activities and ways to adjust oneself to the new reality constraints. Task-irrelevant thoughts concern issues that behaviorally or cognitively distract people from the frustrating situation and emotionally distance them from the threatening failure. These thoughts have nothing to do with the task situation. People imagine other possible situations and think about other people, inanimate objects, tasks, or goals that are irrelevant to their current failure.

Three working hypotheses guided the organization of the current chapter. The first hypothesis is that both types of thoughts, state and task-irrelevant ruminations, are aroused during helplessness training. That is, helplessness training leads to the passage from nondeliberative to deliberative thinking and the heightening of both action and off-task thoughts. However, these two types of thoughts may be aroused at different stages of helplessness training and may may have different implications for task performance. On this basis, the second hypothesis is that a small amount of helplessness training would mainly produce action rumination, whereas a large amount of training would mainly produce off-task rumination. The third hypothesis is that action rumination would improve task performance, whereas off-task rumination would lead to performance deficits.

HELPLESSNESS TRAINING AND MENTAL RUMINATION

Theoretical Basis

Helplessness training may be a precursor of heightened cognitive activity and purposive mental rumination. In dealing with the uncontrollable failure, people may search, process, and ruminate on stored and incoming information that could help them to cope with the failure situation. Having encountered a failure and feeling the need to cope with it, people should adopt a "mindful" state of mind rather than their habitual "mindless" attitude. This idea fits the Martin and Tesser (1989) proposal that "Consciousness is often a troubleshooting process. . . . Consciousness becomes consequential when the environment does not permit behavioral scripts to unfold in their expected way" (p. 311).

Heightened cognitive activity after uncontrollable failure may also result from the fact that helplessness training generates ambiguity about the causes and meaning of environmental events and increases the need to understand the meaning of the situation. The exposure to uncontrollable failures is generally an unexpected event and people may not understand why they have failed in the task. They therefore focus their thoughts on trying to understand their current experience and to incorporate it to their stored schemata, and purposively ruminate on the meaning and implications of the frustrating situation.

The exposure to helplessness training may also lead people to stop current actions and delay any further action until they find more appropriate ways of coping with the uncontrollable failure. Helplessness training symbolically means that the individual's response repertoire is ineffective to deal with the failure and to manage the resulting distress and that its automatic repetition may only augment rather than reduce the distress. Therefore, people may feel that they should think before acting in order to organize new programs of actions and more effective coping means. This attitude may in turn be reflected in heightened cognitive activity, which may facilitate the programming of new coping strategies by bringing remotely associated contents into direct juxtaposition and creating new associative paths among them. Following this reasoning, Pittman and D'Agostino (1989) suggested that "an experience with failure to control one's outcomes is a danger signal that produces an increased desire to construe subsequent situations accurately. Toward this end subjects engage in effortful information acquisition . . . and new information is processed carefully and deeply (a style that could be characterized as more systematic, bottom up, or data-driven)" (p. 479).

In this way, failure may open the cognitive system in order to construct and test new and more valid knowledge. People may put aside inappropriate coping devices and replace them with more suitable plans and strategies. Individuals may also learn something new about themselves, reorganize their stored schemata about the world and the self, and construe substitute goals and projects. In other words, failure may refute knowledge, create cognitive confusion, and increase the need for new answers that could end ambiguity and distress. Failure indicates that one's response repertoire does not fit reality and that one should open the cognitive system and ruminate on the implications of the situation as well as on one's action programs and priorities.

Empirical Evidence

There is extensive evidence on the heightening of cognitive activity following helplessness training. For example, several studies have found that the frequency of self-reported ruminative thoughts increases after the experience or anticipation of failure (e.g., Klinger, 1984; Morris, Davis, & Hutchings, 1981). Research conducted in the author's laboratory also provides direct evidence that the exposure to repeated uncontrollable failures increases the reported frequency of ruminative thoughts (Mikulincer, 1989a, 1989b, 1989c; Mikulincer, Glaubman, Ben-Artzi, & Grossman, 1991; Mikulincer & Marshand, 1991; Mikulincer & Nizan, 1988). The author also found that these failures increased any tendency to engage in off-task thoughts, both for people who habitually engage in mental rumination and for those who were diagnosed as suffering from depression.

Another series of studies has focused on other aspects of effortful cognitive activity: the search, encoding, and retrieval of information. In the first study, Pittman and Pittman (1980) found that if helplessness training activated deliberative thinking, it would make people attentive to attribution-relevant cues and prone to process and use them when making causal judgments. Then they exposed subjects to no, two, or six unsolvable problems, and gave them a written essay and information on the motives for its creation. Half of the subjects were told that the essay was written for payment; a cue leading to external attribution ("mand" condition). The other half were told that it was not written for publication; a cue leading to internal attribution ("tact" condition). The dependent variable was the extent to which subjects attributed the essay's writing to external or internal causes. Results showed that failure subjects tended to encode and use attributional-relevant cues efficiently. The information about the motives for the essay's writing had greater impact on internal-external attributions among subjects exposed to two or four uncontrollable failures than among no-feedback subjects. While subjects in the no-feedback condition were not influenced by the attributional information, subjects exposed to small or large amounts of helplessness training attributed the writing to more internal and fewer external causes in the tact than in the mand condition. These findings were conceptually replicated by Liu and Steele (1986).

Helplessness training was also found to foster the active search for information (Swann, Stephenson, & Pittman, 1981). In interviewing another person, subjects exposed earlier to helplessness training asked more questions that increase the knowledge about the interviewee than subjects exposed to no feedback. Moreover, while no-feedback subjects tended to end the examination after the interviewee answered the questions, subjects exposed to uncontrollable failures tended to continue the interview and to select diagnostic issues to examine beyond those that the interviewee had already answered.

Pittman and D'Agostino (1989) found that helplessness training also increases the effortful encoding and retrieval of stored information. Subjects previously exposed to no or six unsolvable problems were given a list of sentence pairs to study, followed by a recognition test consisting of sentences from the list, inferences based on these sentences, and new sentences. Results showed that subjects exposed to uncontrollable failures were more accurate in recognizing inferences as either old or new sentences than no-feedback subjects. Similar results were obtained in regard to the learning and recognition of a short text (Pittman & D'Agostino, 1989, experiment 2).

In general, the reviewed studies suggest that exposure to uncontrollable failures triggers the effortful search, encoding, and retrieval of information. However, one can also propose that the cognitive effect of helplessness training may depend on an array of situational and personal factors. For example, this effect may depend on the extent to which existing knowledge has been violated, the centrality of this violation to the person's schemata and goals, and the level of the resulting distress. It may also depend on dispositional factors, such as the individual's tendency to ruminate, his or her tolerance of ambiguity, and his or her need for cognitive closure. In addition, the complexity of the cognitive structure and the availability of cognitive resources may also moderate the heightening of cognitive activity after helplessness training. The more complex the cognitive structures and the more available the resources, the more intensive the elaboration of information pertinent to the failure situation. One can also propose a "stop-rule" that goes into effect whenever the failure is understood and new action programs are generated. At this time, it is possible to cease effortful information processing and begin to act in a nondeliberative way.

A CYCLE OF MENTAL RUMINATION DURING HELPLESSNESS TRAINING

Having produced heightened cognitive activity, helplessness training may also activate a specific cycle of mental rumination. That is, different types of ruminative thoughts will be elicited by different amounts of helplessness training. Initially, a small amount of failure may heighten action rumination in order to cope with the failure by trying to solve the problem and remove the source of the mismatch. However, if the failure continues despite the person's persistent problem solving efforts, and no action program can solve the problem, people begin to engage in off-task rumination. This rumination may help individuals to cope with what they recognize as irreversible failures by trying either to remove the painful reality from their awareness, or to reorganize their schemata in accordance to the new reality constraints. Similar ideas have been proposed by Kuhl (1981) and Martin and Tesser (1989), who emphasized the shift from action to off-task thinking during helplessness training. Though there is no direct evidence on the hypothesized cycle of mental rumination, studies that have assessed the impact of small and large amounts of failure on information processing provide some indirect support.

Cue Utilization and the Cycle of Mental Rumination

Indirect support for the hypothesized cycle of mental rumination was provided by Mikulincer, Kedem, and Zilkha-Segal (1989) in their study on cue utilization following different amounts of helplessness training. Subjects were exposed to either no, one or four unsolvable problems, and then asked to perform a letter cancellation task under three conditions. One group of subjects received the test task with no additional cues. A second group received task-relevant cues the utilization of which could improve performance (pairs of parentheses that signaled the space which held the target letters). A third group received the same task with task-irrelevant cues which the utilization of could impair performance (randomly located pairs of parentheses).

Based on the theory of cue utilization (e.g., Easterbroock, 1959; Geen, 1980), Mikulincer et al. (1989) hypothesized that people's rumination should be reflected in the way they employ the cues. Those who engage in action rumination, search for problem solving cues, and inhibit the diversion of their thoughts from the task at hand, may make use of relevant cues and ignore irrelevant cues.

Therefore, they should exhibit (a) performance facilitation with the addition of task-relevant cues, and (b) no performance change with the addition of task-irrelevant cues. On the other hand, subjects who engage in off-task thoughts and draw attention away from task features may use neither task-relevant nor task-irrelevant cues. That is, their off-task thoughts may be reflected in no performance change with the addition of relevant or irrelevant cues.

Therefore, if subjects exposed to a small amount of failure engage in action rumination, task-relevant cues would improve their performance while task-irrelevant cues would lead to no performance change. Moreover, if subjects exposed to a large amount of failure engage in off-task rumination, neither task-relevant nor task-irrelevant cues would change their performance. Indeed, subjects exposed to one failure were found to be more accurate in the task-relevant cue condition than in the no cue condition. However, the addition of task irrelevant cues did not affect their performance. Moreover, subjects exposed to four failures showed no performance change with the addition of either task-relevant or task-irrelevant cues. In all the conditions, subjects exposed to four failures performed worse than no-feedback subjects.

The findings suggest that people react to small amounts of failure with action thoughts and to larger amounts with off-task thoughts. In support of this view, the frequencies of off-task thoughts, as assessed by the Cognitive Interference Questionnaire (CIQ; Sarason, Sarason, Keefe, Hayes, & Shearin, 1986), were higher after four failures than after one or no failure. Lamentably, there is no adequate scale of action rumination that could test whether action thoughts are increased after a small amount of helplessness training.

Judgmental Behavior and the Cycle of Mental Rumination

Indirect support for the hypothesized cycle of rumination is also provided in two experiments conducted by Dekel (1993) on stereotypical thinking and the primacy effect. Dekel analyzed the cognitive operations that underlie stereotypical thinking and the primacy effect and concluded that both of them reflect the engagement in off-task rumination and the consequent depletion of resources for analyzing task-relevant information. Stereotypical thinking reflects the tendency to evaluate another person through the commonly accepted features of that person's group, without expending the effort needed to analyze his or her unique personal characteristics. The primacy effect reflects the reluctance to spend the effort needed to retest a hypothesis built on the basis of an initial impression, even after receiving contradictory information (Kruglanski & Freund, 1983).

In Experiment 1, subjects previously exposed to no, one, or four unsolvable problems were asked to evaluate an essay written by a fourth grader and were provided information about the child's socioeconomic status (low vs. high). In Experiment 2, subjects were also exposed to no, one, or four unsolvable problems, and then they were given a two-paragraph description of a person and were asked to rate the person's level of sociability. In order to examine the primacy effect, the information depicted in the first paragraph contradicted the data presented in the second paragraph. Half of the subjects received an information sequence that first described the person as highly sociable and then as reluctant to initiate social contacts. The other half of the subjects were given a reversed sequence of information. In the two experiments, subjects also answered the CIQ tapping the frequency of their off-task thoughts during the experiment.

Results indicated that subjects exposed to only one failure did not differ from no-failure subjects in their reported frequencies of off-task thoughts. In addition, their judgments in the test task were found to be less influenced by stereotypes and initial impressions than those of the no-failure subjects. In contrast, relative to no-failure subjects, those exposed to four failures reported more off-task thoughts and their evaluations were found to be more influenced by stereotypes and initial impressions. In general, subjects initially reacted to failure with task-relevant information processing, as manifested in a reduction of stereotypical thinking and primacy effect. However, after a large amount of helplessness training, they became reluctant to invest effort in processing task-relevant data, as reflected in increased stereotypical thinking and primacy effect.

The reduction in stereotypical thinking and primacy effect observed after one failure may reflect the individual's engagement in action rumination, which involves the processing of task-relevant information. In Dekel's study, this cognitive activity might have lead people to revise hypotheses derived from preconceptions and initial impressions. The increase in stereotypical thinking and primacy effect observed after four failures may reflect the individual's engagement in off-task rumination, which draws cognitive resources away from the processing of incoming task-relevant material and therefore leads one to rely on preconceptions and initial impressions.

Cognitive Appraisal and the Cycle of Mental Rumination

On the whole, helplessness training seems to activate a cycle of mental rumination. However, this is not to say that people necessarily go through a fixed ruminative sequence. In fact, any of the stages of the cycle may be skipped. For example, a person with a tendency to depression may, after only a single failure, move directly to off-task thinking. What is proposed is that, in adequately functioning people, off-task rumination is more likely to occur after repeated failure, when people perceive action programs to be ineffective for solving the problem. This appraisal may result from actual experiences with repeated failures or from generalized expectancies and limited response repertoire. Indeed, Wicklund and Braun (1987) found that failure leads to off-task rumination mainly among persons with a small repertoire of instrumental actions.

In the author's terms, the shift from action to off-task rumination during helplessness training may result from the person's subjective appraisal of the failure situation. After one failure, individuals may still expect to overcome failure by their own problem solving actions. Therefore, they would engage in action rumination as an aid for problem-focused coping. In fact, action rumination can be seen as a cognitive tool that facilitates problem-focused coping. Problem-focused coping requires a systematic analysis of the problem, the retrieval of both declarative knowledge on problem solving situations and of procedural knowledge of problem solving strategies, as well as deliberative thinking about how the situation can be altered. In support of this view, Erwin and Marcus-Mendoza (1987) found that the frequency of action thoughts was related to the reliance on problem-focused coping in a midterm exam.

After repeated failures, people may recognize the uncontrollability of the failure, and therefore engage in off-task rumination. They may conclude that they should either avoid the confrontation with the uncontrollable failure by engaging in distracting, task-irrelevant thoughts, or accommodate their mental structures to the new reality constraints by engaging in state rumination. In fact, task-irrelevant rumination can be seen as a cognitive tool that facilitates avoidance coping. To disengage from a threat, people should stop thinking about it, suppress all related thought and affect, and think about irrelevant, distracting issues. Accordingly, state rumination may accomplish an editing function in that it allows the evaluation and reorganization of damaged self-schemas and goal hierarchies. In Kuhl's terms (1984), state rumination can be viewed "... as serving a similar purpose as the editing of a program ... reflecting on ineffective parts of the program without executing any of the steps that are being analyzed" (p. 144).

Similar ideas have been raised by Kuhl (1984), who proposed that the "perceived surmountability" of failure may underlie the passage from action to state rumination. Action rumination occurs whenever the failure is perceived as surmountable. If the failure is perceived as irreversible, people may end problem solving attempts and engage in state rumination as a device for reorganizing mental structures.

Beyond these ideas once can locate the underlying action of the appraisal of control. In fact, the perceived surmountability of failure is synonymous with the appraisal of control: the stronger the belief that one's actions can change outcomes, the stronger the expectancy of failure reversibility. Correlational evidence is available on the link between appraisal of control and rumination. Several studies found that the frequency of off-task worries was inversely related to success expectations of high school and college students taking academic exams (Doctor & Altman, 1969; Liebert & Morris, 1967; Morris & Liebert, 1970, 1973). Other studies found that changes in off-task worries over time were a function of changes in success expectancy (e.g., Doctor & Altman, 1969). Accordingly, Heckhausen (1982) found that the frequency of off-task thoughts during an exam was inversely related to subjects' success expectancy. Similar results were reported by Mikulincer (1989b) and Stiensmeier-Perlster (1989) in a laboratory LH setting. Klinger, Barta, and Maxeiner (1980) also demonstrated that the expectancy of goal attainment is positively related to the frequency of action thoughts, as measured in a thought-sampling method.

Another important piece of evidence was provided by Mikulincer and Nizan (1988). In two studies, the authors found that subjects who attributed failure to global causes (i.e., causes that recur in different tasks and settings) and thus expected no control in the test task reported more frequent off-task thoughts (as measured by the CIQ) after helplessness training than those who made task-specific attributions. Moreover, it was only among subjects who made global attributions for failure that the frequency of off-task thoughts increased after repeated failures.

AUTONOMIC RUMINATION DURING HELPLESSNESS TRAINING

Though mental rumination is viewed as a purposive activity during helplessness training, it could be sometimes accompanied by autonomic failure-related thoughts (e.g., Horowitz, 1982; Martin & Tesser, 1989). These thoughts run ballistically on to completion, are hard to suppress, and may exacerbate tension and distress. Horowitz (1982) called this cognitive material an "uninvited intruder," Uleman and Bargh (1989) called it "unintended thoughts," and Logan (1989) "autonomic cognitions." These autonomic thoughts, which are the basic component of what Horowitz (1982) calls "intrusion states," typically alternate with avoidance and denial and can be found after every type of serious failure. These thoughts may be accompanied by uncontrollable pangs of emotion, somatic hyperactivity, excessive alertness, reenactments of personal responses to the failure, bad dreams, intrusive sensations and images while trying to sleep, and misperceptions. In general, the cognitive system seems to be flooded by autonomic thoughts and affects that the person cannot stop from intruding into consciousness.

When people ruminate on a failure situation, stored material relevant to this issue is purposively activated in the "associative memory network" (Anderson & Bower, 1973), and can be incorporated into the thought flow. However, this activation may also spread over other nodes of information connected with the failure-related material by existing pathways in the associative network. In this way, cognitive material that is not purposively activated is made accessible for processing and may intrude into conscious thinking. In some cases, the autonomic spread of activation may be overridden by inhibitory mechanisms that selectively incorporate into conscious thinking only material that can help people to cope with the failure (Clark & Isen, 1982). In other cases, however, autonomic memory activation overwhelms conscious thinking with associations and images that are irrelevant to the coping task. Here, inhibitory mechanisms are weakened and autonomic thoughts intrude into consciousness, creating a state of cognitive autonomy and mental disorganization.

The main question is how this state of cognitive autonomy can be created after helplessness training. In the author's terms, the mere occurrence of a personally important failure may activate autonomic failure-related thoughts. This is what Horowitz (1979) called a period of "outcry," in which the activation of the "failure" node in the associative memory network may spread to other related thoughts, affects, and sensations. At this stage, people who have insufficient resources to master this onslaught of intrapsychic events may become overwhelmed by failure-related thoughts. However, adequately functioning people may be able to channel these thoughts into purposive mental rumination and to selectively control their conscious processing. Alternatively, they may totally inhibit the access of failure-related thoughts into consciousness by distracting themselves with task-irrelevant thoughts. Either way, they could put an end to the brief state of cognitive autonomy.

The problem is that some purposive attempts to cope with the failure may lead to the recurrence of the autonomic intrusion of failure-related thoughts into consciousness. Here, the activation of these autonomic thoughts may result from a choice of coping strategies that involve bad tradeoffs. These coping strategies may produce short-term relief, but may subsequently lead to the intrusion of autonomic thoughts. One of these coping strategies is excessive, prolonged avoidance. Avoidance coping intends to suppress direct or symbolic confrontation with a threat. However, when important self-schemas and goals are damaged by the failure, suppression may be unsuccessful and the suppressed material may return to consciousness. The to-be-suppressed thoughts may remain active in memory and any related stimuli may automatically call them into mind. Now these thoughts return to consciousness, but as autonomous intruders rather than as wanted material. In Horowitz' (1982) terms, autonomic failure-related thoughts are inherent products of every avoidance attempt, even the most successful, because the to-be-suppressed material exerts a constant demand for processing, and intrudes into consciousness every time internal or external stimuli call it up.

The above ideas are based on both theoretical and empirical data. Freud (1957/1914) suggested that attempts to repress unwanted thoughts lead to preoccupation with those thoughts and to the intrusive return of the repressed material. Lazarus (1983) observed that suppression of thought can result in subsequent obsessive concern. The same pattern was found among people who inhibit the expression of thoughts about a traumatic experience (e.g., Foa & Kozak, 1986; Silver, Boon, & Stones, 1983) and among people who were asked to suppress a particular thought (Wegner, Schneider, Carter, & White, 1987; Wegner, Schneider, Knutson, & McMahon, 1991).

In the LH context, there is a recent study that suggests that a state of cognitive autonomy may follow a large amount of helplessness training (Schor, 1994).

According to Zbrodoff and Logan (1986), cognitive autonomy refers to any cognitive operation that is unintentionally set in motion by a stimulus and which interferes with other operations. Cognitive autonomy has been demonstrated, for example, by Zbrodoff and Logan in a study that asked subjects to verify associative lures and nonassociative lures. Associative lures are false equations that would have been true had subjects performed a different operation (e.g., $5 + 4 = 20$, $5 \times 4 = 9$) and nonassociative lures are false equations that would not have been true under any arithmetic operation (e.g., $5 + 4 = 8$, $5 \times 4 = 21$). Cognitive autonomy is apparent when subjects take more time to verify associative than nonassociative lures. In this case, the irrelevant operation in the associative lures is initiated by the stimulus presentation, it is hard to suppress, it inevitably evokes the tendency to say that the equation is true, and it interferes with the appropriate response.

Schor (1994) integrated Zbrodoff and Logan's (1986) reasoning and methodology into a classic LH experiment. After being exposed to no, one, or four failures, subjects were asked to check 80 simple arithmetic equations of the form $a + b = c$ or $a \times b = c$. Half of the equations were true and half were false. Half of the false equations were associative lures; the other half were nonassociative lures. The dependent variable was the difference in reaction time and accuracy between associative and nonassociative lures. Upon completing the test phase, all subjects answered the CIQ which assessed the frequencies of their off-task thoughts while performing the task.

Results indicate that subjects exposed to a large amount of failure showed signs of difficulty in suppressing the irrelevant operation in associative lures, reflecting cognitive autonomy. Though accuracy was generally lower in associative lures than in nonassociative lures, this difference was greater after four failures than after one or no failure. This finding implies that a large amount of helplessness training weakened inhibitory processes, leading some cognitive operations to run on autonomically. Interestingly, this cognitive autonomy was accompanied by increased frequencies of off-task thought.

Schor's findings imply that the autonomic thoughts after failure are not only failure related. In fact, the cognitive autonomy in this study was observed in relation to arithmetic operations, while the prior failures were in a totally different area (verbal concept formation). The findings therefore seem to reflect a change in mental structures: a weakening of inner controls. The mental apparatus begins to operate autonomically, and any material that intrudes into consciousness will remain active despite efforts to inhibit it.

However, although the weakening of inner controls may allow the intrusion of all kinds of thoughts, the most common thoughts after helplessness training tend to be related to the failure experience. There are two reasons for this. First, uncontrollable failure is the most salient and meaningful event that people encounter in LH settings and it is therefore a powerful external stimulus. Second, the heightened intentional rumination on the task situation that generally follows uncontrollable failure may be an internal stimulus that also activates failure-related material. This is not to say that people cannot be distracted by other failure-irrelevant material, but that failure-related thoughts are the most frequent intruders.

At first sight, Schor's findings may contradict Pittman's results on controlled information processing after helplessness training. In the author's view, this apparent contradiction can be resolved by proposing a cycle of coping disorganization. That is, people may initially react to control deprivation failure with purposive information processing and only after repeated failure will they become overwhelmed by autonomic thoughts. At first, people try to cope with failure through problem-focused coping and then engage in purposive action rumination. After repeated failure, people rely more and more on off-task coping, such as avoidance, which may have some dysfunctional side effects. At some point, avoidance may weaken inhibitory mechanisms and may lead to the intrusion into consciousness of autonomic failure-related thoughts elicited by the failure or by other external or internal stimuli.

Summing up, three general cognitive shifts can be found during helplessness training: one, the passage from nondeliberative to deliberative thinking; two, the passage from action rumination during a small amount of helplessness training to off-task rumination after a large amount of training; and three, the passage from purposive to autonomous rumination. While the first and second changes each are a reflection of the individual's attempts to cope with the failure, the third change seems to be an unwanted by-product of off-task coping.

Mental Rumination and Task Performance Following Helplessness Training Theoretical Ideas

There are theoretical statements suggesting that mental rumination is a precursor of performance changes following helplessness training. It affects task performance by providing the cognitive context to, and facilitating the organization of, coping strategies that improve or impair task performance. On the one hand, action rumination may improve task performance because it enables full concentration on the problem at hand and facilitates the organization of task-relevant, problem-solving strategies. On the other hand, off-task rumination may impair task performance, because it draws away resources from the processing of task-relevant information and from the generation of problem-solving plans. In addition, off-task rumination may be accompanied by autonomic thoughts that overwhelm the cognitive system and may therefore foster a passive attitude toward the task at hand. In Kuhl's (1982) terms, "A person is passive ... when he or she is preoccupied with activities that are not intended to transform a present state into a desired future state" (p. 148).

According to Kuhl (1984, 1985), mental rumination may influence task performance through its effects on information processing, emotional control, and the replacement of frustrating activities. While action rumination may optimize the processing of information, off-task rumination might make this processing difficult and delay action. While action rumination may facilitate the regulation of interfering emotions, off-task rumination cannot prevent these emotions from overwhelming the cognitive system. While action rumination fosters persistence in reaching only attainable goals, off-task rumination may lead people to remain slack with unattainable goals.

In the author's view, if rumination is directed to restoring control and overcoming failure (action rumination), it has a positive effect on task performance. Attention is directed to task-relevant features, working memory filled with task-relevant ideations, cognitive resources fully allocated in task-relevant activities, and a complex context facilitating the generation of problem-solving plans is created. At the same time, attention is purposely drawn away from off-task features, relatively few cognitive resources and little working memory space are available for processing off-task material, and the cognitive context inhibits the generation of knowledge irrelevant to solving the problem.

If rumination is oriented away from the task, it has a negative effect on task performance. Attention is directed to off-task stimuli, working memory filled with off-task ideations, cognitive resources allocated in off-task activities, and a complex cognitive context facilitating the generation of knowledge about task-irrelevant matters is created. At the same time, attention is purposely drawn away from task relevant stimuli, relatively few cognitive resources and little working memory space are available for processing problem-focused material, and the cognitive context makes difficult the generation of problem-solving plans. These deleterious effects may be exacerbated by the instigation of autonomic failure-related thoughts, which compete for resources and working memory space with task-relevant activities.

Empirical Evidence

Correlational studies generally support the hypothesized association between mental rumination and task performance. Peterson, Swing, Braverman, and Buss (1982) found that the frequency of action thoughts during achievement tests was associated with performance improvement. In addition, traitlike measures of off-task worry were found to be inversely related to cognitive and psychomotor performance, and the frequency of off-task rumination while working on a task was found to be inversely correlated with task performance in both natural and laboratory settings (see Deffenbacher, 1980, for a review). Most important, these correlations were also found when there were controls for emotionality and other components of distress and anxiety (Deffenbacher, 1980).

Using the Action-State Scale, Kuhl and his colleagues demonstrated the hypothesized effects of mental rumination on information processing. Kuhl (1984) revealed that action-oriented persons had a higher ability to focus efficiently on task-relevant cues than state-oriented persons. Kuhl and Eisenberger (1986) found that the predisposition to state rumination seems to "stick" people with unattractive and frustrating activities. Kuhl and Wassiljaw (1983) found that the stronger the predisposition to state rumination, the less complex the strategies used for solving a problem.

Assessing the effects of rumination after helplessness training, Brunstein and Olbrich (1985) measured the reactions to unsolvable problems of subjects who habitually tend to engage in action rumination or state rumination. As expected, while action- and state-oriented subjects did not differ in their use of efficient or inefficient hypothesis-testing strategies during solvable problems, they showed a significant difference after failure. Action-oriented subjects showed a reactance effect, as evidenced in the increased use of efficient, problem-solving strategies. State-oriented subjects showed LH deficits, as evidenced in the increased use of inefficient strategies. Brunstein (1989) replicated these effects following a delay of 24 hours between the training and test sessions and when task performance was measured in a test task that was dissimilar from the training task.

One of the author's LH studies (Mikulincer, 1989a) also provided direct support for the hypothesized performance effects of mental rumination. Subjects were preselected according to their habitual tendency to engage in off-task rumination, were exposed to failure or no feedback on four unsolvable cognitive problems, and their performance was assessed in a letter cancellation task. Results showed that failure, as compared to no feedback, impaired performance accuracy only among subjects who habitually engaged in off-task rumination. Subjects who did not were impervious to helplessness training. However, not every type of off-task rumination was equally related to LH deficits. A regression analysis revealed that the predisposition to engage in task-irrelevant thoughts, particularly when these thoughts denote an escape from the task, made a stronger contribution to LH deficits than the predisposition to engage in state rumination.

Three other findings refine the conditions and processes by which off-task rumination impairs performance after failure. First, mind wandering during the experimental task was inversely associated with performance accuracy after helplessness training. Second, subjects predisposed to engage in off-task rumination made more errors than subjects not so predisposed, but did not scan fewer letters. This finding indicates that off-task rumination impairs performance by drawing attention away from task features rather than by reducing speed. Third, subjects predisposed to engage in off-task rumination were less accurate than subjects not so predisposed only in the 6-letter version, but not in the 2- and 4-letter versions, of the letter cancellation task. It is possible that their reduced attentional resources remained sufficient for the less demanding versions, but proved inadequate when the demands were increased.

Experimental evidence for the effects of mental rumination was provided by Kuhl (1981), who exposed subjects to either no feedback or failure in a concept learning task, induced either state rumination (asking subjects to describe and evaluate their current emotional state) or action rumination (asking subjects to engage in a nonachievement activity), and measured task performance in a subsequent cognitive task. As expected, failure subjects performed worse than controls only under the state rumination condition. The induction of action rumination made the failure ineffective in producing LH deficits. These findings were extended by Kuhl and Weiss (1983) and Mikulincer and Nizan (1988, Experiment 3). Kuhl and Weiss found that LH deficits were prevented by the induction of action rumination. Mikulincer and Nizan found that asking subjects to verbalize their hypothesis-testing strategies while working on unsolvable problems eliminated the performance deficit produced by helplessness training.

CONCLUSIONS

In this chapter, the role of rumination in human LH was explored and cognitive shifts during helplessness training and their effects on test task performance were discussed. With respect to the antecedents of rumination, the author's view is that rumination is a coping device elicited in response to a threatening, person-environment mismatch. This idea is supported by the research findings reviewed throughout the chapter that demonstrate that failure activates mental rumination and that this activation occurs along with coping activity. A small amount of failure seems to elicit task-relevant, action rumination, that is used in problem solving attempts. A large amount of failure seems to elicit off-task thoughts, with state rumination facilitating the adjustment to reality constraints and task-irrelevant rumination facilitating avoidance coping. In addition, a large amount of failure may lead to the intrusion of autonomic, failure-related thoughts into consciousness, which may be a side effect of excessive avoidance coping.

On the whole, action rumination seems to improve task performance after helplessness training. Off-task rumination seems to impair task performance. In addition, off-task rumination has an autonomic facet that may overwhelm the cognitive system, disorganize thought and action, and exacerbate performance deficits. On this basis, it is possible to outline the mediating role of rumination in human LH. First, a small amount of failure may activate action rumination, that, in turn, may lead to improved performance. Second, enough additional failure will eventually activate off-task rumination, that, in turn, will lead to LH deficits.

REFERENCES

Anderson, J. R., & Bower, G. H. (1973). *Human associative memory*. Washington DC: Winston.

Brunstein, J. C. (1989). Action-oriented vs state-oriented reactions to experimentally-induced failure. *Zeitschrift fur Experimentelle und Angewandte Psychologie, 36*, 349–367.

Brunstein, J. C., & Olbrich, E. (1985) Personal helplessness and action control: analysis of achievement-related cognitions, self-assessment, and performance. *Journal of Personality and Social Psychology, 48*, 1540–1551.

Clark, M. S., & Isen, A. M. (1982). Toward understanding the relationship between feeling states and social behavior. In A. H. Hastorf & A. M. Isen (Eds.), *Cognitive social psychology* (pp. 73–108). New York: Elsevier.

Deffenbacher, J. L. (1980). Worry and emotionality in test anxiety. In I. G. Sarason (Ed.), *Test anxiety: Theory, research, and applications* (pp. 111–128). Hillsdale, NJ: Lawrence Erlbaum Associates.

Dekel, A. (1993). *The learned helplessness phenomenon: Information processing in an exhausted cognitive system*. Unpublished master's thesis. Bar-Ilan University, Israel.

Doctor, R. M., & Altman, F. (1969). Worry and emotionality as components of test anxiety: Replication and further data. *Psychological Reports, 24*, 563–568.

Easterbrook, J. A. (1959). The effect of emotion on cue utilization and the organization of behavior. *Psychological Review, 66*, 183–201.

Erwin, T. D., & Marcus-Mendoza, S. (1987). *Action control and academic problems*. Unpublished manuscript, Texas A & M University.

Foa, E. B., & Kozak, M. S. (1986). Emotional processing of fear: Exposure to corrective information. *Psychological Bulletin, 99*, 20–35.

Freud, S. (1957). Repression. In Strachey, J. (ed. and trans.), *The standard edition of the complete psychological works of Sigmund Freud* (Vol. 14, pp. 146–158). London: Hogarth. (Original work published in 1914)

Geen, R. G. (1980). Test anxiety and cue utilization. In I. G. Sarason (Ed.), *Test anxiety: Theory, research, and applications* (pp. 43–61). Hillsdale, NJ: Lawrence Erlbaum Associates.

Heckhausen, H. (1982). Task-irrelevant cognitions during an exam: Incidence and effects. In H. Khrone & L. Laux (Eds.), *Achievement, stress, and anxiety* (pp. 247–274). Washington, DC: Hemisphere.

Horowitz, M. (1979). Psychological response to serious life events. In V. Hamilton & D. M. Warburton (Eds.), *Human stress and cognition: An information processing approach* (pp. 237–265). Chichester, England: Wiley.

Horowitz, M. (1982). Psychological processes induced by illness, injury, and loss. In T. Millon, C. Green, & R. Meagher (Eds.), *Handbook of clinical health psychology*. New York: Plenum.

Klinger, E. (1984). A consciousness sampling analysis of test anxiety and performance. *Journal of Personality and Social Psychology, 46*, 1376–1390.

Klinger, E., Barta, S. G., & Maxeiner, M. E. (1980). Motivational correlates of thought content frequency and commitment. *Journal of Personality and Social Psychology, 39*, 1222–1237.

Kruglanski, A., & Freund, T. (1983). The freezing and unfreezing of lay-inferences: Effects on impressional primacy, ethnic stereotyping, and numerical anchoring. *Journal of Experimental Social Psychology, 19*, 448–468.

Kuhl, J. (1981). Motivational and functional helplessness. The moderating effect of stat versus action orientation. *Journal of Personality and Social Psychology, 40*, 155–170.

Kuhl, J. (1982). The expectancy-value approach in the theory of social motivation: Elaborations, extensions, critique. In N. T. Feather (Ed.), *Expectations and actions: Expectancy-value models in psychology* (pp. 407–432). Hillsdale, NJ: Lawrence Erlbaum Associates.

Kuhl, J. (1984). Volitional aspects of achievement motivation and learned helplessness: Towards a comprehensive theory of action control. In B. Maher (Ed.), *Progress in experimental personality research* (Vol. 13, pp. 99–171). New York: Academic Press.

Kuhl, J. (1985). Volitional mediators of cognition-behavior consistency: Self-regulatory processes and action versus state orientation. In J. Kuhl & R. Beckmann (Eds.), *Action control: From cognition to behavior* (pp. 101–128). New York: Springer-Verlag.

Kuhl, J., & Eisenberger, T. (1986). Mediating versus meditating cognitions in human motivation: Action control, inertial tendencies, and the alienation effect. In J. Kuhl & J. W. Atkinson (Eds.), *Motivation, thought, and action* (pp. 126–151). New York: Praeger.

Kuhl, J., & Wassiljaw, I. (1983). *Intrinsic task involvement coping with failure, and problem-solving: Motivational and emotional determinants of the complexity of action plans*. Unpublished manuscript. Max Plank Institute, Munich.

Kuhl, J., & Weiss, J. (1983). *Performance deficits following uncontrollable failure: Impaired action control or global attributions and generalized expectancy deficits*. Unpublished manuscript. Max Plank Institute, Munich.

Lazarus, R. S. (1983). The costs and benefits of denial. In S. Breznitz (Ed.), *The denial of stress* (pp. 1–30). New York: International Universities Press.
Liebert, R. M., & Morris, L. W. (1967). Cognitive and emotional components of test anxiety: A distinction and some initial data. *Psychological Reports, 20*, 975–978.
Liu, T. J., & Steele, C. M. (1986). Attributional analysis as self-affirmation. *Journal of Personality and Social Psychology, 51*, 531–540.
Logan, G. D. (1989). Automaticity and cognitive control. In J. S. Uleman & J. A. Bargh (Eds.), *Unintended thought* (pp. 52–74). New York: Guilford.
Martin, L. L., & Tesser, A. (1989). Toward a motivational and structural theory of ruminative thought. In J. S. Uleman & J. A. Bargh (Eds.), *Unintended thought* (pp. 306–326). New York: Guilford.
Mikulincer, M. (1989a). Cognitive interference and learned helplessness: The effects of off-task cognitions on performance following unsolvable problems. *Journal of Personality and Social Psychology, 57*, 129–135.
Mikulincer, M. (1989b). Causal attribution, coping strategies, and learned helplessness. *Cognitive Therapy and Research, 13*, 565–582.
Mikulincer, M. (1989c). Coping and learned helplessness: Effects of coping strategies on performance following unsolvable problems. *European Journal of Personality, 3*, 181–194.
Mikulincer, M., Glaubman, H., Ben-Artzi, E., & Grossman, S. (1991). The cognitive specificity of learned helplessness and depression deficits: The role of self-focused cognitions. *Anxiety Research, 3*, 273–290.
Mikulincer, M., Kedem, P., & Zilcha-Segal, H. (1989). Learned helplessness, reactance, and cue utilization. *Journal of Research in Personality, 23*, 235–247.
Mikulincer, M., & Marshand, O. (1991). An excuse perspective of the learned helplessness paradigm: The self-protective role of causal attribution. *Journal of Social and Clinical Psychology, 10*, 134–151.
Mikulincer, M., & Nizan, B. (1988). Causal attribution, cognitive interference, and the generalization of learned helplessness. *Journal of Personality and Social Psychology, 55*, 470–478.
Morris, L. W., Davis, M. A., & Hutchings, C. H. (1981). Cognitive and emotional components of anxiety: Literature review and a revised Worry-emotionality Scale. *Journal of Educational Psychology, 73*, 541–555.
Morris, L. W., & Liebert, R. M. (1970). Relationship of cognitive and emotional components of test anxiety to physiological arousal and academic performance. *Journal of Consulting and Clinical Psychology, 35*, 332–337.
Morris, L. W., & Liebert, R. M. (1973). Effects of negative feedback, threat of shock, and level of trait anxiety on the arousal of two components of anxiety. *Journal of Counseling Psychology, 20*, 321–326.
Peterson, P. L., Swing, S. R., Braverman, M. T., & Buss, R. R. (1982). Students' aptitudes and their reports of cognitive processes during direct instruction. *Journal of Educational Psychology, 74*, 535–547.
Pittman, T. S., & D'Agostino, P. R. (1989). Motivation and cognition: Control deprivation and the nature of subsequent information processing. *Journal of Experimental Social Psychology, 25*, 465–480.
Pittman, T. S., & Pittman, N. L. (1980). Deprivation of control and the attribution process. *Journal of Personality and Social Psychology, 39*, 377–389.
Sarason, I G., Sarason, B. R., Keefe, D. E., Hayes, B. E., & Shearin, E. N. (1986). Cognitive interference: Situational determinants and traitlike characteristics. *Journal of Personality and Social Psychology, 51*, 215–226.
Schor, A. (1994). *Learned helplessness and cognitive autonomy.* Unpublished master's thesis. Bar-Ilan University, Israel.
Seligman, M. E. P. (1975). *Helplessness: On depression, development and death.* San Francisco: Freeman.

Silver, R. L., Boon, C., & Stones, M. H. (1983), Searching for meaning in misfortune: Making sense of incest. *Journal of Social Issues, 39*, 81–101.
Stiensmeier-Pelster, J. (1989). Attributional style and depressive mood reactions. *Journal of Personality, 57*, 581–599.
Swann, W. B., Stephenson, B., & Pittman, T. S. (1981). Curiosity and control: On the determinants of the search for social knowledge. *Journal of Personality and Social Psychology, 40*, 635–642.
Uleman, J. S., & Bargh, J. A. (Eds.). (1989). *Unintended thought.* New York: Guilford.
Wegner, D. M., Schneider, D. J., Carter, S., & White, L. (1987). Paradoxical effects of thought suppression. *Journal of Personality and Social Psychology, 53*, 5–13.
Wegner, D. M., Schneider, D. J., Knutson, B., & McMahon, S. R. (1991). Polluting the stream of consciousness: The effect of thought suppression on the mind's environment. *Cognitive Therapy and Research, 15*, 141–152.
Wicklund, R. A., & Braun, O. L. (1987). Incompetence and the concern with human categories. *Journal of Personality and Social Psychology, 53*, 373–382.
Zbrodoff, N. J., & Logan, G. D. (1986). On the autonomy of mental processes: A case study of arithmetic. *Journal of Experimental Psychology: General, 115*, 118–130.

CHAPTER

11

COGNITIVE INTERFERENCE AND SOCIAL INTERACTION: THE CASE OF SHYNESS AND NONASSERTIVENESS

Monroe A. Bruch
University at Albany, State University of New York

This chapter is concerned with cognitive variables that are associated with the social interaction problems of shyness and nonassertiveness. Recent conceptualizations have emphasized the important role of cognitive processes (Cheek & Melchior, 1990; Galassi & Bruch, 1992) in the etiology, maintenance, and treatment of these problems. The focus in the chapter is on cognitive self-statements or internal dialogue and cognitive structures, such as self-schemata, and their role in shyness and nonassertiveness.

Self-statements reflect what Ingram and Kendall (1986) refer to as cognitive propositions in their taxonomy of cognitive constructs. Cognitive propositions are defined as information that is easily and immediately represented in consciousness and that is considered by the individual. Self-schemata fit the category of cognitive structures which involve the manner in which cognitive content is internally encoded and stored in memory. Although cognitive structures, such as self-schemata, may be associated with a greater or lesser frequency of certain self-statements, self-statement content is of interest in its own right.

Shyness and nonassertiveness are probably the two most widely researched types of social interaction problems (cf. Galassi & Bruch, 1992). Although shyness refers to a personality dimension and nonassertion to a domain of interpersonal behavior, theory and research show that shyness is synonymous with difficulties in initiating relationships, which is a domain that can be distinguished from assertiveness. Buhrmester, Furman, Wittenberg, and Reis (1988) conceptualized interpersonal competence in peer relations to be comprised of five domains of functioning: initiating relationships, asserting one's needs and rights, self-disclosure, providing emotional support, and managing interpersonal conflicts. They suggest that different competencies are required to behave effectively in each of these domains and provide evidence for the utility in distinguishing among these domains. Although Buhrmester et al. (1988) found that shyness was inversely related to perceived competence in assertion situations ($r = -.32$), shyness was more strongly related to perceived competence in initiating interactions and relationships with others ($r = -.69$). Consequently, when reviewing the literature on cognitive variables in shyness and nonassertiveness, it is important to recognize the type of interpersonal task being negotiated. Each interpersonal domain may generate its own unique set of difficulties, which in turn may or may not be related to specific patterns of dysfunctional cognition.

COGNITIVE SELF-STATEMENTS

Cognitive self-statements refer to internal speech that is self-referent and that typically accompanies any type of information-processing task. As Kendall and Hollon (1981) noted, self-referent does not mean that the individual is always the object of the statement, but rather that the primary audience for the covert speech is the individual him or herself.

There are a number of reasons for wanting to assess an individual's self-statements. Kendall (1981) was one of the first theorists to articulate several purposes for assessing self-statements, and these reasons remain relevant today. He proposed that self-statements be examined in order to study their relationship with the experience and expression of affective responses as well as of overt behaviors. Second, he suggested that self-statements be studied to investigate their role in the development of various types of psychopathology as well as in different types of successful coping processes. Third, he suggested that self-statements be studied to evaluate whether treatments designed to alter specific cognitions in fact lead to change in the targeted thoughts.

As previously mentioned, the construct of cognitive self-statements fits Ingram and Kendall's (1986) category of cognitive proposition, which included any surface level thought content. When assessing self-statements, responses must be scored or coded in some meaningful manner for clinical or research purposes. To date, the valence (i.e., positive and negative, or facilitative and inhibitory nature) of a self-statement is the dimension of interest in most cognitive self-statement measures. Relative to a social interaction, an example of a positive self-statement would be, "I'm interested in seeing if we have things in common," since such a self-statement should presumably facilitate effective performance; it is task oriented and does not direct attention toward possible feelings of anxiety. An example of a negative self-statement would be, "What if I can't think of anything to say?" This kind of self-statement could inhibit performance, because it is self rather than task oriented, and might direct attention to subjectively perceived deficits and negative affect.

Self-Statement Assessment Methodology

Glass (1993) has suggested that self-statement measures differ on at least four properties: (a) degree of structure (e.g., endorsement of questionnaire items vs. production), (b) response mode (e.g., oral vs. written), (c) timing (e.g., concurrent vs. retrospective), and (d) nature of stimuli evoking self-statements (e.g., imagined, videotape replay, role played, or naturalistic situation). Measures like the Social Interaction Self-Statement Test (SISST; Glass, Merluzzi, Biever, & Larsen, 1982), in the case of shyness, and the Assertion Self-Statement Test (ASST; Schwartz & Gottman, 1976) in the case of nonassertiveness, are examples of endorsement measures. Such measures ask respondents to rate how frequently they experienced any of the listed thoughts and usually contain an equal number of positive and negative (facilitative and inhibitory) thoughts. The representativeness of the thought content for the situation of interest is controlled by item-generation techniques such as Goldfried and D'Zurilla's (1969) behavioral-analytic method as in the case of the SISST.

The most commonly used production method is thought listing (Cacioppo & Petty, 1981). This technique asks subjects to list any thoughts they had during a preceding period of time, ignoring concerns about spelling and grammar in order to get a close approximation to the actual "cognitive verbiage." Subjects are given only 2 to 3 minutes to complete the protocol and are asked to put each thought in a separate box to allow the subject to determine how many thoughts had occurred. Using predeveloped coding rules that differentiate the content of positive, negative, neutral, and irrelevant thoughts, trained raters code the written responses. Presumably, this less structured method should elicit a subject's idiosyncratic thoughts and hence provide a more sensitive measure of his or her self-statements.

Aside from the degree of structure and the type of response format, self-statement measures have also varied as to the timing of the assessment. When applied to social interaction problems, self-statement measures may be administered immediately (i.e., following termination of the interaction) or retrospectively, as in the case of a daily diary (e.g., Hope, Heimberg, Zollo, Nyman, & O'Brien, 1987). Presumably the more concurrent the administration the more sensitive and accurate the sample of thoughts. However, the often spontaneous and short-lived nature of most social interactions can make it difficult to conduct concurrent assessments except in the case of simulated interactions. In the one study that directly compared the predictiveness of concurrent versus retrospective (1 week later) self-statement responses (Myszka, Galassi, & Ware, 1986), there were no effects due to time of assessment.

Finally, for the dimension of evoking stimulus, it has been assumed that the closer the approximation to in vivo stimuli the more accurate (and hence predictive) the data collected (Kendall & Hollon, 1981). However, for the SISST, expected differences in the frequency of positive and negative thoughts between shy and nonshy persons have been found both for in vivo (e.g., Bruch, Gorsky, Collins, & Berger, 1989; Turner, Beidel, & Larkin, 1986) and for imagined stimuli (Zweig & Brown, 1985).

Issues in Self-Statement Assessment

Before reviewing the research on self-statements and social interaction problems, it is important to consider several unresolved conceptual and methodological problems with this type of assessment. The first issue involves assumptions about the veridicality of self-statements. Based on Meichenbaum's (1977) theorizing, Kendall and Hollon (1981) discussed the notion that seemingly negative self-statements may serve an adaptive function depending on the subjective meaning the individual attaches to such thoughts. In other words, for some individuals the seemingly negative self-statement of "I'm getting anxious and tongue-tied" may serve as a goad to get more involved in a conversation if we can presume that the individual believes he or she is capable of effective interaction. While most investigators would agree that veridicality should be assessed rather than assumed, no widely accepted method for such an evaluation has emerged.

Earlier investigators such as Cacioppo, Glass, and Merluzzi (1979) suggested that following thought listing, subjects mark the valence of their thoughts, and that the discrepancy between judges' and subjects' valence codings be evaluated to appraise veridicality. Subsequent experience has shown, however, that the number of discrepancies is relatively small and that both indexes are equally predictive of certain behaviors. In a study involving test anxiety, Bruch, Kaflowitz, and Kuethe (1986) assessed the veridical and nonveridical nature of subjects' self-statements. They audiotaped subjects' responses to a series of questions (e.g., "What effect did this thought have on you?") asked after completing a thought-listing protocol during and following a pseudoacademic test. Results showed that the subjective meaning attached to the thought rather than the coded valence was substantially more predictive of test performance. However, similar research for social interaction situations has not been conducted. Whether self-statements are more veridical in interpersonal contexts because of the presence of others and the more spontaneous nature of the performance (compared to academic exams) is not known. Obviously, much more research is needed to understand the factors that influence the degree of veridicality in subjects' self-statements.

A second issue involves the question of what additional self-statement dimensions, other than valence, should be assessed. In the case of social interaction problems, the individual's focus of attention may be an important dimension to consider, because theoretical accounts of both shyness (Carver & Scheier, 1986) and nonassertiveness (Gallasi, Gallasi, & Fulkerson, 1984) have pointed to problems evoked by preoccupation with one's interaction partner. Although some theorists (e.g., Cheek & Melchior, 1990) suggest that evaluative concern is associated with subjects' excessive self-focusing, evaluative concern also may be initiated by self-statements regarding qualities possessed by the partner. Excessive focusing on the partner's attractiveness and poise could, for instance, lead to creation of unrealistic performance standards for oneself in the situation (Wallace & Alden, 1991).

Another dimension of importance may be the sequence of subjects' thoughts. For instance, Meichenbaum (1977), has argued that socially competent subjects may follow negative self-statements with positive self-statements, in contrast to less adjusted subjects who get locked-into a string of negative thoughts. Although investigators such as Schwartz and Gottman (1976) and Glass and Arnkoff (1982) conducted initial tests of this notion, little additional published research has appeared addressing the value of assessing this dimension.

A third issue is whether self-statement questionnaires and thought-listing protocols yield similar data. In a review of the validity of self-statement measures, Glass and Arnkoff (1994) found little evidence that these two methods produce equivalent data. For instance, in studies that directly compared the SISST and a thought-listing procedure, positive thoughts on the two measures were not associated (Dodge, Hope, Heimberg, & Becker, 1988; Glass & Furlong, 1990; Myszka et al., 1986) and negative thoughts showed only small correlations in some studies (e.g., Glass & Furlong, 1990). Although the lack of convergence may in part be attributable to administering measures at different points in time (e.g., thought listing before and the SISST after an interaction, Glass & Furlong, 1990), Myszka et al.'s (1986) study provided for a direct comparison of these two methods and results suggested very little convergence. In discussing their results, Myszka et al. (1986) offered an intriguing explanation for the lack of convergence in the data. They suggested that thought-listing responses, in comparison to self-statement inventories, reflect more idiosyncratic and transitory forms of covert thought content. In contrast, they argue that self-statement inventories, which force a subject to make judgments when rating items, may elicit more general thought content (e.g., global self-evaluations), which is a function of existing cognitive structures, such as self-efficacy beliefs. Consequently, there may be a lack of veridicality or parallel direction in the responses generated by these two methods despite their common purpose.

Patterns and Correlates of Self-Statements in Shyness

Compared to nonshy individuals, shy persons (based on self-report measures) have reported more negative, as well as fewer positive, self-statements relative to a social interaction (Beidel, Turner, & Dancu, 1985; Bruch et al., 1989; Glass & Arnkoff, 1982; Johnson & Glass, 1989; Myszka et al., 1986; Turner et al. 1986; Zweig & Brown, 1985). This pattern has been found using both endorsement and thought-listing methods, assessed prior to or following an interaction (Glass &

Arnkoff, 1994). Although these studies were largely conducted with undergraduates, similar self-statement patterns have been found with adult social phobics diagnosed according to DSM-III-R criteria (American Psychiatric Association, 1987). As a type of anxiety disorder, social phobia involves a similar concern with negative evaluation but, compared with shyness, results in greater impairment in daily functioning (Bruch, 1989). In two studies by Heimberg and his colleagues (Dodge et al., 1988; Heimberg, Bruch, Hope, & Dombeck, 1990), social phobics with fears of social interaction were compared with those who only feared public-speaking situations on self-statement measures relevant to interaction situations. In both studies, the former group manifested a significantly greater frequency of negative thoughts, but only one study (i.e., Heimberg et al.) suggested that this group experienced significantly fewer positive thoughts.

Research on the correlates of self-statement responses of shy persons has focused on a variety of criterion variables. One set of criteria involves the shy person's own evaluation of his or her affective experiences and performance during an interaction. Studies by Garcia, Stinson, Ickes, Bissonnette, and Briggs (1991), Glass et al. (1982), Mahone, Bruch, and Heimberg (1993), and Myszka et al. (1986) found a reliable relation between frequency of negative thoughts and greater report of subjective anxiety. Melchior and Cheek (1990) and Bruch, Hamer, and Heimberg (1995) found that a greater frequency of negative thoughts also was associated with rating oneself as performing ineffectively during an interaction and spending a greater amount of time focusing on oneself in contrast to one's interaction partner.

Another set of criteria involves partners, judges, or other independent means of assessing the shy person's responses in an interaction. When behavioral manifestations of anxiety have been coded from videotaped interaction, Bruch et al. (1989) and Glass and Furlong (1990) found a relation between negative and positive thought frequencies and such behaviors as avoidance of eye contact, fidgeting, and nervous laughter. In addition, the frequency of negative and positive thoughts was found to correlate in the expected direction with partners' and judges' global rating of the subject's manifest anxiety and performance during an interaction. Interestingly, Bruch et al. (1989) also found that the frequency of negative thoughts was related to the size of the discrepancy between subjects' report of the visibility of their anxious behavior (e.g., hands trembling) and judges' coding of such behaviors. The more negative thoughts reported, the greater the tendency of subjects to overestimate the visibility of their anxiety. Finally, among the few studies to include a measure of physiological reactivity (Bruch et al., 1989; Dodge et al., 1988; Beidel et al., 1985), there has been no evidence that thought patterns correlate with indices such as heart rate. This finding may be illustrative of the veridicality problem discussed earlier or it may reflect the fact that self-statement patterns are driven by a variety of internal and external factors.

Patterns and Correlates of Self-Statements in Nonassertiveness

Schwartz and Gottman's (1976) analysis of the cognitive, behavioral, and physiological differences between groups who were high and low in assertive expression revealed that low assertive individuals reported more negative and fewer positive self-statements in situations involving refusal of unreasonable requests. Using the same self-statement measure (i.e., the ASST) as Schwartz and Gottman, Bruch (1981) also found that subjects low in self-reported assertiveness obtain higher negative and lower positive self-statement frequencies. However, neither of these studies examined the relation between self-statement patterns and aspects of assertive behavior such as the effectiveness of assertive responses.

Based on a rational grouping of ASST items, Pitcher and Meikle (1980) replicated the previous research showing that concerns about being disliked, negative self-image, and other-directed self-statements were characteristic of nonassertives. However, self-statement frequencies were uncorrelated with the effectiveness of subjects' role-play responses for a series of unreasonable request situations. Frequencies from a measure of self-statements for positive assertion situations (i.e., complementing, expressing feelings of liking and affection) were, however, significantly related to effective performance of positive assertive responses. In contrast to Pitcher and Meikle, Bruch, Haase, and Purcell (1984) employed factor analysis to identify the underlying content dimensions of the ASST. Three factors were interpretable: (a) concern with the other's negative emotional reactions, (b) focusing on the rational basis for refusing, and (c) violating one's moral duty to others if requests are refused. Bruch et al. (1984) found that the first two factors, but not the third, were significantly related to the effectiveness of subjects' written responses to a series of unreasonable requests.

From the review of self-statement research, it appears that negative and positive self-statements are correlated with the maladaptive behavior of shy and nonassertive persons. However, the design of most studies has provided relatively little information about the potential correlates of self-statements and precludes any meaningful interpretation about their causal role. In particular, this area of cognitive-behavioral research is lacking a theoretical model that can specify outcomes that should result from particular self-statement patterns.

States of Mind Model—An Integrative Approach to Self-Statement Processes

The lack of theory to guide self-statement research has been addressed in part by the introduction of the states of mind (SOM) model by Schwartz and Garamoni (1986). Their model is a theoretically developed and empirically testable formulation of the optimal balance between positive and negative thoughts and affect. Although previous research suggested that treatment effects and prediction of criterion behaviors were more often associated with negative rather than positive self-statements—a pattern Kendall and Hollon (1981) labeled the "power of nonnegative thinking"—Schwartz and Garamoni (1986, 1989) have argued that it is the relative balance between positive and negative thoughts that is important. According to Schwartz and Garamoni, optimal adjustment is represented in an asymmetrical balance of positive and negative cognition such that the ratio of positive thoughts to the sum of positive and negative thoughts $[P / (P + N)]$ approaches 0.62. In developing the SOM model, they suggest that there are potentially five different states-of-mind categories, each characterized by different SOM values. As previously stated, optimal adjustment, or the SOM of *positive dialogue*, is associated with a set point of 0.62 and possible range of 0.56 to 0.68. This SOM represents the most adaptive combination of optimism and necessary attention to possible negative events. As a result, possible negative events are salient but not overwhelming, enabling one to cope with stress. A second SOM, *internal dialogue of conflict* with a set point of 0.50 and a range of 0.45 to 0.55, is associated with mild pathology, as may be seen in analogue samples of socially anxious or nonassertive college students. A third SOM, *negative dialogue* with a set point of 0.38 and a range of 0.32 to 0.44, is associated with moderate pathology which may characterize clinical samples of depressed or anxious persons.

The final two SOM categories do not have specific set points because either positive or negative cognitions predominate such that any dialectical process is relatively absent. The SOM of *negative monologue* involves values ranging from 0.31 to 0.00. Because it is characterized by extreme negativity, negative monologue is said to be associated with severe pathology such as that manifested in profound depression or acute panic. The SOM of *positive monologue* involves values ranging from 0.69 to 1.00, is characterized by insufficient attention to negative events, and is hypothetically related to pathological states such as acute mania.

Although empirical evaluation of the SOM model is just beginning, Schwartz and Garamoni (1986, 1989) present evidence from reanalyses of self-statement data in previous research which supports their theorizing. From these reanalyses they showed that functional individuals manifested thought patterns that typically fell in the SOM category of positive dialogue, while mildly dysfunctional individuals manifested patterns that fell in the category of internal dialogue of conflict. Recently, the author has employed the SOM model in studies of shyness, social phobia, and nonassertiveness. In a study of shyness (Bruch & Pearl, 1995), male undergraduates' attributional style for outcomes of heterosocial interactions was used to predict symptoms of shyness in an actual interaction. The cognitive symptom consisted of the relative balance of positive and negative thoughts (i.e., SOM) and was assessed via a thought-listing procedure following a conversation with a female confederate. Affective and behavioral symptoms consisted of subjects' reports of subjective feelings of anxiety during the interaction and the length of time before subjects chose to terminate the conversation. Results showed that subjects who believed that failed interactions were due to factors under their control manifested a more adaptive balance of positive and negative thoughts. When subjects were divided into groups reflecting an adaptive versus maladaptive attributional style based on a median split of their controllability ratings, the adaptive group had a mean SOM of 0.56, while the maladaptive group had a mean of 0.39 ($t(78) = 3.27$, $p < .01$). The SOM of 0.56 is at the lower end of the positive dialogue range, while 0.39 is in the midrange for negative dialogue. However, the attributional dimensions of locus and stability were unrelated to SOM. Subjects' SOM was negatively related to feelings of anxiety and positively related to the length of the conversation. Thus, subjects who reported greater or equal numbers of negative relative to positive thoughts (i.e., SOM of negative dialogue or internal dialogue of conflict) manifested more subjective discomfort and terminated the conversation more quickly.

Within a sample of untreated social phobics, Heimberg et al. (1990) found that individuals with this disorder obtained an SOM of 0.28 ($SD = 0.16$), which is in the negative monologue range. The predictive utility of the SOM was compared to the use of percent of negative thoughts (relative to total thought-listed responses). Self-statement data were collected following a behavioral simulation in which patients are exposed to the phobic situation that is most anxiety provoking to them. SOM ratio was a better predictor than percent of negative thoughts and was significantly related to subjects' oral report of discomfort during the behavior simulation and a measure of state anxiety at the end.

In a study that examined the impact of treatment on SOM, Bruch, Heimberg, and Hope (1991) found that a sample of social phobics had a pretreatment SOM of 0.29. Subsequently, half of the group received a cognitive-behavioral group treatment and the other half an educational-supportive group treatment. After treatment, the two groups did not differ; both improved somewhat, having achieved mean SOM ratios in the range of internal dialogue of conflict. However, when they were assessed at a 6-month follow-up, those receiving the cognitive treatment evidenced continued improvement, having reached SOMs in the positive dialogue range. In contrast, those receiving the supportive treatment fell back to negative monologue, similar to their pretreatment status.

Finally, in a study involving assertive behavior, Bruch, Hamer, and Kaflowitz-Linder (1992) conducted an explicit test of the construct validity of the SOM categories. Following their role-play responses to videotaped rights assertion situations, female undergraduates completed a thought-listing protocol. Audiotaped role-play responses were subsequently coded for effectiveness using Pitcher and Meikle's (1980) components coding scheme. Contingency table analyses among the five SOM categories and four levels of behavioral effectiveness (e.g., refusal, qualified refusal, etc.) were highly significant for each of five role-played situations. These analyses indicated that a number of the SOM categories were associated with expected qualitative differences in assertive behavior (e.g., internal dialogue of conflict with qualified refusal response). However, in contrast to Schwartz and Garamoni's (1986) theorizing, positive monologue, rather than positive dialogue, was more frequently associated with coding of refusal components, suggesting that positive monologue may not always be a dysfunctional cognitive state.

Although continued research is needed to refine the theoretically predicted outcomes for the various SOM setpoints, this model provides a useful approach for integrating positive and negative thought content and how the relative balance of the two relates to adaptive and maladaptive functioning. In a more recent paper, Schwartz (1991) theorized about how the SOM model (and hence self-statement patterns) can be used to define specific treatment goals (e.g., restoring optimal balance) and to monitor situational shifts in balance in order to make informed treatment decisions. These notions hold substantial promise for improving evaluation of the effects of cognitive treatments.

COGNITIVE STRUCTURE

In Ingram and Kendall's (1986) taxonomy of cognitive elements, cognitive structures consist of variables that influence the manner in which social information is discriminated, encoded, and organized in memory. However, investigations of the relation between hypothesized cognitive structures and the problems of shyness and nonassertiveness have been limited. Initial applications of information-processing approaches to social interaction problems focused on the role of semantic schema (Merluzzi, Rudy, & Glass, 1981). A semantic schema refers to the verbal concepts used to characterize one's experiences with specific situations, and such schema assist individuals in encoding events within these situations. Presumably, people who differ in shyness and assertiveness may employ different semantic schema in social situations which could relate to what information is encoded and, in turn, what response is made. In the case of assertiveness, Rudy, Merluzzi, and Henahan (1982) had subjects who differed in assertiveness compare the similarity of various rights assertion situations on the basis of how difficult it would be to respond assertively. Multidimensional scaling analyses revealed that all subjects construed assertive situations in terms of four dimensions (e.g., status of the other, amount of emotional arousal, etc.); however, low compared to high assertives tended to employ the emotional arousal dimension much more frequently in their ratings, suggesting that this schema was more dominant in their processing of situations.

In a similar manner, Goldfried, Padawer, and Robins (1984) had subjects differing in social anxiety (similar to shyness) sort a variety of heterosocial situations for their similarity in evoking subjective discomfort. Results from the multidimensional scaling yielded three dimensions: intimacy, chance of being evaluated, and academic relevance (i.e., whether the interaction related to school activities). Compared to nonanxious subjects, socially anxious subjects gave a greater weight to the evaluative dimension and lesser weight to intimacy, while nonanxious subjects were just the reverse.

While semantic schema tend to reflect the content of self-statements, presumably because they underlie the self-statements, the assessment of semantic schema involves complex measurement procedures. Unfortunately, use of such complex psychometric techniques can shift the focus away from the development of theoretical models of how cognitive structures relate to affective and behavioral responses. In contrast, more recent approaches to the role of cognitive structures in psychopathology (e.g., Kendall & Ingram, 1987; Shaw, 1985) have focused on whether cognitive structures contribute to the onset or maintenance of clinical disorders (or both), and whether specific structures are related to different types of emotional disorders (e.g., anxiety vs. depression; Kendall & Ingram, 1989).

The latter issue is particularly important because of Ingram's (1989a, 1989b) evidence that affective confounding may distort the relation between cognitive and affective variables. Specifically, he showed that subjects high in both social anxiety and depression reported more negative self-statements than subjects high only in social anxiety. The social anxiety group did not differ from nonanxious/nondepressed control subjects in negative thoughts, suggesting that depression may have accounted for past correlations between measures of social anxiety and negative cognitions. In the following sections, research involving the application of three specific cognitive structures to social interaction problems will be presented. In the case of shyness, the application of Higgins' (1987) self-discrepancy theory will be described, while for nonassertiveness, the author's application of conceptual complexity and self-schema theory to aspects of assertive behavior will be described.

Cognitive Structures and Shyness

Studies of self-discrepancy theory (Higgins, 1987; Higgins, Strauman, & Klein, 1986) focused on the cognitive determinants of self-evaluations and how they impact emotional functioning. The theory distinguishes among domains of the self, including the *actual* self, the *ideal* self (i.e., the attributes that the person or others wish or hope he or she possesses), and the *ought* self (i.e., the attributes that the person or others believe the person ought to possess). In turn, each of these selves can be examined from two *points of view*: the subject's own and from the point of view the subject thinks is held by a significant other. The combination of domains and points of view results in six possible representations of the self with the two types of actual self constituting the traditional notion of self-concept. The four remaining categories constitute what Higgins et al. (1986) refer to as *self-guides* or self-evaluative standards against which the actual self is compared. Discrepancies between the actual self and various self-guides represent specific types of cognitive conflict that are associated with particular emotional states.

According to Higgins (1987), specific types of actual self/self-guide inconsistency are predicted to relate to vulnerability to depression versus anxiety. For instance, an *actual:ideal* discrepancy is one in which the individual's perceived actual attributes do not match the ideal state that he or she (or others) wishes or aspires to attain. The person is predicted to be vulnerable to sadness, disappointment, and perhaps depression because such emotions are associated with people believing that they have failed to achieve their personal desires. An **actual:ought** discrepancy is one in which the person's perceived attributes do not match the state that someone (self or significant other) believes it is the individual's duty or obligation to fulfill. This person is predicted to be vulnerable to fear, worry, and anxiety because violation of prescribed duties and obligations is usually associated with threat of punishment.

Of importance to our discussion is that shyness is a type of social anxiety (Leary, 1986) and, therefore, the actual:ought discrepancy may be a factor that could mediate problems of shyness. To determine the relevance of this cognitive structure to shyness, it is necessary to answer two questions. First, can it be shown that a particular actual/self-guide discrepancy is associated with the specific anxiety syndrome of shyness or social anxiety? Second, can it be shown, as predicted by self-discrepancy theory, that a greater degree of actual/self-guide discrepancy is associated with a greater degree of distress in a particular emotional state? In a study designed to test whether particular actual/self-guide discrepancies could predict self-reported social anxiety versus depression, Strauman and Higgins (1988) argued that an actual-own/ought-other (AOO) discrepancy reflected the fear of negative evaluation component underlying social anxiety and shyness. In Study 2 of Strauman and Higgins (1988), these investigators used structural equation modeling to test whether the AOO discrepancy compared to the actual-own/ideal-own (AI) discrepancy (presumed to relate to depression) related more to social anxiety than depression on measures collected several months later. A model in which *AOO* was more strongly associated with social anxiety but not depression and *AI* was more strongly associated with depression but not social anxiety, accounted for the greatest amount of predicted variance. In a more rigorous test of whether particular self-discrepancies are associated with a specific emotional disorder, Strauman (1989) compared groups of social phobics, major depressive disorder patients, and normal controls for differences in self-discrepancy. Results revealed that social phobics evidenced a significantly greater *AOO* discrepancy than depressives and controls, while depressives showed a greater *AI* discrepancy than social phobics and controls.

Strauman's (1989) study also included a substantial test of the second question—whether a greater magnitude of a particular self-discrepancy is associated with the intensity of a particular emotional response. Based on the results from the first study, social phobics and depressives were considered to possess a high degree of discrepancy in *AOO* and *AI*, respectively. In a second study, subjects were exposed to laboratory tasks that seemingly were unrelated to self-evaluation. However, the tasks actually were designed to prime relevant self-discrepancies by presenting subjects with relevant actual self-ideal own and actual self-ought other attributes collected from data previously provided by the subject. In the experiment, skin conductance responses were monitored as a physiological index of anxiety versus dysphoria. Based on previous research, it was expected that exposure to *AOO* mismatched attributes would relate to increased amplitude while an *AI* mismatch should relate to a decreased amplitude. Variation in the length of time subjects verbalized during the experiment served as a behavioral indicator of intensity of emotional response with decreased length associated with exposure to *AI* mismatch and an increased length associated to the *AOO* mismatch. Results showed a significant interaction for subject group by domain of priming in which social phobics, compared to depressives and normal controls, showed both a greater increase in arousal and length of verbalization in response to *AOO* versus *AI* priming and control priming stimuli. In similar fashion depressives, compared to social phobics and controls, when exposed to *AI* priming versus other types, showed the expected pattern of results.

The experimental induction of actual self/self-guide discrepancies and the use of nonself-report measures of emotional response bolsters the validity of the finding that magnitude of the discrepancy is related to the intensity or severity of one's emotional response. Although caution is necessary in generalizing from social phobia to shyness, self-discrepancy as a type of cognitive structure could prove useful in predicting various cognitive, behavioral, and affective consequences of shyness.

Cognitive Structures and Assertive Behavior

The application of operationalized cognitive structures in predicting antecedents and consequences of assertive behavior has been limited. However, the author and his colleagues (Bruch, 1981; Bruch, Heisler, & Conroy, 1981; Bruch, Kaflowitz, & Berger, 1988) have examined the role of two cognitive structure variables—conceptual complexity as an information-processing style and self-schemata for assertiveness.

Conceptual complexity (CC) refers to the number and interrelatedness of rules or semantic schemata used for discriminating, encoding, and retrieving information about the social environment (Schroder, Driver, & Streufert, 1967). In contrast to the work on semantic schemata (e.g., Goldfried et al., 1984), which emphasized content, CC focuses more on the approaches individuals use when processing social stimuli. According to Schroder et al. (1967), high CC individuals can make finer discriminations of situational attributes, can view situations from a greater number of perspectives, and rely more on internally developed standards for problem solving, thereby increasing tolerance for interpersonal as well as intrapsychic conflict. Given that rights assertion situations involve interpersonal conflict, Bruch (1981) argued that one component that may differentiate high from low assertives is greater conceptual complexity. Using a semiprojective measure to assess CC in which subjects provide written reactions to conflict statements such as "When someone disagrees with you . . . ," Bruch (1981) found that assertives were significantly more conceptually complex than nonassertives. In an extension of this research (Bruch et al., 1981), subjects who differed in CC level were compared on various components known to relate to effective assertive behavior to test whether this cognitive structure mediates assertive behavior. High compared to low CC subjects evidenced greater knowledge of an effective response (including content that reflected consideration of the needs of others), better oral delivery skill, and fewer negative self-statements that would inhibit refusal. In a second study subjects were exposed to rights assertion role-play situations that varied on two dimensions which increased the difficulty of behaving assertively. One dimension was the use of an extended interaction rather than single response format where subjects were exposed to persistent attempts to get them to comply with the request, while the second dimension was the nature of the relationship with the requestor (i.e., friend or loved one vs. stranger, mere acquaintance). Results showed that high compared to low CC individuals responded more assertively in extended interactions and when responding to requests from significant others.

In contrast to conceptual complexity, which involves differences in one's general information-processing style (e.g., abstract vs. concrete), self-schema refers to the cognitive representations of one's past behavior and experience relative to a particular characteristic that is important to one's self-description or identity (e.g., independent, soccer player). When activated in a situation, a self-schemata serves to assist individuals in constructing their perception of events in subsequent schemata-relevant situations.

In the application of self-schema processes to assertiveness by Bruch et al. (1988), the information processing approach of individuals who possessed a self-schema for assertiveness was compared to individuals who were aschematic for assertiveness. Based on the endorsement of seven pairs of bipolar adjectives that reflected assertion, subjects were classified as assertive schematic if they endorsed the adjective *assertive*, and four of the six related adjectives, as being both highly self-descriptive and important. In contrast, aschematics had mid-range endorsement ratings on both importance and self-description.

In the first of two studies, Bruch et al. (1988) tested the construct validity of a self-schema for assertiveness. Using an incidental recall task, the author found that assertion schematics remembered significantly more assertion-related adjectives but did not differ from aschematics on recall of adjectives in domains unrelated to assertion (e.g., creativity). In the second study the author tested whether an assertion schema would relate to particular information-processing approaches on tasks relevant to effective assertive behavior. Results from this study showed that schematics differed from aschematics in a number of ways: They recalled more past instances of assertive behavior; they were more certain of responding assertively in situations where assertion was appropriate; and they were more certain of responding assertively in situations where the appropriateness of assertion was ambiguous, reflecting the bias created by a self-schema. In addition, schematics were more likely to judge moderately legitimate (ambiguous) requests as more unreasonable, and when asked to generate expected consequences for assertion, they focused more on self than on other-person consequences, again reflecting the assertion schema bias. Although these results have yet to be replicated and extended, they suggest that the self-schema construct as a type of cognitive structure may be useful in describing how cognitive processes mediate dysfunctional as well as effective responses in social interactions.

SUMMARY AND CONCLUSIONS

Despite a growing literature showing that cognitive variables relate to social interaction problems, a number of concerns are evident from the research just discussed. Although studies have shown that shy and nonassertive subjects manifest maladaptive self-statement patterns, there has been no evaluation of whether self-statements directly influence social interaction problems. This may be due in part to the lack of comprehensive models of how positive and negative thoughts coexist and their resultant impact on subsequent responses. Schwartz and Garamoni's (1986) SOM model is the one exception to this situation, and given the growing evidence for the model's validity, should be used as a framework for future investigations of the role of self-statements in social interaction problems.

A second concern is that thus far there are no studies that have attempted to directly test for a particular set of relations between a specific cognitive structure (e.g., self-schemata) and self-statement patterns. Despite calls to test such a relationship (e.g., Meichenbaum, 1977), the absence of developed assessment procedures necessary to make operational social-cognitive variables of interest has led to limited progress in this area. With the exception of self-discrepancy theory, few models of cognitive structure have well-developed theoretical propositions. Although Bruch et al. (1981) found that a higher level of conceptual complexity was inversely related to frequency of negative self-statements for assertion situations, this result was merely suggestive of a relationship between cognitive structure and self-statement content and pattern. Bruch et al.'s (1988) finding that assertive schematics generated more self-relevant consequences when asked to write about possible consequences to a series of assertion vignettes, while aschematics focused equally on both self and other relevant consequences, tested a more specific hypothesis of how a cognitive structure may relate to particular cognitive content (e.g., self-focused attention).

A third concern evident from the review is that interest in nonassertiveness has peaked, while interest in shyness and related constructs (e.g., social phobia) is on the rise (see Galassi & Bruch, 1992). While the growing research interest in cognitive aspects of shyness is welcome, Buhrmester et al.'s (1988) emphasis on distinguishing among different domains of interpersonal competence should not be neglected. Prior attempts (Kirschner & Galassi, 1983; Russell, Cutrona, & Jones, 1986) to test person-situation models of nonassertiveness and shyness have not been followed up. To increase our understanding of how cognitive processes relate to social interaction, it will be important to show that the operations of particular cognitive structures play a similar role across multiple domains of interpersonal functioning as well as a unique role in a specific domain. For instance, an actual self/ought other discrepancy might have a similar impact on one's thoughts relative to situations involving initiating a conversation, responding assertively, and whether self-disclosure is reciprocated (cf. Buhrmester et al., 1988). Assessment of self-statements relative to these three situations might yield similar SOM ratios which should fall in negative dialogue or internal dialogue of conflict. In contrast, if one's self-efficacy beliefs (another cognitive structure) are high for initiating interactions, sharing feelings (e.g., being supportive), and self-disclosing, but low for assertion and conflict management, we would expect SOM ratio differences across these situations. Research that incorporates more person-situation analyses of how particular cognitive processes impact the effectiveness of one's responses in various interpersonal domains is greatly needed.

ACKNOWLEDGMENT

The author greatly appreciates feedback provided by Ronald J. Hamer and Richard G. Heimberg on an earlier draft of this chapter.

REFERENCES

American Psychiatric Association. (1987). *Diagnostic and statistical manual of mental disorders* (3rd ed.). Washington, DC: Author.

Beidel, D. C., Turner, S. M., & Dancu, C. (1985). Physiological, cognitive, and behavioral aspects of social anxiety. *Behaviour Research and Therapy, 23*, 109–117.

Bruch, M. A. (1981). A task analysis of assertive behavior revisited: Replication and extension. *Behavior Therapy, 12*, 217–230.

Bruch, M. A. (1989). Familial and developmental antecedents of social phobia: Issues and findings. *Clinical Psychology Review, 9*, 34–47.

Bruch, M. A., Gorsky, J. M., Collins, T. F., & Berger, P. A. (1989). Shyness and sociability reexamined: A multicomponent analysis. *Journal of Personality and Social Psychology, 57*, 904–915.

Bruch, M. A., Haase, R. F., & Purcell, M. J. (1984). Content dimensions of self-statements in assertive situations: A factor-analysis of two measures. *Cognitive Therapy and Research, 8*, 173–186.

Bruch, M. A., Hamer., J., & Heimberg, R. G. (1995). Shyness and public self-consciousness: Additive or interactive effects on social interactions? *Journal of Personality, 63*, 47–63.

Bruch, M. A., Hamer, J., & Kaflowitz-Linder, N. G. (1992). Cognitive balance and assertiveness: Testing the construct validity of the States of Mind categories. *Cognitive Therapy and Research, 16*, 653–667.

Bruch, M. A., Heimberg, R. G., & Hope, D. A. (1991). States of Mind Model and cognitive change in treated social phobics. *Cognitive Therapy and Research, 15*, 429–441.

Bruch, M. A., Heisler, B., & Conroy, C. (1981). Effects of conceptual complexity on assertive behavior. *Journal of Counseling Psychology, 28*, 377–385.

Bruch, M. A., Kaflowitz, N. G., & Berger, P. (1988). Self-schema for assertiveness: Extending the validity of the self-schema construct. *Journal of Research in Personality, 22*, 424–444.

Bruch, M. A., Kaflowitz, N. G., & Kuethe, M. (1986). Beliefs and the subjective meaning of thoughts: Analysis of the role of self-statements in academic test performance. *Cognitive Therapy and Research, 10*, 51–69.

Bruch, M. A., & Pearl, L. (1995). Attributional style and symptoms of shyness in a heterosocial interaction. *Cognitive Therapy and Research, 19*, 91–107.

Buhrmester, D., Furman, W., Wittenberg, M. T., & Reis, H. T. (1988). Five domains of interpersonal competence in peer relationships. *Journal of Personality and Social Psychology, 55*, 991–1008.

Cacioppo, J. T., Glass, C. R., & Merluzzi, T. V. (1979). Self-statements and self-evaluations: A cognitive-response analysis of heterosocial anxiety. *Cognitive Therapy and Research, 3*, 249–262.

Cacioppo, J. T., & Petty, R. E. (1981). Social psychological procedures for cognitive response assessment: The thought-listing technique. In T. J. Merluzzi, C. R. Glass, & M. Genest (Eds.), *Cognitive assessment* (pp. 309–342). New York: Guilford.

Carver, C. S., & Scheier, M. F. (1986). Analyzing shyness: A specific application of broader self-regulatory principles. In W. Jones, J. M. Cheek, & S. R. Briggs (Eds.), *Shyness: Perspectives on research and treatment* (pp. 173–185). New York: Academic Press.

Cheek, J. M., & Melchior, L. A. (1990). Shyness, self-esteem, and self-consciousness. In H. Leitenberg (Ed.), *Handbook of social and evaluation anxiety* (pp. 47–82). New York: Plenum.

Dodge, C. S., Hope, D. A., Heimberg, R. G., & Becker, R. E. (1988). Evaluation of the Social Interaction Self-Statement Test with a social phobic population. *Cognitive Therapy and Research, 12*, 211–222.

Galassi, J. P., & Bruch, M. A. (1992). Counseling with social interaction problems: Assertion and social anxiety. In S. D. Brown & R. W. Lent (Eds.), *Handbook of Counseling Psychology* (2nd ed., pp. 757–791). New York: Wiley.

Galassi, J. P., Galassi, M. D., & Fulkerson, K. (1984). Assertion training in theory and practice: An update. In C. M. Franks (Ed.), *New developments in practical behavior therapy: From research to clinical application* (pp. 319–376). Binghamton, NY: Haworth.

Garcia, S., Stinson, L., Ickes, W., Bissonnette, V., & Briggs, S. R. (1991). Shyness and physical attractiveness in mixed-sex dyads. *Journal of Personality and Social Psychology, 61*, 35–49.

Glass, C. R. (1993). A little more about cognitive assessment. *Journal of Counseling and Development, 71*, 546–548.

Glass, C. R., & Arnkoff, D. B. (1982). Think cognitively: Selected issues in cognitive assessment and therapy. In P. C. Kendall (Ed.), *Advances in cognitive-behavioral research and therapy* (Vol. 1, pp. 35–71). New York: Academic Press.

Glass, C. R., & Arnkoff, D. B. (1994). Validity issues in self-statement measures of social phobia and social anxiety. *Behaviour Research and Therapy, 32*, 255–267.

Glass, C. R., & Furlong, M. (1990). Cognitive assessment of social anxiety: Affective and behavioral correlates. *Cognitive Therapy and Research, 14*, 365–384.

Glass, C. R., Merluzzi, T. B., Biever, J. L., & Larsen, K. H. (1982). Cognitive assessment of social anxiety: Development and validation of a self-statement questionnaire. *Cognitive Therapy and Research, 6,* 37–55.

Goldfried, M. R., & D'Zurilla, T. J. (1969). A behavioral-analytic model for assessing competence. In C. D. Spielberger (Ed.), *Current topics in clinical and community psychology* (Vol. 1, pp. 151–196). New York: Academic Press.

Goldfried, M. R., Padawer, W., & Robins, C. (1984). Social anxiety and the semantic structure of heterosocial interactions. *Journal of Abnormal Psychology, 93,* 87–97.

Heimberg, R. G., Bruch, M. A., Hope, D. A., & Dombeck, M. (1990). Evaluating the States of Mind Model: Comparison to an alternative model and effects of method of cognitive assessment. *Cognitive Therapy and Research, 14,* 543–557.

Higgins, E. T. (1987). Self-discrepancy: A theory relating self and affect. *Psychological Review, 94,* 319–340.

Higgins, E. T., Strauman, T. J., & Klein, R. (1986). Standards and the process of self-evaluation: Multiple affects from multiple stages. In R. Sorrentino & E. T. Higgins (Eds.), *Handbook of motivation and cognition: Foundations of social behavior* (pp. 23–63). New York: Guilford.

Hope, D. A., Heimberg, R. G. Zollo, L. J., Nyman, D. J., & O'Brien, G. T. (1987). *Thought listing in the natural environment: Valance and focus of listed thoughts among socially anxious and nonanxious subjects.* Paper presented at the meeting of the Association for Advancement of Behavior Therapy, Boston.

Ingram, R. E. (1989a). Affective confounds in social-cognitive research. *Journal of Personality and Social Psychology, 57,* 715–722.

Ingram, R. E. (1989b). Unique and shared cognitive factors in social anxiety and depression: Automatic thinking and self-appraisal. *Journal of Social and Clinical Psychology, 8,* 198–208.

Ingram, R. E., & Kendall, P. C. (1986). Cognitive clinical psychology: Implications of an information processing perspective. In R. E. Ingram (Ed.), *Information processing approaches to clinical psychology* (pp. 3-21). New York: Academic Press.

Johnson, R. L., & Glass, C. R. (1989). Heterosocial anxiety and direction of attention in high school boys. *Cognitive Therapy and Research, 13,* 509–526.

Kendall, P. C. (1981). Assessment and cognitive-behavioral interventions: Purposes, proposals, and problems. In P. C. Kendall & S. D. Hollon (Eds.), *Assessment strategies for cognitive-behavioral interventions* (pp. 1–12). New York: Academic Press.

Kendall, P. C., & Hollon, S. D. (1981). Assessing self-referent speech: Methods in the measurement of self-statements. In P. C. Kendall & S. D. Hollon (Eds.), *Assessment strategies for cognitive-behavioral interventions* (pp. 85–118). New York: Academic Press.

Kendall, P. C., & Ingram, R. (1987). The future for cognitive assessment of Anxiety: Let's get specific. In L. Michelson & L. M. Ascher (Eds.), *Anxiety and stress disorders: Cognitive-behavioral assessment and treatment* (pp. 89–104). New York: Guilford.

Kendall, P. C., & Ingram, R. (1989). Cognitive-behavioral perspectives: Theory and research on depression and anxiety. In P. C. Kendall & D. Watson (Eds.), *Anxiety and depression: Distinctive and overlapping features* (pp. 27–53). New York: Academic Press.

Kirschner, N. M., & Galassi, J. P. (1983). Person, situational and interactional influences on assertive behavior. *Journal of Counseling Psychology, 30,* 355–360.

Leary, M. R. (1986). Affective and behavioral components of shyness. In W. H. Jones, J. M. Cheek, & S. R. Briggs (Eds.), *Shyness: Perspectives on research and treatment* (pp. 27–38). New York: Plenum.

Mahone, E. M., Bruch, M. A., & Heimberg, R. G. (1993). Focus of attention and social anxiety: The role of negative self thoughts and perceived positive attributes of the other. *Cognitive Therapy and Research 17,* 209–224.

Meichenbaum, D. (1977). *Cognitive behavior modification: An integrative approach* (pp.). New York: Plenum.

Melchior, L. A., & Cheek, J. M. (1990). Shyness and anxious self-preception during a social interaction. *Journal of Social Behavior and Personality, 5,* 117–130.

Merluzzi, T. V., Rudy, T. E., & Glass, C. R. (1981). The information processing paradigm: Implications for clinical science. In T. V. Merluzzi, C. R. Glass, & M. Genest (Eds.), *Cognitive assessment* (pp. 77–126). New York: Guilford.

Myszka, M. T., Galassi, J. P., & Ware, W. B. (1986). Comparison of cognitive assessment methods with heterosocially anxious college women. *Journal of Counseling Psychology, 33*, 401–407.

Pitcher, S. W., & Meikle, S. (1980). The topography of assertive behavior in positive and negative situations. *Behavior Therapy, 5*, 375–388.

Rudy, T., Merluzzi, T., & Henahan, P. (1982). Construal of complex assertion situations: A multidimensional analysis. *Journal of Consulting and Clinical Psychology, 80*, 125–137.

Russell, D., Cutrona, C., & Jones, W. G. (1986). A trait-situational analysis of shyness. In W. H. Jones, J. M. Cheek, & S. R. Briggs (Eds.), *Shyness: Perspectives on research and treatment* (pp. 238–249). New York: Plenum Press.

Schroder, H. M., Driver, M. J., & Streufert, O. (1967). *Human information processing*. New York: Holt, Rinehart & Winston.

Schwartz, R. M. (1991, November). *The idea of balance in psychotherapy*. Paper presented at the Association for Advancement of Behavior Therapy, New York.

Schwartz, R. M., & Garamoni, G. L. (1986). A structural model of positive and negative states of mind: Asymmetry in the internal dialogue. In P. C. Kendall (Ed.), *Advances in cognitive-behavioral research and therapy* (Vol. 5, pp. 1–62). New York: Academic Press.

Schwartz, R. M., & Garamoni, G. L. (1989). Cognitive balance and psychopathology: Evaluation of an information processing model of positive and negative states of mind. *Clinical Psychology Review, 9*, 271–294.

Schwartz, R. M., & Gottman, J. M. (1976). Toward a task analysis of assertive behavior. *Journal of Consulting and Clinical Psychology, 44*, 910–920.

Shaw, B. (1985). Depression and social cognition: Closing commentary. *Social Cognition, 3*, 100–105.

Strauman, T. J. (1989). Self-discrepancies in clinical depression and social phobia: Cognitive structures that underlie emotional disorders? *Journal of Abnormal Psychology, 98*, 5–14.

Strauman, T. J., & Higgins, E. T. (1988). Self-discrepancies as predictors of vulnerability to distinct syndromes of chronic emotional distress. *Journal of Personality, 56*, 685–707.

Turner, S. M., Beidel, D. C., & Larkin, K. T. (1986). Situational determinants of social anxiety in clinic and non-clinic samples: Physiological and cognitive correlates. *Journal of Consulting and Clinical Psychology, 54*, 523–527.

Wallace, S. T., & Alden, L. E. (1991). Discrepancies between standard and perceived ability in social interactions. *Cognitive Therapy and Research, 15*, 237–254.

Zweig, D. R., & Brown, S. D. (1985). Psychometric evaluation of a written stimulus presentation format for the Social Interaction Self-Statement Test. *Cognitive Therapy and Research, 9*, 285–295.

CHAPTER

12

When Is Self-Focused Attention an Adaptive Coping Response?: Rumination and Overgeneralization Versus Compensation

Joanne V. Wood
Philip G. Dodgson
University of Waterloo

It was a bad week for two academics. Each learned that a manuscript she had submitted for publication was rejected, and that a grant proposal that she had been led to believe was especially promising was not funded. Understandably, both were distressed to hear this news. However, they handled their distress differently. Rhonda found herself brooding about her failure, unable to keep her mind off the bad news. She also brooded about her mood, wondering why she continued to feel depressed. She reminded herself of other areas of inadequacy (e.g., her writing ability), worried that perhaps her career was a failure, and even dwelled upon failures in other realms of her life. Carla, in contrast, took a day off to take her daughter to the zoo, devoted considerable time to cooking a five-course gourmet meal for a dinner party, and delved into a chapter she was excited about writing. In short, Carla turned her attention to tasks and areas of her life that gave her reassurance that she was competent and successful. Two weeks later, Rhonda was still depressed and found it difficult to concentrate on her work, whereas Carla was enthusiastically launched into revisions of her manuscript.

This chapter focuses on two contrasting methods of coping with personal failure. The method that Rhonda used will be called the "rumination/overgeneralization" response. She ruminated about her depressed mood and overgeneralized from specific failures to the point of worrying that her career, as well as other areas of her life, were a failure. Research is just beginning to accumulate on the method that Carla used, which will be called "compensation." She tried to reverse her feelings of failure by overturning the failure itself (revising her manuscript) and also by focusing on other talents and strengths (parenting, cooking). What is intriguing about these two very different methods of coping is that they share a critical feature, namely self-focused attention. Rhonda focused on herself and her emotions in particular as she ruminated; Carla reminded herself of her areas of competence and focused on them as she compensated. This commonality introduces a paradox: Self-focused attention is associated with a maladaptive response that perpetuates distress in the rumination case, yet is associated with what appears to be a very adaptive response in the case of compensation. How can self-focused attention be associated with two such different means of coping?

In its focus on methods of coping with failure, this chapter differs from others in this volume. Whereas most of the other chapters concern intrusive thoughts that occur during the performance of tasks, this chapter concerns cognitions that follow performance, particularly failure experiences. The chapter examines the nature of those cognitions and their impact on subsequent performance and emotions, especially feelings about the self. This chapter has four parts. First is a description of the construct of self-focused attention. Second is a review of evidence on rumination/overgeneralization and its association with self-focused attention. Third is a review of the smaller, just-emerging literature on compensation. Finally, possible resolutions to the self-focused attention and coping paradox are proposed.

SELF-FOCUSED ATTENTION

Drawing from various theories and reviews of self-focused attention (Carver & Scheier, 1981; Gibbons, 1990; Hull & Levy, 1979; Wicklund, 1975), self-focus is defined as a state of information processing in which one is especially attentive to some aspect of the self or to the self-relevance of information received from the environment. Self-focus may involve a "private" aspect of oneself, such as one's thoughts and feelings, or a "public" aspect, such as one's appearance or the impression that one is creating. The present chapter concerns private self-focus.

A massive literature indicates that self-focused attention has powerful effects on one's thoughts, affect, and behavior (for reviews, see Carver & Scheier, 1981; Gibbons, 1990). These effects may be grouped generally into two categories. First, self-focused attention often increases responsiveness to whatever dimension of the self is the current object of self-focus. For example, self-focused attention can heighten one's moods (Scheier & Carver, 1977), and enable one to perceive one's bodily symptoms more accurately (Gibbons, Carver, Scheier, & Hormuth, 1979).

The second category of effects of self-focus, and the topic of most studies of self-focus, concerns self-regulation processes. People often behave more in accordance with personal standards when they are self-focused than when they are not. For example, self-focus has been shown to reduce cheating on tests, to increase helping behavior, and to increase the validity of self-reports (see Carver & Scheier, 1981 for references). Why would such effects occur? According to the dominant contemporary theory (Carver & Scheier, 1981), self-focus heightens a process of self-evaluation and self-regulation. Self-regulation processes involve comparing one's current state with a salient goal or standard. If there is a discrepancy, one may either adjust one's behavior to meet the standard, or abandon attempts to meet it and avoid self-focused attention. The determinant of whether one tries to match the standard or avoids self-focus is one's confidence that one can reach the standard in a timely fashion. If one's expectancy is favorable, self-focus will heighten attempts to match the standard and one will be pleased; if expectancy is unfavorable, self-focus will heighten the aversiveness of the situation, one will be displeased, and one will try to escape the self-focused state (see Carver & Scheier, 1990).

People vary in the degree to which they are characteristically self-focused, and this dispositional variable is referred to as "self-consciousness" (Fenigstein, Scheier, & Buss, 1975). One's degree of self-focus also varies from situation to situation. In the laboratory, private self-focused attention is manipulated by stimuli that remind one of the self, such as mirrors or tape recordings of one's own voice (for validity evidence, see Carver & Scheier, 1981).

Self-Focused Attention, Failure, and Distressed Moods

People are more self-focused immediately after they have failed than after they have succeeded (Greenberg & Pyszczynski, 1986). As Greenberg and Pyszczynski (1986) pointed out, such self-focus may serve a self-regulatory function; by becoming self-focused and comparing one's current state with salient standards, one can begin to remedy the failure. In addition, Wood, Saltzberg, and Goldsamt (1990) examined the possibility that unpleasant moods, which often accompany failure, induce self-focused attention. Affect may signal that something is wrong and that one must attend to the self and engage in self-regulation. Wood, Saltzberg, and Goldsamt also argued that self-regulation processes following stressors may aim not only toward achieving one's goal, but also toward controlling the affect itself. People use a variety of strategies to prolong their pleasant moods or to alleviate their unpleasant ones, such as whistling in the dark (Clark & Isen, 1982). Like other self-regulation processes, such affect control strategies may require attending to the self.

To examine the hypothesis that affect induces self-focused attention, Wood, Saltzberg, and Goldsamt (1990) conducted two experiments. In each, subjects participated in a mood induction procedure and then completed measures of self-focused attention. Across the two studies, care was taken to (a) minimize demand characteristics and experimenter bias; (b) measure mood via not only self-report measures, but via measures that are less susceptible to faking, such as speed of counting; and (c) measure self-focus using various measures. For example, Experiment 2 included a measure of self-focus based on subjects' "thought samples," in which subjects wrote freely for 2½ minutes (cf. Greenberg & Pyszczynski, 1986). Self-focused responses mentioned self-evaluations, physical characteristics or states, personality traits, emotions, and the subject's own performance. For example, self-focused responses included, "I'm tired because I had a restless night's sleep" and "I'm fat," whereas external-focused responses included, "How long does this experiment go on?" The two experiments—one that used an imagination mood induction procedure and one that used music—indicated that unpleasant moods heighten private self-focused attention.

Several other laboratory studies have indicated that sad or negative moods induce self-focused attention (Salovey, 1992; Saltzberg, Wood, & Bonvino, 1994; Sedikedes, 1992). Field studies of natural variations in moods also have indicated that unpleasant moods and self-focus are associated (Csikszentmihalyi & Figurski, 1982; Larsen & Cowan, 1988; Wood, Saltzberg, Neale, Stone, & Rachmiel, 1990).[1]

Clearly, then, failure experiences and distressed moods induce self-focused attention. Returning to the example opening this chapter, this evidence suggests that both Rhonda and Carla experienced a state of self-focus after learning about their rejected manuscripts and grant proposals.

Self-Focused Attention and Psychological Disorder

If unchecked, such self-focused attention sometimes appears to result in—or at least intensify—psychological disorder. Depression and private self-focus are positively correlated (e.g., Ingram, Lumry, Cruet, & Sieber, 1987; Smith & Greenberg, 1981). In addition, studies have suggested that self-focus is associated with cognitive, affective, and behavioral correlates of depression (e.g., Gibbons et al., 1985; Ingram et al., 1987). Two theories of depression accord self-focus a central role (Lewinsohn, Hoberman, Teri, & Hautzinger, 1985; Pyszczynski & Greenberg, 1987); both suggest that self-focus contributes to the self-blame, sadness, and poor self-image of depressed people. In addition, theory and evidence link self-focus with other disorders, such as anxiety (e.g., Ingram, 1990; Sarason, 1975).

What determines whether the self-focused attention that often results from failure and from unpleasant affect leads to depression and anxiety disorders? Certainly, not everyone who experiences failure or sadness becomes depressed or clinically anxious. Rhonda became depressed, Carla did not. Part of the answer, though certainly not all of it, may rest in different coping styles. These different coping methods are considered next.

[1]Evidence concerning happy moods is more mixed; some studies have indicated that happy moods do not induce self-focused attention (Saltzberg, Wood, & Bonvino, 1994; Sedikedes, 1992), and some studies have indicated that they do (Salovey, 1992). There appear to be good arguments in support of either view (Salovey, 1992; Wood, Saltzberg, & Goldsamt, 1990).

THE RUMINATION/OVERGENERALIZATION COPING RESPONSE

Self-Focused Attention and Coping

How might self-focused attention contribute to psychopathology? Studies have suggested that self-focus may increase negative thinking (e.g., Ingram et al., 1987; Pyszczynski, Holt, & Greenberg, 1987), amplify negative affect (Gibbons et al., 1985), and impair performance (Strack, Blaney, Ganellen, & Coyne, 1985). Wood, Saltzberg, Neale, et al. (1990) examined a different mechanism by which self-focus may exacerbate distress. Specifically, they proposed that self-focus encourages certain strategies of coping with stressors that heighten and perpetuate distress.

They based this proposal, in part, on Nolen-Hoeksema's (1987) response-styles explanation for sex differences in the prevalence of depression. Women are twice as likely as men to become depressed. Nolen-Hoeksema (1987) proposed that although both women and men become sad, they cope with sadness differently. Whereas women tend to be inactive and to ruminate about the causes and implications of their depressed mood, men tend to avoid thinking about their problems and to engage in distracting activities such as sports. Nolen-Hoeksema argued that women's ruminative response style amplifies and prolongs their depressive moods, whereas men's active, distracting style shortens theirs. Consequently, women have a higher prevalence of depression.

A ruminative response style, as defined by Nolen-Hoeksema, involves "repetitively focusing on the fact that one is depressed; on one's symptoms of depression and on the causes, meanings, and consequences of depressive symptoms" (Nolen-Hoeksema, 1991, p. 569). One may think about how tired and unmotivated one feels, wonder "Why do I get depressed when other people don't?" and worry, "I'm not going to be able to finish my work if I keep feeling this way" (see Lyubomirsky & Nolen-Hoeksema, 1993, p. 340; Nolen-Hoeksema, 1991, p. 569). Ruminative behaviors include, "isolating oneself to think about how one is feeling, writing in a diary about how one is feeling, or repeatedly telling others how badly one feels" (Morrow & Nolen-Hoeksema, 1990, p. 519).

Wood, Saltzberg, Neale, et al. (1990) reasoned that the self-focused attention that accompanies depression may encourage the self-preoccupied, ruminative response style that Nolen-Hoeksema suggested contributes to depression. Wood, Saltzberg, Neale, et al. also proposed that self-focus may interfere with problem-focused coping. Problem-focused coping is activity directed at alleviating the stressor itself, and is distinguished from emotion-focused coping, which is directed at making oneself feel better (Folkman & Lazarus, 1980). Depressed people appear to engage in less problem-focused coping than do nondepressed people (e.g., Billings & Moos, 1984). Wood, Saltzberg, Neale, et al. reasoned that self-focused attention may impede problem-focused coping under three conditions. First, when one has low expectations for achieving a goal, self-focus weakens one's motivation to try to achieve it (e.g., Carver, Blaney, & Scheier, 1979). Second, self-focus heightens emotional states (e.g., Scheier & Carver, 1977), and research has indicated that intense emotions may lead one to retreat from a goal (e.g., Scheier & Carver, 1982). Third, if self-focus promotes ruminating about one's moods and one's problems, it may reduce cognitive capacity to generate plans of action to improve the situation (Kuhl, 1981; cf. Hermann & Wortman, 1985). These three conditions—pessimistic expectations, intense affect, and tendencies to ruminate—appear to be common in depressed people (e.g., Alloy & Ahrens, 1987; Kuhl & Helle, 1986). It seems possible, then, that depressives' heightened self-focus may interfere with problem-focused coping.

Wood, Saltzberg, Neale, et al. (1990) examined these hypotheses—that self-focus is associated with a ruminative response style and with less problem-focused coping—in a sample of middle-aged married male community residents. Although Nolen-Hoeksema proposed that a ruminative response style is especially characteristic of women, the predictions concerning the relation for self-focus and rumination should hold for men as well, if some men do ruminate to some degree. In Wood et al.'s sample, men were not selected for being clinically depressed; rather, the association between self-focus and coping was examined in connection with the normal ups and downs of moods.

Participants in the study completed daily records of their moods, stressors, and coping responses. Self-focus was measured in a way similar to the thought samples that were used in the earlier laboratory experiments. In their daily records, respondents were asked to describe "the most bothersome event or issue of the day." Respondents typically wrote several short sentences, describing stressors that ranged from minor events, such as hassles related to commuting or disagreements with children, to major events, such as being fired or the death of a friend. These descriptions were content analyzed in the same way as the thought samples had been.

The men were also asked whether they had engaged in various strategies "to try to feel better or handle the problem." One such coping strategy was direct action ("thought about solutions to the problem, gathered information about it, or actually did something to try to solve it"), which served as the measure of problem-focused coping. Rumination was measured by the question, "Regarding the problem or situation that you described, did you find yourself dwelling on it, focusing on how bad it was and even intensifying its negative aspects in your own mind?" which was rated on a five-point scale (*not at all* to *a great deal*).[2]

[2]This operationalization of rumination differs somewhat from Nolen-Hoeksema's conception of rumination, as reflected in Nolen-Hoeksema's definition and examples of rumination presented earlier. Whereas our operationalization involves dwelling on the stressor itself, Nolen-Hoeksema has increasingly emphasized focusing on one's depressive *symptoms*. Nevertheless, her Ruminative Responses Scale does have items that focus on the stressor itself (i.e., "analyze recent events to try to understand why you are depressed," "think about a recent situation, wishing it had gone better"; Nolen-Hoeksema & Morrow, 1994). The scale also includes items that may tap into overgeneralization (e.g., "think about your shortcomings, failings, faults, and mistakes," "think back to other times you have felt depressed"). We suspect that ruminating about one's symptoms, the problem itself, and one's inadequacies (overgeneralization) often co-occur, but we know of no evidence to support this suspicion.

For each respondent, the researchers examined 30 days of reporting. Associations between self-focus and coping were examined on both within-subject and between-subjects levels. For the between-subjects case, which psychological researchers are most accustomed to, we obtained a single self-focus score and a single coping score for each subject (i.e., the average self-focus and coping scores across the 30 days), and then correlated these two scores across the sample. A between-subjects association would imply that people who are dispositionally high in self-focused attention also are dispositionally high in a tendency to ruminate or to refrain from problem-focused coping. In contrast, a within-subject association was examined by computing, for each subject separately, a correlation between his 30 daily self-focus scores and his 30 daily coping scores. These individual correlations were then averaged across the whole sample. A correlation between self-focus and coping at the within-subject level would imply that most people—regardless of their level of dispositional self-focus—tend to engage in rumination when they are self-focused.

There were no significant within-subjects associations, implying that fluctuations in daily self-focus are not associated with daily fluctuations in rumination and direct action. Between-subject results indicated self-focus was associated (at the $p = .06$ level) positively with rumination, and inversely with direct action. This between-subjects finding implies that people who tend to be high in their self-focus also tend to ruminate about their problems and to be less likely to take direct action to deal with them. Because these results are correlational, it is, of course, impossible to know whether self-focus promotes these coping styles, or whether these coping styles lead one to focus attention on the self. The results are at least consistent, however, with the view that self-focus encourages a contemplative, self-preoccupied coping style (cf. Strack et al., 1985).

Ruminative, Self-Preoccupied Coping and Depression

Does a ruminative coping style in turn perpetuate depression, as Nolen-Hoeksema (1987) proposed? Several studies suggest that the answer is "yes." Wood, Saltzberg, Neale, et al. (1990) obtained between-subjects effects for direct action (problem-focused coping) and negative mood, indicating that respondents who tend to use less direct action also tend to be unhappiest. Even stronger were the results for rumination, which showed both within-subjects and between-subjects associations. These results suggest that most people tend to ruminate when they are in a negative mood, but also that people who have a dispositional tendency to ruminate also tend to be more sad and anxious.

The finding that the men who engaged in rumination were especially distressed provides a stringent test of Nolen-Hoeksema's hypothesized mediator of sex differences in depression—namely, ruminative, passive coping. At the same time, Wood et al. also found that ruminative, passive coping was associated with anxiety as well as sadness, suggesting that Nolen-Hoeksema's ideas may be relevant not only to depression, but also to anxiety.

Additional evidence that rumination prolongs distress has emerged from several experimental and correlational studies (see Nolen-Hoeksema, 1993, for a review). For example, one field study showed that the more ruminative responses that respondents engaged in, the longer their depressed moods lasted, even after taking into account the initial severity of their moods (Nolen-Hoeksema, Morrow, & Fredrickson, 1993). In addition, Nolen-Hoeksema and Morrow (1991) found that students who exhibited a ruminative response style before the 1989 San Francisco area earthquake had more depression and stress symptoms 7 weeks after the earthquake.

Overgeneralization

In addition to ruminating about the problem and their own reactions to it, depressed people exhibit a second response to stressors that is relevant to the present discussion, namely overgeneralization. Overgeneralization concerns responses to the specific stressor of failure, and involves either: (a) inferring from single failures in specific domains that one has global deficiencies, or (b) extending unfavorable thoughts about oneself to areas unrelated to the stressor (e.g., Epstein, 1992). Rhonda, for example, worried about how failure in getting her article published and her grant funded might mean that she was not well-suited to do research, and even brooded about how she was incompetent in other areas, such as teaching and managing her personal finances.

Although much less systematic research has concerned overgeneralization than rumination, they do seem to be close cousins. Like rumination, overgeneralization is a self-preoccupied response that involves magnifying a failure or stressor. Whereas rumination dwells on and intensifies the stressor or one's emotional reactions, overgeneralization dwells on and intensifies the unfavorable implications of the failure for one's self-image.

Research has indicated that depressed people (e.g., Carver & Ganellen, 1983; Carver, La Voie, Kuhl, & Ganellen, 1988) and people with low self-esteem (Kernis, Brockner, & Frankel, 1989) are most likely to overgeneralize following failure. However, most of this evidence consists of correlations between measures of depression or self-esteem and self-report measures of overgeneralization. These studies demonstrate that depressed people *believe* that following failure, they think about themselves negatively. There are only a couple of demonstrations of overgeneralization in action—that depressed persons' thoughts following failures extend to areas of the self unrelated to the failure (e.g., Hammen & Krantz, 1976). For example, depressed subjects who had been told that they performed poorly on a test of social perceptiveness lowered their self-evaluations not only of their social perceptiveness, but also their general proficiency (Wenzlaff & Grozier, 1988).

In summary, self-focus is associated with ruminative, inactive coping, which in turn appears to perpetuate distress. Overgeneralization also may accompany ruminative responses to failures. It, too, seems to be a self-focused response, and it, too, appears to be a maladaptive response.

THE COMPENSATION COPING RESPONSE

In recent years, our research efforts have turned toward a strategy of coping likely to be adaptive rather than maladaptive, one which we call compensation. There are two important differences between our earlier work on rumination and our current work on compensation. One difference is that whereas the rumination research concerned responses to stressors of any nature, the newer research concerns specifically threats to the individual's view of self, including unfavorable feedback about personal attributes and failures.

A second difference is a shift in focus from depressed moods to self-esteem. However, this is not such a big leap, because there is substantial overlap between depression and low self-esteem. Depressed people often have low self-esteem (e.g., Beck, 1967; Nadich, Gargan, & Michael, 1975), even when their depression is in remission (Altman & Wittenborn, 1980). Estimates of the inverse correlation between self-esteem and depression range from about .40 to about .60 (Crandall, 1973). Low self-esteem people and depressed people often respond to failures in similar ways (e.g., Kernis et al., 1989). For example, measures of self-esteem and of depression are equally predictive of the use of self-serving biases (Blaine & Crocker, 1993). In addition, people with low self-esteem have high levels of self-consciousness (Turner, Scheier, Carver, & Ickes, 1978), just as depressed people do.

The shift from depression to self-esteem seems reasonable as the latter appears to be more fundamental, for two reasons. First, self-esteem is associated with many behavioral problems and behavioral disorders other than depression, such as anxiety disorders, paranoid schizophrenia, and substance abuse (see Brockner & Hulton, 1978, and Solomon, Greenberg, & Pyszczynski, 1991, for references). Second, several theorists have suggested that a foundation of low self-regard may make one vulnerable to depression (e.g., see Becker, 1979, and Alloy & Abramson, 1988, for reviews), and some evidence supports this suggestion.

Self-Esteem Differences in Reactions to Failure

A great deal of research documents the differences between people with low and with high self-esteem in their responses to esteem-threatening feedback. Whereas low self-esteem people tend to accept such feedback, high self-esteem people are inclined to use strategies to minimize its impact. For example, people with high self-esteem are more likely to attribute negative outcomes to external factors, devalue tasks on which they fail, and discredit negative feedback (see Blaine & Crocker, 1993; Taylor & Brown, 1988, for reviews).

Research on the strategy of compensation is just beginning to accumulate. In contrast to the other strategies of self-enhancement, compensation does not involve minimizing unfavorable feedback or attributing it elsewhere. Rather, it involves attempting to generate an experience that will reflect positively on the self and thereby counterbalance the negative feedback (Giordano-Beech & Wood, 1995). Compensation may take either of two forms. One form, which Giordano-Beech and Wood (1995) called "direct compensation," challenges the negative feedback. For example, one may behave in ways that contradict that feedback. Subjects told that they were "self-oriented and apathetic to the concerns of others" became especially helpful toward others (Steele, 1975). People also may challenge failures by trying to improve their performance on a second attempt at the failed task (e.g., McFarlin, Baumeister, & Blascovich, 1984).

Instead of trying to overturn unfavorable feedback, the second form of compensation, which Giordano-Beech and Wood (1995) called "indirect," focuses attention on other favorable attributes of the self. For example, subjects who had received a negative personality profile later rated themselves very favorably on characteristics that were unrelated to that profile (Baumeister & Jones, 1978). Similarly, subjects who had failed on a test of intellectual ability rated their social abilities especially highly, and were especially helpful toward other people (Brown & Smart, 1991). The idea of indirect compensation is consistent with Steele's (1988) theory of self-affirmation. Self-affirmation theory holds that people are not motivated to refute each specific threat to self-esteem that arises, but to try to restore an overall self-image that is positive and efficacious. Hence, after failing in one domain, one may restore one's self-image by affirming important aspects of oneself—aspects that may be related or unrelated to the domain in which one failed.

The authors have studied a means of compensation that differs from those described earlier that does not involve rating oneself highly on related or unrelated dimensions or behaving in ways that contradict the feedback. Specifically, they have examined social comparison as a means of compensation. After failing, people may make downward comparisons—they may focus on other people who are inferior to themselves. Although people seem to usually prefer to measure themselves against others who are superior, because of the information or inspiration such upward comparisons can provide, people may prefer downward comparisons when their self-esteem is threatened (Wills, 1981; Wood & Taylor, 1991). Such downward comparisons can be self-enhancing (Wills, 1981; Wood, 1989). After receiving her rejection letter, then, Carla could console herself by considering a colleague who has received several rejections lately. She also could make downward comparisons in domains unrelated to the failure. She could, for example, focus on her special talent as a parent by lingering at the supermarket, watching miserable parents battling with their screaming toddlers. Downward comparisons such as these may provide an especially effective means of compensating after failure. One not only sees the self in a positive light, one sees oneself as superior to another person, and hence one's self-esteem can receive an extra boost.

High Self-Esteem and Compensation

Three previous studies have suggested that people with high self-esteem are more likely than people with low self-esteem to engage in compensation strategies following failure (Baumeister, 1982; Brown & Smart, 1991; Josephs, Markus, & Tafarodi, 1992, Experiment 3). Research by Wood, Giordano-Beech, Taylor, Michela, and Gaus (1994) confirmed these findings within a social comparison context. Specifically, subjects participated in pairs, and received feedback such that one subject succeeded and the other failed. Subjects were then given an opportunity to seek comparisons with the other subject on a variety of tasks. By choosing tasks on which they thought they would perform better than the other, they could hope to compensate for the failure. The results yielded an interaction between self-esteem and success/failure in subjects' rate of comparison-seeking: High self-esteem subjects were especially likely to seek comparisons after they failed, whereas low self-esteem subjects were especially likely to seek comparisons after they succeeded. This interaction was obtained in two studies, despite different manipulations of success/failure, different measures of self-esteem, and other differences in procedure.

Wood, Giordano-Beech, Taylor, Michela, and Gaus (1994, Experiment 2) obtained evidence that these subjects did not seek comparisons merely because they were puzzled or skeptical about their test results. Instead, Wood et al. argued that low self-esteem/success subjects were seeking to compare with the person who had failed against them so that they could revel in their success, and high self-esteem/failure subjects were seeking to compensate for their failure. Evidence supportive of this interpretation was that low self-esteem/success subjects and high self-esteem/failure subjects expected to outperform the other, which suggests that they were seeking self-enhancing social comparisons.

However, because it was uncertain that subjects' desires to perform better than the other motivated their comparison-seeking, more direct evidence was sought (e.g., Wood et al., 1994, Experiment 3). Most relevant to the present topic, Giordano-Beech and Wood (1995) conducted two studies to establish more definitively that high self-esteem/failure subjects seek comparisons so as to compensate for failure. Both studies involved providing failure feedback to subjects with high self-esteem and then manipulating available opportunities for compensation. In one experiment, dimensions for potential comparisons concerned either subjects' self-perceived strengths or weaknesses, which had been identified beforehand. It was predicted that subjects would seek more comparisons if they could do so in their areas of strength than if they could do so only in their areas of weakness, because they could hope to outperform the other, and thereby compensate for the failure, only on their strengths. This prediction was confirmed. In addition, a condition was included in which subjects received success feedback and then had an opportunity to compare on their strengths, to control for the possibility that subjects may seek comparisons on their strengths simply because they are more interested in them. It was predicted that success/strength subjects would seek fewer comparisons than would failure/strength subjects, because success/strength subjects should have no need to compensate. This prediction also was confirmed.

The second experiment tested the compensation hypothesis in a different way. Before subjects had an opportunity to compare themselves with the other, half of the high self-esteem/failure subjects were provided with a different means of compensating for their failure. Specifically, they completed a "self-affirmation" task, as is used in Steele's research, which involved completing a scale concerning a value that was especially important to them. Previous research had illustrated the value of this self-affirmation task (e.g., Steele & Liu, 1981). Giordano-Beech and Wood (1995) found that high self-esteem subjects who failed but then had an opportunity to self-affirm in this manner sought fewer comparisons than did subjects who had not had this opportunity. Subjects in the self-affirmation condition presumably did not need to make comparisons any longer, because they had already compensated for their failure through the self-affirmation task.

This research adds social comparison to the roster of strategies by which people may compensate for unfavorable feedback. In addition, it supports previous suggestions that compensation strategies are more common among high self-esteem people than among low (e.g., Baumeister, 1982). Why would this be so? High self-esteem people may be more able to focus on their talents after failure because they believe that they have more talents on which they can focus, whereas low self-esteem people have fewer and less distinct positive aspects of their self-image to which they can turn (Spencer, Josephs, & Steele, 1993). However, this does not seem to be the whole story. People who are labeled "low self-esteem" in most studies do not dislike themselves; they just like themselves less than do high self-esteem people (Baumeister, Tice, & Hutton, 1989). Even those lowest in self-esteem have at least one attribute that they prize (Pelham & Swann, 1989). These findings suggest that people with low self-esteem have the resources to compensate, if they would only try.

Recruiting Positive Thoughts About Oneself

One mechanism that may underlie high self-esteem people's attempts to compensate for failure is that following failure people with high self-esteem recruit positive conceptions of themselves. Other researchers have expressed very similar ideas. To explain the finding that subjects who failed at an achievement task exaggerated their social qualities, Brown and Smart (1991) suggested that these subjects tried to counter the negative feedback "by actively recruiting positive perceptions of their social qualities" (p. 370). Similarly, Steele, Spencer, and Lynch (1993) suggested that self-affirmation processes following threats to self-esteem involve "recruiting self-knowledge and other beliefs that ... affirm [one's] overall adequacy" (pp. 885–886). Both Brown and Smart (1991) and Steele et al. (1993) argue that such processes should be easier for people with high self-esteem than for low, because people with high self-esteem should have more positive aspects of their self-image from which to draw.

Interestingly, recruiting positive self-conceptions following failure runs counter to the phenomenon of mood-congruent cognition, in which moods make similarly valenced thoughts more accessible. Bower's (1981) associative-network theory suggested that moods activate or cue similarly toned material in memory. Effects consistent with this theory have been well documented. For example, people in sad moods selectively recall memories of unhappy events from their pasts and interpret their own behavior more negatively than do people in happy moods (see Singer & Salovey, 1988; Blaney, 1986, for reviews). At the same time, others have argued that people may at times recall events that are incongruent with their negative moods, to try to "repair" their negative moods (e.g., Isen, 1984). Such a self-regulatory process would help explain why affect is not always intensified—why one sad thought does not necessarily lead to an unending, downward spiral into depression. However, this process of mood-incongruent recall has not been demonstrated until recently; in both field quasi-experiments and two laboratory experiments, Parrott and Sabini (1990) found that subjects in bad moods recall events with more positive affective tone than those in happy moods. As part of their explanation for why they obtained results counter to the mood-congruency research, Parrott and Sabini (1990) offered that mood-incongruent recall seems to occur in memory retrieval tasks possessing the "potential for regulating mood, for balancing subjects' perspectives of their selves and their lives" (p. 334). They argued that in contrast to previous research showing mood-congruent recall for material supplied by the experimenter, the autobiographical memories used in their studies, being more detailed, vivid, and personal, are far more suitable for self-regulation.

This latter process of mood-incongruent recall in reaction to negative mood states is consistent with the present notion of compensation. However, it is not simply argued that individuals with higher levels of self-esteem react to esteem-threatening events by retrieving positively toned material. Instead, following such events as failure, high self-esteem people may turn toward positive features of the self, such as special abilities. Memories and thoughts within these domains, more likely to be positively toned, are also able to redress damage to self-esteem.

Some research on motivated reasoning bears on this idea. Markus and Kunda (1986) led subjects to see themselves to a disturbing degree as either very similar to others or as unique. Subjects then seemed to recruit memories or conceptions of themselves that contradicted these self-views. This was evidenced, for example, by the finding that subjects made to feel unique were faster to endorse as self-descriptive words related to similarity than subjects made to feel similar. This finding suggests that the "unique" subjects brought to mind examples from their lives that illustrated their similarity to others. More recently, Sanitioso, Kunda, and Fong (1990) have shown that when certain traits are made to appear desirable, subjects recruit autobiographical memories that are congruent with these traits. Such studies suggest that people are endowed with the ability to actively build and maintain a positive sense of self.

Clearly, some individuals are able to maintain more positive views of the self than are others—namely, those high in self-esteem. The authors have begun a series of studies designed to test the idea that for people with high self-esteem, failure experiences may actually serve to cue memories and thoughts relating to their strengths. Such a process enables further attempts at compensation in that it rallies a person's full resources and inspires greater self-confidence. A person able to bring such positive self-thoughts to mind following failure would be far more likely to make a second attempt at a task, or perhaps engage in social comparison, with the expectation it will counteract the failure experience.

One such study (Dodgson & Wood, 1994) exposed individuals with either high or low self-esteem to failure or success feedback, and then measured changes in accessibility of thoughts pertaining to pretested strengths and abilities. Participants had been pretested for self-esteem, as well as their self-reported ability in 12 different domains, such as intellectual/academic ability, social skills/social competence, and artistic/musical ability. Upon arrival at the experiment, subjects were led to believe that they would participate in two studies. In the first "study," a test of "Verbal Problem Solving" was administered which purportedly strongly predicted academic performance. Participants were then given false feedback that they had performed better than 92% (success) or 38% (failure) of a large sample of other first-year university students. Other participants received no feedback at all, as a control condition. Subjects were then taken to another room, where a new researcher explained that the second study involved "how people describe themselves." Subjects were required to make me or not me judgments about 96 trait adjectives presented on a personal computer. These adjectives were derived from the 12 pretested domains of ability, and included such words as "athletic" and "clever." The length of time subjects took to decide whether a particular adjective described them was recorded as an index of the accessibility of the domain corresponding to that word.

The prediction that high self-esteem people recruit strength-related thoughts about themselves following failure was supported by an interaction among level of self-esteem, condition (success, failure, no-feedback), and ability domain (ranked in order of self-rated ability). The reaction times for both strengths and weaknesses were fairly similar following success and no feedback for both high and low self-esteem subjects. However, following failure, reaction times were faster for stimuli associated with more highly rated abilities (strengths) for people with high self-esteem, consistent with the idea that such people's strengths had become relatively more accessible. The finding that their self-perceived strengths were more accessible after failure than after success is especially surprising; the mood-cognition congruency literature would predict that the happiness resulting from success would make positive thoughts about the self more accessible.

These results, then, are consistent with the idea that following failure, people with high self-esteem recruit positive thoughts about themselves. Specifically, they call upon their strengths.

Is Compensation Adaptive?

Compensation and recruiting positive aspects of oneself would appear to be an adaptive response to stressors that have negative implications for the self. The high self-esteem person is attempting to reverse failures and repair his or her wounded self-esteem. There is no strong evidence yet, however, that it is adaptive. It is known, however, that people with high self-esteem tolerate failures better than do people with low self-esteem (e.g., Shrauger & Rosenberg, 1970). Such evidence is consistent with the idea that the responses high self-esteem people exhibit following failure—including compensation—lift their moods and benefit their self-esteem.

THE PARADOX OF SELF-FOCUSED ATTENTION AND COPING

Self-Focus, Rumination, and Overgeneralization Versus Compensation

The two areas of research summarized share certain features. Both the rumination/overgeneralization research and the compensation research concern individual differences in cognitive ways of coping with stressors. Depressed people are more likely than nondepressed people to exhibit the rumination/overgeneralization response. People high in self-esteem are more likely than people low in self-esteem to compensate for failures. These findings are consistent with the idea that personality differences are manifested and perpetuated in coping responses to the stressors of everyday life (cf. Bolger & Schilling, 1991).

Indeed, personality differences may link the two areas of research quite closely. In the field study of self-focus and rumination, Wood, Saltzberg, Neale, et al. (1990) found both a within-person and between-persons association between rumination and distress. The combination suggests that there may be an almost universal tendency to ruminate when upset by a stressor, but that some people are able to "snap out" of this preoccupation, whereas others do not. Hence, the question becomes, what is it that people do who "snap out of it"? It may be that people with high self-esteem are such people, and that their tendency to compensate for failures, plus their tendency to actively recruit positive thoughts about themselves, contributes to their ability to "snap out of it."

Another central similarity between the two areas of research is self-focused attention. Self-focus is clearly associated with rumination (Wood, Saltzberg, Neale, et al., 1990). It also seems central to overgeneralization, in that overgeneralization requires thinking intensively about the self. The individual infers from failure negative implications for various areas of self, and might bring to mind past failures to embroider a negative self-conception. Self-focused attention is also implied in compensation. To compensate directly, people must think about past successes in the area of the failure, so as to have confidence that they can overturn the failure. To compensate indirectly, people must focus on the self to think of other domains in which they are strong or talented. Both require attention to the self. In addition, because a number of studies have suggested that self-focused attention heightens the accessibility of self-schemata (Hull & Levy, 1979; see Carver & Scheier, 1981, pp. 99–116, for a review), self-focus should facilitate the recruiting of positive self-conceptions for high self-esteem people.[3]

This commonality between the two responses of self-focused attention introduces a paradox: How could self-focused attention be associated, perhaps even encourage, maladaptive coping in one case, yet be associated with and perhaps promote adaptive coping in the other? The rest of this chapter is devoted to trying to resolve this puzzle. The resolutions proposed are not mutually exclusive, and indeed, the answer likely lies in some combination of them.

The reader is asked to bear with certain liberties being taken in this section. First, the distinction is ignored between depression, which rumination research has concerned, and self-esteem, which compensation research has concerned. It is recognized that these are overlapping but distinct constructs, but it is assumed for the moment that the people who were chronically distressed in the authors' rumination work were also low in self-esteem. Second, the rumination research concerned stressors that were not limited to personal failures. It seems a safe assumption, however, that rumination would be as likely a response to personal failures as to most stressors. The focus here is stressors that have negative implications for one's self-evaluation, which are referred to here simply as "failures." A third liberty being taken is the assumption that compensation is an adaptive coping response.

[3]Steele et al. (1993) also have suggested that in order for people to access their self-esteem resources, they have to be self-focused. They argued that immediately following a threat, one's attention is often directed toward diminishing or rationalizing the threat itself, and something may have to direct one's attention to oneself to bring their self-esteem resources "on line." Steele et al. (1993) obtained some support for this idea; in a free-choice dissonance paradigm, high self-esteem subjects did not show the usual postdecisional rationalization effect if they had just completed a self-esteem scale (see also Spencer et al., 1993). However, filling out a self-esteem scale is likely more than a self-focus manipulation; it reminds the individual of his or her strengths. Hence, this study does not demonstrate that self-focused attention by itself primes one's self-evaluative resources.

Possible Resolutions to the Self-Focused Attention and Coping Paradox

1. Self-Focused Attention Is Not Necessarily an Unpleasant Experience. The original self-focus theorists believed self-focused attention to be aversive, because it makes salient discrepancies from one's standards (Duval & Wicklund, 1972). Hence, it was thought to necessarily lower one's self-esteem (Ickes, Wicklund, & Ferris, 1973). Contemporary thinking about self-focus does not hold that it is necessarily aversive. According to Carver and Scheier's (1981; 1990) theory, self-focus leads to negative affect only when the person is aware of a discrepancy and believes that he or she cannot attenuate that discrepancy quickly enough. Self-focused attention may even heighten positive affect (Scheier & Carver, 1977).[4] People even seem to seek out self-focused attention when they are successful, possibly to prolong their positive moods (Greenberg & Musham, 1981; Pyszczynski & Greenberg, 1985).

The idea that a self-focused state can be a positive or negative one does not offer a complete resolution to the question of why self-focused attention can be associated with both a maladaptive and an adaptive coping response, because it merely changes the question: When is self-focused attention a positive experience and when is it a negative one?

2. Self-Focus Heightens One's Current State. As stated earlier, one effect of self-focus is that it tends to exaggerate whatever state one is already experiencing. Hence, self-focus should promote a positive state when one's thoughts are already happy, and a negative state when one's thoughts are already unhappy. Evidence of this effect was found by Ickes et al. (1973, Experiment 3). Subjects who received negative feedback and who then rated themselves in the presence of a self-focusing stimulus (namely, a mirror) had lower self-evaluations than did subjects not exposed to a mirror. There also was a tendency for positive feedback subjects to have more positive self-evaluations when self-focused than when not. Similarly, Berkowitz (1987, Experiment 2) induced positive, negative, or neutral moods in subjects and then manipulated self-focused attention. Self-focus increased the frequency of positive ideas about the self in the happy subjects and increased the frequency of negative ideas about the self in the unhappy subjects.

Because people with high self-esteem are generally happier than those with low self-esteem (e.g., Campbell, Chew, & Scratchley, 1991), a self-focused state may

[4]Gibbons' (1990) review indicates that in almost all studies of the effect of self-focus on emotion, it was negative emotion, such as fear or anger, that was intensified by self-focus. Of the five or so studies that have examined the effect of self-focus on positive emotions, the effects have been marginal or absent. Although studies that manipulate self-focus and then measure mood do not strongly support the idea that positive moods are enhanced by self-focus, nonetheless it is likely that this effect often occurs, because of the other evidence cited under points 1 and 2 in the resolutions section.

magnify such differences, making highs especially happy and feeling especially good about themselves, and lows especially unhappy and feeling especially inadequate (cf. Ingram, 1990). There is evidence that this is the case (e.g., Brown, 1989, cited in Brown & Mankowski, 1993; Sedikedes, 1992). Similarly, Brockner (1979a) has suggested that people who are low in self-esteem experience self-focus as especially aversive and anxiety-provoking. This idea makes sense in view of self-focus theory; low self-esteem people should be aware of more negative aspects of themselves and more discrepancies from their ideal state than high self-esteem people, and self-focus should heighten that awareness.

The possibility that the state of self-focused attention is generally more pleasant for people with high self-esteem than people with low does not provide a full account, however, for their differences in coping with failure. After failure, even people with high self-esteem should be unhappy, and their self-worth should dip, if only temporarily. Hence, if failure induces self-focused attention (Greenberg & Pyszczynski, 1986), and if self-focus heightens one's current state, it should intensify distress and unfavorable thoughts about the self even among people with high self-esteem.

3. A Negative Self-Focused State Should Be More Aversive and Prolonged for People With Low Self-Esteem Than for People With High Self-Esteem. Part of the resolution to the paradox may be that even though self-focus heightens one's current state, and even though this state should be unpleasant for both high and low self-esteem people following a stressor, the state should be especially aversive and prolonged in the case of low self-esteem people. In line with spreading activation theorizing and research (Bower, 1981; Isen, 1984), people with low self-esteem should have a richer web of negative associations to stress and failure. They should recall more past experiences that involved failure or personal inadequacy, and they should be reminded of what they perceive to be their many current deficiencies.

Indeed, failure seems to hit people with low self-esteem especially hard. They accept negative feedback more readily and regard it as more credible than do people with high self-esteem (e.g., McFarlin & Blascovich, 1981; Shrauger, 1975), their self-ratings are more responsive to failure (Shrauger & Rosenberg, 1970; cf. Pyszczynski & Greenberg, 1985), they feel more shame and humiliation (Brown & Dutton, 1995), and their performance on subsequent tasks is more impaired (e.g., Shrauger & Rosenberg, 1970). In addition, as discussed earlier, they are more likely to overgeneralize negative feedback in one domain to other domains of the self. Moreover, Brockner (1979a; 1979b) has found that following failure feedback, self-focusing stimuli debilitate the performance of low self-esteem people more than that of high self-esteem people.

The possibility that the self-focused state induced by failure is especially aversive for low self-esteem people suggests a reason why they would be "stuck" longer in a cycle of rumination and self-recrimination (cf. Pyszczynski & Greenberg, 1987). However, this possibility cannot account for compensation processes. For high self-esteem people, their distress following failure does not merely dissipate more quickly than does low self-esteem people's. Rather, people with high self-esteem seem to be actively doing something to stop their negative moods and to reverse the failure. It is difficult to understand how self-focused attention, which should perpetuate their current mood, would allow this to happen.

4. High Self-Esteem People Actively Avoid Self-Focused Attention After Failure. Recall that in addition to intensifying current thoughts and feelings, self-focused attention also yields another category of effects—namely, effects revolving around self-regulation processes in the pursuit of goals. If one's expectations are high that one can achieve a goal, one will try to do so, but if one's expectations are low, then one will try to exit the situation and avoid self-focused attention (Carver & Scheier, 1981). Evidence has indicated that people may attempt to avoid a state of self-focus when they have experienced a failure (e.g., Greenberg & Musham, 1981). For example, Gibbons and Wicklund (1976) showed that after receiving a negative evaluation, subjects avoided self-focus by spending less time listening to tape recordings of their own voices.

Such evidence may seem to conflict with evidence that both failure and negative moods induce self-focused attention (Greenberg & Pyszczynski, 1986; Wood, Saltzberg, & Goldsamt, 1990). Greenberg and Pyszczynski's (1986) study, which indicated that failure does induce self-focused attention, showed that when people seemed to avoid self-focus, they did so only after an initial period of self-focus. It is consistent with current self-focus theory that initially, failure or negative mood should induce self-focused attention so as to prompt self-regulation or affect-control processes, but that these processes may then result in the avoidance of self-focus.

People with high self-esteem may be more adept at avoiding self-focus than people with low self-esteem. Greenberg and Pyszczynski (1986) found that the self-focused attention induced by failure declined rapidly among nondepressed people, but not among depressed people. There is even some indication that nondepressed people seek self-focus when they have succeeded but attempt to escape self-focused attention following failure, but that depressed people exhibit the opposite pattern (Pyszczynski & Greenberg, 1985, 1986). Perhaps, then, one of the actions that high self-esteem/nondepressed people take to short-circuit their negative moods following failure is to avoid self-focused attention.

How can this evidence that high self-esteem people avoid self-focus be reconciled with evidence that they use compensation strategies after failure? One possibility is that avoidance of self-focus may be the most adaptive response in some circumstances, but not others. Specifically, avoidance is the wisest response when the setting offers no opportunity to compensate for the failure. A review of the avoidance studies supports this reasoning. In the Gibbons and Wicklund (1976) study, subjects had no opportunity to rectify their previous negative evaluation (see also Greenberg & Musham, 1981). The same seems to be true of the Greenberg and Pyszczynski (1986) study, in which subjects' self-focus was measured immediately after their failure or success and again after reading ten pages of a novel, which should have offered a distraction, but no means of compensation. In the Pyszczynski and Greenberg studies (1985, 1986), subjects who have succeeded or failed had an opportunity to work on puzzles either in front of a mirror or not. Successfully solving puzzles could have offered an opportunity to compensate for failure. However, in one study (Pyszczynski & Greenberg, 1985), subjects worked for only 3 minutes each on two puzzle sets, one in front of a mirror and one not, without recording their solutions. Because their time was so short on each puzzle and because their performance was not evaluated, subjects likely saw little opportunity for compensation. When asked about their preferences, nondepressed subjects showed the usual finding; they clearly liked the mirror-associated puzzle more after success than after failure. In contrast, in the other study (Pyszczynski & Greenberg, 1986), subjects were given 10 minutes which they could allocate as they wished toward either puzzle set. More emphasis was placed on performance, and as subjects recorded their puzzle solution, they probably expected evaluation. In this study, the time that nondepressed subjects spent in front of the mirror did not depend on whether they had succeeded or failed. It seems quite possible that nondepressed subjects did not avoid self-focus after failure in this case because the puzzles offered a means of compensating for the failure. As Pyszczynski and Greenberg (1986) themselves put it in terms of the self-focus theory, "the nondepressed subjects ... may have viewed the puzzle task as a way to reduce the negative discrepancy created by the failure" (p. 103).

More direct evidence that people will not prefer avoidance if subjects have an opportunity to compensate is offered by a study by Steenberger and Aderman (1979), who found that subjects escaped self-focus more quickly after receiving negative feedback if they had been led to expect that their performance could not be improved than if they believed their performance could be remedied. Although people with high self-esteem are capable of avoiding self-focus after failure, then, we believe that if they see an opportunity to compensate for the failure, they will remain self-focused and will invest energy into doing so.

5. The Goals of People With High and Low Self-Esteem Differ Following Failure. Recall that self-focused attention can fuel one's goals if one expects that one can attenuate the discrepancy between one's current state and one's ideal state. Perhaps the difference in the self-focused states of high and low self-esteem people following failure, then, lies in their differing goals or in their differing expectations for achieving their goals. This section considers the possibility that their goals differ, and in the next possible resolution, their expectations will be considered.

Baumeister et al. (1989) proposed that, in general (not just following failure), people with high self-esteem seek self-*enhancement*; they seek ways of drawing attention to their skills. They are bold, willing to take risks to achieve gains in self-esteem. In contrast, people with low self-esteem seem to focus on *self-protection*. Rather than trying to achieve gains for their self-esteem, they seek to avoid losses. They "focus not on their good points but on trying to minimize their weaknesses" (Schlenker, Weigold, & Hallam, 1990, p. 856). Consequently, they avoid risks that may lead to humiliation. This view of the cautious, self-protective, low self-esteem person is growing, as is supportive evidence (e.g., Arkin, 1981; see Baumeister, 1993, for reviews).

Failure should accentuate these differences between low and high self-esteem people (cf. Wood et al., 1994). Following failure, low self-esteem people should be even more likely than usual to shrink from further evaluation, to avoid exacerbating their already wounded self-esteem. If their goal is to avoid further exposure of their deficiencies, self-focus could lead them to focus on their deficiencies. They could be trying to identify their deficiencies in the hopes of also identifying ways of avoiding their exposure, just as having a map that indicates roadblocks can help one to avoid them. Perhaps this need to scrutinize the self following failure could contribute to depressed people's "depressive self-focusing style," in which they self-focus more after failure than after success (Pyszczynski & Greenberg, 1985, 1986).

In contrast, failure should heighten high self-esteem people's usual goal of self-enhancement. Their goal should be to counteract their failures, both to redeem themselves in the eyes of others and to feel better about themselves (Baumeister, 1982; Baumeister & Tice, 1985). If the goal of high self-esteem people is to compensate, self-focus could lead them to focus not on their weaknesses, but on their assets, as they struggle to identify ways in which they can overturn the failure or substitute a compensatory talent.

6. People With Low Self-Esteem Are Less Goal-Oriented Following Failure. Another possibility is not that the goals of high and low self-esteem people differ following failure, but that people with high self-esteem have a goal, whereas people with low self-esteem do not. It seems likely that people with low self-esteem may not be focused on the goal of feeling better about themselves. Recall that Wood et al. (1990b) identified three conditions under which self-focused attention may interfere with problem-focused coping: when affect is too intense, when one's expectations for achieving the goal are unfavorable, and when one's cognitive capacity for generating plans of action is low. If these conditions are met, self-focus may interfere not only with problem-focused coping, but with any goal-directed action. Following failure, low self-esteem people appear to meet all of these conditions, whereas people with high self-esteem do not.

First, as described earlier, people with low self-esteem react more strongly to failure than do high self-esteem people. Their stronger affect may lead them to withdraw from any goal they might have to feel better (e.g., Scheier & Carver, 1982). Second, people with low self-esteem should have low expectations following failure that they can feel better about themselves. Their generally low self-confidence should be especially low following a failure, when the discrepancy between their current state of failure and their ideal state of feeling competent and lovable should be especially pronounced.

In contrast, high self-esteem people seem to be surprisingly confident in the face of failure: They still expect to perform successfully on a second try at the same task (McFarlin & Blascovich, 1981), and they exhibit greater effort and performance after failure than do low self-esteem people (McFarlin, Baumeister, & Blascovich, 1984; Shrauger & Sorman, 1977). They sometimes even have higher expectations after failure than after success (see Brockner, 1983, for references). Although these studies concern expectations for performance on a task, such expectations may be closely related to high self-esteem people's confidence that they can restore their own self-esteem. In addition, even if their confidence about one area of themselves is truly shaken, they may perceive themselves as having many other talents on which they can draw (Spencer et al., 1993). Hence, the goal of feeling better about themselves should be quite reachable. As discussed earlier, when people are self-focused and their expectations are favorable, they vigorously apply themselves to the goal (Carver & Scheier, 1981). Hence, people with high self-esteem should exert considerable effort to restore their self-worth, whereas people with low self-esteem, even when they entertain such a goal, should retreat from that goal quickly because of their low expectations.

The third condition under which self-focus may interfere with problem-focused coping is when it reduces a person's cognitive capacity for generating solutions. There are two reasons why people with low self-esteem may have a diminished cognitive capacity for devising ways of feeling better about themselves after they fail. First, as mentioned earlier, people with low self-esteem should have an especially complex and intricate web of associations to failure. Low self-esteem people's cognitive capacity may well be overwhelmed, then, with negative thoughts about themselves, whereas people with high self-esteem should be less burdened by such thoughts. Second, high self-esteem people should require less cognitive capacity for figuring out how to feel better about themselves. The routes toward feeling better about themselves should be clear and well-practiced. The evidence that following failure they can readily access domains of strength (Dodgson & Wood, 1994) supports this reasoning.

CONCLUSION: RESOLUTION TO THE SELF-FOCUSED ATTENTION AND COPING PARADOX

Resolving the self-focus/coping paradox—that self-focused attention can be associated with both adaptive and maladaptive coping responses to stressors—requires invoking a variety of factors related to self-focus and to self-esteem. It seems that the self-focused attention induced by failure is of a different character when it is experienced by someone with low self-esteem, like Rhonda, than when it is experienced by someone with high self-esteem, like Carla. Near the beginning of this chapter, a distinction was made between two categories of effects of self-focus: one that involves intensifying one's responses, and one that facilitates goal-directed behavior. These two effects seem often contradictory, yet other researchers have not appeared to be disturbed by this contradiction. In any case, Rhonda's self-focused attention seems to be the type that intensifies one's responses, whereas Carla's self-focus seems to be the type of self-focus that facilitates goal-directed behavior. In overgeneralization and rumination, people with low self-esteem are not focused on arriving at a solution to their problem, but are focused on their failure, their emotional reactions to it, and their own weaknesses. In compensation, people with high self-esteem are goal-directed and are focused on a solution for feeling better about themselves. If self-focus can both intensify one's current state as well as facilitate progress toward a goal, it should exacerbate the ruminative/overgeneralization tendency of low self-esteem people, but also energize the attempts of high self-esteem people to recoup their losses.

Why do the self-focused states induced by failure differ so greatly between low and high self-esteem people? There are several possibilities. First, even though the initial self-focused state induced by failure is likely to be unpleasant for both high and low self-esteem people, that state is likely to be especially damaging to the self-image of people with low self-esteem. Less burdened by negative associations to their failures, people with high self-esteem should be able to move on more quickly to thoughts not focused on the failure. Second, specifically, the self-focused attention of people with high self-esteem should quickly begin to serve a self-regulatory function: High self-esteem people will direct their energies toward repairing their self-esteem. They should be more likely to do so than people with low self-esteem, for several reasons: They are generally more likely to harbor self-enhancement goals, these goals are likely to be heightened when their self-esteem is threatened, their confidence that they can restore their self-esteem should fuel this goal, and their efforts toward achieving this goal should be facilitated by their previous practice in doing so.

Future work on resolving the self-focus and coping paradox should focus on what may be a key difference between these two different types of self-focus—namely the object of self-focused attention in early responses to failure. Rhonda's self-focus focused on unfavorable areas of herself, whereas Carla's self-focus quickly shifted to favorable aspects of herself. The thoughts that take center stage when one is self-focused may not be merely concomitants of the different self-focused states that were described earlier. Rather, those thoughts may be intimately tied to, and even enable, the coping responses that follow. The tendency of low self-esteem people to think about their shortcomings may serve only to diminish their morale further and to interfere with any coping attempts aimed at solving their problems or feeling better about themselves. In contrast, the tendency of high self-esteem people to recruit positive thoughts about themselves may assist, first, their emotion-focused coping. It should allow them to soothe their own egos and to shore up their confidence. Second, reminding themselves of their strengths should in turn increase their capacity to enact problem-focused coping strategies, such as attempts at compensation (e.g., trying the task again). Individuals capable of bringing to mind areas of strength and competence after failure are thereby most likely to take actions to remedy the failure and to restore a positive self-image.

ACKNOWLEDGMENTS

This chapter was written while the first author was on sabbatical at the University of Amsterdam. She thanks the Vakgroep Sociale Psychologie (especially Tony Manstead and Joop van der Pligt) and the Dutch Science Foundation (Nederlandse Organisatie voor Wetenschappenlijk Onderzoek) for providing resources and support. Philip Dodgson was supported by a Social Science and Humanities Research Council Doctoral Fellowship.

REFERENCES

Alloy, L. B., & Abramson, L. Y. (1988). Depressive realism: Four theoretical perspectives. In L. B. Alloy (Ed.), *Cognitive processes in depression* (pp. 223–265). New York: Guilford.

Alloy, L. B., & Ahrens, A. H. (1987). Depression and pessimism for the future: Biased used of statistically relevant information on predictions for self versus others. *Journal of Personality and Social Psychology, 52*, 366–378.

Altman, J. H., & Wittenborn, J. R. (1980). Depression-prone personality in women. *Journal of Abnormal Psychology, 89*, 303–308.

Arkin, R. M. (1981). Self-presentational styles. In J. I. Tedeschi (Ed.), *Impression management theory and social psychological research.* (pp. 311–333). San Diego, CA: Academic Press.

Baumeister, R. F. (1982). Self-esteem, self-presentation, and future interaction: A dilemma of reputation. *Journal of Personality, 50*, 29–45.

Baumeister, R. F. (1993). Understanding the inner nature of low self-esteem: Uncertain, fragile, protective, and conflicted. In R. F. Baumeister (Ed.), *Self-esteem: The puzzle of low self-regard* (pp. 201–218). New York: Plenum.

Baumeister, R. F., & Jones, E. E. (1978). When self-perception is constrained by the target's knowledge: Consistency and compensation. *Journal of Personality and Social Psychology, 36*, 608–618.

Baumeister, R. F., & Tice, D. M. (1985). Self-esteem and responses to success and failure: Subsequent performance and intrinsic motivation. *Journal of Personality, 53*, 450–567.

Baumeister, R. F., Tice, D. M., & Hutton, D. G. (1989). Self-presentational motivations and personality differences in self-esteem. *Journal of Personality, 57*, 547–579.

Beck, A. T. (1967). *Depression: Clinical, experimental, and theoretical aspects.* New York: Harper & Row.

Becker, J. (1979). Vulnerable self-esteem as a predisposing factor in depressive disorders. In R. A. Depue (Ed.), *The psychobiology of depressive disorders: Implications for the effects of stress* (pp. 317–324). New York: Academic Press.

Berkowitz, L. (1987). Mood, self-awareness, and willingness to help. *Journal of Personality and Social Psychology, 52*, 721–729.

Billings, A. G., & Moos, R. M. (1984). Coping, stress, and social sources among adults with unipolar depression. *Journal of Personality and Social Psychology, 46*, 877–891.

Blaine, B., & Crocker, J. (1993). Self-esteem and self-serving biases in reactions to positive and negative events: An integrative review. In R. F. Baumeister (Ed.), *Self-esteem: The puzzle of low self-regard* (pp. 55–85). New York: Plenum.

Blaney, P. (1986). Affect and memory: A review. *Psychological Bulletin, 99*, 229–246.

Bolger, N., & Schilling, E. A. (1991). Personality and the problems of everyday life: The role of neuroticism in exposure and reactivity to daily stressors. *Journal of Personality, 59*, 355–386.

Bower, G. H. (1981). Mood and memory. *American Psychologist, 36*, 129–148.

Brockner, J. (1979a). Self-esteem, self-consciousness, and task performance: Replications, extensions, and possible explanations. *Journal of Personality and Social Psychology, 37*, 447–461.

Brockner, J. (1979b). The effects of self-esteem, success-failure, and self-consciousness on task performance. *Journal of Personality and Social Psychology, 37*, 1732–1741.

Brockner, J. (1983). Low self-esteem and behavioral plasticity: Some implications. In L. Wheeler & P. Shaver (Eds.), *Review of personality and social psychology* (Vol. 4, pp. 237–271). Beverly Hills: Sage.

Brockner, J., & Hulton, A. J. B. (1978). How to reverse the vicious cycle of low self-esteem: The importance of attentional focus. *Journal of Experimental Social Psychology, 14*, 564–578.

Brown, J. D., & Dutton, K. A. (1995). The thrill of victory, the complexity of defeat: Self-esteem and emotional reactions to success and failure. *Journal of Personality and Social Psychology, 68*, 712–722.

Brown, J. D., & Mankowski, T. A. (1993). Self-esteem, mood, and self-evaluation: Changes in mood and the way you see you. *Journal of Personality and Social Psychology, 64*, 421–430.

Brown, J. D., & Smart, S. A. (1991). The self and social conduct: Linking self-representations to prosocial behavior. *Journal of Personality and Social Psychology, 60*, 368–375.

Campbell, J. D., Chew, B., & Scratchley, L. S. (1991). Cognitive and emotional reactions to daily events: The effects of self-esteem and self-complexity. *Journal of Personality, 59*, 473–505.

Carver, C. S., Blaney, P. H., & Scheier, M. F. (1979). Focus of attention, chronic expectancy, and responses to a feared stimulus. *Journal of Personality and Social Psychology, 37*, 1186–1195.

Carver, C. S., & Ganellen, R. J. (1983). Depression and components of self-punitiveness: High standards, self-criticism, and overgeneralization. *Journal of Abnormal Psychology, 92*, 330–337.

Carver, C. S., La Voie, L., Kuhl, J., & Ganellen, R. J. (1988). Cognitive concomitants of depression: A further examination of the roles of generalization, high standards, and self-criticism. *Journal of Social and Clinical Psychology, 7*, 350–365.

Carver, C. S., & Scheier, M. F. (1981). *Attention and self-regulation: A control theory approach to human behavior.* New York: Springer-Verlag.

Carver, C. S., & Scheier, M. F. (1990). Origins and functions of positive and negative affect: A control-process view. *Psychological Review, 97*, 19–35.

Clark, M. S., & Isen, A. M. (1982). Toward understanding the relationship between feeling states and social behavior. In A. Hastorf & A. Isen (Eds.), *Cognitive social psychology* (pp. 73–108). New York: Elsevier/North-Holland.

Crandall, R. (1973). The measurement of self-esteem and related constructs. In J. Robinson & P. Shaver (Eds.), *Measures of social psychological attitudes* (pp. 45–167). Ann Arbor, MI: Institute for Social Research.

Csikszentmihalyi, M., & Figurski, T. J. (1982). Self-awareness and aversive experience in everyday life. *Journal of Personality, 50*, 15–28.

Dodgson, P. G., & Wood, J. V. (in press). *If at first you don't succeed . . . you're better off: Heightened accessibility of positive thoughts following failure among people with high self-esteem*, University of Waterloo.

Duval, S., & Wicklund, R. A. (1972). *A theory of objective self-awareness*. Orlando, FL: Academic Press.

Epstein, S. (1992). Coping ability, negative self-evaluation, and overgeneralization: Experiment and theory. *Journal of Personality and Social Psychology, 62*, 826–836.

Fenigstein, A., Scheier, M. R., & Buss, A. H. (1975). Public and private self-consciousness: Assessment and theory. *Journal of Consulting and Clinical Psychology, 43*, 522–527.

Folkman, S., & Lazarus, R. S. (1980). An analysis of coping in a middle-aged community sample. *Journal of Health and Social Behavior, 21*, 219–239.

Gibbons, F. X. (1990). Self-attention and behavior: A review and theoretical update. In M. Zanna (Ed.) *Advances in experimental social psychology* (Vol. 23, pp. 249–303). San Diego: Academic Press.

Gibbons, F. X., Carver, C. S., Scheier, M. F., & Hormuth, S. E. (1979). Self-focused attention and the placebo effect: Fooling some of the people some of the time. *Journal of Experimental Social Psychology, 15*, 263–274.

Gibbons, F. X., Smith, T. W., Ingram, R. E., Pearce, K., Brehm, S. S., & Schroeder, D. J. (1985). Self-awareness and self-confrontation: Effects of self-focused attention on members of a clinical population. *Journal of Personality and Social Psychology, 48*, 662–675.

Gibbons, F. X., & Wicklund, R. A. (1976). Selective exposure to self. *Journal of Research in Personality, 10*, 98–106.

Giordano-Beech, M., & Wood, J. V. (1995). *Compensating for failure through social comparison: A self-enhancement strategy used by people with high self-esteem*. Unpublished manuscript, University of Waterloo.

Greenberg, J., & Musham, C. (1981). Avoiding and seeking self-focused attention. *Journal of Research in Personality, 15*, 191–200.

Greenberg, J., & Pyszczynski, T. (1986). Persistent high self-focus after failure and low self-focus after success: The depressive self-focusing style. *Journal of Personality and Social Psychology, 50*, 1039–1044.

Hammen, C. L., & Krantz, S. (1976). Effect of success and failure on depressive cognitions. *Journal of Abnormal Psychology, 85*, 577–586.

Hermann, C., & Wortman, C. B. (1985). Action control and the coping process. In J. Kuhl & J. Beckman (Eds.), *Action control: From cognition to behavior* (pp. 151–180). New York: Springer.

Hull, J. G., & Levy, A. S. (1979). The organizational functions of the self: An alternative to the Duval and Wicklund model of self-awareness. *Journal of Personality and Social Psychology, 37*, 756–768.

Ickes, W. J., Wicklund, R. A., & Ferris, C. B. (1973). Objective self-awareness and self-esteem. *Journal of Experimental Social Pscychology, 9*, 202–219.

Ingram, R. E. (1990). Self-focused attention in clinical disorders: Review and a conceptual model. *Psychological Bulletin, 107*, 156–176.

Ingram R. E., Lumry A. E., Cruet, D., & Sieber, W. (1987). Attentional processes in depressive disorders. *Cognitive Therapy and Research, 11*, 351–360.

Isen, A. M. (1984). Toward understanding the role of affect in cognition. In R. S. Wyer & T. K. Srull (Eds.), *Handbook of social cognition* (Vol. 3, pp. 179–236). Hillsdale, NJ: Lawrence Erlbaum Associates.

Josephs, R. A., Markus, H. R., & Tafarodi, R. W. (1992). Gender and self-esteem. *Journal of Personality and Social Psychology, 63*, 391–402.

Kernis, M. H., Brockner, J., & Frankel, B. S. (1989). Self-esteem and reactions to failure: The mediating role of overgeneralization. *Journal of Personality and Social Psychology, 57*, 707–714.

Kuhl, J. (1981). Motivational and functional helplessness: The moderating effect of state versus action orientation. *Journal of Personality and Social Psychology, 40*, 155–170.

Kuhl, J., & Helle, P. (1986). Motivational and volitional determinants of depression: The degenerated-intention hypothesis. *Journal of Abnormal Psychology, 95,* 247–251.

Larsen, R. J., & Cowan, G. S. (1988). Internal focus of attention and depression: A study of daily experience. *Motivation & Emotion, 12,* 237–249.

Lewinsohn, P. M., Hoberman, H., Teri, L., & Hautzinger, M. (1985). An integrative theory of depression. In S. Reiss & R. Bootzin (Eds.), *Theoretical issues in behavior therapy* (pp. 331–359). Orlando, FL: Academic Press.

Lyubomirsky, S., & Nolen-Hoeksema, S. (1993). Self-perpetuating properties of dysphoric rumination. *Journal of Personality and Social Psychology, 65,* 339–349.

Markus, H., & Kunda, Z. (1986). Stability and malleability of the self-concept. *Journal of Personality and Social Psychology, 51,* 858–866.

McFarlin, D. B., Baumeister, R. F., & Blascovich, J. (1984). On knowing when to quit: Task failure, self-esteem, advice, and nonproductive persistence. *Journal of Personality, 52,* 138–155.

McFarlin, D. B., & Blascovich, J. (1981). Effects of self-esteem and performance feedback on future affective preferences and cognitive expectations. *Journal of Personality and Social Psychology, 40,* 521–531.

Morrow, J., & Nolen-Hoeksema, S. (1990). Effects of responses to depression on the remediation of depressive affect. *Journal of Personality and Social Psychology, 58,* 519–527.

Nadich, M., Gargan, M., & Michael, L. (1975). Denial, anxiety, locus of control, and the discrepancy between aspirations and achievements as components of depression. *Journal of Abnormal Psychology, 84,* 1–9.

Nolen-Hoeksema, S. (1987). Sex differences in unipolar depression: Evidence and theory. *Psychological Bulletin, 101,* 259–282.

Nolen-Hoeksema, S. (1991). Responses to depression and their effects on the duration of depressive episodes. *Journal of Abnormal Psychology, 100,* 569–582.

Nolen-Hoeksema, S. (1993). Sex differences in control of depression. In D. M. Wegner & J. W. Pennebaker (Eds.), *Handbook of mental control* (pp. 306–324). Englewood Cliffs, NJ: Prentice Hall.

Nolen-Hoeksema, S., & Morrow, J. (1991). A prospective study of depression and posttraumatic stress symptoms after natural disaster: The 1989 Loma Prieta earthquake. *Journal of Personality and Social Psychology, 61,* 115–121.

Nolen-Hoeksema, S., & Morrow, J. (1994). *Self-focus and the maintenance of depressed mood: Different viewpoints.* Unpublished manuscript, Stanford University.

Nolen-Hoeksema, S., Morrow, J., & Fredrickson, B. L. (1993). Response styles and the duration of episodes of depressed mood. *Journal of Abnormal Psychology, 102,* 20–28.

Parrott, W. G., & Sabini, J. (1990). Mood and memory under natural conditions: Evidence for mood incongruent recall. *Journal of Personality and Social Psychology, 59,* 321–336.

Pelham, B. W., & Swann, W. B., Jr. (1989). From self-conceptions to self-worth: On the sources and structures of global self-esteem. *Journal of Personality and Social Psychology, 57,* 672–680.

Pyszczynski, T., & Greenberg, J. (1985). Depression and preference for self-focusing stimuli after success and failure. *Journal of Personality and Social Psychology, 49,* 1066–1075.

Pyszczynski, T., & Greenberg, J. (1986). Evidence for a depressive self-focusing style. *Journal of Research in Personality, 20,* 95–106.

Pyszczynski, T., & Greenberg, J. (1987). Self-regulatory perseveration and the depressive self-focusing style: A self-awareness theory of the development and maintenance of depression. *Psychological Bulletin, 102,* 122–138.

Pyszczynski, T., Holt, K., & Greenberg, J. (1987). Depression, self-focused attention and expectancies for future positive and negative events for self and others. *Journal of Personality and Social Psychology, 52,* 994–1001.

Salovey, P. (1992). Mood induced self-focused attention. *Journal of Personality and Social Psychology, 62,* 699–707.

Saltzberg, J., Wood, J. V., & Bonvino, L. J. (1994). *A second look at sad versus happy mood in inducing self-focused attention*. Under editorial review.

Sanitioso, R., Kunda, Z., & Fong, G. T. (1990). Motivated recruitment of autobiographical memories. *Journal of Personality and Social Psychology, 59*, 229–241.

Sarason, I. G. (1975). Anxiety and self-preoccupation. In I. G. Sarason & C. D. Spielberger (Eds.), *Stress and anxiety* (Vol. 2, pp. 27–44). New York: Wiley.

Scheier, M. F., & Carver, C. S. (1977). Self-focused attention and the experience of emotion: Attraction, repulsion, elation, and depression. *Journal of Personality and Social Psychology, 35*, 625–636.

Scheier, M. F., & Carver, C. S. (1982). Cognition, affect, and self-regulation. In M. S. Clark & S. T. Fiske (Eds.), *Affect and cognition: The Seventeenth Annual Carnegie Symposium on Cognition* (pp. 157–183). Hillsdale, NJ: Lawrence Erlbaum Associates.

Schlenker, B. R., Weigold, M. E., & Hallam, J. R. (1990). Self-serving attributions in social context: Effects of self-esteem and social pressure. *Journal of Personality and Social Psychology, 58*, 855–863.

Sedikedes, C. (1992). Attentional effects on mood are moderated by chronic self-conception valence. *Personality and Social Psychology Bulletin, 18*, 580–584.

Shrauger, J. S. (1975). Responses to evaluation as a function of initial self-perception. *Psychological Bulletin, 82*, 581–596.

Shrauger, J. S., & Sorman, P. B. (1977). Self-evaluations, initial success and failure, and improvement as determinants of persistence. *Journal of Consulting and Clinical Psychology, 45*, 784–795.

Shrauger, J. S., & Rosenberg, S. E. (1970). Self-esteem and the effects of success and failure feedback on performance. *Journal of Personality, 38*, 404–417.

Singer, J. A., & Salovey, P. (1988). Mood and memory: Evaluating the network theory of affect. *Clinical Psychology Review, 8*, 211–251.

Smith, T. W., & Greenberg, J. (1981). Depression and self-focused attention. *Motivation and Emotion, 5*, 323–331.

Solomon, S., Greenberg, J., & Pyszczynski, T. (1991). A terror management theory of social behavior: The psychological function of self-esteem and cultural worldviews. In M. P. Zanna (Ed.), *Advances in experimental social psychology* (Vol. 21, pp. 261–302). New York: Academic Press.

Spencer, S. J., Josephs, R. A., & Steele, C. M. (1993). Low self-esteem: The uphill struggle for self-integrity. In R. F. Baumeister (Ed.), *Self-esteem: The puzzle of low self-regard* (pp. 21–36). New York: Plenum.

Steele, C. M. (1975). Name calling and compliance. *Journal of Personality and Social Psychology, 31*, 361–369.

Steele, C. M. (1988). The psychology of self-affirmation: Sustaining the integrity of the self. In L. Berkowitz (Ed.), *Advances in experimental social psychology* (Vol.21; pp. 261–302). San Diego, CA: Academic Press.

Steele, C. M., & Liu, T. J. (1981). Making the dissonant act unreflective of self: Dissonance avoidance and the expectancy of a value-affirming response. *Personality and Social Psychology Bulletin, 7*, 393–397.

Steele, C. M., Spencer, S. J., & Lynch, M. (1993). Self-image resilience and dissonance: The role of affirmational resources. *Journal of Personality and Social Psychology, 64*, 885–896.

Steenberger, B. N., & Aderman, D. (1979). Objective self-awareness as a nonaversive state: Effect of anticipating discrepancy reduction. *Journal of Personality, 47*, 330–339.

Strack, S., Blaney, P. H., Ganellen, R. J., & Coyne, J. C. (1985). Pessimistic self-preoccupation, performance deficits, and depression. *Journal of Personality and Social Psychology, 49*, 1076–1085.

Taylor, S. E., & Brown, J. D. (1988). Illusion and well-being: A social psychological perspective on mental health. *Psychological Bulletin, 103*, 193–210.

Turner, R. G., Scheier, M. F., Carver, C. S., & Ickes, W. (1978). Correlates of self-consciousness. *Journal of Personality Assessment, 42*, 285–289.

Wenzlaff, R. M., & Grozier, S. A. (1988). Depression and the magnification of failure. *Journal of Abnormal Psychology, 97*, 90–93.

Wicklund, R. A. (1975). Objective self-awareness. In L. Berkowitz (Ed.), *Advances in experimental social psychology* (Vol. 8, pp. 233–275). Orlando, FL: Academic Press.

Wills, T. A. (1981). Downward comparison principles in social psychology. *Psychological Bulletin, 90*, 245–271.

Wood, J. V. (1989). Theory and research concerning social comparisons of personal attributes. *Psychological Bulletin, 106*, 231–248.

Wood, J. V., Giordano-Beech, M., Taylor, K. L., Michela, J. L., & Gaus, V. (1994). Strategies of social comparison among people with low self-esteem: Self-protection and self-enhancement. *Journal of Personality and Social Psychology, 67*, 713–731.

Wood, J. V., Saltzberg, J. A., & Goldsamt, L. A. (1990). Does affect induce self-focused attention? *Journal of Personality and Social Psychology, 58*, 899–908.

Wood, J. V., Saltzberg, J. A., Neale, J. M., Stone, A. A., & Rachmiel, T. B. (1990). Self-focused attention, distressed mood, and coping responses in everyday life. *Journal of Personality and Social Psychology, 58*, 1027–1036.

Wood, J. V., & Taylor, K. L. (1991). Serving self-relevant goals through social comparison. In J. Suls & T. A. Wills (Eds.), *Social comparison: Contemporary theory and research* (pp. 23–49). Hillsdale, NJ: Lawrence Erlbaum Associates.

CHAPTER

13

PERFORMANCE ANXIETY, COGNITIVE INTERFERENCE, AND CONCENTRATION ENHANCEMENT STRATEGIES IN SPORTS

Ronald E. Smith
University of Washington

In all achievement domains, the ability to identify, attend to, and process task-relevant cues is a key to optimal performance. Factors that interfere with concentration almost invariably result in performance decrements, and the identification and control of such factors has long been of interest to psychologists from both theoretical and practical perspectives.

Disruption of attentional processes may occur as a result of situational factors, internal processes, or an interaction of the two. Situations that contain strong competing external stimuli clearly increase attentional demands, but competing cues can also be produced by internal processes such as emotional reactions and task-irrelevant thinking. Moreover, individual difference factors may make individuals particularly vulnerable to concentration disruption in certain classes of situations. For example, it is well established that people who are high in test anxiety are susceptible to task-irrelevant thinking that can interfere with their performance in academic achievement situations (Sarason & Sarason, 1990). Similarly, individuals having low self-esteem are at risk for self-deprecating thinking that can interfere with effective behavior in social situations (Cheek & Melchior, 1990). In each case, the personality variable constitutes a vulnerability factor that increases the likelihood that cognitive interference will disrupt effective behavior in a particular class of situations. In contrast, other individuals respond to similar "pressure" situations with enhanced attention and task-relevant thinking that results in superior performance. The study of such person-by-situation interactions has significantly increased our understanding of both personality variables and the cognitive processes that underlie effective and ineffective behavior.

In the achievement domain, the bulk of the research on cognitive interference has focused on academic test-like situations. As Sarason, Sarason, and Pierce (1995) have noted, there is a need for analysis of the role of cognitive interference in other situations as well. The focus of this chapter is another important performance domain, namely competitive sports. First, recent theoretical and empirical advances in our understanding of attentional processes that affect sport performance are considered. Next, the role of performance anxiety as an individual difference variable that can produce performance-disrupting cognitive interference is discussed, and finally, a number of intervention procedures used by sport psychologists in their attempts to enhance concentration skills in athletes are described.

ATTENTIONAL PROCESSES IN SPORTS

Information processing theories have provided a useful framework for the analysis of attentional processes. Attention is by its very nature a selective process in which certain cues are focused on while other stimuli are screened out or ignored (Broadbent, 1958; Parasuraman, 1984). At any given time, an organism is being bombarded by countless stimuli from both the external and internal environments. Because of the limited capacity of the information processing system, a person can process only a very limited sample of these stimuli at any given point in time. Selectivity is therefore necessary, for, in the words of William James, "without selective interest, experience is an utter chaos" (1890, p. 402). Selection can be voluntary, as when a person chooses to attend to certain cues, or it can be involuntary to the extent that certain intense, novel, or meaningful stimuli demand attention and cannot be selectively ignored. Attention can thus be viewed as a figure-ground phenomenon, with certain stimuli being focal at any given point in time, while others recede into the background but are potentially capable of becoming focal stimuli.

Attentional processes are critical determinants of task performance. During the performance of a task, certain internal and external cues are task relevant in the sense that they evoke or guide instrumental behaviors that facilitate performance. Others are task irrelevant, and a focus on these cues can interfere with effective processing of task relevant stimuli or can evoke task irrelevant behaviors, such as maladaptive cognitive or emotional responses. Cognitions have both stimulus and response properties, and cognitive interference occurs when the stimulus properties of task irrelevant cognitions interfere with the effective processing of task-relevant cues, or when they evoke responses (e.g. emotional arousal) that are incompatible with task-relevant responses.

Automatic and Controlled Processing

An explicit and voluntary focus on task-relevant cues is not always in the best interests of the performer. Cognitive psychologists distinguish between controlled processing and automatic processing of information (Schneider, Dumais,

& Shiffrin, 1984). Controlled processing is an effortful process in which the performer voluntary focuses on specific cues and exercises conscious control over the performance of task behaviors. Such processing is relatively slow, effortful, and capacity-limited, and it requires high levels of attention and awareness. Controlled processing is characteristic of the initial stages of learning. For example, a novice basketball player who is dribbling the ball may have to devote considerable attention to the act of dribbling, leaving few attentional resources available for scanning the court, locating teammates and defensive players, or planning a drive to the basket.

As skills become well learned, information processing becomes less effortful and requires less conscious awareness. Automatic processing is far more efficient and leaves more attentional capacity available for task-relevant cues. Thus, an experienced basketball player can dribble the ball "without thinking," making it possible for him or her to process task-relevant cues such as the positions of other players on the court, the amount of time on the shot clock, and instructions being shouted from the sidelines by the coach. Like other performers, athletes spend countless hours of practice overlearning skills so they can respond automatically to specific cues. Subjective accounts of peak performance by athletes commonly contain references to being on automatic pilot or in a zone where performance occurs automatically and without conscious guidance (Williams, 1986). One way in which cognitive interference degrades performance is by disrupting automatic processing of task-relevant cues. On the other hand, by leaving attentional resources available, automatic processing may sometimes make performers more susceptible to the influence of internal or external task-irrelevant cues, such as task-irrelevant cognitions, that would not enter consciousness if the performer were having to focus on performing the task (Boutcher, 1993). In this sense, automatic processing can be a two-edged sword, having the potential to degrade as well as to enhance performance.

Attentional Dimensions

As noted earlier, attention may be directed toward either internal or external sources of stimulation. Likewise, attention may be narrowly focused on a particular internal or external cue, such as a single object or thought, or it may be broadly deployed, as when a person scans the environment or considers a broad concept. These attentional dimensions of direction (internal-external) and breadth (narrow-wide) have figured prominently in several theories of attention (e.g. Bacon, 1974, Easterbrook, 1959; Wachtel, 1967). More recently, Nideffer (1989, 1993) has incorporated them into a comprehensive model of attentional processes in sport.

Nideffer regards direction and breadth as orthogonal dimensions that yield four basic classes of attention and attentional demands: broad-external, narrow-external, broad-internal, and narrow-internal. A broad-external focus requires the individual to scan a wide portion of the external environment, as when a football quarterback "reads" the defense as he drops back to pass. A narrow-external focus is typified by a batter in baseball who focuses closely on the thrown ball as it leaves the pitcher's hand. A golfer who is developing a "game plan" for a difficult hole by drawing upon his or her knowledge of the course and past experiences would be engaging in a broad-internal attentional focus. On the other hand, a narrow-internal focus is exemplified by a basketball player who is forming a specific image of his or her shot dropping through the net.

A key to successful performance, according to Nideffer, is the ability to match one's attentional focus to the momentary attentional demands of the task situation. These demands can change quickly. For example, once a quarterback has "read" the defense and spotted an open receiver, he must focus narrowly on the moving receiver as he throws the ball, ignoring the sight and sounds of onrushing defenders who are about to tackle him. In this sense attention may be regarded as a state phenomenon, and athletes must be able to shift attentional focus quickly in order to comply with task demands.

Attention also has trait properties, according to Nideffer. That is, individual differences exist in the ability to adopt the four attentional foci and in the ability to shift quickly from one to the other. In this respect, people may be regarded as having attentional strengths and weaknesses. For example, some individuals are better at analyzing large amounts of information than are others. People with broad attentional and analytical abilities would be expected to perform more effectively on tasks that require the ability to integrate internal or external cues or both, and formulate a "plan of action." Successful trial lawyers and expert medical diagnosticians, as well as coaches who are capable of adapting to rapidly changing game situations with strategic decisions, all seem to possess this skill. On the other hand, some people have attentional skills that enable them to focus very narrowly on internal or external cues. The ability to concentrate on a specific idea or to focus narrowly on a moving ball or on a target is a reflection of such skills.

Individual differences also occur in individuals' ability to attend to internal versus external cues. Certain people appear to be more sensitive to environmental information than are others. For example, individual differences are evident in the ability to perceive and interpret the emotional expressions of others or, on the other hand, to concentrate on one's thoughts and retrieve specific information from memory even in the face of strong external distractions. A common example of the latter is students who claim that they can perform cognitive tasks effectively while the stereo is blaring and other people are conversing nearby.

The ability to rapidly shift attentional breadth or direction or both in response to situational demands is another important individual difference factor. With regard to internal cues, this includes the ability to to control the focus of attention on a temporal dimension as well. The ability to focus one's thinking in the present is instrumental to effective performance. Ruminating about past mistakes or preoccupation with future consequences are common forms of cognitive interference because they reduce the capacity of working memory to process current task-relevant cues effectively (Eysenck & Calvo, 1992).

Applying the Hull-Spence concept of a hierarchy of responses to attentional skill differences, Nideffer (1989) has invoked the classical Habit Strength × Drive formulation to derive the prediction that in pressure (high Drive) situations, people have a tendency to utilize their preferred (high Habit Strength) attentional styles. Thus, a person with well-developed broad-internal skills will tend to become even more analytical (and, perhaps, even obsessive) as pressure (and arousal) increases, whereas a skilled narrow-external focuser may become even more concrete and stimulus bound. To the extent that the tendency to play to one's attentional strengths corresponds to the attentional demands of the task at hand, such people will perform at a high level in pressure situations. On the other hand, their performance may deteriorate markedly as arousal increases if their attentional preferences are incongruent with task demands.

With these attentional principles in mind, the role of performance anxiety in attentional disruption and cognitive interference is now considered.

PERFORMANCE ANXIETY AND ATTENTIONAL DISRUPTION

Disruption of attentional processes can be brought about by a variety of factors, with a resultant decline in performance. Intense, novel, and otherwise compelling external stimuli can disrupt attentional focus on both internal and external task-relevant cues. In sports, a roaring, banner-waving crowd can provide a strong "home court" advantage by disrupting the concentration of a visiting team at critical times in a contest. Perceptually ambiguous situations can also result in the necessity of dividing attention, thereby reducing attentional resources that should be applied to the task at hand (Navon, 1985).

Intraindividual factors can also contribute to attentional deficits. As an example, the deleterious effects of fatigue on the performance of tasks that require vigilance or sustained attention are well documented (Bartley & Chute, 1947; Hirst, 1986; Parasuraman, 1984). Equally well established are the deleterious effects of emotional arousal on certain forms of attention. Easterbrook's (1959) hypothesis that increases in arousal result in a narrowing of the perceptual field has received strong support in subsequent research (Bacon, 1974; Landers, 1980, Wachtel, 1967). Thus, individuals who are in a state of high physiological arousal may lose sensitivity to peripheral cues and suffer a decrement in performance if the task requires a broad-external focus. Under such conditions, performers may also have difficulty in shifting their focus of attention (Boutcher, 1993).

In general, the disruptive effects of divided attention are greater for novel or newly learned tasks that require controlled processing of information than for well-learned or overlearned tasks in which automatic processing of information occurs. As noted earlier, automatic processing occupies fewer attentional resources, leading some theorists to conclude that the ability to divide attention is influenced more by the performer's skill level than by the number of cues or tasks requiring attention (Hirst, 1986). However, distracting internal or external cues can cause a performer to shift from automatic to controlled processing, providing an important mechanism for decreased performance.

Such distraction can take many forms. For example, Carver and Scheier (1981) have noted that self-awareness (attending to oneself while performing) can have a detrimental effect on the processing of task-relevant cues. In sports, the term "paralysis by analysis" is used to denote the detrimental effects of focusing on the mechanics of an otherwise automated skill. When athletes are performing poorly, they tend to start analyzing what they are doing, resulting in a shift from the generally more efficient automatic processing to the less efficient controlled processing. Thus, Hall of Fame baseball player Yogi Berra once stated, "You can't think and hit at the same time." Conversely, athletes commonly report that when they are enjoying a peak performance, they experience themselves as being on automatic pilot and are able to react effortlessly and with little if any forethought (Williams, 1986). They report being in a zone or cocoon, detached from the external environment and any potential external or internal distractions.

Performance decrements can thus be brought about by situational, physiological, and cognitive influences that disrupt attentional processes. In the case of skilled task performance, an important mechanism of degraded performance is interference with automatic processing and responding. Of the intraindividual factors that are capable of producing performance decrements, anxiety has received perhaps the greatest amount of theoretical and empirical attention.

A Model of Sport Performance Anxiety

Anxiety has been conceptualized in a number of ways. First, it may be regarded as either a transitory emotional state or as a stable personality trait (Spielberger, 1966). As a trait, anxiety has been regarded by some theorists as a global transituational personality trait (e.g., Spence & Spence, 1966) and by others as a situation-specific construct, for example, a tendency to become anxious in tests, social situations, or during sport competition (see Leitenberg, 1990). Finally, many theorists have come to view anxiety as a multidimensional construct having cognitive, physiological, and behavioral facets (e.g., Davidson & Schwartz, 1976; Liebert & Morris, 1967; Sarason, 1984; Smith, 1986).

As a trait construct, sport performance anxiety may be defined as a learned tendency to respond with cognitive or somatic state anxiety (or both) to competitive sport situations in which the adequacy of the athlete's performance can be evaluated (Smith, 1986; Smith & Smoll, 1990). Although a number of specific sources of threat (including the possibility of physical harm) may reside in the sport situation, the most salient sources of threat are the possibilities of failure and of disapproval by significant others who are evaluating the athlete's performance in relation to some standard of excellence, as well as the threat of self-disparagement. Athletic performance anxiety is thus part of a family of performance-related fear of failure constructs that include test anxiety, speech anxiety, and the "stage fright" that actors, musicians, and dancers can experience within their evaluative performance situations (Steptoe & Fidler, 1987; Kendrick, Craig, Lawson, & Davidson, 1982). Like other forms of anxiety, sport performance anxiety has separate but related cognitive, affective, and behavioral components.

A conceptual model of athletic performance anxiety is presented in Fig. 13.1. This model, derived from conceptions of emotionality and anxiety advanced by Arnold (1960), Ellis (1962), Lazarus and Folkman (1984), Mandler and Sarason (1952), Smith (1986), and Spielberger (1966), includes both the trait-state distinction and the differentiation between situational, cognitive, physiological, and behavioral components of the process of anxiety.

The cognitive and somatic components of competitive state anxiety are shown within the appraisal and physiological response panel of the figure. The

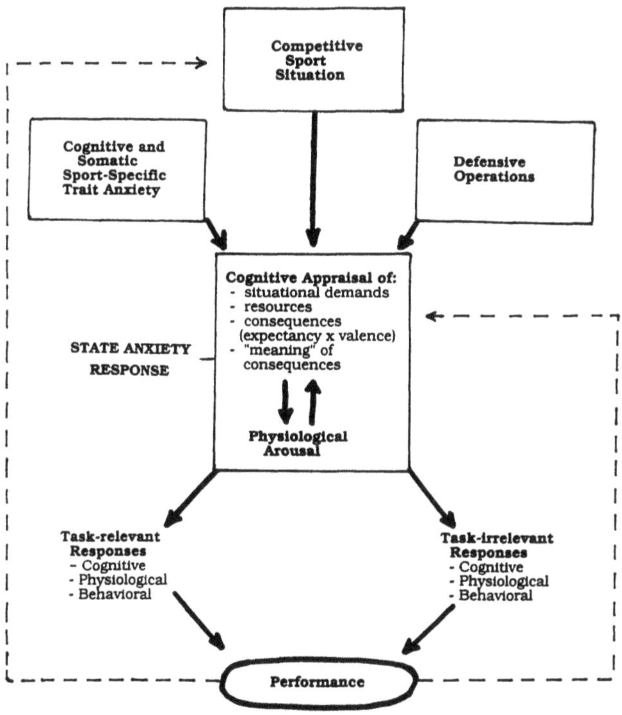

FIG. 13.1. A conceptual model of sport performance anxiety and its relation to cognitive interference.

intensity and duration of the state anxiety response are assumed to be influenced by three major factors. The first of these factors is the nature of the competitive sport situation in which the athlete is involved. Obviously, such situations differ in the demands they place upon the athlete, as well as the degree of threat that they pose to successful performance. Such factors as strength of opponent, importance of the contest, presence of significant others, and degree of social support received from coaches and teammates can affect the amount of threat that the situation is likely to pose for the individual.

Two classes of intrapersonal factors are also important determinants of the level of state anxiety experienced by the athlete. One of these is the performer's level of sport-specific cognitive and somatic trait anxiety. As noted earlier, this individual difference variable involves the individual's tendency to experience cognitive and somatic state anxiety reactions within competitive situations. The second intraindividual factor is the psychological defenses that the athlete may have developed to cope with anxiety-arousing competitive situations. As Spielberger (1966) has noted, defensive processes may be mobilized to avoid or reduce anxiety. These defensive processes operate at the level of appraisal and in some way modify or distort the perception or appraisal of the situation. To the extent that a defensive operation is successful, the competitive sport situation would be seen as less threatening, with a resulting decrease in state anxiety. Thus, defensive processes may at times balance or mitigate the effects of the high level of sport-specific trait anxiety.

The objective situation, level of trait anxiety, and the individual's defenses are all assumed to influence the performer's appraisal processes. Four classes of appraisal are particularly important: appraisal of the situational demands; appraisal of the resources available to deal with them; appraisal of the nature and likelihood of potential consequences if the demands are not met (that is, the expectancies and valences relating to potential consequences); and the personal meaning that the consequences have for the individual. The meanings attached to the consequences derive from the person's belief system, and they often involve the individual's criteria for self-worth (Ellis, 1962; Rogers, 1959). Thus, an athlete who defines the present situational demands as overwhelming, who appraises his or her resources and skills as insufficient to deal with the demands, who anticipates failure or disapproval or both as a result of the demands/resources imbalance, and who defines his or her self-worth in terms of success or the approval of others will clearly perceive this competitive situation as threatening or dangerous. Such appraisals are likely to generate high levels of physiological arousal, and this arousal, in turn, feeds back into the ongoing process of appraisal and reappraisal. High levels of arousal may convince the athlete that he or she is "falling apart" and help generate even more negative appraisals that create cognitive interference.

As Mandler and Sarason (1952) have noted, motivational and emotional states may generate two broad classes of task-related responses. Some of these responses facilitate task performance (task-relevant), whereas others are detrimental to performance (task-irrelevant responses). These task-relevant and task-irrelevant responses may be cognitive, physiological, or behavioral in nature. Thus, cognitive responses such as concentration on the task and strategic planning may be facilitated by certain levels of state anxiety and would thereby contribute to performance. On the other hand, task-irrelevant cognitive responses such as worry and catastrophic thinking could readily interfere with task performance by disrupting attentional and problem-solving processes. Likewise, certain classes and intensities of physiological responding might facilitate task performance, whereas other types and intensities of physiological responding might interfere with task performance. Finally, behavioral responses such as persistence and smooth execution of motor responses would facilitate performance, while impulsive or inappropriate behaviors would interfere with it. The balance between task-relevant and task-irrelevant responses and the manner in which they are affected by the performer's anxiety level will thus affect the adequacy of performance. It should also be noted that ongoing appraisal of performance adequacy will influence the four basic appraisal elements shown in Fig. 13.1 and thereby produce additional task-relevant or interfering cognitions.

The Dynamics of "Choking"

The term "choking" is commonly used in sports to refer to a marked deterioration in performance that can occur when an athlete is unable to cope with high levels of anxiety evoked by strong situational demands. The cognitive-affective model of anxiety presented earlier provides a framework within which to make this term and the processes that cause it operational.

As anxiety increases beyond an optimal level for performance of the task at hand, a variety of cognitive, physiological, and behavioral task-irrelevant responses occur. Cognitive appraisals of the situation as threatening and of oneself as incapable of coping successfully with the situation not only increase physiological arousal, but also command attention in their own right. Cognitions concerning the terrible consequences that might occur ("catastrophizing") and the negative personal implications of failure are also likely to occupy the performer's attention and produce cognitive interference (Blankstein, Toner, & Flett, 1989). As individuals become more self-oriented and preoccupied with the threatening aspects of the performance situation and their possible impending failure, they become less capable of processing task-relevant environmental and internal information. Their focus of attention narrows and becomes more internal (Sarason, 1984), but their self-preoccupation interferes with successful performance even if their normal attentional strength is narrow-internal and the task calls for such processing. This occurs because the negative cognitions compete for processing resources and thereby negate the athletes' normal attentional skills.

The negative cognitions that produce cognitive interference are also likely to cause increases in physiological arousal that produce additional task-irrelevant responses. The effects of arousal on performance are generally couched in terms of the venerable Yerkes-Dodson law (Yerkes & Dodson, 1908), which has two postulates. First, it is assumed that there is an optimal level of arousal for the performance of any task (the so-called inverted-U function), and that increases in physiological arousal beyond that optimum results in a performance decrement. Second, it is postulated that the more complex the task, the lower is the optimal level of arousal for performing it. Thus, motor tasks that require delicate movements and high demands for timing and coordination, such as complex gymnastics routines or hitting a golf ball, are more likely to be disrupted by high levels of arousal than are simple tasks such as running or lifting a weight.

High levels of physiological arousal can produce performance decrements on motor performance in a number of ways. First, arousal has negative effects on complex motor responses by producing muscle tension that interferes with motor coordination and reduces power and timing (Schmidt, 1982). High arousal also contributes in two ways to cognitive interference through the physiological feedback it provides. First, these internal cues may themselves become a focus of the performer's attention, commanding attentional resources that are needed to focus on task-relevant cues. Second, the feedback may evoke additional cognitions of being overwhelmed by situational demands that increase cognitive interference and arousal in a recursive fashion. Finally, as noted earlier, increased arousal results in a narrowing of the perceptual field and a subsequent failure to process peripheral cues that may be important to performance (Easterbrook, 1959). Whether some or all of this perceptual narrowing is independent of the self-preoccupation processes described above is not known at this point, but it is clear that narrowing that accompanies high levels of arousal can markedly interfere with performance on tasks that require a broad focus of attention (Cratty, 1989; Nideffer, 1993).

Sport-specific multidimensional measures of both state and trait anxiety have recently been developed, making it possible to assess the relative effects of cognitive and somatic anxiety on athletic performance. The Competitive State Anxiety Scale II (CSAI-2; Martens, Vealey, & Burton, 1990) contains separate cognitive and somatic scales, as well as a self-confidence scale. A study by Burton (1988) assessed relations between the CSAI-2 subscales and swimming performance in two samples of college and elite swimmers. The first sample completed the anxiety measure shortly before competing in three meets. This design involving three repeated measures, thus fulfilled the minimal conditions required to assess curvilinearity. In the sample of 28 collegiate swimmers, CSAI-2 scores accounted for 18%, 25%, and 57% of the variance in performance at the three meets, respectively. Using an intrasubject analytic method introduced by Sonstroem and Bernardo (1982), Burton found that somatic anxiety was related to swimming performance in a curvilinear fashion, with the athletes' own moderate level of anxiety across the three meets being associated with their best performance. In contrast, cognitive anxiety bore a negative linear relation to performance, and self-confidence a positive linear relation. On the basis of regression analyses in which somatic anxiety, cognitive anxiety, and self-confidence scores were used as predictor variables for performance in a variety of different swimming events (e.g., breaststroke, freestyle), Burton concluded that cognitive anxiety bore a more consistent negative relation to performance than did somatic anxiety, since it generally accounted for far more variance in the regression equations.

A recently developed trait measure of sport performance anxiety is the Sport Anxiety Scale (SAS; Smith, Smoll, & Schutz, 1990). Developed through a process of confirmatory factor analysis, the SAS consists of three subscales: Somatic Anxiety, Worry, and Concentration Disruption. The SAS thus permits a comparison of two components of cognitive anxiety: worry (e.g., "I'm concerned about choking under pressure") and disruption of concentration (e.g., "I have lapses in concentration during competition because of nervousness"). In one study of athletic performance by college football players over the course of a season, Concentration Disruption bore a significant negative relation to performance; the other two scales were unrelated (Smith, Smoll, & Schutz, 1990). Thus, studies using both state and trait measures of anxiety indicate that cognitive interference is a significant predictor of poor athletic performance.

Anxiety can produce not only task-irrelevant cognitive and physiological responses, but also behavioral ones. For example, athletes have been known to "freeze" or otherwise fail to react respond appropriately in performance situations. Anxiety may also trigger escape or avoidance responses that harm performance. For example, a gymnast found himself unable to perform a parallel bar routine after a humiliating performance in a televised meet, and he begged his coach to allow him to compete on another apparatus instead. Risk-taking during performance may also be affected; anxious athletes who fear failure may become excessively cautious or, on the other hand, may take foolhardy risks during competition (Atkinson & Birch, 1978).

Thus, cognitive interference is one of a number of related cognitive-physiological mechanisms that can impair athletic performance, and it appears to be a potent one. These processes are state phenomena that are more likely to occur in athletes who are high in the trait of performance anxiety. Such athletes would also be expected to have a lower environmental pressure threshold for responding with cognitive interference, heightened physiological arousal, and dysfunctional behaviors.

We now turn to the practical question that has occupied many sport psychologists: Given the crucial role of attentional factors in sport performance, what can be done to train athletes to control their attentional processes more effectively?

ATTENTION CONTROL INTERVENTIONS

Because of the central importance of attentional processes in athletic performance, coaches, athletes, and sport psychologists have long been interested in methods for improving concentration. Many of the techniques to be discussed are explicitly intended to reduce the negative impact of cognitive interference and other task irrelevant responses, including physiological arousal. It should be noted, however, that relatively few methodologically sound outcome studies of attention control interventions are currently available in the sport psychology literature. Consequently, the absolute and the relative efficacy of these interventions is in many cases unknown. Clearly, this is a research area that deserves a good deal of empirical attention.

Concentration enhancement procedures that have been described or proposed in the sport psychology literature can be broadly divided into two classes. The first class consists of situational interventions, some of which have been employed by coaches for generations. The second includes a variety of psychoeducational techniques that are designed to teach athletes specific attention-relevant psychological skills.

Situational Interventions

Physical Conditioning. The deleterious effects of physical and mental fatigue on sustained attention is well documented in the human factors literature (Bartley & Chute, 1947; Cratty, 1989). Physical fatigue produces aversive internal cues that compete for attention with task-relevant ones. Mental fatigue also drains attentional resources and decreases attentional efficiency (Posner & Snyder, 1975). Achieving optimum physical fitness has long been emphasized by coaches as a means of countering the negative effects of fatigue. Even competitors who engage in cognitive rather than physical activities seem to recognize the potential value of physical fitness. Many world class chess masters, who engage in sustained periods of mental competition, practice rigorous physical conditioning regimens. To this point, however, the effects of physical conditioning regimens on sport-specific attentional abilities have not been empirically evaluated.

Effective Skill Instruction. Effective instruction in sport skills should include not only training in the physical aspects of the sport, but also instruction and practice in identifying and reacting to task relevant cues. Thus, defensive players in football are taught to read offensive keys so they can quickly and automatically respond to a developing offensive play. Nideffer's (1993) attention-control training heavily emphasizes teaching athletes to identify and learn to attend to the most task-relevant situational cues.

Repetitive skill instruction has another attention-enhancing consequence: It helps to automatize the skill and reduce the need for controlled processing of information, thereby freeing attentional resources for attention to task-relevant cues.

Exposure to Laboratory Training Tasks. Attention control exercises can be conducted outside of the competition site as well. One such exercise that has been used extensively in the training of Eastern European athletes involves a 10×10 grid that contains in each block a two digit number ranging from 00 to 99 (Harris & Harris, 1984). The digits are arranged in random order and the athlete's task is to scan the grid and within a given time period to put a slash through as many of the digits as possible in ascending order. This task, which requires the ability to attend and focus on task-relevant cues, has been used not only as a training device, but also as a measure of concentration skills. To this point, scores on this exercise have not been studied in relation to athletic performance.

Any number of laboratory tasks used in vigilance and attention studies by experimental psychologists might fruitfully be employed as training exercises for specific concentration skills. Examples might include the Stroop test, reaction time tasks, and signal detection tasks (Boutcher, 1993). Computer simulations of attentional tasks could easily be tailored to specific sports and used as training devices as well. This would appear to be a promising focus for research by experimental as well as sport psychologists, for performance outcome measures of high ecological validity can easily be obtained in athletics and related to scores on laboratory tasks.

Simulating Competitive Stressors. Competitive situations can contain numerous stimuli that distract attention and increase arousal. Jeering crowds, unfamiliar surroundings, and verbally abusive opponents all must be dealt with, particularly by a visiting team. It has long bean a practice in both Europe and North America to introduce such stimuli during practice sessions so as to habituate athletes to them and allow them to develop and practice skills in screening out these distractors. Tape recordings of crowd noise, unexpected actions from competitors, verbal abuse from the coach and other players, and displacement of equipment have all been used to simulate stressors that athletes may have to deal with during competition (Cratty and Hanin, 1980; Vanek & Cratty, 1970). Coaches have also obtained photos and videotapes showing the unfamiliar competitive environment so that athletes can become familiar with the setting in which they will be competing. Such practices are designed to help athletes prepare to deal with stressors, but they may have the additional performance-enhancing effect of increasing self-efficacy expectancies by demonstrating to athletes that they are capable of coping with the anticipated stressors.

Modeling Interventions. A common practice in sports training is to have novice athletes observe more experienced ones who model the ability to respond adaptively to distractors. The models may also instruct the novices concerning the methods they use to attend to task-relevant cues and ignore irrelevant ones. Although this practice has not been formally evaluated in sports, several empirical studies of modeling influences have been conducted in other settings. For example, Sarason (1972, 1973) exposed subjects about to perform a test-like anagrams task to models who, using a talk-out-loud technique, exhibited facilitative and task-relevant cognitions that involved focusing attention on the task at hand. High test anxious subjects who were exposed to the adaptive model subsequently performed at a higher level than did control groups who did not have the benefit of the modeled task-relevant cognitions. Systematic use of cognitive modeling by means of the talk-aloud technique may have useful application in sports, and systematic studies in the athletic context are clearly warranted.

Social Support Interventions. Several studies have revealed that people who are low in perceived social support are especially prone to self-devaluative cognitions that can generate negative emotions and task-irrelevant cognitions (Lakey & Heller, 1988; Miller, Sarason, & Sarason, 1987). These findings raise the interesting possibility that interventions designed to provide social support may reduce such cognitions and thereby enhance performance. In the sport context, this could be one benefit of team-building interventions designed to develop team cohesion. A recent study by Smith, Smoll, and Barnett (1995) showed that a training program for youth baseball coaches that was designed to increase the amount of social support that characterized coach-athlete and athlete-athlete interactions resulted in significant decreases in performance anxiety as measured by the Sport Anxiety Scale. These findings are consistent with the results of an experimental study by Sarason (1981) which revealed that a supportive group discussion of concerns and solutions to students' problems with evaluative anxiety resulted in lowered self-preoccupation during performance of a subsequent anagrams task, as well as enhanced performance on the task. Sarason and Sarason (1986) later demonstrated similar salutary effects on cognitive interference and task performance using experimentally-induced social support. It thus appears that future research on the effects of team building and other cohesion-related intervention should assess the impact of such treatments on cognitive interference as well as subsequent task performance, particularly on the part of subjects who are high in sport performance anxiety.

Psychological Skills Training

A second class of interventions involve training in self-regulation skills that are designed to give athletes greater control over attentional processes. These involve interventions that focus specifically on attentional control as well as those that do so indirectly by removing impediments to attention. Examples of the latter are arousal and cognitive control interventions that are designed to reduce the negative effects of high physiological arousal and cognitive interference.

Refocusing Techniques. Refocusing techniques are designed to teach athletes specific strategies for redirecting their attention from task-irrelevant internal or external cues to task-relevant ones. One commonly used refocusing technique for dealing with cognitive interference is to direct one's attention to a compelling external stimulus instead. For example, a baseball pitcher who is experiencing cognitive interference might turn to the outfield and focus intently on a particular sign on the outfield wall, or, perhaps, count the bulbs on one of the light towers (Smith, 1992). This strategy results in a quick switch from an internal focus of attention to an external one which helps to "shut off" the interfering cognitions. The pitcher can then redeploy attention to task-relevant cues.

Nideffer (1993) taught athletes a refocusing technique called centering as a foundation attention control skill. Derived from the martial arts, centering is useful both in regaining attentional control and in reducing physiological arousal. The latter has the effect of producing arousal-induced thoracic breathing that raises the center of gravity in the athlete's body and causes a sense of being unbalanced, as well as increasing muscle tension in the upper body. In centering, the athlete breathes slowly and deeply into the abdomen and focuses attention on a spot immediately behind the navel, which is the body's natural center of gravity. The abdominal breathing helps reduce arousal and reestablish an appropriate center of gravity, and the shift in attentional focus directs attention away from task-irrelevant internal or external cues. As centering is established (within one breath in a trained athlete), the athlete refocuses attention on task-relevant cues. This procedure can be repeated as often as needed, and many athletes include it as part of a performance routine that they use in competition. In a study designed to evaluate the effects of several cognitive strategies on the tennis serves of advanced and novice athletes, Weinberg, Gould, and Jackson (1980) found centering to be one of the strategies associated with improved performance.

Mental Rehearsal. Imagery-based procedures have been shown to have considerable value in enhancing athletic performance (Murphy & Jowdy, 1993). They can be used in a variety of ways, one of which is to enhance comcentration and to resist cognitive interference. Athletes can mentally rehearse concentrating on task-relevant cues and ignoring distractors as a means of preparing for competition. In training the U.S. rhythmic gymnastics team for international competition, Schmid and Peper (1982) paired up the athletes. One member of the dyad would relax and mentally rehearse his or her routine while the other would introduce distracting stimuli (which could be anything except touching). Through exercises of this kind, athletes can learn how to detach or dissociate themselves from task-irrelevant stimuli while focusing on task-relevant ones. Biofeedback devices can be utilized in conjunction with this training to provide athletes with direct feedback concerning their ability to resist the stressful distractors as well as practice in doing so and maintaining low arousal (Schmid & Peper, 1993).

Mental rehearsal can also be used as a means of resisting cognitive interference during competition. When task-irrelevant or interfering cognitions occur, athletes can shift their attention to an imagery routine in which they mentally rehearse how they wish to perform. This represents an internal-internal shift from task-irrelevant to task-relevant stimuli. Mentally rehearsing a successful performance also may help to reduce negative cognitions and increase self-efficacy.

Soft Focus–Hard Focus. In some sports, such as baseball and tennis, the athlete must focus narrowly on a particular stimulus, such as a pitched or served ball. Unfortunately, however, most people can maintain an intense narrowed focus of attention for only a brief period of time. Athletes therefore need an attentional routine that enables them to "zoom in" on the relevant stimulus at just the right moment. The soft focus-hard focus routine involves maintaining a broad external focus that is "soft" or even slightly blurred until the specific moment at which the player needs to lock in on the specific stimulus. At that moment, the athlete switches to the hard, or narrow, external focus. The subjective experience when this is done is a contrast in detail that provides a vivid focus on task-relevant cues. Five-time American League batting champion Wade Boggs stated that this technique resulted in a focus on the pitcher's release point that was so good that he could literally see the ball's spin as it came off the pitcher's fingers. The soft focus-hard focus technique can be practiced in many contexts until it becomes a well-learned skill. Moreover, because it involves a focus on external cues, it can be used to counter cognitive interference.

Stress Management Training. As discussed earlier, anxiety responses involve cognitive and physiological elements that can interfere with task performance. Stress management programs teach athletes self-regulation skills that are designed to help counter these classes of task-irrelevant responses. One such program, known as cognitive-affective stress management training (Smith, 1980), trains athletes in relaxation skills as well as cognitive restructuring and self-instructional strategies, then has athletes rehearse these skills under high emotional arousal created by an induced affect technique (Smith & Ascough, 1985).

Although it is basically a somatic technique, relaxation training has a number of useful functions in countering cognitive interference. First, the ability to relax under stress reduces potentially distracting physiological feedback cues produced by high levels of physiological arousal. In addition to being distracting in their own right, such cues are also capable of generating interfering negative cognitions if interpreted by the athlete as indicating loss of control, helplessness, or impending failure. Finally, a reduction in arousal should reduce the tendency toward attentional narrowing and the tendency to become self-preoccupied as attention becomes internally focused (Nideffer, 1993).

Cognitive techniques such as cognitive restructuring and self-instructional training are directly targeted at the negative cognitions that produce cognitive interference in stressful situations. Cognitive restructuring counters the irrational elements of self-defeating cognitions, whereas self-instructional training is often used to provide self-instructions that direct attention to the task at hand (Meichenbaum, 1985). Nideffer (1993) has emphasized the importance of training athletes to focus on process-oriented self-talk (i.e., cognitions that direct attention to the specific athletic task or strategy) rather than to focus on outcome-related cognitions, which have a tendency to become negative during the stress of competition.

Rehearsal of the coping skills gained through these somatic and cognitive training techniques under induced affective arousal provides an opportunity for athletes to practice their use in a context that approximates the performance situation and leads not only to greater efficiency, but also to increases in self-efficacy that help counter anxiety (Smith & Nye, 1989).

In contrast to most of the techniques described earlier, there is empirical evidence that stress management training procedures can reduce cognitive interference. Crocker, Alderman, and Smith (1988) administered the cognitive-affective program to elite male and female volleyball players. Among the dependent variable measures was a thought-listing procedure that was administered after subjects watched videotapes of successful and unsuccessful performances. Compared with control subjects, the men and women who received the stress management program reported significantly fewer negative thoughts after watching the "failure" tapes. They also showed a significant improvement in volleyball performance following the intervention.

In a 6-month followup study (Crocker, 1989), the athletes were administered the outcome measures again. Females showed a significant decrease in sport-specific trait anxiety from pretreatment to followup, a decrease in negative thoughts in response to failure-relevant videotaped incidents, and a maintenance of their performance improvement from pretreatment levels. On the other hand, males maintained only their performance improvement over time; Their decrease in negative thoughts was not maintained at followup. Clearly, additional research is needed, particularly on the role of gender in response to such training. Nonetheless, there are indications that the types of negative thoughts that are characteristic of cognitive interference can be reduced by training in stress management coping skills.

Performance Routines. Many top performers develop ritualized routines that are designed to produce a state of mind and body that facilitates performance. Experimental studies have shown that in most instances, this state involves a level of optimal arousal, task-relevant cognitions (or, in some instances, a blank mind), a state of focused concentration on task-relevant cues, and a reliance on automatic as opposed to controlled processing. From a behavioral perspective, a performance routine that becomes overlearned through constant use can be likened to a chain of behaviors, each of which cues the next. Over time, the performance routine or protocol will serve as a set of attentional cues or triggers for eliciting the appropriate focus of attention.

During a performance routine, the focus of attention may change at various times. An example of this is shown in Table 13.1, which presents a prototypic performance routine designed for batters in professional baseball (Smith, 1992).

This performance routine is designed to bring hitters to an end state in which they are relaxed, focused in a narrow-external fashion, and engaged in automatic processing. If we apply the attentional dimensions described earlier (broad-narrow; internal-external) to this performance routine, it can be seen that all four combinations are represented at various points in the chain of behaviors. For example, developing a plan before facing a particular pitcher requires a broad-internal focus during which many bits of information are integrated. Generating visual images of specific pitches during the mental rehearsal components of the routine involves a narrow-internal focus. The soft focus-hard focus sequence as the pitcher prepares to deliver represents a timed shift from a broad-external focus to the narrow-external focus needed to pick up the ball as it leaves the pitcher's hand. Given the fact that the batter has only about one fifth of a second to detect the flight of a ball and to swing the bat at a 90 mph pitch (Adair, 1990), the ability to pick up the flight of the ball as soon as possible is an essential ingredient of success.

It should also be noted that several measures included in the performance routine are designed to reduce anxiety and cognitive interference. These include the prescribed relaxation inductions and abdominal breathing and the explicit mandate to clear the mind and not think about mechanics once in the batter's box. (This protocol is part of a psychological skills training program, and the hitters who use it have already been trained in the component skills such as relaxation and imagery.)

Experimental evidence indicates that consistently applied performance routines can enhance sport performance. For example, Boutcher and Crews (1987) demonstrated that a preshot attentional routine significantly increased the putting performance of female golfers.

Intervention as a Person x Situation Strategy

The attentional control procedures described here have been categorized as situational or athlete-centered interventions. Obviously, all are ultimately aimed at increasing the ability of athletes to focus successfully on task-relevant internal or external cues (or both) and to minimize cognitive interference. When applied to individual athletes, the choice of attention-control strategies should be based upon an assessment of the nature of the processes that produce cognitive interference, the current coping weaknesses and resources of the athlete, and the demands of the performance situations that the athlete will be expected to confront.

TABLE 13.1
A Performance Routine for Professional Baseball Players Designed to Facilitate Appropriate Attentional Foci

The Hitter's Success Chain

Before the Game:

Watch the opposing pitcher warm up, focusing on his speed and pitches. Note whether he seems to be having any difficulty controlling one of his pitches. If, for example, he seems to be having trouble with his breaking ball, you may expect to see more fast balls as he goes to his strength.

In the Dugout:

Study the pitcher, noting what he is throwing and what you can handle. Talk to teammates about his pitches and visualize how he's pitched you in the past and what you're likely to see. Develop your plan, taking into account game circumstances. Visualize past successes and your own strengths--how you match up best and how you can get your pitch, and not his.

On-Deck Circle:

Get relaxed, and take practice swings with any necessary self-reminders about mechanics. This is the only time you should think about mechanics unless you need to adjust after a pitch. Time the pitcher's delivery as you take your practice swings.

Visualize what you will see, and see/feel/hear yourself hitting your pitch hard. Mentally rehearse taking bad pitches. Allow only positive thoughts and images: what you want to do, not what you *don't* want to do. Program yourself for success.

Outside the Batter's Box:

Relax yourself with breathing and your trigger word for relaxation. Combine your trigger word with the exhalation or outbreath. Breathe into your stomach, not into your chest. Clear your mind by focusing on your breathing.

In the Batter's Box:

Step into the box and do a set preswing routine that is compatible with relaxation and a relaxed rhythm. For example, you might swing the bat back and forth in a loose, relaxed swing. Do not vary this routine. If anything disrupts it, step out of the batter's box and start over. Remember, the batter's box is your domain as a hitter. Take charge of it and of yourself.

Concentrate only on seeing the ball. Use a soft focus/hard focus to the release point. Your mind should be clear and focused on the only thing that matters: seeing *this* pitch from the release point into the hitting zone. Let yourself be on automatic pilot, so that your reflexes operate freely and take your hands to the ball.

Reprinted by permission from R. E. Smith (1992), *Psychological skills in professional baseball.* Houston, TX: Houston Astros Baseball Club, pp. 73-74.

Where concentration difficulties are based on high levels of performance state anxiety, it may be necessary to first develop effective cognitive and physiological coping skills through stress management training before the athlete can profit fully from the more situationally based interventions, such as simulation and modeling procedures. Where anxiety is not excessive, the athlete may respond well to the use of laboratory tasks, competition stress simulations, or the development of a specific performance routine that serves as a means of focusing attention on task-relevant cues at the critical junctures of task performance. Likewise, the demands of particular competitive situations may govern the choice of intervention strategy. For example, a soft focus-hard focus strategy might be more useful to a tennis player who has to pick up the opponent's serve quickly than it is for a football lineman whose perceptual and information processing demands are more global. For the latter, a cognitive refocusing approach may prove helpful as a means of gaining control over potentially interfering self-oriented cognitions. In essence, the tailoring of interventions to the needs and current resources of the athlete as well as the situational demands of the competitive setting involves a person × situation approach. At the present time, there is little in the way of systematic research on such person × situation interventions, but the many empirical questions generated by such an approach provide an inviting context for future research in the area of sport psychology.

CONCLUSION

Attentional processes are of great importance in athletic performance, and cognitive interference produced by stressful situations and anxiety responses is a major contributor to poor performance. It is therefore somewhat surprising that in spite of theoretical advances in the understanding of attentional factors and the factors that create concentration disruption, research on the effects of most of the intervention techniques described in this chapter awaits the attention of sport scientists. It seems likely that such research will not only advance our understanding of performance anxiety, cognitive interference, and attentional processes, but will have important practical applications as well.

REFERENCES

Adair, R. K. (1990). *The physics of baseball*. New York: Harper & Row.

Arnold, M. B. (1960). *Emotion and personality*. New York: Columbia University Press.

Atkinson, J. W., & Birch, D. (1978). *An introduction to motivation*. New York: Van Nostrand.

Bacon, S. J. (1974). Arousal and the range of cue utilization. *Journal of Experimental Psychology, 103*, 81–87.

Bartley, S. H., & Chute, E. (1947). *Fatigue and impairment in man*. New York: McGraw-Hill.

Blankenstein, K. R., Toner, B. B., & Flett, G. R. (1989). Test anxiety and the contents of consciousness: Thought-listing and endorsement measures. *Journal of Research in Personality, 23,* 269–286.
Boutcher, S. H. (1993). Attention and athletic performance: An integrated approach. In T. Horn (Ed.), *Advances in sport psychology* (pp. 267–284). Champaign, IL: Human Kinetics.
Boutcher, S. H., & Crews, D. H. (1987). The effect of a preshot routine on a well-learned skill. *International Journal of Sport Psychology, 18,* 30–39.
Broadbent, D. E, (1958). *Perception and communication.* London: Pergamon.
Burton, D. (1988). Do anxious swimmers swim slower? Reexamining the elusive anxiety-performance relationship. *Journal of Sport and Exercise Psychology, 10,* 45–61.
Carver C. S., & Scheier, M. F. (1981). *Attention and self-regulation.* New York: Springer-Verlag.
Cheek, J. M., & Melchior, L. A. (1990). Shyness, self-esteem, and self-consciousness. In H. Leitenberg (Ed.), *Handbook of social and evaluation anxiety* (pp. 47–84). New York: Plenum.
Cratty, B. J. (1989). *Psychology in contemporary sport* (3rd ed.). Englewood Cliffs, NJ: Prentice-Hall.
Cratty, B. J., & Hanin, Y. (1980). *The athlete and the sports team.* Denver, CO: Love.
Crocker, P. R. E. (1989). A follow-up of cognitive-affective stress management training. *Journal of Sport and Exercise Psychology, 11,* 236–242.
Crocker, P. R. E., Alderman, R. B., & Smith, M. R. (1988). Cognitive-affective stress management training with high performance youth volleyball players: Effects on affect, cognition, and performance. *Journal of Sport and Exercise Psychology, 10,* 461–470.
Davidson, R. J., & Schwartz, G. E. (1976). The psychobiology of relaxation and related states: A multi-process theory. In D. Mostofsky (Ed.), *Behavioral control and modification of physiological activity.* Englewood Cliffs, NJ: Prentice-Hall.
Easterbrook, J. A. (1959). The effect of emotion on cue utilization and the organization of behavior. *Psychological Review, 66,* 183–201.
Ellis, A. (1962). *Reason and emotion in personality.* New York: Lyle Stuart.
Eysenck, M. W., & Calvo, M. G. (1992). Anxiety and performance: The processing efficiency theory. *Cognition and Emotion, 6,* 256–273.
Harris, D. V., & Harris, B. L. (1984). *The athlete's guide to sport psychology: Mental skills for physical people.* New York: Leisure Press.
Hirst, W. (1986). The psychology of attention. In J. LeDoux & W. Hirst (Eds.), *Mind and brain* (pp. 105–141). Cambridge, England: Cambridge University Press.
James, W. (1890). *Principles of psychology* (Vol. 1). New York: Holt.
Kendrick, M. J., Craig, K. D., Lawson, D. M., & Davidson, P. O. (1982). Cognitive and behavioral therapy for musical-performance anxiety. *Journal of Consulting and Clinical Psychology, 50,* 353–362.
Lakey, B., & Heller, K. (1988). Social support from a friend, perceived social support, and social problem solving. *Americal Journal of Community Psychology, 16,* 811–824.
Landers, D. M. (1980). The arousal-performance relationship revisited. *Research Quarterly, 51,* 77–90.
Lazarus, R. S., & Folkman, S. (1984). *Stress, appraisal, and coping.* New York: Springer.
Leitenberg, H. (Ed.). (1990). *Handbook of social and evaluation anxiety.* New York: Plenum.
Liebert, R. M., & Morris, L. W. (1967). Cognitive and emotional components of test anxiety: A distinction and some initial data. *Psychological Reports, 20,* 975–978.
Mandler, G., & Sarason, S. B. (1952). A study of anxiety and learning. *Journal of Abnormal and Social Psychology, 47,* 166–173.
Martens, R., Vealey, R. S., & Burton, D. (1990). *Competitive anxiety in sport.* Champaign, IL: Human Kinetics.
Meichenbaum, D. (1985). *Stress inoculation training.* New York: Pergamon.
Miller, G., Sarason, I. G., & Sarason, B. R. (1987). *Social support and cognitive interference.* Paper presented at the Western Psychological Association, Long Beach, CA.
Murphy, S. M., & Jowdy, D. P. (1993). Imagery and mental practice. In T. Horn (Ed.), *Advances in sport psychology* (pp. 217–248). Champaign, IL: Human Kinetics.

Navon, D. (1985). Attention division or sharing? In M. I. Posner & O. S. M. Martin (Eds.), *Attention and performance XI* (pp. 103–117). Hillsdale, NJ: Lawrence Erlbaum Associates.

Nideffer, R. M. (1989). Anxiety, attention, and performance in sports: Theoretical and practical considerations. In D. Hackfort & C. D. Spielberger (Eds.), *Anxiety in sports: An international perspective* (pp. 117–136). New York: Hemisphere.

Nideffer. R. M. (1993). Concentration and attention control training. In J. M. Williams (Ed.), *Applied sport psychology: Personal growth to peak performance* (2nd ed., pp. 243–261). Palo Alto, CA: Mayfield Press.

Parasuraman, R. (1984). Preface. In R. Parasuraman & R. Davies (Eds), *Varieties of attention* (pp. xi–xvi). Orlando, FL: Academic Press.

Posner, M. I., & Snyder, C. R. R. (1975). Attention and cognitive control. In R. L. Solso (Ed.), *Information processing and cognition: The Loyola Symposium* (pp. 113–137). Hillsdale, NJ: Lawrence Erlbaum Associates.

Rogers, C. R. (1959). A theory of therapy, personality and interpersonal relationships as developed in the client-centered framework. In S. Koch (Ed.), *Psychology: A study of a science* (Vol. 3). New York: McGraw-Hill.

Sarason, I. G. (1972). Test anxiety and the model who fails. *Journal of Personality and Social Psychology, 22*, 410–413.

Sarason, I. G. (1973). Test anxiety and cognitive modeling. *Journal of Personality and Social Psychology, 28*, 58–61.

Sarason, I. G. (1981). Test anxiety, stress, and social support. *Journal of Personality, 49*, 101–114.

Sarason, I. G. (1984). Stress, anxiety, and cognitive interference: Reactions to tests. *Journal of Personality and Social Psychology, 46*, 929–938.

Sarason, I. G., & Sarason, B. R. (1986). Experimentally provided social support. *Journal of Personality and Social Psychology, 50*, 1222–1225.

Sarason, I. G., & Sarason, B. R. (1990). Test Anxiety. In H. Leitenberg (Ed.), *Handbook of social and evaluation anxiety* (pp. 475–496). New York: Plenum.

Sarason, I. G., Sarason, B. R., & Pierce, G. R. (1995). Cognitive interference: At the intelligence-personality crossroads. In D. Saklofske & M. Zeidner (Eds.), *International handbook of personality and intelligence* (pp. 285–296). New York: Plenum.

Schmid, A. B., & Peper, E. (1982). *Mental preparation for optimal performance in rhythmic gymnastics.* Paper presented at the Western Society for Physical Education of College Women, Asilomar, CA.

Schmid, A. B., & Peper, E. (1993). Training strategies for concentration. In J. M. Williams (Ed.), *Applied sport psychology: Personal growth to peak performance* (pp. 262–273). Palo Alto, CA: Mayfield Press.

Schmidt, R. A. (1982). *Motor control and learning.* Champaign, IL: Human Kinetics.

Schneider, W., Dumais, S. T., & Shiffrin, R. M. (1984). Automatic and control processing and attention. In R. Parasuraman & R. Davies (Eds.), *Varieties of attention.* Orlando, FL: Academic Press.

Smith, R. E. (1980). A cognitive-affective approach to stress management training for athletes. In C. H. Nadeau, W. Halliwell, K. M. Newell, & G. C. Roberts (Eds.), *Psychology of motor behavior and sport—1979* (pp. 54–72). Champaign, IL: Human Kinetics.

Smith, R. E. (1986). A component analysis of athletic stress. In M. R. Weiss & D. Gould (Eds.), *Sport for children and youths* (pp. 107–111). Champaign, IL: Human Kinetics.

Smith, R. E. (1992). *Psychological skills in professional baseball.* Houston, TX: Houston Astros Baseball Club.

Smith, R. E., & Ascough, J. C. (1985). Induced affect in stress management training. In S. R. Burchfield (Ed.), *Stress: Psychological and physiological interactions* (pp. 359–378). New York: Hemisphere.

Smith, R. E., & Nye, S. L. (1989). Comparison of induced affect and covert rehearsal in the acquisition of stress management coping skills. *Journal of Counseling Psychology, 36*, 17–23.

Smith, R. E., & Smoll, F. L. (1990). Sport performance anxiety. In H. Leitenberg (Ed.), *Handbook of social and evaluation anxiety* (pp. 417–454). New York: Plenum.

Smith, R. E., Smoll, F. L., & Barnett, N. (1995). Reduction of children's sport performance anxiety through social support and stress-reduction training for coaches. *Journal of Applied Developmental Psychology, 16*, 125–142.

Smith, R. E., Smoll, F. L., & Schutz, R. W. (1990). Measurement and correlates of sport-specific cognitive and somatic trait anxiety: The Sport Anxiety Scale. *Anxiety Research, 2*, 263–280.

Sonstroem, R. J., & Bernardo, P. (1982). Intra-individual pregame state anxiety and basketball performance: A reexamination of the inverted-U curve. *Journal of Sport Psychology, 4*, 235–245.

Spence, J. T., & Spence, K. W. (1966). The motivational components of manifest anxiety: Drive and drive stimuli. In C. D. Spielberger (Ed.), *Anxiety and behavior* (pp. 291–326). New York: Academic Press.

Spielberger, C. D. (1966). Theory and research on anxiety. In C. D. Spielberger (Ed.), *Anxiety and behavior* (pp. 3–20). New York: Academic Press.

Steptoe, A., & Fidler, H. (1987). Stage fright in orchestral musicians: A study of cognitive and behavioural strategies in performance anxiety. *British Journal of Psychology, 78*, 241–249.

Vanek, M., & Cratty, B. J. (1970). *Psychology and the superior athlete.* New York: Macmillan.

Wachtel, P. L. (1967). Conceptions of broad or narrow attention. *Psychological Bulletin*, 68, 417–429.

Weinberg, R. S., Gould, D., & Jackson, A. (1980). Cognition and motor performance: Effects of psyching-up strategies on three motor tasks. *Cognitive Therapy and Research, 4*, 239–245.

Williams, J. M. (1986). Psychological characteristics of peak performance. In J. M. Williams (Ed.), *Applied sport psychology: Personal growth to peak performance* (pp. 121–132). Palo Alto, CA: Mayfield Press.

Yerkes, R. M., & Dodson, J. D. (1908). The relationship of strength of stimulus to rapidity of habit formation. *Journal of Comparative Neurology and Psychology, 18*, 459–482.

CHAPTER

14

COGNITIVE INTERFERENCE AND PERSONALITY: THEORETICAL AND METHODOLOGICAL ISSUES

Gregory R. Pierce
Ciarda A. Henderson
John H. Yost
Cynthia M. Loffredo
Hamilton College

Numerous studies have documented the debilitating effects of cognitive interference on task performance. The term *cognitive interference* refers to intrusive thoughts individuals may have that compete for attentional resources while performing a task (Sarason & Stoops, 1978). Intrusive thoughts appear to play a significant role in day-to-day events (e.g., automobile accidents), in important life tasks (e.g., academic, athletic, and social situations), and in clinical disorders (e.g., anxiety, depression, and sexual dysfunction). It has been demonstrated that individuals who had recently experienced a relatively high number of negative life events (and may therefore have been subject to high levels of intrusive thoughts) were more likely than others to be in automobile accidents. Students whose cognitions during actual course examinations are characterized by intrusive off-task thoughts achieve lower grades than do more task-focused students, a finding that has been replicated in several countries (Communian, 1993; van der Ploeg, 1982).

Conceptualizations of cognitive interference and related phenomena have increasingly adopted an information processing approach (see, e.g., Klinger, this volume). This framework is particularly helpful in focusing attention on the specific mechanisms (e.g., distraction, failure to retrieve pertinent information from memory) by which intrusive thoughts might influence task performance. Yet, by emphasizing the link between cognitive information and performance outcomes, we may overlook the fact that intrusive thoughts per se are a distressing event and are worthy of empirical and theoretical attention, regardless of their role in performance. The performance of a student who is plagued by anxious, intrusive thoughts while working on an examination in a mathematics course might suffer from these distracting cognitions; yet we suspect that this student would wish to be freed from these intrusive thoughts even if he or she did not undermine his or her performance. The present chapter, therefore, focuses primarily on the cognitive interference construct itself, with less attention being devoted to its possible consequences for task outcomes.

Sarason and Stoops (1978) developed the Cognitive Interference Questionnaire (CIQ) to assess the following three categories of attentional difficulties: task-relevant thoughts (e.g., "I thought about how poorly I was doing"), task-irrelevant thoughts (e.g., "I thought about something that made me feel guilty"), and mind wandering (rated using a single 7-point scale). The CIQ has been used extensively in research on test anxiety and academic performance and in cross-cultural research. Finally, the CIQ has been adapted for research in other task domains (e.g., athletics). As was the case with the Reactions to Tests Questionnaire (RTT), development of the CIQ was guided by a cognitive approach to the study of test anxiety and its consequences (Sarason, 1978). As an inspection of the CIQ items reveals, however, not all of the possible thoughts a person might have during an examination (or similar task) are assessed; instead, the CIQ scales focus on those cognitions that are likely to be associated with negative affect, in particular, worry.

This focus is not surprising given the fact that interest in cognitive interference grew out of research on anxiety, particularly with respect to the test anxiety construct. As with the concept of anxiety, distinctions can be drawn between state and trait aspects of cognitive interference. The bulk of research on cognitive interference has focused on its manifestation in particular classes of situations (e.g., academic, athletic). In particular, cognitive interference has been shown to occur in evaluative situations in which the person believes his or her performance is being scrutinized.

Given this emphasis on situation-specific approaches to cognitive interference, it is not surprising that theory and research on cognitive interference has largely ignored the possibility that the propensity to experience intrusive thoughts in one type of situation might be related to the occurrence of intrusive thoughts in other contexts. Thus, a primary goal of this chapter is to argue that cognitive interference might profitably be conceptualized and investigated as a personality characteristic with transituational implications. Put differently, the authors suspect that individuals who are plagued by distracting thoughts in one context also experience intrusive thoughts in other domains as well. While the notion that cognitive interference has trait-like characteristics is not new, the supposition that the predisposition to experience cognitive interference might extend across categories of situations has not previously been considered in any systematic manner.

In this chapter, research on cognitive interference is examined, both as it arises in specific classes of situations and as it manifests itself across diverse settings.

The first section is a review of research on cognitive interference in three domains: academic, social, and athletic situations. Next is an examination of the few studies that have conceptualized and investigated cognitive interference as a personality characteristic, one that is presumed to influence cognitive and overt behavior across a broad range of situations. Finally, an agenda is developed for future research and theory development in the area of cognitive interference.

SITUATIONAL APPROACHES TO COGNITIVE INTERFERENCE

Research on cognitive interference has tended to be domain specific; in other words, investigators have typically been concerned with conceptualizing cognitive interference as it manifests itself in a particular class of situations. For example, much of the work on intrusive thoughts has stemmed from studies of test anxiety; cognitive interference was conceptualized as a mediating mechanism by which test anxiety might influence performance in academic situations. Similarly, investigations of social anxiety have, understandably, focused primarily on the effects of cognitive interference in settings with a strong interpersonal element. Studies of cognitive interference in athletic situations have also been characterized by a domain specific approach. Common to each of these areas of research is an emphasis on an individual differences variable that determines whether a person experiences cognitive interference in a particular type of situation.

Test Anxiety

The bulk of research on cognitive interference has examined its role in test taking situations (Sarason, 1980; Smith, this volume). Intrusive thoughts occurring in academic situations are hypothesized to be a function of test anxiety—people's characteristic level of anxiety in academic situations. The construct of test anxiety is multidimensional. For instance, Sarason (1984) developed a factorially derived, self-report instrument, the RTT Questionnaire, to assess four facets of individuals' habitual responses to test taking situations: (a) tension, (b) worry, (c) test-irrelevant thinking, and (d) bodily symptoms. The RTT tension, worry, and test-irrelevant thinking scales—but not the Bodily Symptoms Scale—have been shown to be good predictors of intrusive thoughts experienced in academic situations (Hunsley, 1987; Sarason, 1984; Sarason, Sarason, Keefe, Hayes, & Shearin, 1986). These findings are consistent with the observation that physiological arousal in test situations is universal, rather than specific to those who are highly test anxious (Hollandsworth, Glazeski, Kirkland, Jones, & Van Norman, 1979; Holroyd, Westbrook, Wolf, & Badhorn, 1978); it also fits with a cognitive orientation to the conceptualization of test anxiety.

A substantial body of evidence indicates that individuals differ in the manner in which they construe and subsequently respond to evaluative features of academic situations. Highly test-anxious individuals, compared with others, appear to be overly attuned to this evaluative component; they report having many more thoughts concerning how others are performing and concerning how the experimenter (or instructor) will view their performance. In addition, those high in test anxiety describe themselves as experiencing many more off-task thoughts about their relationships with family members or friends, and about past, current, and anticipated events. Finally, persons high in test anxiety experience more mind wandering than do others.

Evidence indicates that individuals vary reliably in the degree to which they report experiencing cognitive interference in academic settings. For example, Hunsley (1987) found that students' ratings of cognitive interference assessed after each of five examinations in a particular course were positively related; students who experienced high levels of intrusive thoughts during one examination also reported high levels of intrusive thoughts during other examinations in that course (see also, Zatz & Chassin, 1983). These results are in accord with those of other investigators showing that trait measures of test anxiety (such as the RTT) successfully predict levels of cognitive interference experienced in academic situations, both in actual classroom settings as well as laboratory settings.

Research on test anxiety and cognitive interference provides compelling evidence that the tendency to experience intrusive thoughts in test-taking situations reflects a stable individual differences variable. This conclusion is based on (a) links between trait measures of test anxiety and indices of cognitive interference reported while completing academic tasks, and (b) interrelations among assessments of cognitive interference obtained during several similar academic situations. Thus, a high level of consistency is observed when intrusive thoughts are sampled across situations that fall within the same domain (in this case, academic settings).

Sport Anxiety

Research on sport anxiety has often been conducted in applied settings with the goal of developing interventions for improving athletes' performance and decreasing their vulnerability to injuries. These studies have documented the negative role of cognitive interference in athletic situations (see Smith, this volume, for a review of this literature). For example, Coddington and Troxell (1980) showed that football players who had recently experienced relatively high levels of stressful life events sustained more injuries on the playing field than did other football players, presumably because the players experiencing the highest levels of stress were more preoccupied with the recent occurrence of these stressors.

Researchers have also examined the role of self-confidence in athletics (Feltz, 1988; Gould, Petlichkoff, & Weinberg, 1984; Martens, Burton, Vealey, Bump, & Smith, 1990). Athletes who are confident in their ability to perform effectively in sport-oriented situations experience fewer intrusive thoughts and concerns about the possible outcome of their performance when engaged in such tasks (Martin & Gill, 1991).

Some researchers in the area of sport anxiety have suggested that difficulties in attentional processes experienced by some athletes have trait-like characteristics (Martin & Gill, 1991). Individuals are hypothesized to differ in their capacity to process various aspects of task-relevant information. Cognitive interference undermines performance by diverting attentional resources to processing intrusive thoughts. Other definitions of sport anxiety focus on the athlete's predisposition to attend to the potential evaluative features of sport situations (Smith, 1986). Thus, research on test anxiety and sport anxiety are consistent with the idea that the propensity to experience intrusive thoughts within a particular domain reflects a personality characteristic.

Social Anxiety

Research on social anxiety—like that on test anxiety and sport anxiety—reflects a strong cognitive orientation (Sarason, Sarason, & Pierce, 1990). Socially anxious individuals are more likely than their less socially anxious counterparts to perceive situations as evaluative (Emmelkamp & Van Oppen, 1994), and to place more emphasis on this aspect of social situations (Goldfried, Padawer, & Robins, 1984). Lucock and Salkoskis (1988) explored differences in the expectations of a clinical sample of subjects (each of whom had been referred to a clinic for social skills training) and a control group. Results suggested that, compared with control subjects, the clinical sample expected future socially oriented interactions to be more negative and expected to be evaluated more critically by others in these situations.

Research suggests that socially anxious individuals do not suffer from a skills deficit, per se, but rather they may be so distracted by negative thoughts that these skills are actually inhibited (Trower, 1981). For example, investigations of cognitive interference in social situations have demonstrated that preoccupying thoughts have a greater impact on social behavior than does the lack of social skills (Clark & Arkowitz, 1975; Leary, 1983). Although earlier studies posited that those who experienced social anxiety (e.g., social phobics) lacked the appropriate social skills to avoid anxiety in social interactions, more recent studies have revealed that social phobics can exhibit adequate social skills (in terms of eye contact and length of speaking time) but fail to do so once they perceive themselves to be in a situation that could lead to evaluation and embarrassment (Monti et al., 1984). At the point at which social phobics deem themselves to be in a possibly embarrassing situation, cognitive activity in the form of negative self thoughts increase in frequency and draw attention away from existing social skills, resulting in an inability to interact without experiencing high levels of anxiety (Myszka, Galassi, & Ware, 1986).

Despite clear similarities, the literature on social anxiety differs from that on test anxiety and sport anxiety in the breadth of related constructs that have been linked to social anxiety vs. test anxiety and sport anxiety. Research on cognitive interference in academic and athletic settings has focused almost exclusively on the possible contributions of situation-specific anxiety; in contrast, studies of intrusive thoughts in social situations have considered, in addition to social anxiety, such constructs as shyness, social phobias, nonassertiveness, and low self-esteem (Cheek & Melchior, 1990; Bruch, this volume). Thus, considerably more is known about the manner in which social anxiety ties in with other individual differences variables as they influence behavior in social circumstances than is known about linkages between either test anxiety or sport anxiety and other features of personality that might also play a role in behavior in relevant settings. It is therefore not surprising that social anxiety is typically conceptualized as part of a larger constellation of personality characteristics, whereas test anxiety and sport anxiety are usually viewed as isolated aspects of personality with little attention being given to their possible relations to other important personal characteristics.

In summary, studies of cognitive interference in academic, athletic, and social situations have highlighted the important role played by the way in which individuals appraise particular classes of situations. Those who experience cognitive interference in a specific domain appear to be especially attentive to the possible evaluative features of the situation; this concern about evaluation, in turn, leads to poor performance, regardless of available responses in their behavioral repertoire. The point being emphasized here is that cognitive interference arises from a view of situations that exaggerates their evaluative features and distracts the individual from task-oriented responses. On the whole, however, this body of research has neglected the possible links between cognitive interference experienced in each of these classes of domains. Is the highly test anxious individual also prone to distraction in athletic situations? Is the social phobic also likely to be fearful in testing or athletic contexts?

A TRANSITUATIONAL APPROACH TO COGNITIVE INTERFERENCE

The propensity of researchers to adopt a situation-specific approach to cognitive interference is understandable, given the problems associated with investigations of global features of adjustment such as anxiety (Sarason, 1980). Another strength of this approach is that each of the settings in which cognitive interference has been studied has high face validity for people; in other words, individuals can relate easily to the thoughts, feelings, and behaviors of those who experience high levels of anxiety in these situations.

This approach has clearly been valuable. For instance, we know quite a bit about some of the properties of these situations that elicit cognitive interference, and some of the individual differences variables that render some persons more vulnerable than others to experiencing intrusive thoughts. The downside of this approach, however, is that, in emphasizing the role of cognitive interference in particular situations, the possibility that the tendency to experience intrusive thoughts might be transituational may not be considered.

Several researchers have proposed that cognitive interference occurring in a particular situation may reflect the influence of a general tendency to experience intrusive thoughts across situations. Sarason et al., (1986) found significant and positive associations between subjects' reports of the frequency of occurrence of intrusive thoughts while completing laboratory tasks and the Thought Occurrence Questionnaire (TOQ), a trait measure of their habitual tendency to experience cognitive interference. Hunsley (1987) extended these findings by showing that students' ratings of cognitive interference assessed after each of five examinations in a course were positively related; that is, students who experienced high levels of intrusive thoughts on one examination also reported high levels of intrusive thoughts during other examinations in that course (see also, Zatz & Chassin, 1983). The correlations among the ratings of cognitive interference occurring across the five examinations ranged from .47 to .75, and remained essentially unchanged when a measure of test anxiety was partialled out of these correlations. The latter finding suggests that the cross-situational consistency in cognitive interference reported by these students did not reflect the contribution of a situation-specific feature of personality (in this case, test anxiety). Instead, the co-occurrence of intrusive thoughts across examinations was apparently influenced by a broader feature of personality, one that was not specific only to test-related situations. A significant feature of these studies is that, within a particular study, the occurrence of intrusive thoughts was examined in only one class of situations (e.g., those involving academic examinations or test-like tasks completed in a laboratory setting).

Pierce, Ptacek, Henderson, Joseph, and Loffredo (1995) reported two studies in which the possibility that intrusive thoughts experienced in academic situations might be related to cognitive interference occurring in either athletic or self-evaluative situations was investigated. In one study, 96 students completed the CIQ after each of two examinations (randomly selected for each subject such that the examinations occurred in different courses) and following their completing a packet of questionnaires assessing personality characteristics and the quality of family and peer relationships. Subjects' reports of task-relevant and task-irrelevant intrusive thoughts and mind wandering experienced while completing each of the examinations were positively correlated (*rs* = .57, .60, and .26, respectively, all $ps < .05$). These findings are consistent with results from Hunsley's (1987) study, while at the same time providing a more stringent evaluation of the issue by exploring links between cognitive interference occurring in two different courses (rather than examining links across examinations taken in the same course).

Subjects who reported high levels of cognitive interference while taking examinations also described themselves as having experienced more intrusive thoughts while completing questionnaire packets in the laboratory session than did other subjects. Interestingly, the magnitude of the correlations between CIQ scores obtained following each of the course examinations was comparable to the correlations computed between examination CIQ scores and those obtained after subjects had completed the questionnaire packets. These results suggest that the tendency to experience intrusive thoughts in academic and self-evaluative situations may reflect a common individual differences variable.

Further support for this hypothesis was found when subjects' CIQ scores were correlated with TOQ scores (which assessed subjects' habitual tendency to experience intrusive thoughts in evaluative situations). Subjects who described themselves as predisposed to cognitive interference, in general, reported more intrusive thoughts following the examinations and the questionnaire session than did other subjects.

In the second study reported by Pierce et al. (1995), cognitive interference was examined in academic and athletic situations. Fifty-eight members of a college football team completed the CIQ following each of two regular season games and after two course examinations (occurring in different courses). Subjects' CIQ scores for the two course examinations were significantly and positively related (and were similar in magnitude to those found in the first study). CIQ scores obtained following each of two football games were also significantly and positively related. More importantly, CIQ scores assessing intrusive thoughts experienced during the course examinations and the football games were also interrelated. Subjects' TOQ scores successfully predicted their CIQ scores assessing intrusive thoughts in both academic and athletic situations.

These findings provide evidence suggesting that individuals who are vulnerable to experiencing cognitive interference in a particular domain are also particularly likely to experience intrusive thoughts in other contexts as well. They also suggest that the TOQ assesses this general predisposition to experience cognitive interference across different task domains. Although further research is clearly warranted to replicate and extend these findings, results from the Pierce et al. (1995) study provide an initial evaluation of the hypothesis that cognitive interference reflects a personality characteristic with transituational properties.

Taken together, findings from both studies reported by Pierce et al. (1995) suggest that the predisposition to experience cognitive interference reflects a personality characteristic. Particularly important is the finding that this predisposition has transituational implications. Thus, individuals appear not to be vulnerable to cognitive interference in only a single domain; instead, they appear likely to experience cognitive interference across types of situations, especially those situations with a salient evaluative component.

THEORETICAL AND METHODOLOGICAL NEEDS IN COGNITIVE INTERFERENCE RESEARCH

The observation that cognitive interference reflects a personality characteristic that influences thought and action across diverse domains has important implications for further research on the topic. Studies of cognitive interference have repeatedly demonstrated that individuals who are vulnerable to intrusive thoughts are particularly likely to experience them in evaluative settings. This suggests that more information is needed about the manner in which individuals construe the situations they confront. Experimental studies are valuable because they afford the opportunity to investigate the ways in which individuals respond to objectively similar situations. On the other hand, because cognitive processes are likely to play an important role in these responses, incorporation of the assessment of subjects' subjective appraisals of these situations is also needed. Thus, an adequate understanding of cognitive interference and its effect on individuals' responses in evaluative situations will require attention to both the objective and subjective aspects of situations.

More information is also needed about the mechanisms by which cognitive interference influences performance. For example, studies have shown that intrusive thoughts compete for attentional resources, thereby decreasing performance. But other mechanisms might also come into play. Individuals who perform poorly on a task (e.g., as a result of intrusive thoughts), might avoid similar situations in the future, with the result that they deny themselves the opportunity to gain experience that might enhance their skills. These individuals, if and when they encounter the task in the future, will probably be especially likely to perform poorly on the task, thereby strengthening their avoidance response.

Individuals who are particularly attentive to the evaluative component of situations (i.e., those who are high in cognitive interference) may have different goals that guide their behavior in certain situations. Dweck (1986) has postulated two different goals that may influence behavior in situations that are potentially evaluative. Individuals with a learning goal orientation view situations as opportunities to acquire skills and knowledge regarding particular tasks; those with a performance goal orientation see situations primarily in terms of their implications for evaluating their abilities. Several studies have shown that individuals with learning goal orientations outperform their performance goal oriented counterparts. The important point here is that intrusive thoughts may stem from schemas that shape the way in which individuals construe situations. We need to know more about differences in the ways that people view situations and the consequences these construals have for subsequent thought and action.

If intrusive thoughts do stem from cognitive models or schemas, we need to determine the sequelae of such cognitive structures. For example, what are the developmental histories of individuals who are especially vulnerable to cognitive interference, and how do these experiences differ from those of individuals who are less vulnerable to intrusive thoughts? When the tendency to experience cognitive interference is viewed as a domain-specific personal characteristic, it may overemphasize the possible role played by previous experiences related to that domain. For example, we may assume that cognitive interference in testing situations arises from an unusually high number of failure experiences related to test taking. On the other hand, when the predisposition to experience intrusive thoughts is viewed as a general trait that influences behavior in many different settings, it directs attention towards developmental experiences that are not necessarily tied to a particular domain of activities. For instance, it may be that those who are especially sensitive to the evaluative features of situations have failed to develop a sense that they are loved and valued by others; such a developmental history might reflect poor attachment experiences in childhood. In this regard, the authors suspect that one major contributor to the development of vulnerabilities to intrusive thoughts is parent-child relationships that fail to foster children's beliefs that they are cared about regardless of their accomplishments in any domain.

Efforts are also needed to explore links between the predisposition to experience cognitive interference and other enduring individual differences. A substantial body of evidence has accumulated documenting the role of intrusive thoughts in clinical disorders. By far, the majority of this research has examined cognitive interference in depression and anxiety (Kendall & Ingram, 1989; see Klinger, this volume, for an excellent review of this literature). However, studies have also indicated that problems related to intrusive thoughts are a major feature of other disorders such as sexual dysfunction, depression and affective disorders (Ishiyama & Munson, 1993), obsessive-compulsive disorder (Emmelkamp & Van Oppen, 1994), and posttraumatic stress disorder (Watson et al., 1991). By investigating such linkages, we will be able to develop a more comprehensive theory regarding the nature and consequences of cognitive interference.

CONCLUSION

Research on cognitive interference has shown its debilitating effects in specific domains. The authors have argued for the need to conceptualize the construct of cognitive interference as a personality characteristic that influences thought and behavior across a wide range of situations. Such an approach would direct attention toward diverse developmental experiences and possible links with other features of personality. Further research is needed to delineate the mechanisms by which vulnerability to cognitive interference arises and its consequences in particular task domains.

REFERENCES

Cheek, J. M., & Melchior, L. A. (1990). Shyness, self-esteem, and self-consciousness. In H. Leitenberg (Ed.), *Handbook of social and evaluation anxiety* (pp. 47–84). New York: Plenum.

Clark, J. V., & Arkowitz, H. (1975). Social anxiety and self-evaluation of interpersonal performance. *Psychological Reports, 36*, 211–221.

Coddington, R. D., & Troxell, J. R. (1980). The effect of emotional factors on football injury rates: a pilot study. *Journal of Human Stress, 6*, 3–5.

Communian, A. L. (1993). Anxiety, cognitive interference, and school performance of Italian children. *Psychological Reports, 73*, 747–754.

Dweck, C. S. (1986). Motivational processes affecting learning. *American Psychologist, 41*, 1040–1048.

Emmelkamp, P. M. G., & van Oppen, P. (1994). Anxiety disorders. In V. B. Van Hasselt & M. Hersen (Eds.), *Advanced abnormal psychology* (pp.). New York: Plenum.

Feltz, D. (1988). Self-confidence and sport performance. *Exercise and Sport Sciences Reviews, 16*, 423–457.

Goldfried, M. R., Padawer, W., & Robins, C. (1984). Social anxiety and the semantic structure of heterosocial interactions. *Journal of Abnormal Psychology, 93*, 87–97.

Gould, D., Petlichkoff, L., & Weinberg, R. S. (1984). Antecedents of, temporal changes in, and relationships between CSAI-2 subcomponents. *Journal of Sport Psychology, 6*, 289–304.

Hollandsworth, J. G., Jr., Glazeski, R. C., Kirkland, K., Jones, G. E., & Van Norman, L. R. (1979). An analysis of the nature and effects of test anxiety: Cognitive, behavioral, and physiological components. *Cognitive Therapy and Research, 3*, 165–180.

Holroyd, K. A., Westbrook, T., Wolf, M., & Badhorn, E. (1978). Performance, cognition, and physiological responding in test anxiety. *Journal of Abnormal Psychology, 87*, 442–451.

Hunsley, J. (1987). Internal dialogue during academic examinations. *Cognitive Therapy and Research, 11*, 653–664.

Ishiyama, F. I., & Munson, P. A. (1993). Development and validation of a self-critical cognition scale. *Psychological Reports, 72*, 147–154.

Kendall, P. C., & Ingram, R. E. (1989). Cognitive-behavioral perspectives: Theory and research on depression and anxiety. In P. C. Kendall & D. Watson (Eds.), *Anxiety and depression: Distinctive and overlapping features* (pp. 27–53). San Diego, CA: Academic Press.

Leary, M. R. (1983). *Understanding social anxiety: Social, personality and clinical perspectives*. Beverly Hills, CA: Sage.

Lucock, M. P., & Salkoskis, P. M. (1988). Cognitive factors in social anxiety and its treatments. *Behavioral Research and Therapy, 26*, 297–302.

Martin, J. J., & Gill, D. L. (1991). The relationships among competitive orientation, sport confidence, self-efficacy, anxiety, and performance. *Journal of Sport & Exercise Psychology, 13*, 149–159.

Martens, R., Burton, D., Vealey, R. S., Bump, L. A., & Smith, D. E. (1990). Development and validation of the Competitive State Anxiety Inventory-2. In R. Martens, R. S. Vealey, & D. Burton (Eds.), *Competitive anxiety in sport* (pp. 117–190). Champaign, IL: Human Kinetics.

Monti, P. M., Boice, R., Fingeret, A. L., Zwick, W. R., Kolko, D., Munroe, S., & Grunberger, A. (1984). Midi-level measurement of social anxiety in psychiatric and psychiatric samples. *Behaviour Research and Therapy, 22*, 651–660.

Myszka, M. T., Galassi, J. P., & Ware, W. B. (1986). Comparison of cognitive assessment methods with heterosocially anxious college women. *Journal of Counseling Psychology, 33*, 401–407.

Pierce, G. R., Ptacek, J. T., Henderson, C. A., Joseph, H. J., & Loffredo, C. (1995). *Exploring the transituational nature of cognitive interference*. Manuscript submitted for publication.

Sarason, I. G. (1978). The Test Anxiety Scale: Concept and research. In C. D. Spielberger & I. G. Sarason (Eds.), *Stress and anxiety* (Vol. 5). New York: Halsted.

Sarason, I. G. (1980). Introduction to the study of test anxiety. In I. G. Sarason (Ed.), *Test anxiety: Theory, research, and applications* (pp. 3–14). Hillsdale, NJ: Lawrence Erlbaum Associates.

Sarason, I. G. (1984). Stress, anxiety and cognitive interference: Reactions to tests. *Journal of Personality and Social Psychology, 46*, 929–938.

Sarason, I. G., Sarason, B. R., Keefe, D. E., Hayes, B. E., & Shearin, E. N. (1986). Cognitive interference: Situational determinants and traitlike characteristics. *Journal of Personality and Social Psychology, 31*, 215–226.

Sarason, I. G., Sarason, B. R., & Pierce, G. R. (1990). Anxiety, cognitive interference, and performance. *Journal of Social Behavior and Personality, 5*, 1–18.

Sarason, I. G., & Stoops, R. (1978). Test anxiety and the passage of time. *Journal of Consulting and Clinical Psychology, 46*, 102–109.

Smith, R. E. (1986). A component analysis of athletic stress. In M. R. Weiss & D. Gould (Eds.), *Sport for children and youths* (pp. 107–111). Champaign, IL: Human Kinetics.

Trower, P. (1981). Social skills disorder: Mechanisms of failure. In R. Gilmore & S. Duck (Eds.), *Personal Relationships in Disorder* (pp.). London, England: Academic Press.

Van der Ploeg, H. M. (1982). The relationship of worry and emotionality to performance in Dutch school children. In R. Schwazer, H. M. van der Ploeg, & C. D. Spielberger (Eds.), *Advances in test anxiety research* (Vol. 1, pp. 55–66). Lisse: Swets & Zeitlinger.

Watson, C. G., Kucala, T., Juba, M., Manifold, V., Anderson, P. E. D., & Anderson, D. (1991). A factor analysis of the DSM-III posttraumatic stress disorder criteria. *Journal of Clinical Psychology, 47*, 205–214.

Zatz, S., & Chassin, L. (1983). Cognitions of test-anxious children under naturalistic test-taking conditions. *Journal of Consulting and Clinical Psychology, 53*, 393–401.

PART

III

Cognitive Interference and Clinical Problems

CHAPTER

15

COGNITIVE INTERFERENCE AND COPING STRATEGIES IN VULNERABILITY TO NEGATIVE AFFECT

Mark J. Dombeck
Greg J. Siegle
San Diego State University and University of California, San Diego

Rick E. Ingram
San Diego State University

INTRODUCTION

Kierkegaard, a nineteenth century Danish philosopher, discusses the "Knight of Faith," whose unshakably consistent world view allows him to accept stressors such as negative life events without cognitive distress or other negative consequences. In contrast to the Knight of Faith, Kierkegaard further discusses other character types less well equipped to handle stress who end up depressed (e.g., "infinitely resigned" with a "sickness unto death") or anxious (with "fear and trembling"). Kierkegaard's identification of people's attitudes towards stressors as casual contributors in the formation of mood states has important similarities to contemporary cognitive theory. Seen through the modern lens of Lazarus and Folkman's (1984) idea of coping as the mediator between stress and distress, Kierkegaard's precedent suggests an understanding of euthymic, anxious and depressive states as products of alternative coping strategies for dealing with common stressful occurrences, such as cognitive interference. Cognitive interference, the presence of intrusive, negatively valenced cognitions often concerning themes of danger or failure (Sarason, 1984), is one of a core of cognitive features often present in people who are depressed or anxious (e.g., Ingram, 1990; Clark & Watson, 1991).

The goal of this chapter is to link differential vulnerability to various psychopathologies together with alternate methods of coping with cognitive interference. To achieve this goal the chapter begins by outlining a variety of theoretical assumptions that guide a conceptualization of cognition as it pertains to self-related functioning. These guiding assumptions encompass ideas about how beliefs are cognitively represented, the structure of the self, the impact of life events on self-related functioning, and finally, strategies for coping with the rise of inconsistent beliefs which, it is proposed, engender cognitive interference. These assumptions are brought together to form the basis of a theoretical foundation which has previously been referred to as the "threats to identity framework." Within the context of this approach, cognitive interference and processes for coping with this interference as they apply to vulnerability to psychopathology, are discussed. Specifically, some forms of anxiety, depression, and repression are considered. Finally, directions for future research based on the approach are examined.

THEORETICAL ASSUMPTIONS

To examine the theoretical assumptions that link cognitive interference and vulnerability to psychopathology, several constructs are addressed. These include the representation of beliefs, the idea of how self-related constructs are structured, the impact of stressful life events, and finally proposals concerning coping with the cognitive interference that is engendered by stressful circumstances.

Representation of Beliefs

A model of information processing in which memories and beliefs are considered clusters of nodes (Bower, 1981) in an associative network (Collins & Loftus, 1975) of concepts and descriptive propositions serves as an important theoretical basis for understanding cognitive interference. This associative network model has been used extensively in explaining information processing in both nonemotional (Collins & Loftus, 1975) and emotional (Bower, 1981; Ingram, 1984) domains. For information in the cognitive network to reach awareness, propositional nodes in the network must become activated (see Bower, 1981, and Collins & Loftus, 1975, for descriptions of this activation). Environmental stimuli or internal reflection are hypothesized to begin a process of *spreading activation* in which activation from one node is propagated to other nodes to which it is connected, allowing chains of nodes to become activated sequentially, resulting in the stream of consciousness. For example, beliefs such as "I am worthless" may activate other related concepts such as feelings of sadness (Bower, 1981; Segal & Ingram, 1995).

Theoretical accounts of spreading activation do not typically consider the structure or semantic content of the involved propositions or nodes. While this fact makes spreading activation a very general theory for explaining information processing, it means that implications of specific propositional structures (e.g., beliefs) in the development of psychopathology have largely been ignored in the literature. Ingram and Kendall (1986) argued that the content of propositions is potentially as important as their structure and the processes which serve to activate them. For example, they propose that anxiety and depression may be differentiated to a loose degree on the basis of the content of semantic propositions. In this spirit, a phenomenon which may prove particularly interesting in explaining psychopathology involves the existence within a network of logically contradictory propositions, or beliefs which cannot both be considered true at the same time. For example, the beliefs "I am likable" and "I am unlikable" would seem contradictory if held by the same person. Given inconsistent information of this type it is difficult or impossible to draw firm conclusions from beliefs based on either of these conflicting propositions (Da Costa, Henschen, Lu, & Subrahmanian, 1990). Practically, this means that when propositions underlying beliefs regarding what to do in a given situation are contradictory, no clear course of action may be apparent, potentially resulting in conflicted inaction.[1] Such conflicts may lead to substantial stress in individuals (MacReynolds, 1991). Similarly, researchers such as Ellis (1989, 1991) and Higgins (1987) noted that many individuals report distressing cognitive inconsistencies stemming from conflict between their implicit beliefs that the world should be some way and their perception that it is, in fact, some other way (e.g., "the world should be fair" and also "the world is not being fair to me"). Such implicit beliefs regarding individuals' identification of the way things should be with the way things are become sources of conflict and stress when things are not as they should be.

MacReynolds (1991) and cognitive-dissonance theorists (Aronson, 1992) provide a basis for a theory of cognitive interference, which will be followed in this chapter, by assuming that cognitive inconsistencies cause some degree of upset or stress. Attentional resources may thus be directed towards resolving this incompatibility of propositions, potentially to the detriment of other cognitive processes which also depend on these resources. That is, if there is a finite amount of attention which may be allocated to cognitive tasks at a given time (Broadbent, 1958; Neisser & Becklen, 1975; Triessman, 1964) attention to internal conflict may pre-empt attention usually allocated to other information processing tasks (Siegle, Harrow, Sands, Miller, & Jobe, 1993). Such processes stemming from propositional incompatibilities may constitute cognitive interference. That is, given certain conditions, propositional incompatibility is assumed to be stressful, and if not adequately resolved, leads to acute distress and negative affect. This distress forms the motivational basis for cognitive interference producing processes directed at resolving discrepancies.

---

[1]A great deal of theory regarding the organization of computer databases composed of such linked contingent semantic propositions is devoted to drawing conclusions in situations in which some propositions are inconsistent (e.g., da Costa et al., 1990; Pimentel & Rodi, 1991; Murata, Subrahmanian, & Wakayama, 1991; da Costa & Subrahmanian, 1989). Thus, many of the ideas developed in this chapter have parallels in this literature which this chapter does not afford space to discuss.

Self-Structure

Intuitively, if a person's entire propositional network is not attended to at all times, not all instances of propositional incompatibility are expected to be noticed as soon as they arise. Similarly, if few beliefs in a person's propositional network depend on conflicting beliefs, the conflicting beliefs may be thought of as rather isolated, and not central to the way the person views the world. Thus such isolated conflicted beliefs may not be occasions for distress even if they are noticed. It is therefore suggested that the stressfulness of a given instance of belief incompatibility will be dependent upon the degree to which one or more conflicting propositions is important to the structural integrity of the network, that is, how central the conflicting beliefs are in the person's propositional network. Threats to the validity of such centralized propositions in the network strongly impact relationships among propositions throughout the network, since by definition, the evaluation of many propositions in the network are based on the unambiguous interpretation of more central propositions. Thus, when a centralized proposition is modified (e.g., to alleviate inconsistency), a great deal of the network may be forced to undergo revision to maintain internal consistency.[2]

Because of their unique placement within the network, centralized propositions are in the position to summarize, or be integral to, themes distributed among the many propositions comprising the network. In this context, the term *central* is used to refer to beliefs which are both connected to many other propositions in the network and also integral to one's notion of the self. Centralized propositions may thus act in many ways as "core" beliefs (Beck, 1967, 1976) which, according to some theorists, form the basis for the self-concept (Carver & Scheier, 1990; Rosenberg, 1979). Therefore, to the extent that beliefs about the self tend to be centralized propositions, conflicts involving beliefs about the self will tend to be perceived as stressful and threatening to the integrity of the self-concept, while conflicts among propositions which are more peripheral to the self-concept will tend not to be sources of stress (e.g., James, 1892; Kihlstrom & Cantor, 1984; Markus, 1977).

Impact of Life Events

Collins and Loftus (1975) proposed that initial activation of nodes in the propositional network occurs when the content of propositions are attended to in the environment. Theorists such as Ortony, Collins, and Clore (1988) and Lazarus (1966, 1968, 1982) clarified this notion by suggesting that an *appraisal* process

[2]This chapter intentionally does not discuss how propositions in the network are modified. Theoretical mechanisms governing belief revision have been covered from both psychological (e.g., Evans & Hollon, 1988) and database-theoretic (e.g., Dubois & Prade, 1994; Levy, 1994; Pimentel & Rodi, 1991) perspectives elsewhere.

serves to link environmental stimuli, or life events, to such cognitive structures. Intuitively then, appraisal of life events may also be hypothesized to govern the occasions on which propositional inconsistencies are activated (hence, noticed), and the degree of activation which takes place. For example, by providing or failing to provide an eliciting context, life events may temporarily raise or lower individuals' awareness of existing propositional inconsistencies. That is, until interpersonal interactions occur, latent conflicted beliefs concerning the likability of the self by others may not be noticed. Over time, life events may also cause propositions to become more or less important within the core self-concept. Exposure to life events has been suggested to alter the relative salience (centrality in the current terminology) of certain aspects of depressive schema in formerly depressed individuals' propositional networks (Teasdale, 1988). Accordingly, the experience of a series of failures at initiating interpersonal relationships may act to strengthen a depressive belief that one is not likable and thus should not initiate attempts at forming friendships. The interaction between life events and beliefs may additionally act as a crucible within which belief inconsistancies can be formed or resolved. Experiences such as psychotherapy, education, or religious conversion can encourage belief modification such that preexisting belief conflicts are resolved or preexisting beliefs come into conflict with new beliefs, creating a new propositional conflict. For example, assertiveness training might help instill in a previously socially avoidant individual new beliefs concerning personal worthyness that conflict with older beliefs concerning personal worthlessness.

Strategies for Coping With Inconsistency and the Emergence of Cognitive Interference

As noted earlier, propositional inconsistencies involving beliefs that are core to the self-concept are hypothesized to pose a threat to the internal consistency of the cognitive network. Individuals experiencing such inconsistencies are therefore hypothesized to be likely to perceive them as stressful and threatening, and will thus be motivated to find some way to resolve the situation and restore the internal consistency of the self. The behaviors and mental processes used to resolve conflict can be thought of as attempts at coping. As noted by Lazarus (1993) and Scheier, Weintraub, and Carver (1986), individuals may characteristically, but not exclusively, favor certain strategies and use these strategies more often than other comparable coping strategies; factors such as individual life-event histories, social conditioning, and temperament, all converge to make one coping strategy appear as a path of least resistance (Lazarus, 1993). Many potential strategies exist for coping with propositional inconsistency, each of which may be favored by different individuals. The following discussion suggests links between some of these strategies and creation of vulnerability to various psychopathologies involving negative affect and its avoidance. Figure 15.1 shows

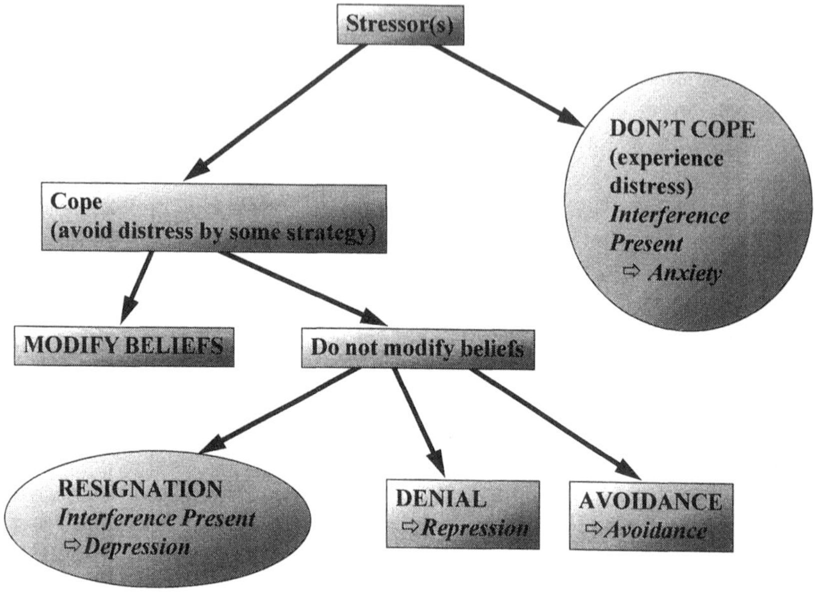

FIG. 15.1. Taxonomy of coping styles.

a taxonomy of these strategies with psychopathologies which could, theoretically, result from their chronic use, and the choices of coping strategies which, it will be suggested, may lead to cognitive interference. Figure 15.1 is intended merely as a taxonomic representation of various forms of coping and not as a diagram of the process by which coping unfolds.

The first level of the taxonomy presents a distinction between situations in which coping occurs and situations in which coping does not occur, and presumably, distress ensues. In this context cognitive interference may be understood as emerging when coping strategies are not employed and hence, attention, which was previously allocated to other tasks, is allocated to anxious contemplation of the discrepancy. Negative thoughts regarding the nature of the inconsistency, and potentially the self for not resolving the inconsistency, may also be present (e.g., as *automatic thoughts*, Beck, 1967, 1976, or *automatic questioning*, Kendall & Ingram, 1989). For example, an individual faced with the decision of whether or not to introduce him or herself to a potential friend, and burdened with simultaneous beliefs regarding his or her likableness and unlikableness, may be indecisive and unable to settle on a path of action. This situation may result in inaction and consequent stress regarding the life situation and the conflicting beliefs (e.g., "I don't know whether I should introduce myself and there's nothing I can do about it"). If, on the other hand, the individual does have the cognitive tools and motivation to alleviate this stress, many different coping strategies, illustrated on lower levels of the taxonomy, may be used. Notably, pure *cope* and *not-coping* reactions represent extreme end points on a continuum of possibilities for dealing with propositional inconsistency in which combinations of coping and not coping may be employed.

The second level of the taxonomy presents the distinction between coping strategies in which beliefs or propositions are modified to resolve cognitive discrepancies, and strategies in which beliefs are preserved, and other methods of avoiding the distress caused by the discrepancies are employed. This distinction is particularly important because strategies in which propositions are modified fundamentally resolve discrepancy and distress. Teasdale and Barnard (1993) suggested that belief modification, used to resolve cognitive discrepancies, is a central mechanism in developmental change, and controls many of the dynamics of information processing. Yet, coping strategies involving belief modification are potentially problematic since, if the beliefs to be modified are at all central to the cognitive network their modification will likely provoke a reorganization of many dependent beliefs in the network. Such network reorganization would itself be expected to be stressful. For this reason some individuals are expected to choose coping strategies that do not require belief modification so as to avoid the stress of network reorganization. Coping strategies which do not modify propositions may moderate, but do not fundamentally resolve, underlying inconsistencies in the network. Thus the integrity of the network may still be disturbed even while the individual is coping, leaving the individual open to potentially chronic distress and vulnerability to psychopathology. Examples of such strategies, illustrated on the third level of the taxonomy, include resignation to the presense of the conflict, denial of the conflict, avoidance of thoughts or actions leading to consideration of the conflict. The examples provided on level 3 of the taxonomy are not meant to be exhaustive, but were chosen for their potential roles in the development of psychopathology.[3]

Each of the capitalized coping strategies depicted in Fig. 15.1 require that the cognitive network undergo certain alterations which may be tolerated to different degrees by different individuals. Individuals are hypothesized to prefer the use of coping strategies requiring cognitive alterations they are best able to tolerate. *Modifying beliefs* necessitates the changing of propositions in the cognitive network so as to preserve true internal consistency. *Resignation* necessitates living with chronic cognitive interference and subsequent distress produced by cognitive inconsistency. *Denial* involves the preservation of an appearance of internal consistency through inaccurate representation of the environment. *Avoidance* involves environmental and cognitive restriction of

[3]Though these strategies are discussed separately in this chapter, they could be used in combination or one after another, depending on the coping individual's tolerances for different strategies and the particular conflict involved. Notably, additional coping strategies such as modification of the outside environment so as to eliminate the eliciting context for activation of the inconsistent propositions (Teasdale & Barnard, 1993) are plausible alternatives but are not explicitly discussed in this chapter.

stimulation which would activate conflicting propositions. The remainder of the chapter is devoted to an investigation of situations in which each of these strategies might be used, and types of psychopathology which may result from their continued use.

VULNERABILITY TO PSYCHOPATHOLOGY

The following section discusses three alternative strategies for coping with propositional inconsistancy. The chronic use of each of these strategies is proposed to contribute to vulnerability to the development of different forms of psychopathology. After a short treatment of the role of propositional inconsistency and consequent cognitive interference in factors leading jointly to anxiety and depression, both propositional inconsistency and consequent cognitive interference specifically with regard to anxiety, depression, and the personality style of repression will be discussed. Coping strategies proposed to promote vulnerability to each form of psychopathology are discussed. As an aid to understanding, a running example is given in which a student, faced with conflicting occupational alternatives, is shown using each coping strategy. In this fictional but realistic example, a young college student is torn between a personal desire to train as an artist and a parental demand to train as an accountant. Propositionally, the student's dilemma is between beliefs that self-actualization (i.e., training as an artist) and parental approval, a result of becoming an accountant, are necessary (for fulfilment), and mutually exclusive posibilities. Finally, conditions which might lead individuals to cope using each particular strategy are considered.

Commonalities Between Cognitive Interference and Propositional Inconsistency in Depression and Anxiety

Ingram and Kendall (1987) proposed that involuntary, predominantly negatively toned, self-focused cognitions are integral to both anxious and depressive disorders. These involuntary cognitions disrupt ongoing cognitive processes and attract attentional resources.

One explanation for this cognitive interference is the hypothesized personality trait known as "negative affectivity," which is characterized by being "distressed and upset" and "being high in feelings of nervousness, tension, and worry" (Watson & Clark, 1984, p. 465). Individuals who develop anxiety and depressive disorders tend to be high in negative affectivity (Watson & Clark, 1984). These observations of similar experiences of cognitive interference and negative affect across anxiety and depressive disorders are consistant with the proposal that the phenomena are common outcomes of employing coping strategies which are incapable of resolving belief inconsistancy (i.e., not belief modification). This follows from the current proposal that people with propositional conflicts respond to a basic distressed and upset state produced by the unresolved state of beliefs core to their thinking and by the allocation of their attention away from other important moment-to-moment tasks. The use of coping strategies which operate without producing fundamental resolution of inconsistent beliefs (e.g., avoidance and resignation), is proposed to prolong the presense of underlying propositional inconsistencies. The presense of these inconsistencies in their cognitions may cause interference with other cognitions, and may leave individuals vulnerable to the development of psychopathology. Similarly, Watson and Clark (1984) found that people high in negative affectivity report high incidence of negative emotional states including unresolved or ambiguous states such as guilt and anger. Such feelings of unresolvedness and ambiguity seem likely consequences of agonizing central inconsistencies, which are not fundamentally resolved by coping strategies involving belief revision.

Anxiety

Anxiety and Interference. In addition to its role in negative affectivity, cognitive interference has long been maintained to be an integral part of anxiety (Sarason, 1985), specifically, anxiety in response to performance evaluation. According to Sarason and Sarason (1981), the evaluative setting is a stressful event calling the individual to attention. In susceptible individuals, preexisting introjected preoccupations may be elicited by this stress (e.g., "I must do well on this test"). These preoccupations produce an increase in intrusive, self-focused, task-irrelevant cognitions and performance deficits (Sarason, 1984; Sarason, Sarason, Keefe, Hayes, & Shearin, 1986). The idea of an introjected preoccupation as a root of cognitive interference fits quite well with the notion that life events elicit latent propositional conflicts which produce cognitive interference.

Many other cognitive theories of anxiety have recognized the role of cognitive interference or similar phenomena in their accounting of anxiety processes (Dombeck & Ingram, 1993). Consistent with the current explanation of anxiety as resulting from upsetting central propositional inconsistencies, many of these models (e.g., Barlow, 1988; Beck & Emery, 1985; Carver & Scheier, 1990, Higgins, 1987) hold that involuntary cognitive interference occurs as a warning signal acting to override ongoing behavior and cognition and focus attention towards aspects of the environment that are perceived as posing a danger to the self. This involuntary warning signal is vital to the operation of anxiety, for without it the reallocation of attention to perceived danger could not be accomplished.

Across many models, anxiety is suggested to occur when beliefs forming the self-concept are conflicted by the implications of life events. For instance, according to the control-process model (Carver & Scheier, 1990) threat and danger are perceived when ongoing goal-driven behavior (e.g., obtaining food) is perceived to have deviated from the aims of hierarchically higher level goals and beliefs (e.g., preserving the self from harm). Anxiety, according to the control-process model, thus stems from belief conflict, with a form of cognitive interference occurring during the process of conflict resolution. A similar explanation of anxiety as stemming from belief conflict occurs in the self-discrepancy model (Higgins, 1987) which holds that anxiety occurs when individuals become aware of a discrepancy between perceptions of their actual qualities and those qualities they expect they ought to possess in order to satisfy others. Such a discrepancy between actual and ought qualities reflects an implied threat to the internal consistency and integrity of the self in that the self has failed to meet its internalized standards. Cognitive interference occurs as this discrepancy is elaborated and punishment is anticipated. In Barlow's (1988) anxious apprehension model, anxiety is produced when discrepancy forms between individuals' appraisals of the demands of actions and their appraisals of their ability to meet these demands. The centrality of low efficacy beliefs in the self-concepts of individuals vulnerable to anxiety may act to form a preexisting latent discrepancy within the self-concept between a belief in lack of ability ("I can't perform this action") and a belief in accountability ("If called upon, I must perform this action"). Cognitive interference will thus occur when such latent discrepancies are activated (e.g., when individuals with such discrepancies make appraisals of their ability to perform the action).

In contrast to the view of anxiety as a response to belief conflict, schema theories of anxiety (e.g., Beck & Emery, 1985) suggest that anxiety occurs in response to belief confirmation. According to Beck and Emery (1985), the cognitive mechanism responsible for anxiety is the anxiety schema; interconnected collections of cognitive propositions concerned with the degree of danger posed by the environment. In cases of pathological anxiety, the information in the anxiety schema is exaggerated and out of proportion to the objective dangers posed by the environment. Pathological anxiety is generated when distorted appraisals of danger confirm erroneously that innocuous situations pose real danger. In response, an anxiety reaction is initiated to force the anxious individual to take immediate steps to deal with the danger.

Avoidance as a Mechanism for Coping With Inconsistency. Clearly, cognitive interference and anxiety are aversive and distressing. The anxious individual's experience of inability to cope with perceived danger and threat may even feed back upon itself, resulting in greater levels of interference and performance deficits and increasing self-focus. In order to minimize the amount of interference and distress they experience, anxiety prone individuals may learn to systematically avoid situations they find threatening (Barlow, 1988). Through the use of avoidance as a coping strategy, the anxious affect and cognitive interference resulting from cognitive propositional discrepancies may be evaded for extended periods of time. The success of an avoidance coping strategy will depend upon the degree to which the conflicting beliefs underlying the anxiety are specific to an avoidable set of circumstances (Higgins, 1987). For example, anxiety concerning public speaking can be avoided by avoidance of situations in which public speaking is a possibility. To the extent that public speaking cannot be avoided, a strategy of avoidance will not be effective.

An avoidance strategy functions by sidestepping existing propositional conflicts as well as closely linked propositions. Individuals may escape from anxiety through the use of an avoidance strategy, but do not in this manner fundamentally resolve or modify the propositional conflict from which they are escaping. Thus, whenever life events occur that elicit the avoided conflict, the strategy of avoidance is temporarily overcome and anxiety occurs. In this manner, the use of an avoidance strategy acts to prolong and solidify vulnerability to the anxious negative affect proposed to occur when coping strategies are unavailable or ineffective. The more dependent an individual becomes on the use of avoidance to cope with anxiety, the more vulnerable the individual is to anxious affect when avoidance cannot be used effectively.

Anxiety as the Student's Response. Conflicted and anxious over the course of study that should be undertaken, the student might attempt to find refuge by avoiding situations that remind him or her of the conflict. While in the short run this strategy might prove quite effective in banishing conflict from the student's mind, relatively insurmountable hurdles such as the approach of semester registration and parental telephone conversations would intrude upon avoidance and likely elicit episodes of painful conflict and anxiety. Due to the time-limited nature of the academic schedule, before long the student would probably be forced into making a choice of some kind and would then need to cope with the consequences of this decision. However, under other circumstances, such as anxiety over dating, or public speaking, avoidance could go on indefinitely, with anxiety being experienced whenever situational constraints conspire to make dating or public speaking unavoidable.

Specific Vulnerability to Anxiety. The four coping strategies shown in Fig. 15.1 each require certain cognitive alterations to occur before they can work effectively. Individuals particularly reluctant to modify their cognitive network in any fashion may use avoidance as their coping strategy of choice since it requires little or no cognitive alteration. Yet, use of an avoidance strategy perpetuates the continued existence of underlying propositional conflict and therefore is proposed to promote vulnerability to continuing anxious affect and distress. With chronic use of avoidance, conflict-driven anxiety may resurface repeatedly in response to unavoidable or unanticipated situations.

Depression

Depression and Interference. Cognitive interference seems to play a broad role in a manner specific to depression, independent of its role in negative affectivity. Considering cognitive interference from the perspective of propositional inconsistency allows the integration of aspects of theories and data that attempt to explain depression. For example, information processing deficits such as slower reaction times to cognitive tasks, and problem solving difficulties are common in people who are depressed (MacLeod & Matthews, 1991). Theorists such as Ellis and Ashbrook (1987) have suggested that these deficits are due to allocation of attention to interferering depressive cognitions and hence lowered attention to the complex information processing tasks at hand. This theory of attentional allocation in depression is consistent with an explanation of cognitive interference as stemming from inconsistent beliefs or propositions; presumably, ongoing failed attempts to deal with underlying conflict could consume cognitive resources. Potentially, rumination on failure associated with such unsuccessful attempts to resolve inconsistent propositions becomes "negative automatic thoughts" (Beck, 1967, 1976). These constant attempts to provide consistent explanation for contradictory information would explain why such negative cognitions seem to be the focus of much rumination (Nolen-Hoeksema & Morrow, 1993) in depression. Similarly, theorists such as Hartlage, Alloy, Vazquez, and Dykman (1993) explained the same deficits by suggesting that usually automatic tasks (taking no attentional resources) become effortful processes in depression and thus, less attentional capacity may be devoted to specific information processing tasks. Propositional inconsistency may be thought of as a factor which disrupts "automatic" spreading activation between propositions when they are in conflict with one another, forcing them to be contemplated in order to be resolved, thereby transforming ordinarily automatic processes into effortful processes.

The link between cognitive interference and inconsistency becomes stronger in cognitive models of depressive information processing which account for negative cognitions in terms of activation spreading through propositional networks (e.g., Bower, 1981; Ingram, 1984). Ingram (1984) hypothesized that maintenance of existing depression occurs by reciprocal spreading activation between negative "emotion nodes" in the cognitive network and semantic propositions to which they are linked. Inconsistency, viewed as a cause of stress, would then have reason to be strongly linked to these negative emotion nodes. Since more central inconsistencies are hypothesized to be attended to a great deal in order to resolve them, Ingram's (1984) reciprocal feedback loop of increasing negative affect is strengthened in proportion to the centrality of inconsistency.

Inconsistency has also been explicitly addressed in literature which attempts to explain the etiology and maintenance of depression. For example, Higgins' (1987) self-discrepancy theory proposed that depression occurs as a reaction to individuals' perception of discrepancy between their actual qualities and their idealized conception of desirable qualities. The importance of discrepancy in cognitive conceptions of depression is also illustrated by Ellis' (1989, 1991) notion of irrational or contradictory thoughts as serving to augment depressive cognitions. More indirectly, researchers such as Greenberg and Alloy (1989) noted that people who are depressed seem to have coexistent positive and negative schemas and posited a role for such seemingly mutually exclusive schemas in the etiology of depression. One explanation for their role is that the conflicting valences of these schemas (e.g., allowing both positive and negative self statements to occur) produces cognitive inconsistently valenced beliefs about the same subjects and hence stress. Finally approaches growing out of the Abramson, Seligman, and Teasdale's (1978) learned helplessness model of depression (e.g., Abramson, Metalsky, & Alloy, 1989) are founded on the premise that depression is a learned response to an individual's perception of helplessness to make the outside world conform to internal standards. The proposed discrepancy between internal expectations and their presumed failure to be attained in the outside world may be thought of as creating inconsistencies between beliefs about the the way the world should and does work, and thus may indirectly contribute to maintenance of depression.

Resignation as a Mechanism for Coping With Inconsistency

Each of the descriptions of the relationship between depression and inconsistency described earlier presupposes that when propositions are inconsistent, they are not immediately resolved by modifying belief systems (otherwise, depression would not be prolonged). Potentially then, another method of coping is used which preserves inconsistencies but does not cause a great amount of anxiety. This coping style could be characterized by acceptance of the propositions as inconsistent and thus not necessitate anxious worrying, but instead, create a resignation to the constant internal turmoil of non-integration of self-structure. This proposed coping-by-resignation would occur through the development of a sense of resignation or helplessness to resolve discrepancy. Resignation would thus serve to normalize the experience of discrepancy and to discourage further energy-expending attempts at coping. While such a strategy of resignation cannot resolve discrepancy or eliminate distress it can potentially serve to blunt the acuteness and intensity of experienced negative affect.

Another aspect of depression explained by resignation is its prolonged ruminative character. Conflicting propositions are proposed to be ruminated upon passively in depression, creating stress. Listless reiteration of the same unworkable arguments and chastisement of the self may ensue. Attention is implicitly allocated to the contradiction, but due to inability to equitably resolve the contradictory propositions the cognitive network is not changed as a result. Such a ruminative coping style is discussed by Nolen-Hoeksema and Morrow (1993) as being particularly detrimental to recovery from depression. They suggested that distraction from such rumination (in the current terminology, lessening attentional focus on the contradictory propositions) may actually serve to alleviate depressive resignation and consequent cognitive interference, at least in the short run.

Depression as the Student's Response. The student, torn between the beliefs that he or she must pursue art yet that parents must be obeyed, could respond to the dilemma by resignation to the sad situation that he or she will not be able to accomplish all of his or her goals. One option or the other may be chosen, but neither solution will be satisfactory; knowledge that "I have failed in my goals," precisely because they are contradictory, will continue to haunt the student. This resignation may breed contingent negative thoughts in the student about self-worth (e.g., "I am worthless if I cannot accomplish my goals") and the student may, before long, sink deeper and deeper into the ruminative morass of depression. Attention will continue to be allocated to the inconsistency because it is not resolved, but resignation will prevent the student from experiencing profound anxiety at the situation.

Specific Vulnerability to Depression. Resignation might be chosen as a coping strategy of choice when conflicting propositions are so central that any modification of the cognitive network is intolerable, and so global/independent of situational context that the eliciting situations cannot be avoided, for example, the triad of negative self-worth, negative evaluation of the world, and dim prospects for the future (Beck, 1967) frequently found in depressed people. Learned hopeless reactions to negative situations (Abramson, Metalsky, & Alloy, 1989), also observed in people who are depressed, could breed such a resistance to cognitive modification, and passive resignation. Resignation is thus seen as a method to dull the intense pangs of ever-present cognitive interference.

Similarly, Carver and Scheier (1981) suggested that when the subjective probability of a successfully resolving cognitive discrepancies between the perceived self and an internal standard for the self is low, the discrepancy resolution process is abandoned, leading to alternative coping strategies such as resignation. They further suggested that such an abandonment avoids negative cognitive interference caused by hopeless pursuit of an apparently unreachable goal.

Repression

Repression and Cognitive Interference. Repression is the name given to one polar extreme of a bipolar dimension of personality describing a continuum of coping with threatening or disturbing information, termed repression-sensitization (Byrne, 1961; Weinberger, 1990). The term *sensitizer* has historically been used to describe individuals predisposed to anxiety. As the name suggests, sensitizers are sensitive to threatening information and prone to cognitive interference and anxious affect. Repression, the polar opposite of sensitization, refers to individuals characterized by a lack of cognitive interference and a propensity to deny anxious symptomatology. Repression thus appears to function as a strategy for avoiding or ignoring the cognitive implications of potentially anxiety or depression formenting information.

Importantly, repressors are not simply nonanxious individuals. In comparison to normal nonanxious individuals, repressors admit to less flexibility (Sincoff, 1992) and spontaneity (Weinberger, 1990) in their thinking and are measurably more uncomfortable and cognitively inefficient in situations where negative emotion is unavoidable (Davis, 1987; Davis & Schwartz, 1987; Hansen & Hansen, 1988; Hansen, Hansen, & Shantz, 1992; Neilson & Fleck, 1981; Ward, Leventhal, & Love, 1988). Repressors describe themselves as valuing internal consistency and prizing their ability to avoid becoming upset by life stressors (Weinberger, Schwartz, & Davidson, 1979). Despite having been shown to have elevated physiological indices of anxiety similar to those characteristic of anxious individuals, repressors characteristically deny experiencing anxious symptomatology (Newton & Contrada, 1992; Weinberger, Schwartz, & Davidson, 1979). Rather than being non-anxious individuals, repressors appear to share in common with highly anxious individuals a preoccupation with negative affect (Weinberger, 1990).

These findings suggest that repression may involve a mechanism or series of mechanisms that function to inhibit repressors' awareness of inconsistencies within cognitive processes. Repressors thus may not explicitly experience cognitive interference or distress in that they appear to habitually avoid examination of their propositions for signs of inconsistency. This mechanism may involve repressors having a disposition to focus their attention externally to the environment (e.g., Baumeister & Cairns, 1992). In support of this hypothesis, some research suggests that repressors perform better on complex attentionally demanding tasks than nonrepressors (Bonanno, Davis, Singer, & Schwartz, 1991; Dombeck, 1994). This attentional effect appears to be facilitated when repressors are placed in evaluative situations (e.g., Newton & Contrada, 1992).

Repression as a Mechanism for Coping With Inconsistency. Accumulated evidence from the study of repression suggests that repressors use a strategy of denial and self-deception in order to cope with stressful internal cognitive conflict. In essence, repressors may only infrequently or never become cognitively aware of one or more conflicted propositions. Such repressed or denied propositions will likely remain implicit or latent a great percentage of the time. In their implicit or latent state, these propositions do not impact the functioning of the cognitive system and will not contribute to the formation of distress. Potentially, conflicted propositions may be elicited and result in physiological arousal and anxiety. Although repressors will acknowledge becoming anxious, they will tend to describe their anxiety in purely affective and physiological terms, maintaining their cognitive distance from the event (Weinberger, Schwartz, & Davidson, 1979). Even though denial of awareness of the existence of conflict does not eliminate actual structural conflict, it does functionally remove conflicting propositions from the cognitive system and in so doing, returns the cognitive system to the appearance of internal consistency. As far as the repressor is concerned there is no inconsistency and no reason to become aroused.

Denial as the Student's Response. Provided the student is cognitively inclined to repression, he or she might cope with the conflict over career direction by failing to recognize that a conflict exists. More specifically, the student might consistently fail to attend to his or her own feelings concerning art, or to feelings concerning letting parents down. By denying the importance of one or more propositions involved in the conflict, (for instance, a denial that art is his or her preferred career, or a denial that he or she dislikes accounting) the student manages to avoid the cognitive aspects of this conflict (e.g., cognitive interference, distress, etc.). At a more purely physiological and emotional level, mere inability to recognize affect does not make it any less real. Thus, the student's conflict may express itself behaviorally (e.g., through elevations in arousal level) even while it is not expressed on a cognitive level. The student might agree to train as an accountant and never end up acknowledging that it was not, on an affective level, the choice he or she wanted to make. Theoretically, the student could sustain such a strategy of repression indefinitely.

Specific Vulnerability to Repression. It is proposed that individuals use denial as a strategy for coping with propositional inconsistencies when they are unwilling or unable to tolerate propositional change but have little difficulty tolerating inaccurate representation of themselves and their environment. Part of this latter ability to tolerate inaccurate representation may involve cognitive features specific to a particular repressive personality style (Bonanno & Singer, 1990; Weinberger, 1990).

Summary

The preceding review suggests that several ideas are relatively constant across a variety of literatures concerned with negative affect and its avoidance. Literature concerning anxiety and depression highlights cognitive interference as an important factor in the experience of negative affect. Given the presence of cognitive interference, the type and character of experienced negative affect appears to involve the attitudes and modes of coping taken by individuals towards salient conflict. It has been proposed that attitudes of resignation, failure and hopelessness underlie depression while attitudes of acute desire for avoidance of danger are associated with anxiety. If, because of personality-based cognitive and behavioral dispositions, individuals are able to either integrate or deny awareness of cognitive discrepancies, it appears that cognitive interference and negative affect are evaded.

Some of the coping strategies just described may appear to be more desirable than others, perhaps because they more fundamentally resolve propositional inconsistency than do other strategies, resulting in less overall distress. For example, the denial of propositional inconsistency preserves the fundamental underlying inconsistency, while belief modification involves its resolution. Assuming they are successful, however, both coping strategies will result in the cessation of threats to identity.

A THREATS-TO-IDENTITY APPROACH

As previous discussion indicates, the identification of propositional inconsistency with the emergence of cognitive interference, and the assumption that different coping strategies essentially offer alternative means for reorganizing relationships among propositions provide a means to understand what predisposes different individuals to develop different psychopathologies in response to similar stressors. The collection of working assumptions, strategies for coping with inconsistency/interference, and the resultant conception of vulnerability to psychopathology presented in this chapter is termed the "threats-to-identity framework" (TIF; Dombeck, 1994), to reflect the role of propositional consistency in preserving the identity of the self. Inconsistent beliefs, as discussed above, are hypothesized to threaten the structural integrity of the cognitive semantic network, presumably the location of one's conception of his or her identity or self. When the network's structural integrity is threatened (as in propositional inconsistancy), basic beliefs and convictions are pitted against one another. An individual in such a situation is left without an unambiguous set of basic convictions or beliefs on which to act and thus may be unable to act using rational, reasoned, principles. Strategies for coping with such inconsistencies are then seen as efforts at repairing the structural integrity of the self, so as to leave one with an unambiguous identity. Yet, as has been discussed, such strategies may often lead to vulnerability to psychopathology.

The assumptions underlying the TIF, taken from the discussion above, are as follows. Using Collins and Loftus' (1975) spreading activation model, beliefs are assumed to be represented in a semantic network as propositions. Attention to environmental or internally generated stimuli activate such propositions. Activation then spreads in a rapidly decaying manner among propositions, activating other semantically related propositions with some strength. Inconsistency among propositions is hypothesized to be occasion for cognitive interference, as the individual's ability to produce reasoned and emotionally consistant conclusions given inconsistent beliefs is impaired, serving as a source of stress. The relative importance of the inconsistent propositions to the structural integrity of the semantic network governs the magnitude of stress generated by the inconsistency. If the resultant stress is of sufficient magnitude, coping is assumed to ensue. Coping may take many forms, including modification of inconsistent propositions, avoidance of situations which activate the inconsistent propositions, resignation to hopeless resolution of the inconsistency, denial of the inconsistency, etc. Of the strategies examined in this chapter, only belief modification is assumed to fundamentally alleviate the underlying inconsistency, thus eliminating cognitive interference generated by that inconsistancy. However, other forms of coping may reduce or stall the emergent cognitive interference. To the extent that they are unable to provide lasting relief from cognitive interference, coping strategies are posited to lead to vulnerability to various psychopathologies including anxiety, depression, and repression. Cognitive interference is preserved to some extent in anxiety and depression because of the focus on the underlying inconsistent beliefs. It is alleviated in repression because inconsistencies cease to be a focus of attention.

The TIF is thus an approach to explaining vulnerability to some forms of psychopathology involving negative affect as resulting from chronic reliance on particular strategies for coping with cognitive interference. The framework is intended to provide an integration of factors common to some forms of anxiety, depression, and repression which will be useful in future research and therapeutic practice. Hopefully, the TIF will be useful in conceiving of these psychopathologies as related, and moreover, will aid clinical conceptualization of individual cases of psychopathology, and allow clinicians to recognize early factors predisposing clients to one psychopathology or another.

FUTURE DIRECTIONS FOR RESEARCH

If strategies for coping with inconsistency help to determine vulnerability to negative affect, it is important to understand the factors that influence individuals' choice of coping strategies. While the strategies hypothesized in this chapter to lead to anxiety and to depression have already been the subject of much empirical work, the strategies hypothesized to lead to more successful discrepancy resolutions are less well understood. In this final portion of the chapter three major areas that require further attention if cognitive interference and discrepancy reduction are to be more fully understood, are presented.

Empirical Validation of the TIF

Given that a threats-to-identity framework has been employed for conceptualizing cognitive interference and vulnerability to psychopathology, an important direction for future research is to provide empirical support to this framework, and to further clarify its clinical and theoretical implications. Results from preliminary research have provided empirical support for the existence of self-concept integration as a factor that may contribute to vulnerability to depression and anxiety (Dombeck, 1993, 1994; McLaughlin & Bernet, 1994; McKellar, 1994; Siegle, 1994). These studies involve the use of a self-report form called the Threats to Identity Questionnaire (TIQ; Bernet & Dombeck, 1994; Dombeck, 1993), a factor analytically derived measure assessing facets of self-concept integration. The TIQ is comprised of three subscales measuring factors hypothesized to covary with poorly integrated self-structures; Fear of Emotion, Identity Fragmentation and Lack of Confidence in Coping, with higher scores on these scales indicating greater levels of the named factors. An omnibus TIQ score, reflecting the overall elevation of the three TIQ factors has been shown to covary with negative affectivity and with measures of anxiety and depression. Despite this correlation, however, self-structure integration, as measured by the omnibus TIQ, exists independently of anxiety. In one study highly anxious subjects, scoring both high and low on the omnibus TIQ scale, were asked to rate adjectives as to the degree the words described their idealized and actual selves. Although all subjects were highly anxious, high TIQ scoring subjects produced larger ideal-actual discrepancies than low-TIQ scoring subjects (Bernet & Dombeck, 1994; Dombeck, Ingram, Gray, Jeffers, & Jorgensen, 1994).

Further research is needed to validate a number of assumptions of the TIF. For instance, the amount of stress associated with central versus peripheral propositional inconsistencies should be explicitly measured. Correlations between the presence of centralized inconsistencies and the presence of psychopathology should be examined. Along this line, studies are planned to examine the TIQ's ability to longitudinally predict psychopathology, in accordance with the TIF's hypothesized link between discrepant self-beliefs and vulnerability to psychopathology. Empirical study will also prove useful in determining the validity of the TIF's proposed linkage between specific forms of coping and specific forms of psychopathology (or lack of psychopathology, e.g., the hypothesis that belief modification, as described in the TIF, should be associated with a lack of psychopathology).

Self-Structure Organization

Also in need of further study are the factors governing individuals' choice of coping strategies. Reconciling inconsistent beliefs by modifying some or all of those beliefs permanently resolves conflict among beliefs whereas the other coping strategies mentioned thus far do not share this property. Although belief modification would appear to be the most effective and permanent strategy discussed, its cost, in terms of the amount of cognitive change it requires in order to produce relief from cognitive interference, may bias individuals with highly inconsistant beliefs towards choosing alternative strategies. Although the idea that the structure of self has ramifications for cognitive flexibility and rigidity is not new (e.g., Erickson, 1959; Horowitz, 1991; Kegan, 1982; Marcia, 1980), few empirical studies have been conducted in this area. Thus, an empirical investigation of self-structure organization as a mediator of the relationship among stressors, choice of coping strategies, and experienced cognitive interference is in order.

Default Focus of Attention

As noted earlier, some individuals may cope with cognitive inconsistencies by denying inconsistent propositions central to their self-concept. This denial would involve sustained aversion of attention (cognitive avoidance) from the inconsistent propositions or beliefs (e.g., towards other stimuli in the attentional field). For this reason it is proposed that individuals using a denial strategy may be predisposed to an external focus of attention while people who do not choose denial as their coping strategy of choice are not similarly predisposed. Thus, premorbid predisposition to an external or internal focus of attention may guide individuals towards or dissuade them from choosing a coping strategy involving denial, which might require such an external focus of attention. Repressors have been noted to be sensitive to social appearances and to lack awareness of their internal processes (Weinberger, 1990). They thereby appear to be predisposed to an external, environmental focus of attention. Contrasted with the repressor, anxious and depressed individuals are known to experience internally oriented, self-focused cognitive interference. These individuals may thus be predisposed to attend internally, making it difficult for them to sustain cognitive avoidance of propositional inconsistency. Empirical investigation of factors underlying attentional disposition and the role they play in fostering choice of coping strategies may facilitate understanding of the mechanisms underlying successful instances of repression and affect avoidance.

CONCLUSIONS

The central aspect of the theoretical ideas presented here are their provision of a framework for conceptualizing anxiety, depression, repression and more adaptive belief modification. Much work has previously discussed the common and unique features of anxiety and depression (Watson & Kendall, 1989). Additionally, the conception of repression-sensitization implies a connection between repression and anxiety. Yet, these phenomena have not previously been conceptualized as representing variations on the common theme of approaches to the resolution of salient cognitive discrepancy and corresponding cognitive interference. In the threats-to-identity framework, anxiety, depression, and repression represent alternative possible outcomes of cognitive inconsistency. Thus, these ideas account for many methods of coping with a single stressor and differential outcomes of these strategies. Coping strategies that prevent cognitive interference from occurring (i.e., tolerance of flexible belief modification and tolerance of invalid representation of experience) produce positive outcomes, inasmuch as negative affect does not occur. Coping strategies providing only temporary or partial relief from cognitive interference (resignation to inconsistency and avoidance of situationally triggered dissonance) produce the "negative" outcome of leaving individuals vulnerable to painful negative affect of varying tones. Discussion of factors governing when vulnerability to psychopathology actually leads to psychopathology are beyond the scope of this chapter.

The threats-to-identity framework hypothesizes an active etiological role of cognitive interference in the formation of psychopathology. Specifically, it proposes that cognitive interference can occur as the result of inconsistent beliefs, and that strategies for eliminating the interference without resolving the beliefs may lead to psychopathology. To the extent that these ideas provide an accurate accounting of vulnerability, a shift is indicated from a research focus on cognitive interference itself to a focus on factors proposed to determine the expression of cognitive interference, such as the structure of self, and dispositional attentional focus. The results of this research will hopefully produce an expanded understanding of cognitive interference, a more fine-grained understanding of vulnerability processes, and a clinically useful framework for conceptulizing the evaluation and treatment of depression, anxiety, and repression.

REFERENCES

Abramson, L. Seligman, M., & Teasdale, J. (1978). Learned helplessness in humans: Critique and reformulation. *Journal of Abnormal Psychology, 87*, 40–47.

Abramson, L. Y., Metalsky, G. I., & Alloy, L. B. (1989). Hopelessness depression: A theory-based subtype of depression. *Psychological Review, 96*, 358–372.

Aronson, E. (1992). The return of the repressed: Dissonance theory makes a comeback. *Psychological Inquiry, 3*(4), 303–311.

Barlow, D. H. (1988). *Anxiety and its disorders: The nature and treatment of anxiety and panic.* New York: Guilford.

Baumeister, R. F., & Cairns, K. J. (1992). Repression and self-presentation: When audiences interfere with self-deceptive strategies. *Journal of Personality and Social Psychology, 62*, 851–862.

Beck, A. T. (1967). *Depression: Clinical, experimental and theoretical aspects.* New York: Harper & Row.

Beck, A. T. (1976). *Cognitive therapy and the emotional disorders.* New York: International Universities Press.

Beck, A. T., & Emery, G. (1985). *Anxiety disorders and phobias: A cognitive perspective.* New York: Basic Books.

Bernet, C., & Dombeck, M. (1994). Measurement of self-structure integration: the Threats to Identity Questionnaire. In M. Dombeck (Chair), *Self structure and vulnerability to psychopathology.* Symposium conducted at the meeting of the Rocky Mountain Psychological Association, Las Vegas.

Bonanno, G. A., Davis, P. J., Singer, J. L., & Schwartz, G. E. (1991). The repressor personality and avoident information processing: A dichotic listening study. *Journal of Research in Personality, 25*, 386–401.

Bonanno, G. A., & Singer, J. L. (1990). Repressive personality style: Theoretical and methodological implications for health and pathology. In J. L. Singer (Ed.), *Repression and dissociation* (pp. 435–470). Chicago: University of Chicago Press.

Bower, G. (1981). Mood and memory. *American Psychologist, 36*, 129–148.

Broadbent, D. E. (1958). *Perception and communication*. New York: Pergamon.

Byrne, D. (1961). The repression-sensitization scale: Rationale, reliability and validity. *Journal of Personality, 29*, 334–349.

Carver, C. S., & Scheier, M. F. (1981). *Attention and self-regulation: A control theory approach to human behavior*. New York: Springer Verlag.

Carver, C. S., & Scheier, M. F. (1990). Origins and functions of positive and negative affect: A control process view. *Psychological Review, 97*, 19–35.

Clark, L. A., & Watson, D. (1991). Tripartite model of anxiety and depression: Psychometric evidence and taxonomic implications. *Journal of Abnormal Psychology, 100*, 316–336.

Collins, A., & Loftus, E. (1975). A spreading-activation theory of semantic processing, *Psychological Review, 82*, 407–428.

da Costa, N. C. A., Henschen, L. J., Lu, J. J., & Subrahmanian, V. S. (1990). Automatic theorem proving in paraconsistent logics: Theory and implementation. In M. E. Stickel (Ed.), *10th International Conference on Automated Deduction Proceedings* (pp. 72–86). Berlin: Springer-Verlag.

da Costa, N. C. A., & Subrahmanian, V. S. (1989). Paraconsistent logics as a formalism for reasoning about inconsistent knowledge bases. *Artificial Intelligence in Medicine, 1*(4), 167–174.

Davis, P. J. (1987). Repression and the inaccessibility of affective memory. *Journal of Personality and Social Psychology, 53*, 585–593.

Davis, P. J., & Schwartz, G. E. (1987). Repression and the inaccessibility of affective memories. *Journal of Personality and Social Psychology, 52*, 155–162.

Dombeck, M. J. (1993). *Development and validation of the Threats to Identity Questionnaire: A means to study the relationship between self-structure and vulnerability to psychopathology*. Unpublished doctoral dissertation proposal, San Diego State University, University of San Diego, California, Joint Doctoral Program in Clinical Psychology.

Dombeck, M. J. (1994). *Self-structure integration: A vulnerability factor for negative affect*. In M. J. Dombeck (Chair), Self-structure integration and vulnerability to negative affect. Symposium conducted at the meeting of the Rocky Mountain Psychological Association, Las Vegas.

Dombeck, M. J., & Ingram, R. E. (1993). Cognitive conceptions of anxiety. In P. Kendall & K. Dobson (Eds.), *Psychopathology and cognition* (pp. 53–81). San Diego: Academic Press.

Dombeck, M. J., Ingram, R. E., Gray, J. A., Jeffers, M., & Jorgensen, K. W. (1994). *Self-structure mediates anxiety coping style*. Paper presented at the annual convention of the American Psychological Association, Los Angeles.

Dubois, D., & Prade, H. (1994) A survey of belief revision and updating rules in various uncertainty models. *International Journal of Intelligent Systems, 9*(1), 61–100.

Ellis, A. (1991). Suggestibility, irrational beliefs, and emotional disturbance. In J. F. Schumaker (Ed.), *Human suggestibility: Advances in theory, research, and application* (pp. 309–325). New York: Routledge.

Ellis, A. (1989). Rational-emotive therapy. In R. J. Corsini & D. Wedding (Eds.), *Current psychotherapies* (4th ed., pp. 197–238). Itasca, IL: Peacock.

Ellis, H. C., & Ashbrook, P. W. (1987). Resource allocation model of the effects of depressed mood states on memory. In K. Fiedler & J. Forgas (Eds.), *Affects, cognition and social behaviour*. Toronto: Hogrefe.

Erickson, E. H. (1959). Identity and the life cycle. *Psychological Issues Monograph Series. 1*. New York: International Universities Press.

Evans, M. D., & Hollon, S. D. (1988). Patterns of personal and causal inference: Implications for the cognitive therapy of depression. In L. B. Alloy (Ed.), *Cognitive processes in depression* (pp. 344–377). New York: Guilford.

Goodwin, F. K., & Jameson, K. R. (1990). *Manic depressive illness.* New York: Oxford University Press.

Greenberg, M., & Alloy, L. (1989). Depression and anxiety: Processing of self- and other-referent information. *Cognition and Emotion, 3,* 207–223.

Hansen, R. D., & Hansen, C. H. (1988). Repression of emotionally tagged memories: The architecture of less complex emotions. *Journal of Personality and Social Psychology, 55,* 811–818.

Hansen, C. H., Hansen, R. D., & Shantz, D. W. (1992). Repression at encoding: Discrete appraisals of emotional stimuli. *Journal of Personality and Social Psychology, 63,* 1026–1035.

Hartlage, S., Alloy, L., Vazquez, C., & Dykman, B. (1993). Automatic and effortful processing in depression. *Psychological Bulletin, 413*(2), 247–278.

Higgins, E. T. (1987). Self-discrepancy: A theory relating self and affect. *Psychological Review, 94,* 319–340.

Horowitz, M. J. (1991). Person schemas. In M. J. Horowitz (Ed.), *Person schemas and maladaptive interpersonal patterns* (pp. 13–31). Chicago: University of Chicago Press.

Ingram, R. (1984). Towards an information processing analysis of depression, *Cognitive Therapy and Research, 8,* 443–478.

Ingram, R. (1990). Self-focused attention in clinical disorders: Review and a conceptual model, *Psychological Bulletin, 107,* 156–176.

Ingram, R. E., & Kendall, P. C. (1986). Cognitive clinical psychology: Implications of an information processing perspective. in R. Ingram (Ed.), *Information processing approaches to clinical psychology* (pp. 3–21). San Diego: Academic Press.

Ingram, R. E., & Kendall, P. C. (1987). The cognitive side of anxiety. *Cognitive Therapy and Research, 11,* 523–536.

James, W. (1908). *Psychology: The briefer course,* London, England: Macmillan.

Kegan, R. (1982). *The evolving self.* Cambridge, MA: Harvard University Press.

Kendall, P. C., & Ingram, R. E. (1987). The future for cognitive assessment of anxiety: Let's get specific. In L. Michelson & L. M. Ascher (Eds.), *Anxiety and stress disorders: Cognitive-behavioral assessment and treatment* (pp. 89–104). New York: Guilford.

Kendall, P. C., & Ingram, R. E. (1989). Cognitive behavioral perspectives: Theory and research on depression and anxiety. In P. C. Kendall & D. Watson (Eds.), *Anxiety and depression: Distinctive and overlapping features* (pp. 27–53). San Diego: Academic Press.

Kierkegaard, S. (1954). *Fear and trembling.* Garden City, NY: Doubleday.

Kihlstrom, J. F., & Cantor, N. (1984). Mental representations of the self. In L. Berkowitz (Ed.), *Advances in experimental social psychology* (Vol 15, pp. 1–47). New York: Academic Press.

Lazarus, R. S. (1966). *Psychological stress and the coping process.* New York: McGraw-Hill.

Lazarus, R. S. (1968). Emotions and adaptation: Conceptual and empirical relations. In W. J. Arnold (Ed.), *Nebraska symposium on motivation,* (pp. 175–266). Lincoln: University of Nebraska Press.

Lazarus, R. S. (1982). Thoughts on the relations between emotion and cognition. *American Psychologist, 37,* 1019–1024.

Lazarus, R. S. (1993). Coping theory and research: Past, present, and future. *Psychosomatic Medicine, 55*(3), 234–247.

Lazarus, R. S., & Folkman, S. (1984). *Stress, appraisal, and coping.* New York: Springer.

Levy, F. (1994). A survey of belief revision and updating in classical logic. *International Journal of Intelligent Systems, 9*(1), 29–59.

MacLeod, C., & Mathews, A. M. (1991) Cognitive-experimental approaches to the emotional disorders. In P. R. Martin (Ed.), *Handbook of behavior therapy and psychological science: An integrative approach* (Vol. 164, pp. 116–150). New York: Pergamon.

MacReynolds, P. (1991). The nature and logic of intrapsychic conflicts. In C. D. Spielberger, I. G. Sarason, J. Strelau, & J. Brebner (Eds.), *Stress and anxiety* (Vol. 13, pp. 73–83). Washington, DC: Hemisphere.

Marcia, J. E. (1980). Identity in adolescence. In J. Adelson (Ed.), *Handbook of adolescent psychology* (pp. 159–187). New York: Wiley.

Markus, H. (1977). Self-schemata and processing information about the self. *Journal of Personality and Social Psychology, 35*, 63–78.

McKellar, J. (1994). Self focussed attention and self-structure. In M. Dombeck (Chair), *Self structure and vulnerability to psychopathology*. Symposium conducted at the meeting of the Rocky Mountain Psychological Association, Las Vegas.

McLaughlin, S., & Bernet, C. (1994). Self-structure in a sample of sexually and physically abused college students. In M. Dombeck (Chair), *Self structure and vulnerability to psychopathology*. Symposium conducted at the meeting of the Rocky Mountain Psychological Association, Las Vegas.

Murata, T., Subrahmanian, V. S., & Wakayama, T. (1991). A Petri net model for reasoning in the presence of inconsistency. *IEEE Transactions on Knowledge and Data Engineering, 3*, 281–292.

Newton, T. L., & Contrada, R. J. (1992). Repressive coping and verbal-autonomic response dissociation: The influence of social context. *Journal of Personality and Social Psychology, 62*, 159–167.

Nielsen, L. E., & Fleck, J. R. (1981). Defensive repressors and empathic impairment. *Psychological Reports, 48*, 615–624.

Neisser, U., & Becklen, R. (1975). Selective looking: Attending to visually specified events. *Cognitive Psychology, 7*, 480–494.

Nolen-Hoeksema, S., & Morrow, J. (1993). Effects of rumination and distraction on naturally occurring depressed mood. *Cognition and Emotion, 7*, 561–570.

Ortony, A., Clore, G., & Collins, A. (1988). *The cognitive structure of emotions*. Cambridge, England: Cambridge University Press.

Pimentel, S. G., & Rodi, W. L. (1991) Belief revision and paraconsistency in a logic programming framework. In A. Nerode, W. Marek, & V. S. Subrahmanian (Eds.), *Logic Programming and Non-Monotonic Reasoning. Proceedings of the First International Workshop* (pp. 228–242). Cambridge, MA: MIT Press.

Rosenberg, M. (1979). *Conceiving the self*. New York: Basic Books.

Sarason, I. G. (1984). Stress, anxiety, and cognitive interference: Reactions to tests. *Journal of Personality and Social Psychology, 46*, 929–938.

Sarason, I. G. (1985). Cognitive processes, anxiety and the treatment of anxiety disorders. In A. H. Tuma & J. Maser (Eds.), *Anxiety and the anxiety disorders* (pp. 87–107) Hillsdale, NJ: Lawrence Erlbaum Associates.

Sarason, I. G., & Sarason, B. R. (1981). The importance of cognition and moderator variables in stress. In D. Magnusson (Ed.), *Towards a psychology of situations: An interactional perspective* (pp. 195–210). Hillsdale, NJ: Lawrence Erlbaum Associates.

Sarason, I. G., Sarason, B. R., Keefe, D. E., Hayes, B. E., & Shearin, E. N. (1986). Cognitive interference: Situational determinants and traitlike characteristics. *Journal of Personality and Social Psychology, 51*, 215–226.

Scheier, M. F., Weintraub, J. K., & Carver, C. S. (1986) Coping with stress: Divergent strategies of optimists and pessimists. *Journal of Personality and Social Psychology, 51*, 1257–1264.

Segal, Z. V., & Ingram, R. E. (1995). Mood priming and construct activation in tests of cognitive vulnerability to depression. *Clinical Psychology Review, 14*, 663–695.

Siegle, G., Harrow, M., Sands, J., Miller, A., & Jobe, T. (1993). *Does stimulus difficulty play a role in thought pathology: Schizophrenics vs. depressives*. Poster presented at the annual meeting of the Society for Research in Psychopathology, Chicago.

Siegle, G. (1994). Integration of self as a modulator for depressive rumination. In M. Dombeck (Chair), *Self structure and vulnerability to psychopathology*. Symposium conducted at the meeting of the Rocky Mountain Psychological Association, Las Vegas.

Sincoff, J. B. (1992). Ambivalence and defense: Effects of a repressive style on normal adolescents' and young adults' mixed feelings. *Journal of Abnormal Psychology, 101*, 251–256.

Teasdale, J. (1988). Cognitive vulnerability to persistent depression, *Cognition and Emotion, 2*, 247–274,

Teasdale, J., & Barnard, P. (1993). *Affect, cognition, and change: Remodelling depressive thought*, Hillsdale, NJ: Lawrence Erlbaum Associates.

Triessman, A. M. (1964). Selective attention in man. *British Medical Bulletin, 20*, 12–16.

Ward, S. E., Leventhal, H., & Love, R. (1988). Repression revisited: Tactics used in coping with a severe health threat. *Personality and Social Psychology Bulletin, 14*, 735–746.

Watson, D., & Clark, L. A. (1984). Negative affectivity: The disposition to experience aversive emotional states. *Psychological Bulletin, 96*, 465–490.

Watson, D., & Kendall, P. C. (1989). Understanding anxiety and depression: Their relation to negative and positive affective states. In P. C. Kendall & D. Watson (Eds.), *Anxiety and depression: Distinctive and overlapping features. Personality, psychopathology, and psychotherapy* (pp. 3–26). San Diego: Academic Press.

Weinberger, D. A. (1990). The construct validity of the repressive coping style. In J. L. Singer (Ed.), *Repression and dissociation* (pp. 337–386). Chicago: University of Chicago Press.

Weinberger, D. A., Schwartz, G. E., & Davidson, R. J. (1979). Low-anxious, high-anxious, and repressive coping styles: Psychometric patterns and behavioral and physiological responses to stress. *Journal of Abnormal Psychology, 88*, 369–380.

CHAPTER

16

COGNITIVE INTERFERENCE IN DEPRESSIVE AND ANXIETY-BASED DISORDERS

Zindel V. Segal
University of Toronto

Viewed from the vantage point of cognitive models of psychopathology, the concept of cognitive interference has been defined through both clinical and experimental avenues. Starting with a description of symptoms, the magnitude of interference phenomena has been an oft used yardstick for determining whether changes in mental functioning reported by patients are transitory or sufficiently severe to warrant a clinical diagnosis. This is implicitly acknowledged by the inclusion of such features as recurrent ideation (suicidal or guilt) or diminished ability to think or concentrate in formal diagnostic criteria for various psychiatric disorders (American Psychiatric Association, 1995, *DSM–IV*). From the perspective of cognitive science, interference phenomena are bona fide experimental findings that have contributed to development of models of knowledge representation in normal populations, and allowed for more recent extensions of this work to pathological groups (Williams, Watts, MacLeod, & Mathews, 1988). This chapter examines the mutual influence of these two domains in current notions of cognitive interference in depression and anxiety.

COGNITIVE INTERFERENCE IN DEPRESSION

Leslie T. was a 45-year-old female grocery store owner who had been battling depression for the past 20 years. She had experienced, on average, one episode of major depression a year and was recovering from her most recent bout of the disorder. In the past year, Leslie and her husband had purchased a grocery store

> in a northern community and were working hard at earning a living and building a group of friends in their new town. This work pace took a toll on Leslie's husband, who was 13 years older and who suffered a mild heart attack after the store had been open for 9 months. Leslie now spent a good deal of the time commuting the 40 km between the store and the hospital in which her husband was recuperating. One day in the late fall, while driving this route in broad daylight, Leslie found that her car lost control and she hit a tree. Her car was wrecked and she was quite badly hurt. When asked how she had lost control of the automobile, she replied that "she did not know where her mind was at the time, but she remembers being lost in thought about one thing or another." By the time she saw the tree it was too late for her to do anything about it.

If we accept a definition of cognitive interference "as thoughts that intrude on task-related activity and serve to reduce the quality and level of performance" (Sarason, Sarason, & Pierce, 1995), then the example provided above suggests that Leslie may have been engaged in this type of thinking to the detriment of her driving ability. This type of interference in cognitive functioning is easily observed in the ruminations, obsessive doubting, and memory difficulties which accompany the mood changes seen in affective disorder, but the difficulty with accepting these signs as a sufficient definition is that they make no reference to the consequences which these symptoms have on behavior. In order to speak meaningfully about cognitive interference in depression, one must describe the process(es) being interfered with and, perhaps, also specify what a noninterfered cognitive process would look like following treatment or recovery.

A tentative definition of cognitive interference in depression is the allocation of attention (either intentionally or automatically) to negative thought streams, in the midst of task-related activity. Cognitive interference would be said to occur if a person experienced intrusions of negative evaluative thoughts, for example, that hindered ongoing performance. One advantage of this definition is that it is of sufficient scope to encompass phenomena such as momentary lapses of attention or more prolonged periods of rumination that may intrude into the awareness of depressed persons.

Cognitive Responses to Depressed Mood

A number of researchers have commented on the nature of individual differences in response to depressed mood (Kuhl & Helle, 1986; Nolen-Hoeksema, Morrow, & Fredrickson, 1993; Teasdale, 1983). More specifically, variation in the patterns of thinking that are activated during a depressive state has been suggested as a contributing factor to the maintenance of the disorder. There a number of intriguing commonalities in these models which posit different reasons for essentially similar content coming to mind.

According to Nolen-Hoeksema (1987), depressed persons react to their mood states by engaging in either ruminative or distracting responses. Ruminative responses are thoughts and behaviors that bring the individual's attention to his or her symptoms or the possible causes and consequences of those symptoms (Nolen-Hoeksema et al., 1993). Distracting responses take the depressed person's mind off his or her symptoms and focus it instead on other activities. It is proposed that ruminative responses to depressed mood prolong depression, whereas distracting responses shorten the interval of depressed mood and reduce its severity. Interestingly, since women are said to engage in more ruminative activity than men, we would expect a greater incidence of cognitive interference among females.

Whereas response style theory tries to account for the type of cognitive interference elicited in response to symptom cues as well as map its consequences, the work of Kuhl and his colleagues (1981; Kuhl & Helle, 1986) has examined interference phenomena in depression from the standpoint of an analysis of motivations and intentions. Kuhl (1981) distinguished individuals who have a "state orientation" from those with an "action orientation." This personality dimension refers to the extent to which a person focuses their attention on the state of mind engendered by a difficult situation, as opposed to devising or carrying out a plan for dealing with it. These tendencies are assessed by the Action Control Scale (Kuhl, 1981) with high scores on state orientation being a response to a hypothetical situation such as "when I notice that I have been used" by endorsing "I can't stop thinking about it." High scores on action orientation would be reflected in a response such as "I soon forget about it" to the same item.

In support of this model, Kuhl (1981) described a study in which he experimentally induced state or action orientation in a group of subjects and then had them perform a learned helplessness task, that was followed by a subsequent task. Following exposure to the uncontrollable failure, the state oriented subjects performed significantly more poorly than did the action oriented subjects, but they were able to improve their performance if they were prevented from self-focusing or considering the causes of their failures. The difficulties these subjects had seemed to be due to an inability to let go of thinking about concepts related to solving the original task while they were engaged with the second task. An assessment of the subjects' own thoughts indicated that the state-oriented subjects were quite motivated to solve the second task, but had trouble keeping failure-related thoughts from entering awareness. This seems to be a clear example of cognitive interference arising from the difficulty in inhibiting state-oriented information.

Pyszcznski and Greenberg (1987) have proposed a model of depression emphasizing the role of self-focused attention, which shares a number of similarities with the two accounts just described. In their view, people focus on discrepancies between their goals and their current behavior in an ongoing effort to self-regulate. Depression may occur when a person is unable or unwilling to relinquish a desired but unattainable goal, and so gets stuck in an escalating cycle of negative affect, produced in response to the awareness of a negative discrepancy (what one has is less than what one wants), fueling the unproductive pursuit of a goal that cannot be reached. The assumption here is that normal efforts to reduce the discrepancy would involve renouncing the goal after a number of failed attempts to achieve it, but that self-focused attention (much like a state orientation) prevents the person from exiting this self-regulatory cycle and pursuing other goals.

As is the case with action and state orientation, the development of depression is tied to difficulties in abandoning efforts to achieve a goal, especially when the nature of the goal would indicate that doing so is adaptive. One implication from this work for cognitive interference is that the content of intrusions should reflect intentions to keep working towards the desired goal along with recall of past failures to attain important outcomes.

Broadly speaking, the three theories reviewed posit that as individuals become more preoccupied with themselves, attention-demanding but task irrelevant cognitions will; (1) be harder to ignore, (2) amplify existing negative affective states, and (3) hinder disengagement from unproductive intentions. Cognitive interference in depression would, therefore, be most likely to occur under conditions of affective arousal (a chronic condition in depression) interacting with information that is self-referent, especially with respect to goals or outcomes that the person still strives for (Teasdale & Barnard, 1993).

Associative Networks, Negative Thoughts and Depressed Mood

Attempts to understand the effects of depressed mood on information processing have been largely influenced by associative network theories of knowledge representation (Bower, 1981; Collins & Loftus, 1975). In depression, negative concepts and negative events are rehearsed, leading to extensive elaboration of related mnemonic structures highly interconnected with depression (Ingram, 1984, Teasdale & Barnard, 1993; Williams, Watts, MacLeod, & Mathews, 1988). Changes in the network over time, such as increases in the strength of links or decreases in activation thresholds lead to the representation of individual events and concepts that have been associated together and with depressed mood in the past. In time these can come to form a strongly interconnected unit, such that activation of one element in the unit is enough to activate the entire structure. So, for example, individuals who have, through early adverse life experiences or other means, strongly associated sadness with the activation of intensely negative constructs related to profound loss, lack of self-worth, or global hopelessness will have formed a relatively durable and stable elaborative structure around the emotion of sadness. This structure, which could alternatively be described as a "depression schema," ties together the associated items so closely that experiencing the emotion in a variety of contexts may serve to activate the entire structure, and call to mind notions of self-denigration, profound loss, and other cognitions commonly found in depression (Segal, Williams, Teasdale, & Gemar, in press).

In line with this account, a number of studies have reported that depressed mood is associated with greater recall of negative personal memories, and the selective recall of material learned in the depressed state. Clark and Teasdale (1982), for example, studied the effects of diurnal variations in mood in depressed patients and reported that subject recalled more unhappy and fewer happy memories at the most depressed point of their diurnal cycle than at the least depressed point (excellent reviews of this work can be found in Blaney, 1986; Matt, Vazquez, & Campbell, 1992; and Singer & Salovey, 1988).

If we refer back to the original definition of cognitive interference as the allocation of attention to negative thought streams in the midst of task related performance, then the foregoing analysis suggests that these effects are mediated by the extent to which the elements comprising the negative thought streams are interconnected or organized in the depressed person's associative network. We may also wonder whether information relevant to task completion or re-engagement is not as tightly interconnected. The relevant studies for exploring this issue are those in which changes in online cognitive processing illuminate aspects of cognitive organization in depression.

Empirical Studies of Cognitive Interference in Depression

Within the overall literature on cognitive processing in depression, relatively few studies have examined how task performance changes as a result of cognitive intrusions, and what the content of these intrusions is. While there is good evidence that self-referent information processing is negatively biased, the majority of tasks compare content differences between groups of depressed and control subjects, without inquiring into whether the content differences were arrived at by similar or differing factors. Perhaps depressed subjects show poorer recall for positive information due to increased interference from previously memorized negative cues. Analyses of content alone would not be able to answer this question. In this section studies are reviewed that have tried to assess interference effects in depressive processing.

Krames and MacDonald (1985) examined the extent to which repetitive thoughts occupy short-term memory (STM) space in depressed and nondepressed subjects. Competition for available short-term memory capacity was studied by having subjects perform two tasks concurrently; listening to a list of words read to them while looking at a series of digits presented one at a time. The variables of interest were the number of digits written down just after being seen (an STM task) and delayed recall of the words (a long-term memory task). Results indicated that depressed subjects had the same short-term memory capacity as controls, but that there was interference with the processing of information held in STM. As the list of words read to subjects increased in length (to a maximum of six), the task became more difficult to perform and more STM capacity was devoted to it. Depressed patients performed at equal levels to controls under the longer list length conditions, but showed inferior performance when the list was shorter. The authors reasoned that interference by repetitive or ruminative thinking occurred when STM capacity was greatest. Shorter lists left more space in STM for distracting thoughts and this hindered recall. As the task became harder, less space in STM was available and so performance was not impaired.

An analogue study by Zuroff, Colussy, and Weilgus (1983) pointed to the possibility that cognitive interference may comprise information which the subject has been previously exposed to, as well as that which is similar but has not been previously seen. High and low scorers on the Beck Depression Inventory were asked to examine 20 positive and 20 negative adjectives, rate them for self-descriptiveness and then select 10 items from each category that described them best. Recall was then tested at 1-hour, 2-day and 7-day intervals and results indicated that the more dysphoric group recalled more negative items and also showed more negative intrusions of previously unpresented material. In addition, a recognition test administered following the final recall showed that dysphoric subjects recognized more negative items and also gave more false positive responses.

Dichotic listening tasks have been used in creative ways to examine the types of distractor stimuli which are capable of capturing depressed subjects' attention. How attention is allocated is thought to be a schema-driven process that functions to structure information processing (Neisser, 1976; Williams et al., 1988) and processing errors might shed light on the type of cognitive structures that are momentarily activated into operation. The general strategy is to present subjects in one ear with a story to which they are instructed to attend, while in the other ear distractor words were presented, some representing positive stimuli and some representing negative stimuli. Tracking errors serve as an index of the diversion of attentional capacity to task irrelevant stimuli a process presumably controlled by the activation of various cognitive structures.

McCabe and Gotlib (1993) tested 15 depressed patients and 10 nondepressed controls twice over a 3-month interval on a dichotic listening task with a concurrent light probe reaction time task. They report that at Time 1 depressed subjects took longer to respond to the light probe when negative distractors were presented in the unattended channel than when positive or neutral words were presented. When subjects were retested at Time 2, when a number of the depressed subjects were presumably no longer in episode, their performance was no longer disrupted by the negative distractors. Control subjects' reaction times did not differ across conditions or time of testing.

Ingram, Bernet, and McLaughlin (1994) used the standard version of a dichotic listening task to examine tracking errors in recovered depressed patients and never depressed controls, under two different mood states. Results indicated no differences between subjects in the normal mood control condition, but when induced into a sad mood, formerly depressed subjects made more tracking errors for both negative and positive stimuli than did never depressed subjects. That is, relative to a normal mood, tracking errors for formerly depressed subjects increased when they experienced a sad mood. The number of tracking errors for never depressed subjects, however, was quite similar in both the normal and sad mood conditions.

These data suggest that the occurrence of a negative mood does appear to activate a process in vulnerable people that has been suggested to be schema-controlled, that is, the allocation of attention, and that this may contribute to increasing the accessibility for emotional information in recovered patients. As suggested by the McCabe and Gotlib (1993) study, perhaps for patients who are currently depressed this information is filtered so that negative self-referent information receives enhanced elaborative processing, while more positive or benign self-referent information is discarded or ignored.

Another measure currently in use within mainstream cognitive psychology which can yield evidence of cognitive organization for specific stimuli is the modified Stroop color-naming test (Mills & Tyrrell, 1983; Warren, 1972). The specific modification of this paradigm entails the presentation of affectively laden stimuli (such as adjectives or nouns) in lieu of the color names traditionally employed with this procedure (Stroop, 1935; MacLeod, 1991).

Gotlib and McCann (1984) and Williams and Nulty (1986), using this procedure both reported that mildly dysphoric subjects took significantly longer to color name negative words, than positive or neutral (Gotlib & McCann, 1984) or only neutral (Williams & Nulty, 1986) control words. Nondysphoric controls showed no differences in color-naming speed as a function of the valence of the word. With respect to clinical samples, Williams and Broadbent (1986) compared a group of depressed patients, all of whom had recently attempted suicide by overdose, with hospital control and community based subjects. They reported that all groups took longer to color name negative words than neutral words, but that the level of interference for the negative words was greatest for depressed subjects when the word was specifically related to an overdose theme (e.g., blackout, drug) than when it was negative in more general terms (e.g., immature, helpless).

What is needed is a task on which performance is affected as a result of this increased accessibility. This can be achieved by adding a priming condition to the modified Stroop test. A more direct test of the organization of negative material in depression comes from a further modification of the Stroop test that involves the a priori presentation of one element of the cognitive structure, so that the effects of element interrelation on subsequent responding can be studied.

Gotlib and Cane (1987) utilized such a primed-Stroop test with a group of depressed patients while they were in episode and again at discharge. Subjects listened to and repeated a series of either positive or negative words following which they were asked to color name either depressed, manic, or neutral targets (which matched the valence of the prime). Results indicated that, while in episode, depressed subjects showed more interference for depressed content than nondepressed content words, but that this difference was no longer apparent when subjects were retested at discharge. These findings are tempered by the lack of a significant priming effect, although primes and targets were not selected for their self-reference.

In a series of related studies (Segal, Hood, Shaw, & Higgins, 1988; Segal & Vella, 1990; Segal et al., 1995) the authors adapted Warren's (1972) category-priming paradigm to examine the organization of self-referent constructs in depression. In these studies, subjects were asked to keep a prime word in mind and to repeat it following the color naming of the target word. The relatedness of the prime and target was the variable of interest and comparisons were made between conditions in which both prime and target were self-descriptive (as determined by the subject's earlier self-ratings) to conditions where the target was self-descriptive but the prime was not. Slower color naming latencies for self-descriptive prime and target pairs (compared to nondescriptive pairs) would support the idea that when both elements belong to the same cognitive representation, exposure to the prime automatically increases the accessibility of the target word's meaning, which interferes with naming the color in which it is presented.

Results indicated that depressed subjects had significantly longer response latencies for self-descriptive prime-target pairs than for nondescriptive pairs. Furthermore, this effect was strongest in depressed subjects compared to normal control or patients with an anxiety disorder (Segal et al., 1988) or normal controls alone, but not a group of nondepressed subjects who were made to experience elevated levels of self-focused attention (Segal & Vella, 1990). Finally, neither depressed subjects nor controls showed evidence for interference effects with positively valanced material (Segal et al., 1995; see Table 16.1).

In summary, cognitive interference in depression can be characterized as occurring when a person has an unwanted thought due to cognitive processing that is not under intentional control. We hypothesized that the tight interconnection among negative constructs might make it easier for intrusion to come to mind and we cited evidence that supported the greater tendency for intrusions in online processing to be of a negative valence and that negatively valenced material is more likely to be organized as a cognitive unit than is positive information.

COGNITIVE INTERFERENCE IN ANXIETY

A tentative definition of cognitive interference in anxiety is the allocation of attention (either automatically or intentionally) to threat-related stimuli. Cognitive interference is said to occur if an individual experienced intrusive thoughts

TABLE 16.1
Mean Color Naming Latencies

	Group			
	Depressed (n = 58)		Controls (n = 44)	
Condition	M	SD	M	SD
	Negative			
SS: Self-descriptive prime/self-descriptive target	898	(183)	804	(154)
SN: Self-descriptive prime/non self-descriptive target	864	(173)	788	(33)
NS: Non self-descriptive prime/self-descriptive target	874*	(169)	809	(166)
NN: Non self-descriptive prime/non self-descriptive target	880*	(189)	794	(127)
	Positive			
SS: Self-descriptive prime/self-descriptive target	843	(172)	769	(154)
SN: Self-descriptive prime/non self-descriptive target	842	(176)	751	(143)
NS: Non self-descriptive prime/self-descriptive target	846	(176)	751	(147)
NN: Non self-descriptive prime/non self-descriptive target	848	(176)	755	(129)

Note. *Superscript denotes means which differ significantly from the SS Condition.
From Segal et al., (1995).

related to threat which hindered ongoing performance. One advantage of this definition is that it is of sufficient scope to encompass a wide range of phenomena. That is, threat-related intrusive thoughts may cause momentary lapses of attention or may intrude into the awareness of anxious individuals causing prolonged periods of obsession. As in the depression literature, both clinical and experimental observations provide evidence of cognitive interference associated with anxiety.

Cognitive Responses to Anxiety

Each of the anxiety disorders have interference-based clinical symptoms. For example, individuals with posttraumatic stress disorder (PTSD) experience intrusive thoughts, flashbacks, and nightmares of the traumatic event. Panic-disordered patients experience thoughts about possible catastrophe, such as having a heart attack or "going crazy." Obsessive-compulsive disorder (OCD) patients experience unwanted, recurrent obsessions regarding contamination, doubt, and so forth. Social phobics experience thoughts that he or she may appear foolish. And generalized anxiety disorder (GAD) patients experience worrisome thoughts about various life circumstances, such as finances, family, work, school, and health.

Although the specific content of these thoughts varies across the anxiety disorders, unrealistic thoughts concerning personal risk and danger are a general characteristic that unites them. Such thoughts are highly prevalent in the thinking of anxious individuals; they can be attentionally demanding, reduce the ability to focus on tasks, and impair performance. The occurrence of these thoughts often brings the individual's attention to his or her fears and increases anxious mood. For example, a PTSD patient who was sexually assaulted in an elevator may experience thoughts such as "if I go into an elevator again, I will be attacked"; a panic patient may think "if my heart beats rapidly, I will have a heart attack"; or a social phobic may think "if I speak aloud in class, everyone will think I'm stupid." Threat-related thoughts such as these increase anxiety and interfere with the individual's performance on ongoing tasks.

Moreover, threat-related thoughts may lead to avoidance, another characteristic common to all the anxiety disorders. The PTSD patient might avoid elevators or similar places in which escape would prove difficult; the panic patient might avoid activities in which heart rate increases; the social phobic might avoid situations in which he or she may be the focus of attention. While avoidance behavior decreases the likelihood that an individual will encounter feared situations, such behavior similarly reduces the opportunity to demonstrate to anxious individuals that their feared consequences will not be realized. Whether behavioral (i.e., physically avoiding the feared stimulus) or cognitive (i.e., trying not to think of the feared stimulus), avoidance may be a contributing factor to the maintenance of anxiety (Foa & Kozak, 1986).

Associative Networks, Threat-Related Thoughts, and Anxiety

Several cognitive theories have been developed to explain interference phenomena in anxiety. These theories rest on the view that anxious individuals differentially attend to and retrieve threat-related information, whereas nonanxious individuals do not exhibit such differences in cognitive processing. The more that threat-related information is attended to and the easier it is retrieved from memory, the more likely it will interfere with cognitive functioning.

The tendency for individuals to selectively attend to objective threat cues can be adaptive. Such a bias might function as an early warning system, enabling individuals to avoid danger. However, if the criterion for classifying threatening input is inappropriately low, early detection would prove maladaptive for the individual (McNally, 1990). For example, a tendency to selectively attend to mildly threatening stimuli may give rise to frequent occurrences of threat-related intrusive thoughts and a high level of anxiety. This possibility has a potential role in the development and maintenance of anxiety disorders.

Lang (1977, 1979) has advanced an information-processing theory of fear and anxiety in which threat-relevant stimuli are encoded in propositional form in memory (Anderson & Bower, 1974) in anxious individuals. He posits that a highly coherent "fear network" contains information about the feared stimulus situation, fear responses, and their meanings. This fear network is an enduring system that develops based on past experience. According to this theory, the network can be activated by objective threat stimuli and by symbolic stimuli, such as ambiguous stimuli or threat-related words. Such activation is thought to lead to intrusive thoughts, as well as other manifestations of anxiety.

From an experimental perspective, there are a number of information processing paradigms to help elucidate how threat-related information is represented in memory. Moreover, these paradigms can be used to study cognitive interference or the mechanism underlying the occurrence of intrusive thoughts. If threat-related information is organized in an associative network in anxious individuals that makes it easier for intrusions to come to mind, then they should evidence interpretive, attentional, and memory biases for threat relative to normal control subjects.

Empirical Studies of Cognitive Interference in Anxiety

Interpretive Bias for Threat. In everyday life, individuals encounter many situations whose meanings are ambiguous, that is, they can be interpreted both as nonthreatening and as threatening. For example, rapid heart rate may be dismissed as simply due to a recent walk up a steep flight of stairs, or it may be interpreted as a sign of an impending heart attack. Similarly, a friend who passes you without saying hello may do so because he is simply preoccupied with other matters, or it may signify rejection. In accordance with the cognitive theories of anxiety, anxious individuals should have a tendency to interpret ambiguous stimuli as threatening.

In a study on interpretive bias (Butler & Mathews, 1983), anxious patients and normal control subjects provided the first explanation that came to mind after reading ambiguous scenarios (e.g., "You wake with a start in the middle of the night, thinking you heard a noise, but all is quiet. What do you think woke you up?"). For each scenario, subjects then ranked three experimenter-provided explanations (one threatening) in terms of their likelihood of coming to mind in a similar situation. In contrast to normal control subjects, anxious patients more often provided threatening interpretations for the ambiguous scenarios, and they more often ranked the threatening experimenter-provided explanation as the one most likely to come to mind. Similar results have been obtained with panic-disordered patients (McNally & Foa, 1987).

These findings have been extended in subsequent studies on interpretive bias. Other experiments have revealed that anxious subjects tend to choose the more threatening interpretation of ambiguous sentences (e.g., "The doctor examined little Emily's growth" Eysenck, Mogg, May, Richards, & Mathews, 1991; MacLeod & Cohen, 1993), the more threatening meaning of ambiguous homophones (e.g., DIE/DYE; Eysenck, MacLeod, & Mathews, 1987; Mathews, Richards, & Eysenck, 1989), and the more threatening meaning of ambiguous homographs (e.g., STROKE; Richards & French, 1992).

Attentional Bias for Threat. Employing detection, interference, and facilitation tasks, several studies have provided evidence that anxious individuals are characterized by an attentional bias for threat (for a review, see Logan & Goetsch, 1993). The tendency to attend selectively to threat-related stimuli takes attention away from an ongoing task, thereby interfering with performance.

In detection paradigms, the subject's task is to detect threat words and neutral words that are presented under conditions that make their perception difficult. An attentional bias for threat is inferred when subjects' detect more threat words than neutral words, and more threat words relative to normal control subjects.

In one experiment, Burgess, Jones, Robertson, Radcliffe, and Emerson (1981) used a dichotic listening paradigm. In this paradigm, threat words and neutral words were embedded in prose passages presented to the unattended channel. Agoraphobics, social phobics, and normal control subjects were asked to shadow aloud the passage presented in the attended channel, and to press a button whenever they detected a phobia-related or neutral target word. The patients evidenced an attentional bias for threat stimuli as shown by higher detection rates for phobic words, relative to neutral words; in contrast, the normal control subjects evidenced no difference in detection rates. Similar results have been obtained with GAD patients (Mathews & MacLeod, 1986) and with OCD patients (Foa & McNally, 1986).

One limitation inherent in detection paradigms is that the results could be attributable to a response bias. In response to this potential problem, researchers have developed interference paradigms. Like detection paradigms, interference paradigms involve the presentation of threat words and neutral words. However, response biases are rendered irrelevant because subjects are not required to detect the stimuli. In fact, they are asked to ignore them, and to focus on performing another primary task. In these paradigms, threat-related attentional biases are inferred from impaired performance on the primary task due to the presence of threat distractors.

The most commonly used interference paradigm in research on anxiety disorders is the modified Stroop (1935) color-naming paradigm. In this paradigm, subjects are shown words of varying affective significance, and are asked to name the colors in which the words are printed while ignoring the meanings of the words. A delay in color naming, or "Stroop interference," occurs when the word's meaning captures the subject's attention despite the subject's effort to attend to the color of the word. If anxious individuals are characterized by an attentional bias to threat stimuli, they should evidence longer color-naming latencies for threat words relative to neutral words. That is, the meaning of the threat word should interfere with the primary task of color naming.

In the original demonstration of the effect, Mathews and MacLeod (1985) applied the modified Stroop color-naming paradigm to investigate selective processing of words related to social and physical threat with GAD patients. They found that GAD patients, relative to normal control subjects, evidenced greater interference for threat-related words than for neutral words. Moreover, although anxious subjects showed interference effects with social threat words, only those with physical concerns were equally disrupted by physical threat words. Accordingly, the bias for selective processing of threat information seems specific to a particular threat and not to threatening information in general.

Evidence of Stroop interference for threat has been found in all the anxiety disorders. In each case, patients have evidenced delayed color-naming for disorder-specific, threat-related words. For example, Stroop interference has been found in patients with GAD (Mathews & MacLeod, 1985; Mogg, Mathews, & Weinman, 1989), simple phobia (Lavy, van den Hout, & Arntz, 1993; Watts, McKenna, Sharrock, & Trezise, 1986), social phobia (Hope, Rapee, Heimberg, & Dombeck, 1990; Mattia, Heimberg, & Hope, 1993), OCD (Foa, Ilai, McCarthy, Shoyer, & Murdock, 1993; Lavy, van Oppen, & van den Hout, 1994), panic disorder (Ehlers, Margraf, Davies, & Roth, 1988; McNally, Riemann, & Kim, 1990; McNally, Riemann, Louro, Lukach, & Kim, 1992), and PTSD (Cassiday, McNally, & Zeitlin, 1992; Foa, Feske, Murdock, Kozak, & McCarthy, 1991; McNally, English, & Lipke, 1993; McNally, Kaspi, Riemann, & Zeitlin, 1990; Thrasher, Dalgleish, & Yule, 1994). Evidence of delayed color naming of threatening words has also been found in individuals with test anxiety (Ray, 1979), and high trait anxiety (Richards & Millwood, 1989).

Research using masked presentations of Stroop stimuli has provided evidence that the bias towards threat information occurs at an early, preattentive stage, prior to subjective awareness. Subject groups that have been tested using this paradigm include students before exams (MacLeod & Rutherford, 1992), women waiting for a coloscopy examination (MacLeod & Hagan, 1992), GAD patients (Mogg, Bradley, Williams, & Mathews, 1993), and high and low trait anxious individuals (Mogg, Kentish, & Bradley, 1993). Overall, these studies indicate that anxious subjects display an interference effect to threat-related words when presented at a level that does not permit conscious recognition of the words.

Additional evidence of an attentional bias for threat has been obtained from studies in which the presence of threat stimuli facilitates performance, as in the attention deployment paradigm. In a standard attention deployment task, subjects see brief exposures of word pairs on a computer monitor, with one word presented in the upper part of the monitor, and the other word in the lower part. Following the termination of these displays, a small dot appears, sometimes replacing the top word, other times replacing the bottom word. Subjects are told simply to read the top word aloud, and to press a button whenever a dot replaces one of the words. Research with this paradigm has demonstrated that reaction time to this neutral dot is decreased if it happens that subjects' attention was already directed toward the area of the monitor where the dot appears.

MacLeod, Mathews, and Tata (1986), employing this paradigm, presented word pairs consisting of threat and neutral words to GAD patients and normal control subjects. If GAD patients are characterized by an attentional bias for threat, then their attention should be drawn to the threat word. Therefore, when the dot replaces the threat word, reaction times should be decreased, relative to when the dot replaces the neutral word. The result of this study confirmed this prediction—GAD patients, in comparison to normal control subjects, were quicker to detect the dot when it was preceded by a threat word, suggesting that GAD patients shifted their attention to the threat words. Similar results have been obtained with panic-disordered patients (Asmundson, Sandler, Wilson, & Walker, 1992) and high trait anxious individuals (MacLeod & Mathews, 1988).

Memory Bias for Threat. Researchers have also investigated whether anxious individuals exhibit memory biases for threat. Clinically, enhanced memory for threat appears to occur, at least for some of the anxiety disorders. For example, involuntary retrieval of traumatic memories is one of the hallmark symptoms of PTSD patients. Threat-related thoughts also often seem to pop into mind for panic patients and for GAD patients. Such thoughts interfere with performance on other tasks.

Researchers have used explicit and implicit memory paradigms (for a review, see Graf & Schacter, 1985) to investigate memory biases in anxiety disorders. Explicit memory paradigms, such as free recall, cued recall, and recognition, have been employed to examine whether anxious individuals are better able to remember threatening information than normal control subjects. Explicit memory is demonstrated when performance on a task requires conscious recollection of previous experiences, in these cases, recollection of previously-presented experimental stimuli. For example, subjects might be shown threat words and neutral words, and then later be asked to recognize or recall them. An explicit memory bias for threat would be revealed by subjects recalling more threat words than neutral words, controlling, of course, for response bias.

Implicit memory paradigms, such as word stem completion, have been employed to examine whether anxious individuals are better able to remember threatening information in the absence of awareness than normal control subjects. Implicit memory is demonstrated when previous experience enhances performance on a task that does not require deliberate or conscious recollection of that experience. For example, subjects might be shown threat words and neutral words, and then later be asked to complete a series of 3-letter stems with the first word that comes to mind. An implicit memory effect would be indicated by subjects disproportionately completing stems with words that had been presented previously. An implicit memory bias for threat would be revealed by subjects completing more threat stems than neutral stems. Implicit memory biases for threat may explain the occurrence of threat-related memories automatically coming to mind in some anxious individuals.

Explicit memory studies with simple phobics (Watts, Trezise, & Sharrock, 1986; Watts & Dalgleish, 1991) and with GAD patients (Mogg, Mathews, & Weinman, 1987) found that such patients were not characterized by disorder-specific recognition and recall biases for threat. However, patients with agoraphobia (Nunn, Stevenson, & Whalan, 1984), panic disorder (Becker, Rinck, & Margraf, 1994; Cloitre & Liebowitz, 1991; Cloitre, Shear, Cancienne, & Zeitlin, 1994; McNally, Foa, & Donnell, 1989), and posttraumatic stress disorder (PTSD) (Zeitlin & McNally, 1991) were characterized by such biases. Implicit memory studies with GAD patients (Mathews, Mogg, May, & Eysenck, 1989), panic patients (Cloitre et al., 1994), and PTSD patients (Zeitlin & McNally, 1991) found that such patients were characterized by disorder-specific retrieval biases for threat.

Memory biases for threat in the anxiety disorders appears to depend on the disorder and on the memory paradigm. One possible explanation for the differences in explicit memory performance is that simple phobic patients and GAD patients may be better able than panic patients and PTSD patients to avoid elaborative processing of threat-related stimuli (Mogg et al., 1987). That is, although all the anxiety disorders appear to be characterized by an early stage, attentional bias for threat, further processing of threat-related stimuli might vary across the anxiety disorders, thereby producing differences in explicit memory for such stimuli. If patients are able to engage in postattentional cognitive avoidance, then they are unlikely to evidence an explicit memory bias for threat, although they may evidence an implicit memory bias. Alternatively, if patients are either unwilling or unable to avoid further elaborative processing, then they are likely to evidence an explicit memory bias for threat. Such an inability may characterize the more severe anxiety disorders, such as panic disorder and PTSD.

The studies described above are only a representative subset of recent cognitive-experimental research on the anxiety disorders. Nevertheless, these studies suggest some conclusions. The existing evidence indicates that anxious individuals are characterized by interpretive, attentional, and (in some cases) memory biases for threat. These biases in cognitive processing increase the intake of information concerned with possible risk and danger, and therefore have the potential for maintaining or increasing anxiety levels. A consequence of these biases toward threat is interference with other ongoing tasks, leading to performance decrements. It appears that these effects may be initiated automatically, prior to subjective awareness, and may cause only momentary lapses in attention. In some cases, however, they result in individuals becoming aware of the threatening stimuli. This would allow further intentional or control processes, that could either enhance the biases, or possibly reduce them. Cognitive interference associated with anxiety may thus arise from a combination of automatic and controlled processes.

In summary, cognitive interference in anxiety can be characterized as occurring when an individual has an unwanted thought due to biased cognitive processing. There is good evidence to support the notion that threat-related information is organized in an associative network in anxious individuals which makes it easier for intrusions to come to mind. There is also evidence that supports the tendency for such intrusions to be related to threat.

DISCUSSION

The past two decades have witnessed a burgeoning interest in understanding the interference phenomena seen in depressive and anxiety-based disorders. Researchers have sought to isolate the mechanisms underlying such intrusive phenomena because they appear to constitute the core cognitive pathology. Indeed, unwanted, negative thoughts are common to depressed and anxious patients alike. Such thoughts are "ego-dystonic," that is, patients do not want to selectively attend to disorder-related stimuli and do not want to have distressing memories arise so easily.

Researchers have only just begun to understand the mechanisms underlying interference phenomena. Indeed, several questions remain. First, are the interference phenomena seen in depression and the anxiety disorders causes or consequences of the disorders? To determine whether cognitive biases contribute to their etiology, investigators must establish that the cognitive biases precede the occurrence of the disorders. There is some evidence in the anxiety area that suggests that cognitive biases do precede the disorder. MacLeod and Mathews (1988) and Mogg et al. (1993), for example, have shown that normal subjects with high trait anxiety—possibly a group at risk for GAD—evidence some of the attentional biases shown by GAD patients. Longitudinal studies of such high-risk populations employing cognitive experimental paradigms would provide a method for further investigating this question.

Second, can treatments be designed to prevent the occurrence of unwanted thoughts that interfere with task performance? A number of cognitive-behavioral therapy (CBT) interventions, for example, provide patients with cues for initiating more controlled or effortful processing of information in situations where automatic processing predominated (Moretti & Shaw, 1989). Studies which have examined the effects of treatment on cognitive processing have found that an attentional bias for disorder-related stimuli is reduced or eliminated following CBT. For example, a dichotic listening task administered to patients with OCD showed an attentional bias for threatening stimuli before but not after treatment (Foa & McNally, 1986). Stroop interference for disorder-specific threat words by spider phobics (Watts et al., 1986), PTSD patients (Foa et al., 1991), and social phobics (Mattia et al., 1993) was attenuated following treatment. We know very little about the effects of different types of treatment on the selective processing of threat cues. It is possible that some types of treatment will be more successful than others in modifying these cognitive networks.

The empirical research has several clinical implications. For example, the cognitive experimental measures described in this chapter may be useful in evaluating the effectiveness of treatment. They are attractive in this connection as they are much less subject to response biases by the patient than are self-report measures.

Until recently, thought suppression techniques were advocated in the treatment of depression and anxiety. Patients were instructed to try not to think of their distressing thoughts. Indeed, given the aversive nature of these thoughts, individuals often try to suppress them on their own. Despite their efforts, however, they frequently continue to experience such thoughts. In a series of studies (for a review, see Wegner, 1994 it has been shown that attempts to suppress a thought have a paradoxical effect, producing a subsequent increase in thought frequency and a subsequent disruption of ongoing performance. Effort to suppress unwanted thoughts and the subsequent rebound effect may be another mechanism underlying cognitive interference. Perhaps this is due to the fact that these tactics discourage elaborative processing of material, as might occur with thought monitoring, generating alternatives or gathering evidence. It would be interesting to know whether relapse in these disorders is associated with the greater use of suppression-based strategies on the part of patients, who unwittingly contribute to a return of the very thoughts they are trying to banish. One prediction might be that strategies which address the interference, perhaps by exploring it more fully or recording aspects of it, should lead to superior clinical outcomes.

In conclusion, in this chapter the clinical symptoms in depressive and anxiety-based disorders that are interference based were highlighted. Some of the cognitive experimental paradigms that have been used to identify possible mechanisms underlying cognitive interference were reviewed, and the theoretical and clinical implications of these findings were discussed. In light of the ramifications interference phenomena have on individuals who experience them, additional work is needed to fully understand the mechanism by which they influence behavior in order to develop improved treatment procedures.

ACKNOWLEDGMENTS

Preparation of this manuscript was supported in part by the MacArthur Foundation Mental Health Research Network, Grant #1011 awarded to the first author.

REFERENCES

American Psychiatric Association (1994). *Diagnostic and Statistical Manual of mental disorders* (4th ed., rev.). Washington, DC: Author.

Anderson, J. R., & Bower, G. H. (1974). A propositional theory of recognition memory. *Memory and Cognition, 2*, 406–412.

Asmundson, G. J. G., Sandler, L. S., Wilson, K. G., & Walker, J. R. (1992). Selective attention toward physical threat in patients with panic disorder. *Journal of Anxiety Disorders, 6*, 295–303.

Becker, E., Rinck, M., & Margraf, J. (1994). Memory bias in panic disorder. *Journal of Abnormal Psychology, 103*, 396–399.

Blaney, P. H. (1986) Affect and memory: A review. *Psychological Bulletin, 99*, 229–246.

Bower, G. H. (1981). Mood and memory. *American Psychologist, 36*, 129–148.

Burgess, I. S., Jones, L. M., Robertson, S. A., Radcliffe, W. N., & Emerson, E. (1981). The degree of control exerted by phobic and non-phobic verbal stimuli over the recognition behaviour of phobic and non-phobic subjects. *Behaviour Research and Therapy, 19*, 233–242.

Butler, G., & Mathews, A. (1983). Cognitive processes in anxiety. *Advances in Behavior Research and Therapy, 5*, 51–62.

Cassiday, K. L., McNally, R. J., & Zeitlin, S. B. (1992). Cognitive processing of trauma cues in rape victims with post-traumatic stress disorder. *Cognitive Therapy and Research, 16*, 283–295.

Clark, D. M., & Teasdale, J. D. (1982). Diurnal variation in clinical depression and accessibility of memories of positive and negative experiences. *Journal of Abnormal Psychology, 91*, 87–95.

Cloitre, M., & Liebowitz, M. R. (1991). Memory bias in panic disorder: An investigation of the cognitive avoidance hypothesis. *Cognitive Therapy and Research, 15*, 371–386.

Cloitre, M., Shear, M. K., Cancienne, J., & Zeitlin, S. B. (1994). Implicit and explicit memory for catastrophic associations to bodily sensation words in panic disorder. *Cognitive Therapy and Research, 18*, 225–240.

Collins, A. M., & Loftus, E. (1975). A spreading-activation theory of semantic processing. *Psychological Review, 82*, 407–428.

Ehlers, A., Margraf, J., Davies, S., & Roth, W. T. (1988). Selective processing of threat cues in subjects with panic attacks. *Cognition and Emotion, 2*, 201–219.

Eysenck, M. W., MacLeod, C., & Mathews, A. M. (1987). Cognitive functioning in anxiety. *Psychological Research, 49*, 189–195.

Eysenck, M. W., Mogg, K., May, J., Richards, A., & Mathews, A. M. (1991). Bias in interpretation of ambiguous sentences related to threat in anxiety. *Journal of Abnormal Psychology, 100*, 144–150.

Foa, E. B., Feske, U., Murdock, T. B., Kozak, M. J., & McCarthy, P. R. (1991). Processing of threat-related information in rape victims. *Journal of Abnormal Psychology, 100*, 156–162.

Foa, E. B., Ilai, D., McCarthy, P. R., Shoyer, B., & Murdock, T. (1993). Information processing in obsessive-compulsive disorder. *Cognitive Therapy and Research, 17*, 173–189.

Foa, E. B., & Kozak, M. J. (1986). Emotional processing of fear: Exposure to corrective information. *Psychological Bulletin, 99*, 20–35.

Foa, E. B., & McNally, R. J. (1986). Sensitivity to feared stimuli in obsessive-compulsives: A dichotic listening analysis. *Cognitive Therapy and Research, 10*, 477–485.

Gotlib, I. H., & Cane, D. B. (1987). Construct accessibility and clinical depression: A longitudinal investigation. *Journal of Abnormal Psychology, 96*, 199–204.

Gotlib, I. H., & McCann, C. D. (1984). Construct accessibility and depression: An examination of cognitive and affective factors. *Journal of Personality and Social Psychology, 47*, 427–439.

Graf, P., & Schacter, D. L. (1985). Implicit and explicit memory for new associations in normal and amnesic subjects. *Journal of Experimental Psychology: Learning, Memory, and Cognition, 13*, 45–53.

Hope, D. A., Rapee, R. M., Heimberg, R. G., & Dombeck, M. J. (1990). Representations of the self in social phobia: Vulnerability to social threat. *Cognitive Therapy and Research, 14*, 177–189.

Ingram, R. E. (1984). Toward an information-processing analysis of depression. *Cognitive Therapy and Research, 8*, 443–478.

Ingram, R. E., Bernet, C. Z., McLaughlin, S. C. (1994). Attention allocation processes in depressed individuals. *Cognitive Therapy and Research, 18*, 317–332.

Krames, L., & MacDonald, M. R. (1985). Distraction and depressive cognitions. *Cognitive Therapy and Research, 9*, 561–573.

Kuhl, J. (1981). Motivational and functional helplessness: The moderating effects of state versus action orientation. *Journal of Personality and Social Psychology, 40*, 5–17.

Kuhl, J., & Helle, L. (1986). Motivational and volitional determinants of depression: The degenerated intentions hypothesis. *Journal of Abnormal Psychology, 95*, 247–251.

Lang, P. J. (1977). Imagery in therapy: An information processing analysis of fear. *Behavior Therapy, 8*, 862–886.

Lang, P. J. (1979). A bio-informational theory of emotional imagery. *Psychophysiology, 16*, 495–512.

Lavy, E., van den Hout, M., & Arntz, A. (1993). Attentional bias and spider phobia: Conceptual and clinical issues. *Behaviour Research and Therapy, 31*, 17–24.

Lavy, E., van Oppen, P., & van den Hout, M. (1994). Selective processing of emotional information in obsessive-compulsive disorder. *Behaviour Research and Therapy, 32*, 243–246.

Logan, A. C., & Goetsch, V. L. (1993). Attention to external threat cues in anxiety states. *Clinical Psychology Review, 13*, 541–559.

MacLeod, C. M. (1991). Half a century of research on the Stroop Effect: An integrative review. *Psychological Bulletin, 109*, 163–203.

MacLeod, C., & Cohen, I. (1993). Anxiety and the interpretation of ambiguity: A text comprehension study. *Journal of Abnormal Psychology, 102*, 238–247.

MacLeod, C., & Hagan, R. (1992). Individual differences in the selective processing of threatening information, and emotional responses to a stressful life event. *Behaviour Research and Therapy, 30*, 151–161.

MacLeod, C., & Mathews, A. (1988). Anxiety and the allocation of attention to threat. *The Quarterly Journal of Experimental Psychology, 40A*, 653–670.

MacLeod, C., Mathews, A., & Tata, P. (1986). Attentional bias in emotional disorders. *Journal of Abnormal Psychology, 95*, 15–20.

MacLeod, C., & Rutherford, E. M. (1992). Anxiety and the selective processing of emotional information: Mediating roles of awareness, trait and state variables, and personal relevance of stimulus materials. *Behaviour Research and Therapy, 30*, 479–491.

Mathews, A., & MacLeod, C. (1985). Selective processing of threat cues in anxiety states. *Behaviour Research and Therapy, 23*, 563–569.

Mathews, A., & MacLeod, C. (1986). Discrimination of threat cues without awareness in anxiety states. *Journal of Abnormal Psychology, 95*, 131–138.

Mathews, A., Mogg, K., May, J., & Eysenck, M. (1989). Implicit and explicit memory bias in anxiety. *Journal of Abnormal Psychology, 98*, 236–240.

Mathews, A., Richards, A., & Eysenck, M. (1989). Interpretation of homophones related to threat in anxiety states. *Journal of Abnormal Psychology, 98*, 31–34.

Matt, G. E., Vazquez, C., Campbell, W. K. (1992). Mood-congruent recall of affectively toned stimuli: A meta-analytic review. *Clinical Psychology Review, 12*, 227–255.

Mattia, J. I., Heimberg, R. G., & Hope, D. A. (1993). The revised Stroop color-naming task in social phobics. *Behaviour Research and Therapy, 31*, 305–313.

McCabe S. B., & Gotlib, I. H. (1993). Attentional processing in clinically depressed subjects: A longitudinal investigation. *Cognitive Therapy and Research, 17*, 359–377.

McNally, R. J. (1990). Psychological approaches to panic disorder: A review. *Psychological Bulletin, 108*, 403–419.

McNally, R. J., English, G. E., & Lipke, H. J. (1993). Assessment of intrusive cognition in PTSD: Use of the modified Stroop paradigm. *Journal of Traumatic Stress, 6*, 33–41.

McNally, R. J., & Foa, E. B. (1987). Cognition and agoraphobia: Bias in the interpretation of threat. *Cognitive Therapy and Research, 11*, 567–581.

McNally, R. J., Foa, E. B., & Donnell, C. D. (1989). Memory bias for anxiety information in patients with panic disorder. *Cognition and Emotion, 3*, 27–44.

McNally, R. J., Kaspi, S. P., Riemann, B. C., & Zeitlin, S. B. (1990). Selective processing of threat cues in post-traumatic stress disorder. *Journal of Abnormal Psychology, 99*, 398–402.

McNally, R. J., Riemann, B. C., & Kim, E. (1990). Selective processing of threat cues in panic disorder. *Behaviour Research and Therapy, 28*, 407–412.

McNally, R. J., Riemann, B. C., Louro, C. E., Lukach, B. M., & Kim, E. (1992). Cognitive processing of emotional information in panic disorder. *Behaviour Research and Therapy, 30*, 143–149.

Mills, C. J., & Tyrrell, D. J. (1983). Sex-stereotypic encoding and release from proactive interference. *Journal of Personality and Social Psychology, 45*, 772–781.

Mogg, K., Bradley, B. P., Williams, R., & Mathews, A. M. (1993). Subliminal processing of emotional information in anxiety and depression. *Journal of Abnormal Psychology, 102*, 304–311.

Mogg, K., Kentish, J., & Bradley, B. P. (1993). Effects of anxiety and awareness on color-identification latencies for emotional words. *Behaviour Research and Therapy, 31*, 559–567.

Mogg, K., Mathews, A., & Weinman, J. (1987). Memory bias in clinical anxiety. *Journal of Abnormal Psychology, 96*, 94–98.

Mogg, K., Mathews, A., & Weinman, J. (1989). Selective processing of threat cues in anxiety states: A replication. *Behaviour Research and Therapy, 27*, 317–323.

Moretti, M. M., & Shaw, B. F. (1989). Automatic and dysfunctional cognitive processes in depression. In J. S. Uleman & J. A. Bargh (Eds.), *Unintended thought* (pp. 383–424). New York: Guilford.

Neisser, U. (1976). *Cognition and reality*. San Francisco: Freeman.

Nolen-Hoeksema, S. (1987). Sex differences in unipolar depression: Evidence and theory. *Psychological Bulletin, 101*, 259–282.

Nolen-Hoeksema, S., Morrow, J., & Fredrickson, B. L. (1993). Response styles and the duration of episodes of depressed mood. *Journal of Abnormal Psychology, 102*, 20–28.

Nunn, J. D., Stevenson, R. J., & Whalan, G. (1984). Selective memory effects in agoraphobic patients. *British Journal of Clinical Psychology, 23*, 195–201.

Pyszczynski, T., & Greenberg, J. (1987). Self-regulatory perseveration and the depressive self-focusing style: A self-awareness theory of reactive depression. *Psychological Bulletin, 102*, 122–138.

Ray, C. (1979). Examination stress and performance on a color word interference task. *Perceptual and Motor Skills, 49*, 400–402.

Richards, A., & French, C. C. (1992). An anxiety-related bias in semantic activation when processing threat-neutral homographs. *Quarterly Journal of Experimental Psychology, 45*, 503–525.

Richards, A., & Millwood, B. (1989). Colour-identification of differentially valenced words in anxiety. *Cognition and Emotion, 3*, 171–176.

Sarason, I. G., Sarason, B. R., & Pierce, G. R. (1995). Cognitive interference: At the intelligence personality crossroads. In D. Saklofske & M. Zeidner (Eds.), *International handbook of personality and intelligence* (pp.). New York: Plenum.

Segal, Z. V., Hood, J. E., Shaw, B. F., & Higgins, E. T. (1988). A structural analysis of the self-schema construct in major depression. *Cognitive Therapy and Research, 12*, 471–485.

Segal, Z. V., Gemar, M., Truchon, C., Guirguis, M., & Horowitz, L. (1995). A priming methodology for studying self-representation in major depressive disorder. *Journal of Abnormal Psychology, 104*, 205–213.

Segal, Z. V., & Vella, D. D. (1990). Self-schema in major depression: Replication and extension of a priming methodology. *Cognitive Therapy and Research, 14*, 161–176.

Segal, Z. V., Williams, J. M., Teasdale, J. D., & Gemar, M. C. (in press). A cognitive science perspective on kindling and episodic sensitization in recurrent affective disorder. *Psychological Medicine.*

Singer, J. A., & Salovey, P. (1988) Mood and memory: Evaluating the network theory of affect. *Clinical Psychology Review, 8,* 211–251.

Stroop, J. R. (1935). Studies of interference in serial verbal reactions. *Journal of Experimental Psychology, 18,* 643–662.

Teasdale, J. D. (1983). Negative thinking in depression: Cause, effect or reciprocal relationship? *Advances in Behaviour Research and Therapy, 5,* 3–25.

Teasdale, J. D., & Barnard, P. J. (1993). *Affect, cognition, and change.* Hillsdale, NJ: Lawrence Erlbaum Associates.

Thrasher, S. M., Dalgleish, T., & Yule, W. (1994). Information processing in post-traumatic stress disorder. *Behaviour Research and Therapy, 32,* 247–254.

Warren, R. E. (1972). Stimulus encoding and memory. *Journal of Experimental Psychology, 94,* 90–100.

Watts, F. N., & Dalgleish, T. (1991). Memory for phobia-related words in spider phobics. *Cognition and Emotion, 5,* 313–329.

Watts, F. N., McKenna, F. P., Sharrock, R., & Trezise, L. (1986). Colour naming of phobia-related words. *British Journal of Psychology, 77,* 97–108.

Watts, F. N., Trezise, L., & Sharrock, R. (1986). Processing of phobic stimuli. *British Journal of Clinical Psychology, 25,* 253–259.

Wegner, D. M., (1994). Ironic processes of mental control. *Psychological Review, 101,* 34–52.

Williams, J. M. G., & Broadbent, K. (1986). Distraction by emotional stimuli: Use of a Stroop task with suicide attempters. *British Journal of Clinical Psychology, 25,* 101–110.

Williams, J. M. G., & Nulty, D. D. (1986). Construct accessibility, depression and the emotional stroop task: Transient mood or stable structure. *Personality and Individual Differences, 7,* 485–491.

Williams, J. M. G., Watts, F. N., MacLeod, C., & Mathews, A. (1988). *Cognitive psychology and emotional disorders.* Chichester, England: Wiley.

Zeitlin, S. B., & McNally, R. J. (1991). Implicit and explicit memory bias for threat in post-traumatic stress disorder. *Behaviour Research and Therapy, 29,* 451–457.

Zuroff, D. C., Colussy, S. A., & Weilgus, M. S. (1983). Selective memory and depression: A cautionary note concerning response bias. *Cognitive Therapy and Research, 7,* 223–232.

CHAPTER

17

COGNITIVE INTERFERENCE IN DEPRESSION

Ian H. Gotlib
John E. Roberts
Eva Gilboa
Northwestern University

Of all the psychiatric disorders, depression is by far the most common. Each year, more than 100 million people worldwide develop clinically recognizable depression. During the course of a lifetime, it is estimated that between 8% and 18% of the general population will experience at least one clinically significant episode of depression (Karno et al., 1987), and that approximately twice as many women than men will be affected by this disorder (Frank, Carpenter, & Kupfer, 1988). Moreover, for a significant proportion of these individuals, the depressive episode will result in death by suicide (Hirschfeld & Goodwin, 1988) or other causes (cf. Murphy, Monson, Olivier, Sobol, & Leighton, 1988).

The term *depression* has a number of meanings, covering a wide range of emotional states that range in severity from normal, everyday moods of sadness, to psychotic episodes with increased risk of suicide. The current diagnostic system in North America, the Diagnostic and Statistical Manual of Mental Disorders (DSM-IV; American Psychiatric Association, 1994), divides depression, or mood disorders, into depressive disorders and bipolar disorders. A diagnosis of depressive disorder, the focus of this chapter, requires one or more periods of clinically significant depression without a history of either manic or hypomanic episodes. Because of the absence of manic episodes, depressive disorders are often referred to as "unipolar depression." Depressive disorders are characterized by at least a 2-week period of depressed mood or a loss of interest or pleasure in almost all daily activities, as well as a number of other symptoms, such as weight loss or gain, loss of appetite, sleep disturbance, psychomotor agitation or retardation, fatigue, feelings of guilt or worthlessness, and difficulties in thinking and concentration.

In this chapter, we focus on cognitive functioning, an area with which depressed persons report particular difficulty. More specifically, we examine the effects of depression on *cognitive interference*, that is, the disruptive impact of depression on attention, learning, and memory. Cognitive difficulties are so pervasive and troublesome in depression that they are included in the diagnostic criteria of the disorder. Depressed patients frequently report being bothered by poor concentration, forgetfulness, and intrusive negative thoughts. It is critical to note, however, that the *subjective* experience of such cognitive difficulties does not imply that *objective* deficits necessarily exist (cf. Watts, 1993). In this regard, numerous empirical studies have been conducted in an attempt to provide objective documentation of reported difficulties in attention, learning, and memory in depression. Furthermore, investigators have also attempted to examine the specific nature and locus of these difficulties. This research is slowly beginning to identify the processes that may be responsible for particular cognitive difficulties, and to suggest potential strategies for rehabilitation (e.g., Hertel & Hardin, 1990; Hertel & Rude, 1991a). Finally, some aspects of cognitive interference, such as mood congruent biases, have been postulated to be more than a symptom of depression, and to play a role in the etiology and maintenance of this disorder (cf. Blaney, 1986; Teasdale, 1988).

This chapter begins with an examination of research assessing the effects of depression on the processing of nonvalenced, or neutral, material. Essentially, studies in this area examine whether depression interferes with general learning and memory functioning. In this literature, therefore, cognitive interference would be observed as depression-associated deficits or difficulties in concentration, learning, memory, and problem solving. The next area examined is another large body of research, spawned largely from Beck's (1976) cognitive theory of depression and Bower's (1981) network theory of emotion. Investigations in this area examine the effects of depression on the processing of valenced (i.e., positive- and negative-content) material. In this literature, cognitive interference would be observed as depression-associated *biases* in attention, judgment, and memory. Finally, explanations for the patterns of deficits and biases in cognitive functioning that have been observed in depression are examined, and fruitful directions for further research are offered.

It should be noted that investigations of cognitive interference in depression have examined a wide range of conditions under the rubric of depression. Thus, studies using experimental mood manipulations, as well as investigations examining cognitive interference in individuals with mild depressive symptoms and with more severe, clinically significant, levels of depression are discussed. In the case of depressive mood inductions, various experimental manipulations are used to create a depressed mood in normal, nondepressed subjects. Although in some of these studies it is possible that demand characteristics might account for performance differences between induced depressed and nondepressed subjects, in general these differences can be more readily attributed to mood state than to other factors often associated with naturally occurring depression (e.g., other symptoms, medications). Furthermore, these studies are potentially informative in terms of localizing the deficit or bias. For example, by manipulating mood at various stages in the information processing sequence, the influence of depressed mood on encoding versus retrieval could be more readily differentiated than would be the case with naturally occurring mood.

Investigations of cognitive interference in mildly depressed, nonclinical subjects typically involve samples of college students who are classified as depressed according to their scores on self-report psychometric instruments, most commonly the Beck Depression Inventory (BDI; Beck, Rush, Shaw, & Emery, 1979). Generally, these subjects have not sought treatment for their dysphoria, and most would not meet diagnostic criteria for major depression. In contrast, investigators examining the impact of more severe, clinically significant, depression on cognitive functioning select subjects who are in treatment for their depressions and who meet formal diagnostic criteria for depressive disorders. In fact, there is evidence to suggest that severity of depression may be an important factor in understanding difficulties in cognitive functioning in this disorder (e.g., Hartlage, Alloy, Vazquez, & Dykman, 1993). Finally, although many investigators explicitly attempt to test patients during medication-free periods, there is little evidence that antidepressants are responsible for cognitive impairments (Wright & Salmon, 1990), and this issue is not addressed further.

COGNITIVE INTERFERENCE WITH NONVALENCED STIMULI

Attention and Concentration

As noted, depressed patients frequently complain about concentration problems and difficulties in maintaining attention. Despite the prevalence of this complaint, there has been relatively little empirical investigation into its specific nature and impact. This state of affairs is particularly surprising given that disruptions and biases in attention are potential explanations for other forms of cognitive interference in depression, such as memory disturbances.

In two experiments, Siebert and Ellis (1991) demonstrated that both sad and happy mood inductions were associated with an increased frequency and intensity of irrelevant thoughts during a memory task. In their first study, Siebert and Ellis asked subjects to list these irrelevant thoughts after the memory task was completed. In contrast, in their second study subjects were asked to "think aloud" during the memory task. Irrelevant thoughts were highly negatively correlated with performance on the memory task in both studies.

Investigators have also begun to examine "thought suppression" (i.e., the ability to not think certain thoughts) as an individual difference variable that might be associated with depression (Wenzlaff, Wegner, & Roper, 1988). An individual's skill at suppressing thoughts would reflect one aspect of his or her attentional capacity, namely the ability to filter out unwanted or task-irrelevant thoughts. Conway, Howell, and Giannopoulos (1991, Study 2) instructed mild depressed and control subjects to "not think of a white bear." These investigators found that dysphoric subjects exhibited more intrusions than did control subjects, but only during the fifth, final minute of suppression. Research with valenced stimuli has similarly found greater negative intrusions in the latter portions of suppression tasks in mild depressives (e.g., Wenzlaff et al., 1988; Conway et al., 1991, Experiment 1). Together, these findings suggest that attentional difficulties involving the inability to suppress unwanted thoughts might be related to reduced cognitive effort in depression or to difficulties in sustaining attention.

Finally, Watts and Sharrock (1985) developed a structured interview and an "online" measure to assess concentration problems in clinical depression. The online measure involved subjects reporting each occasion that they lost their concentration while reading a passage. Watts and Sharrock found that problems in reading and watching television were the most common occasions of concentration difficulty and, further, that the two were highly correlated. Moreover, "mind wandering" was the most commonly reported source of concentration difficulty. Lapses in concentration were primarily attributed to thinking about something else, particularly unpleasant personal events from the past, rather than to distraction from external factors or to blanking out. Most interestingly, similar to Siebert and Ellis' (1991) findings, concentration lapses were negatively correlated with memory performance.

Memory

The literature examining memory for nonvalenced stimuli in depression is both large and complex. Many investigations of the effects of depression on memory have examined memory functioning in the context of a stage model of memory formulated by Atkinson and Shiffrin (1968). An important distinction in this model is that between short-term and long-term memory. Short-term memory is essentially a temporary storage system, in which information is held anywhere from a few seconds to a few minutes before being transferred to long-term memory.

Another important distinction with respect to types of memory involves the degree of intentionality associated with memory (Jacoby, 1991). More specifically, researchers have begun to examine possible dissociations between two particular types of memory. For example, investigators have now demonstrated that some persons (e.g., amnestic patients) can experience profound impairment in *explicit* memory ("intentional" memory under conscious control), but remain relatively unimpaired in *implicit* memory (nonintentional, or "automatic," memory not influenced by conscious control) (Tobias, Kihlstrom, & Schacter, 1992).

To date, the literature on depression and memory for nonvalenced stimuli has been concerned primarily with the study of explicit memory functioning, in which subjects are specifically instructed to recall experimentally presented information, primarily of a semantic nature. More recently, however, the literature on depression and memory has expanded to encompass implicit memory tasks. In the following sections evidence is reviewed concerning possible deficits in both explicit and implicit memory for nonvalenced stimuli in depressed persons.

Explicit Memory

In a widely cited paper, Ellis, Thomas, and Rodriguez (1984) conducted three studies examining memory functioning in persons who were exposed to the Velten (1968) mood induction procedure. The results of all three studies indicated that persons who were in an induced depressed mood state during encoding of the stimuli demonstrated poorer recall than did those in a neutral mood. Further, depressed subjects were most impaired on more difficult tasks, possibly because they demanded greater attention than did the easier tasks. Hertel and Rude (1991b, Experiment 2) also found that mood-induced depressed subjects showed an overall deficit in recall of words that were used previously in a sentence completion task. Finally, similar findings were reported by other investigators (e.g., Hasher & Zacks, 1979; Siebert & Ellis, 1991), and by Hertel and Hardin (1990) for recognition memory.

In each of these studies, mood was manipulated prior to the learning task, suggesting that depressed mood might interfere with the encoding of information. It is possible, however, that depressed mood also interferes with retrieval processes. In fact, it is unclear whether mood affected encoding or retrieval processes in these studies. Indeed, although mood manipulations were conducted prior to encoding, their effects likely persisted during the recall stages. Consequently, memory impairment could have been due to the impact of depressed mood on encoding, retrieval, or both. In this regard, it is important to note that Ellis, Thomas, McFarland, and Lane (1985) found that depressive mood induced subsequent to a learning task also resulted in memory impairment, suggesting that depressed mood can interfere with retrieval processes independent of mood at encoding.

Hasher, Rose, Zacks, Sanft, and Doren (1985) conducted a series of experiments examining memory for positive, negative, and neutral stories in subjects with naturally occurring, mild levels of depression. Across three studies, no evidence was found for memory impairment in depressed students in either short- or long-term memory conditions. Surprisingly, in one study (Experiment 3) depressed subjects exhibited better overall memory of the passage than did nondepressed subjects. Importantly, these null findings cannot be attributed to a lack of statistical power because this research involved some of the largest sample sizes in the literature (N's = 109 to 356).

In attempting to understand the lack of objective memory deficits in Hasher et al.'s (1985) studies, it is important to note that, unlike the majority of studies in this area, which are based on incidental memory paradigms, Hasher et al. informed subjects at the beginning of the studies that their memory for the stories would be tested. It is possible, therefore, that mildly depressed persons are able to shore up their cognitive resources when they know that they will be tested, even though they would likely exhibit deficits if they were not actively attempting to retain information. In contrast to this possibility, Hertel and Rude (1991b, Experiment 1 and Experiment 3) and Potts, Camp, and Coyne (1989) failed to find impairment in naturally occurring, mild depression in experiments examining incidental recall of words previously used in sentence completion tasks.

In contrast to these studies, which deal primarily with long-term memory, Colby and Gotlib (1988) found that mild depression was associated with impairment in short-term memory (measured by a digit-span task). Interestingly, short-term memory deficits were greatest when recall was delayed by 20 and 30 seconds. Colby and Gotlib interpreted this latter finding as suggesting that short-term memory deficits were due in part to deficient rehearsal, which, as will be seen in a later section of this chapter, may itself be due to depressed persons' inability to inhibit task-irrelevant thoughts.

In terms of clinical depression, Stromgren (1977) found that a variety of memory measures were negatively correlated with severity of depression. Further, memory improved following symptom remission with electroconvulsive therapy. Cohen, Weingartner, Smallberg, Pickar, and Murphy (1982) also found memory deficits to be correlated with severity of clinical depression. These researchers investigated motor effort and memory over multiple occasions in inpatients with affective disorders and in normal controls, and found that increasing severity of depression was associated with decrements in performance on both cognitive and motor tasks. When data were analyzed categorically, only severely depressed patients exhibited cognitive deficits; normal controls, euthymic patients, and moderately depressed patients did not differ. Further, consistent with Colby and Gotlib's (1988) findings, severely depressed patients showed significant increases in recall deficits with increases in recall delay.

Other researchers have examined more specific cognitive processes and strategies involved in memory. For example, research conducted by Weingartner, Cohen, Murphy, Martello, and Gerdt (1981) suggests that depressive deficits result from the use of weak encoding strategies. Depressed patients showed impairment in long-term free recall of semantically processed information, but not in cued recall or in memory for acoustically processed material (Experiment 1). Further, compared with nondepressed controls, depressed subjects imposed less structure on information and showed poorer recall of less structured material (Experiment 2). Finally, depressed patients did not differ from controls in recall of word-lists that were highly organized, but showed deficits when the word-list structure was removed (Experiment 3).

More recent investigations have found that depression-associated impairments are most evident on learning materials that involve medium levels of structure (Channon, Baker, & Robertson, 1993; Watts, Dalgleish, Bourke, & Healy, 1990). For example, Backman and Forsell (1994) demonstrated that whereas nondepressed older persons tended to benefit from learning material that was potentially organizable, slowly presented, and cued at time of recall, clinically depressed older persons failed to show these benefits. Findings such as these suggest that depressed persons fail to organize material in a manner conducive to recall. Indeed, some researchers have found that memory deficits could be corrected by structuring the learning task such that subjects focused on the material to be learned (Hertel & Rude, 1991a). Together, these findings suggest that depressives fail to spontaneously initiate strategies that facilitate learning, but can make use of such techniques when explicitly instructed to do so, and indicate that at least some forms of cognitive interference in the depressed can be reduced through specific training programs.

Finally, Hartlage et al. (1993) suggested that depressed persons are more impaired on tasks requiring greater cognitive effort, and are relatively unimpaired on more automatic tasks. Consistent with this formulation, investigators have found that, within intentional tasks, those that require greater effort tend to be associated with the larger depressive deficits. For example, Tancer et al. (1990), Hart, Kwentus, Taylor, and Harkins (1987), Calev and Erwin (1985), and Channon et al. (1993) all found depressed patients to demonstrate greater impairment in learning and recall than in recognition memory (but see also Watts, Morris, & MacLeod, 1987).

Summary. The empirical literature suggests that depression adversely affects explicit memory. It is important to note, however, that deficits are not exhibited on all cognitive measures. More specifically, depressed persons appear weakest on tasks that are difficult and require conscious and effortful retrieval strategies. Furthermore, the severity of depression also appears to be critically important. Deficits are most apparent in studies employing depressive mood inductions and in severe, clinical depression, but are generally absent in naturally occurring mild depression. Although there are relatively few studies, there is no evidence that mild depression is associated with robust deficits in explicit memory.

In attempting to make sense of the null findings associated with mild depression, some investigators have suggested that persons suffering from mild depression learn to adapt to cognitive difficulties over time (Hasher et al., 1985). In this regard, it is important to observe that although these "subclinical depressions" are typically mild affective disturbances, they are often quite longstanding (Depue & Monroe, 1986). If mild depression is initially associated with cognitive impairments, as it is in the case of experimental manipulations, it seems reasonable that people might learn to compensate for these difficulties over time, perhaps by exerting greater effort. This hypothesis suggests that the duration of mild depressive episodes is critically important, and that future studies need to examine individuals at various stages in the development and course of their depressive episodes.

Implicit Memory

In the earliest study of implicit memory in depression, Hertel and Hardin (1990) employed a spelling test of homophones (words that sound alike but that have different meanings and spellings, such as "pear" and "pair"). Subjects were asked questions about the words that reflected the homophones' less common meaning, and were later given a spelling test. Participants' implicit memory would be demonstrated by their use of the less common spelling. Hertel and Hardin found that mood-induced depressed and nondepressed subjects did not differ in the frequency with which they used the less common spelling, indicating that depressive mood is not associated with interference in implicit memory. In contrast, and as mentioned earlier, depressive deficits were found in this study in explicit (recognition) memory.

Danion, Willard-Schroeder, Zimmermann, Grange, and Singer (1991) examined the effects of clinical depression on both explicit (incidental recall) and implicit (word-stem-completion) memory tasks. Both depressed and nondepressed subjects tended to complete wordstems with previously exposed words, thus demonstrating an overall effect of priming. The depressed and nondepressed groups did not differ from each other, however, indicating that implicit memory was intact in the depressed patients. In contrast, and consistent with our conclusions regarding explicit memory, Danion et al. found depressed patients to be significantly impaired in explicit memory.

In a similar study, Watkins, Mathews, Williamson, and Fuller (1992) found no significant differences between depressed and nondepressed subjects in an implicit memory task (word completion), although there was a nonsignificant trend for depressed patients to recall fewer words overall (positive and negative) on a measure of explicit memory (cued recall). Denny and Hunt (1992), too, found lower recall in depressed patients' explicit memory (free recall), but no difference in implicit memory (word fragment completion). These findings concerning explicit memory were stronger when the valence of stimuli was considered.

In contrast to these findings, two studies have reported deficits in implicit memory (Bradley, Mogg, & Williams, 1994; Elliott & Greene, 1992). Interestingly, Bazin, Perruchet, De Bonis, and Feline (1994) pointed out that subjects in Elliott and Greene's study might have become aware that the word-stem completion task measured memory. Specifically, Elliott and Greene's implicit memory task involved only previously presented stimuli at recall. Thus, subjects might have recognized this pattern and employed intentional recall strategies. In contrast, all of the other studies that documented dissociations between explicit and implicit memory in depression used a combination of old and new material in the implicit task, thus preventing the subjects from making a conscious association between exposure and the memory tasks. This explanation, however, is unlikely to account for Bradley et al.'s (1994) finding of implicit memory deficits in high negative affect (NA) college students. These investigators assessed implicit memory with a primed lexical decision task. Implicit memory would be represented in this study by increased speed in lexical decisions for those words to which the subjects had been previously exposed. Explicit memory was assessed by an incidental recall task. Bradley et al. reported that the low NA subjects demonstrated quicker decisions for neutral material that had been subliminally primed, whereas the high NA (likely both mildly depressed and anxious) subjects failed to exhibit this advantage. This finding suggests a deficit in implicit memory in these psychologically distressed individuals.

Summary. Whereas depressive mood inductions and clinical depression appear to be associated with memory deficits when subjects are explicitly asked to recall test material, depressed and nondepressed subjects do not seem to differ on measures of implicit memory. Although implicit memory has been evaluated in various ways, each method involves examining the effects of previous exposure to stimuli on subsequent performance. In general, both depressed and nondepressed subjects show advantages from such priming. Interestingly, one of the few studies that did find depressive impairment in implicit memory (Bradley et al., 1994) involved naturally occurring, mild depression, which tends not to be associated with deficits in explicit memory. We should note here, however, that Roediger and McDermott (1992) argued that these studies of implicit memory "mismatched" their encoding and retrieval tasks in terms of conceptual versus perceptual processing. That is, whereas the encoding task was conceptual (e.g., judging whether adjectives were self-descriptive), the retrieval task relied on perceptual processing (e.g., word-stem completions). Therefore, none of these studies provided an adequate test of whether depression is characterized by a deficit in implicit memory. In contrast, explicit tasks typically use congruent encoding and retrieval tasks (i.e., both tasks are conceptual in nature). In order to assess deficits or biases in implicit memory adequately, therefore, a different set of tests is required, with a closer match between the encoding and the retrieval tasks.

Problem Solving and Decision Making

In contrast to the generally nonsignificant effects of mild levels of depression on memory, there is some evidence that mild depression affects other aspects of cognitive functioning. Smith, Tracy, and Murray (1993, Experiment 1) examined the impact of mild depression on category learning. They hypothesized that depressives' performance would be impaired on tasks that have one particular diagnostic feature that discriminates among categories (criterial-attribute tasks;

CA), because these require flexible attention and analysis. In contrast, depressives' performance would be unimpaired on tasks that benefit from holistic processing (family resemblance tasks; FA) because these are less affected by perseveration and rigid thinking.

Smith et al. (1993, Experiment 1) reported results consistent with these predictions. Whereas depressed subjects performed worse than nondepressed subjects on a CA task, performance on a FA task did not differentiate the two groups. Furthermore, subjects took longer to learn the FA than the CA task, suggesting that it was more difficult. In a second study (Experiment 2), Smith et al. essentially replicated these results in a sample of male psychiatric and medical patients at a Veterans Administration hospital. These findings are intriguing because they imply that it is not overall level of difficulty that is important in understanding depressives' cognitive deficits, but rather the specific nature of the underlying processes involved.

Edwards and Weary (1993) presented evidence that mild depressives tend to engage in a relatively effortful, detailed, and complex analysis of information in a person perception task. Mildly depressed subjects tended to engage in "piecemeal" processing, in which judgments are based on particular attributes, as opposed to "categorical" processing, in which judgments are based on category information. Similarly, mild depression has also been associated with increased production of social inferences (Gleicher & Weary, 1991), and with increased sensitivity to social information in making evaluations (Weary, Jordan, & Hill, 1985). Interestingly, mild depression also has been associated with the use of more limited information in nonsocial decision making (Conway & Giannopoulos, 1993). Taken together, these findings suggest that mildly depressed individuals might process social and nonsocial information very differently (see also Gotlib & Asarnow, 1979). Specifically, mild depression appears to be associated with a more in-depth and vigilant style of processing social information, and a more cursory processing of nonsocial information.

Finally, Silberman, Weingartner, and Post (1983) assessed performance on a visual discrimination task in patients with affective disorders (bipolar-depressed and unipolar depression patients) and in normal controls. Affective disorder patients experienced performance deficits in learning the task and appeared to be hampered by difficulties in their ability to narrow down the set of possible solutions (poor focusing) and perseveration on disconfirmed hypotheses.

Summary. Both mild and severe depression appear to be associated with certain forms of difficulty in learning and problem solving in nonsocial domains. In contrast to the deficits and impairment often found in nonsocial domains, depression seems to be related to a style of highly effortful and detailed analysis of social information. Future research is required to determine whether such hypervigilance might account for deficits in nonsocial domains and whether these findings generalize to clinical depression.

COGNITIVE INTERFERENCE WITH VALENCED STIMULI

As this review of the literature indicates, cognitive interference for neutral, or nonvalenced, material in depression appears to be related to the severity and nature of depression. As will become apparent in the following sections, there is less consensus regarding the influence of severity of depression on the processing of valenced stimuli.

Two influential theories of emotion and cognition, those of Beck (e.g., Beck et al., 1979; Beck & Clark, 1988) and Bower (1981), predict that depression should be associated with cognitive biases that operate in three important areas of information processing: attention, interpretation, and memory. In contrast, other theorists (e.g., Hartlage et al., 1993; Williams, Watts, MacLeod, & Mathews, 1988; Mathews & MacLeod, 1994) proposed that depression is associated primarily with biases in controlled or effortful processing, such as interpretation and memory, but not in areas that involve relatively automatic processing, such as attention. In the following sections, we review empirical evidence concerning the association of depression with biases in attention, judgment, and memory for valenced stimuli.

Attention

Although some contemporary theories of emotion and cognition predict that depression should be associated with an attentional bias for mood-congruent information (e.g., Beck & Clark, 1988; Bower, 1981; see Williams et al., 1988, for a review), the empirical evidence for this formulation is equivocal. One of the paradigms utilized to examine the relation between depression and attention is the emotion Stroop task. In a typical study using this task, subjects are presented with several types of words, some neutral and some disorder-related. The subjects' task is to name the *color* of each word as quickly as possible, while ignoring the word's *content*. The relative interference associated with a delayed naming of disorder-related words compared with neutral words is assumed to reflect an attentional bias favoring negatively valenced (i.e., disorder-related) information.

In the first study in this area, Gotlib and McCann (1984) tachistiscopically presented depressed, neutral, and manic words to mildly depressed and nondepressed college students. They found that the depressed students were slower to color name depressed-content than neutral words; in contrast, the nondepressed students did not exhibit differential response latencies to the three types of words. In a second experiment, nondepressed students performed the emotion Stroop task following a negative, positive, or neutral mood-induction procedure. Because no differential response latencies were found among these three groups of subjects, Gotlib and McCann argued that the negative cognitive interference found in mildly depressed persons could not be explained by transient mood (but see also Gilboa and Revelle, 1994). Similar results were obtained by Williams and Nulty (1986), who found that mildly depressed subjects were slower to color name negative emotion words than neutral words. Interestingly, this effect was most pronounced for subjects who were chronically depressed. In contrast, another study (Hill & Knowles, 1991) found no evidence for selective interference with negative stimuli (self-esteem threatening and negative adjectives) in mildly depressed subjects. Instead, depression was associated with a general retardation in color-naming.

Gotlib and Cane (1987) assessed clinically depressed psychiatric patients on the emotion Stroop task at two different time points: first when the subjects were hospitalized, and second within a week following discharge, when they were no longer clinically depressed. While depressed, the patients exhibited the predicted interference with depression-related words. After discharge, however, this bias was no longer evident. These results suggest that depression-induced interference is state, rather than trait, related and, combined with the findings of Gotlib and McCann (1984, Study 2), suggest that a state of naturally occurring depression, rather than an experimentally induced negative mood, is required for this interference to be manifested.

Using a somewhat different paradigm, Gotlib, McLachlan, and Katz (1988), demonstrated an association between depression and mood-related information using a "color perception" task. Gotlib et al. presented subjects with a series of word pairs differing in emotional valence (e.g., negative paired with neutral), followed by a simultaneous presentation of two color bars, replacing both of the original words. The subjects' task was to indicate which color bar appeared first. If subjects are attending to a particular word in the word pair, they are more likely to perceive it as appearing first. Because this task relies less on strategic processes (i.e., processes that take place serially and are influenced by such factors as capacity limitations and practice), it is assumed to provide a purer measure of attentional deployment than the Stroop task. The results of this study indicated that *nondepressed* subjects showed an attentional bias favoring positive words, whereas *mildly depressed* individuals demonstrated an even-handedness in their deployment of attention, attending equally often to positive, neutral, and negative stimuli. In a follow-up to this study, Mogg et al. (1991, Experiment 3) sought to replicate these results, and concluded that this attentional bias was more closely related to anxiety than to depression (but see also McCabe & Gotlib, 1995).

Investigators have also used lexical decision tasks to examine attentional biases in depression, but these studies have generally found only weak support for biases. In these studies, subjects were requested to make a judgment about a target word (for example, subjects were asked to judge whether the target word is a legitimate English word). If affect automatically activates semantically congruent stimuli, individuals in depressed affective states should be faster and more accurate in identifying words that are associated with their affective state (cf. Bower, 1981). Yet, most lexical decision tasks have not supported such an association. For example, Clark, Teasdale, Broadbent, and Martin (1983) reported a failure to find effects of induced depression on lexical decision tasks regarding negative and neutral personality trait words. Similarly, Challis and Krane (1988) had subjects in a positive or a negative mood perform a lexical decision task for positive or negative trait adjectives, neutral nontrait adjectives, or nonwords. Although subjects in a positive mood showed facilitated processing of positive words, this mood-congruent facilitation was not obtained for negative-mood subjects.

Dichotic listening tasks have also been utilized in examining attentional processes in depression. Ingram, Bernet, and McLaughlin (1994), for example, administered a dichotic listening task to college students with a previous episode of major depression and to never depressed subjects. The task involved repeating, or shadowing, an affectively neutral story that was presented in one ear, while positive, neutral, or negative distractor words were presented in the other ear at 10-second intervals. Prior to the dichotic listening task subjects received either a depressive or a neutral mood induction. Interestingly, depressive mood inductions differentially affected the remitted and never depressed subjects. In the case of remitted depressives, depressed mood resulted in attentional disruptions (defined as errors on the verbal tracking task) for both positive and negative stimuli, whereas depressive mood failed to influence attention in never depressed individuals. In a similar study, McCabe and Gotlib (1993) assessed clinically depressed and nondepressed subjects on a dichotic listening task with a secondary reaction time task to an external light. McCabe and Gotlib found that, whereas clinically diagnosed depressed subjects showed slower reaction times to pressing a button to the light when negative words were presented in the unattended channel than when neutral or positive words were presented, nondepressed subjects did not demonstrate differential reaction times. These studies suggest that attentional interference effects for depression are state dependent, but also raise the interesting possibility that mood might affect aspects of cognition more powerfully in persons who are vulnerable to depression (see Segal & Ingram, 1994, for a recent review).

Finally, we should note here that the association between depression and biases in attentional processing is complicated by the high comorbidity between depression and anxiety. Given the well-documented association between anxiety and attentional biases (see Williams et al., 1988, for a review), and the high degree of comorbidity between depression and anxiety (cf. Maser & Cloninger, 1990), it is possible that the relation between depression and attentional biases is mediated by concomitant anxiety. Indeed, Mogg, Bradley, Williams, and Mathews (1993) recently found that anxious, but not depressed, patients exhibited interference with both supraliminal and subliminal Stroop presentation of negative materials. Because most studies of depressed subjects have generally not assessed the role that concomitant anxiety may be playing in the deployment of attention, the nature of the relation between depression and attentional biases is unclear.

Summary. Studies attempting to document a relation between depression and attentional biases for valenced materials present a rather mixed pattern of results, some supporting the existence of this association, and some failing to do so. It is unclear whether severity of depression is associated with more pronounced attentional biases. Similarly, the relation between degree of self-relevance of valanced stimuli and attentional deployment has yet to be examined. And finally, it is unclear whether the association between depression and attentional bias is mediated by anxiety. As outlined in greater detail later, these are all important areas for further investigation.

Judgment and Interpretation

Environmental stimuli can rarely be unambiguously categorized as either positive or negative. Ultimately, it is the process of interpretation that assigns valence to these stimuli. Interpretative and judgment biases are central to Beck's (1976) theory of depression because it is the interpretation and the incorporation of novel information into a person's knowledge base that helps perpetuate depressive schemata. Given the theoretical importance of the interpretative process, surprisingly few experimental studies have assessed the relation between depression and interpretative biases.

One major line of research on interpretative biases is concerned with causal attributions for hypothetical positive and negative events. Miller and Morretti (1988) reviewed a number of studies comparing such attributions across depressed and nondepressed individuals. They concluded that the most reliable finding is that depressives take more personal responsibility for negative outcomes than do nondepressed individuals. Depressed and nondepressed persons generally do not differ in their attributions for positive outcomes: both tend to make more internal than external attributions. In contrast, Forgas, Bower, and Moylan (1990; Experiment 1) found that depressive mood inductions can influence judgments concerning both success and failure. Specifically, sad subjects were more likely to attribute success to external sources and failure to internal sources than were either happy or control subjects.

Studies of judgments of real-life performance on tasks involving achievement and interpersonal performance suggest similar conclusions: Depressives seem to be "harsher" in performance judgments than nondepressed individuals (e.g., Cane & Gotlib, 1985; Forgas, Bower, & Krantz, 1984). For example, Forgas et al. (1984) found that experimentally induced depressive mood affected subjects' judgment of their interpersonal performance. These subjects were asked to observe their previously videotaped social interaction and monitor and identify skilled (positive) and unskilled (negative) behavior in both themselves and their partners. Sad subjects were more critical of their own, than their partner's behavior. Cane and Gotlib (1984) reported similar findings with naturally occurring mild depression. They found that depressives' ratings of their own performance were negatively biased compared to objective ratings. Similarly, Forgas (1994) reported that subjects in whom sad mood was induced tended to blame themselves for interpersonal conflicts to a greater extent than did happy subjects. With respect to achievement tasks, Forgas, Bower and Moylan (1990) found that following a negative mood induction, individuals demonstrated self-critical attributions for performance on an exam.

Another important line of research has examined subjects' expectancies of future life events. For example, depressive mood inductions appear to lead to inflated subjective probabilities for adverse future life events and lower probabilities for positive events (e.g., Constans & Mathews, 1993). Similarly, other studies have found that naturally occuring mild depression is associated with a tendency to expect more negative and fewer positive life events in the future (e.g., Anderson, Spielman, & Bargh, 1992; Gaschke, Braveman, & Evans, 1992). Finally, depressive affect has been demonstrated to influence person perception, stereotyping, judgments of conflicts and relationships, and effectiveness of persuasion in a similar manner (e.g., Forgas, 1991). Forgas (1994) proposed an intriguing framework, the Affect Infusion Model, to understand such effects. He suggested that the presence and magnitude of the effects of affect on social judgment depend on the complexity and constructiveness of the processes involved in making a judgment. Forgas argued that affect infusion into judgment is more likely to occur when making constructive and substantive judgments (e.g., judgments of serious interpersonal conflict) than when making relatively more simple judgments based on direct retrieval of previously made evaluations (e.g., evaluation of living quarters).

Summary. Whereas the association between depression and biases in judgment/interpretation is well documented (albeit based almost exclusively on self-report measures of judgment), the nature of the relation between these constructs is still unclear. Some researchers argue that these biases are stable and increase risk for developing depression subsequent to life stressors (e.g., Abramson, Metalsky, & Alloy, 1989). Another, not necessarily incompatible, view holds that biases in the interpretation of events is a *concomitant* of the depressed mood. Consistent with this possibility, the literature just reviewed suggests that biased event interpretation and event expectancies are due, at least in part, to mood-congruent biases. Given the likely importance of depressives' tendency to negative attributions, negative self-evaluations, and self-blame, the study of judgment and interpretative biases clearly warrants more extensive attention. Finally, it is not difficult to see how biased interpretation of information can perpetuate depression and contribute to cognitive interference. For example, as depressed persons engage in tasks, they might experience some difficulties or encounter some dead ends. If those experiences are interpreted as excessively negative, or indeed, as representative of future events, the depressed individuals might begin to ruminate and engage in task-irrelevant thoughts. These cognitions, in turn, would not only further impair performance, but could contribute to the maintenance or exacerbation of dysphoria.

Memory

As noted earlier in this chapter, studies examining depressed persons' memory for nonvalenced material have examined both explicit and implicit memory for experimentally-presented neutral stimuli. In contrast, investigations assessing depression-associated deficits or biases in memory for valenced material typically examine either autobiographical memory or memory for experimentally-presented valenced stimuli.

Memory for Autobiographical Experiences

Several recent investigations have examined the relation between depression and the time taken to retrieve autobiographical memories (e.g., Richards & Whittaker, 1990; Williams & Scott, 1988). In a typical experiment, subjects are presented with neutral, positive, and negative word cues, and are asked to retrieve a specific autobiographical memory. The results of these studies suggest that depressed individuals, but not normal controls, take longer to respond to positive than to negative cues, and retrieve positive memories that are less specific. These findings are also consistent with the results of earlier studies on personal memory and depression (e.g., Lloyd & Lishman, 1975; Teasdale & Fogarty, 1979).

Although the finding that depressed individuals have a biased retrieval pattern for autobiographical materials is reliable, the explanation for this bias remains problematic. On the one hand, it might be argued that differential retrieval effects between depressed and nondepressed subjects reflect differences in actual memory content (the "past experiences" hypothesis). On the other hand, it is also plausible that affective states influence the retrieval of personal memories (the "mood congruency" hypothesis). Of course, these two hypotheses are not necessarily incompatible: depressed individuals may have experienced more negative events in their past *and* depressive mood may enhance retrieval of these past events (Williams, 1992).

Consistent with the mood congruency hypothesis, studies employing within-subject designs (i.e., examined the same individuals on several occasions) find that the pattern of autobiographical recall changes with fluctuations in affect (see Williams, 1992, for a review). Clark and Teasdale (1982), for example, found that diurnal variations in the intensity of depressed mood in clinically depressed persons affected the probability of their retrieving a happy memory: as the depressed mood intensified, the probability of retrieving a positive memory decreased. More recently, Bullington (1990) assessed university students on two occasions. In the first session subjects generated their own stimuli by reporting autobiographical experiences. During the second session, 24 hours later, and following a mood induction, subjects were asked to recall the same personal experiences. Bullington found that subjects recalled a greater number of pleasant experiences when they were in a positive rather than in a negative mood state.

Studies that have employed between-subject designs (i.e., examined different individuals in various affective states) have yielded a less consistent pattern of results. Mood congruency findings have been reported in a number of laboratory studies (e.g., Parrott, 1991; Richards & Whittaker, 1990; see Singer & Salovey, 1988 for a review), in a naturalistic study using a recognition-memory test (Barclay, Pettitto, Larbum, & Carter-Jessop, 1991), and in a study using depressed and nondepressed older individuals (Yang & Rehm, 1993). In contrast, several naturalistic quasi-experiments conducted by Parrott and Sabini (1990) revealed mood-incongruent biases in autobiographical recall. Furthermore, Seidlitz and Diener (1993) found that retrieval mood did not make a significant independent contribution to recall differences. (However, the latter finding should be interpreted with caution because only a single-item measure of mood was used.) Although the reason for this inconsistent pattern of findings is unclear, it appears that the particulars of the memory tasks used and the type of affective state induced are important. For example, mood congruence is observed when subjects are made aware of the relevance of their moods to the experiment, and when the task involves retrieving a specific memory to a specific cue (typically, an emotion word). In contrast, mood-incongruent findings are observed in experiments with more subtle mood manipulations (e.g., sunny or rainy weather), and when no given cues are presented; in these studies subjects were asked to recall events that had occurred during a particular time interval (e.g., during their high school years).

Taken together, the results of both between- and within-subject studies suggest that autobiographical retrieval biases are at least partly a function of affective states, although actual memory content is also likely to play a role. Depressives exhibit a biased pattern of recall of personal experiences, tending to have decreased availability and less specific memory for positive materials (Williams, 1992). However, the degree to which this bias is the result of differences in actual experiences, automatic memory processes, strategic deficiencies in depressives' use of mood-repair techniques, or differences in the interpretation of ambiguous episodic information, is still unclear.

Memory for Experimentally Presented Materials

Explicit Memory. Studies examining depression-associated deficits or biases in memory for experimentally presented valenced stimuli typically have subjects rate words that vary in affective content for degree of self-descriptiveness, and later ask subjects to recall as many of the words that they rated as possible. Numerous studies have demonstrated that clinically depressed subjects show a strong bias to recall negative, especially self-referential, information, while nondepressed subjects tend to demonstrate a bias in recalling positive material (cf. MacLeod & Mathews, 1991; Matt, Vazquez, & Campbell, 1992). Interestingly, and consistent with the severity issue described earlier, subclinically depressed subjects tend to show an intermediate even-handed memory, remembering approximately equal amounts of positive and negative material (Matt et al., 1992).

The substantial literature regarding memory for experimentally-presented, valenced materials has been the subject of several recent reviews and analyses (e.g., MacLeod & Mathews, 1991; Matt et al., 1992); therefore, this literature is not reviewed here. However, the conclusion that the mood-congruent memory bias is specific to depression-relevant words is noteworthy. For example, Watkins et al. (1992) included physical threat words as well as depression-relevant words in their experimental materials, and found depressed subjects to demonstrate a bias only for the depression-relevant words. Similarly, Bellew and Hill (1990) found a recall bias in depressed subjects for self-esteem threatening words, but not for negative words in general. The disorder specific nature of memory biases (i.e., enhanced memory for depression specific material) can be contrasted with a general negativity bias in attention (i.e., enhanced attention to negative material in general), and is consistent with Williams et al.'s (1988) emphasis on depressive biases in later stages of the information-processing sequence (i.e., after attention but before memory).

Finally, the literature on memory for experimentally presented words is supplemented by studies assessing memory for nonverbal materials, such as recall of positive and negative task-performance feedback. Gotlib (1983), for example, found that mildly and more severely depressed persons tended to underestimate their positive performance feedback and to negatively distort their recall of self-relevant personality feedback. Thus, memory for various types of experimentally presented materials seems to be influenced by a common depression-associated bias.

Implicit Memory. In the past several years researchers have begun to address the question of whether depressed subjects show mood-congruency effects in implicit memory, as they do in explicit memory. Demonstration of implicit mood-congruent memory biases in depression would help to account for the phenomenon of intrusive thoughts: because negative information may be activated automatically, that is, independent of a person's strategic efforts to recall (or suppress) such information, it may appear to come to mind spontaneously. However, consistent with the findings described earlier in the discussion of implicit memory for nonvalenced stimuli, studies in this area have found no evidence of a implicit mood-congruent memory bias for negative information, although they all replicated the standard explicit mood-congruency effects (Bradley et al., 1994; Danion et al., 1991; Denny & Hunt, 1992; Hertel & Hardin, 1990; Watkins et al., 1992). As noted earlier, however, Roediger and McDermott (1992) contended that none of these studies provided an adequate test of whether depression is characterized by a bias in implicit memory, and future research needs to match more closely the characteristics of encoding and retrieval tasks used in examinations of implicit memory.

Summary. The evidence for attentional biases in depression seems to be mixed, and its interpretation complicated particularly by the high comorbidity between depression and anxiety. Although evidence for interpretative or judgment biases in depression seems to be relatively solid, too few experimental studies using objective (e.g., reaction-time) measures have been conducted. Indeed, at present, the most robust finding in this area is that depression is associated with negative mood-congruent biases in explicit memory; related evidence regarding implicit memory biases is inconclusive.

What are the implications of these biases for cognitive interference in depression? Teasdale (1988) and others have argued that memory biases for negative self-referential material, in combination with the interpretative and judgmental biases, are important because they can be seen as creating a "vicious cycle of depression." The addition of negative memory and judgment/interpretative biases to an already existing depressive episode can easily perpetuate the depression. Furthermore, interpretative, and especially memorial, biases are likely to lead to the subjective experience of negative intrusions, in which recollection of unpleasant past experiences and negative interpretations of present experiences spontaneously come to mind. Consistent with this formulation, Howell and Conway (1992) found that mood-congruent thoughts are more likely to intrude during a period of thought suppression than are mood-incongruent thoughts. In another set of experiments Wenzlaff, Wegner, and Roper (1988) found that depressed college students frequently experience intrusion of unpleasant thoughts, even if they attempt to exercise mental control to suppress this negative material. Thus, it is plausible that biases in attention, judgment, and memory can interact both to produce cognitive interference in depression, and to perpetuate the depressive episode.

EXPLANATIONS FOR COGNITIVE INTERFERENCE IN DEPRESSION

A number of theories have been proposed in attempt to explain cognitive interference in depression. The basic premise of most of these theories is that depressed individuals direct fewer attentional resources towards external tasks than do their nondepressed counterparts, resulting in impaired performance on these tasks (e.g., Ellis & Ashbrook, 1988; Hasher & Zacks, 1979; Hartlage et al., 1993). Overall, these theories were primarily developed to explain deficits and biases in memory functioning in depression. Nevertheless, several can also be extended in attempts to account for depression-associated interference in attention, judgment, and learning.

Motivation

In his early review of the literature, Miller (1975) concluded that cognitive impairment in depression was likely due to motivational deficits: depressives (as well as psychiatric patients in general) simply did not exert as much effort on cognitive tasks as did normal controls. Similarly, Weingartner et al. (1981) concluded that depressives' poor cognitive performance was due to motivational factors. In their study deficits were most apparent when sustained effort was required. It is also possible that clinically inexperienced test administrators, who are frequently used in research settings, are simply less able to elicit optimal performances from less motivated depressed patients (Grossman, Kaufman, Mednitsky, Scharff, & Dennis, 1994).

In an attempt to test this motivational hypothesis directly, Richards and Ruff (1989) compared the performance of depressed outpatients and normal controls on neuropsychological tests. Motivation was manipulated by providing monetary incentives to half of the subjects in each group for putting forth their best effort. Results showed that, although measures of verbal performance did not discriminate depressed subjects from nondepressed controls, the depressed subjects demonstrated impairment on visuospatial attention and learning, as well as on verbal learning. Moreover, in contrast to Cohen et al.'s (1982) conclusions, these differences could not be attributed to motivation.

Studies reporting specific or localized depressive deficits are also inconsistent with the motivational hypothesis. For example, much of the research we reviewed above concerning processing of valenced stimuli has found that depressed persons show cognitive deficits primarily with respect to the processing of positive information; indeed, they are actually advantaged when processing negative material. If depressives simply were not exerting as much effort, we would expect general deficits across content domains. Nevertheless, it is important to note here that depressive deficits that have been obtained on more difficult, effortful tasks, as opposed to easier, automatic tasks (e.g., Hartlage et al., 1993) are consistent with motivational explanations. At this point, therefore, it can be concluded that although the role of effort remains uncertain, it is unlikely to account for all of the different types of cognitive interference reviewed in this chapter. Further, it is possible that the role of effort might be more important in particular stages and processes, such as initiative in spontaneously employing learning strategies (e.g., Hertel & Hardin, 1990).

Capacity Reduction

According to capacity reduction theories, total cognitive capacity is reduced in depressed individuals, resulting in fewer attentional resources directed towards an external task (e.g., Hasher & Zacks, 1979; see Hartlage et al., 1993 for review). This formulation suggests that depressed subjects should consistently perform worse than controls on effortful, resource-demanding, tasks. However, as our review indicates, such global performance decrements are the exception rather than the rule. The existence and magnitude of cognitive deficits in depression depends critically on task instructions (i.e., whether or not subjects were explicitly instructed to remember specific material) and on the type of stimuli (e.g., neutral, negative, social). Furthermore, an important difficulty in evaluating results from studies purporting to test capacity reduction theories is the lack of an independent measure of cognitive capacity. Although there are methodologies capable of assessing this construct (e.g., secondary task procedures; Hasher & Zacks, 1988; McCabe & Gotlib, 1993), they have been used only rarely to test these theories.

In contrast to relatively global cognitive-capacity-reduction theories, other theorists propose that capacity is not reduced, but *reallocated* (or redistributed) between criterion task processing and extra-task processing (e.g., Ellis & Ashbrook, 1988; Ingram & Wisnicki, 1991). Because of this redistribution, fewer resources are allocated to the criterion task, resulting in depression-associated deficits (Hartlage et al., 1993). Indeed, the following three explanations in somewhat different ways all implicate resource allocation difficulties in accounting for depression-associated cognitive interference.

Strategy Initiation

Hertel and Hardin (1990) proposed that depressives' deficits in memory occur mainly when tasks permit variation in the control of processing. Whereas nondepressed subjects spontaneously generate elaborative heuristics to assist them in task performance, depressed subjects seem to do only what they are told. The cognitive initiation hypothesis goes beyond proposing that depressed individuals are impaired at controlled, but not at automatic, types of information processing (e.g., Hartlage et al., 1993). Instead, it suggests that the difference in performance between depressed and nondepressed individuals has more to do with the extent to which controlled procedures are *initiated* by the subjects than with task automaticity (Hertel, 1994). In other words, depressed subjects might be impaired on relatively automatic tasks if these tasks have to be spontaneously initiated. Similarly, depressed subjects may not be impaired on relatively resource-intensive (and, thus, nonautomatic) tasks if given specific instructions that facilitate memory.

Support for the "reduced initiative" account of depressive deficits comes from studies in which the degree to which controlled procedures can be spontaneously initiated by the subjects is varied. For example, Channon et al. (1993) varied the degree of structure of to-be-remembered lists. They reasoned that if depressive deficits are due to a failure to initiate learning strategies spontaneously, the deficits would be greatest when the benefits from such strategies are most pronounced (i.e., ease of encoding is high and prior organization is low). Thus, impairment should be greatest with material of medium structure, rather than with materials of either high or low structure. Consistent with the initiative account, Channon et al. found that clinically depressed subjects were more impaired in a medium-structure condition than they were in high- or low-structure conditions. Hertel (1994) similarly varied the degree to which self-initiated strategies in attending to word meanings could influence implicit tests of word identification. Her results suggested that whereas nondepressed subjects spontaneously integrated letters into words even when not specifically required to do so, depressed subjects did not. Hertel argued that these results are inconsistent with the cognitive capacity accounts: the capacity model suggests that depressive deficits should be most pronounced with resource-demanding tasks, but the deficits in Hertel's study occurred with a relatively simple task (i.e., the integration of letters into words).

Failures of Inhibition

Some theorists maintain that depression-associated memory impairments could result from difficulties in inhibiting task-irrelevant thoughts (e.g., Hertel & Rude, 1991a; Siebert & Ellis, 1991). Such thoughts would interfere with performance due to distraction because they would compete for attentional resources. This hypothesis implies that there are individual differences in the ability to inhibit, or suppress, thoughts that come to mind, and that these individual differences mediate the relation between depression and memory. Depression would be associated with memory difficulties only indirectly through its relation with poor inhibitory mechanisms. Indeed, consistent with this hypothesis, test anxiety appears to be related to poorer performance through the mediating role of cognitive intrusions and distraction (e.g., Sarason, 1984; Sarason, Sarason, Keefe, Hayes, & Shearin, 1986). More directly, Siebert and Ellis (1991) found that induced depressed mood was associated with thoughts that subjects rated as task irrelevant and distracting. Most importantly, these thoughts were related to poorer recall in a memory task. This investigation, however, failed to assess subjects' ability to control such thoughts and, consequently, was unable to test Hertel and Rude's (1991a) hypothesis that depression is associated with disturbances in central inhibitory processes that make any thoughts that come to mind distracting.

A related theory of depression has been proposed by Nolen-Hoeksema (1987, 1991), who emphasized the critical importance of ruminative response styles in depression. She posits that individuals who tend to repetitively dwell on the causes, meanings, and consequences of depression experience more prolonged periods of dysphoria, compared to individuals who tend to actively distract themselves. This model has been supported empirically in laboratory studies in which responses to depression are manipulated (Morrow & Nolen-Hoeksema, 1990), as well as in prospective field studies (e.g., Nolen-Hoeksema, Morrow, & Fredrickson, 1993; Nolen-Hoeksema, Parker, & Larson, 1994). Overall, the results of this research indicate that individuals who respond to depressed mood with rumination tend to remain depressed for longer periods of time. Further, Nolen-Hoeksema (1987; Nolen-Hoeksema et al., 1993) suggested that gender differences in depression might be accounted for by females being more likely than males to respond to depressive affect with rumination.

Interestingly, this model is also consistent with other recent theoretical and empirical work suggesting that depression is associated with heightened self-focused attention (e.g., Ingram, 1990; Pyszczynski & Greenberg, 1987). If depression is indeed marked by intense self-focus and rumination, it is easy to understand how memory deficits might arise. Because depressives are so attuned to internal matters, they would allocate less attention to external stimuli during encoding. As a consequence, depressives would have less material in memory storage available for potential retrieval. On the other hand, rumination and self-focused attention models have more difficulty with negative memory biases in depression. In particular, it is not clear how they would explain *enhanced* memory for negative stimuli. It is possible that, whereas depressives pay relatively little attention to external stimuli in general, they are hypervigilant to negative stimuli. Indeed, studies employing attentional measures, such as the emotional Stroop task, support the viability of this hypothesis (e.g., Gotlib & McCann, 1984). Such vigilance would lead to greater storage of negative material in memory, facilitating recall of this material during retrieval. In turn, increased attention and memory for negative material may also influence the interpretation of incoming ambiguous stimuli. Thus, depressed persons' increased accessibility of negative recollections and negatively toned ruminations may bias their online judgments of events occurring in their lives.

Extensive Elaboration

The Williams et al. (1988) model is based on the idea that there may be unique modes of cognitive operation associated with each primary emotion (Oately & Johnson-Laird, 1987). Because depression involves significant reflective consideration of life events involving failure and loss (e.g., Beck, 1976; Bowlby, 1980), it should also be associated with an extensive elaboration of past (especially negative) events. Accordingly, Williams et al. proposed that depression is characterized by a tendency to process mood-congruent material to a disproportionate degree, but not by any special early activation of this material. This formulation accounts for the consistent evidence observed in the depression literature for mood-congruent explicit memory biases, where material has already been processed and elaborated (but not implicit memory biases), and for the relatively inconsistent evidence for attentional biases for negative information. Although this theory does not directly offer predictions regarding depressives' performance with neutral materials, one may postulate that the process of extensive elaboration may deplete cognitive resources, thereby diverting attention from neutral to negative materials. In addition, this theory is able to account for variations in patterns of depressive deficits across different levels of severity. For example, some theorists suggest that as depressed mood worsens or becomes more chronic, mood-congruent biases may become increasingly automated, and thus affect not only elaborative, but also attentional and integrative processes (e.g., Mathews & MacLeod, 1994).

FUTURE DIRECTIONS

A "bold strokes" summary of the literature reviewed so far suggests several conclusions. First, although cognitive *deficits* in depression appear to be related to the severity of the disorder, the issue of severity and nature of depression (induced, mild, or clinical) has been less thoroughly examined in terms of cognitive *biases*. Second, depressive deficits are more pronounced with controlled, effortful, and elaborative memory tasks than with automatic and relatively easy tasks. Third, depressives have better memory for negative material than they do for either neutral or positive material. Finally, depression appears to negatively bias interpretation and judgment processes. Unfortunately, too few studies have been conducted to make general conclusions about social information processing and problem solving.

Thus far, the lines of research addressing questions of severity, process, and valence have proceeded with little integration. For example, there are very few single studies in which memory biases were examined with different depressive populations (e.g., mood-induced, mildly depressed, and clinically depressed individuals). Although these groups are examined in *different* studies, it is clear that a *single* study that examines different groups with same materials within the same task is more sensitive than across-studies comparisons. Thus, in order to provide a more complete account of the mechanisms that mediate cognitive interference in depression, as well as to help elucidate the etiology and maintenance of this disorder, these lines of research need to be integrated.

The first set of questions that could be addressed by such an integrated approach concerns the nature of the circumstances under which cognitive interference becomes potent. Do some deficits and biases emerge only at severe levels of depressed mood? Are these deficits and biases stable, that is, evident at multiple time points (e.g., after the intensity of the negative affective state associated with a depressive episode decreases)? In contrast, is cognitive interference merely a concomitant of depression that completely disappears following recovery? Or are these deficits and biases latent, as Beck postulated, and potentially activated by stressful life events and dysphoric mood? Studies with remitted depressives seem to be especially useful in addressing such questions. Indeed, the results of such studies indicate that mood-congruent attention and memory biases appear to remit following recovery from depression (Gotlib & Cane, 1987; MacLeod & Mathews, 1991; McCabe & Gotlib, 1993). However, given that at least some of these biases can be observed with induced depressed mood in normal subjects, it will be important to determine whether remitted depressives show an even more powerful mood-congruent memory bias than do normals under a depressive mood induction procedure (cf. Teasdale & Dent 1987). The existing pattern of results suggests that remitted depressives would be more vulnerable to the effects of depressed mood on memory than would normals, which could, in turn, partially mediate their vulnerability for future episodes of depression.

The second set of questions concerns the interaction between cognitive strategies and the nature of the information that is affected by these processes. For example, are similar cognitive strategies applied to the processing of different types of material (i.e., neutral, positive, and negative)? Addressing this question directly requires a study that includes materials differing in structure as well as in valence. If depressives exhibit deficits in strategy initiation with respect to the neutral, but not the negative, materials, theories implicating *global* difficulties in strategy initiation would need to be revised.

There is also a lack of studies testing particular causal mechanisms that might produce cognitive interference in depression directly. For example, how are cognitive resources reallocated in depression? Is failure at inhibiting task-irrelevant thoughts related to decreased memory performance? Finally, although it is abundantly clear from the research reviewed and discussed in this chapter that certain patterns of cognitive deficits are *associated* with depression, we know much less about the *causal status* of cognitive interference in depression. For example, to what extent does enhanced memory for negative information actually serve to maintain or exacerbate depressed mood? Do biases in attentional and memory functioning have predictive validity with respect to the onset or course of depression? Do these biases represent a vulnerability in currently nondisordered individuals?

Interestingly, although biases in attentional and memory functioning appear to normalize following recovery from depression, there is promising evidence indicating that these biases may predict the course of depression (e.g., Brittlebank, Scott, Williams, & Perrier, 1993; Dent & Teasdale, 1988). In addition, the results of a number of studies suggest that information processing biases may also predict onset of depression (e.g., Bellew & Hill, 1990, 1991). Future studies might examine a broader set of causal hypotheses and their relation to depression onset, maintenance, recovery, and relapse. For example, thought suppression mechanisms might be studied from a longitudinal perspective. Is propensity to be distracted by irrelevant thoughts correlated with the onset of depression, with the length of the depressive episode (maintenance), or with susceptibility to relapse? Such research is needed because, in spite of the significant progress in understanding cognitive deficits and biases in depression, the causal mechanisms underlying this interference remain to be elucidated. Research examining depressed, as well as depression-prone individuals, combined with an assessment of the processes, materials, and cognitive strategies used by these individuals, is likely to provide answers to these important questions.

REFERENCES

Abramson, L. Y., Metalsky, G. I., & Alloy, L. B. (1989). Hopelessness Depression: A theory based subtype of depression. *Psychological Review, 96*, 358–372.

American Psychiatric Association. (1994). *Diagnostic and statistical manual of mental disorders, 4th ed.* Washington, DC: Author. American Psychiatric Association.

Andersen, S. M., Spielman, L. A., & Bargh, J. A. (1992). Future-event schemas and certainty about the future: Automaticity in depressives' future-event predictions. *Journal of Personality and Social Psychology, 63*, 711–723.

Atkinson, R. C., & Shiffrin, R. (1968). Human memory: A proposed system and its control processes. In K. Spence & J. Spence (Eds.), *The psychology of learning and motivation* (Vol. 2). New York: Academic Press.

Backman, L., & Forsell, Y. (1994). Episodic memory functioning in a community-based sample of old adults with major depression: Utilization of cognitive support. *Journal of Abnormal Psychology, 103*, 361–370.

Barclay, C. R., Pettito, A., Larbum, A. H., & Carter-Jessop, L. (1991). Mood-related self-schemata and mood congruity effects in autobiographical memory: A study of women with premenstrual syndrome. *Applied Cognitive Psychology, 5*, 461–481.

Bazin, N., Perruchet, P., De Bonis, M., & Feline, A. (1994). The dissociation of explicit and implicit memory in depressed patients. *Psychological Medicine, 24*, 239–245.

Beck, A. T. (1976). *Cognitive therapy and the emotional disorders*. New York: International Universities Press.

Beck, A. T., & Clark, D. A. (1988). Anxiety and depression: An information processing perspective. *Anxiety Research 1*, 23–36.

Beck, A. T., Rush, A. J., Shaw, B. T., & Emery, G. (1979). *Cognitive therapy of depression*. New York: Guilford.

Bellew, M., & Hill, B. (1990). Negative recall bias as a predictor of susceptibility to induced depressive mood. *Personality and Individual Differences, 11*, 471–480.

Bellew, M., & Hill, B. (1991). Negative recall bias as predictor of susceptibility of depression following childbirth. *Personality and Individual Differences, 12*, 943–949.

Blaney, P. H. (1986). Affect and memory: A review. *Psychological Bulletin, 99*, 229–246.

Bower, G. H. (1981). Mood and memory. *American Psychologist, 36*(2), 129–148.

Bowlby, J. (1980). *Loss: Sadness and depression*. New York: Basic Books.

Bradley, B. P., Mogg, K., & Williams, R. (1994). Implicit and explicit memory for emotional information in non-clinical subjects. *Behavioral Research and Therapy, 32*, 65–78.

Brittlebank, A. D., Scott, J., Williams, J. M., & Perrier, I. N. (1993). Autobiographical memory in depression: State or trait marker? *British Journal of Psychiatry, 162*, 118–121.

Bullington, J. C. (1990). Mood congruent memory: A replication of symmetrical effects for both positive and negative moods. *Journal of Social Behavior and Personality, 5*, 123–134.

Calev, A., & Erwin, P. G. (1985). Recall and recognition in depressives: Use of matched tasks. *British Journal of Clinical Psychology, 24*, 127–128.

Cane, D. B., & Gotlib, I. H. (1985). Depression and the effects of positive and negative feedback on expectations, evaluations, and performance. *Cognitive Therapy and Research, 9*, 145–160.

Challis, B. H., & Krane, R. V. (1988). Mood induction and the priming of semantic memory in lexical decision task: Asymmetric effects of elation and depression. *Bulletin of the Psychonomic Society, 26*(4), 309–312.

Channon, S., Baker, J. E., & Robertson, M. M. (1993). Effects of structure and clustering on recall and recognition memory in clinical depression. *Journal of Abnormal Psychology, 102*, 323–326.

Clark, D. A., & Teasdale, J. D. (1982). Diurnal variation in clinical depression and acccessibility of memories of positive and negative experiences. *Journal of Abnormal Psychology, 91*, 95–97.

Clark, D. M., Teasdale, J. D., Broadbent, D. E., & Martin, M. (1983). Effect of mood on lexical decisions. *Bulletin of the Psychonomic Society, 21*, 175–178.

Cohen, C. M., Weingartner, H., Smallberg, S. A., Pickar, D., Murphy, D. L. (1982). Effort & cognition in depression. *Archives of General Psychiatry, 39*, 593–597.

Colby, C. A., & Gotlib, I. H. (1988). Memory deficits in depression. *Cognitive Therapy and Research, 12*, 611–627.

Constans, J. I., & Mathews, A. M. (1993). Mood and the subjective risk of future events. *Cognition and Emotion, 7*, 545–560.

Conway, M., & Giannopoulos, C. (1993). Dysphoria and decision making: Limited information use for evaluations of multiattribute targets. *Journal of Personality and Social Psychology, 64,* 613–623.

Conway, M., Howell, A., & Giannopoulos, C. (1991). Dysphoria and thought suppression. *Cognitive Therapy and Research, 15,* 153–166.

Danion, J. M., Willard-Schroeder, D., Zimmerman, M. A., Grange, D., Schlienger, J. L., & Singer, L. (1991). Explicit memory and repitition priming in depression. *Archives of General Psychiatry, 48,* 707–711.

Denny, E. B., & Hunt, R. R. (1992). Affective valence and memory in depression: Dissociation of recall and fragment completion. *Journal of Abnormal Psychology, 101,* 575–580.

Dent, J., & Teasdale, J. D. (1988). Negative cognition and the persistence of depression. *Journal of Abnormal Psychology, 97,* 29–34.

Depue, R. A., & Monroe, S. M. (1986). Conceptualization and measurement of human disorder in life stress research: The problem of chronic disturbance. *Psychological Bulletin, 99,* 36–51.

Edwards, J. A., & Weary, G. (1993). Depression and the impression-formation continuum: Piecemeal processing despite the availability of category information. *Journal of Personality and Social Psychology, 64,* 636–645.

Elliott, C. L., & Greene, R. L. (1992). Clinical depression and implicit memory. *Journal of Abnormal Psychology, 101,* 572–574.

Ellis, H. C., & Ashbrook, P. W. (1988). Resource allocation model of the effects of depressed mood states on memory. In K. Fiedler & J. Forgas (Eds.), *Affect, cognition and social behavior.* Toronto, Canada: Hogrefe.

Ellis, H. C., Thomas, R. L., McFarland, A. D., & Lane, J. W. (1985). Emotional mood states and retrieval in episodic memory. *Journal of Experimental Psychology, 11,* 363–370.

Ellis, H. C., Thomas, R. L., & Rodriguez, I. A. (1984). Emotional mood states and memory: Elaborative encoding, semantic processing, and cognitive effort. *Journal of Experimental Psychology, 10,* 470–482.

Forgas, J. P. (1991). Affect and social judgment: An introductory review. In J. P. Forgas (Ed.), *Emotion and social judgments* (pp. 3–30). Elmsford, NY: Pergamon.

Forgas, J. P. (1994). Sad and guilty? Affective influences of the explanation of conflict in close relationships. *Journal of Personality and Social Psychology, 66,* 56–68.

Forgas, J. P., Bower, G. H., & Krantz, S. E. (1984). The influence of mood on perception of social interactions. *Journal of Experimental Social Psychology, 20(6),* 497–513.

Forgas, J. P., Bower, G. H., & Moylan, S. J. (1990). Praise or blame? Affective influences on the attributions for achievement. *Journal of Personality and Social Psychology, 59,* 809–819.

Frank, E., Carpenter, L. L., & Kupfer, D. J. (1988). Sex differences in recurrent depression: Are there any that are significant? *American Journal of Psychiatry, 145,* 41–45.

Gilboa, E., & Revelle, W. (1994). *Emotion duration: Cognitive and self-report measures.* Manuscript in preparation.

Gleicher, F., & Weary, G. (1991). The effect of depression on the quantity and quality of social inferences. *Journal of Personality and Social Psychology, 61,* 105–114.

Gotlib, I. H. (1983). Perception and recall of interpersonal feedback: Negative bias in depression. *Cognitive Therapy and Research, 7,* 399–412.

Gotlib, I. H., & Asarnow, R. F. (1979). Interpersonal and impersonal problem-solving skills in mildly and clinically depressed university students. *Journal of Consulting and Clinical Psychology, 47,* 86–95.

Gotlib, I. H., & Cane, D. B. (1987). Construct accessibility and clinical depression: A longitudinal investigation. *Journal of Abnormal Psychology, 96,* 199–204.

Gotlib, I. H., & McCann, C. D. (1984). Construct accessibility and depression: An examination of cognitive and affective factors. *Journal of Personality and Social Psychology, 47,* 427–439.

Gotlib, I. H., McLachlan, A. L., & Katz, A. N. (1988). Biases in visual attention in depressed and nondepressed individuals. *Cognition and Emotion, 2,* 185–200.

Grossman, I., Kaufman, A. S., Mednitsky, S., Scharff, L., & Dennis, B. (1994). Neurocognitive abilities for a clinically depressed sample versus a matched control group of normal individuals. *Psychiatry Research, 51*, 231–244.

Hart, R. P., Kwentus, J. A., Taylor, J. R., & Harkins, S. W. (1987). Rate of forgetting in dementia and depression. *Journal of Consulting and Clinical Psychology*, 55, 101–105.

Hartlage, S., Alloy, L. B., Vazquez, C., & Dykman, B. (1993). Automatic and effortful processing in depression. *Psychological Bulletin, 113*, 247–278.

Hasher, L., Rose, K. C., Zacks, R. T., Sanft, H., & Doren, B. (1985). Mood, recall, and selectivity effects in normal college students. *Journal of Experimental Psychology: General, 114*, 104–118.

Hasher, L., & Zacks, R. T. (1979). Automatic and effortful processes in memory. *Journal of Experiemntal Psychology: General, 109*, 356–388.

Hasher, L., & Zacks, R. T. (1988). Working memory, comprehension, and aging: A review and a new view. In G. Bower (Ed.), *The Psychology of Learning and Motivation, 22*, (pp. 193–225). San Diego, CA: Academic Press.

Hertel, P. (1994). Depressive deficits in word identification and recall. *Cognition and Emotion, 8*, 313–327.

Hertel, P. T., & Hardin, T. S. (1990). Remembering with and without awareness in a depressed mood: Evidence of deficits in the initiative. *Journal of Experimental Psychology: General, 119*, 45–59.

Hertel, P. T., & Rude, S. S. (1991a). Depressive deficits in memory: Focusing attention improves subsequent recall. *Journal of Experimental Psychology: General, 120*, 301–309.

Hertel, P. T., & Rude, S. S. (1991b). Recalling in a state of natural or experimental depression. *Cognitive Therapy and Research, 15*, 103–127.

Hill, A. B., & Knowles, T. H. (1991). Depression and the 'emotional' Stroop effect. *Personality and Individual Differences, 12*, 481–485.

Hirschfeld, R. M. A., & Goodwin, F. K. (1988). Mood disorders. In J. A. Talbott, R. E. Hales, & S. C. Yudofsky (Eds.), *Textbook of psychiatry* (pp. 403–441). Washington, DC: American Psychiatric Press.

Howell, A., & Conway, M. (1992). Mood and the suppression of positive and negative self-referent thoughts. *Cognitive Therapy and Research, 16*, 535–555.

Ingram, R. E. (1990). Self-focused attention in clinical disorders: Review and a conceptual model. *Psychological Bulletin, 107*, 156–176.

Ingram, R. E., Bernet, C. Z., & McLaughlin, S. C. (1994). Attentional allocation processes in individuals at risk for depression. *Cognitive Therapy and Research, 18*, 317–332.

Ingram, R. E., & Wisnicki, K. (1991). Cognition in depression. In P. A. Magaro (Ed.), *Annual review of psychopathology* (pp. 187–230). Newbury Park, CA: Sage.

Jacoby, L. L. (1991). A process dissociation framework: Separating automatic and intentional uses of memory. *Journal of Memory and Language, 30*, 513–541.

Karno, M., Hough, R. L., Burnam, A., et al. (1987). Lifetime prevalence of specific psychiatric disorders among Mexican Americans and non-Hispanic whites in Los Angeles. *Archives of General Psychiatry, 44*, 695–701.

Llyod, G. C., & Lishman, W. A. (1975). Effects of depression on the speed of recall of pleasant and unpleasant experiences. *Psychological Medicine, 5*, 173–180.

MacLeod, C., & Matthews, A. (1988). Anxiety and the allocation of attention to threat. *Quarterly Journal of Experimental Psychology: Human Experimental Psychology, 38*, 659–670.

MacLeod, C., & Matthews, A. (1991). Cognitive experimental approaches to the emotional disorders. In P. R. Martin (Ed.), *Handbook of behavior therapy and psychological science: An integrative approach* (pp. 116–150). New York: Pergamon.

Maser, J. D., & Cloninger, C. R. (Eds.). (1990). *Comorbidity in anxiety and mood disorders*. Washington, DC: American Psychiatric Press.

Matt, G. E., Vazquez, C., & Campell, W. K. (1992). Mood-congruent recall of affectively toned stimuli: A meta-analytic review. *Clinical Psychology Review, 12*, 227–255.

Matthews, A., & MacLeod, C. (1994). Cognitive approaches to emotions and emotional disorders. *Annual Review of Psychology, 45,* 25–50.

Mayer, J. D., Gaschke, Y. N., Braveman, D. L., & Evans, T. W. (1992). Mood-congruent judgment is a general effect. *Journal of Personality and Social Psychology, 63,* 119–132.

McCabe, S. B., & Gotlib, I. H. (1993). Attentional processing in clinically depressed subjects: A longitudinal investigation. *Cognitive Therapy and Research, 17,* 359–377.

McCabe, S. B., & Gotlib, I. H. (1995). Selective attention and clinical depression: Performance on a deployment-of-attention task. *Journal of Abnormal Psychology, 104,* 241–245.

Miller, D. T., & Morretti, M. M. (1988). The causal attributions of depressives: Self-serving or self-deserving? In L. B. Alloy (Eds.), *Cognitive biases in depression* (pp. 266–289). New York: Guilford.

Miller, W. R. (1975). Psychological deficit in depression. *Psychological Bulletin, 82,* 238–260.

Mogg, K., Bradley, S. D., William, R., & Mathews, A. (1993). Subliminal processing of emotional information in anxiety and depression. *Journal of Abnormal Psychology, 102,* 304–312.

Mogg, K., Mathews, A., May, J., Grove, M., Eysenck, M., & Weinman, H. (1991). Assessment of cognitive bias in anxiety and depression using a colour perception task. *Cognition and Emotion, 5,* 221–238.

Morrow, J., & Nolen-Hoeksema, S. (1990). Effects of responses to depression on the remediation of depressive affect. *Journal of Personality and Social Psychology, 58,* 519–527.

Murphy, J. M., Monson, R. R., Olivier, D. C., Sobol, A. M., & Leighton, A. H. (1987). Affective disorders and mortality. *Archives of General Psychiatry, 44,* 473–480.

Nolen-Hoeksema, S. (1987). Sex differences in unipolar depression: Evidence and theory. *Psychological Bulletin, 101,* 259–282.

Nolen-Hoeksema, S. (1991). Responses to depression and their effects on the duration of depressive episodes. *Journal of Abnormal Psychology, 100,* 569–582.

Nolen-Hoeksema, S., Morrow, J., & Fredrickson, B. L. (1993). Response styles and the duration of episodes of depressed mood. *Journal of Abnormal Psychology, 102,* 20–28.

Nolen-Hoeksema, S., Parker, L. E., & Larson, J. (1994). Ruminative coping with depressed mood following loss. *Journal of Personality and Social Psychology, 67,* 92–104.

Oatley, K., & Johnson-Laird, P. (1987). Towards a cognitive theory of emotions. *Cognition and Emotion, 1,* 29–50.

Parrott, W. G. (1991). Mood induction and instrructions to sustain moods: A test of the subject compliance hypothesis of mood congruent memory. *Cognition and Emotion, 5*(1), 41–52.

Parrott, W. G., & Sabini, J. (1990). Mood and memory under natural conditions: Evidence for mood incongruent recall. *Journal of Personality and Social Psychology, 59,* 321–336

Potts, R., Camp, C., & Coyne, C. (1989). The relationship between naturally occurring dysphoric moods, elaborative encoding, and recall performance. *Cognition and Emotion, 3,* 197–205.

Pyszczynski, T., & Greenberg, J. (1987). Self-regulatory perseveration and the depressive self-focusing style: A self-awareness theory of reactive depression. *Psychological Bulletin, 201,* 122–138.

Richards, A., & Whittaker, T. M. (1990). Effects of anxiety and mood manipulation in autobiographical memory. *British Journal of Clinical Psychology, 29,* 145–153.

Richards, P. M., & Ruff, R. M. (1989). Motivational effects on neuropsychological functioning: Comparison of depressed versus nondepressed individuals. *Journal of Consulting and Clinical Psychology, 57,* 396–402.

Roediger, H. L., & McDermott, K. B. (1992). Depression and implicit memory: A commentary. *Journal of Abnormal Psychology, 101,* 587–591.

Sarason, I. G. (1984). Stress, anxiety, and cognitive interference: Reactions to tests. *Journal of Personality & Social Psychology, 46,* 929–938.

Sarason, I. G., Sarason, B. R., Keefe, D. E., Hayes, B. E., & Shearin, E. N. (1986). Cognitive interference: Situational determinants and trait-like characteristics. *Journal of Personality & Social Psychology, 51,* 929–938.

Segal, Z. V., & Ingram, R. E. (1994). Mood priming and construct activation in tests of cognitive vulnerability to unipolar depression. *Clinical Psychology Review*, 14, 663–695.

Seidlitz, L., & Diener, E. (1993). Memory for positive versus negative life events: Theories for the differences between happy and unhappy persons. *Journal of Personality and Social Psychology, 64*, 654–664.

Siebert, P. S., & Ellis, H. C. (1991). Irrelevant thoughts, emotional mood states, and cognitive task performance. *Memory and Cognition, 19*, 507–513.

Silberman, E. K., Weingartner, H., & Post, R. M. (1983). Thinking disorder in depression. *Archives of General Psychiatry, 40*, 775–780.

Singer, J. A., & Salovey, P. (1988). Mood and memory: Evaluating the network theory of affect. *Clinical Psychology Review, 8*, 211–251.

Smith, J. D., Tracy, J. I., & Murray, M. J. (1993). Depression and category learning. *Journal of Experimental Psychology: General, 122*, 331–346.

Stromgren, L. S. (1977). The influence of depression on memory. *Acta Psychiatrica Scandinavia, 56*, 109–128.

Tancer, M. E., Brown, T. M., Evans, D. L., Ekstrom, D., Haggerty, J. J., Pedersen, C., & Golden, R. N. (1990). Impaired effortful cognition in depression. *Psychiatry Research, 31*, 161–168.

Teasdale, J. D. (1988). Cognitive vulnerability to persistent depression. *Cognition and Emotion, 2*, 247–274.

Teasdale, J. D., & Dent, J. (1987) Cognitive vulnerability to depression. An investigation of two hypotheses. *British Journal of Clinical Psychology, 26*, 113–126.

Teasdale, J. D., & Fogarty, S. J. (1979). Differential effects of induced mood on retrieval of pleasant and unpleasant events from episodic memory. *Journal of Abnormal Psychology, 88*, 248–257.

Tobias, J. F., Kihlstrom, J. F., & Schacter, D. L. (1992). Emotion and implicit memory. In S. A. Christianson (Ed.), *The handbook of emotion and memory: Research and theory* (pp. 67–92). Hillsdale, NJ: Lawrence Erlbaum Associates.

Velten, E. (1968). A laboratory task for induction of mood states. *Behavior Research and Therapy, 6*, 473–482.

Watkins, P. C., Mathews, A., Williamson, D. A., & Fuller, R. D. (1992). Mood-congruent memory in depression: Emotional priming or elaboration? *Journal of Abnormal Psychology, 101*, 581–586.

Watts, F. N. (1993). Problems of memory and concentration. In C. G. Costello (Ed.), *Symptoms of depression* (pp. 113–140). New York: Wiley.

Watts, F. N., Dalgleish, T., Bourke, P., & Healy, D. (1990). Memory deficit in clinical depression: Processing resources and the structure of materials. *Psychological Medicine, 20*, 345–349.

Watts, F. N., Morris, L., & MacLeod, A. K. (1987). Recognition memory in depression. *Journal of Abnormal Psychology, 96*, 273–275.

Watts, F. N., & Sharrock, R. (1985). Description and measurement of concentration problems in depressed patients. *Psychological Medicine, 15*, 317–326.

Weary, G., Jordan, J. S., & Hill, M. G. (1985). The attributional norm of internality and depressive sensitivity to social information. *Journal of Personality and Social Psychology, 49*, 1283–1293.

Weingartner, H., Cohen, R. M., Murphy, D. L., Martello, J., & Gerdt, C. (1981). Cognitive Processes in Depression. *Archives of General Psychiatry, 38*, 42–47.

Wenzlaff, R. M., Wegner, D. M., & Roper, D. W. (1988). Depression and mental control: The resurgence of unwanted negative thoughts. *Journal of Personality and Social Psychology, 55*, 882–892.

Williams, J. M. G. (1992). Autobiographical memory and emotional disorders. In S. A. Christianson (Eds.), *The handbook of emotion and memory* (pp. 451–476). Hillsdale, NJ: Lawrence Erlbaum Associates.

Williams, J. M., & Nulty, D. D. (1986). Construct accessibility, depression and the emotional stroop task: Transient mood or stable structure? *Personality and Individual Differences, 7*, 485–491.

Williams, J. N., & Scott, J. (1988). Autobiographical memory in depression. *Psychological Medicine, 18*, 689–695.

Williams, M. J., Watts, F. N., MacLeod, C., & Mathews, A. (1988). *Cognitive psychology and the emotional disorders*. Chichester, England: Wiley.

Wright, J. H., & Salmon, P. G. (1990). Learning and memory in depression. In C. D. McCann & N. S. Endler (Eds.), *Depression: New directions in theory, research, and practice* (pp. 211–236). Toronto, Canada: Wall & Emerson.

Yang, J. A., & Rehm, L. P. (1993). A study of autobiographical memories in depressed and nondepressed elderly individuals. *International Journal of Aging and Human Development, 36*, 39–55.

CHAPTER

18

TOWARD A NETWORK MODEL OF DISSOCIATIVE MECHANISMS

William Nasby
Jean L. Yates
Pacific Graduate School of Psychology

Since approximately 1970, dissociative processes and disorders that implicate functional "disruption in the usually integrated functions of consciousness, identity, memory, or perception of the environment" (American Psychiatric Association, 1994, p. 477) have sparked renewed interest among clinical psychologists (e.g., Greaves, 1980; Yates & Nasby, 1993). Not surprisingly, dissociative identity disorder (DID), which entails "the presence of two or more distinct identities or personality states" (American Psychiatric Association, 1994, p. 484), has received the lion's share of attention.[1] The volume of case reports (e.g., Beer, Beer, & Beer, 1993; Davidson, Allen, & Smith, 1987); quantitative case studies (e.g., Dick-Barnes, Nelson, & Aine, 1987; Lowenstein, Hamilton, Alagna, Reid, & deVries, 1987; Nissen, Ross, Willingham, Mackenzie, & Schacter, 1988; Schacter, Kihlstrom, & Kihlstrom, 1989); annotated bibliographies (e.g., Boor & Coons, 1983; Damgaard, Benschoten, & Fagen, 1985); books and edited volumes (e.g., Beahrs, 1982; Bliss, 1986; Braun, 1986; Cohen, Giller, & W., 1991; Confer & Abeles, 1983; Kenny, 1986; Kluft, 1985; Putnam, 1989; Quen, 1986; Ross, 1990); and special issues of professional journals (e.g., Braun, 1983, 1984a; Dell, 1988; Rome, 1984; Sanders & Hall, 1986; Thigpen & Cleckley, 1984) that present clinical accounts of DID, and

[1]All of the literature we cite that concerns pathological dissociation actually refers to Multiple Personality Disorder (MPD). Although the diagnostic label has recently changed from MPD (American Psychiatric Association, 1987) to DID (American Psychiatric Association, 1994), the essential features of the disorder remain the same. Therefore, we consider appropriate both the substitution of the current label and the citation of previous literature that refers to MPD.

the treatment or management thereof, has indeed dramatically increased. Although nomothetic research still lags behind, a number of controlled and comparative investigations (e.g., Lowenstein & Putnam, 1988; Silberman, Putnam, Weingartner, Braun, & Post, 1985) have also recently appeared.

Unfortunately, the recent flurry of interest has yet to generate theories that serve other than descriptive functions (e.g., Braun, 1984b, 1988; Braun & Sachs, 1985; Kluft, 1984b). More specifically, the clinical accounts lack theoretical explanations of the processing mechanisms that produce initial development and subsequent articulation of dissociated and dissociative identities or personality states.

To increase theoretical precision, some investigators have reviewed clinical and empirical literature that concerns either DID specifically, or dissociative problems more broadly, from the vantage of cognitive psychology (e.g., Andorfer, 1985; Kihlstrom & Hoyt, 1990; Kihlstrom, Tataryn, & Hoyt, 1993; Schacter & Kihlstrom, 1989). Unfortunately, the reviews promise more than they deliver, deferring to a later date specification of a bona fide theory. Clearly, the comparative dearth of controlled investigations that specifically examine memory explains some reluctance to formulate cognitive explanations. The limited progress, however, may also prove inherent to the primary source of theoretical insight: information processing models of human memory. Because the models have stressed excitatory learning (Wagner, 1981), the approach may not readily accommodate critical, indeed essential, features of the phenomena under scrutiny, that is, inhibitory processes.

Elsewhere, the authors (Yates & Nasby, 1993) argued that network models of memory (e.g., Anderson, 1983; Bower, 1981; Rumelhart, McClelland, & the PDP Research Group, 1986) may provide a profitable means to conceptualize DID. Although this model did not exclude or ignore excitatory processes, the authors maintained that inhibitory processes contribute substantially to DID. (To anticipate the subsequent discussion, network models often assume that excitatory and inhibitory processes increase and decrease, respectively, the sensitivity of recipient nodes when initiating nodes have become activated. Referring to the relative difficulty or ease of activating recipient nodes, excitatory processes create facilitation, whereas inhibitory processes create interference.)

The authors' model, however, did not specify a *learning rule* (e.g., Rumelhart et al., 1986) to provide a defensible and principled means of identifying the network conditions under which inhibitory, rather than excitatory, connections between nodes would form. How the external conditions that promote DID—most notably, recurrent but unpredictable trauma (e.g., physical and sexual abuse) during childhood—would lead the network to dissociate through inhibition also lacked precision.

The previous model is refined in this chapter to accomplish both ends, drawing from not only network models of human memory but also infrahuman models of respondent conditioning that incorporate network constructs and principles. The infrahuman models offer many insights about the inhibitory processes that contribute to dissociation. After outlining the assumptions of the revised model, *splitting* and *switching*, related but distinguishable processes of dissociation, and the contributions of each to DID are explained. Both forms of dissociation operate through inhibitory processes, from which cognitive interference ensues.

The authors apply the model to describe how an initial split forms during the etiology of DID, then explore the structure and function of dissociated alters, and examine how switching among dissociated alters might occur. This application considers also how recurrent and unpredictable trauma dramatically impacts the elaboration and organization of memory among infants and young children through the proposed mechanisms. Before presenting and applying the actual model, a descriptive account of DID that emphasizes mental representations of the self is outlined.

SELF, DISSOCIATION, AND DID

Specifying and exploring the dissociative processes whereby trauma disrupts the "usually integrated functions of consciousness, identity, memory, or perception" (American Psychiatric Association, 1994, p. 477) requires consideration of how network models (a) represent the self (e.g., Kihlstrom & Cantor, 1984; Kihlstrom, Cantor, Albright, Chew, Klein, & Niedenthal, 1988; Nasby, 1994; Nasby & Kihlstrom, 1986), and (b) conceptualize the relation between the self and conscious experience.

Consider first the representational issue. A node that mentally represents the self, as some network models (e.g., Kihlstrom et al., 1993) proposed, would send associative links to and receive associative links from other nodes. Certainly, for example, the other nodes would include representations of autobiographical memories, generic beliefs and knowledge about physical and psychosocial attributes, and the like. Under normal circumstances, active memory contains mental representations of not only the current environment and episode, but also the self—the cognitive, emotional, and motivational states that coexist when the event occurs.

Conscious thought, experience, and action (James, 1890; Kihlstrom & Hoyt, 1990) require *self-reference*: The mental representation must specify that the agent of or the one who experiences an event refers to the individual, to the self. Stated differently, when linked to an activated representation of the self, thoughts, feelings, motives, and goals enter consciousness or occupy phenomenal awareness. Routinely, then, the self becomes linked to some, but not all, contents of memory. Absent the link to self, activated but dissociated nodes or constellations may still influence behavior and experience. The influence and expression, however, would occur automatically, preconsciously, or subconsciously, outside self-consciousness or phenomenal awareness and beyond voluntary control (Kihlstrom & Hoyt, 1990).

Many clinicians accept a definition of dissociation that emphasizes, implicitly or explicitly, the *general* disconnectedness, independence, or separation between one part of memory and another (e.g., Braun, 1984b, 1988; Braun & Sachs, 1985; Kluft, 1984b; cf. Yates & Nasby, 1993). Reviewing empirical research, however, Kihlstrom and Hoyt (1990; see also Kihlstrom et al., 1993) concluded that dissociated memories specifically lack associative linkages to mental representations of the self. Dissociation, therefore, specifically involves activated contents of the cognitive system that lack excitatory connections to and from the self.

Putnam (1988), from a different but complementary perspective, has noted intriguing similarities between the dissociations of DID and the state-changes of normal infancy. According to Putnam (1988), a state-change would:

> encompass the psychobiological events associated with shifts in state of consciousness as manifest by changes in state-related variables such as affect, access to memories, sense of self, cognitive and perceptual style, and often reflected in alterations of facial expression, speech and motor activity, and interpersonal relatedness. (p. 26)

Although state-change refers to a discontinuous, hence nonlinear, process during which a discrete state of consciousness shifts to another, normal infants and young children gradually develop smooth (or smoother) transitions between states (Wolff, 1987).

Arguably, smooth transitions emerge when developmental conditions, especially during infancy and early childhood, have fostered establishment and strengthening of excitatory connections between previously disparate (dissociated) states. Over time, the structure of memory would increasingly become integrated or interconnected, many excitatory links having formed between elements, including memories, that cross distinguishable states. The development of an integrated memory requires the establishment of excitatory links that can activate a new state by spreading activation (Anderson, 1983; Bower, 1981) between nodes, thereby producing smooth transitions.

Akin to infants and even young children, the state changes that characterize dissociative patients (especially individuals who suffer from DID) lack an integrative basis. Consequently, dissociative patients exhibit rough, rather than smooth, transitions from one self-state to another. Indeed, individuals who suffer from DID usually cannot, from the dominant or primary self, access or retrieve information that pertains to an alter. For example, DID patients often cannot remember specific events that occurred while an alter occupied consciousness. The inaccessibility may entail lack of excitatory connections: Having attained consciousness, the alter lacks excitatory connections to the dominant self, and the dominant self lacks excitatory connections to the alter. The authors contend that dissociative processes operate through inhibition, producing a form of cognitive interference. Among pathological cases, the extensive inhibition (interference) undermines the integrative establishment and strengthening of excitatory links between nodes.

Clinicians who treat DID, when characterizing pathological dissociation, frequently distinguish between the processes of splitting and switching (e.g., Clary, Burnstin, & Carpenter, 1984; Gruenewald, 1984; Kluft, 1984a; Yates & Nasby, 1993; Young, 1988). Descriptively, splitting refers to the process that initiates the development of an alter self, whereas switching refers to the process in which an individual changes state from dominant to alter self (or vice versa), as well as from one alter to another.

Traumatic events—most often, physical and sexual abuses—that occur during early childhood apparently trigger splitting, whereas reactivation of an existing split through recurrent trauma epitomizes switching (e.g., Braun, 1984b, 1988; Kluft, 1985). More specifically, splitting occurs when trauma of a *novel* form floods consciousness, producing levels of stimulation beyond developmental limits to assimilate or accommodate the information (Mandler, 1982; Yates & Nasby, 1993). Having surpassed assimilative or accommodative capacities, an automatic process may nevertheless produce an isolated encoding of the trauma that lacks excitatory connections to the dominant self. Conversely, switching refers to a process in which an emerging or established alter that lacks excitatory connections to the dominant or primary self attains consciousness (e.g., Clary et al., 1984; Gruenewald, 1984; Kluft, 1984a; Yates & Nasby, 1993; Young, 1988).

Gradually, from the initial split and a series of related switches, an alter personality could develop. A recurrent trauma would not only reactivate but also elaborate an emerging alter: The reactivated alter and new but related memories, behaviors, and affects would become linked. Eventually, the repeated elaborations would produce a complex structure that resembles a distinct personality or personality state (American Psychiatric Association, 1987, 1994; Putnam, 1988, 1989).

The creation of alter selves usually occurs early (Bliss, 1980; Greaves, 1980; Putnam et al., 1986), suggesting that (a) trauma, splitting, and switching undermine the normal attainment or development of the ability to move smoothly between states (Putnam, 1988; Wolff, 1987), and (b) having successfully elaborated and integrated a dominant self actually might afford a means of insulating an older child (or adult) from responding to trauma through dissociation.

Conceivably, the establishment and segregation of discrete or dissociated selves would serve adaptive functions among young children who experience recurrent but unpredictable trauma (e.g., Braun & Sachs, 1985; Kluft, 1984b; Ludwig, 1983). The dissociations would protect the child against overwhelming affects (e.g., terror, rage) and disturbing recollections during nontraumatic periods, as well as provide *some* means to cope during traumatic periods when alternatives have yet to develop (Putnam, 1988).

Although internally elaborated, alter selves relate less to the remainder of the cognitive system through excitatory links than do normal states. Psychologically, the pathological dissociations exact an exorbitant price: The isolated pockets of memory actually might weaken the ability of the dominant self to develop and extend capabilities. Rather than acquiring and refining appropriate and effective skills to solve problems and to cope when stress (even mild discomfort) arises, the individual dissociates instead.

Successfully integrating alter selves and the remainder of the cognitive system, including the dominant self, presages developmental leaps. During effective therapy and treatment, an interrelated structure that incorporates memories from both the alter/alters and the dominant self emerges (e.g., Bliss, 1986; Braun, 1986; Kluft, 1984c, 1986; Putnam, 1989; Ross, 1990).

A MODEL OF DISSOCIATIVE MEMORY ORGANIZATION

Over the years, cognitive psychologists (e.g., Anderson, 1983; Anderson & Bower, 1973; Bower, 1981; Rumelhart et al., 1986) have frequently proposed network models of human memory. Structurally, networks consist of nodes that represent the units of cognition (thought) and links that specify the relations between units (see Yates & Nasby, 1993, who described the assumptions shared by network models of human memory). Networks also provide the structural framework according to which certain theorists (e.g., Konorksi, 1967; Wagner, 1981) have modeled infrahuman memory and respondent conditioning. Interestingly enough, cognitive models have almost exclusively concerned the *excitatory* learning that occurs (through the establishment and strengthening of excitatory links) when activated nodes enter short-term memory, or undergo rehearsal, but have offered little delineation of inhibition. Unlike cognitive models, conditioning models have more often articulated explicit rules to identify joint states of relative activation between nodes that differentially produce inhibitory or excitatory learning. Assuming that dissociation necessarily entails inhibitory processes (Yates & Nasby, 1993), the conditioning models offer much promise to refine theoretical understanding of dissociative mechanisms. Other assumptions, which concern fatigue and arousal, mental representations of self, and disinhibition, identify the conditions that lead the network to dissociate through inhibitory processes. More specifically, to refine the earlier model (Yates & Nasby, 1993), the following specific assumptions are added to that model.

Assumption I: States of Activation. Wagner (1981) has proposed a network model of respondent conditioning that heuristically distinguishes among three ranges or states of nodal activation: (1) a primary state of full activation, corresponding to focal short-term memory (STM); (2) a secondary state of partial activation, corresponding to marginal working memory (MWM); and (3) an inactive state. Wagner assumed further that a node must pass through MWM either to become fully activated from the inactive state or to become fully inactive from focal STM.

Assumption 2: Excitatory and Inhibitory Links. A 2 × 2 matrix can illustrate the relation between a pair of active nodes from the larger network (see Table 18.1). Two active nodes, *X* and *Y*, may each occupy either focal STM or MWM. If *X* and *Y* both occupy focal STM, then bidirectional excitatory connections would form between the two nodes. If, instead, *X* and *Y* both occupy MWM, then no connection between the nodes would form. When one unit occupies focal STM and the other MWM, the relation between *X* and *Y* becomes directionally inhibitory (Wagner, 1981). More specifically, the direction of the inhibitory connection extends from the unit that occupies focal STM to the unit that occupies MWM. No connection, however, would extend from the node that occupies MWM to the node that occupies focal STM.

Although Wagner (1981) originally proposed the associative rules of Table 18.1 to model respondent conditioning, notably Pavlovian inhibition (e.g., Konorski, 1948; Wagner, 1981), one may also recast Assumption 2 from a cognitive perspective. For example, the upper left and lower right cells of Table 18.1 basically reaffirm the established principle that attention, corresponding to nodes that jointly occupy focal STM, fosters (excitatory) learning, whereas peripheral awareness, corresponding to nodes that jointly occupy MWM, does not.

Referring to the upper right and lower left cells next, consider what partial activation of one node may signal, given that a contrasting node simultaneously occupies focal STM. The node that occupies MWM has either already decayed from focal STM or has only attained partial activation. Conversely, the contrasting node will already have passed from MWM to focal STM (see Assumption 1).

TABLE 18.1
Joint States of Relative Activation Between Nodes *X* and *Y* That Differentially Produce Inhibitory or Excitatory Links

		Node Y	
		Focal Short-Term Memory	*Marginal Working Memory*
Node *X*	Focal Short-Term Memory	Symmetric: Excitatory, bi-directional links between Nodes *X* and *Y*	Asymmetric: Inhibitory link from Node *X* to Node *Y*; no link from Node *Y* to Node *X*
	Marginal Working Memory	Asymmetric: No link from Node *X* to Node *Y*; inhibitory link from Node *Y* to Node *X*	Symmetric: No links between Nodes *X* and *Y*

Among several meanings of the *juxtaposition* between a node that occupies MWM and one that occupies focal STM (e.g., Grossberg & Levine, 1987), two concern us.

If the first node has decayed, then memory retains through the inhibitory link the inverse course that the activation of the two nodes has just followed. Alternatively, the first node may have only achieved partial activation because of inhibitory input from other sources. The node that simultaneously occupies focal STM should, therefore, also send an inhibitory link to the node that occupies MWM. Again, the inhibitory link signals an inverse relation between the two nodes—one receives inhibitory input that prevents the transition to focal STM while the other simultaneously has attained full activation. Either scenario would create interference: The inhibition renders the recipient node more difficult to activate. Suppose, for example, that the recipient node represents a particular memory. Because of the interference, which the inhibition creates, the memory may become less accessible, hence more difficult to retrieve.

Notice finally that the upper right and lower left cells specify asymmetric relations between *X* and *Y*. The asymmetries result because insufficient activation prevents a partially active node from establishing *any* linkages.[2]

Assumption 3: Fatigue and Arousal. Intense and/or prolonged stimulation of a node leads to fatigue (e.g., Martindale, 1980, 1981, 1991). During the process of fatigue, the node would pass from focal STM to MWM, and thence to inactivity. While occupying MWM, the fatigued node becomes subject to the establishment or strengthening of inhibitory (interfering) connections from nodes that occupy focal STM. Having decayed fully and while inactive, the fatigued node would not contribute to associative learning, whether excitatory or inhibitory.

Fatigue proves especially relevant to an exploration of DID, given the particular nature of abuse that DID patients routinely and consistently report (e.g., Coons, Bowman, & Milstein, 1988; Putnam, Guroff, Silberman, Barban, & Post, 1986). Abuse would entail extraordinarily intense stimulation, from which a massive release of the arousal system would follow (e.g., Martindale, 1981, 1991; Shallice, 1978). Prolonged abuse would simply compound the problem. In addition, unpredictability often characterizes the pattern of abuse that DID patients report. Prototypically, the child receives love and affection from a parent or

[2]Even a broader range of perspectives can readily accommodate the second assumption. For example, if activation level equals rate of neural firing, then the assumption captures the circumstances that will produce excitatory or inhibitory connections between synapses (e.g., Levy, 1985; Singer, 1983). Similarly, the assumption summarizes a major component of the Hebb Rule. (The Hebb rule extends and refines the original proposal that Hebb [1949] formulated to explain associative learning and development of neural assemblies. Network theorists [e.g., Grossberg & Levine, 1987; McClelland, Rumelhart, & the PDP Research Group, 1986] now routinely invoke some variation of the rule.) Interestingly enough, Thorndike (1911) long ago proposed that the second assumption characterized instrumental learning.

caretaker one moment, and provides the target for physical or sexual abuse (or both) the next (e.g., Coons et al., 1988; Putnam et al., 1986; Spiegel, 1986). Unpredictable events, especially if meaningful, also serve to elicit arousal (e.g., Martindale, 1981, 1991; Shallice, 1972). Furthermore, abuse would elicit panic and terror, emotional responses that mediate additional input from the arousal to the cognitive system. Therefore, several factors would insidiously conspire to maximize arousal of a child who experiences recurrent and unpredictable trauma through physical or sexual abuse, or both.

We know also that the arousal system projects throughout the cortex. Many architects of network models (e.g., Martindale, 1981, 1991; Shallice, 1972), therefore, assume that most—perhaps all—nodes receive excitatory input from the arousal system. In addition, some nodes receive mediated arousal through connections from the emotion system (Bower, 1981). Evidence also suggests that arousal input *multiplies* (rather than merely adds to) the activation that cognitive units receive from other sources (e.g., Martindale, 1980, 1981, 1991; cf. Hull, 1943). To the extent, then, that nodes receive prolonged input via strong connections not only from cognitive sources, but also from the arousal and emotion systems, the likelihood of fatigue increases.

Therefore, prolonged and recurrent trauma, especially when unpredictable, would fatigue certain nodes. The most susceptible would receive the "extra" input from the emotion system, and specifically would pertain to the self.

Assumption 4: Mental Representations of Self. Some nodes refer to the self (Kihlstrom & Cantor, 1984; Kihlstrom et al., 1988; Nasby, 1994; Nasby & Kihlstrom, 1986). Structurally and functionally, a subset would meet the definitional criteria of chunking units (Wickelgren, 1979). Most broadly, a chunking unit mediates the link between stimulus and response or situation and behavior. More specifically, a chunking unit that represents the self both receives input from and sends output to numerous sources throughout and beyond the network: episodic—notably, autobiographical—memories that preserve spatiotemporal as well as other information about the context of events and experiences, semantic memories that represent generic knowledge and beliefs about oneself (self-concept), others (person categories or prototypes), and situations (settings plus persons), dispositions and motives, as well as the emotion and arousal systems (e.g., Bower, 1981; Nasby, 1994).

Abuse specifically and trauma generally would, of course, involve both the self and arousal, direct as well as emotionally mediated. (Direct arousal would stem from the intensity and unpredictability of the abuse or trauma. Mediated arousal would stem from the emotional reactions of panic and terror.) Because of prolonged and possibly intense stimulation, self nodes—most likely the ones that receive input from emotional sources that pertain to trauma—may decay through fatigue, declining from focal STM to MWM. A decayed self node, fatigued to inactivation, may lack excitatory connections to and from other nodes, or configurations thereof, that occupy focal STM. Furthermore, before full deactivation, a self node that occupies MWM may acquire inhibitory (interfering) links from other nodes that have attained full activation. Fatigue of self nodes would provide one means—albeit extreme and costly—of managing or regulating overwhelming stimulation of the network.

Assumption 5: Disinhibition. If Node *X* sends an inhibitory link to Node *Y*, then deactivation or even decay of the former (e.g., through fatigue) may disinhibit the latter (e.g., Martindale, 1981, 1991). Stated differently, having removed or even lessened the inhibitory impact of Node *X*, Node *Y* may overcome interference, and hence become activated (e.g., through excitatory input from other sources).

APPLYING THE MODEL TO DID

Referring to Table 18.1, when either *X* or *Y* represents the self (or some element thereof), psychological explanations of the dissociative processes that can produce DID become possible. The processes of both splitting and switching operate through inhibition to produce cognitive interference.

Splitting

During normal consciousness, STM includes mental representations of the dominant or primary self, including the internal context (e.g., cognitive, emotional, and motivational states) as well as current representations of the external context or environment (Kihlstrom et al., 1993). The dominant self and many representations of current thought, experience, and action would, then, become associated via excitatory links.

Some representations, however, may not share excitatory links to self, and when activated fully would occur outside phenomenal awareness. According to our model, links may nevertheless exist between self and the dissociated representations, but of an inhibitory nature. Inhibitory links would form when the self representation occupied MWM, whereas the dissociated representations occupied focal STM, or vice versa. More specifically, if the self unit occupied focal STM, while the mental representations occupied MWM, then inhibitory links would form directionally from the self unit to the mental representations, and activation of the self would inhibit the mental representations. If, however, the self unit occupied MWM, whereas the mental representations occupied focal STM, then inhibitory links would form directionally from the mental representations to dominant self, and activation of the mental representations would inhibit the self.

Subjecting a young child to trauma causes rapid fatigue of nodes that occupy focal STM. The trauma almost certainly produces extreme arousal and hence maximal activation of the dominant self, however nascent or rudimentary, and related nodes, leading to rapid fatigue and deactivation. Concurrently, unoccupied or unbound (e.g., Konorski, 1967; Martindale, 1981; Wickelgren, 1979) nodes not only encode the event, but also establish associative links to other nodes—specifically, to the dominant self. Because extreme stimulation from trauma forces the dominant self and related nodes to fatigue and hence to pass through MWM, the new, trauma-induced fragment of an alter would send directionally inhibitory (interfering) links to the dominant self. In addition, no links form between the deactivated self and the activated nodes that encode the traumatic event or the sequelae. Conversely, excitatory connections would form among the various nodes that encode the trauma. The result, an isolated (dissociated) constellation of interconnected nodes (a) encodes and hence represents the memories of the trauma, and (b) sends directionally inhibitory (interfering) links to the dominant self, and (c) lacks excitatory links to other nodes. The authors suggest that among infants and young children, memory has not yet sufficiently developed to prevent or counteract the formation of distinct or dissociated constellations of nodes that lack excitatory connections to the dominant self. While memory structures mature, growing more elaborate, the complex interconnections of the dominant self to memory limit the likelihood that isolated encodings of events will result.

Among DID patients, the development of alter personalities most often occurs sequentially. Clinical investigations (e.g., Kluft, 1986; Yates & Nasby, 1993) suggest that a given alter usually encodes memories from a certain period of time during which the same (or a similar) trauma has recurred. Pattern matching reactivates an alter, each reactivation further elaborating and strengthening the structure through excitatory learning. Once established, the alter provides an adaptive mechanism to handle a familiar trauma. After all, the structure contains much trauma-relevant information. Moreover, while the trauma continues, the alter serves a protective function, stimulating inhibitory links to the dominant self. The inhibitory input from the alter creates interference, preventing or rendering more difficult the reactivation of the dominant self as long as the trauma persists. Each reactivation of the alter also strengthens the inhibitory links from alter to dominant self.

When the trauma ceases, the primary self could again become regnant through disinhibition. The alter no longer receives excitatory input, and inhibitory input from the alter to the primary self wanes. Given excitatory input from other sources, the dominant self again becomes activated.

The splitting mechanism may engender a new alter while existing alters continue to develop. A new alter emerges when a new trauma (different setting, perpetrator, method, or the like) fails to match an existing alter sufficiently. Instead of reactivating an existing alter, splitting ensues. Overwhelming stimulation floods the dominant self, engendering fatigue. While activation of the dominant self decays, dissociated nodes that encode the new trauma lay the foundation of a new alter.

Inhibitory links would isolate distinct alters, thereby fragmenting memory further. If fragmentation weakens the integrative function and organization of memory, then splitting might retard, or possibly even preclude, other means to handle extreme stress from developing. Indeed, splitting might lead to more splitting. Therefore, although initially adaptive, splitting becomes a major obstacle to realizing the integrative function and organization of memory.

Switching

When the environment presents distinct stresses, DID patients switch between alter personalities (e.g., Putnam, 1988, 1989; Yates & Nasby, 1993). (Indeed, among adults who have developed DID, coping almost exclusively consists of switching.) The alter that corresponds to the prevailing circumstances most closely becomes activated (occupies consciousness) and assumes control.

Dissociative switching might represent a special case of state-change (Putnam, 1988). A split encodes a new, hence distinct, constellation or distribution of activated nodes, thereby representing a new state of the network. Reactivation of the state through switching adds information to the state, elaborating the new structure, but does not, according to the authors' definition, evoke a new split. Although splitting represents a reaction to novel trauma, switching more commonly involves pattern matching through recurrent trauma. Switching occurs when information activates, or more accurately reactivates, a dissociated state to consciousness. Circumstances that sufficiently match the split reinvoke the alter (or fragment thereof). Recurrence of the trauma that initially produced the dissociated state would provide the optimal circumstances.

That alters typically exhibit different affective ranges, vocal and speech patterns, perceptual and cognitive styles, dispositional or motivational profiles, and even ages (e.g., Beahrs, 1982; Putnam et al., 1986), becomes more understandable. The glaring distinctions (even discrepancies) between alters bear the stamp of fatigue, inhibition, and interference.

Moreover, one cannot usually access every alter from the dominant self (Kluft, 1986; Putnam, 1988). Occasionally, access to a particular alter may only occur through another alter, or even through a succession of alters (Kluft, 1986; Lowenstein et al., 1987; Putnam, 1988). Conceivably, a hierarchy of alter selves might develop as well as a complex and evolving pattern of excitatory and inhibitory connections among alters that results from repeated, but differential, evocation over time. An isolated alter may nevertheless develop excitatory connections to other alters, and a complex organization may ensue, mimicking certain properties that would characterize an integrated structure of self and memory.

Often, while probing memory, clinicians also observe among various alters the phenomenon of coconsciousness: One personality may know about the actions, feelings, or thoughts of another (e.g., Kluft, 1984a; Prince, 1906; Taylor & Martin, 1944). Should excitatory connections form between the two states, coconsciousness might result: The alters would overlap, each matching the pattern of a trauma sufficiently to achieve consciousness jointly.

Many clinicians assume that integrating alter personalities to achieve a cohesive self constitutes a superordinate goal during the treatment of DID (e.g., Bliss, 1986; Braun, 1986; Kluft, 1984c, 1986; Putnam, 1989; Ross, 1990). Switching plays a role here, because therapy would seek to establish and strengthen excitatory connections between personality states, thereby overcoming the inhibition and interference that prevents dissociated material from attaining consciousness. Gradually, therapeutic interventions seek to render conscious simultaneously dissociated memories from each alter and the dominant or primary self. When therapy progresses, the switches between alters increasingly resemble normal state-changes, coconsciousness among and multiconsciousness of alters replacing the dissociative amnesia. Eventually, one hopes, the therapeutic outcome consists of an integrated structure. The current approach to modeling the organization of self and memory perhaps may inspire new methods of evoking alters simultaneously. More specifically, the methods would seek to foster the development of excitatory links among alters that could successfully counteract interference and effect integration.

CONCLUSION

The authors' conviction has strengthened (cf. Yates & Nasby, 1993) that network models of memory (e.g., Anderson, 1983; Bower, 1981; McClelland et al., 1986; Rumelhart et al., 1986) provide a profitable means to conceptualize DID specifically and dissociation generally. The concepts of nodal fatigue and inhibitory learning have particularly enriched the analysis of DID from a perspective that emphasizes cognitive interference, and the authors intend to pursue that approach.

Given the understandable difficulties and costs of conducting empirical research that concerns DID, however, it is not advisable to rush pell-mell to nomothetic and comparative investigations. Instead, a prudent course first requires making formal through computer simulation the cognitive model outlined here. Of course, the proposed shift to formal modeling will require additional refinements and decisions. Should the authors' efforts to construct a network architecture that dissociates and manifests dissociative amnesia succeed, there will be better justification of the costs of programmatic research to test specific hypotheses. No doubt, however, the eventual program will judiciously emphasize an interplay among chronic arousal, negative affectivity, and self-reference—

an interplay that acts dynamically through inhibitory mechanisms and cognitive interference to produce and reinforce pathological dissociation.

REFERENCES

American Psychiatric Association. (1987). *Diagnostic and statistical manual of mental disorders* (3rd ed., rev.). Washington, DC: Author.

American Psychiatric Association. (1994). *Diagnostic and statistical manual of mental disorders* (4th ed.). Washington, DC: Author.

Anderson, J. R. (1983). *The architecture of cognition*. Cambridge, MA: Harvard University Press.

Anderson, J. R., & Bower, G. H. (1973). *Human associative memory*. Washington, DC: Winston & Sons.

Andorfer, J. C. (1985). Multiple personality in the human information-processor: A case history and theoretical formulation. *Journal of Clinical Psychology, 41*, 309–324.

Beahrs, J. O. (1982). *Unity and multiplicity: Multilevel consciousness of self in hypnosis, psychiatric disorder and mental health*. New York: Brunner/Mazel.

Beer, D., Beer, J., & Beer, J. (1993). Multiple personality: A persecutor sees opposites as "smeared" together. *Journal of Social Behavior and Personality, 8*, 471–480.

Bliss, E. L. (1980). Multiple personalities: A report of 14 cases with implications for schizophrenia and hysteria. *Archives of General Psychiatry, 37*, 1388–1397.

Bliss, E. L. (1986). *Multiple personality, allied disorders, and hypnosis*. New York: Oxford University Press.

Boor, M., & Coons, P. M. (1983). A comprehensive bibliography of literature pertaining to multiple personality disorder. *Psychological Reports, 53*, 295–310.

Bower, G. H. (1981). Mood and memory. *American Psychologist, 36*, 129–148.

Braun, B. G. (Ed.). (1983). Communicating about multiple personality [Special issue]. *American Journal of Clinical Hypnosis, 26*(2).

Braun, B. G. (Ed.). (1984a). Symposium on multiple personality [Special issue]. *Psychiatric Clinics of North America, 7*(1).

Braun, B. G. (1984b). Towards a theory of multiple personality and other dissociative phenomena. *Psychiatric Clinics of North America, 7*, 171–193.

Braun, B. G. (Ed.). (1986). *Treatment of multiple personality disorder*. Washington, DC: American Psychiatric Press.

Braun, B. G. (1988). The BASK model of dissociation. *Dissociation, 1*(1), 4–23.

Braun, B. G., & Sachs, R. G. (1985). The development of multiple personality disorder: Predisposing, precipitating, and perpetuating factors. In R. P. Kluft (Ed.), *Childhood antecedents of multiple personality* (pp. 37–64). Washington, DC: American Psychiatric Press.

Clary, W. F., Burnstin, K. J., & Carpenter, J. S. (1984). Multiple personality and borderline personality disorder. *Psychiatric Clinics of North America, 7*, 89–99.

Cohen, B. M., Giller, E., & W., L. (Eds.). (1991). *Multiple personality disorder from the inside out*. Baltimore, MD: Sidran Press.

Confer, W. N., & Abeles, B. S. (1983). *Multiple personality: Etiology, diagnosis, and treatment*. New York: Human Sciences.

Coons, P. M., Bowman, E. S., & Milstein, V. (1988). Multiple personality disorder: A clinical investigation of 50 cases. *Journal of Nervous and Mental Disease, 176*, 519–527.

Damgaard, J., Benschoten, S., & Fagen, J. (1985). An updated bibliography of literature pertaining to multiple personality. *Psychological Reports, 53*, 295–310.

Davidson, J., Allen, J. G., & Smith, W. H. (1987). Complexities in the hospital treatment of a patient with multiple personality disorder. *Bulletin of the Menninger Clinic, 51*, 561–568.

Dell, P. F. (Ed.). (1988). Professional skepticism about multiple personality. *Journal of Nervous and Mental Disease, 176*(9).

Dick-Barnes, M., Nelson, R. O., & Aine, U. (1987). Behavioral measures of multiple personality: The case of Margaret. *Journal of Behavioral Therapy and Experimental Psychiatry, 18*, 229–239.

Greaves, G. B. (1980). Multiple personality 165 years after Mary Reynolds. *Journal of Nervous and Mental Disease, 168*, 577–596.

Grossberg, S., & Levine, D. S. (1987). Neural dynamics of attentionally modulated Pavlovian conditioning: Blocking, inter-stimulus interval, and secondary reinforcement. *Applied Optics, 26*, 5015–5030.

Gruenewald, D. (1984). On the nature of multiple personality disorder: Comparisons with hypnosis. *International Journal of Clinical and Experimental Hypnosis, 32*, 170–190.

Hebb, D. O. (1949). *The organization of behavior.* New York: Wiley.

Hull, C. L. (1943). *Principles of behavior.* New York: Appleton-Century-Crofts.

James, W. (1890). *The principles of psychology* (Vol. 1). New York: Dover.

Kenny, M. G. (1986). *The passion of Ansel Bourne: Multiple personality in American culture.* Washington, DC: Smithsonian Institution Press.

Kihlstrom, J. F., & Cantor, N. (1984). Mental representations of self. In L. Berkowitz (Ed.), *Advances in experimental social psychology* (Vol. 17, pp. 1–47). New York: Academic Press.

Kihlstrom, J. F., Cantor, N., Albright, J. S., Chew, B. R., Klein, S. B., & Niedenthal, P. M. (1988). Information processing and the study of the self. In L. Berkowitz (Ed.), *Advances in experimental social psychology* (Vol. 21, pp. 145–177). San Diego: Academic Press.

Kihlstrom, J. F., & Hoyt, I. P. (1990). Repression, dissociation, and hypnosis. In J. L. Singer (Ed.), *Repression and dissociation: Implications for personality theory, psychopathology, and health* (pp. 181–208). Chicago: University of Chicago Press.

Kihlstrom, J. F., Tataryn, D. J., & Hoyt, I. P. (1993). Dissociative disorders. In P. B. Sutker & H. E. Adams (Eds.), *Comprehensive handbook of psychopathology* (2nd ed., pp. 203–229). New York: Plenum.

Kluft, R. P. (1984a). An introduction to multiple personality disorder. *Psychiatric Annals, 14*(1), 19, 22–24.

Kluft, R. P. (1984b). Multiple personality in childhood. *Psychiatric Clinics of North America, 7*, 121–134.

Kluft, R. P. (1984c). Treatment of multiple personality disorder. *Psychiatric Clinics of North America, 7*, 9–29.

Kluft, R. P. (Ed.). (1985). *Childhood antecedents of multiple personality.* Washington, DC: American Psychiatric Press.

Kluft, R. P. (1986). Personality unification in multiple personality disorder: A follow-up study. In B. G. Braun (Ed.), *Treatment of multiple personality disorder* (pp. 31–60). Washington, DC: American Psychiatric Press.

Konorski, J. (1948). *Conditioned reflexes and neuron organization.* Cambridge, England: Cambridge University Press.

Konorski, J. (1967). *Integrative activity of the brain.* Chicago: University of Chicago Press.

Levy, W. B. (1985). Associative changes at the synapse: LTP in the hippocampus. In W. B. Levy, J. Anderson, & S. Lehmkuhle (Eds.), *Synaptic modification, neuron selectivity and nervous system organization* (pp. 5–33). Hillsdale, NJ: Lawrence Erlbaum Associates.

Lowenstein, R. J., Hamilton, J., Alagna, S., Reid, N., deVries, M. (1987). Experiential sampling in the study of multiple personality disorder. *American Journal of Psychiatry, 144*, 19–24.

Lowenstein, R. J., & Putnam, F. W. (1988). A comparison study of dissociative symptoms in patients with complex partial seizures, DID, and posttraumatic stress disorder. *Dissociation, 1*(4), 17–23.

Ludwig, A. M. (1983). The psychobiological functions of dissociation. *American Journal of Clinical Hypnosis, 26*, 93–99.

Mandler, G. (1982). The structure of value: Accounting for taste. In M. S. Clark & S. T. Fiske (Eds.), *Affect and cognition: The 17th Annual Carnegie Symposium on Cognition* (pp. 3–36). Hillsdale, NJ: Lawrence Erlbaum Associates.

Martindale, C. (1980). Subselves: The internal representation of situational and personal dispositions. In L. Wheeler (Ed.), *Annual review of personality and social psychology, Vol. 1* (pp. 193–218). Newbury Park, CA: Sage.

Martindale, C. (1981). *Cognition and consciousness*. Homewood, IL: Dorsey.

Martindale, C. (1991). *Cognitive psychology: A neural-network approach*. Pacific Grove, CA: Brooks/Cole.

McClelland, J. L., Rumelhart, D. E., & the PDP Research Group. (Eds.). (1986). *Parallel distributed processing: Explorations in the microstructure of cognition. Volume 2: Psychological and biological models*. Cambridge, MA: MIT Press.

Nasby, W. (1994). Moderators of mood-congruent encoding: Self-/other-reference and affirmative/nonaffirmative judgement. *Cognition and Emotion, 8*, 259–278.

Nasby, W., & Kihlstrom, J. F. (1986). Cognitive assessment of personality and psychopathology. In R. E. Ingram (Ed.), *Information-processing approaches to psychopathology and clinical psychology* (pp. 217–239). New York: Academic Press.

Nissen, M. J., Ross, J. L., Willingham, D. B., Mackenzie, T. B., & Schacter, D. L. (1988). Memory and awareness in a patient with multiple personality disorder. *Brain and Cognition, 8*, 21–38.

Prince, M. (1906). *The dissociation of a personality: A biographical study in abnormal psychology*. New York: Longmans Green.

Putnam, F. W. (1988). The switch process in multiple personality disorder and other state-change disorders. *Dissociation, 1*(1), 24–32.

Putnam, F. W. (1989). *Diagnosis and treatment of multiple personality disorder*. New York: Guilford.

Putnam, F. W., Guroff, J. J., Silberman, E. K., Barban, L., & Post, R. M. (1986). The clinical phenomenology of multiple personality disorder: Review of 100 recent cases. *Journal of Clinical Psychiatry, 47*, 285–293.

Quen, J. M. (Ed.). (1986). *Split minds/split brains: Historical and current perspectives*. New York: New York University Press.

Rome, H. P. (1984). Reflections on the concept of multiple personality [Special issue]. *Psychiatric Annals, 14*(1).

Ross, C. A. (1990). *Multiple personality disorder: Diagnosis, clinical features, and treatment*. New York: Wiley.

Rumelhart, D. E., McClelland, J. L., & the PDP Research Group. (Eds.). (1986). *Parallel distributed processing: Explorations in the microstructure of cognition. Volume 1: Foundations*. Cambridge, MA: MIT Press.

Sanders, S., & Hall, J. (Eds.). (1986). Dissociation [Special issue]. *American Journal of Clinical Hypnosis, 29*(2).

Schacter, D. L., & Kihlstrom, J. F. (1989). Functional amnesia. In F. Boller & J. Grafman (Eds.), *Handbook of neuropsychology* (Vol. 3, pp. 209–231). New York: Elsevier Science.

Schacter, D. L., Kihlstrom, J. F., & Kihlstrom, L. C. (1989). Autobiographical memory in a case of multiple personality disorder. *Journal of Abnormal Psychology, 98*, 508–514.

Shallice, T. (1972). Dual functions of consciousness. *Psychological Review, 79*, 383–393.

Silberman, E. K., Putnam, F. W., Weingartner, H., Braun, B. G., & Post, R. M. (1985). Dissociative states in multiple personality disorder: A quantitative study. *Psychiatry Research, 15*, 253–260.

Singer, W. (1983). Neuronal activity as a shaping factor in the self-organization of neuron assemblies. In E. Basar, H. Flohr, H. Haken, & A. J. Mandell (Eds.), *Synergetics of the brain* (pp. 89–101). New York: Springer-Verlag.

Spiegel, D. (1986). Dissociation, double binds, and posttraumatic stress in multiple personality disorder. In B. G. Braun (Ed.), *Treatment of multiple personality disorder* (pp. 63–77). Washington, DC: American Psychiatric Press.

Taylor, W. S., & Martin, M. F. (1944). Multiple personality. *Journal of Abnormal and Social Psychology, 39*, 281–300.

Thigpen, C. H., & Cleckley, H. M. (Eds.). (1984). On the incidence of multiple personality disorder [Special issue]. *International Journal of Clinical and Experimental Hypnosis, 32*(2).

Thorndike, E. L. (1911). *Animal intelligence: Experimental studies*. New York: Macmillan.

Wagner, A. R. (1981). SOP: A model of automatic memory processing in animal behavior. In N. E. Spear & R. R. Miller (Eds.), *Information processing in animals: Memory mechanisms* (pp. 5–43). Hillsdale, NJ: Lawrence Erlbaum Associates.

Wickelgren, W. A. (1979). Chunking and consolidation: A theoretical synthesis of semantic networks, configuring in conditioning, S-R versus cognitive learning, normal forgetting, the amnesic syndrome, and the hippocampal arousal system. *Psychological Review, 86*, 44–60.

Wolff, P. H. (1987). *The development of behavioral states and the expression of emotions in early infancy*. Chicago: University of Chicago Press.

Yates, J. L., & Nasby, W. (1993). Dissociation, affect, and network models of memory: An integrative proposal. *Journal of Traumatic Stress, 6*, 305–326.

Young, W. C. (1988). Psychodynamics and dissociation: All that switches is not split. *Dissociation, 1*(1), 33–38.

CHAPTER

19

INTRUSIVE THOUGHT AND THE MAINTENANCE OF CHRONIC STRESS

Karrie J. Craig
Jennifer A. Heisler
Andrew Baum
University of Pittsburgh

Stressful and traumatic life events are often followed by intrusive thoughts about these events or their aftermath (Goodhart, 1985; Ingram, 1984; Sarason, Potter, & Sarason, 1986). Defined as repetitive thoughts, images, memories, or impulses that are usually uncontrollable, or both, unwanted, intrusive thoughts have been linked with subjective and psychophysiological disturbances and may be triggered by both internal and external stimuli (Horowitz, 1970; Rachman, 1981). Intrusive thoughts have been associated with a wide range of stressors and have been linked to distress in studies of disasters (Horowitz, 1985), bereavement (Lehman, Wortman, & Williams, 1987), physically disabled traffic accident victims (Silver, Wortman, & Klos, 1982), women who were incest victims (Silver, Boon, & Stones, 1983), and young women following hysterectomy (Vincent, Vincent, Griess, et al., 1975; Kaltreider, Wallace, & Horowitz, 1979). It can be concluded, then, that intrusive thoughts are associated with the experience of stress, and a link between such intrusions and chronic distress is evident. However, the nature and mechanisms of these effects on chronic stress are not clearly drawn. This chapter considers some of the basic links between intrusive thoughts or memories and chronic stress.

The authors' investigations of intrusive thought center on the relationship between intrusive thoughts and the stress process. The maintenance of chronic stress has often been difficult to explain: Theories of adaptation and habituation suggest that stress should abate at some point following a stressful event, and common sense suggests that stress responding should cease soon after the stressor ends. However, people often experience chronic stress long after a stressor has occurred. Mechanisms underlying the persistence of distress beyond the life of the stressor remain largely uninvestigated. Recent findings and analysis suggest that intrusive thoughts may play a role in the maintenance of long-term stress and that constant or recurrent reliving of a stressor associated with intrusive thoughts is a possible mechanism underlying stress that persists long after the stressor has ended (Baum, Cohen, & Hall, 1993). The authors are evaluating the stress-intrusive thought relationship in several groups including victims of natural and technological disasters (e.g., Hurricane Andrew and Three Mile Island), Vietnam veterans, victims of motor vehicle accidents, and parents of critically ill children. Findings reflecting on specific aspects of the persistence of stress have varied, but consistent across most or all of these studies has been a robust relationship between the experience of intrusive thoughts and symptoms of chronic stress.

INTRUSIVE THOUGHTS

Intrusive thoughts have been of interest for years, as a symptom of psychological disorders, as a means of communication between realms of consciousness, and as a mechanism in several psychological syndromes. More recently the focus has been on posttraumatic stress disorder (PTSD) and victimization. Intrusive thoughts play an important role in posttraumatic stress disorder and intrusions are often considered a hallmark symptom of the disorder (DSM IV; APA, 1994). PTSD is an anxiety disorder that may occur following an extreme traumatic stressor involving oneself or someone else. One of the characteristics of PTSD is frequent reexperiencing of the event, which can occur in several ways; through recurrent and intrusive recollections, recurrent dreams, or dissociative states. These thoughts about traumatic events may generate intense psychological distress or physiological arousal, and this appears to contribute to distress and withdrawal. The experience of PTSD can also be debilitating because victims may be subject to feelings of guilt, emotional numbing, hypervigilance, and an exaggerated startle response, as well as difficulties with sleeping, controlling anger, and concentrating. However, a major component of the disorder is the persistence of intrusive thoughts and motivation to avoid any person, place, or object that may serve as a reminder of the traumatic event (DSM IV, 1994). The authors and others have suggested elsewhere that these associations may become broad and diffuse through repeated pairing with neutral stimuli and that an increasingly large and varied network of stimuli that can evoke stressful reminiscence result in more stressful experience and withdrawal.

The frequency of PTSD within the general population has been estimated at 1% (Helzer, Robins, & McEvoy, 1987) though estimates vary (Breslau, 1991). Research on the number of people who exhibit PTSD following the experience of a disaster has yielded a broader estimate, suggesting that 3–58% may develop

PTSD (Smith & North, 1993), while the prevalence (15.2%) and lifetime prevalence (30%) of PTSD among Vietnam veterans were established by the National Vietnam Veterans Readjustment Study (Kulka et al., 1988; Kulka et al., 1991). However, rates in Vietnam veterans that range as high as 75% have been reported by other researchers (Rosenheck & Fontana, 1994). In these and other cases, intrusive and avoidant thoughts appear to be early and enduring symptoms of distress and adjustment difficulties.

While investigation of PTSD and traumatic stress has been an important vehicle for research on intrusive thoughts, it is not the only way to characterize intrusive thoughts and memories. Intrusions are not always disruptive or negative; they may be about neutral or positive events or feelings, and may be nothing more than a fleeting thought about something one has to do. However, they may also be more disruptive and have stronger affective tone and may consist of dreams and nightmares that disrupt sleep, racing thoughts that keep people awake, or persistent images or memories of situations or stimuli that are aversive or evocative. These unbidden thoughts can occur immediately after a stressful event or some time later, may persist briefly or for several years, and may or may not be experienced as upsetting or aversive. With this great variety of manifestations and characteristics, it has been challenging to formulate clear conceptual and methodological analyses of intrusive experience. However it does appear that there is a core of properties that most or all intrusive thoughts share: they are uncontrollable, aperiodic, and are often related to sources or experiences of stress or demand (Goodhart, 1985; Horowitz et al., 1980; Sarason et al., 1986). They also appear to be arousing and can interfere with ongoing behavior.

To some extent, thoughts about stressful situations appear to be normal and predictable aspects of poststressor experience. Even routine stressors may be followed by some thoughts and a few thoughts experienced casually may be benign and hardly noticed. As the frequency and intensity of these thoughts increase, distress is more likely. Their strength, capacity to interrupt and upset, and their frequency are probably determined by the magnitude of the stressor and one's appraisal of it. Similarly, the intensity, frequency, and unwanted or uncontrollable qualities of the experience are probably influenced by the intensity and demand associated with the stressor and the effectiveness of coping and adaptation to the stressor. Routine stressors such as commuting to work, dealing with crowded stores and markets, or other daily hassles are so brief, so predictable, and pose so little demand as to be barely perceived (Lazarus & Folkman, 1984). If one commute was unusually difficult, it might be associated with more thoughts about it, but in general, these thoughts should be transient and mild. However, more substantial stressors, particularly those involving loss or threats to freedom and self-esteem, probably generate more frequent thoughts and may prove challenging enough to evoke uncontrollable, intrusive thoughts.

Anticipation of a noxious event or concern and worry about something that may happen seem particularly likely to be associated with stress, but any stressors strong enough to overwhelm or severely tax adaptive skills are also potent sources of intrusive thoughts. Horowitz (1975) viewed these thoughts as adaptive, suggesting that they represent the process of integration of the content and implications of major stressors with preexisting assumptions and world views. Some stressors are violations of assumptions associated with one's world view and part of coping and recovery is the integration of these jarring violations. When the fit between new information and old is poor, reconciliation may be difficult and painful. In such cases, intrusive thoughts and images may help by permitting continued processing of the stressful situation, with periods of reflection and avoidance of reminiscent stimuli cycling with these forced exposures (Horowitz, 1975).

This suggests that in cases like PTSD, the persistence of intrusive memories and thoughts about a trauma reflects basic conflict between one's basic assumptions about the world and the implications or apparent meaning of a trauma. Lasting intrusions would then reflect stalled or slowly evolving adaptation and integration of discrepant information and become a symptom of continuing threat or demand. As such, intrusions could be the mechanism by which unresolved conflict is translated into negative affect and arousal. Alternatively, intrusions may be a symptom of exaggerated or overly generalized coping and defense, or could reflect stressor interactions with appraisal and memory processes. Whatever their causes, it is when intrusive thoughts about an event become abnormally persistent, intrusive, and bothersome that they suggest underlying conditions and unhealthy outcomes. Many recent investigations of intrusive experience have focused on the most profound cases of stressful exposure, but there is some evidence that suggests a continuum of intrusive experience that reflects both the frequency and aversiveness of the stressor. In other words, intrusive thoughts are common and not only associated with the most extreme instances of poststressor response (e.g., PTSD). More benign or manageable stressors may also give rise to intrusive thoughts, and many people may experience these thoughts.

We are not suggesting that intrusive thoughts and memories are a consequence of stressor characteristics alone. The magnitude of the stressor is but one of several potential determinants of this experience, and it is likely that interactions among these factors determine the nature of intrusive thoughts. As Horowitz (1975) suggested, they may reflect adaptation and cognitive restructuring, coping, and growth. They may also be affected by memory consolidation processes that can alter the quality of one's memories, or may be related to personality variables or one's characteristic ways of dealing with threats or problems. Research on intrusive experience must pursue the identification of the extent and strength of predictors of intrusive thoughts, including causal and mediating processes.

Measurement

With the evolution of theory about intrusive thoughts came the need to develop reliable measures of hard-to-assess constructs such as thoughts and images. Measures of intrusive experience must consider problems associated with self-presentation biases in memory and reporting as well as difficulties in defining and interpreting intrusive experience. The Impact of Event Scale (IES) was developed by Horowitz, Wilner, and Alvarez (1979) and is the most commonly used measure of intrusions. The IES is used to assess subjective distress to a specific stressor and consists of two subscales to measure intrusive thinking and avoidance as stress responses. Collins and Clark (1989) used a 6-item version of the intrusive-thinking subscale of the IES and found that frequency of intrusive thoughts regarding past love relationships was positively correlated with reported anger, anxiety, depression, and perceived stress. Using the 50-item IES (prior to revision), Kaltreider, Wallace, and Horowitz (1979) found that following hysterectomy, 17 of 28 premenopausal women reported experiencing persistent intrusive thoughts and images. Five of these women were rated as experiencing serious levels of intrusive and avoidant symptoms. An interview 1 year later revealed that those women who experienced the most severe intrusive experience were still exhibiting signs of stress. Other scales and instruments to assess intrusive thoughts have or are being developed, but the IES remains the most widely used measure.

Intrusions and Interference

Intrusive thoughts have also been examined in relationship to cognitive interference, and evidence suggests that intrusive thoughts can divide attention, create cognitive overload, and cause people to perform more poorly on complex tasks, especially under challenging conditions (Sarason, 1984; Sarason et al., 1986). The tendency to experience intrusive thoughts has been associated with deficits in interpersonal experience such as poor childhood relationships with parents (Yee & Pierce, 1989), lack of social support (Sarason, 1981; Sarason & Sarason, 1986), and emphasis on negative thoughts (Sarason, Potter, & Sarason, 1989). Sarason hypothesized that if the tendency to experience cognitive interference was a stable, trait-like condition then it may have predictive value when evaluating behavior, examining personality styles, and performing clinical assessments.

Another account of how intrusive thoughts develop depicts them as responses to goal blocking or interference (Millar, Tesser, & Millar, 1988). When an individual experiences an interruption of goal-directed behavior he or she will attempt to resume the same activity or a conceptually similar activity. When an instrumental means of resuming this behavior is not available, the need will persist and the person will engage in thought or fantasy about people or objects related to that need. The occurrence of a disruptive or stressful event could interrupt an organized behavior sequence and result in intrusive thought if the individual cannot find suitable alternative ways to complete the sequence.

Intrusions and Stress

The authors' current focus on the maintenance of stress and the role that intrusions may play in the stress process led them to examine stressful events and the responses that follow with a specific interest in intrusive thought. When stressors are followed by intrusive thoughts, these unwanted, unbidden thoughts may contribute to the experience of stress and its maintenance. The selective vulnerability to long-term intrusive thoughts, the dynamics of how these thoughts are fixed, and the overall relationship among intrusive thoughts and other stress risk factors are of interest. In this chapter, the authors summarize their findings and nascent model and suggest that by better understanding this relationship and the mechanisms underlying chronic stress responding we may better understand cognitive interventions and stress-reduction techniques.

Research findings are consistent in showing that emotional distress is accompanied by an increased number of intrusive cognitions, a worsening of cognitive performance, and heightened sensitivity to stress-related stimuli. This work also makes clear the links among anxiety and dysphoric mood and the occurrence of intrusive thoughts. Stressful events can intensify existing intrusive activity or create new sources of intrusions. As these cognitions become more intense they appear to cause increased distress and discomfort, and decreased perceptions of control. Thus, removal of ongoing stressors may lead to a reduction in intensity and frequency of intrusive activities (Parkinson & Rachman, 1981). Additionally, intrusions may occur when goal-directed or normal patterns of behavior, or both, are blocked. These intrusions may allow individuals to attempt to reconcile these inconsistent assumptions and experiences and resolve conflicts associated with this integrative process.

CONSEQUENCES OF INTRUSIONS

The consequences of intrusive thoughts range from mild distress to chronic stress (Baum, Cohen, & Hall, 1993). As noted earlier, intrusive thoughts can divide attention and increase cognitive overload, conditions that make it more difficult to focus attention on the task at hand and cause people to perform poorly on complex tasks (Sarason, Sarason, Keefe, Hayes, & Shearin, 1986). Cognitive interference impairs performance and may cause problems in relationships and social behavior (Clark & Arkowitz, 1975), test-taking situations (Sarason, 1984), behavior during depression (Beck, 1976; Beck, Rush, Shaw, & Emery, 1979), and accidents and injuries (Coddington & Troxell, 1980; Selzer & Vinokuur, 1974). These performance deficits may be associated with stress.

A series of studies by Sarason (1984) illustrated some of the effects of cognitive interference. Sarason examined test anxiety and its relationship to performance and intrusive thinking, hypothesizing that anxiety causes intrusive thinking which then interferes with task-centered thought and results in impaired performance. In one study, Sarason administered a difficult digit task to 385 college students. After the task, subjects were given questionnaires that evaluated any cognitive interference and worrying that they experienced. Results indicated that worrying was negatively correlated with performance and positively correlated with cognitive interference. Sarason concluded that in evaluative situations cognitive interference was related to fears of failure and comparison to others rather than to intrusions unrelated to the situation. The complexity of these consequences was revealed in another study comparing anagram performance by subjects given attention-directing statements, reassurance, or given no comment before the task. Findings indicated that reassurance enhanced performance in high test anxiety subjects but lowered performance in low test anxiety subjects. Performance of all subjects given attention-directing instructions was high and cognitive interference was low. Control subjects with high test anxiety performed poorly on the anagram task and experienced high levels of cognitive interference.

Cognitive fear structures may also be related to the impact of intrusive thoughts (e.g., Foa & Kozak, 1986). Fear structures are activated when people are exposed to information relevant to their anxiety, making them sensitive to threat-related stimuli. To test this hypothetical increased sensitivity and decreased threshold, Foa, Feske, Murdock, Kozak, and McCarthy (1991) administered a modified version of the Stroop test to 15 rape victims with PTSD, 13 rape victims without PTSD, and 16 nonvictimized controls. The Stroop test was originally designed to evaluate performance with interfering stimuli; modification of it was made to evaluate the cognitive processing associated with emotional disturbance. In the original Stroop, color-name words were written in different colors of ink. Subjects were asked to identify the color of the ink while ignoring the word itself. This caused problems as the dominant response (reading the word) interfered with the naming of the ink color. In the modification of the Stroop task, some words were inserted that were trauma or stressor related instead of color names. The time it took to name the color of ink of stress-related words and non-stress-related words was then compared. Studies showed that stress-related words were associated with longer response times in subjects with anxiety disorders (Mathews & MacLeod, 1985; Watts, McKenna, Sharrock, & Trezise, 1986; Ehlers, Margraf, Davies, & Roth, 1988).

Four categories of words were inserted into the modified Stroop: specific rape-related words (e.g., rape, assault, trapped), general threat words (e.g., death, cancer, funeral), neutral words (the names of fruits), and nonsense or nonwords (e.g., gosp, shet, shorry) (Foa et al., 1991). Results showed that the PTSD group scored higher on all measures of psychopathology and took longer to name colors for rape-related words, supporting the hypothesis that rape victims with PTSD would show selective processing for rape-related information. Specific threat-related material may thus be represented differently among people with PTSD than those without it. Results also suggested that responses to this task were related to PTSD and not just exposure to a trauma. McNally, Kaspi, Riemann, and Zeitlin (1990) also used the Stroop task in studying PTSD, and reported that there were delays in naming stress-related words among Vietnam veterans with PTSD.

These studies suggest that intrusive thoughts about stressors, depending on their nature and the setting people are in, can cause people to feel upset, threatened, or anxious, or a combination of all three emotions. In some cases the thoughts may cause people to relive some of the feelings and fears associated with the actual stressful experience. While design and measurement issues characterizing most studies in this area preclude making strong causal inferences about intrusive thoughts and distress, several theories predict such a relationship and available data provide some support for the notion that intrusive reliving of a stressor or interference and frustration associated with this experience can cause stress. Research on disasters, which can be associated with life threat, loss, and considerable challenges to one's worldview (and interference with ongoing behavior), provides some support for such a hypothesis.

DISASTERS AND INTRUSIONS

Studies have linked disasters with heightened experience of a number of symptoms of distress, including anxiety, depression, anger, guilt, sleep disturbance, somatic symptoms, and intrusive thoughts (Cohen & Ahearn, 1980; Davidson & Baum, 1986; Escobar, Canino, Rubio-Stipec, & Bravo, 1992; Phifer, Kaniasty, & Norris, 1988; Shore, Tatum, & Vollmer, 1986b; Wood & Bootzin, 1992). Studies of major storms and floods show that victims experience elevated levels of distress following these disasters (Canino, Bravo, Rubio-Stipec, & Woodbury, 1990; Lima et al., 1993; Milne, 1977; Parker, 1975). The human-made flood at Buffalo Creek following failure of a dam was associated with stronger and longer-lasting effects than are most floods, in part because of its suddenness and devastating power (e.g., Green et al., 1990). The eruption of Mt. St. Helen's volcano, tornadoes, and other forms of natural disasters have also been linked to distress and short-term mental health effects (e.g., Shore, Tatum, & Volmer, 1986b). Several of these studies have found evidence of posttraumatic stress disorder (PTSD) in substantial numbers of disaster victims, representing profound stress effects of the disaster and its aftermath (e.g., Canino et al., 1990; Smith & North, 1993). Estimates of PTSD rates for disaster victims range from 2.3% to 53% (Smith & North, 1993), and Steinglass and Gerrity (1989) found that up to 20% of tornado victims exhibited signs of PTSD, including intrusive thoughts. Symptoms of PTSD have also been noted in victims of mud slides and floods (Canino et al., 1990), and people living near the Mt. St. Helen's volcano (Shore, Tatum, & Vollmer, 1986a).

A recent study of victims of Hurricane Andrew in South Florida in 1992 provided further evidence of a link between disaster stress and intrusive thoughts (Craig et al., in preparation). Hurricane Andrew provided the opportunity to study victims of a devastating natural disaster that left 250,000 people homeless and many without electricity or water for months. Data from a sample of 180 hurricane victims indicated that intrusive thoughts, as measured by the Impact of Event Scale (IES) and a questionnaire developed by the authors to assess frequency, unwantedness, and triggers of intrusions, were related to stress. Those individuals who reported experiencing more intrusive thoughts up to 4 months after the storm also reported more physical and psychological stress symptoms, exhibited higher urinary epinephrine and resting heart rate levels, and had lower urinary cortisol levels than did victims reporting fewer intrusive thoughts. Multiple regression analyses revealed that intrusive thoughts predicted up to 26% of the variance in symptom reporting after the effects associated with gender, education, injury, and damage were removed (Craig et al., in preparation).

Research involving technological disasters has provided findings similar to those involving natural disasters although the effects may be longer lasting after human-made disasters. In particular, studies of disasters involving toxic substances appear to be associated with long-term worry and distress. In March, 1979, an accident occurred at the Three Mile Island (TMI) nuclear power station involving the release of radiation. Radioactive gas was trapped during the accident, some of which was reported to have leaked into the environment. This gas was eventually released into the environment in controlled bursts more than 1 year later. In addition, considerable solid and liquid radioactive waste remained for years before it was removed. Contradictory information regarding the possible dangers and the amount of radiation involved contributed to confusion and fear among area residents.

Researchers reported that residents experienced significant distress following the accident, as evidenced by increased threat perception, fear, depression, and symptom reporting (Bromet, 1980; Dohrenwend, Dohrenwend, Kasl, & Warheit, 1979; Flynn, 1979). Some reports suggested that distress peaked within a few months after the accident and then returned to control levels (Dohrenwend et al., 1979), while others showed evidence of stress lasting up to a year following the accident (Bromet, 1980). Still other researchers found that these symptoms of distress continued for years after the event (Baum, Gatchel, & Schaeffer, 1983; Davidson, Fleming, & Baum, 1984; Dew et al., 1987). The authors' research has suggested that TMI-area residents reported greater somatic and emotional distress and exhibited behavioral and physiological symptoms of stress for up to 6 years following the accident. Measured repeatedly over this time, symptom reporting and physiological markers of stress were elevated among TMI-area residents relative to controls while task performance was poorer among TMI-area residents.

The experience of intrusive thought following the accident at TMI was of interest initially as part of a study of PTSD symptoms among TMI-area residents. In this study, 87 subjects completed the IES in addition to several stress measures. Fifty-two of these individuals lived within 5 miles of the damaged plant and 35 subjects were part of a comparison group that lived more than 80 miles away from the reactor. As had been found before, TMI-area residents exhibited more symptoms of stress than did control subjects. In addition, PTSD symptoms were related to stress among TMI-area residents. Those residents who reported more intrusive thoughts on the IES also experienced higher levels of chronic stress several years after the accident. Individuals who were exposed to the accident and reported frequent intrusive thoughts about it reported more symptom distress, and exhibited poorer proofreading performance, higher systolic blood pressure levels, and increased levels of urinary norepinephrine. These results suggested a pattern of chronic stress responding following the accident. It is interesting to note that variables such as perceived control, social support, and coping were associated with distress during the first 2 years after the TMI accident but intrusive thought remained a reliable predictor of stress almost 5 years later (Baum, 1990).

VIETNAM VETERANS AND INTRUSIVE THOUGHT

Similar results of a study of combat veterans provided further evidence of a chronic stress-intrusive thoughts link. A study examining intrusive thoughts and stress in Vietnam veterans who did not have PTSD (Davidson & Baum, 1993) suggested that reported combat experience was not associated with chronic stress but an interaction of intrusions and combat exposure predicted chronic stress responding more than 14 years after the significant event. Sixty-seven men, ages 33–49, participated in this study of combat exposure, chronic stress, and intrusive recall. Thirty-four of these men served in combat in Vietnam, 18 of the men were noncombat Vietnam-era veterans and 15 comprised an age-matched comparison group with no military experience. Combat veterans reported more intrusive thoughts on the IES than either noncombat or nonmilitary comparison groups, but did not necessarily exhibit more symptoms of chronic stress. In fact, irrespective of combat exposure, those individuals who reported more intrusive thoughts were more likely to exhibit symptoms of chronic stress. The interaction of combat and reported intrusive thought was significantly related to the experience of chronic stress as indicated by symptom endorsement and proofreading performance. There were no significant relationships found among intrusions, combat, and catecholamine variables.

Another study also bears on this issue. Rosenheck and Fontana (1994) compiled information regarding PTSD symptoms, as indicated on the Structured Clinical Interview for DSM III (SCID; Spitzer & Williams, 1985), among veterans of World War II, the Korean Conflict, and the Vietnam War. No differences were found in intrusive symptomatology and hyperarousal across groups, but Vietnam veterans more often met criteria for numbing and manifested more guilt. The percentage of veterans reporting intrusive symptoms ranged from 83% (Korea) to 87% (Vietnam), with 85% of WWII veterans also reporting intrusive thoughts. Symptoms of numbing and guilt were reported as diminishing in intensity over time while intrusive symptoms and hyperarousal were more persistent.

INTRUSIONS AND PARENTS OF CRITICALLY ILL CHILDREN

In a study examining the relationship between frequency of intrusions and susceptibility to reminiscent stimuli, Hall and Baum (in press) compared performance on a modified Stroop task between parents of children with cancer and parents with healthy children. The researchers administered the test to 17 parents of children who had been battling cancer for a year or more and to 10 parents of healthy children. The cancer group was then split into high and low intrusive experience groups based on a median split of score on the IES. The task consisted of five Stroop pages: two original Stroop task pages, one cancer page consisting entirely of cancer-related words, one page consisting of 60% color words and 40% cancer words, and one page of asterisks printed in different colors. In addition, physiological and self-report measures were taken.

After completing the Stroop task, parents of children with cancer experienced more intrusive thoughts and reported more avoidance behaviors than did the parents of healthy children. High IES parents reported more thoughts about their child's illness and were more distressed about these thoughts after the task than were the low IES and control group subjects. After a rest period, both high and low IES groups reported more intrusive thoughts and distress than did the control group, suggesting that once subjects had an opportunity to think about the task they completed, all parents of cancer patients became more distressed (Hall & Baum, in press). It is also possible that the frequency of intrusive material is influenced by the ability to focus on a task and eliminate emotion-laden thoughts such that once the low IES parents completed the task they were then cognitively available for the intrusions to return. The low IES parents may have been able to focus on the task and reduce intrusions only to have the intrusions increase following the task.

MOTOR VEHICLE ACCIDENTS AND INTRUSIVE THOUGHT

The authors are currently conducting a study of victims of serious motor vehicle accidents (MVAs) in order to examine the effects of a smaller-scale, more personal trauma than the more collective disasters that we have studied previously. Natural disasters and human-made catastrophes, such as tornadoes, floods, and war involve large areas or numbers of victims or potential victims, and occur in the context of a community under stress. Smaller-scale stressors, such as MVAs, may be as threatening and traumatic but do not ordinarily happen to large groups. (One could argue on this basis, that the shared experience of disaster may make it easier to cope with than are MVAs, but the actual facilitating role of extent of victimization is not clear.) The consequences of MVAs pose a significant social and economic burden with an expected death toll of 3 million by the mid-1990s (National Safety Council, 1987). Not only are millions of people involved in MVAs each year, but billions of dollars are spent for health care or other needs due to accidents. There is a striking lack of information about adjustment and stress following MVAs and most of the available information is in the form of case studies or clinical reports. Prospective analysis of sequelae of MVAs or psychosocial factors that predict recovery may provide another context for examination of the role of intrusive thoughts in chronic stress.

The authors' work with accident victims focused mainly on stress and the psychological sequelae of the accident, with special attention paid to the examination of intrusive thoughts. Participants were selected from among patients admitted to a regional trauma center following a serious MVA. These individuals were free from head injury and exhibited no signs of CNS damage. Participants were seen initially 14–21 days after the accident, and were seen again at 3, 6, 12, and 18 months after the accident. Stress was measured using self-report instruments, a structured interview (The SCID), and the examination of physiological, biochemical, and behavioral changes often associated with stress. Preliminary analyses indicated that the victims of MVAs experienced more stress than did control subjects (people who visited the emergency room in the same hospital for a minor, non-MVA injury). Data for 159 people were available for these analyses, 120 MVA victims and 39 control subjects, though data for some were available only for two or three assessments.

These preliminary analyses suggest that intrusions, as measured by the IES, were correlated with symptom distress (measured on the SCL-90-R, Derogatis, 1983) throughout the first year following the accident. Those MVA victims reporting more intrusive thoughts also reported more symptom distress. This relationship did not hold for the control group in which a relationship between intrusions and symptoms was evident for the first 6 months but disappeared after that. The MVA victims also reported more intrusions than did control subjects throughout the first year postaccident, reported more symptoms on the SCL-90-R 3 months after their accident, and scored higher on most of the SCL-90-R subscales including; somatization, obsessive-compulsive, interpersonal sensitivity, anxiety, and psychoticism. Proofreading performance was also different between the MVA victims and the comparison group, with the comparison group performing better on the task (finding more errors) than the MVA victims at the initial visit and 3 months postaccident. Performance on the proofreading task, a behavioral measure that taps concentration and attentiveness, was inversely related to intrusions at the initial session (for the MVA group) and was positively associated with intrusion in the comparison group, indicating that more intrusions were associated with poorer performance among MVA victims but with better performance for control subjects. The negative relationship between intrusions and performance among MVA victims was still evident 12 months after the accident.

These exploratory analyses provide some additional evidence of a link between intrusions and long-term reactions to a traumatic event, in this case, a motor vehicle accident. Clearly, definitive conclusions about these relationships must await completion of the study and data analysis. However, the preliminary analyses were based on a substantial number of participants and they are consistent with the idea that individuals who experience a traumatic event experience more intrusive thoughts for up to 1 year following the event. They also suggest that intrusions are associated with a greater level of physical and psychological symptom reporting and with higher heart rate and poorer performance on the proofreading task for victims of MVAs. While more systematic analyses of these data will clarify these issues, the findings to date suggest that intrusions are an important component of emotional reactions to major stressors.

SUMMARY AND CONCLUSIONS

This brief review of research involving intrusive thoughts and stress suggests that this is a potentially rich area for further exploration. It is fairly clear that intrusions and stress often occur together and the findings indicate that intrusive thoughts may serve as an important mechanism in the maintenance of chronic stress. The authors have consistently found a relationship between the occurrence of intrusive thought and the persistence of stress symptoms. This association was observed in a variety of samples including victims of natural and human-caused disasters, victims of motor vehicle accidents, Vietnam veterans, and in parents of terminally ill children. Studies of all of these groups provided evidence of a relationship between intrusions and chronic stress.

By assessing stress with a variety of measures it is possible to obtain a more comprehensive view of stress responding. The authors' studies have provided such a picture and have led to the conclusion that intrusive thoughts are related to both acute and chronic stress following traumatic events. These findings suggest that intrusions may be a mechanism by which the stress reaction is prolonged but it is unclear exactly how this potential mechanism works. The idea of intrusions yielding a sense of reliving of the traumatic event may play a part in the maintenance of the stress response because the individual is unable to fully process the event and reconcile it with existing mental schemas.

While the association of these constructs seems evident, causal analyses of them can yield very different conclusions. The authors believe that intrusive thoughts cause people to feel stress, that is, to experience symptoms of stress such as GI distress, hypervigilance, anxiety, and arousal. The thoughts are caused by some combination of stressor characteristics and appraisal variables or memory processes and intervene between cognitive work related to adaptation and the experience of distress. However, they may also be viewed as a symptom of distress, no different than anxiety or arousal, that is caused by some other cognitive or affective processes. The authors' view of the origin and effects of intrusive thoughts is consistent with existing theories of stress and intrusions and is based largely on their observations of temporal as well as magnitude relationships between intrusive thoughts and chronic stress. Ultimately, the most useful way of viewing these events and evaluating what causes what will become apparent as researchers consider these and other issues related to the phenomenology of chronic stress.

Future research in this area should include more detailed examination of the role of intrusions following traumatic or stressful events. Development of new measurement techniques for intrusive thought would add important information to this field, particularly behavioral measures of the effects of intrusions to complete the picture provided by self-report and physiological measures that are currently in use. Further investigation of the relationship between intrusive thought and chronic stress will provide valuable clues to help understand the stress process also and possibly the means of altering the pathway of chronic stress through cognitive interventions and stress-reduction techniques involving intrusions.

REFERENCES

American Psychiatric Association. (1994). *Diagnostic and statistical manual of mental disorders; fourth edition (DSM IV).* Washington, DC: American Psychiatric Association.

Baum, A. (1987). Toxins, technology, and natural disasters. In G. R. Van den Bos & B. K. Bryant (Eds.), *Cataclysms, crises, and catastrophes* (pp. 5–53). Washington, DC: American Psychological Association.

Baum, A. (1990). Stress, intrusive imagery, and chronic distress. *Health Psychology, 9*, 653–675.

Baum, A., Cohen, L., & Hall, M. (1993). Control and intrusive memories as possible determinants of chronic stress. *Psychosomatic Medicine, 55*, 274–286.

Baum, A., Gatchel, R. J., & Schaeffer, M. A. (1983). Emotional, behavioral, and physiological effects of chronic stress at Three Mile Island. *Journal of Consulting and Clinical Psychology, 51*, 565–572.

Beck, A. T. (1976). *Cognitive therapy and the emotional disorders.* New York: International Universities Press.

Beck, A. T., Rush, A. J., Shaw, B. F., & Emery, G. (1979). *Cognitive therapy of depression.* New York: Guilford Press.

Breslau, N. (1991). Traumatic events and posttraumatic stress disorder in an urban population of young adults. *Archives of General Psychiatry, 48*(3), 216–222.

Bromet, E. (1980). *Three Mile Island: Mental health findings.* Pittsburgh, PA: University of Pittsburgh, Western Psychiatric Institute and Clinic.

Canino, G., Bravo, M., Rubio-Stipec, M., & Woodbury, M. (1990). The impact of disaster on mental health: Prospective and retrospective analyses. *International Journal of Mental Health, 19*, 51–69.

Clark, J. V., & Arkowitz, H. (1975). Social anxiety and self-evaluation of interpersonal performance. *Psychological Reports, 36*, 211–221.

Coddington, R. D., & Troxell, J. R. (1980). The effect of emotional factors on football injury rates—a pilot study. *Journal of Human Stress, 6*, 3–5.

Cohen, R. E., & Ahearn, F. L. (1980). *Handbook for mental health care of disaster victims*. Baltimore, MD: Johns Hopkins University Press.

Collins, J. E., & Clark, L. F. (1989). Responsibility and rumination: The trouble with understanding the dissolution of a relationship. *Social Cognition, 7*, 152–173.

Craig, K. J., Liegey-Dougall, A., Carver, C., Ironson, G., Scheiderman, N., & Baum, A. (in preparation). *Stress, intrusive thoughts, and loss of resources due to Hurricane Andrew*.

Davidson, L. M., & Baum, A. (1986). Chronic stress and post-traumatic stress disorders. *Journal of Consulting and Clinical Psychology, 54*, 303–308.

Davidson, L. M., & Baum, A. (1993). Predictors of chronic stress among Vietnam veterans: Stressor exposure and intrusive recall. *Journal of Traumatic Stress, 6*, 195–212.

Davidson, L. M., Fleming, I., & Baum, A. (1984, August). *Chronic stress and TMI: The role of toxic exposure and uncertainty*. Paper presented at the annual meeting of the American Psychological Association, Toronto, Ontario, Canada.

Derogatis, L. R. (1977). *The SCL-90 Manual I: Scoring, administration, and procedures for the SCL-90*. Baltimore, MD: Johns Hopkins University School of Medicine, Clinical Psychometrics Unit.

Derogatis, L. R. (1983). *SCL-90-R: Administration, scoring, and procedures manual-II*. Towson, MD: Clinical Psychometric Research.

Dew, M. A., Bromet, E. J., Schulberg, H. C. (1987). A comparative analysis of two community stressors' long-term mental health effects. *American Journal of Community Psychology, 15*(2), 167–184.

Dohrenwend, B. P., Dohrenwend, B. S., Kasl, S. V., & Warheit, G. J. (1979, October). *Technical staff analysis report on behavioral effects*. Paper presented to the President's Commission on the Accident at Three Mile Island, Washington, DC.

Ehlers, A., Margraf, J., Davies, S., & Roth, W. T. (1988). Selective processing of threat cues in subjects with panic attacks. Special issue: Information processing and the emotional disorders. *Cognition and Emotion, 2*(3), 201–219.

Escobar, J. I., Canino, G., Rubio-Stipec, M., & Bravo, M. (1992). Somatic symptoms after a natural disaster: A prospective study. *American Journal of Psychiatry, 149*, 965–967.

Flynn, C. B. (1979). *Three Mile Island telephone survey* (Contract No. NUREG/CR-1093). Washington, DC: U.S. Nuclear Regulatory Commission.

Foa, E. B., Feske, U., Murdock, T. B., Kozak, M. J., & McCarthy, P. R. (1991). Processing of threat-related information in rape victims. *Journal of Abnormal Psychology, 100*, 156–162.

Foa, E. B., & Kozak, M. J. (1986). Emotional processing of fear: Exposure to corrective information. *Psychological Bulletin, 99*(1), 20–35.

Goodhart, D. E. (1985). Some psychological effects associated with positive and negative thinking about stressful event outcomes: Was Pollyanna right? *Journal of Personality and Social Psychology, 48*, 216–232.

Green, B. L., Grace, M. C., Lindy, J. D., Gleser, G. C., Leonard, A. L., Karol, M., & Winget, C. (1990). Buffalo Creek survivors in the 2nd decade—comparison with unexposed and nonlitigant groups. *Journal of Applied Social Psychology, 20*, 1033–1050.

Hall, M. H., & Baum, A. (in press). Intrusive thoughts as predictors of distress in parents of children with cancer. *Journal of Applied Social Psychology*.

Helzer, J. E., Robins, L. N., & McEvoy, L. (1987). Post-traumatic stress disorder in the general population: Findings of the Epidemiologic Catchment Area Survey. *The New England Journal of Medicine, 317*(26), 1630–1634.

Horowitz, M. J. (1970). *Image formation and cognition*. New York: Appleton-Century-Crofts.

Horowitz, M. J. (1975). Intrusive and repetitive thoughts after experimental stress. *Archives of General Psychiatry, 32*, 1457–1463.

Horowitz, M. J. (1985). Disasters and psychological responses to stress. *Psychiatric Annals, 15*, 161–167.

Horowitz, M., Wilner, N., & Alvarez, W. (1979). Impact of Event Scale: A measure of subjective stress. *Psychosomatic Medicine, 41*, 209–218.

Horowitz, M. J., Wilner, N., Kaltreider, N., & Alvarez, W. (1980). Signs and symptoms of posttraumatic stress disorder. *Archives of General Psychiatry, 37*, 85–92.

Ingram, R. E. (1984). Toward an information-processing analysis of depression. *Cognitive Therapy and Research, 8*, 443–478.

Kaltreider, N. B., Wallace, A., & Horowitz, M. J. (1979). A field study of the stress response syndrome. *Journal of the American Medical Association, 242*, 1499–1503.

Kulka, R. A., Schlenger, W. E., Fairbank, J. A., Hough, R., Jordan, K., Marmar, C., & Weiss, P. (1988). *Contractual report of findings from the National Vietnam veterans readjustment study*. Research Triangle Park, North Carolina, Research Triangle Institute.

Kulka, R. A., Schlenger, W. E., Fairbank, J. A., Jordan, K. B. (1991). Assessment of posttraumatic stress disorder in the community: Prospects and pitfalls from recent studies of Vietnam veterans. *Psychological Assessment, 3*(4), 547–560.

Lazarus, R. S., & Folkman, S. (1984). *Stress, appraisal, and coping*. New York: Springer.

Lehman, D. R., Wortman, C. B., & Williams, A. F. (1987). Long-term effects of losing a spouse or child in a motor vehicle crash. *Journal of Personality and Social Psychology, 52*, 218–231.

Lima, B. R., Shaila, P., Toledo, V., Caris, L., Haro, J. M., & Santacruz, H. (1993). Emotional distress in disaster victims. *The Journal of Nervous and Mental Disease, 181*, 388–393.

Mathews, A., & MacLeod, C. (1985). Selective processing of threat cues in anxiety states. *Behaviour Research & Therapy, 23*(5), 563–569.

McNally, R. J., Kaspi, S. P., Riemann, B. C., & Zeitlin, S. B. (1990). Selective processing of threat cues in posttraumatic stress disorder. *Journal of Abnormal Psychology, 99*, 398–402.

Millar, K. U., Tesser, A., & Millar, M. G. (1988). The effects of a threatening life event on behavior sequences and intrusive thought: A self-disruption explanation. *Cognitive Therapy and Research, 12*, 441–457.

Milne, G. (1977). Cyclone Tracy: Some consequences of the evacuation in adult victims. *Australian Psychology, 12*, 39–54.

National Safety Council. (1987). *Accident Facts*, 45–78.

Parker, G. (1975). Psychological disturbance in Darwin evacuees following Cyclone Tracy. *The Medical Journal of Australia, 21*, 650–652.

Parkinson, L., & Rachman, S. (1981). Intrusive thoughts: The effects of an uncontrived stress. *Advances in Behaviour Research and Therapy, 3*, 111–118.

Phifer, J. F., Kaniasty, K. Z., & Norris, F. H. (1988). The impact of a natural disaster on the health of older adults. *Journal of Health and Social Behavior, 29*, 65–78.

Rachman, S. (1981). Unwanted intrusive cognitions. *Advances in Behaviour Research and Therapy, 13*, 89–99.

Rosenheck, R. T., & Fontana, A. (1994). Long-term sequelae of combat in World War II, Korea, and Vietnam: A comparative study. In R. J. Ursano, B. G. McCaughey, & C. S. Fullerton (Eds.), *Individual and community responses to trauma and disaster: The structure of human chaos*. Cambridge, England: Cambridge University Press.

Sarason, I. G. (1981). Test anxiety, stress, and social support. *Journal of Personality, 49*, 101–114.

Sarason, I. G. (1984). Stress, anxiety, and cognitive interference: Reactions to tests. *Journal of Personality and Social Psychology, 46*, 929–938.

Sarason, I. G., Potter, E. H., & Sarason, B. H. (1986). Recording and recall of personal events: Effects on cognitions and behavior. *Journal of Personality and Social Psychology, 51*, 347–356.

Sarason, I. G., & Sarason, B. R. (1986). Anxiety and interfering thoughts: Their effect on social interaction. In W. H. Jones, J. M. Cheek, & S. R. Briggs (Eds.), *Shyness: Perspectives on research and treatment.* New York: Plenum.

Sarason, I. G., Sarason, B. R., Keefe, D. E., Hayes, B. E., & Shearin, E. N. (1986). Cognitive interference: Situational determinants and traitlike characteristics. *Journal of Personality and Social Psychology, 51*, 215–226.

Selzer, M. L., & Vinokur, A. (1974). Life events, subjective stress, and traffic accidents. *American Journal of Psychiatry, 131*, 903–906.

Shore, J., Tatum, E., & Vollmer, W. (1986a). Psychiatric reactions to disaster: The Mount St. Helen's experience. *American Journal of Psychiatry, 143*, 590–595.

Shore, J. H., Tatum, E. L., & Vollmer, W. M. (1986b). Evaluation of mental effects of disaster, Mt. St. Helen's eruption. *American Journal of Public Health, 76*, 76–83.

Silver, R. L., Boon, C., & Stones, M. H. (1983). Searching for meaning in misfortune: Making sense of incest. *Journal of Social Issues, 39*, 81–102.

Silver, R. L., Wortman, C. B., & Klos, D. S. (1982). Cognitions, affect, and behavior following uncontrollable outcomes: A response to current human helplessness research. *Journal of Personality, 50*, 480–514.

Smith, E. M., & North, C. S. (1993). Posttraumatic stress disorder in natural disasters and technological accidents. In J. P. Wilson & B. Raphael (Eds.), *International handbook of traumatic stress syndromes.* New York: Plenum.

Spitzer, R. L., & Williams, J. B. W. (1985). *Structured Clinical Interview for DSM-III.* New York: New York State Psychiatric Institute.

Steinglass, P., & Gerrity, E. (1989). Natural disasters and post-traumatic stress disorder: Short-term vs. long-term recovery in two disaster affected communities. *Journal of Applied Social Psychology, 20*, 1746–1765.

Vincent, C., Vincent, B., Griess, F. C., & Linton, E. B. (1975). Marital-sexual concomitants of carcinoma of the cervix. *Southern Medical Journal, 68*, 552–558.

Watts, F. N., McKenna, F. P., Sharrock, R., & Trezise, L. (1986). Colour naming of phobia-related words. *British Journal of Psychology, 77*(1), 97–108.

Wood, J. M., & Bootzin, R. R. (1992). Effects of the 1989 San Francisco earthquake of frequency and content of nightmares. *Journal of Abnormal Psychology, 101*(2), 219–224.

Yee, P. L., & Pierce, G. R. (1989). *Cognitive interference as a personality characteristic.* Paper presented at the annual meeting of the American Psychological Association, New Orleans, LA.

Author Index

C

L

N

Q-R

Subject Index

T

For Product Safety Concerns and Information please contact our EU representative GPSR@taylorandfrancis.com
Taylor & Francis Verlag GmbH, Kaufingerstraße 24, 80331 München, Germany

www.ingramcontent.com/pod-product-compliance
Ingram Content Group UK Ltd.
Pitfield, Milton Keynes, MK11 3LW, UK
UKHW022114190926
475702UK00013B/1430
* 9 7 8 1 1 3 8 9 9 1 4 5 3 *